Financial Crises
Volume II

# The International Library of Macroeconomic and Financial History

*Series Editor:* Forrest H. Capie

*Professor of Economic History*
*and Head of the Department of Banking and Finance*
*The City University Business School, London*

1. Major Inflations in History
   *Forrest H. Capie*

2. Multinational and International Banking
   *Geoffrey Jones*

3. Monetary Regime Transformations
   *Barry Eichengreen*

4. Financing Industrialization (Volumes I and II)
   *Rondo Cameron*

5. Financial Crises (Volumes I and II)
   *Michael Bordo*

Future titles will include:

Debt and Deficits (Volumes I, II and III)
*Geoffrey E. Wood and Lakis C. Kaounides*

Price Controls
*Hugh Rockoff*

Central Banking in History
*Michael Collins*

Protectionism in the World Economy
*Forrest H. Capie*

Stock Market Crashes and Speculative Manias
*Peter M. Garber*

Free Banking
*Lawrence H. White*

# Financial Crises
# Volume II

*Edited by*

# Michael Bordo

*Professor of Economics*
*Rutgers University*

An Elgar Reference Collection

Published by
Edward Elgar Publishing Limited
Gower House
Croft Road
Aldershot
Hants GU11 3HR
England

Edward Elgar Publishing Company
Old Post Road
Brookfield
Vermont 05036
USA


A CIP catalogue record for this book is available from the British Library

**Library of Congress Cataloguing in Publication Data**
Financial crises/edited by Michael Bordo.
       p.   cm. – (The International library of macroeconomic and
financial history; 5) (An Elgar reference collection)
    1. Panics (Finance)  I. Bordo, Michael D.  II. Series.
III. Series: An Elgar reference collection.
HB3722.F53  1992
338.5′42–dc20                                                                                    91–47704
                                                                                                              CIP


ISBN 1 85278 432 6 (2 volume set)


Printed in Great Britain at the University Press, Cambridge.

# Contents

# Acknowledgements

The editor and publishers wish to thank the following who have kindly given permission for the use of copyright material.

Academic Press, Inc. for article: Georg Rich (1989), 'Canadian Banks, Gold and the Crisis of 1907', *Explorations in Economic History*, **26** (2), 135–60.

American Enterprise Institute for Public Policy Research for article: Marvin Goodfriend and Robert G. King (1988), 'Financial Deregulation, Monetary Policy and Central Banking', in William S. Haraf and Rose Marie Kushmeider (eds.), *Restructuring Banking and Financial Services in America*, 216–53.

Basil Blackwell Ltd. for article: Julian Hoppit (1986), 'Financial Crises in Eighteenth-century England', *Economic History Review*, 2nd Series, **XXXIX** (1), 39–58.

Cambridge University Press for article and excerpt: Eugene N. White (1981), 'State-Sponsored Insurance of Bank Deposits in the United States, 1907–1929', *Journal of Economic History*, **XLI** (3), 537–57; Barry Eichengreen and Richard Portes (1987), 'The anatomy of financial crises', in Richard Portes and Alexander K. Swoboda (eds.), *Threats to International Financial Stability*, 10–58. (In addition the publishers would like to thank the authors of the diagrams featured in this latter article).

Federal Reserve Bank of Chicago for article: Charles Calomiris (1989), 'Deposit insurance: Lessons from the record', *Economic Perspectives*, 10–30.

Federal Reserve Bank of Richmond for article: Michael Bordo (1990), 'The Lender of Last Resort: Alternative Views and Historical Experience', *Federal Reserve Bank of Richmond Economic Review*, **76** (1), 18–29.

Macmillan Press Ltd. for excerpts: Hugh Rockoff (1980), 'Walter Bagehot and the Theory of Central Banking', in Forrest Capie and Geoffrey E. Wood (eds), *Financial Crises and the World Banking System*, 160–80; Roy A. Batchelor (1986), 'The Avoidance of Catastrophe: Two Nineteenth-century Banking Crises', in Forrest Capie and Geoffrey E. Wood (eds), *Financial Crises and the World Banking System*, 41–73.

Ohio State University Press for article: Gary Gorton and Donald J. Mullineaux (1987), 'The Joint Production of Confidence: Endogenous Regulation and Nineteenth Century Commercial Bank Clearinghouses', *Journal of Money, Credit and Banking*, **19** (4), 457–68.

Oxford University Press for article: C.A.E. Goodhart (1987), 'Why do Banks Need a Central Bank?', *Oxford Economic Papers*, **39**, 78–89.

Rivista di Storia Economica for article: Michael D. Bordo (1985), 'The Impact and International Transmission of Financial Crises: Some Historical Evidence, 1870–1933', *Rivista di Storia Economica*, Second Series, **2**, International Issue, 41–78.

University of Chicago Press for excerpts: Rudiger Dornbusch and Jacob A. Frenkel (1984), 'The Gold Standard and the Bank of England in the Crisis of 1847', in Michael D. Bordo and Anna J. Schwartz (eds), *A Retrospective on the Classical Gold Standard 1821–1931*, 233–64; Ben Bernanke and Harold James (1991), 'The Gold Standard, Deflation, and Financial Crisis in the Great Depression: An International Comparison', in R. Glenn Hubbard (ed.), *Financial Markets and Financial Crises*, 33–68.

v. Hase & Koehler Verlag, Mainz for excerpt: Charles Kindleberger (1985), 'International Propagation of Financial Crises: The Experience of 1888–93', *Keynesianism vs. Monetarism and Other Essays in Financial History*, 226–39.

In addition the publishers wish to thank the library of the London School of Economics and Political Science and The Alfred Marshall Library, Cambridge University for their assistance in obtaining these articles.

# Part I
# Financial Crises in Other Countries

# [1]

*Economic History Review*, 2nd ser. XXXIX, 1 (1986), pp. 39-58

# Financial Crises in Eighteenth-century England[1]

## By JULIAN HOPPIT

In describing the causes and course of English economic growth during industrialization historians have frequently used a medium or long-term approach. Looking at average growth rates or the contribution of various key sectors to the economy as a whole, over long periods of time, has often been seen as the best way of outlining and explaining the growth process. Such an approach has clear enough links with postwar development economics. Growth, however, rarely conforms to a golden mean or a mythical average. It comes and goes, especially over the short term. An accurate picture of any economy must balance micro and macro aspects, calling on short, medium and long-term perspectives. In this article I want to employ this approach by looking at a part of one of the key factors behind early industrialization: finance. In particular, financial crises are examined not just in the belief that they were important, but that as short-term phenomena they tell us significant things about the role of finance, and more especially about credit.

## I

There has never been much doubt that financial crises occurred all too often in eighteenth-century England. But what has caused concern and disagreement has been attempts to chronicle crises and to assess their importance. All agree that crises blighted the developing economy, but how frequent and catastrophic was the disease? Contemporary onlookers, such as Chalmers and Macpherson, saw that the financial system of the day was remarkably prone to moments of great instability.[2] Recent historians have been similarly impressed.[3] Yet it is difficult to extract from their observations a simple list of crisis years. While agreement exists for certain years, confusion reigns for others. Chalmers, for example, was struck in 1794 by the limited impact the bursting of the South Sea Bubble had on the financial systems of the domestic economy in 1720, while Carswell in 1960 believed the crisis to be both deep and pervasive.[4] Similarly, Clapham argued in 1944 that in 1763 "There was

---

[1] Many thanks to Donald Coleman for all his help.

[2] G. Chalmers, *An Estimate of the Comparative Strength of Great Britain* (1794); D. Macpherson, *Annals of Commerce* (1805), III & IV.

[3] T. S. Ashton, *Economic Fluctuations in England, 1700-1800* (Oxford, 1959), ch. 5 (hereafter Ashton, *Fluctuations*); J. H. Clapham, *The Bank of England* (Cambridge, 1944), I, ch. VII; C. P. Kindleberger, *Manias, Panics, and Crashes* (1978); M. C. Lovell, 'The Role of the Bank of England as Lender of Last Resort in the Crises of the Eighteenth Century', *Explorations in Entrepreneurial History*, X (1957), pp. 8-21; P. E. Mirowski, 'The Birth of the Business Cycle' (unpublished Ph.D. thesis, University of Michigan, 1979), ch. IV; L. S. Pressnell, *Country Banking in the Industrial Revolution* (Oxford, 1956), ch. 15.

[4] Chalmers, *An Estimate*, p. xliii; J. Carswell, *The South Sea Bubble* (1960), p. 191.

no true crisis", yet a little over ten years later Lovell firmly believed that there was.[5] As a final example Ashton, whose study of crises in the century remains the most comprehensive, was in no doubt that there was a crisis of sorts in 1788; yet Mirowski flatly denies it, stating that "the year 1788 was no crisis or depression year at all, but the early part of an expansion".[6] Discordant opinion is general, both among and between contemporary observers and modern economic historians.

Conflict has arisen for three broad reasons: because of the different sorts of evidence employed; because of the varying definitions of "crisis" utilized; and, most importantly, because the financial system in the eighteenth century was evolving and becoming more sophisticated, with the result that the nature of crises developed and changed.

Much of the discord and strife can be settled by constructing a definition of "financial crisis" that takes into account the problems of evidence surrounding the eighteenth-century financial world. Financial crises are, in fact, notoriously difficult to define. They are not exact phenomena which can be precisely identified by measuring the intensity of fluctuations in financial series. They are also states of mind of those involved. At the time, people surveying a financial arena that was strained used impressionistic standards when deciding whether the dislocation amounted to a crisis. They felt, quite rightly, that they knew a crisis when they saw one.[7] Unsurprisingly, historians have been nervous about relying on such variable, indeterminate criteria. While not rejecting the literary evidence they have usually preferred to place considerable weight upon statistical indicators. Ashton called upon four such series: the volume of Bank of England discounting and its bullion holdings; the price of consols and Bank and East India stock; numbers of bankrupts; and the course of the exchanges.[8] With more specific intentions in mind, Lovell called on just the first of Ashton's series. Mirowski, who while concerned with general macro-economic instability never shied away from joining the fray over when crises happened, used a share price and profit index he had constructed.[9] Disagreement over the timing and nature of crises has arisen both because different weight has been put on the pieces of evidence and because the various series and items of impressionistic evidence are rarely in total agreement. Although historians will always disagree about the emphasis that should be given to various pieces of evidence, it is the apparently conflicting evidence presented which has been at the centre of the dispute. Discord has been produced because it has been loosely assumed that crises were reasonably homogeneous entities, sharing a range of common characteristics. However, by accepting that crises were both similar and dissimilar it is possible to reconcile some of the differences of opinion; there was no single type of

---

[5] Clapham, *The Bank of England*, I, p. 237; Lovell, 'The Role of the Bank of England', p. 14.

[6] Ashton, *Fluctuations*, pp. 131-2; Mirowski, thesis, p. 574.

[7] This is made clear in a recent discussion of the problems of definition by C. P. Kindleberger and J. P. Laffargue, eds. *Financial Crises: Theory, History, and Policy* (Cambridge and Paris, 1982), p. 2.

[8] Ashton, *Fluctuations*, pp. 112-14.

[9] Mirowski, thesis, ch. IV. These indices have been published in two articles: 'The Rise (and Retreat) of a Market: English Joint Stock Shares in the Eighteenth Century', *Journal of Economic History*, XLI (1981), pp. 559-77 and 'Adam Smith, Empiricism, and the Rate of Profit in Eighteenth-century England', *History of Political Economy*, XIV (1982), pp. 178-98.

FINANCIAL CRISES 41

crisis in the eighteenth century, their heterogeneity was as important as their homogeneity.

Financial crises are usually defined as those moments when the financial system(s) or network(s) of the area under discussion suddenly becomes markedly unstable. Important parts of the structure become very strained, perhaps to the point of collapse. Certain types of financial transactions might virtually disappear, evaporating in the heat of the moment. A recent definition has proposed that crises are

> associated with changed expectations that led owners of wealth to try to shift quickly out of one type of asset into another, with resulting falls in prices of the first type of asset, and frequently bankruptcy. The crisis is particularly acute if the asset newly sought is limited in quantity, so that one's chances of getting it are increased by being early.[10]

It is worth stressing a few points here. First, crises are produced by sudden alterations of expectations that are rooted partly in reality and partly in the imagination. Often enough alterations of those expectations are associated with speculative tendencies. Second, crises can be generated within a financial system alone or by articulating growth and speculation in the economy as a whole, or both. Equally, crises have causes some of which determine their precise timing while others create the general conditions favourable to crisis. Third, crises may be generated throughout the whole financial system or in some parts only; consequently, their effect on the wider economy is likely to vary. Depending on the strength of the links within the financial sector and the links between that sector and others a crisis might be either specific or general or somewhere in between. In the eighteenth century the financial system was not static, it developed both in itself and within the context of all economic activity. Certain parts of it grew more vigorously and speculatively than other areas. It is hardly to be expected that the crisis of 1788, for example, should run a similar course to that of 1720. We would expect that as the decades passed crises would probably become more general and less specific as the financial system both increased in size and in the extent of its ties to all economic activity. This expectation can be examined by sketching the possibilities for crises in the eighteenth century before testing them against the historical record to discover whether reality confirms or contradicts such a pattern.

II

Eighteenth-century finance divides far from neatly into three areas: public finance, corporate finance and private finance. Crises could occur in each, but crises on the public and private side were the most important. As Mirowski has recently reiterated, corporate finance was seldom used in enterprise at the time. Between 1688 and 1720 there was considerable speculative activity in joint-stock companies, but many of these were either stillborn or had very short lives. Although before 1720 crises of corporate finance were very possible they were of negligible significance. After 1720 non-governmental corporate

[10] Kindleberger and Laffargue, eds. *Financial Crises: Theory, History and Policy*, p. 2.

finance centred on the insurance companies, the turnpike trusts and the canal companies. The Bubble Act helped to ensure that the speculative element in their formation was kept to a minimum. Moreover, none tied up large amounts of money compared to public and private finance.[11] Corporate finance grew relatively slowly and steadily for the bulk of the eighteenth century, consequently the speculative impetus was small. Although it would be foolish to dismiss corporate finance it seems that in general it probably played a secondary role in causing crises, and for this reason the main focus of attention will be with public and private finance.

How likely was it that public or private finance could experience crises? Kindleberger and Laffargue argued that a crisis happens when there is a rapid and sudden shift from one type of asset to another. On this basis it is possible to outline the changing desirability of the key assets within the financial system. The desirability of any asset depends upon the profit it can generate and the security that is attached to it. Profit (which can be social as well as economic) results from the uses which any asset can be put to, and when the asset is a credit instrument to the rate of interest it generates. An asset's security rests on both its legal position and, crucially, on the guarantees attached to it. Such guarantees, or securities, may be either real or personal— a commodity or an opinion. However, crises are sudden and unexpected occurrences and only some assets can experience such a swift alteration in their desirability to make this possible. By and large, those assets heavily dependent on confidence and most closely associated with speculation would be the most vulnerable. Bearing this matrix of factors in mind, short-term changes in the desirability of financial assets in the public and private sphere can be suggested.

Ever since the onset of inflation in the early sixteenth century the crown had found it ever more difficult to obey that medieval maxim and "live of its own". After the Restoration, crown finances did take some steps along a new path in an attempt to solve the problem but it was the Glorious Revolution and the subsequent wars that necessitated a financial revolution. The national debt was born, and with war so common and so expensive in the eighteenth century public finance tended to grow. Only Walpole was able to resist the tide.[12] The national debt enabled parliament to borrow money from pools of savings by offering interest, short or long dated assets, various financial rewards and a parliamentary guarantee that the debt would be provided for in the future. Investors in the national debt were bound hand and foot to the regime. Consequently, the desirability of assets in public finance depended not just on the rewards being offered relative to other assets but, vitally, to the security of the regime. Over the long term, as the uncertainty of the Revolution Settlement gave way to certainty, confidence in the national debt mounted. But that confidence did not grow unchecked, for it was peculiarly vulnerable to short-term influences: notably the outbreak of war, defeat in

[11] Mirowski, 'The Rise (and Retreat) of a Market'; W. R. Scott, *The Constitution and Finance of English, Scottish and Irish Joint-stock Companies to 1720* (Cambridge, 1912), I, especially chs. XVI-XXII; A. B. Du Bois, *The English Business Corporation after the Bubble Act, 1720-1800* (New York, 1938); G. H. Evans, *British Corporate Finance, 1775-1850* (Baltimore, 1936).

[12] P. G. M. Dickson, *The Financial Revolution in England* (1967); A. C. Carter, *Getting, Spending and Investing in Early Modern Times* (Assen, 1975).

battle and Jacobite threats. Running alongside these factors lay the experimental nature of the form of the national debt in the early days, a speculative element that helped create uncertainty in the desirability of the assets on offer.

In the realm of private finance crises were most likely in the area of paper instruments. Unless very heavily clipped, coinage was highly desirable at moments of stress largely because of its metallic content. It was an almost perfectly liquid asset which could satisfy any debt. Because of the quality of the securities attached to them, mortgages and the pawn—two of the main ways in which credit was raised—were unlikely to suffer crises. However, the same could not be said of paper money and credit instruments. Within private finance in the eighteenth century the rush from one asset to another, described by Kindleberger and Laffargue, was in the direction of increasing the liquidity of one's credit holdings. Usually when it was possible the shift was from bills of exchange to cash. We would expect crises in private finance to be in the area of credit networks, where interconnexions were forged by bills of exchange and, to a lesser extent, promissory notes and accommodation bills. At moments of pressure these assets were unattractive because they were unable to generate much interest (the usury laws stood in the way) and, more important, because they were highly dependent upon personal security. Such security was simply a *belief*, based on an assessment of the individual's creditableness (where issues of character meshed with financial acumen), that repayment would be made. Confidence was a cornerstone of the whole system.

Bills and credit, which of necessity had been a commonplace in overseas trade during the seventeenth century, did not have to pervade all corners of the domestic economy until the eighteenth century. Bills were used to overcome problems caused by the shortage of cash, the uncertainties and risks of transport and the considerable delays that existed in and between production and distribution. Bills were most commonly used in the most advanced regions, and depended on key individuals, such as merchants, along with the banks to ensure that the system worked. But because relationships in bill networks were so dependent upon confidence, marriages between creditor and debtor were likely to be volatile. If prosperity was checked, or perceived as suffering a setback, or if those central individuals or banks had to retrench, then confidence would ebb and the system might collapse.[13]

Discussion so far has stressed that in the eighteenth century financial crises would emanate either from public or private finance, or from both where the two parts were linked closely enough. Nothing has been said of the possible consequences of such crises. That depended on the severity of the crisis and the effectiveness of the ties between the crisis and other areas of the economy. The two immediate tasks are to categorize eighteenth-century crises and to assess their significance.

### III

Because crises happen in financial reality and in peoples' perceptions of financial conditions at the time, it is impossible to present a definitive list of

[13] T. S. Ashton, *An Economic History of England: The Eighteenth Century* (1955), ch. VI. 'The Bill of Exchange and Private Banks in Lancashire, 1790-1830', *Economic History Review*, 2nd ser. XV (1945), pp. 25-35. B. L. Anderson, 'Money and the Structure of Credit in the Eighteenth Century', *Business History*, XII (1970), pp. 85-101.

crisis years. However, by mixing together facts, figures and opinions, Ashton produced a list which both contemporary observers and modern historians would agree included all the main crises and most of the possible ones. He suggested that crises happened in 1701, 1710, 1715, 1720, 1726, 1745, 1761, 1763, 1772, 1778, 1788, 1793, and 1797 (thirteen in all). Which of these were crises of public finance, which of private finance, which of both?

Statistically, crises in public finance can be seen by looking at movements in the prices of Bank, East India Company and South Sea Company shares, as well as the price of consols.[14] Sharp falls in their prices showed a desire to move from them to other assets. Such indicators tell us little or nothing about private finance. Indeed, on the side of private finance the indicators are less satisfactory because of the dominance of London. Pressure to sell bills of exchange is partly evidenced by a decline of the Bank of England's bullion holding and a rise in its discounting. There are also two series which reflect on both public and private sides. First, the course of the exchanges; crises were usually associated with upward movements in exchange rates, though it is impossible to say from this evidence which area of the financial system was suffering a crisis. Second, the incidence of bankruptcy; sharp rises in the figures by themselves can help pinpoint crises, but by looking at the sectoral and geographical composition of bankruptcy at the key moments the nature and importance of the crises can also be detailed. It is the flexibility of the bankruptcy material which is valuable in describing with some accuracy the changing nature of financial crises in eighteenth century England. Bankruptcy figures are not a perfect indicator of the incidence or type of crises but used carefully and cautiously they provide the most useful way of both describing changes in the type of crises and changes in their impact on the economy.[15]

In eighteenth-century England the legal process of bankruptcy was just one of a number of means by which creditors and debtors could deal with insolvency or indebtedness. Moreover, the conditions attached to it made it distinctive and rather different from our modern definition. It could, for example, only be used to deal with the debts of members of the business community who owed at least £100. As a measure of insolvency, therefore, it does not include farmers and landowners unless they also traded; nor does it include the very small craftsman or artisan, the pedlar, petty chapman or hawker.[16] Nevertheless, the scope of bankruptcy was wide, catching the merchant princes alongside small shopkeepers, the large west country clothier and his poorer cousin in the West Riding, the once great goldsmith and the unassuming jeweller. Only those at the very base of the pyramid of enterprise were excluded.

As crises were often short and sudden, it is best to begin by looking at quarterly totals of bankruptcies. The seasonal element which exists in the data has been removed to allow measurement of the extent of other deviations

---

[14] Other series could be employed but these are all conveniently available.

[15] These statistical indicators are discussed in Ashton, *Fluctuations*, pp. 112-14; Lovell, 'The Role of the Bank of England', pp. 8-12, 18-20; Miroswki, thesis, pp. 520-3.

[16] I. P. H. Duffy, 'English Bankrupts, 1571-1861', *American Journal of Legal History*, XXIV (1980), pp. 283-305; 'Bankruptcy and Insolvency in London in the Late Eighteenth and Early Nineteenth Centuries' (unpublished Ph.D. thesis, University of Oxford, 1973), chs. 1-3; J. Hoppit, 'Risk and Failure in English Industry, c. 1700-1800' (unpublished Ph.D. thesis, University of Cambridge, 1984), ch. 1.

FINANCIAL CRISES                                                45

in the quarterly totals from a 61 quarter moving average. This can be presented as a percentage deviation from the trend and reveals clearly the chronology and amplitude of the fluctuations (fig. 1).[17]

Recalling the list of crisis years produced earlier it is clear from Figure 1 that such crises sometimes resulted in only a slight increase in the numbers of bankrupts (1715, 1745, and 1761). Sometimes the rise was not great but was nonetheless marked (1720 and 1763). Finally, there were those occasions when crises coincided with large and dramatic rises in the numbers of bankrupts (1710, 1726, 1772, 1778, 1788, 1793, and 1797).[18] Such crude totals of bankrupts help to describe the effect of crises on the general business environment. By and large the bulk of the crises before 1770 had a limited effect whereas after that date their effect was both general and spectacular. The explanation of this pattern lies, as has already been suggested, in the type of crisis, in the nature of the links between the epicentre of the crisis and the more remote parts of the economy and, finally, in developments within the financial system. The crises of 1701, 1715, 1720, 1745, and 1761 can be shown to have been primarily crises of public finance, the causes of which were largely divorced from the manufacturing and trading economy and the consequences of which were largely contained within the ambit of high finance. Similarly, the crises of 1772 and 1788 were solely of private finance. The remainder—1710, 1726, 1763, 1778, 1793, and 1797—were either crises in both public and private finance, or a crisis in one which coincided with a depression in the other. Corporate finance also made an occasional contribution.

In the bankruptcy material crises of public finance alone are shown by their limited effect on the total number of bankrupts and by the fairly specific sectoral and geographical impact of bankruptcy in those years. Such crises tended to influence London and certain groups within the capital, while others elsewhere were left remarkably untouched. In the three great crises of public finance—1715, 1720, and 1745—the proportion of bankrupts coming from the capital was always higher in the crisis year than in the previous three years. Before 1715 the proportion was 52·0 per cent but in 1715 it was 65·0 per cent. Similarly for the crisis of 1720 the figures were 47·8 per cent and 53·8 per cent, while in the crisis of 1745 the figures were 40·7 per cent and 50·7 per cent.

The limited geographical impact of the crises of 1715, 1720, and 1745 can be explained by the origins of the crises being restricted to the sphere of public finance; by the nature of the links between public and private finance which at that time were relatively weak and poorly formed; and finally by the lack of integration nationally, which largely insulated private finance from a crisis of confidence on a large scale. In 1715, 1720, and 1745 those groups and occupations working in London with close relations with those in the arena of high finance were inevitably strained by crises of public credit. But if these

---

[17] The data has been drawn from the *London Gazette* for the years before 1711 and those after 1764 and from P.R.O. B4/1-20 for the period in between. Adjustments to these figures and a fuller discussion of methods, figures and findings is in my thesis, chs. 2 and 3 and app. 2. There is a break in the data from mid 1723 to the end of 1724.

[18] Because the law of bankruptcy was changed in 1706 it is difficult to use data about bankruptcy when looking at the crisis of 1701.

Figure 1. *Quarterly Fluctuations in Bankruptcy, 1708-1801*

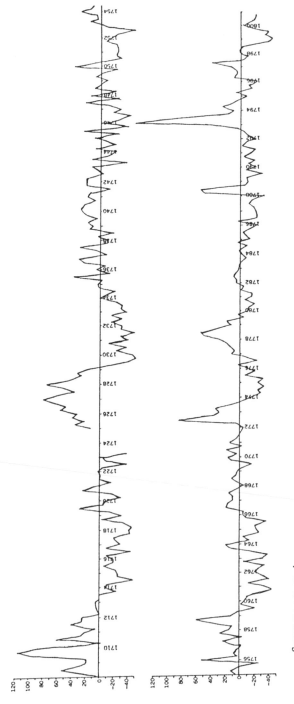

*Source:* see note 17 above.

private financiers did fail, the shock waves that they generated, while intense, went downwards rather than outwards, shaking the bedrock of the City, rather than the surface of the country. This process may be demonstrated clearly by examining the effect of the South Sea Bubble on bankruptcy.

"The economic confusion of the last three months of 1720 has perhaps no parallel in the history of England. A tangle of ruined credit sprawled over the country like a vast, overgrown beanstalk, withering."[19] Public credit was ruined, but the effect of this crisis on private credit is easily exaggerated. It is not true that "The whole system of credit . . . collapsed".[20] Only public credit suffered a true crisis. When the Bubble burst in August 1720 the price of assets in public credit plummeted and notable heads rolled, ensuring the place of the Bubble in the common folklore of English economic history. Between July 1720 and January 1721 the price of Bank stock fell to 59 per cent of its peak value, East India Company stock to 38 per cent and South Sea Company stock to just 15 per cent.[21] The crisis of the national debt was catastrophic. But it is too easy to assume that when the Bubble burst that the whole of trade and industry was afflicted by a similar fit and languished in the depths of depression. Given the extent of the collapse, what is surprising is how few businesses seem to have been pushed to the wall. The numbers of

Table 1. *Quarterly and Annual Totals of Bankruptcy, 1715-22*

| Year | I | II | III | IV | Total |
|------|-----|-----|-----|-----|-------|
| 1715 | 40 | 40 | 36 | 41 | 157 |
| 1716 | 43 | 47 | 21 | 48 | 159 |
| 1717 | 38 | 40 | 31 | 29 | 138 |
| 1718 | 32 | 29 | 26 | 54 | 141 |
| 1719 | 38 | 47 | 54 | 54 | 193 |
| 1720 | 55 | 40 | 36 | 75 | 206 |
| 1721 | 69 | 50 | 46 | 61 | 226 |
| 1722 | 66 | 61 | 28 | 56 | 211 |

*Source:* P.R.O. B4/2-3.
*Note:* These figures have not been de-seasonalized.

bankrupts to be found in 1720 and 1721 (Table 1) suggest that there is only limited validity to the claim that "There was a very marked contraction of business after the South Sea Bubble burst".[22] Although numbers did rise they did so less sharply and to a lesser degree than might have been expected. Throughout 1720 and 1721 the quarterly totals corrected for seasonal influences moved above their trend level only once, in the final quarter of 1720. More telling is the fact that levels of bankruptcy indicate that the depressions of 1709-10 and of the late 1720s were much worse than that caused by the pricking of the Bubble.

In 1720 and 1721 the crisis forced into the pages of the *London Gazette* those whose links with the edifice of public credit were strongest, in particular the goldsmiths and the substantial merchants who played with the funds. Both groups suffered more bankruptcies in 1720 than in the previous year whereas

[19] Carswell, *The South Sea Bubble*, p. 191.
[20] Ibid.
[21] J. E. T. Rogers, *A History of Agriculture and Prices in England* (Oxford, 1902), VII, pt. II, pp. 706-7, 724-5, 817-18.
[22] Mirowski, thesis, p. 545.

virtually all other occupations suffered less. In short, the suddenness and the severity of the crisis was kept within bounds; elsewhere the impact was both slighter and more gradual. For the business community as a whole, through the length and breadth of England, the Bubble was not a catastrophe.

The South Sea Bubble burst because the speculative momentum which inflated it in the first place had, at some time, to pause.[23] It was a crisis caused by an experiment that tried to provide the immature national debt with greater solidity and respectability. With the cause of the crisis so specific to public credit it is hardly surprising that private finance was only slightly affected. Money did become somewhat tighter, but without a specific challenge to the manufacturing and trading base of the economy—such as the onset of a war or a disastrous harvest—it was hardly likely that bill networks would collapse. Moreover, there had been little rapid expansion in trade and industry which otherwise might have been stopped dead in its tracks, crisis fashion. As Chalmers recognized "The South-sea-year, 1720, appears to have involved our merchants in the burst of the bubbles, though it was public, rather than private, credit, which was chiefly affected".[24] Beyond the city financiers and the merchant princes (only a portion of whom tried to sell too late) the greatest sufferers must have been the relatively inexperienced investors, the gentry who had involved themselves in matters about which they knew little and for whom Defoe wept.[25] "It was the small speculator, the petty country gentleman or substantial farmer, jealous of the gains of his wealthy neighbours, who came late into the game, without experience and without London advisers, who was most likely to lose his all."[26] By virtue of the law, insolvent farmers and landowners could not be dealt with via bankruptcy, though their fate could perhaps be seen in the volume of land sales that perhaps followed the Bubble. Yet without them, there would have been no Bubble. It was their inexperience and lack of inside knowledge which fuelled the absurdities of the speculative expansion. The bulk of merchants, who played such a vital role in the bill networks, probably sold their shares before the collapse, limiting the transmission of the shock waves to ordinary businessmen.

Both causes and effects of the crises of 1701, 1715, 1745 and 1761, like that of 1720, were largely contained within the sphere of public finance. In 1701 it was the struggle between the two East India Companies (the old and the new) that was so upsetting; in 1715 and 1745 the Jacobite Rebellions exercised a disturbing influence. In 1761 the growing threat of war against Spain brought the slump in the stocks. On each occasion conditions for enterprise as a whole were not similarly threatened. Taking 1761 as an example, businessmen were probably even faced by an encouraging scene: exports were 25 per cent higher in 1761 than they had been at the onset of the war in 1756; the harvest of 1761 was good, wheat in southern England selling well below normal price; and the war had been going well on land and sea.[27] Because businessmen had

---

[23] Dickson, *The Financial Revolution*, chs. 5 and 6; J. G. Sperling, *The South Sea Company* (Cambridge, Mass. 1962); Carswell, *The South Sea Bubble*.

[24] Chalmers, *An Estimate*, p. xliii.

[25] D. Defoe, *A Tour through the Whole Island of Great Britain*, edited by P. Rogers (Harmondsworth, 1971), p. 111; J. V. Beckett, 'Cumbrians and the South Sea Bubble, 1720', *Transactions of the Cumberland and Westmorland Antiquarian and Archaeological Society*, LXXXII (1982), pp. 141-50.

[26] E. P. Thompson, *Whigs and Hunters* (1975), p. 114.

[27] Ashton, *Fluctuations*, pp. 149-50; P. Deane and W. A. Cole, *British Economic Growth, 1688-1959* (Cambridge, 2nd edn. 1969), p. 320; B. R. Mitchell and P. Deane, *Abstract of British Historical Statistics* (Cambridge, 1962), p. 487; I. R. Christie, *Wars and Revolutions: Britain, 1760-1815* (1982), pp. 45-6.

little reason to feel that opportunities were about to disappear rapidly, the bill market did not experience the short-lived crisis in the securities market.

Before 1770 crises in public finance did not inevitably infect private finance with the same jitters. Crises which did appear to happen in both spheres (1710, 1726, and 1763) were usually crises of public finance which coincided with depressions of trade and industry. Straitened conditions in private finance in 1710 were in large part caused by the bad harvests of 1708 and 1709, which led to an increasing export of specie in 1709.[28] Pressure on private credit may well have been further intensified by a diversion of resources to take advantage of the speculation in insurance that took place in 1709 and 1710.[29] It is hardly surprising, therefore, that the number of bankrupts peaked in the second half of 1709 *before* the crisis in public finance of late 1710, when numbers peaked once again though less dramatically. The crisis of public finance in 1710 coincided with a severe depresion in private finance (though the evidence of a large scale loss of confidence is slight), which had largely run its course before the slump in Exchange Alley.

Similar factors are relevant in explaining the crises of 1726 and 1763. As in 1710, in 1726 the crisis in the area of high finance was unmistakeable. When war with Spain was threatened in 1726 assets of the national debt were sold in considerable amounts; corporate finance was similarly checked. The threat of war also led businessmen to cut back on the credit they had been offering and to seek liquidity in the justified belief that war would hit trade (by 1727 exports were nearly 20 per cent lower than in 1725). A shortage of cash ensued, but as in 1710 evidence of a crisis of confidence is lacking.[30] The depression was intensified in 1727 and 1728 by harvest failure and mortality crises.[31] High numbers of bankrupts throughout 1726-8 reflect not just financial pressures but deep depression arising from a series of unhappy coincidences. What the crisis of 1726 shows, moreover, is that war could precipitate a simultaneous crisis in public, corporate and private finance, even though connexions between them were, as yet, insubstantial. Thus, 1726 brought three crises rather than one, though the real extent of economic dislocation owed much to the bad harvests and crisis mortality that came in the following year.

In 1763 Britain found itself at peace after seven years of war, a war which had established it as the dominant power in Europe. How was it possible for public finance to suffer a crisis if, as was suggested earlier, the usual cause of slumps in the price of stocks were threats to the regime? Alone among the crises of the eighteenth century 1763 was largely Continental in origin, arising from two main sources: the raising of loans for Prussian postwar

---

[28] Wheat prices in 1709 suffered their most severe upward fluctuation of the whole period from 1620 to 1759. W. G. Hoskins, 'Harvest Fluctuations and English Economic History, 1620-1759', *Agricultural History Review*, XVI (1968), p. 16; E. B. Schumpeter, *English Overseas Trade Statistics, 1697-1808* (Oxford, 1960), p. 15.

[29] Scott, *Joint-stock Companies*, I, ch. XIX.

[30] Deane and Cole, *British Economic Growth*, pp. 320-1; Ashton, *Fluctuations*, p. 122; J. de L. Mann, 'Clothiers and Weavers in Wiltshire during the Eighteenth Century', in L. S. Pressnell, ed. *Studies in the Industrial Revolution* (1960), pp. 67-8; Mirowski, thesis, p. 527.

[31] Hoskins, 'Harvest Fluctuations', p. 23; E. A. Wrigley and R. S. Schofield, *The Population History of England, 1541-1871* (1981), p. 333.

reconstruction, and the collapse in Amsterdam of key lynchpins of the international monetary order. The most prominent failure was Gebroeders Neufville, but a total of about twenty major houses collapsed in Amsterdam.[32] However, repeating Clapham, "There was no true crisis and no collapse in London".[33] The crisis was largely limited to international monetary links. Unsurprisingly, numbers of bankrupts did not rocket, but they did become much more common in London. Over the years 1760-2 only 33 per cent of bankrupts had come from the capital, but in 1763 and 1764 the figures were 41 per cent; similarly, the numbers of merchants failing tripled over the same period. That the crisis was not felt over a large area says much about the rather specific cause of the crisis and the limited means by which the shock waves could be communicated to the domestic economy.

Crises which happened before the last third of the century appear either to have created few bankrupts or to have created them for a short period of time in limited areas of the economy. There is little evidence before *c.* 1770 of crises being generated by the workings of private finance, and the impression is that the system was for the most part too little developed to suffer a widespread loss of faith arising from a simple and specific cause such as in public finance. Political factors and the financial innovation of the national debt rendered significant crises probable only on the public side, their specific timing resulting either from a loss of faith in the regime, usually because of war, or rebellion, but occasionally because of the failure of experiments in the financial mechanisms themselves. Crises of public finance did not affect the whole economy and if widespread dislocation did occur then it arose from a coincidence, rather than the communication, of panic. A collapse of the price of shares in Jonathan's Coffeehouse was hardly likely to worry the businessman living and working beyond the shadow of high finance.

As time passed so crises in public finance became less spectacular and less significant. Not only did the Hanoverian regime become more secure internally but high finance allowed victory in war, which established it internationally as a major power. Moreover, whereas at the start of the eighteenth century the new instruments of public credit were experimental and novel, time and experience allowed their testing and eventual acceptance as institutions (though the outbreak of war or defeat in battle continued to exert a depressing effect on the value of assets in the national debt). By the end of the Seven Years War in 1763 the spectre of crises of public credit was less daunting than ever; in their place, however, the fearful apparitions of crises of private finance emerged before the public eye.

## IV

During the last thirty years of the eighteenth century financial crises became almost commonplace, occurring on average every six years. But it was not

[32] C. Wilson, *Anglo-Dutch Commerce and Finance in the Eighteenth Century* (Cambridge, 1941), pp. 167-9.

[33] Clapham, *The Bank of England*, I, 237; Ashton, *Fluctuations*, pp. 125-7; Lovell, 'The Role of the Bank of England', p. 14; L. S. Sutherland, 'Sir George Colebrooke's World Corner in Alum, 1771-3', *Economic History*, III (1934-7), p. 237; F. C. Spooner, *Risks at Sea* (Cambridge, 1983), pp. 77-86. This crisis is nicely detailed in the *London Chronicle*, 9-11 Aug. 1763, pp. 141, 144; 13-16 Aug. 1763, pp. 154, 158; 25-27 Aug. 1763, p. 198, 27-30 Aug. 1763, pp. 202, 207. There is no mention in the paper's reports of a crisis in Britain.

their frequency alone which caused such dismay at the time. Worryingly, their complexion differed from those earlier crises and cast serious doubts on the strength of one part of the financial structure underpinning the growth process, for the later crises not only began to involve the whole business community, but also were mainly caused and structured by the very nature of private credit.

From 1772 crises were always marked by a substantial and quick surge in the numbers of bankrupts, an increase moreover that was not limited to

Table 2. *Proportion of Bankrupts from London, 1769-97*

| Year | % | Year | % |
|------|-----|--------|------|
| 1769-71 | 50·2 | 1790-2 | 42·3 |
| 1772 | 52·6 | 1793 | 34·4 |
| 1775-7 | 45·2 | 1794-6 | 36·9 |
| 1778 | 45·2 | 1797 | 35·9 |
| 1785-7 | 34·1 | | |
| 1788 | 38·8 | | |

*Source: London Gazette.*

London nor to those with the strongest links to high finance. Table 2 demonstrates how even handed the last five crises of the eighteenth century were in their geographical impact. Similarly, the crises of 1778, 1793, and 1797 were very even across the sectors. In 1772 and especially in 1788 there was a tendency for the crisis to concentrate in the textile sector. In 1772-3 the proportion of bankrupts from that sector was 28 per cent, whereas over the previous three years the figure had been 23 per cent. Much the same was true in 1788. Nevertheless, the overriding impression is that crises after 1770 spread well beyond London to engulf the provinces and affected most occupational groups. This can best be explained by looking at the two main crises of this period, 1772 and 1793.

What distinguishes financial crises after 1770 from those before is that they were in large part caused by economic growth. Growth encouraged speculative business expansion funded by trade credit, which occasionally interacted to very damaging effect. Because of the business community's heavy dependence on credit instruments, the stability of which was largely maintained by confidence, because those instruments were easy to create and, finally, because growth encouraged risk-taking and speculation, genuine expansion found itself periodically beset by a debility in private finance that bordered on complete paralysis. Real economic opportunities encouraged an over dependence on unstable financial mechanisms, and real economic fluctuations often generated the specific causes of crises. In particular it was the strengths and weaknesses of bills of exchange that were problematic, being at one moment advantageous but at the next destructive. The growth of foreign trade, agriculture, population, urbanization and industry all encouraged businessmen to expand, usually by increasing their credit relative to their capital base, leaving them exposed if their expectations were not fulfilled rapidly enough to bear the costs of that credit creation. After 1770 financial crises usually resulted from private finance getting out of hand, after the initial foundations for growth had been overtaken by speculation.

In the 1760s and 1770s there were many areas of economic advance in

England. Capital was invested through corporate finance in fixed capital projects such as turnpikes and canals, though other methods were used for financing enclosures and building construction. 1770 saw a marked peak in the number of turnpike acts while seven canals, which eventually raised finance valuing £2·4 million, were initiated between 1766 and 1771.[34] For both canals and turnpikes there was a noticeable setback between 1772 and 1776. But that was not true of enclosures or construction, both of which experienced only a mild check to expansion in 1772 and 1773.[35] All four of these areas experienced some expansion due to speculation. Because the gestation period of capital in all four was relatively long, unrealistic expectations about the timing and volume of returns may have been created. But the check to those expectations in 1772 does not appear to have amounted to a crisis. The speculative tendencies in these four areas was nowhere near as marked as that in individual business expansion. It was the coincidence of this check in fixed capital formation with a crisis in working capital which in 1772 brought such a severe interruption to the trend development of the economy.

Expansion in the late 1760s and early 1770s was not restricted to large-scale, lumpy capital projects. Naturally, growth in transport, agriculture and building did help create a suitable environment for development elsewhere, as did rising population and urbanization. Domestic industry and trade expanded rapidly under these conditions, and were accompanied at the same time by significant growth in overseas trade. The crisis of working capital was generated in both domestic and overseas spheres. Large amounts of unstable finance were linked to what was frequently highly risky expansion. Trade with America in particular helped to fan the flames of instability.[36] America, where population and economy were growing rapidly at this time, was virtually a captive market for British suppliers before the War of Independence. Exports rose dramatically down to 1771, as British merchants extended more and more credit to the planters. That credit was unstable, however; because of the possibilities of a saturated market in the colonies; because credit was often extended for a long period, and because it was poorly secured. It is impossible to quantify accurately the extent of this credit creation, but British merchants claimed that £5 million of debts incurred before 1775 were still unpaid after 1783—an impressively high figure when compared with the £1·3 million invested in canals between 1761 and 1770.[37] In 1771 exports to America surged, glutting the market and necessitating some sort of depression, though

[34] E. Pawson, *Transport and Economy: The Turnpike Roads of Eighteenth-century Britain* (1977), pp. 113, 127, 132; J. R. Ward, *The Finance of Canal Building in Eighteenth-century England* (Oxford, 1974), pp. 29-37.

[35] M. Turner, *English Parliamentary Enclosure* (Folkestone, 1980), pp. 68-70. I have used timber imports as a surrogate measure of construction here. See Mitchell and Deane, *British Historical Statistics*, p. 286.

[36] There were other areas of trade involved, notably the East Indies. See Sutherland, 'George Colebrooke'.

[37] R. B. Sheridan, 'The British Credit Crisis of 1772 and the American Colonies', *J. Econ. Hist.* xx (1960), pp. 161-86; J. M. Price, *Capital and Credit in British Overseas Trade* (Cambridge, Mass. 1980), ch. 7. On p. 122 Price quotes a figure of £6 million owed by the colonists to British merchants in 1774; K. A. Kellock, 'London Merchants and the pre-1776 American Debts', *Guildhall Studies in London History*, I (1974), pp. 109-49; C. H. Feinstein, 'Capital Formation in Great Britain', in P. Mathias and M. M. Postan, eds. *The Cambridge Economic History of Europe*, VII, pt. I, *The Industrial Economies* (Cambridge, 1978), p. 41.

## FINANCIAL CRISES 53

not necessarily a crisis.[38] The crisis element developed out of the financial arrangements on which much of the expansion of domestic and overseas industry was based. Extensive trade credit combined with the improved links within the world of private finance created the possibility of a general collapse of such business credit when confidence vanished. Through the rise of the country banks, the continued dominance of the London discount market, and the importance of London middlemen, strong bonds tied provincial credit networks to one another.

As is well known, the modest amounts of finance needed by most businessmen in the early stages of industrialization were often provided by ploughing back profits from earlier successes and borrowing from friends and relations. There were, however, limits to how much money could be raised by such methods. To seize the opportunities that were emerging in the late 1760s often demanded greater financial freedom than they allowed. A new means of raising funds was developed whereby businessmen paid more attention to the future than to the past: "raising money by circulation" was the process by which businessmen created credit, drawing and redrawing bills of exchange and accommodation notes upon one another without actually having traded goods at all.[39] Economic growth preceding the early 1770s encouraged people to speculate and to take risks. Sometimes the financial underpinning was well considered and unlikely to collapse crisis fashion, usually because of the very nature of the type of finance; most obviously with the use of mortgages or similarly low-risk methods used to fund turnpikes, canals and enclosures. But the successful funding of infra-structural investment stimulated the attention of investors in sectors which lacked a comparable institutional basis to sustain similar expansion. Credit creation was the alternative chosen by individual businessmen as the easiest route to expansion; in times of prosperity the willingness to give credit and to contract debts increases. Such an expansion of credit, however, might be "dangerously easy and attractive".[40]

Credit is dangerous because it is costly, because it has conditions attached to it, and because it is so dependent upon confidence. A system of drawing and redrawing could only have worked if the profits being sought were reaped quickly, before the heavy costs of interest and commission fell due. It is significant, therefore, that activity in two of the main growth sectors just before the onset of the crisis were typically slow to yield returns: overseas trade, where distance caused the delay, and capital intensive projects for which the gestation period was long. A month after the crisis began the *London Chronicle* carried this explanation of the main initiating cause:

> Bills became so universally accepted in *lieu* of Specie, became almost equal in value: and it being in *every one's power* to draw a Bill who could not raise a *shilling* in specie, hence a door was opened for schemers of every denomination, a knot of whom assuming the external semblance of honesty and fair dealing, could *create* that capital they never possessed . . . . And indeed, when Paper-currency gains

---

[38] Exports to the thirteen colonies fell by nearly one-half between the peak of 1771 and trough of 1773. J. J. McCusker, 'The Current Value of English Exports, 1697 to 1800', *William and Mary Quarterly*, 3rd ser. XXVIII (1971), Table IIIA.

[39] A. Smith, *An Inquiry into the Nature and Causes of the Wealth of Nations*, ed. E. Cannan (Chicago, 1976), I, p. 329.

[40] R. G. Hawtrey, *Currency and Credit* (4th ed. 1950), p. 169.

such a footing as to be in *universal use*, it is a matter of no small difficulty so to discriminate as to distinguish the *good* from the *bad* . . . .[41]

Two banks were particularly guilty, the London bank of Neale, James, Fordyce & Down and the Ayr Bank of Douglas, Heron & Co. It was the London bank, largely under the control of Fordyce, that broke first, creating a widespread loss of confidence that determined the timing of the crisis. Fordyce, who had gambled in East India stock and the commodity markets, and who later admitted raising extensive sums by fictitious bills, fled to the Continent. His bank stopped payment on 10 June.[42] News of his failure quickly reached Edinburgh; the old aphorism that no news is good news could never have been truer. The Ayr Bank, which had been particularly guilty of misusing bills of exchange, was thunderstuck.[43] Everywhere, the confidence, which had hitherto kept credit's house of card intact, disappeared. Panic set in and trust vanished. Bankers, new and old, weak and strong, were faced with crowds clamouring at their doors for repayment in cash. With some glee, Horace Walpole wrote on 1 July that "Will you believe, in Italy, that one rascally and extravagant banker had brought Britannia, Queen of the Indies, to the precipice of bankruptcy! It is very true, and Fordyce is the name of the caitiff. He has broke half the bankers".[44] In truth, others had been as foolish as Fordyce and it was not just confidence in the bankers that evaporated but confidence in all debtors in the sphere of private finance; the London representative of an American firm wrote to his partners in Maryland "every man seems afraid of each other".[45] In Leeds by September there was "scarce any Money to be got on personal Secur.y".[46]

Two Scots neatly summarized the novelty of the crisis of 1772. The first saw that "like a company connected by an electrical wire, the people in every corner of the country have almost instantaneously received the same shock".[47] The second, David Hume, wrote to Adam Smith in June 1772, complaining that "We are here in a very melancholy Situation: Continual Bankruptcies, universal Loss of Credit, and endless Suspicions".[48] Although Hume exaggerated by claiming that the crisis was universal—in public finance only the price of East India stock fell significantly—he was very close to the truth. The crisis of 1772 was general, as the causes were all too effectively communicated throughout the prospering economy.

Conditions in 1793 were remarkably similar to those in 1772 and contemporaries advanced strikingly similar explanations for the two crises. Economic growth since 1788 in the rapidly expanding cotton industry (the crisis of 1788

[41] 16-18 July 1772, p. 58. Adam Smith provides a similar analysis, *Wealth of Nations*, I, pp. 327-35. See also Clapham, *The Bank of England*, I, pp. 242-3.

[42] Ashton, *Fluctuations*, p. 128; *Scots Magazine*, XXXIV (1772), p. 311; *London Chronicle*, 20-3 June, 1772, pp. 598-600; *Gentleman's Magazine*, XLII (1772), p. 292.

[43] The Scottish side of 1772 has been given more attention. H. Hamilton, 'The Failure of the Ayr Bank, 1772', *Econ. Hist. Rev.* 2nd ser. VIII (1955-6), pp. 405-17; F. Brady, 'So Fast to Ruin. The Ayr Bank Crash', *Ayrshire Archaeological and Natural History Society Collections*, XI (1973), pp. 25-44; Anon. *The Precipitation and Fall of Mess. Douglas, Heron, and Company, Late Bankers in Air* (Edinburgh, 1778).

[44] P. Cunningham, ed. *The Letters of Horace Walpole* (1891), V, p. 395.

[45] J. M. Price, ed. *Joshua Johnson's Letterbook, 1771-1774* (1979), p. 40.

[46] Quoted in M. Miles, 'The Money Market in the Early Industrial Revolution: The Evidence from the West Riding Attornies, c. 1750-1800', *Bus. Hist.* XXIII (1981), p. 144.

[47] J. Boswell, *Reflections on the Late Alarming Bankruptcies in Scotland* (Edinburgh, 1772), p. 1.

[48] E. C. Mossner and I. S. Ross, eds. *The Correspondence of Adam Smith* (Oxford, 1977), p. 162.

had largely been contained within that area) and over a longer period in other sectors had begun by being well founded, but as growth continued so the inadequacies of safe and sure finance became ever greater. More and more weight came to be put on drawing and redrawing; golden opportunities clouded men's memories of earlier crises.

> A spirit of commercial speculation and commerce had been for some time increasing in every part of the kingdom. . . . The circulating specie being by no means sufficient to answer the very increased demands of trade, the quantity of paper currency brought into circulation, as a supplying medium was so great and disproportionate, that a scarcity of specie was produced which threatened a general stagnation in the commercial world.[49]

Some onlookers at the time were convinced that the villains of the piece were the country bankers who, by investing in the funds and issuing large amounts of paper notes, both created the crisis and ensured that public and private finance were disastrously linked.[50] Prof. Pressnell has clearly demonstrated the error of ascribing the cause of the crisis to the country banks.[51] Nevertheless, they were key players on the stage, helping to determine the way the crisis spread.

In November 1792 the first clouds on the horizon were seen. The wheat harvest had been poor and prices rose to nearly 25 per cent above the previous year. War with France was an immediate threat. In November 1792 a momentary but marked peak in the numbers of bankrupts was accompanied by signs of panic in Exchange Alley.[52] As such the optimism of 1789-91 could hardly continue unrestrained. The check in November 1792 was real enough, though felt mostly in the area of public finance. But it was not until France declared war on Britain on 1 February 1793 that the full weight of a crisis was felt. War hit confidence at every level in public, private and, less significantly perhaps, corporate finance. Most of the fall in price of assets in public finance was experienced during the period when war threatened, before its actual declaration, but the crisis of private finance took place almost exclusively after 1 February. Numbers of bankrupts peaked in April and June 1793. As in 1726, war created more than one crisis in 1793.

The reason why the crisis of 1793 proved to be the worst of the century was not simply the coincidence of massive dislocation in public and private finance, nor because "confidence in their Banks vanished, every creditor was clamourous for payment"; but because there was a very general failure of paper credit that reduced "many respectable, prudent, and, ultimately, very solvent persons to the mortifying necessity of stopping payment".[53] The intensity of the rush for liquidity was allowed by the better communications that had been established in the financial world by the rise of the country

[49] W. Cobbett, ed. *The Parliamentary History of England*, xxx (1817), p. 739.

[50] Ibid. p. 741; W. Playfair, *Better Prospects to the Merchants and Manufacturers of Great Britain* (1793), p. 4; *London Chronicle*, 27-9 Nov. 1792, p. 520; 23-5 April 1793, p. 396; Macpherson, *Annals of Commerce*, IV, p. 266.

[51] Pressnell, *Country Banking*, pp. 457-9.

[52] Mitchell and Deane, *British Historical Statistics*, p. 487; *London Chronicle*, 22-4 Nov. 1792, p. 497; 27-9 Nov. 1792, p. 520; 29 Nov.-1 Dec. 1792, p. 521; Ashton, *Fluctuations*, p. 133.

[53] F. Baring, *Observations on the Establishment of the Bank of England, and on the Paper Circulation of the Country* (1797), p. 20; H. Thornton, *An Enquiry into the Nature and Effects of the Paper Credit of Great Britain*, ed. F. A. von Hayek (1939), p. 187.

banks, greater use of bills and economic growth. The system of private finance had become more systematized.

Just as the causes of the crisis had been fostered by growth so it was the prospering areas of the economy—the ports of Bristol, Liverpool and London, together with the growing centres of industry in Lancashire, Yorkshire and Warwickshire—which felt the full force of the crisis. Merchants, who acted as central coordinators in the credit networks, and those in the building industry, who were famously speculative, were the only groups to suffer disproportionately. Lack of confidence was universal.

Economic growth must in part be the product of speculative decisions, or what is usually called risk-taking. In the late eighteenth century that uncertainty was encouraged by, and in turn encouraged, a particular structure of credit. A vicious spiral leading from growth to crisis emerged. Bills of exchange and other credit instruments were vital in allowing the seizing and the creating of opportunities, but the form which credit took created possibilities for massive instability.[54] In part, the crises of 1772, 1778, 1788, 1793, and 1797 can all be seen as the early growing pains of the first industrializing nation. The nature of those pains and the structure of distress, along with part of the impetus for growth itself, rested on a financial edifice that was so flexible that it was capricious. Substantive growth after 1770 was often founded on solid foundations, but the opportunities that growth generated also encouraged businessmen to exploit them by using methods which increased the risk of instability. The periodic collapses of trade credit, which continued well into the nineteenth century, were not inevitable though. Just as the possibility of such crises was in part caused by growth, the immediate cause usually took the form of a real check to that growth. Credit, like tinderwood, only flared up when caught by a spark such as the outbreak of war, harvest failure, a downturn in foreign trade, a movement in the building cycle or the bankruptcy of central coordinators in credit networks.

## V

Before about 1770 financial crises tended to be restricted to the sphere of public credit and the national debt, where both the origins and the ill effects of the crises were largely concentrated. After 1770 crises were more general, often hitting both public and private finance, sometimes because the loss of confidence originated from the same cause. The background cause of crises of public finance was obviously the growing importance of public credit itself. But the specific cause of the timing of those crises was the loss of confidence in the regime (a factor which never completely disappeared) and from the experimental nature of the system itself. Public credit, immature, experimental and innovative in 1700, naturally took time to find its feet; by George III's reign it had done so. Consequently, crises of public credit became less severe, related to the momentary loss of confidence arising from the onset or progress of war. It was about this time that the various arms of the financial system,

---

[54] On these lines see Price, *Capital and Credit*, p. 122 and Anderson, 'Money and the Structure of Credit', pp. 95-6.

public and private, began to be effectively interlocked for the first time.[55] So that at just the moment when we might have expected to see crises in the public sphere spilling over into the private sphere crises in the former were becoming less significant. Crises did affect more than just public or corporate or private finance, but a crisis in more than one of these three areas simultaneously did not arise from the communication of panic from one to another; the common causal factor was the loss of confidence arising from the same event, usually war. In a single crisis year up to three crises might have occurred. If this is understood then much of the confusion about the appearance and importance of financial crises in the eighteenth century can be removed. Nevertheless, the forging of links within the financial system was vital in ensuring that crises in the world of private credit were as punishing as they were after 1770.

Banks, especially the country banks, together with the great merchants acting as coordinators of bill networks, constituted the main connexions binding the separate parts of the financial world together. Those connexions, loose at first, rapidly became firm. In the second half of the century the number of country banks increased from a handful to around 400.[56] Because they maintained deposits with London bankers, were involved in local bill networks and invested in the funds, these new banks joined public and private finance together and spun a new and more powerful web within private finance itself.[57] Merchants and middlemen, especially those from London, operated in a similar way. By controlling provincial credit networks and being linked to one another they provided a means, just as did the banks, whereby shock waves could hit all those actively involved in the world of credit. It was not until the nineteenth century that some areas of the developing economy managed to liberate themselves from their dependence upon London middlemen and London credit. In the eighteenth century, indeed, as the prospering regions expanded they established more and more credit links between the centre and the periphery.

Such developments allowed crises of private credit, challenging the usual view that credit played a benign and important role in eighteenth-century economic growth. The evidence of the financial crises suggests that credit was an ambiguous blessing. Crises of public and private credit were, in large part, a function of their novelty, most likely where speculation and dependence on confidence were greatest. Crises of private credit were the product of growth, the increasing use of credit to enable growth, and the nature of credit itself. The fundamental cause of crises of private finance was the increasing use of working capital, more specifically trade credit, associated with growth, while the proximate cause which determined their precise appearance was the occurrence of sudden changes in economic conditions, or the over-expansion of the particular mechanisms being employed. Credit, public and private, bred life and death. In the long run, of course, it more than payed its way,

---

[55] R. V. Eagly and V. K. Smith, 'Domestic and International Integration of the London Money Market, 1731-1789', *J. Econ. Hist.* XXXVI (1976), pp. 198-212.

[56] Pressnell, *Country Banking*, ch. 2.

[57] Ibid. ch. 4; K. F. Dixon, 'The Development of the London Money Market, 1780-1830' (unpublished Ph.D. thesis, University of London, 1962); P. Hudson, 'The Role of Banks in the Finance of the West Yorkshire Wool Textile Industry, c. 1780-1850', *Bus. Hist. Rev.* LV (1980), pp. 379-402.

but the short run has shown the problems encountered. We might recall 1 Timothy VI, 9: "But they that will be rich, fall into temptation, and a snare, and into many foolish and hurtful lusts, which drown men in destruction and perdition". Growth provided the temptation, credit the snare, and crises destruction and perdition.

*Magdalene College, Cambridge*

# [2]

Excerpt from *A Restrospective on the Classical Gold Standard 1821–1931*, 233–64

5          # The Gold Standard and the Bank of England in the Crisis of 1847

### Rudiger Dornbusch and Jacob A. Frenkel

> When there occurs a state of panic—a state which cannot be foreseen or provided against by law—which cannot be reasoned with, the government must assume a power to prevent the consequence which may occur.
> —Sir Robert Peel (1847)[1]

## 5.1  Introduction

The acceleration of world inflation during the 1970s along with the rise in the rate of unemployment and the general instability of money and prices have renewed interest in the operation of the gold standard. Recent proposals for a return to some variant of the gold standard stem from the belief that a return to such a standard will restore macroeconomic stability. The belief is based on a casual look at history with the consequent inference that the gold standard contributed to the stability of the system. That view of price stability was supported by Keynes who argued in *Essays in Persuasion*:

> The course of events during the nineteenth century favoured such ideas. . . . The remarkable feature of this long period was the relative *stability* of the price level. Approximately the *same* level of price ruled in or about the years 1826, 1841, 1855, 1862, 1867, 1871, and 1915. Prices were also level in the years 1844, 1881, and 1914. . . . No

Rudiger Dornbusch is professor of economics at the Massachusetts Institute of Technology and a research associate of the National Bureau of Economic Research.

Jacob A. Frenkel is professor of economics at the University of Chicago and a research associate of the National Bureau of Economic Research.

This paper is a revision of one presented at the conference "A Retrospective on the Classical Gold Standard, 1821–1931," at Hilton Head Island, South Carolina in March 1982. An earlier version was presented at the Workshop in Economic History at the University of Chicago in October 1971. The authors are indebted to Eliana Cardoso, Karl Brunner, Charles Goodhart, and the conference participants for helpful comments and to Lauren Feinstone and Alberto Giovannini for research assistance. A special debt is owed to Anna Schwartz for drawing the authors' attention to the important role of public deposits. Financial support was provided by grants from the National Science Foundation. This research is part of the NBER Program in International Studies and Business Fluctuations. The views expressed are those of the authors and not necessarily those of the NBER, Inc.

wonder that we came to believe in the stability of money contracts over a long period. The metal *gold* might not possess all the theoretical advantages of an artificially regulated standard, but it could not be tampered with and had proved reliable in practice. (Keynes 1932, pp. 88–89)

But another view of the history of the gold standard during the nineteenth century reveals a succession of crises of varying length and depth. As documented by Hyndman [1932] 1967, the nineteenth century in the United Kingdom witnessed at least eight serious crises: in 1825, 1836–39, 1847, 1857, 1866, 1873, 1882, and 1890. Given this perspective of the gold standard era the relevant question should be not only how the gold standard worked but also why did it fail.

The origins of the various crises during the gold standard era vary. Some were "real" and some were "financial," some autonomous (like a massive harvest failure), and some induced by mistaken policies. Of course, no proponent of the gold standard has suggested that it would eliminate harvest failures. The question, therefore, is whether and to what extent the policies that are induced by the rules of the game mitigate or exacerbate the severity of crises. Our paper examines the 1847 crisis in Great Britain. That year, well documented by parliamentary inquiries, is of special interest because the origin of the crisis was "real." A harvest failure gave rise to commercial distress and financial panic, the extremity of which was remarkable. Our analysis examines the operation of the gold standard, the policies of the Bank of England, as well as the speed and extent of international adjustment in the form of gold and capital flows.

The paper proceeds as follows: Section 5.2 provides a brief account of the main events in the United Kingdom during 1847. Section 5.3 studies the institutional setting of the gold standard and spells out a formal model of the financial markets. The two crises of April and October 1847 are studied in section 5.4. In section 5.5 we discuss whether suspension of Peel's Act was necessary. The paper concludes with some observations on the gold standard as a monetary system.

## 5.2   Outline of Events

The events of 1847 were initiated by a major harvest failure in Ireland and England in 1846. The shortage of domestic food supplies led to large price increases and trade deficits which in turn brought about an external drain of bullion from the Bank of England. These developments occurred against the background of the "railway mania" which commenced in 1845. The railway mania along with the food shortage resulted in a massive financial crisis, the analysis of which is the subject of this paper. The characteristics of the 1847 crisis were stated by John Stuart Mill:

It is not, however, universally true that the contraction of credit, characteristic of a commercial crisis, must have been preceded by an extraordinary and irrational extension of it. There are other causes; and one of the more recent crises, that of 1847, is an instance, having been preceded by no particular extension of credit, and by no speculations; except those in railway shares. . . . The crisis of 1847 belonged to another class of mercantile phenomena. There occasionally happens a concurrence of circumstances tending to withdraw from the loan market a considerable portion of the capital which usually supplies it. These circumstances, in the present case, were great foreign payments, (occasioned by a high price of cotton and an unprecedented importation of food,) together with the continual demands on the circulating capital of the country by railway calls and the loan transactions of railways companies. . . . This combination of a fresh demand for loans, with a curtailment of the capital disposable for them, raised the rate of interest, and made it impossible to borrow except on the very best security. Some firms . . . stopped payment: their failure involved more or less deeply many other firms which had trusted them; and, as usual in such cases, the general distrust, commonly called a panic, began to set in, and might have produced a destruction of credit equal to that of 1825, had not circumstances which may almost be called accidental, given to a very simple measure of the government (the suspension of the Bank Charter Act of 1844) a fortunate power of allaying panic, to which, when considered in itself, it had no sort of claim. (Mill 1871, bk. 3, chap. 12, section 3)

Table 5.1 reports selected data for the period 1845–48. 1847 was characterized by a deterioration in the balance of trade and the terms of trade as well as by a significant rise in the price of wheat and the other price indexes.

The trade-balance deficit caused gold outflows and an accompanying reduction in the supply of Bank of England liabilities and credit. While

**Table 5.1**            **Selected Data for Great Britain, 1845–48**

|                                | 1845   | 1846   | 1847   | 1848   |
| ------------------------------ | ------ | ------ | ------ | ------ |
| Exports                        | 69.4   | 67.0   | 70.5   | 61.2   |
| Imports                        | 88.4   | 87.3   | 112.1  | 88.2   |
| Trade balance                  | − 19.0 | − 20.3 | − 41.6 | − 27.0 |
| Terms of trade                 | 119.6  | 115.1  | 112.5  | 121.7  |
| Price of wheat                 | 50.8   | 54.7   | 70.0   | 50.5   |
| Price of agricultural products | 120.0  | 118.0  | 125.0  | 107.0  |
| Price of industrial products   | 99.0   | 99.0   | 104.0  | 92.0   |

*Source*: All data are from Mitchell 1962.

*Notes*: The balance-of-payments data are measured in £ million; the terms of trade are an index of the net barter terms (1880 = 100); the price of wheat is in shillings per imperial quarter; and the prices of agricultural and industrial products are the Rousseaux price indexes (1885 = 100).

the external bullion drain was one direct consequence of the harvest failure, a second one was the extensive commercial failures arising from speculative forward purchases of foodstuffs for delivery in mid-1847. By the time these contracts came to maturity, a good harvest for 1847 was expected, and that change in expectations led to a drastic decline in spot prices and default of many trading establishments. In addition, the precarious financial position of many enterprises that had taken part in the railway speculations reduced confidence in the financial integrity of the system and resulted in an internal drain of bank reserves.

Figures 5.1–5.3 show the weekly data for the stock of bullion in the Bank of England, the Bank's note reserve, the stock of notes held outside the Bank, and the price of consols (the sources of the data are listed in the Appendix).

Two major crises occurred during the year. The April crisis arose from the reversal of Bank of England credit policy. Having followed to that date a policy of sterilization of the credit effect of the deficit by lowering its reserve-deposit ratio, the Bank reversed its policy in April by raising the discount rate and only sparingly accommodating the discount market. The suddenness and severity of the action led to a panic as the best houses in the trade found it impossible to obtain domestic credit.

The panic in October by contrast was due to an internal drain that resulted from a loss of confidence in the convertibility of bank deposits into Bank of England notes and was essentially due to the operation of Peel's Act, which is described in the next section. That crisis was overcome by the joint effect of a suspension of the prohibition of fiduciary issue and of a discount rate at an unprecedented level of 8 percent. The

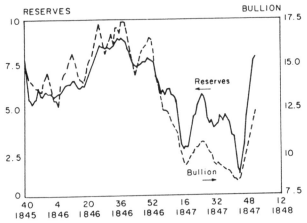

Fig. 5.1          Bank of England holdings of bullion and note reserves (in million £).

**237**     The Bank of England in the Crisis of 1847

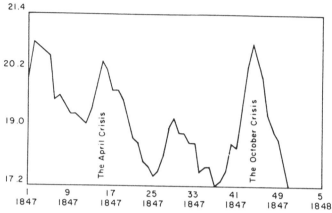

**Fig. 5.2**                 Stock of currency, 1847 weekly data (in million £).

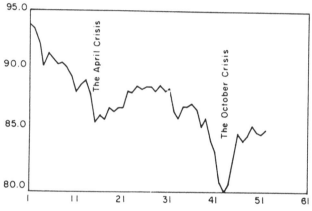

**Fig. 5.3**                 Price of 3 percent consols, 1847 weekly data.

policy led domestically to a full return of confidence and a reduction in defensive liquidity positions while at the same time attracting gold and capital from the rest of the world. By the end of the year the Bank of England had restored its note reserve as well as its stock of bullion to the levels prevailing prior to the year of crisis. Both in April and in October the timing of the public-sector-deposit withdrawals aggravated significantly Bank of England liquidity problems and contributed to precipitating the crises.

   The policies pursued to alleviate the October panic were an early application of by now well-accepted central-banking principles. In the subsequent section we develop an analytical framework to study the interaction of external payments and the financial system.

## 5.3   Institutions and a Model of Financial Markets

In what follows we discuss the events of 1847 in the context of a simple model. The model establishes how the rate of interest is determined by the existing stock of bullion, currency preferences of the public, and reserve behavior of the Bank of England. The analysis starts with the institutional setting, namely the provisions of Peel's Act of 1844.

### 5.3.1   The Provisions of Peel's Act and the Money Supply

Peel's Act, passed by Parliament in 1844, essentially enacted the doctrine of the "currency school."[2] The main provisions were the following:

1. The Bank was separated into Banking and Issue departments.

2. The fiduciary note issue was limited to fourteen million pounds sterling, and the supplementary note issue required a 100-percent marginal bullion reserve.

3. Notes were issued for bullion at 13.17s.9d pound sterling per ounce of gold.

The consolidated balance sheet of the Issue and Banking departments is shown in table 5.2. Several points are worth noting. First, public deposits, including in particular the Exchequer and the account for debt service (entitled "For Payment of Dividends"), are distinguished from private deposits that include bankers' accounts. Second, on the liability side, the item "circulation" refers to Bank of England notes including seven-day and other bills. The latter remain less than one million pounds throughout. On the asset side, the item "bullion" refers to silver and gold bullion as well as coin in the Bank.

To study the Bank of England as it operated under Peel's Act, we show in table 5.3 the corresponding disaggregated balance sheets of the Banking and Issue departments, respectively.

In analyzing the balance sheet two comments are relevant: First, the Issue Department has security holdings in the amount of £14 million that back the fiduciary component, $(F)$, of note issue, $(N)$, but at the margin there is 100 percent backing of note issue. Furthermore, note issue is confined to the Issue Department. Second, the Banking Department holds part of the Bank of England note issue as reserve, $(R)$, against its deposit liabilities, $(D + G)$.

The money supply—by which is meant here the supply of Bank of England liabilities—equals the sum of currency and *private* deposits, and the monetary base equals the sum of currency and reserves. With these definitions we express the proximate determinants of the money supply in equation (1):

$$(1) \qquad M \equiv \frac{1 + c}{c + r\alpha} [B + F] = m(c, r)[B + F],$$

239     The Bank of England in the Crisis of 1847

Table 5.2          The Consolidated Bank of England Balance Sheet,
                   17 April 1847 (in £)

*Assets*

Public securities:
  Advances on Exchequer bills:
    Deficiency                           1,315,000
    Other Exchequer bills                    —
  Exchequer bills purchased                10,000
  Stock and annuities                   9,800,000
                                                          11,125,000

Private securities:
  Bills discounted:
    London                               6,375,000
    Country                              4,280,000
                                                          10,655,000
  East India bonds                         466,000
  City bonds, &c.                        4,140,000
  Mortgage                                 512,000
Advances:
  Bills of exchange                        931,000
  Exchequer bills, stock, &c.              407,000
                                                           6,456,000

                                                          28,236,000
            Bullion                                        9,330,000

  TOTAL                                                   37,566,000

*Liabilities*

Circulation:
  London                                14,274,000
  Country                                6,879,000
                                                          21,153,000

Deposits, public, viz.
  Exchequer account                       712,000
  For payment of dividends              1,232,000
  Savings banks, &c.                      259,000
  Other public accounts                   808,000
                                                           3,011,000

Deposits, private, viz.
  Railways                              1,228,000
  London bankers                        1,695,000
  East India company                      536,000
  Bank of Ireland, Royal Bank
    of Scotland, &c.                      297,000
  Other deposits                        5,129,000
  Deposits at branches                  1,120,000
                                                          10,005,000

  TOTAL                                                   34,169,000

*Source*: United Kingdom, Parliament 1848a, app. 8, p. 131.

240       **Rudiger Dornbusch and Jacob A. Frenkel**

Table 5.3                    **Bank of England Disaggregated Balance Sheet**

| Banking Department | | Issue Department | |
|---|---|---|---|
| Assets | Liabilities | Assets[a] | Liabilities |
| Note reserves ($R$) | Private deposits ($D$) | Gold ($B$) | Notes ($N$) |
| Loans ($L$) | Public deposits ($G$) | Securities ($F$) | |

[a]As usual, we suppress the equity component in the balance sheet.

where $m(c, r) \equiv (1 + c)/(c + r\alpha)$ is the money multiplier. The ratio of total to private deposits is denoted by $\alpha \equiv (D + G)/D$, $c$ denotes the currency–private-deposit ratio of the nonbank public, and $r$ is the actual reserve–total-deposit ratio of the Banking Department.[3] From equation (1) it can be seen that an increase in bullion $B$, given the reserve- and currency-deposit ratios, will increase the money stock as will a reduction of the ratio of total to private deposits and of the reserve- and currency-deposit ratios. Throughout this paper the discussion is confined to the supply of Bank of England note and deposit liabilities.

### 5.3.2   The Financial Model

The currency-deposit ratio is determined by institutional factors as well as by the reserve-deposit ratio. Specifically, a rise in the actual reserve-deposit ratio, $r$, is assumed to enhance confidence in the convertibility of deposits into notes (internal convertibility), and therefore it reduces the desired currency-deposit ratio, $c$. This relation between $c$ and $r$ is expressed by equation (2):

$$(2) \qquad c = c(r), \ c' \leqslant 0.$$

With this assumption the money-supply function (1) becomes:

$$(3) \qquad M = \tilde{m}(r)[B + F]; \ \tilde{m}' \leqslant 0.$$

where $\tilde{m}(r) \equiv m(c(r), r)$.

Our specification implies that a rise in the reserve-deposit ratio exerts two effects on the money multiplier. First, the ratio reduces the multiplier directly through the increased use of high-powered money by the Banking Department; and second, the rise in the reserve-deposit ratio raises confidence and thereby reduces the currency-deposit ratio, which in turn increases the money multiplier. In what follows we assume that the net effect of a higher reserve-deposit ratio is to lower the money multiplier, that is, $\tilde{m}' < 0$. This may appear plausible at first sight but is in fact a strong assumption since it eliminates the possibility of a dominating impact of the internal convertibility problem.

The demand for real balances is assumed to depend on real income, $y$,

**241**   The Bank of England in the Crisis of 1847

as well as on the rate of interest, $i$, in the conventional way. Monetary equilibrium requires that the real money stock, $M/P$, equals the demand for real balances, $L(\ )$ as in equation (4):

(4)             $\tilde{m}(r)[B + F]/P = L(i, y); \qquad L_i < 0, L_y > 0.$

Focusing on the short run of weeks or months rather than a year or more, we take both prices and output as exogenous to the financial sector.[4] With this assumption and with a given fixed stock of fiduciary issue, equation (4) can be solved for the equilibrium interest rate as a function of the reserve-deposit ratio and the stock of bullion:

(4′)             $i = i(r, B; \ldots); \qquad i_r > 0, i_B < 0.$

The adjustment of the Bank's lending policy, motivated by prudence and profit, is described in equation (5). The Banking Department adjusts gradually, raising the reserve-deposit ratio through credit contraction, in proportion to the discrepancy between the desired reserve-deposit ratio $\phi(\ )$ and the actual ratio, $r$. Thus,

(5)             $\dot{r} = v[\phi(i) - r], \phi' < 0.$

In equation (5) the desired reserve-deposit ratio, $\phi(i)$, declines as the rate of interest increases. This decline reflects the behavior of the Banking Department: in response to more profitable loan opportunities the desired liquidity of the balance sheet is reduced.

A specification of the rate of inflow of bullion completes the model. The rate of inflow of bullion or the balance of payments, denoted by $\dot{B}$, depends on the exogenous trade balance as well as on the rate of capital inflow. Capital flows respond positively to the international interest differential, $i - i^*$, and the foreign interest rate, $i^*$, is taken as given:

(6)             $\dot{B} = B(i - i^*; \ldots); \dot{B}_i > 0.$

Again, we concentrate on the short term and therefore leave relative prices and output as exogenous to the model.

### 5.3.3  Formal Dynamics

Equations (4′), (5), and (6) represent a dynamic model of the interaction between the Banking Department's credit policy and the balance of payments. Substituting equation (4′) in equations (5) and (6) yields the following pair of equations:

(7)             $\dot{r} = G(r, B); G_r < 0, G_B > 0.$

(8)             $\dot{B} = H(r, B); H_r > 0, H_B < 0.$

where the signs of the partial derivatives follow from the previous assumptions. It is readily verified that the system shown in figure 5.4 must be stable.

In figure 5.4 the $\dot{r} = 0$ schedule shows the locus of reserve-deposit ratios and levels of bullion at which the Banking Department is in equilibrium with respect to its liquidity position. Therefore, along that schedule the reserve-deposit ratio is neither rising nor falling. At points above the schedule, the high reserve-deposit ratio implies a low real-money supply and thus high interest rates. The preferred reserve-deposit ratio is low, and therefore above the $\dot{r} = 0$ schedule the reserve-deposit ratio is being lowered. Conversely, below the $\dot{r} = 0$ schedule, the Banking Department seeks to become more liquid because interest rates are low, and therefore the reserve-deposit ratio is raised.

Along the $\dot{B} = 0$ schedule the balance of payments is in equilibrium. Points below and to the right of the schedule correspond to high money supplies, low interest rates, capital outflows, and therefore deficits and falling bullion. By contrast, points to the left of the schedule involve high interest rates and growing levels of bullion. Along the $\dot{B} = 0$ schedule the interest rate is compatible with external balance. The interest rate is higher above and to the left of the schedule and lower below and to the right of the schedule. The relative slopes of the two schedules are implied by the previously assumed restrictions.

As the arrows indicate, the dynamic model of the financial sector must be stable and the approach to equilibrium cannot be oscillatory. From any initial reserve-deposit ratio and stock of bullion, the adjustment process leads to the steady state at point A where the Bank's liquidity position is in equilibrium and external payments are balanced.

The response of the Bank's reserve-deposit ratio to the rate of interest is reflected in the slope of the $\dot{r} = 0$ schedule. The less responsive the

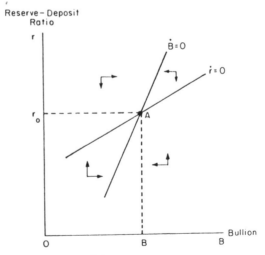

**Fig. 5.4**          Financial model.

**243**     The Bank of England in the Crisis of 1847

Bank, the flatter the schedule; in the extreme, when the Bank is entirely unresponsive, the desired reserve-deposit ratio is constant and the $\dot{r} = 0$ schedule is horizontal. As the reserve-deposit ratio becomes more responsive, the schedule steepens until, in the limit, its slope coincides with that of the $\dot{B} = 0$ schedule. The responsiveness of the reserve-deposit ratio, of course, determines the extent to which interest rates move in the adjustment process. If the reserve-deposit ratio declines in response to high interest rates, then a shortage of bullion will in part be offset by increased lending on the part of the Bank and interest rates therefore will tend to be lower, the balance of payments will be smaller, and the rate of adjustment will be slower. Conversely, if the reserve-deposit ratio is unresponsive, a shortage of bullion implies a sharper reduction in the money stock, high equilibrium interest rates, larger capital flows, and faster adjustment.

### 5.3.4   The Adjustment Process

The traditional model of the price-specie-flow mechanism, originating with David Hume, emphasizes the impact of relative prices on the trade balance and hence on the balance of payments and the international flow of bullion. A deterioration of the external balance due to increased aggregate spending or an adverse development of net exports will lead to bullion export, monetary deflation, declining spending, and price deflation. Both the decline in spending and deflation work to restore external balance.

The model we have sketched here, on the contrary, places emphasis on capital flows and banking policy as the main factors in the adjustment process. The two views of the adjustment mechanism are of course complementary, although they may well correspond to different adjustment periods. In the short run, banking policy and capital flows are likely to be the main factors determining bullion flows, since, in the short run, prices and trade flows do not adjust to the full, possible extent.

The role of capital flows in the adjustment process was recognized by contemporaries. John Stuart Mill, in particular, noted:

> It is a fact now beginning to be recognised, that the passage of the precious metals from country to country is determined much more than was formerly supposed, by the state of the loan market in different countries, and much less by the state of prices. (Mill 1871, bk. 3, chap. 8, section 4)

In addition to the difference between the balance of trade and the capital account in facilitating adjustment, there is another aspect of the adjustment process that deserves emphasis. The traditional representation of the gold standard takes it to be an automatic, nondiscretionary adjustment. Bullion flows are matched one-for-one by changes in the amount of currency outstanding. This is, of course, not the case once the reactions of the Banking Department are taken into account. Changes in the reserve-deposit ratio of the Banking Department affect the money stock independently of the existing stock of bullion. The question then arises whether during the 1847 episode the Banking Department's credit policy might in fact have amounted to partial or even complete *sterilization* of bullion flows. The possibility of credit expansion by the Bank and of loss of note reserves to finance the export of bullion is suggested by the data which reveal a high correlation between weekly changes in bullion and in note reserves.

Consider an autonomous, transitory improvement in the trade balance which leads to an inflow of bullion and therefore to a monetary expansion. The monetary expansion lowers the interest rate, and, with a constant reserve-deposit ratio (or a flat $\dot{r} = 0$ schedule in figure 5.4), the lower interest rate leads to capital outflows and thereby to restoration of the initial equilibrium. Now if, on the contrary, the reserve-deposit ratio rises due to the Banking Department response to the reduced profitability of loans, then the rise in the reserve-deposit ratio dampens the decline in interest rates and therefore slows down the adjustment process. The Banking Department's reaction to the interest rate will only slow the speed of adjustment but will not eliminate the adjustment process. Thus our model is also capable of incorporating a partial sterilization policy with an effect of dampening interest-rate movements and reducing the speed of adjustment.

Changes in the reserve-deposit ratio enter consideration in another respect. If the Bank, perhaps in response to a loss of confidence on the part of the public, decides to raise the reserve-deposit ratio, then this raise, of course, leads to a reduction in the supply of money and credit. Interest rates rise and that state persists until bullion inflows accommodate the desired increase in reserves. The model suggests therefore that changes in the Bank's reserve preferences may be an important source of macroeconomic disturbance.

The possibility of internal inconvertibility turns out to be an important issue in the 1847 crisis. Internal inconvertibility would arise if the Banking Department should become sufficiently illiquid not to be able to redeem its deposit liabilities in notes. Thus there is a clear distinction between external or gold convertibility and internal or note convertibility. Note convertibility involves the Banking Department's reserve-deposit ratio. If the reserve-deposit ratio falls too low, the public loses confidence and reacts by raising the currency-deposit ratio. While our model embodies this reaction of the public, the reaction is for the moment not allowed to exercise a dominating influence.[5]

**245**     The Bank of England in the Crisis of 1847

### 5.3.5  Some Evidence

Before discussing in detail the various crises that occurred during 1847, we look at some evidence that is consistent with the general analytical framework outlined in this section.

The dynamic model was summarized by equations (7) and (8). Changes in the reserve-deposit ratio depend negatively on the level of that ratio and positively on the stock of bullion, while changes in the stock of bullion depend positively on the reserve-deposit ratio and negatively on the stock of bullion. In table 5.4 we report regressions of the changes in the reserve-deposit ratio and bullion on the previous-week levels of these variables. The coefficients have the predicted sign and are statistically significant. We view these estimates as providing support for the analytical framework that was developed in this section, and we turn next to a more detailed analysis of the crises of 1847.

### 5.4  Financial Markets and the Balance of Payments in 1847

### 5.4.1  The April Crisis

The harvest failure of 1846–47 depleted the bullion in the Bank in the fall of 1846 and more so in early 1847. Table 5.5 shows the development of bullion, note reserves, the reserve-deposit ratio, the discount rate, and the stock of notes in the hands of the public during the first half of 1847. The table brings out forcefully the magnitude of this depletion. Indeed, over the period 2 January to 17 April 1847, bullion fell by about 40 percent and note reserves in the Banking Department declined by about 70 percent. The extraordinary decline in the reserve-deposit ratio from 46 percent to 19.6 percent implies that the Bank sterilized substantially the effect of gold outflows. The decline in the reserve-deposit ratio occurred

| Table 5.4 | The Dynamic Model, 1847 Weekly Data (standard errors in parentheses) | | | | | |
|---|---|---|---|---|---|---|
| Dependent Variable | Constant | $r_{t-1}$ | $B_{t-1}$ | $R^2$ | D.W. | $\rho$ |
| $\Delta r_t$ | −0.119 (0.099) | −0.625 (0.151) | $0.301(10^{-7})$ $(0.122)10^{-7}$ | .36 | 1.85 | .75 |
| $\Delta B_t$ | $0.337(10^7)$ $(0.099)10^7$ | $0.262(10^7)$ $(0.118)10^7$ | −0.413 (0.116) | .66 | 2.00 | .85 |

*Notes:* $r_t$ and $B_t$ denote, respectively, reserve-deposit ratio and bullion in the Bank of England; $\Delta r_t$ and $\Delta B_t$ denote the weekly change in these variables. $R^2$ denotes the coefficient of determination and $\rho$ the first-order autocorrelation coefficient.

along with an increasing discount rate. The table reports the weighted average discount rate applied by the Bank. From a level of 3 percent at the beginning of the year, the rate was gradually raised toward 5 percent in early April 1847.

These developments suggest that part of the effects of the external drain on the money supply were sterilized. Whether sterilization was a conscious policy, or whether it was a banking response to increasing interest rates and credit tightness, is open to question. But it is certainly interesting to note that F. T. Baring, the ex-chancellor of the exchequer, argued that the possibility of sterilization was a major defect of the Bank Act of 1844:

> I believe, if we look back, we shall find that the operation of the deposits and the question of reserve was not sufficiently considered, either by those who were favourable or those who were opposed to the bill. I cannot find in the evidence before the committee of 1840 more than a few sentences leading me to suppose that danger arising from such a cause was contemplated or referred to; yet this was a most important consideration; for it was by the reserve, the bank was enabled to do what was contrary to the spirit of the bill when gold was running out, not to reduce their circulation by a single pound. I do not think that the system works satisfactorily in this respect; and in fact, the point did not receive anything like a sufficient consideration. Perhaps it was impossible before the bill was in practical operation to see how the reserve of notes would operate; but it certainly never entered into the contemplation of anyone then considering the subject that £7,000,000 in gold should run off, yet that the notes in the hands of the public would rather increase than diminish. (MacLeod 1896, pp. 141–42)

The relative constancy of notes in the hands of the public, to which Baring refers, is shown in table 5.5. Through late April 1847, notes were practically unchanging while bullion declined by nearly one-third. In this period the Bank of England expansion "financed" the export of bullion.

| Table 5.5 | | The April 1847 Crisis (million £) | | | |
|---|---|---|---|---|---|
| | Note Reserves | Bullion in Issue Department | Reserve-Deposit Ratio (%) | Discount Rate (%) | Notes in Public Hands |
| 2 January | 8.23 | 14.26 | 46.0 | 3.10 | 20.0 |
| 6 March | 5.71 | 10.99 | 36.0 | 4.14 | 19.3 |
| 3 April | 3.70 | 9.55 | 23.9 | 4.25 | 19.9 |
| 17 April | 2.56 | 8.80 | 19.6 | 5.25 | 20.2 |
| 1 May | 2.74 | 8.51 | 23.6 | 5.25 | 19.8 |
| 5 June | 5.09 | 9.43 | 32.0 | 5.20 | 18.3 |

*Sources*: See table 5.2 and Appendix.

**247**      The Bank of England in the Crisis of 1847

Bullion losses did not exert their full contractionary effect on money and credit because the reserve-deposit ratio was declining.[6]

In March and April things became troublesome. The ongoing decline of bullion tightened credit-market conditions, and the failure of the Bank to change its accommodating stance in the face of a deteriorating balance sheet evoked concern about a sudden reversal of policies that would leave the public without notes and without loans. In April, therefore, the ongoing drain of bullion was reinforced dramatically by the seasonal payment of the dividend, which meant a significant run-down of public deposits. During the week of 17 April reserves fell to a level of only £2.56 million; the reserve-deposit ratio fell to less than 20 percent. Consol prices fell in March–April by 4.5 percent and short-term interest rates skyrocketed as the Bank moved vigorously to restore its liquidity position by reduced discounts, consol sales, and high discount rates.

Figure 5.5 shows the series for private and public deposits. The figure makes it clear that whatever influence the bullion drain had on the liquidity position of the Bank, the sharp public-deposit withdrawal could not but accentuate the problem. Table 5.6 shows that the public-sector-deposit withdrawal led only partially to a loss of note reserves and that the money stock (currency held by the public plus private deposits at the Bank of England) did not change substantially. The table confirms that the Bank of England managed to face the runoff by selling securities. Figure 5.6 shows the weekly series of the reserve-deposit ratio during the year. The effects of the extraordinary loss of reserves (by 17 April) and the reaction of the financial markets and the Bank of England have been described by MacLeod (1896, p. 142):

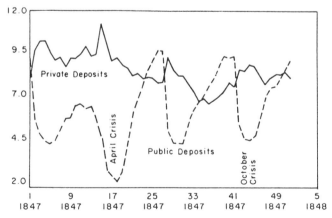

**Fig. 5.5**          Public and private deposits at the Bank of England (in million £).

Table 5.6                **Money, Public Deposits, and Note Reserves in the
                          April 1847 Crisis (million £)**

|          | Money Stock[a] | Public Deposits | Note Reserves | Bullion[b] |
|----------|------------|-----------------|---------------|------------|
| 3 April  | 30.3       | 6.0             | 3.7           | 10.2       |
| 10       | 32.7       | 5.0             | 2.8           | 9.8        |
| 17       | 32.2       | 3.0             | 2.6           | 9.3        |
| 24       | 29.8       | 2.6             | 2.7           | 9.2        |

*Sources*: See table 5.2 and Appendix.
[a]Notes in the hands of the public plus private deposits at the Bank of England.
[b]Total bullion in the Issue and Banking departments including coin.

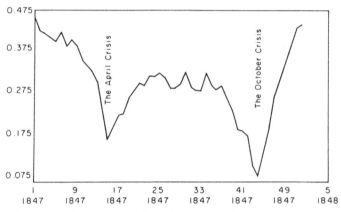

**Fig. 5.6**               Reserve–total-deposit ratio, 1847 weekly data.

When, therefore, the public saw that the whole banking resources of
the bank were reduced to £2,558,000, a complete panic seized both the
public and the directors. The latter adopted severe measures to check
the demand for notes. The rate was not only raised to five percent, but
this was only applicable to bills having only a few days to run, and a
limit was placed upon the amount of bills discounted, however good
they might be. Merchants who had received loans were called upon to
repay them without being permitted to renew them. During some days
it was impossible to get bills discounted at all. These measures were
effectual in stopping the efflux of bullion; and a sum of £100,000 in
sovereigns, which had been actually shipped for America, was re-
landed. During this period the rate of discount for the best bills rose to
nine, ten and twelve percent.

The tightening of credit led to internal dishoarding and to some reflow
of bullion. Accordingly, the Bank's reserve-deposit ratio quickly rose to
about 30 percent. The crisis was overcome and the adjustment process of

tight money was underway. The external part of that adjustment process involved importation of bullion and foreign investment in London as well as English borrowing abroad. In response to high yields on consols, the emperor of Russia decided to substitute foreign securities for gold as backing for the Russian currency and made substantial purchases of consols. These developments and their effect on the restoration of confidence were described by a contemporary as follows:

> Between the 25th and 28th of April confidence in a slight degree revived. The Bank was then discounting more freely; and the important news was announced that the Emperor of Russia had issued a Ukase "ordering an investment of about four and a half million sterling in home and foreign securities." Under the impression that a large amount of the money would find employment in Consols, as ultimately was the case, this circumstance, coupled with greater disposition of the Bank to grant facilities for accommodation, tended to abate the pressure. (Evans 1849, p. 62)

It seems fairly clear from the events that the Bank's policy in the first half of the year was certainly poor. It had all the characteristics of a policy of "too late, and (therefore) too vigorously." The continued expansion of credit in the face of falling reserves and the prospect of further decline in bullion meant that a crunch was quite inevitable. To wait too long before tightening, and ultimately to administer it with severity, led to an unnecessary panic in the money market.

### 5.4.2 The October Crisis

The severe credit tightening following the April crisis restored the Bank's ability to maintain convertibility. Table 5.7 shows that by June the reserve-deposit ratio was again substantial. Currency outstanding was significantly lower than during the April crisis. But during the late summer, and especially in early fall, conditions deteriorated, setting the basis for the October crisis.

**Table 5.7**          **The October 1847 Crisis (million £)**

|  | Note Reserves | Bullion in Issue Department | Reserve-Deposit Ratio (%) | Discount Rate (%) | Notes in Public Hands |
|---|---|---|---|---|---|
| 5 June | 5.09 | 9.43 | 32.0 | 5.2 | 18.3 |
| 4 September | 4.19 | 8.40 | 28.9 | 5.9 | 18.2 |
| 23 October | 1.55 | 7.87 | 11.6 | 8.1 | 20.3 |
| 24 December | 7.79 | 11.61 | 44.5 | 5.7 | 17.8 |

*Sources*: See table 5.2 and Appendix.

The credit tightening starting with the April crisis raised the cost of credit substantially above what it had been in past years, and indeed above anything the public could remember. This raise is the burden of "The Petition of Merchants, Bankers, and Traders of London against the Bank Charter Act" issued in July 1847, in which the opening statement reads: "That there has lately been apparent throughout the commercial and manufacturing community of this country an extent of monetary pressure, such as is without precedent in the memory of the oldest living merchant" (Gregory 1929, 2: p. 3).

Figure 5.7 confirms that 1847 interest rates were at a peak relative to the preceding twenty-five years. In May, first-class bills had been discounted at an all-time high of 7 percent, but by July the rate had in fact returned to 5.5 percent which, as the figure shows, was still very high.

By October the increasing tightness of credit, the extraordinary height of the rate of interest, commercial failures, and the threat of default by financial institutions had increased even further. Sir Charles Wood, the chancellor of the exchequer, is quoted as stating:

> When he came to town in October he found the City in a state of panic. He saw persons of all classes and descriptions from the time he was up until he went to bed, and he never passed so painful a week. The interest of money rose to an exorbitant rate, and 60 percent per annum was charged for what were called "continuations" for one day. It was thought impossible that the loans could be repaid. (Gregory 1929, 2: p. 11)

Developments between June and September resulted in some decline in both bullion and note reserves. The large payments for grain shipments received in June and July from Russia became due and caused a further drain of bullion and reserves. By now, of course, the cumulative external drain had reduced both bullion and note reserves. Bullion in the Issue

Fig. 5.7          Rate of discount on first-class bills, 1824–48 (percent per year).
                  *Source*: United Kingdom, Parliament 1848a, app. C, p. 467.

and Banking departments still remained at a comfortable £8.3 million, but note reserves were down to only £1.55 million, well within the possibility of depletion by a scramble for currency. The same point is evident from the reserve-deposit ratio that had declined from 32 percent in June to only 11.6 percent by late October.

In the October crisis, once again, public-sector-deposit movements played a role, but this time in combination with a scramble for currency by the public. Table 5.8 shows a large decline in public-sector deposits of nearly £4 million between 9 and 16 October. Three-quarters of that deposit reduction is matched by a reduction in Exchequer bills on the asset side. In the week of 23 October, dividend payments further reduced public-sector deposits and showed up in increased currency in circulation. The increase in currency during the first three weeks was only £2 million and as such did not appear large, but that gain must be compared to note reserves in the Issue Department which by the 23rd had fallen to only £1.5 million. The crisis thus involved potential minor increases in currency holdings reducing the Bank to insolvency.

While the external drain set the preconditions for the crisis, it was the internal run and scramble for currency shown in figure 5.8 that caused the panic of October. The poor liquidity position of the Bank deteriorated further as a result of commercial failures. These caused the public to question the soundness of private banks and thus required, on the banks' part, increased liquidity to demonstrate convertibility of their liabilities into Bank of England notes or specie. Again this factor exacerbated the shortage of Bank of England notes and the inadequacy of note reserves.[7]

It is not certain who broke the Old Lady's back. There is some indication in the inquiry that private bankers threatened the withdrawal of deposits from the Bank in excess of the amount of notes on hand (Gregory 1929, 2: p. 113).[8] The Bank, however, put up an admirable stone face and would claim in the inquiry that convertibility was never in question. Thus, in 1848, the governor of the Bank, James Morris, told the House of Lords:

| Table 5.8 | The Bank in October 1847 (million £) | | | | |
|---|---|---|---|---|---|
| | Public Deposits | Private Deposits | Circu-lation[a] | Exchequer[b] Bills | Bul-lion[c] |
| 9 October | 9.4 | 7.7 | 19.5 | 3.9 | 8.4 |
| 16 | 5.5 | 8.7 | 20.3 | 0.8 | 8.4 |
| 23 | 4.8 | 8.6 | 21.3 | 0.7 | 8.3 |
| 30 | 4.7 | 8.9 | 21.8 | 1.2 | 8.4 |

*Sources*: See table 5.2 and Appendix.
[a]Including seven-day bills.
[b]Held by the Banking Department.
[c]Total bullion, including coin in the Issue and Banking departments.

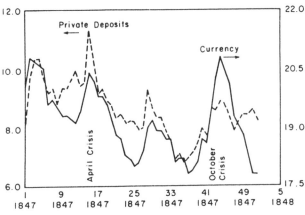

**Fig. 5.8**                  Private deposits and currency.

The Question was put to me over and over again whether we were able to take care of the Bank. I always stated that, so far as the Bank itself was concerned, we had no Difficulty; but that, whether Her Majesty's Government might have any political Reasons, such as Fear of Mills being stopped, or Riots in the Country, was a Question for them to decide, and one which we could not answer. (Gregory 1929, 2: p. 11)

Indeed, the way the Bank proposed to restore its financial position suggests that it might well have been able to maintain convertibility by an extraordinary contraction of credit. Here it is worth quoting what the governor told the House of Lords:

We should have had no Difficulty whatever in meeting all our Liabilities. We should not have been able to give the same Extent of Accommodation that Parties were requiring from us. Parties came and thought they had only to ask for Money and they would have it at once. We might have put into the Account a considerable Amount by selling Consols. We had going off weekly Bills to the Extent of £1,500,000, so that by discounting even at the Rate of £100,000 a Day to give the Public some Accommodation our Reserve would still have increased at the Rate of £900,000 a Week. It is certain that in a very short Period we should have had as large a Reserve as would be necessary for our Purposes, and therefore I maintain that the Bank was never at any Period in Jeopardy. (Evans 1849, p. 89)

Whether the Bank might have been successful or not, the contraction of money and credit was so severe, commercial failure was so widespread and reaching increasingly the banking system, the government felt it was wise to suspend Peel's Act, authorizing the Bank to issue notes without gold backing. The letter of instruction, dated 25 October 1847, is given below (the letter is reproduced in Turner 1897, pp. 159–60 and in Evans 1849, p. 87).

**253** The Bank of England in the Crisis of 1847

Downing Street, Oct. 25th, 1847.

GENTLEMEN,—Her Majesty's Government have seen with the deepest regret the pressure which has existed for some weeks upon the commercial interests of the country, and that this pressure has been aggravated by a want of that confidence which is necessary for carrying on the ordinary dealings of trade.

They have been in hopes that the check given to dealings of a speculative character, the transfer of capital from other countries, the influx of bullion, and a feeling which the knowledge of these circumstances might have been expected to produce, would have removed the prevailing distrust.

They were encouraged in this expectation by the speedy cessation of a similar state of feeling in the month of April last.

These hopes have, however, been disappointed, and Her Majesty's Government have come to the conclusion that the time has arrived when they ought to attempt, by some extraordinary and temporary measure, to restore confidence to the mercantile and manufacturing community.

For this purpose, they recommend to the directors of the Bank of England in the present emergency to enlarge the amount of their discounts and advances upon approved security; but that in order to retain this operation within reasonable limits a high rate of interest should be charged.

In present circumstances they would suggest that the rate of interest should not be less than 8 per cent.

If this course should lead to any infringement of the existing law, Her Majesty's Government will be prepared to propose to Parliament on its meeting a Bill of Indemnity. They will rely upon the discretion of the directors to reduce as soon as possible the amount of their notes if any extraordinary issue should take place within the limits prescribed by law.

Her Majesty's Government are of opinion that any extra profit derived from this measure should be carried to the account of the public, but the precise mode of doing so must be left to future arrangement.

Her Majesty's Government are not insensible of the evil of any departure from the law which has placed the currency of this country upon a sound basis; but they feel confident that, in the present circumstances, the measure which they have proposed may be safely adopted, and at the same time the main provisions of that law, and the vital principle of preserving the convertibility of the bank-note may be firmly maintained.

We have the honour to be, Gentlemen,
Your obedient, humble Servants,
(Signed)  J. RUSSELL.
CHARLES WOOD.

The Governor and Deputy Governor
of the Bank of England.

The authorization for fiduciary issue, coupled with the high discount that the Bank was charging, rapidly restored financial stability. The removal of the restriction of fiat-money issue dissipated the concern for the internal convertibility of deposits into notes. High interest rates, at the same time, brought about very substantial inflows of capital. The capital inflows, in turn, expanded the bullion in the Bank and thus led to internal monetary expansion that over time alleviated the extreme tightness in credit markets. By 24 December 1847, the reserve-deposit ratio had risen substantially while interest rates had declined from their panic peaks of late October.

It is important to recognize the role of international capital flows in the adjustment process. A key aspect, in the eyes of the government, was that suspension of Peel's Act be implemented in a manner in no way prejudicial to external convertibility, as it would be if fiat-money issue financed export of bullion. To prevent such a course of events, a high interest rate was an essential part of the suspension of Peel's Act since the very size of the international interest differential would ensure that gold imports were advantageous. They would in turn provide an external basis for domestic monetary expansion.

The 1847 episode was probably responsible for the popular maxim that "7 percent will draw gold from the moon."[9] That high interest rates do attract gold flows is immediately obvious from the bullion gain. Between October and December the Bank's holdings of bullion rose by more than 50 percent. The interest responsiveness of bullion flows is substantiated by a regression of the flow of bullion on lagged interest rates. To examine the interest responsiveness of bullion flows we regressed the change in the stock of bullion on current and lagged values of the consol yield (up to a lag of eight weeks). We experimented with various lag structures and, consistently, the only significant coefficients were on the fourth and the seventh lag. Equation (9) reports the regression of gold flows on the four- and seven-week lagged interest rate; standard errors are reported below the coefficients:

$$(9) \qquad \Delta B_t = -0.892(10^7) + 0.179(10^9)i_{t-4} + 0.795(10^8)i_{t-7}.$$
$$\qquad\qquad (0.131)10^7 \quad (0.043)10^9 \qquad (0.396)10^8$$

$$R^2 = 0.75, \text{ D.W.} = 2.16, \rho = 0.43.$$

The results are consistent with the expectation that the rate of capital inflow is related positively to the domestic rate of interest. Since in the pretelegraph period information on interest differentials could not be transmitted instantaneously, it is reasonable that gold flows responded to lagged values of interest rates. The length of the lag, in turn, should correspond to the length of time needed for a round trip between the home country and its trading partners. The round trip was necessary since the information on rates of interest had to be transmitted and then the

**255**     The Bank of England in the Crisis of 1847

gold had to be shipped. The four- and seven-week lags that are reported in equation (9) correspond, respectively, to the length of time of the round trip between London and New York and London and St. Petersburg.[10] If this interpretation of the lag structure is correct, one might expect that in subsequent periods, following the introduction of the telegraph, the lag structure would be shortened by a factor of 50 percent.

What the regression bears out is also quite clear from contemporary accounts—capital did move in response to interest rates.

> The season was advanced and the navigation on the Baltic near its close; but even at the disadvantage of a double rate of insurance, orders had been sent to St. Petersburg, under the impulse of an 8 percent rate of interest, which sufficed to bring back all, and more than all the gold which had been exported in the beginning of the year. (Hubbard 1848, p. 23)

That same principle was understood by the Bank of England.

> It was desirable that capital and bullion should be attracted to this country, and it was only by the attraction of a high rate of interest that this desideratum could be accomplished. He [the chancellor of the exchequer] was convinced, therefore, that the mode in which the Government had acted was the one best calculated to attain the end they had in view—namely, the influx of capital and the importation of bullion, and thereby the removal of the panic. (Evans 1849, p. 98)

It is relevant to note in the context of the discussion of capital flows that in the case of a transitory real disturbance, such as a harvest failure, the correct response is indeed financing through the capital account of the balance of payments as opposed to the price-specie-flow mechanism of adjustment which operates through the trade account. The 1847 episode illustrates that principle.

### 5.5   Was the Suspension of Peel's Act Necessary?

The authorization for uncovered note issue, as we already mentioned, immediately removed the panic, so much so that there was almost no need to actually issue uncovered notes. In fact during the period of suspension the Bank issued only £400,000 in notes in excess of the limits set by the Act of 1844. The rapid restoration of confidence and the normalization of affairs allowed the government to revoke the suspension on 23 November (reprinted from Evans 1849, p. 102):

Downing Street, Nov. 23, 1847.
GENTLEMEN,—Her Majesty's Government have watched with the deepest interest the gradual revival of confidence in the commercial classes of the country.
They have the satisfaction of believing that the course adopted by

the Bank of England on their recommendation has contributed to produce this result, whilst it has led to no infringement of the law.

It appears from the accounts which you have transmitted to us, that the reserve of the Bank of England has been for some time steadily increasing, and now amounts to £5,000,000. This increase has in great measure arisen from the return of notes and coin from the country.

The bullion exceeds £10,000,000, and the state of the exchanges promise a further influx of the precious metals.

The knowledge of these facts by the public is calculated to inspire still further confidence.

In these circumstances it appears to her Majesty's Government that the purposes which they had in view in the letter which we addressed to you on the 25th of October has been fully answered, and that it is unnecessary to continue that letter any longer in force.

We have the honour to be, Gentlemen,

Your obedient humble servants,

(Signed)

J. RUSSELL

CHARLES WOOD,

The Governor and Deputy-Governor of the Bank of England.

The rapid normalization led in some quarters (in the Bank and elsewhere) to the belief that there had been no real reason for the panic and no need to suspend Peel's Act. Thus Hubbard (1848, p. 25) commented:

How utterly baseless were the apprehensions of the panic-mongers is now proved by the fact that the Bank not only never availed itself of the power of additional issue, but met from its own resources all the demands made upon it, including the extraordinary applications which would naturally be encouraged by the prospect of their being favourably received.

Of course, the statement reflects, in an exemplary way, the lack of understanding of an *internal* convertibility crisis. A convertibility crisis or run occurs only if in fact not everybody can be paid off. Suspension of the act removed any conceivable basis for panic and therefore immediately restored a measure of financial stability.

The special characteristics of an internal drain and the remedies that are called for were fully perceived by Bagehot ([1873] 1962):

A domestic drain is very different. Such a drain arises from a disturbance of credit within the country, and the difficulty of dealing with it is the greater, because it is often caused, or at least often enhanced, by a foreign drain. . . . What then ought to be done? In opposition to what be at first sight supposed, the best way for the bank . . . to deal with a drain arising from internal discredit, is to lend freely. (P. 23)

Since the key issue underlying an internal drain is lack of confidence, it is clear that what is wanted and what is necessary to stop a panic is to diffuse the impression, that though money may be dear, still money is to be had. If people could be really convinced that they could have money . . . they would cease to run in such a mad way for money. Either shut the Bank at once . . . or lend freely, boldly, and so that the public may feel you mean to go on lending. (P. 31)

Chancellor of the Exchequer Sir Charles Wood told the committee of inquiry that the basis of the panic was indeed a lack of confidence in internal convertibility. He quotes commercial traders and bankers as stating:

We do not want notes—what we desire is that you should give us confidence, it is only for you to say that you will stand by us, and nothing in the world else will give us confidence. We do not want notes, but only to know where we can get them. . . . Charge 10 or 12 percent interest if you like—we do not mean to take notes, but let us know that at some rate of interest we can get them and that will amply suffice. (Evans 1849, p. 96)

Sir Robert Peel for his part expressed the view that the Bank Charter Act had failed in one important respect, namely, it failed to secure a gradual and early, as opposed to severe and sudden, adjustment:

If the Bank had possessed the resolution to meet the coming danger by a contraction of its issue, by raising the rate of discount . . . if they had been firm and determined in the adopting of those precautions, the necessity of extrinsic interference might have been prevented, it might not have been necessary for the Government to authorise the violation of the Act of 1844. (Andreades 1924, p. 339)

Many felt that the act, as opposed to Bank of England policy, had no effect in aggravating the crisis. S. J. Loyd, for example, stated to the committee that

the Act had no effect whatever in aggravating the Pressure. It protected the Public from the additional evil, which would otherwise have occurred, of a Failure in maintaining Convertibility of the Notes, and the consequent complete Destruction of our Monetary System. (Gregory 1929, 2: p. 44)

But this view was not how the House of Lords came to see it. While also agreeing on the fundamental importance of external convertibility, the committee concluded that

the recent panic was materially aggravated by the operation of that statute, and by the proceedings of the Bank itself. This effect may be traced, directly, to the Act of 1844, in the legislative restriction imposed on the means of accommodation, whilst a large amount of bullion was held in the coffers of the Bank, and during a time of

**258      Rudiger Dornbusch and Jacob A. Frenkel**

favourable exchanges; and it may be traced to the same cause, indirectly, as a consequence of great fluctuations in the rate of discount,
and of capital previously advanced at an unusually low rate of interest.
This course the Bank would hardly have felt itself justified in taking,
had not an impression existed that, by the separation of the issue and
the banking departments, one inflexible rule for regulating the Bank
issues had been substituted by law in place of the discretion formerly
vested in the Bank. (Turner 1897, pp. 162–63)

Likewise,

the Committee are fully aware that Alternations of Periods of Commercial Excitement and of Discredit, of Speculation and of Collapse,
are likely to arise under all Systems of Currency; it would be visionary
to imagine that they could be averted altogether, even if the Circulation were exclusively Metallic. But it is on this Account that greater
Care should be taken to avoid increasing an Evil, perhaps inevitable,
by any arbitrary and artificial Enactments.

The Committee are of opinion, that the Principle on which the Act of
1844 should be amended is the Introduction of a discretionary relaxing
Power; such Power, in whomsoever vested, to be exercised only during
the Existence of a favourable Foreign Exchange. (Gregory 1929,
2: p. 40)

The very interesting aspect of the House of Lords' recommendation is
the link between fiat issue and the state of the foreign exchanges. It
represents a departure from strict gold standard rules where only *actual*
gold flows can be monetized. Under the proposal of the committee it is
enough to have the *conditions* for gold flows to take place, as opposed to
actual arrival of gold, for suspension to be allowed. There is money issue,
so to speak, on credit. The compromise of lending freely at high rates—
the high rates ensuring in time the arrival of gold and the validation of the
fiat issue—is important in that it is a remedy specifically for internal
convertibility crises for which Peel's Act had made no allowance.

The model of the gold standard developed in section 5.3 above did not
make provision for issues of stability and crisis. Portfolio adjustment by
the Bank and gold flows in response to interest differentials brought
about smooth adjustment. How can the panic of October be accommodated in such a framework? Here it becomes essential to recognize the
dominating effect of the currency-deposit ratio. When the reserve-
deposit ratio of the Bank is sufficiently low so as to reduce confidence in
the viability of internal convertibility, then further reduction in the
reserve-deposit ratio may bring about changes in the currency-deposit
ratio so large as actually to reduce the money multiplier and the money
stock.

In terms of equation (3), the money multiplier, in that low reserve-de-
posit-ratio region, responds positively to an increase in the reserve-

**259**      The Bank of England in the Crisis of 1847

deposit ratio, and therefore the equilibrium interest rate responds negatively. The sign reversal implies the possibility of multiple equilibria as
shown in figure 5.9. Point A′ is the stable equilibrium studied earlier;
point A is another equilibrium in the region where convertibility concerns
dominate the money-supply process. Point A is an unstable equilibrium
that can be attained only for initial conditions on the GG schedule. Initial
conditions below and to the left of GG lead to unstable paths of the
reserve ratio that decline to zero. From a point such as C, with low bullion
and low reserves, the Bank lowers the reserve-deposit ratio while bullion
is rising. The reserve-deposit ratio keeps falling, the currency-deposit
ratio keeps rising, and the system must collapse.

## 5.6   Concluding Remarks

   In this paper we examined the operation of the gold standard and the
performance of the Bank of England during the crisis of 1847. The key
feature of that crisis was its origin: it began with the instability of the real
sector rather than from monetary disorder. That crisis highlights the role
of confidence in both external and internal convertibility. We presented a
simple model that seems to capture the central characteristics of the crisis
and that emphasizes the role of international capital flows during the
adjustment process. Our analysis suggests that the suspension of Peel's
Act, i.e., the collapse of the rigid rules of the gold standard, was the
correct and the essential policy required for the restoration of confidence.
   We return now to the more general question of the gold standard as a
frame for macroeconomic stability. The monetary system, to work satis-

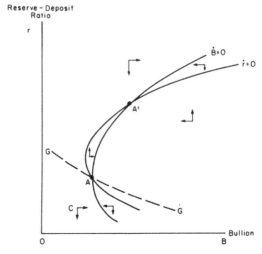

**Fig. 5.9**                 Financial model—the unstable case.

factorily, would have to satisfy three criteria: (1) assure stability and predictability of the general level of prices and output; (2) separate banking and financial problems, to a large extent, from the macroeconomy; and (3) provide a stable financial framework that facilitates financial intermediation and lending, both domestically and in the world economy.

There is considerable doubt now whether the objective of price-level stability was well served by the gold standard. There is evidence of short-term price variability substantially in excess of post–World War II experience. It may also be argued that long-term stability was, to a large extent, accidental—a consequence of fortuitous gold discoveries rather than the systematic operation of the system. But even with these qualifications there can be little question that the gold standard was a system that utterly excluded the extreme monetary instability Europe witnessed, for example, in the 1920s. The system also excluded the accelerating path of inflation that we experienced in the 1970s from the interaction of macroeconomic shocks, inertia, and accommodation.

But on a different account the gold standard was disappointing. Until the principle "during crisis, discount freely" was firmly established, the gold standard provided an exceedingly poor framework for financial markets. The presence of a lender of last resort—whether it be the Treasury or the central bank—is essential with fractional reserve banking. The lack of a lender of last resort was emphasized in the 1847 crisis when the Bank of England, in the midst of a banking panic, *sold* consols and *reduced* discounts, thus assuring confidence in deposit convertibility (not gold convertibility) at the expense of devastating financial distress.

Appendix   Weekly Observations, December 1846–December 1847

| Date | R | D+G | D | B | i | P_c | P_w | C | C/D | R/(D+G) | m |
|---|---|---|---|---|---|---|---|---|---|---|---|
| DEC 26 | 8814 | 18037 | 7696 | 15067 | 3.204 | 93.625 | 63.000 | 20253 | 2.63163 | 0.4887 | 1.69285 |
| JAN 2 | 8227 | 17895 | 7904 | 14952 | 3.196 | 93.875 | 64.333 | 20725 | 2.62209 | 0.4597 | 1.77478 |
| 9 | 6715 | 15645 | 9785 | 14308 | 3.209 | 93.500 | 66.833 | 21593 | 2.20675 | 0.4292 | 1.90170 |
| 16 | 6546 | 15374 | 10340 | 13949 | 3.243 | 92.500 | 70.250 | 21403 | 2.06992 | 0.4258 | 1.87984 |
| 23 | 6167 | 15024 | 10356 | 13443 | 3.320 | 90.375 | 73.250 | 21276 | 2.05446 | 0.4105 | 1.91442 |
| 30 | 5704 | 14123 | 9660 | 12902 | 3.279 | 91.500 | 74.917 | 21198 | 2.19441 | 0.4039 | 2.00846 |
| FEB 6 | 5891 | 13851 | 9183 | 12288 | 3.297 | 91.000 | 73.833 | 20397 | 2.22117 | 0.4253 | 1.96232 |
| 13 | 5747 | 14628 | 9330 | 12299 | 3.315 | 90.500 | 71.583 | 20552 | 2.20279 | 0.3929 | 1.98196 |
| 20 | 5977 | 14707 | 8837 | 12215 | 3.310 | 90.625 | 71.583 | 20238 | 2.29014 | 0.4064 | 1.96267 |
| 27 | 6017 | 15250 | 9322 | 12045 | 3.324 | 90.250 | 74.583 | 20028 | 2.14847 | 0.3946 | 1.91342 |
| MAR 6 | 5715 | 15860 | 9289 | 11596 | 3.347 | 89.625 | 74.333 | 19881 | 2.14027 | 0.3603 | 1.94415 |
| 13 | 5554 | 16252 | 9536 | 11449 | 3.399 | 88.250 | 74.166 | 19895 | 2.08630 | 0.3417 | 1.95036 |
| 20 | 5419 | 16434 | 9962 | 11232 | 3.376 | 88.875 | 75.833 | 19813 | 1.98886 | 0.3297 | 1.93583 |
| 27 | 4876 | 16019 | 9403 | 11016 | 3.361 | 89.250 | 77.000 | 20140 | 2.14187 | 0.3044 | 2.06898 |
| APR 3 | 3700 | 15504 | 9502 | 10246 | 3.409 | 88.000 | 77.083 | 20546 | 2.16228 | 0.2386 | 2.27602 |
| 10 | 2833 | 16242 | 11258 | 9867 | 3.499 | 85.750 | 74.416 | 21034 | 1.86836 | 0.1744 | 2.29168 |
| 17 | 2558 | 13016 | 10005 | 9330 | 3.473 | 86.375 | 74.083 | 20772 | 2.07616 | 0.1965 | 2.44981 |
| 24 | 2719 | 11760 | 9125 | 9214 | 3.488 | 86.000 | 75.833 | 20495 | 2.24603 | 0.2312 | 2.50084 |
| MAY 1 | 2741 | 11611 | 9312 | 9338 | 3.448 | 87.000 | 79.500 | 20597 | 2.21188 | 0.2361 | 2.48146 |
| 8 | 3197 | 11800 | 8930 | 9589 | 3.463 | 86.625 | 81.833 | 20392 | 2.28354 | 0.2709 | 2.41791 |
| 15 | 3793 | 13071 | 8751 | 9870 | 3.448 | 87.000 | 85.166 | 20077 | 2.29425 | 0.2902 | 2.29815 |
| 22 | 4420 | 14430 | 8289 | 9949 | 3.448 | 87.000 | 94.833 | 19529 | 2.35601 | 0.3063 | 2.18884 |
| 29 | 4628 | 15410 | 8432 | 10170 | 3.395 | 88.375 | 102.420 | 19542 | 2.31760 | 0.3003 | 2.14196 |
| JUN 5 | 5089 | 15923 | 8151 | 10237 | 3.399 | 88.250 | 99.833 | 19148 | 2.34916 | 0.3196 | 2.06186 |
| 12 | 5375 | 16922 | 8228 | 10359 | 3.380 | 88.750 | 88.833 | 18984 | 2.30724 | 0.3176 | 2.00044 |
| 19 | 5665 | 17419 | 8160 | 10512 | 3.390 | 88.500 | 91.583 | 18847 | 2.30968 | 0.3252 | 1.95349 |
| 26 | 5625 | 17717 | 7921 | 10526 | 3.380 | 88.750 | 91.833 | 18901 | 2.38619 | 0.3175 | 1.98007 |

(continued overleaf)

Appendix (continued)

| Date | R | D+G | D | B | i | $P_c$ | $P_w$ | C | C/D | R/(D+G) | m |
|---|---|---|---|---|---|---|---|---|---|---|---|
| JUL 3 | 5185 | 17707 | 7968 | 10397 | 3.380 | 88.750 | 87.083 | 19212 | 2.41114 | 0.2928 | 2.06645 |
| 10 | 4331 | 14550 | 9305 | 10086 | 3.380 | 88.750 | 82.250 | 19755 | 2.12305 | 0.2977 | 2.13112 |
| 17 | 4069 | 13200 | 8640 | 9919 | 3.376 | 88.875 | 74.000 | 19850 | 2.29745 | 0.3083 | 2.24172 |
| 24 | 4216 | 12830 | 8326 | 9770 | 3.395 | 88.375 | 75.500 | 19554 | 2.34855 | 0.3286 | 2.22293 |
| 31 | 3775 | 12820 | 8316 | 9331 | 3.385 | 88.625 | 77.250 | 19556 | 2.35161 | 0.2945 | 2.30519 |
| AUG 7 | 3946 | 13457 | 7886 | 9253 | 3.458 | 86.750 | 75.416 | 19307 | 2.44826 | 0.2932 | 2.29826 |
| 14 | 3992 | 13872 | 7514 | 9287 | 3.483 | 86.125 | 66.833 | 19295 | 2.56787 | 0.2878 | 2.33000 |
| 21 | 4488 | 13762 | 6931 | 9240 | 3.443 | 87.125 | 66.500 | 18752 | 2.70553 | 0.3261 | 2.24915 |
| 28 | 4330 | 14299 | 7106 | 9140 | 3.443 | 87.125 | 60.333 | 18810 | 2.64706 | 0.3028 | 2.26618 |
| SEP 4 | 4190 | 14514 | 6791 | 8960 | 3.433 | 87.375 | 56.666 | 18770 | 2.76395 | 0.2887 | 2.32775 |
| 11 | 4467 | 15147 | 6981 | 8915 | 3.453 | 86.875 | 51.333 | 18448 | 2.64260 | 0.2949 | 2.22126 |
| 18 | 4273 | 15934 | 7185 | 8880 | 3.514 | 85.375 | 49.500 | 18607 | 2.58970 | 0.2682 | 2.25100 |
| 25 | 4112 | 16932 | 7484 | 8782 | 3.483 | 86.125 | 53.500 | 18670 | 2.49466 | 0.2429 | 2.25543 |
| OCT 2 | 3409 | 17291 | 7962 | 8565 | 3.556 | 84.375 | 56.750 | 19156 | 2.40593 | 0.1972 | 2.38484 |
| 9 | 3322 | 17129 | 7714 | 8409 | 3.598 | 83.375 | 54.166 | 19087 | 2.47433 | 0.1939 | 2.42851 |
| 16 | 2630 | 14171 | 8675 | 8431 | 3.709 | 80.875 | 54.250 | 19801 | 2.28254 | 0.1856 | 2.51889 |
| 23 | 1547 | 13347 | 8581 | 8313 | 3.750 | 80.000 | 55.166 | 20766 | 2.42000 | 0.1159 | 2.89761 |
| 30 | 1177 | 13607 | 8911 | 8439 | 3.715 | 80.750 | 53.500 | 21262 | 2.38604 | 0.0865 | 2.99098 |
| NOV 6 | 2030 | 13796 | 8804 | 8730 | 3.609 | 83.125 | 52.333 | 20700 | 2.35120 | 0.1471 | 2.72328 |
| 13 | 2798 | 14304 | 8312 | 9259 | 3.535 | 84.875 | 53.666 | 20461 | 2.46162 | 0.1956 | 2.58983 |
| 20 | 4228 | 15086 | 7866 | 10017 | 3.561 | 84.250 | 54.250 | 19789 | 2.51576 | 0.2803 | 2.28667 |
| 27 | 4986 | 15968 | 8239 | 10533 | 3.540 | 84.750 | 52.917 | 19547 | 2.37250 | 0.3122 | 2.10102 |
| DEC 4 | 5583 | 16241 | 8441 | 11033 | 3.504 | 85.625 | 52.083 | 19450 | 2.30423 | 0.3438 | 1.98880 |
| 11 | 6449 | 16667 | 8437 | 11426 | 3.529 | 85.000 | 51.917 | 18977 | 2.24926 | 0.3869 | 1.84160 |
| 18 | 7551 | 17370 | 8607 | 11991 | 3.535 | 84.875 | 52.833 | 18440 | 2.14244 | 0.4347 | 1.67391 |
| 25 | 7786 | 17479 | 8243 | 12237 | 3.519 | 85.250 | 52.750 | 18451 | 2.23838 | 0.4454 | 1.66536 |

*Sources:* Data for R, D+G, D, and B come from United Kingdom, Parliament 1848a, app. 8, pp. 126–43. All other data are from Hubbard 1848.

*Notes:* R, D+G, D, and B denote, respectively, the stock of note reserves held by the Bank of England; total deposits including Exchequer; London Bankers and private deposits; and the total amount of bullion. All are measured in thousand pounds sterling. C denotes currency, which is measured as bullion minus reserves + 14,000 (the fiduciary issue); m denotes the money multiplier. $P_c$ denotes the price of 3-percent consols; $P_w$ the price of wheat; and i is a hundred times the yield on consols, i.e., $(100 \times 3)/P_c$.

**263**     The Bank of England in the Crisis of 1847

## Notes

1. Quoted in Andreades 1924, p. 340.
2. On the banking-and-currency-school controversy, see Mints 1945 and Viner 1937, chap. 5.
3. For the derivation see Friedman and Schwartz 1963. Throughout our discussion we abstract from the existence of private banks, their note issue, their deposit liabilities, or their demand for Bank of England notes.
4. The supply shock—a harvest failure—exerted opposing effects on prices and output so that the net effect on nominal income and thereby on interest rates may in fact be disregarded without obvious strain.
5. If a rise in the reserve-deposit ratio lowers the currency-deposit ratio so much as to *raise* the money multiplier, in contrast with our assumption in equation (3), then a higher reserve-deposit ratio would lower interest rates and thus change the specification in equation (4'). The $\dot{B} = 0$ schedule might then be negatively sloped at low levels of $r$, and so may even the $\dot{r} = 0$ curve. We examine this case in section 5.5 below.
6. The defects of the Bank Act were discussed forcefully by Thomas Tooke (1844) whose views are analyzed by Laidler (1975). For a further analysis see Morgan 1943.
7. It is interesting to note that the developments during the October crisis were part of the evidence that stimulated Jevons's theory of the "frequent autumnal pressure" (see Jevons 1884, chap. 5).
8. On 23 October, when London bankers held deposits of £1.6 million at the Bank of England, the note reserves were only £1.5 million. Balances of all bankers rose from £1.5 to £2.1 million in the week of 16 October, but they declined to only £1.8 million by 23 October.
9. While we could not trace the exact origin of this maxim, it was referred to by Lionel Robbins in a memorandum submitted to the (Radcliffe) Committee on the Working of the Monetary System (United Kingdom, Parliament 1960, p. 218). Robbins ascribes this maxim to "a practical banker." We are indebted to David Laidler for this reference. It is interesting to note that a similar statement can be found in Leaf 1927, p. 34. There it is described as an "old saying in the City." Leaf then goes on to say "but it takes time to bring it even from Paris." We are indebted to Geoffrey Wood for this reference and to Anna J. Schwartz for help in the search for the source of the popular maxim.
10. For some evidence, see Howarth 1974, p. 313.

## References

Acres, W. Marston. 1931. *The Bank of England from within*. Vol. 2. London: Oxford University Press.

Andreades, C. B. E. 1924. *History of the Bank of England, 1640–1903*. 2d ed. London: P. S. King & Sons.

Bagehot, Walter. [1873] 1962. *Lombard Street*. Reprint. London: Richard D. Irwin.

Dornbusch, Rudiger, and Jacob A. Frenkel. 1971. Aspects of adjustment policies and mechanism during the 1847 crisis in Britain. University of Chicago Workshop in Economic History, report 7172–3.

Evans, D. Morier. 1849. *The commercial crisis 1847–1848 being facts and figures illustrative of the events of that important period, considered in relation to the three epochs of the railway mania, the food and money panic and the French revolution.* 2d ed. London: Letts, Son and Steer.

Friedman, Milton, and Anna J. Schwartz. 1963. *A monetary history of the United States, 1867–1960.* Princeton: Princeton University Press.

Gregory, T. E., ed. 1929. *Select statutes, documents, reports relating to British banking, 1832–1928.* London: Oxford University Press.

Howarth, David. 1974. *Sovereign of the seas.* New York: Atheneum.

Hubbard, John G. 1848. *A letter to Sir Charles Wood on the monetary pressure and commercial distress of 1847.* London: Longman.

Hyndman, H. M. [1932] 1967. *Commercial crises of the nineteenth century.* Reprint. New York: Augustus M. Kelley. (First published 1892.)

Jevons, W. Stanley. 1884. *Investigations in currency and finance.* London: Macmillan.

Keynes, John Maynard. 1932. *Essays in persuasion.* New York: Harcourt, Brace & Company.

Laidler, David E. W. 1975. Thomas Tooke on monetary reform. In *Essays on money and inflation*, chap. 11. Chicago: University of Chicago Press.

Leaf, Walter. 1927. *Banking.* New York: Henry Holt and Company.

MacLeod, Henry Dunning. 1896. *A history of banking in Great Britain.* Vol. 2 of *A history of banking in all the leading nations.* New York: *Journal of Commerce and Commercial Bulletin.*

Mill, John Stuart. 1871. *Principles of political economy.* 7th ed. London: Parker & Company.

Mints, Lloyd W. 1945. *A history of banking theory.* Chicago: University of Chicago Press.

Mitchell, B. R. 1962. *Abstract of British historical statistics.* Cambridge: Cambridge University Press.

Morgan, E. V. 1943. *The theory and practice of central banking, 1797–1913.* Cambridge: Cambridge University Press.

Tooke, Thomas. 1844. *An inquiry into the currency principle.* 2d ed. London.

Turner, B. R. 1897. *Chronicles of the Bank of England.* London: Swan Sonnenschein and Company.

United Kingdom. Parliament. 1848a. *Appendix to reports from the secret committee on commercial distress.* Parliamentary papers, 1847–48. Vol. 8, part 2. London: HMSO.

———. 1848b. *First and second reports from the secret committee appointed to inquire into the causes of the distress.* Parliamentary papers 1847–48. Vol. 8, part 1 (395) (584). London: HMSO.

———. Committee on the Working of the Monetary System [Radcliffe Committee]. 1960. *Principal memoranda of evidence.* Vol. 3. London: HMSO.

Viner, Jacob. 1937. *Studies in the theory of international trade.* New York: Harper and Brothers.

# [3]

Excerpt from *Financial Crises and the World Banking System*, 41–73

# 2 The Avoidance of Catastrophe: Two Nineteenth-century Banking Crises

## ROY A. BATCHELOR

### INTRODUCTION

This chapter tells the tale of the two most severe banking crises to trouble Victorian England. The collapse of Overend, Gurney & Co. Ltd in 1866, and the liquidation of Baring Bros in 1890, caused a degree of consternation in the financial community which was quite remarkable in an era when each passing year bought its crop of bank failures. Equally remarkable, however, is the fact that neither of these panics was translated into the sort of domino collapse of the whole banking system so characteristic of the economies at the periphery of the international trading system. Less than ten years before the Overend, Gurney crisis, several hundred banks in the eastern United States were brought down in a single run. The very year before the Baring crisis, and directly contributing to it, the entire financial system of the River Plate republics fell; and only three years later, the Australian banking system suffered a similar fate.

Our analysis of the two episodes must therefore address two issues. First, how did the crises arise? Secondly, how was crisis prevented from becoming catastrophe?

We start by describing the events surrounding the crises of 1866 and 1890. The histories contain many parallels. Both crises were the products of bad asset management. The two great houses concerned

42        *Financial Crises and the World Banking System*

grossly overcommitted their funds to risky enterprises – finance bills for contracting companies, South American securities – which subsequently failed. Each crisis developed in two stages; the failure of bubble companies and utilities at home and abroad, and the succeeding loss of confidence in the financial system. The histories do, however, have very different outcomes. Gurneys failed, never to reappear. In the course of the crisis, interest rates were driven to record levels; and for years after, banks and discount houses held substantial reserves at the Bank of England, fearful that the episode would be repeated. Barings was reconstructed within weeks. Interest rates rose only slightly and briefly; and although the Bank of England subsequently took on a greater responsibility for bank solvency, the crisis made no permanent mark on bank behaviour.

To help sort out the analytical issues surrounding the crises, we develop two theoretical models. Both use in an informal way the language and concepts of 'catastrophe theory'. This is a branch of mathematics which seeks to describe systems which are well behaved under some sets of circumstances (some values of 'control variables'), but in other circumstances can exhibit sudden and irreversible changes. It is a natural vehicle for studying the mechanics of normally quiescent financial systems which periodically experience manic boom or bust phases, and some pioneering work in this area has already been undertaken (Zeeman, 1974; Schott, 1983). Our first model adapts this work to describe the external shocks initiating the Gurney and Baring collapses. Our second model is more novel. It uses catastrophe theory to describe how a subsequent bank run can arise, and to assess the relative contributions of policy and non-policy factors in starting and ending such episodes. The bank run is characterised as a rational reaction on the part of depositors to news arriving in a situation where they are imperfectly informed about the relative solvency of individual banks. The state of the banking system is determined by two control variables – the riskiness of bank assets, and the degree of information about individual bank balance sheets. Both can be affected by non-policy events – the state of the real economy, the track record of each bank – and by the last resort lending policies and balance sheet restrictions imposed by the central bank. The resulting model shares with standard catastrophe models the property of hysteresis, neither the security price collapse nor the sequence of bank failures being easily reversible. The model does of course generate runs, and does so without invoking irrational behaviour on the part of the public. However, as with earlier catastrophe theory models of financial crises, the model yields a genuine catastrophe situation only if some particular assumptions are made about precisely how confidence in individual banks is created and destroyed. Whether financial crises are true catastrophes will only be decided by empirical evidence on the validity of these assumptions. Fortunately, for our present purpose of understanding the Gurney and Baring episodes the general bank run model suffices.

This chapter therefore concludes by offering an interpretation of the two crises in terms of this theoretical framework. Why did the failure of Gurneys' cause such consternation; why did the failure of Barings pass off with such little disturbance? Why did neither trigger a collapse of the whole banking system? There are two competing explanations. One is that these outcomes were determined by the initial conditions. The crimes of the Gurneys were simply greater than those of the Barings. The financial community was too well informed about both to believe that other institutions were being equally irresponsible. The alternative hypothesis is that catastrophe was avoided in both cases only by prompt action of the Bank of England; and that Gurneys failed because assistance was provided only to the major London banks, while Barings survived because they were supported directly. Conventional wisdom attributes considerable responsibility to the Bank for maintaining the integrity of the system through these crises. Our assessment is that the two cases were somewhat different. In 1866 there was suspicion that many finance houses were little better than Gurneys, and consequently there was a genuine danger of a run. The Bank's actions, in temporarily expanding the supply of notes to banks with good security, was appropriate and helpful. In 1890, however, there was no such danger. Barings was known to be a special case; no other house was so heavily committed in Argentina and Uruguay. The actions of its directors in plunging into such securities was no less blameworthy than the actions of Gurneys directors thirty years earlier. The Bank's decision to launch a 'lifeboat' to save this particular bank, where other equally eminent names had earlier been refused, clearly requires some explanation. One possibility is that the Bank acted properly, but on the basis of an incorrect and exaggerated estimate of the probability of a run on London. It seems more probable that the Bank simply felt an obligation towards Barings. Gurneys had been long-standing rivals of the Bank, but the Barings were solid establishment figures, with representatives in Parliament and on the Board of Directors of the Bank itself. The decisions to save Barings but to let Gurneys go seem to have been motivated less by a consistent theory of monetary management than by the politics and personalities of the City.

44        *Financial Crises and the World Banking System*

## GURNEYS' FRIDAY

Overend, Gurney & Company had their origins in the joint activities of
the Gurney Bank of Norwich, and the London bill broking firm of
Richardson, Overend & Company, towards the end of the eighteenth
century. Both firms were run by Quaker families. Samuel Gurney,
cousin of the head of the Norwich bank, Hudson Gurney, joined
Richardsons in 1807. In the ensuing half-century, the firm – soon
reconstructed as Overend, Gurney & Co. with Hudson at its head
– grew enormously in stature and prosperity.

Both of the Gurneys took an active part in public debate on
monetary policy. Their views were, significantly, often at variance with
those of the Bank of England. Hudson, for example, found himself –
along with Alexander Baring, but with few other allies – arguing in
1819 against the resumption of specie payment for notes at pre-war
parity, a measure which had overwhelming official support. In an effort
to persuade the Bank to act consistently with this policy, he subsequently (in 1826) threatened to send £½ million in notes to the Bank
unless they restricted growth of new note issues. Twenty years later,
this sort of discipline was formally imposed by the Bank Charter Act,
which tied the note issue rigidly to the Bank reserve, and insulated the
Bank's commercial banking activities from its responsibilities as the
Chief bank of issue. The Gurneys were still not satisfied. Samuel
Gurney supported his elder's opinions, and had at first been a strong
advocate of Peel's Act. However, the crisis of 1847, in which a reserve
shortage caused monetary contraction and deflation, necessitating the
suspension of the Act, led him to the opinion that the Bank should not
wholly divorce its banking operations from the needs of the rest of the
banking systm. He, and the other managing partner in Gurneys, David
Barclay Chapman, continued to argue the need for temporary last
resort lending above the fiduciary limit, against the security of sound
bills, in times of crises. When the Bank showed no signs of taking on
such a responsibility, Chapman took the unusual step on one occasion,
in October 1856, of going over its head to a Minister of State to seek
assurances that such financial relief would be provided.

Apart from the good sense of their arguments in favour of a system
which, much later, came to be accepted as the proper mode of
operation of a central bank, Gurney and Chapman commanded respect
for the huge commercial success of their company. Their business had
started small and simple. They acted as agents for firms wishing to sell
bills. The firms were carefully vetted for soundness. The buyers of the

bills were generally country bankers, initially concentrated in East Anglia. By the 1820s, all the major London banks were also investing in Gurneys and other finance houses; by the 1830s the Bank of England itself was a regular investor, and on more than one occasion Gurneys bought back bills from the Bank to provide liquidity during a cash squeeze. Gurneys became a huge concern, by far the largest discount house, and one of the City's 'great houses'. By the 1850s, it was each year turning over bills to about half the value of the United Kingdom's National Debt; its profits were £200 000 a year. Its balance sheet was as large as that of the Bank of England; and its Directors clearly felt that this symbiotic relationship should be formally recognised.

In the mid 1850s, however, a change took place in the management of Gurneys which, in the short space of a single decade, reduced the firm to ruins. Samuel Gurney died in 1856; Barclay Chapman retired late in 1857. The new Board still contained Gurneys and Chapmans, but these men, while sharing their elders' ambitions, did not have their good sense. They also wanted an accommodation with the Bank; and they wanted to grow. But they tried to move too fast.

In 1860, they appealed to the Bank for relief after a sharp rise in the Bank rate. By this time, the Bank had a definite policy of *not* assisting the bill brokers in bad times, on the grounds that the brokers put little cash into the Bank during good times, and the request was refused. Gurneys' reply was to demonstrate its power, by organising a well-advertised mass note withdrawal by a group of Quaker-owned banks and brokers, perhaps inspired by Hudson's threatened gold raid of 1826. The Bank found its reserve falling by about £2 million (out of a total of £7 million) in the week of 4–11 April, and it received an anonymous letter claiming that Gurneys was quite capable of pulling out the remaining £5 million. The Bank did not relent. The notes were returned a week later (cut in two), and the bizarre demonstration served only to diminish Gurneys' weight in public affairs, and harden the Bank's heart against the discount houses.

The new management was equally cavalier in the conduct of its private business. High quality bill broking had never been the sole activity of the house, but from 1858 it started taking on extremely dubious bills, and lending on the flimsiest security. After the Act of 1861 authorising limited liability, a large number of speculative companies were floated, and many paid their contracting firms by means of 'finance securities'. The discount on these bills was, of course, considerable and Gurneys saw them as a source of quick profit. Of the precise nature of Gurneys other investments, only dark rumours survive. One story, retailed in *The Economist*, has Ward Chapman boasting that he 'lent money to certain parties "upon shells"' ... at which 'All the country bankers in England began to ask, 'Is our money put out in shells or not?'[1] In spite of such episodes, Gurneys was held in high esteem in the country. Only among insiders in London were its affairs a continual source of concern.

In truth, the firm was slipping heavily into debt, and by 1865 the vast profits of the old firm had been turned into vast losses cumulating to £3–4 million. In a desperate attempt to attract more capital, Gurneys itself was floated as a limited company in July 1865. Ward Chapman was retired. The Gurneys remained, and several more responsible, if optimistic, new directors were appointed. On the strength of the Gurneys' name, an extravagant assessment of the value of partners property and goodwill, and a cosmetic presentation of the bill port-folio, the firm was sold. Outsiders regarded the transaction as a milestone in the advance of limited liability. Insiders were more cynical; *The Economist* suggested its chief virtue was that the firm would now have to publish regular accounts. Outside investors steadily drove Gurneys' shares to a substantial premium. City analysts were puzzled; by early 1866, the 'limited mania' had run its course, and a growing number of bubble companies and their associated contracting firms were failing. The supply of credit to surviving enterprises was curtailed, and interest rates had risen from 3 per cent at the time of Gurneys' flotation to 8 per cent by the year end (Table 2.1). This left the discount houses with heavy contingent liabilities on finance securities and capital losses on liquidated bills. The Joint Stock Discount Company and the Contract Corporation were forced to close, and shares of almost all the others were trading more than 50 per cent below par. It was later remarked of the buoyancy of Gurneys' shares that 'there was a halo about the commodity which made both buyers and sellers fancy it was excellent'.[2]

The public continued to trade Gurneys' shares. Wise depositors, mainly London based, began to withdraw their custom. There were rumours in January that the old partners were personally bankrupt, and that the firm had large liabilities arising from the failure of the eponymous – but actually unrelated – Liverpool railway contractors, Watson, Overend & Company, and Spanish merchants, Pinto, Perez & Co. By early May 1866, the deposits of the limited company had been drawn down from £14½ million to under £10 million. These rumours spread to the stock market, and Gurneys' shares were marked to a discount. The Bank rate itself rose again to 8 per cent. Finally, Gurneys

## Batchelor: Nineteenth-century Banking Crises                47

TABLE 2.1   INTEREST RATES AND SECURITY PRICES 1865–7

| Date | Bank rate (%) | Stock price (£) | | |
|---|---|---|---|---|
| | | Overend, Gurney | Discount Corporation | London and Westminster Bank |
| 1865 Dec | 7 | 21½ | 12 | 95 |
| 1866 Jan | 7 | 20⅛ | 10 | 95 |
| Feb | 7 | 19½ | 11⅛ | 96 |
| Mar | 6 | 15⅞ | 9 | 95¾ |
| Apr | 6 | 14½ | 9 | 96 |
| May  2 | 6 | 14½ | 7 | 96¾ |
| 9 | 9 | failed | 7 | 90 |
| 16 | 10 | | 7 | 90 |
| 23 | 10 | | 7 | 91 |
| 30 | 10 | | 7 | 91 |
| Jun | 10 | | 7 | 91 |
| Jul | 10 | | 7 | 94½ |
| Dec | 3½ | | 9 | 97 |
| 1867 Dec | 2 | | n.a. | 98 |

*Source: Bankers' Magazine 1865–7*

admitted that they could no longer meet their obligations. On Thursday 10 May they sought assistance of £400 000 from the Bank. The Bank was in general not inclined to acquiesce in such arrangements, and in particular had no wish to aid its old, now disreputable, rival. The Gurneys' security was deemed inadequate, and that afternoon they were declared insolvent.

The sheer panic that broke in the City on 'Black Friday', 11 May 1866, is graphically described in the accounts of the time. The *Bankers' Magazine* records a 'terror and anxiety which took possession of men's minds for the remainder of that and the whole of the succeeding day'; 'a mob formed in the neighbourhood of Lombard St, Cornhill, Lothbury and Bartholomew Lane'.[3] *The Economist* was more perceptive, 'the country world, which always trusts the London world largely, became frightened. It was disconcerted beyond example and did not know what to do'. In consequence, 'no-one knew who was sound, and who was unsound. The evil was an overexpenditure of capital . . . not a drain of bullion . . . but a failure of credit from intrinsic defect'.[4]

In fact, the Gurney collapse set in train two processes. The first was the progressive failure of a number of country banks and firms with which it was directly associated. The English Joint Stock Bank, for example, immediately suspended payments. The second, and by far the more serious, was a run on London banks and finance houses by the country banks. This quickly became translated into a run on the Bank of England itself. The failure of the 'great house' of Gurneys led the country to fear that other houses might be in trouble. They liquidated their deposits and demanded Bank of England notes. This action had fatal results for a number of finance houses and banks which were genuinely bad risks. The Imperial Credit Association, the Commercial Bank of India and the East, the European Bank all suspended trading in the course of the next week. A number of basically solvent banks also failed, including Hallett Ommanney and Co. Ltd and the Bank of London, later to be taken over by competitors. The immediate crisis was, however, centred on the Bank of England. The massive demand for notes meant that the Bank lost over £3 million from its already depleted note reserve of £5 million (Table 2.2) in a single day, as it swapped these for the securities of frightened country bankers. Under the Bank Charter Act the Issue Department had no authority to

TABLE 2.2   THE BANK OF ENGLAND, 1865–7 (£ million)

| | | *Liabilities* | | | | *Assets* | |
|---|---|---|---|---|---|---|---|
| *Date* | *Notes* | *Govern-ment deposits* | *Other deposits* | *Notes* | *Bullion* | *Govern-ment securities* | *Other securities* |
| 1865 Dec | 20.9 | 8.5 | 13.2 | 7.6 | 13.4 | 9.9 | 22.5 |
| 1866 Mar | 22.0 | 8.4 | 13.2 | 7.7 | 14.4 | 10.9 | 21.9 |
| Apr | 22.6 | 4.4 | 13.3 | 5.8 | 13.9 | 10.7 | 18.5 |
| May  2 | 23.3 | 4.9 | 13.6 | 4.8 | 13.5 | 10.7 | 20.4 |
| 9 | 22.8 | 5.8 | 13.5 | 5.0 | 13.2 | 10.9 | 20.8 |
| 16 | 26.7 | 5.9 | 18.6 | 0.7 | 12.3 | 10.8 | 30.9 |
| 23 | 26.0 | 6.0 | 18.8 | 1.4 | 11.6 | 10.8 | 31.1 |
| 30 | 26.7 | 6.1 | 20.4 | 0.9 | 11.9 | 10.9 | 33.4 |
| Jun | 25.7 | 7.3 | 21.2 | 4.7 | 14.9 | 11.1 | 31.2 |
| Jul | 25.9 | 2.5 | 18.5 | 3.5 | 13.9 | 9.8 | 26.7 |
| Dec | 22.4 | 8.7 | 18.6 | 12.3 | 19.2 | 13.0 | 20.2 |
| 1867 Dec | 23.9 | 7.2 | 18.8 | 13.6 | 18.3 | 14.1 | 17.5 |

augment the note supply. There was a clear danger that a point would be reached at which the Bank would refuse to lend even on good security. The Bank itself was unwilling to press for a relaxation of the Act, since it would make nonsense of its philosophy of operating the Banking Department as a profit-motivated enterprise rather than an arm of monetary control. Indeed, the Bank added to the panic by hesitating over its normal purchases of the best security of all, new issues of government debt. The Chancellor, Gladstone, was, however, besieged by private deputations of bankers and merchants demanding the suspension of the Bank Charter Act, and this measure was announced late on Friday night. Bank rate, already 9 per cent, went to 10 per cent on Saturday. The suspension provided the necessary assurance of Bank support to the country bankers, and although a small drain on notes continued through the following week the fiduciary limit was never in fact broken. The panic gradually subsided.

Gurneys itself was liquidated, and one of the great names of British banking disappeared in a tangle of litigation brought by furious shareholders who felt that the 1865 prospectus had been fraudulent. With hindsight the company might have been saved, but by the time of its liquidation the loss of confidence in the value of the company's assets was so great that the possibility was never entertained. The discount market as a whole suffered permanent damage. It lost a large part of its country banking clientele to the Bank of England, and these depositors did not return even when the credit market became more settled. Bankers deposits at the Bank of England rose permanently from around 30 per cent to 40 per cent of its total liabilities (Table 2.2). The Bank's status also changed. Apart from this growth in its role as the bankers bank, it had in the course of the crisis taken on the lender of last resort role which had been urged upon it by Samuel Gurney a decade before. Although no formal amendment to the Bank Charter Act was made, and although the Bank had no occasion to intervene on such a grand scale for many years, it was henceforth understood that it would support the rest of the financial community at such times of extreme distress.

## THE BARING CRISIS

Baring Bros & Co., the large international merchant bank which failed in 1890, also had its origins in the eighteenth century, in the bank founded in 1763 by John and Francis Baring to exploit their European

50        *Financial Crises and the World Banking System*

connections in the financing of the textile trade. The family bank grew
rapidly, and the standing of the family itself grew apace. Francis was
ennobled in 1793.

The bank continued to grow in the next generation. The world had
changed after the Napoleonic Wars, however, and Barings business
adapted to exploit the new opportunities for profit which arose. One
change was the lifting of restrictions on international flows of gold and
short term money. Barings quickly became a broker in this market,
with its clients concentrated in Europe, in Paris and St Petersburg.
Another change was the growing need for finance for public development projects. Barings, together with Rothschilds and a few other
London-based merchant banks, became specialised in long-term sterling lending to foreign governments and public bodies. Initially, these
loans were also concentrated in Europe and – to a lesser degree – in
North America. But in 1821–2 the boom in these loans spread to
Mexico and Latin America, with large commitments made to Chile,
Colombia, and Brazil.

In this lending there were, of course, new risks. Barings' European
loans were generally well judged, and became a staple part of their
business. Their North America lending was a little less secure. In 1836,
together with a group of other merchant banks, they were called to
account for the quality of their American assets. By this time, however,
they had opened a New York office, and could mount a display of some
expertise which induced the Bank to support them; in truth they may
have been close to insolvency by the end of the decade. Their early
lending in Latin America was certainly unprofitable. None of the loans
made in 1821–2 was yielding income five years later. The extent of these
losses was small, however, and it was shared with many other reputable
institutions. It is no way tarnished Barings reputation as the pre-
eminent merchant bank in London.

Barings business was not, of course, competitive with the Bank of
England. On the contrary, Barings provided many services to the Bank.
At a time when the Bank could not engage in direct swaps and
borrowings with other central banks in continental Europe, Barings
acted as an intermediary for these operations. The Duc de Richelieu
quipped, in 1819, 'There are in Europe six great powers – England,
France, Russia, Austria, Prussia and Baring Brothers.'⁵ Almost continuously through the nineteenth century there were Barings on the
Bank's Board of Directors. These men were generally also Parliamen-
tarians, and were active in public debate over monetary issues, particularly touching on the conduct of the foreign exchanges. Although, as

we have seen, Alexander Baring was, with Hudson Gurney, an opponent of Resumption, the Barings by and large took the Bank's part in such debates. Francis, for example, argued strongly for an extension of the Banks powers to intervene in the exchanges, following the suspension of the Bank Charter Act during the reserve drain of 1848.

As with Gurneys the middle the century brought a turn in Barings fortunes. The change was not marked by any wild behaviour or dramatic collapse, but its effects were nonetheless appreciable. Barings slowly lost market share to their more energetic rivals, the Rothschilds. As with Gurneys the decline seems to have been a matter of personalities. The dominant figures at the bank in the late nineteenth century – Thomas Charles Baring, Edward Charles Baring (Lord Revelstoke) – put themselves about much less than their predecessors. They were irregular contributors to Parliamentary debate, and – as the Bank had less need of Barings' services – poor attenders at the Bank's Court. Their authority within the bank was considerable, but their judgement of risks was poor. Their most notable acts seem to have been the improvement of their estates and the endowment of numerous (Anglican) churches. It is, all in all, hard to resist the impression that they lived off the social and financial capital of the previous two generations. This was, however, regarded as no bad thing. Of Lord Revelstoke, who led the bank into disaster, it was reported in the *Bankers' Magazine* that

> no dishonourable act has ever been recorded. That he was imprudent; that he neglected the hints of good advisers; that he relied too much upon his own judgement, and was altogether too impetuous and autocratic is probably true; but his uprightness has never been in question. The firm was an honourable firm, conducted by an honourable family.[6]

Almost in spite of the management, the name of Barings continued to be a byword for the quality of bills. As late as 1877, Bagehot welcomed the introduction of Treasury Bills by remarking that they were 'as good as Barings'.

The 'imprudence' which led to the collapse of the bank was a policy of specialising in the promotion and finance of South American public development projects. By the 1880s, the new frontier in South America had shifted to the southern states of Argentina and Uruguay, where the construction of railways promised a boom in urban development and trade with the interior. Between 1880 and 1890 over £100 million of sterling loans were made to the national and provincial governments and associated utilities of the River Plate republics. Undeterred by their

52      *Financial Crises and the World Banking System*

earlier misadventures in South America, Barings took the lead in over
£30 million of this lending, occasionally in partnership with J. P.
Morgan. This was by far the largest involvement of any individual
bank. Between 1888 and 1890, for example, they sponsored £13.6
million in Argentine loans; the next most active bank, C. de Murietta &
Co. took on £4.5 million, and Antony Gibb & Son £1.5 million. These
loans soon crowded out more staple items in the Barings asset
portfolio. To some extent, this was involuntary. Much of the South
American paper proved barely marketable. To a large extent it
reflected a conscious policy decision to ride on the investment boom.
British and European interest rates were low, Bank rate never rising
above 4 per cent after 1883. The productivity of European investments
seemed low by comparison with opportunities in the Americas. Barings
itself took a large equity stake in the Buenos Ayres Water and Drainage
Company. By late 1890, Argentine and Uruguayan loans counted for
well over three-quarters of the bank's total portfolio; European loans
amounted to less than 10 per cent.

As with the 'limited mania' which brought down Gurneys, so
Barings collapse was preceded by the bursting of the bubble in River
Plate financing. The Argentine national government ran into difficulties over interest payments as early as April 1890, and only the sale of
the Western Railway at well above any objective market value to a not
disinterested consortium of European financiers enabled payments to
continue. Inside the country, the National Bank, which had been
heavily involved in speculation on land prices, could pay no dividend
when the property boom ended (land prices fell 50 per cent from 1889
to 1890), and the result was a run on the whole banking system. In
Montevideo, the National Bank of Uruguay faced similar problems as
a result of its own speculations on public works, and was forced to
suspend payments. Both Argentina and Uruguay hurriedly negotiated
short term loans with London (for £10 million and £2 million respectively). The run on the Argentine banks, however, precipitated revolution in Buenos Aires on 26 July, and in August the directors of the
National Bank were dismissed. A representative of the national government, Dr Plaza, was dispatched to London to discuss the reconstruction or River Plate finances.

These events had put Barings under increasing pressure. The value of
their Argentine securities fell by a third, the flow of income from South
America began to dry up, and they had a further large liability arising
out of the failure of the Water Company. Barings initially reacted by
borrowing heavily from their London bankers, but by November –

with the arrival of the Argentine negotiator – the reality of their position became plain to the management. Plaza offered to write off the Water Company liability if Barings could raise additional credit to help the Argentine maintain interest payments on its other debts. Barings refused this, as they had refused a similar, less blunt, request from Uruguay, and on Saturday 8 November – through an intermediary – Revelstoke informed the Governor of the Bank of England, William Lidderdale, of the crisis within his bank.

The Bank and the Government were appalled. Both feared a massive drain of foreign capital if it were learned that the still-revered name of Barings was no longer a guarantee of the quality of a London bill. Both agreed that the position of Barings should be kept secret until this threat could be dealt with. They differed only over what should happen to Barings itself. To avert the drain, Lidderdale and Goschen induced Rothschilds to import £3 million in gold from France, and the Bank itself secured a further £1½ million from Russia. The Bank rate, which had been rising in anticipation of trouble in London since the summer, was raised further to 6 per cent. Goschen offered to suspend the Bank Charter Act, but Lidderdale refused. Goschen was reluctant to support Barings in the event that they were insolvent (and this was the opinion of Rothschilds); Lidderdale felt his reserve was sufficient, and in any case had different plans for Barings. He had before him the example of the Bank of France, which the previous year had organised a consortium to rescue a leading Parisian house which ran into liquidity problems after injudicious speculation in copper. He accordingly set to work one of Barings creditors (B. W. Currie, from Glyn, Mills, Currie & Co) and his own man (Buck Greene) – both close friends of Lord Revelstoke – to establish the true position of the bank. By the next Friday, he received an encouraging report that Barings was fundamentally sound, but needed some £10 million to finance current interest obligations. That same day, Lidderdale invited subscriptions to a fund to guarantee Barings' liabilities for a three-year period. The Bank itself, Rothschilds, and other leading merchant banks built the fund up to £3 million by the end of the day. On Saturday, the fund reached £10 million, with cash pressed from the largest domestic joint stock banks and discount houses. On Sunday it reached £17 million. By this time the 'secret' of Barings' illiquidity was out. Although there was a spasm of activity as country banks switched into cash, and the Bank's holdings of their bills rose temporarily by about 20 per cent, no mobs formed, no capital drain ensued, and the authorities felt well content that they had anticipated any flight from London bills.

54      *Financial Crises and the World Banking System*

Barings itself was put into liquidation. However, a committee had
been set up under Lord Rothschild to address the problem of maintaining the flow of Argentine finances. The committee's report resulted in a
favourable valuation of Barings, with the Buenos Ayres Water and
Drainage Co. debt written off completely. The way was open for
Barings to be refloated as a limited liability company a week later, the
capital of the new firm, Messrs Baring & Co. Ltd, being provided by the
Baring family and friends. Revelstoke retired to his society pursuits,
but an equally testy figure from the bank's past, Thomas Charles
Baring, became chairman.

Although the Baring crisis caused a flurry of activity at the Bank and
the Treasury, its impact on financial markets was small. No other bank
fell in its wake. Interest rates fell sharply in December and again in
January, and by the summer of 1891 Bank rate was below 3 per cent, a
measure of the extent of overkill in the Bank's accumulation of
reserves. Lidderdale's reputation was made by the crisis, and he was
elected a Privy Councillor. Two years later, however, when he again
tried to engineer direct support for the other major Argentinian lender,
Muriettas, he found that the City had reappraised the policy of
selective support, and neither he nor his policies (nor Muriettas)
survived another term in office.


## CATASTROPHES AND RUNS

How best can we analyse the mechanics of crises such as those
described above? Conventional economic theory is of limited use. The
familiar models of economics are designed for a world which satisfies
Marshall's observation that 'natura non facit saltum' – things do not
change in jumps. Most of the time, most markets do indeed seem well
behaved. As demand rises and falls, prices respond in a smooth and
symmetric fashion. Moreover, supply elasticities are generally higher
than demand elasticities, and markets dominated by rational and
profit-seeking reactions to price signals are consequently stable. Some
of the time, however, these laws of demand and supply seem to be suspended. The most obvious instances arise in individual asset markets – for
commodities, currencies, shares – when rising prices increase rather
than decrease demand, thus raising the level of prices further; and
falling prices lead to a cumulative, rapid collapse of the whole market.
The 'bubbles' in finance securities and Argentinian bonds described
above are prime examples. Some less obvious instances arise at the

macroeconomic level when income, rather than price, plays an equili-brating role. A system in which economies gravitate to equilibria at either very low or very high income levels, separated by an unstable region, can arise naturally from the rapid population increase and low savings propensities which attend rising incomes in poor countries. A common feature of all these bubbles, in prices and incomes, is that it is hard to return to normality. Although a large boom or crash may have been initiated by a small change in one variable – a rise in price, a fall in income – an equal and opposite change will not have an offsetting effect. Once a market has collapsed, it takes a long time for confidence to be restored. Once a country has lapsed into poverty it takes a 'big push' to beat the low-level equilibrium trap and return to sustained growth at a high income level.

Frequently, the behaviour of economic systems under normal con-ditions, and their behaviour under crisis conditions, are treated on different levels. The crisis phase is either described by a special model, or by a special case of the conventional model which arises when market participants become irrational. The attraction of catastrophe theory is that this dichotomy is avoided. It suggests that the two conditions described above, one involving gradual symmetric change and a set of stable equilibria, the other involving irreversible step changes and unstable equilibria, are not distinct phenomena, but simply different states of the same system. Catastrophe theory models can function as descriptions of the smooth continuous processes seen in normal times. On the other hand, they do permit the economy to stray into regions where the discontinuities and hysteresis effects so charac-teristic of manias and panics can occur. Catastrophe theory itself, in the form proposed by Thom (1972), has much larger claims that this, of course, and its mathematics have stretched the boundaries of tradi-tional topological theory. Fortunately, largely through the efforts of Zeeman (1977), the language of the theory has been reduced to an accessible form, for use in theoretical – and hopefully empirical – work in describing discrete events in physical and social systems. A number of popular introductions to the subject are now available (Woodcock and Davis, 1978; Saunders, 1980), and the wide range of applications is displayed in Poston and Stewart (1978).

In economics, several attempts have been made to understand speculative markets through the medium of catastrophe theory, start-ing with Zeemans own (1974) analysis of stock markets, and including most recently an account of the mid-1970s UK property boom and collapse by Kerry Schott (1983), and a conjecture about the sources of exchange rate overshooting by de Grauwe (1981). Pertinent to our present paper, Ho and Saunders (1980) present a catastrophe model of bank failure based on inappropriate central bank responses to crisis conditions. Several attempts have also been made to analyse macroeconomic fluctuations in this framework. Varian (1979) and George (1981) adapt Kaldor's growth model to generate catastrophic switches between boom and recession; and the connection between multiple equilibria and catastrophe conditions in a neoclassical general equilibrium model is formally demonstrated by Balasko (1978).

In this section, we explore two catastrophe theory models which are potentially helpful in understanding the Gurney and Baring crisis. One is a model of financial crisis. It is applicable to the bubbles in finance securities and Argentine bonds which preceded the two banking crises. The second is a model of a bank run itself.

## A Catastrophe Theory Model of Financial Crisis

The first model revolves around the reactions of a 'fast' variable, the price of a speculative asset (common stocks, property, finance securities, Argentinian bonds), to slowly rising and falling demand. In normal conditions, defined to be those when the asset is traded for its intrinsic usefulness (or 'fundamental' or 'hedge' purposes) a negative excess demand will induce a falling price, a positive demand a rising price. These cases are illustrated as points $a$ and $b$ in the left panel of Figure 2.1. The conventional law of supply and demand operates, and prices move smoothly along the continuous locus shown. In speculative conditions, defined to be those arising when assets are held for capital gain, the rate of change of price as well as the level of price affects demand. Positive hedge demand will cause prices to rise; the price rise will induce a further speculative pressure and prices will rise still further. On the other hand, falling prices will cause disinvestment, and prices will fall faster than in normal times in response to a given negative demand shock. The result is a bifurcation into a bull market and a bear market, as illustrated in the right panel of Figure 2.1. The greater the speculative interest in a market relative to the hedge interest, the more pronounced will be the separation of the two surfaces be, for a given initial shock.

The speculative scenario admits the possibility of a sharp price fall and hence bankruptcy of the many investors in the market. As soon as a certain number of speculators ('insiders') sell out, and excess demand becomes sufficiently negative, all remaining investors will recognise the

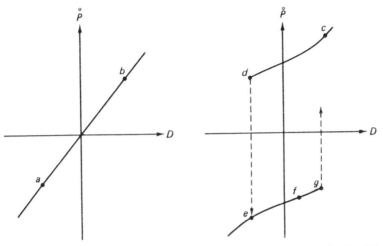

Normal Conditions                          Speculative Conditions

*Key:* P = asset price inflation
      D = excess demand for asset

FIG 2.1   Asset Price Inflation and Excess Demand

probability of price falls, and attempt to sell out. Prices will fall immediately this process starts and the system will jump from the end of the bull market (point *d*) to the start of the bear market (point *e*). The greater the speculative interest in the market, the greater must be the reversal necessary to cause such a market collapse.

Note that a recovery in demand would not necessarily restore bull market conditions. Prices would continue to fall, but at a slower rate (point *f*). Only if some critical excess demand level is reached would confidence be restored and the economy jump from point *g*, say, to point *c*.

The process is an example of a 'cusp catastrophe'. When drawn in three dimensions, the normal and catastrophe situations of Figure 2.1 appear as sections of a continuous three-dimensional surface, taken at increasing values of a splitting variable (in this case, the share of speculators in the market). In Zeeman's stock market model, the splitting variable is the number of 'chartists' trading on price extrapolations, relative to 'fundamentalists'; in Schott's property market model it is the level of borrowing undertaken by investors with no natural position in the property market. The full set-up is shown in Figure 2.2.

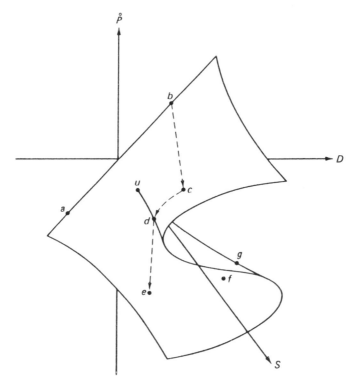

Key: P = asset price inflation
     D = excess demand
     S = degree of speculative interest

FIG. 2.2    Asset Prices – A Cusp Catastrophe

The surface describes all equilibria of a single 'state variable', price
change, corresponding to two 'control variables', excess demand and
speculative interest. The boom, bust and recovery phases of a crisis can
be described as a trajectory on this surface. A positive demand shock
will move the economy to point *b*; rising prices attract speculators and
the system moves towards point *c*; as the underlying demand vanishes,
a few investors start to sell out, pushing prices down further, so that
point *d* is reached; at this point, the catastrophic price fall to *e* occurs,
as all remaining speculators try to sell out. This sort of catastrophic fall
was a possibility from the moment that the speculative interest
exceeded the splitting factor *u*, where the surface became folded. So

long as $S < u$, the system would behave normally, with prices rising when demand is positive, and falling when it is negative. Recovery could be stimulated by some externally generated 'big push' in demand sufficient to move the system to point $g$; but since $S > u$ still, the possibility of catastrophe remains. The safer road to recovery involves reducing the other control variable $S$, reducing the speculative interest and moving from $e$ towards $a$.

This model has a number of nice properties. It has obvious application to the 'limited mania' of the 1860s, and the South American bond speculation of the 1880s. In both instances, the pay-off to the underlying commercial activity was known to be of an uncertain and long-term nature; but the assets were valued for their potential for short-term price movements. The model allows a normal trading situation to degenerate smoothly into a potentially catastrophic situation. It allows small changes in the environment to precipitate sudden large changes in price. This catastrophe, once it occurs, is not simply reversible.

Such models have, however, come in for considerable criticism. Most fundamentally, Sussman and Zahler (1978) argue that the functional form of the cusp catastrophe is not logically implied by the axioms of economic theory. It is a pure self standing assumption and not a testable proposition. Economics is rarely so fussy in its choice of tools. Linear and loglinear functions are used throughout the discipline for their great didactic value, and the catastrophe surface seems no more objectionable than these elementary forms. We should make it clear that in all applications of catastrophe theory in economics, model builders have been obliged to make arbitrary assumptions in order to force the system into a catastrophe. This is true of the model sketched here. The act of trading on extrapolations of prices is not itself irrational, in spite of the arguments of Weintraub (1983); Blanchard and Watson (1982) provide several counter-examples. What is inexplicable in such a model is why a fold rather than, say, a simple discontinuity appears in the surface as this sort of trading grows. Other catastrophe models contain more explicitly irrational elements. De Grauwe (1983) for example, assumes a particular regressive exchange rate expectations scheme. Ho and Saunders (1980), in their bank failure model, assume arbitrary and inappropriate intervention by the banking authority; Flood and Garber (1981), while not working within a catastrophe theory framework, also characterise bank 'runs' as the consequence of unrealistic pegging of a price or exchange rate by the monetary authority.

60        *Financial Crises and the World Banking System*

The remainder of this section is addressed to the problem of constructing a model of a banking run. As we have seen, this may or may not follow from a financial collapse. It proves possible to characterise these possibilities as the stable and unstable facets of a catastrophe model; but a certain element of arbitrariness (though not irrationality) must be imputed to investors if this interpretation is to stand.

**An Uncertainty Model of a Bank Run**

We start by outlining the operations of a single financial intermediary ('bank'). Such an institution attracts deposit and capital liabilities ($D$ and $K$), and invests these in a portfolio consisting of riskless reserves ($R$) and risky loans ($A$). The detail of the actual balance sheets of institutions as different as Gurneys (bill brokers) and Barings (merchant bankers) would, of course, reveal very different items within these broad classes of liabilities and assets. Gurneys' deposits consisted mainly of surplus short-term funds placed in the money market by domestic banks; Barings took the funds of non-bank and individual investors. Barings was a family concern until just after the 1890 crisis, and its capital represented the private wealth of the partners; Gurneys became a public company just before the 1866 crisis, and part of its capital was attracted from outside shareholders. The advances made by Gurneys were largely to English industrial and commercial enterprises, on security of their customers' short-term bills. Barings, on the other hand, provided medium-term bond financing, often to public utilities and governments, throughout the industrialising world – Russia, Europe and the Americas. In spite of these differences, the management problems of both types of institution are essentially the same – to maximise profits from the asset portfolio subject to being able to meet deposit withdrawals with a high probability; and to minimise the cost of raising liabilities subject to the need to reduce the probability of insolvency to some low level.

The risks which make it necessary for such banks to hold low-yielding reserve assets and to raise expensive capital liabilities come from random fluctuations in deposit inflows and the value of the stock of advances. The bank will face a liquidity crisis if its reserves are insufficient to cover a deposit withdrawal ($\Delta D > R$). It will actually be insolvent if its capital and income from assets is insufficient to cover interest payments to depositors. Suppose that in some period liabilities to depositors increase by $\Delta D$, and assets' values change by $\Delta A$. Then the bank is insolvent if

$$A + R + \Delta A < D + \Delta D \tag{1}$$

or $\quad (\Delta D - \Delta A) - (A + R - \,^{\cdot}D) > 0$

$\qquad (\Delta D - \Delta A) - K > 0$

Normalising for size by dividing through by the level of deposits $D$, and writing $\Delta D/D$ as $\Delta d$, $\Delta A/D$ as $\Delta a$ and $K/D$ as $k$, this condition becomes

$$\Delta d - \Delta a - k > 0 \tag{2}$$

or $\qquad\qquad z < 0$

where we define $z$ as the 'safety level' of the bank, where

$$z = k - \Delta d + \Delta a \tag{3}$$

The probability of bankruptcy thus depends on two stochastic factors, the probability distribution of deposit flows and the probability distribution of asset values, and two factors – the reserve and capital ratios – which are decision variables for the bank. For convenience, we assume that $d$ and $a$ have zero mean, so that only their variances enter this calculation. We also assume that banks follow optimal policies with respect to the selection of $r$ and $k$. This means that reserve and capital ratios depend on deposit and loan variances, and on the costs of emergency borrowing and insolvency (Baltensperger, 1980). Since these costs can be taken to be the same for all banks, differences in the probability of insolvency between banks will be (increasing) functions of the deposit and loan variances only.

Consider now a system of $n$ such banks, ranked from 1 to $n$ in decreasing order of riskiness, so that bank 1 is the riskiest (in terms of its $z$-value) and bank $n$ the least risky. For simplicity, we also assume that the $z$ values increase uniformly, so that if $z_1$ is the safety level of the riskiest bank, then the $j$-th bank will have $z_j = jz_1$. Without loss of generality, we can measure risk in terms of units of size $z_1$. Consequently, a fall in all asset values of $j$ units will send banks $1, 2 \ldots j$ into insolvency, but banks $j + 1, \ldots n$ will be safe.

Depositors can hold their (liquid) wealth in two forms – as 'riskless' cash, or as deposits in these risky banks. The distribution of this portfolio will depend on depositors *perceptions* of the risks of each bank. An increase in the perceived risk of a single bank will cause

62          *Financial Crises and the World Banking System*

deposits to flow out of that bank, an increase in the perceived risk in the
whole banking system will cause a general switch from bank deposits
into cash. If a bank is perceived to be insolvent *all* deposits will be
withdrawn.

A key element of our model is that depositors may have less than
complete information on the balance sheets of individual banks.
Typically, depositors in banks are numerous, and do not possess even
shareholders rights to information; on the other hand, the bank
portfolio is often large and complex. Moreover, Leland and Pyle (1977)
have suggested that a degree of confidentiality *must* surround bank
portfolios, or outsiders could capture the returns to the asset manager's
efforts by duplicating his investments. This assumption, of less than
complete information, changes radically the impact of a shock to asset
values on the banking system.

Consider first the case of complete information. A fall in asset values
sufficient to render bank 1 insolvent will have no impact whatsoever on
deposits as other banks, irrespective of the size of the shock to bank 1.
Conversely, a specific increase in the asset values of a single bank will
not cause investors to reappraise the risks of other banks, nor give rise
to an expansion of the banking industry through new entry ('negative
insolvency'). The relation between the change in the degree of insolvency of bank 1 ($z_1$) and the degree of insolvency in the system ($z.$) is
simply a 45° line, as shown on in the left panel of Figure 2.3.

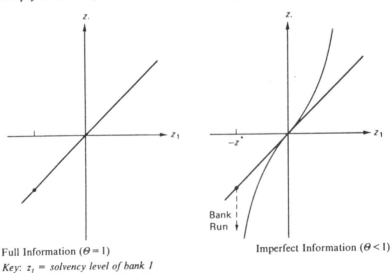

Full Information ($\theta = 1$)                          Imperfect Information ($\theta < 1$)

*Key:* $z_1$ = *solvency level of bank 1*
        $z.$ = *solvency levelof banking system*

FIG. 2.3   Effect of Bank 1 Insolvency on System Solvency

*Batchelor: Nineteenth-century Banking Crises*              63

Consider now a situation where investors are less than fully informed about the individual banks balance sheets for the current year. The depositor can form some estimate of the z-value of each bank on the basis of the limited information which is available about the state of the balance sheet, say $\hat{z}_j = \hat{z}\,(\Omega_j)$. But it will be optimal to use other available information as well. In particular, the $z_j$ estimate can be improved by using information on

   – the z-scores of other banks

   – the z-scores of other years

We look at the optimal use of each type of information in turn.

If differences in z-scores between neighbouring banks are normal random variates, with equal variances, the optimal estimate of the safety level of bank $j$ will take the form of a weighted average of estimates of safety levels of all other banks in the system, with the weights decreasing exponentially according to how distant the bank is from bank $j$ in the safety rank order. So we might say

$$\hat{z}_j = \lambda_j \sum_{i=1}^{n} (1-\theta)^{|i-j|} . (j/i)\hat{z}_i \qquad (4)$$

where $\lambda_j$ is simply a factor scaling the weights $(1-\theta)^{|i-j|}$ to sum to unity, and the estimated value of each bank $i$ must be multiplied by $(j/i)$ to form an estimate of $z_j$ because of our assumption of uniform differences in risk. The crucial parameter is the discount factor $\theta$. This can take values between 0 and 1, and *serves as an index of the amount of information on the relative safety of banks*. If $\theta$ is high, weights decrease quickly as we move away from bank $j$; because so much is known about individual banks, only the information on banks very similar to bank $j$ are used in assessing its safety. If $\theta$ is low, the weights do not fall off so rapidly. Depositors' ignorance of bank performance is so great that even data on banks quite dissimilar from bank $j$ is gratefully seized upon and used in assessing the risk of the bank.

The limiting cases $\theta = 1$ and $\theta = 0$ are of particular interest. When information on the relative standing of banks is complete, $\theta = 1$ and the weights on all z-scores in formula (4) go to zero except that on bank $j$, which tends to 1. When information on the relative standing of banks is wholly absent, $\theta = 0$ and the weights on all z-scores in formula (4) become the same. As a result the solution of the system of equations (4) will produce identical values of $z_j$ for all values of $j$; each bank is assumed no better or worse than its neighbour.

The assumption of limited information about relative riskiness is

sufficient to induce banking 'runs' in the sense that a given shock to
asset values will induce a disproportionate number of bankruptcies.
Suppose asset values at bank 1 fall by $z^*$ units. Depositors in all other
banks will revise downwards their estimates of the safety of these
banks, bank 2 being the worst affected, and bank $n$ the least. There will
be a general switch from deposits into cash. This may be sufficient to
break a number of banks 2, 3, ... $m$ which are objectively solvent. A
rise in asset values and entry of new banks would, conversely, spread
optimism through the system. As a result, the relation between asset
shocks and insolvencies and entries under conditions of incomplete
information will be more highly geared than in the case of complete
information, and will take the form shown in the right panel of Figure
2.3. In the degenerate case of no information on relative bank status
($\theta = 0$), the locus becomes vertical, the failure of bank 1 triggering the
failure of *all* banks (which must be assumed to be identical to the failed
bank), the survival of bank 1 triggering a flood of new entries. This
extreme case of quality uncertainty is the 'lemons' problem discussed in
Akerlof (1970),

So far, we have discussed only the contribution of the estimated
$z$-scores of other banks to the assessment of the $z$-score of an individual
bank. We now consider the contribution of current and past information
on the balance sheet of the bank itself. If the $z$-score of a bank follows a
random walk around a stochastic 'trend', the optimal forecast of $z$ at
time $t$ is known to be an exponentially weighted average of past values of
the variable: thus

$$\hat{z}_t = \varphi \sum_{t=0}^{\infty} (1-\varphi)^t z_{-t}$$

The discount factor in (5) can be shown to depend on the ratio of the
variance of the random walk process to the variance of the underlying
trend (Muth, 1960). The less unpredictable is the time series, the lower
will be $\varphi$, and values of $z$ from the distant past will be given a
substantial weight in the calculation. In the limit, as $\varphi \to 0$, *all* past
information, however distant, is given equal weight. The greater is the
'noise' in the series, the higher will be the optimal value of $\varphi$, and the
less information is there in past values of $z$; only recent safety levels are
used to gauge the solvency of the bank. In the limit, as $\varphi \to 1$, only
current period information is used, and no regard is paid even to recent
safety levels.

The value of $\varphi$ determines the reaction of $z$ to shocks to asset values.
Suppose $z$ has varied randomly around a constant rate $\bar{z}$ for a long
period, so that $\hat{z} = \bar{z}$, but at $t$ there are rumours that the bank is

slipping into serious insolvency. Clearly $\hat{z}$ will fall, and the extent of the fall will depend on the weight given to recent information. If $\varphi$ is large, the insolvency will be instantly recognised, and deposits withdrawn. If $\varphi$ is low, insolvency may not be recognised, and depositors will continue to invest in the bank, though at lower levels. They will be impressed by the bank's 'reputation'. As the insolvency persists, so the perceived safety level of the bank will approach its true, negative value. A recovery in the fortunes of the bank will not necessarily be accompanied by a return of deposits in such circumstances. The longer the period of insolvency and the lower the value of $\varphi$, the greater must be the assurances given to depositors before their rating of the bank rises to a positive level.

These persistence effects introduce an asymmetry into the reactions of the banking system as a whole to rising and falling asset values. Imagine that asset values in bank 1 fall in a situation of incomplete information described by a non-zero parameter $\theta$. A number $(m)$ of additional banks will fail. Imagine now that the initiating change in asset values is reversed. The rating of bank 1 will not immediately improve to a solvency level, since its failure has a non-zero weight in perceptions of its current value. This undervaluation of bank 1 will also keep other banks undervalued. Recovery of the whole system can come about only in two ways. One is through the passage of time. Eventually, memories of the bank 1 insolvency will be forgotten, and one by one its neighbouring banks will be reconstituted starting with bank $m$. Alternatively, bank 1 can be given a positive endowment of assets. For each level of uncertainty $\theta$ and each discount factor $\varphi$ there will be a corresponding change in asset values which will return the whole system to solvency. This endowment must be larger, the larger is $\theta$ and the larger is the initial deficit of bank 1. The endowment must also be larger, the smaller is the discount factor $\varphi$; if memories are long, it will take a large boost to a bank's assets to restore the confidence of investors.

A similar argument can be made for the case of a rise in the assets of bank 1. This will induce a general revaluation upwards in assessments of bank safety, and induce a number of new entrants to the industry. This boom will continue even if the change in the solvency position of bank 1 is immediately reversed; and it will take time, or a collapse of bank 1, to reduce the system to its original size. These pessimistic and optimistic phases of the system are illustrated in the left and right panels of Figure 2.4, for high discount and low discount cases respectively. The return loci show the system z-scores, and implicitly the

66              *Financial Crises and the World Banking System*

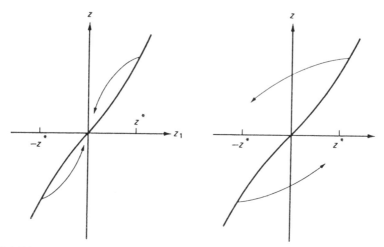

High Discount Factor $\varphi$

Low Discount Factor $\varphi$

*Key*: $z_1$ = solvency level of bank 1
       $z.$ = solvency level of banking system

FIG. 2.4   Banking System Insolvency: Alternative Recovery Paths

number of new/failed banks in the system, at various solvency levels of bank 1, in period $t + 1$, following a shock of size $z^*$ to the asset values of bank 1 in period $t$.

There is an asymmetry in the system, but no genuine catastrophe. No point is reached where the mood of optimism or pessimism is completely broken by the reversal in bank 1's asset position.

In order to generate a catastrophe similar to that of Figure 2.2, we should have to assume that the confidence factor $\varphi$ was itself a systematic variable. Specifically, for any given disturbance $z^*$ there must be some endowment $k\,(\theta)\,z^*$, with $k < 0$ and $k' < 0$, which is sufficient to persuade depositors to forget the track record of the bank. As $z \rightarrow k\,(\theta)\,z^*$, then $\varphi \rightarrow 1$; if $z$ exceeds $k\,(\theta)\,z^*$ the endowment is treated as a 'new' shock and not only will bank 1 recover but the system will expand through the recovery of confidence in neighbouring banks. The feasible states of the system, $z.$, following a shock $z^*$ to bank 1, may then conceivably be described for all values of the splitting parameter $\theta$ by the cusp surface shown on Figure 2.5. The implications of this set-up are spelt out in the next section's discussion of the policy options

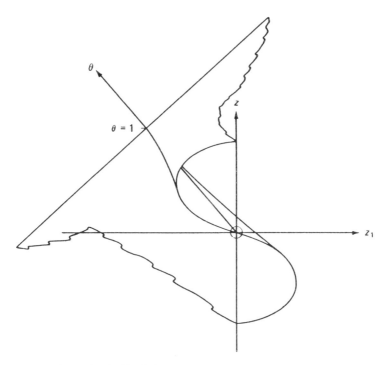

Key: $z_1$ = solvency level of bank 1
     $z.$ = solvency level of banking system
     $\theta$ = information parameter

FIG. 2.5   Banking System Recovery Paths: A Catastrophe Representation

considered by the authorities after the Gurney and Baring crises. Before leaving the theory, however, it is worth noting that this catastrophe framework, rather like the catastrophe model of financial crisis described earlier, is the product of two steps. One is an argument based on a rational, optimising behaviour in the face of limited information; this yielded the prediction of a bank run. The other is a somewhat arbitrary argument based on the assertion that there is some shock to the system which will cause it to switch from one state to another, and that the size of this shock depends on the value of the initiating shock, and the information parameter. This may yield the cusp catastrophe. Whether such behaviour occurs in practice is an empirical issue rather than a consequence of *a priori* theorising.

68          *Financial Crises and the World Banking System*

AN EVALUATION OF THE CRISES

The models sketched above have been developed for two reasons. One is simply to illustrate alternative approaches to the modelling of large and irreversible changes in economic circumstances. The other is to help elucidate the similarities and differences between the two episodes described in our earlier narrative. Our argument is that a banking run may be initiated by a commercial 'catastrophe'; but its dynamics are governed by a somewhat different process. The degree of instability in asset price bubbles arises from the degree of speculative interest in the market. The extent of a banking run depends instead on the quality of information on individual bank liquidity which is available to depositors. In the language of catastrophe theory, speculative interest is the 'splitting factor' in a speculative bubble, information is the splitting factor in a bank run.

The shocks which sent Gurneys and Barings into liquidation share common features which seem well described by the catastrophe model outlined above. If we concede that the possible equilibria for bill and bond prices, asset demands and bank indebtedness exist on a cusp, then even rational behaviour is liable to end in a price collapse. Clearly it was rash of the early investors in bubble companies and Argentine mortgages to subscribe to these ventures. Their expectations were over-optimistic. But as long as there is a probability that such expectations are correct, it is rational for other investors to follow. Only after the expectation has been falsified will it cease to make sense, and all investors will sell out; but by this time many quite reputable banks may be involved.

The outcomes of the Gurney and Baring crises differed greatly, and we would argue that these differences can be equally well described in terms of the bank run model described above. The crucial difference between the two crises lay in the amount of information available to the public at large about the relative state of affairs at the respective banks.

Country bankers had no reason to suppose that Gurneys was any better or any worse than any other discount house. Their track record was long and secure. If anything, current rumour made them look better than many other houses in 1865, and their share price reflected this opinion. Only a few insiders in London were privy to the risks run by Gurneys, and these investors withdrew early in the year, and held their tongues for fear of causing mischief until the collapse had occurred. The upshot of this was that when Overend, Gurney failed, country banks had no means of telling whether the problem was specific to Gurneys or widespread through the money market. Their rational reaction was to assume the worst, and withdraw deposits from the whole system, hitting first those which looked – like Gurneys – overexposed in finance security lending. In terms of our model, the value of $\theta$ was low, and the size of the run consequently high.

The case of Barings was quite different. The extent of Barings involvement in the Argentine was well known. Summaries of bond issues and the sponsoring banks were published as regularly in *The Economist* through the 1880s as are new international bond issues today. The value of the information parameter $\theta$ was high. Only its long history of financial probity, its 'name', prevented its depositors from withdrawing as these assets were accumulated. Because the special position of Barings was well known, there was no mass withdrawal of deposits from private banks when the crisis came. Instead, only those banks known to be most similar to Barings were hit. Muriettas, in particular, suffered badly and finally closed in 1893. Banks with better diversified assets in Europe, North America and North Africa such as Rothschilds, gained rather than lost deposits.

If we regard these events as occurring on a catastrophe surface, we can see from Figure 2.6 that a number of options exist to prevent catastrophe or ameliorate its consequences. Suppose the system is poised on the upper fold of the cusp, at a point such as $a$, where the least suspicion of a fall in bank 1 ( = Gurneys' or Barings') assets will cause a run on other banks and a fall to a point such as $b$. The authorities have two options. They can permit the catastrophe to occur, or they can try to maintain confidence in the system. If the first course is followed the extent of losses in the banking system can be reduced by either increasing information about the true (solvent) condition of most banks, or by giving bank 1 an endowment of assets sufficient to restore confidence. These two policies will move the system in the direction shown by the arrows $B1$ and $B2$. If the second course is followed, the authorities must either *decrease* the amount of information in the system (so that less weight is given to adverse rumours about bank 1), or provide direct assistance to bank 1. These policies shift the system in the directions $A1$ and $A2$.

In the Gurney case, the Bank took the first course $B1$. Its willingness to buy the bills of other leading banks and discount houses was a signal to the country banks that, in the Bank's opinion at least, these institutions were fundamentally sound. This is the sense of 'last resort' lending. In principle, the run could have been avoided by making good Gurneys' losses (policy $A2$), and increasing its solvency by an amount

70          *Financial Crises and the World Banking System*

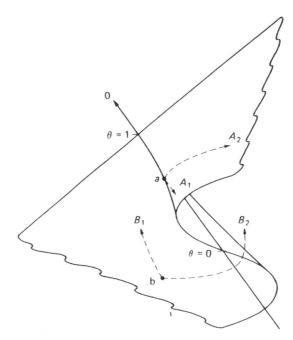

Key: $\Theta$ = information parameter
     $a$ = pre-catastrophe state
     $b$ = post-catastrophe state

FIG. 2.6   The Avoidance of Catstrophe: Policy Alternatives

sufficient to offset the loss in credibility which would follow the disclosure of a decade of reckless management. But this would have been expensive; there would have been no guarantee that the threat of a run would not reappear in the next decade; and the strained relationship between the Bank and Gurneys made such an action in any case unlikely. A third possibility, later pondered by Bagehot, would have been to cover up the Gurney bank's affairs totally, until the new management could recover the losses – in effect, our policy $A1$; but when the bank became public in 1865 that (dubious) option – and the reconstruction option $B2$ – was renounced.

The Bank's intervention in the Barings crisis is much more enigmatic. Superficially, the granting of an excessively large and long-lived guarantee on the assets of an ailing bank is consistent with the second route out of catastrophe described above ($A2$). On further inspection, it is

unclear whether catastrophe was threatened at all. Many early historians of the period (for example, Powell, 1915) emphasise that Barings
deficit was much less than that of Gurneys, and amounted to a liquidity
crisis rather than genuine insolvency. Although there is something in
this argument, it seems to be based on a comparison of the assets of the
two banks at liquidation. It must be remembered that for this purpose
Barings was allowed to write off a large capital loss, and was given a
very favourable value for its surviving Argentine bonds. If true, of
course, this argument vitiates the case for any *long-term* support at all
for the bank, and puts into doubt the need for the monetary authority
to organise further lending. Let us, however, grant that there was a
potential insolvency at Barings; would this have triggered a banking
run? Our reading of public reaction to the crisis is that catastrophe
probably did not threaten, since the system was well informed about
the relative risks being run by the major merchant banks. In terms of
our catastrophe model the value of $\theta$ was high. This, of course, would
vitiate *any* case for a large-scale support operation for the weakest
bank.

The actions of the Bank of England in the Baring crises seem instead
to have been motivated less by a desire to make the banking system
secure than by a desire to save the 'name' of Barings itself. This is the
only explanation for the scale and time span of the assistance given, for
the appointment of auditors for Barings who were bound to produce a
favourable report, and for the haste which was made in the Rothschild
committee to roll over the whole Argentinian debt. There may have
seemed good reasons for helping Barings' name survive. But the name
of Barings was no more nor less reputable in the country than that of
Gurneys before their collapse, and it is hard to resist the conclusion
that it was the difference in political and personal relations between
these institutions and the officials of the Bank of England which
determined who should sink and who should swim.

## NOTES

1. *The Economist*, 15 July 1865, p. 845.
2. *The Economist*, 19 May 1866, p. 1516.
3. *Bankers' Magazine*, June 1866, pp. 45–6.
4. *The Economist*, 19 May 1866, p. 1516.
5. Cited in Powell (1915), p. 340.
6. *Bankers' Magazine*, March 1981, p. 619.

72					*Financial Crises and the World Banking System*

REFERENCES

Akerlof, G. A. (1970) 'The market for "lemons"; quality uncertainty and the market mechanism', *Quarterly Journal of Economics* 89: 488–500.

Balasko, Y. (1978) 'The behaviour of economic equilibria: a catastrophe theory approach', *Behavioural Science* 23: 375–82.

Baltensperger, E. (1980) 'Alternative approaches to the theory of the banking firm', *Journal of Monetary Economics* 6: 1–37.

Blanchard, O. J. and Watson, M. W. (1982) 'Bubbles, rational expectations and financial markets', in P. Wachtel (ed.) *Crises in the Economic and Financial Structure* (New York: Lexington Books).

Fisher, I. (1933) 'The debt-deflation theory of great depressions', *Econometrica* 1: 337–57.

Flood, R. P. and Garber, P. (1981), 'A systematic banking collapse in a perfect foresight world', NBER Working Paper 691.

de Grauwe, P. A. (1983) 'Exchange rate oscillations and catastrophe theory', in E. Claasen and Salin, P. (eds) *Recent Issues in the Theory of Flexible Exchange Rates* (Amsterdam: North-Holland).

George, P. (1981) 'Equilibrium and catastrophes in economics', *Scottish Journal of Political Economy*, 28, 1: 43–61.

Ho, T. and Saunders, A. (1980), 'A catastrophe model of bank failure', *Journal of Finance*, 35, 5, December: 1189–1207.

Kindleberger, C. P. (1978) *Manias, Panics and Crashes: A History of Financial Crises* (London: Macmillan).

Leland, H. and Pyle, D. (1977) 'Information asymmetries, financial structure and financial intermediation', *Journal of Finance* 32: 321–86.

Minsky, H. P. (1977) 'A theory of systematic fragility', in E. I. Altman and A. W. Sametz (eds), *Financial Crises* (New York: Wiley).

Muth, J. F. (1960) 'Optimal properties of exponentially weighted forecasts', *Journal of the American Statistical Association* 55.

Poston, T. and Stewart, I. (1978) *Catastrophe Theory and its Applications* (London: Pitman).

Powell, E. T. (1915) *The Evolution of the Money Market 1385–1915* (London: Frank Cass, 1966, 3rd impression).

Saunders, P. T. (1980) *An Introduction to Catastrophe Theory* (Cambridge: Cambridge University Press).

Schott, K. (1983) 'The British financial crisis in 1974–5: a catastrophe theory approach', *Oxford Economic Papers*.

Sussman, H. J. and Zahler, R. S. (1978) 'A critique of applied catastrophe theory in the behavioural sciences', *Behavioural Science* 23: 383–9.

Thom, R. (1972) *Structural Stability and Morphogenesis* (New York: Benjamin; translated version, 1975).

Varian H. R. (1979) 'Catastrophe theory and the business cycle', *Economic Inquiry* 17: 14–28.

Weintraub, E. R. (1983) 'Zeeman's unstable stock exchange'. *Behavioural Science* 28: 39–83.

Woodcock, A. and Davis, M. (1978) *Catastrophe Theory* (Harmondsworth: Pelican Books).

Zeeman, E. C. (1974) 'On the unstable behaviour of stock exchanges', *Journal of Mathematical Economics* 1: 39–49.

Zeeman, E. C. (1977) *Catastrophe Theory: Selected Papers 1972–1977.* (Reading, Mass.: Addison-Wesley).

In addition to the above journal references, the histories of Overend, Gurney & Co. and Baring Bros & Co. have been pieced together from contemporary accounts in *The Economist* and the *Bankers Magazine.* Additional material on the history and performance of Gurneys came from the summing up of Sir Richard Malins *In re Overend, Gurney and Co. ex parte Oakes and Parke*, Law Reports (Chancery) Vol. III 1866–7; and from Sir John Clapham (1970) *The Bank of England: A History* vol. 2 (Cambridge University Press) and F. W. Fetter (1965) *Development of British Monetary Orthodoxy* (Harvard UP) On Barings, Clapham (1970) and L. S. Presnell (1968) 'Gold flows, banking reserves and the Baring crisis of 1890', in Whittlesley, C. R. and Wilson, J. S. G. (eds) *Essays in Money and Banking in honour of R. S. Sayers* (Oxford University Press) were also helpful.

# [4]

EXPLORATIONS IN ECONOMIC HISTORY **26**, 135–160 (1989)

## Canadian Banks, Gold, and the Crisis of 1907*

GEORG RICH

*Swiss National Bank*

The passive monetary policy of the Canadian government before 1914 was remarkably successful, but came under unusual strain during the crisis of 1907 in New York. This was because the trade credit extended by Canadian exporters to foreigners played a crucial role in generating seasonal movements in Canadian domestic money stock (along with fluctuations in domestic economic activity) and New York interest rates were unusually high in 1907. This contrasts with traditional accounts of the Canadian crisis which emphasize internal factors, especially decreased elasticity of note issue. This is why Viner could argue that Canadian actions made the New York panic worse, when in fact they helped ameliorate it. © 1989 Academic Press, Inc.

An important feature of the pre-1914 Canadian gold standard was its ability to operate with a minimum of government intervention on the money and foreign exchange markets. Prior to 1914, Canada did not operate a central bank.[1] The federal government was empowered to issue notes—commonly known as Dominion notes—which were redeemable in gold upon demand.[2] Dominion notes were used extensively by the chartered banks as cash reserves together with gold.[3] Non-bank holdings

---

* This paper was originally presented at the Thirteenth Conference on Quantitative Methods in Canadian Economic History funded by the Social Science Research Council of Canada and Wilfrid Laurier University. Financial support by the Social Science Research Council of Canada is gratefully acknowledged. I am indebted to Charles Goodhart, Jim Irwin, Anna Schwartz, Geoffrey Wood, and an anonymous referee for very helpful comments. I would also like to thank W. Hermann for computational assistance.

[1] The Bank of Canada was not established until 1935.

[2] United States and British gold coins, as well as Dominion notes were legal tender in Canada. The public was required to accept U.S. ten-dollar pieces (eagles) at 10 Canadian dollars and British one-pound coins (sovereigns) at $4.86 2/3. Thus, the mint par value of the Canadian dollar equalled that of the U.S. dollar. The government was obliged to redeem Dominion notes in eagles or sovereigns. Canadian gold coins were not issued until 1908. See Shortt (1922) for an excellent survey of pre-1914 Canadian monetary and banking legislation.

[3] Banks were required to hold at least one-third of their cash reserves in the form of Dominion notes. Otherwise, the banks were unfettered by reserve requirements. However, the government was subject to a minimum gold reserve requirement on outstanding Dominion notes.

of Dominion notes, by contrast, were small. Over the period 1900–1913, they accounted for less than 3% of the aggregate Canadian money stock.[4] The bulk of Canadian media of exchange was supplied by the chartered banks in the form of notes and deposits. Although the government was able to influence bank cash reserves by varying the supply of Dominion notes, it followed—for the most part—a passive monetary policy stance. Before World War I, monetary policy meant little else than to alter the supply of Dominion notes passively in response to fluctuations in the official gold reserve. The government's laissez-faire approach to monetary policy was remarkably successful. Prior to 1914, the Canadian government and the chartered banks were never compelled to suspend specie payments and bank failures were rare events indeed.

Despite its preference for a laissez-faire approach, the government in a few instances saw fit to depart from its passive monetary policy stance. A highly controversial departure was the emergency measures taken by the government during the crisis of 1907. In order to alleviate a severe credit squeeze, the government undertook to provide temporary liquidity assistance to the chartered banks through an emergency issue of Dominion notes. The crisis of 1907 has received considerable attention in the existing literature since it prompted the Canadian government to assume, for the first time, the role of lender of last resort to the banking system. The emergency measures foreshadowed the fundamental reorientation of Canadian monetary policy that was to result from the passage of the Finance Act of 1914. Under this act, the government acquired the authority to make advances to the chartered banks against specified collateral.

Although various—mostly contemporary—accounts of the crisis of 1907 are available, little is known about the causes of the financial stringency. Inasmuch as the causes of the crisis are discussed at all, existing studies (especially Johnson, 1910) tend to stress various internal factors. A reexamination of the evidence, however, casts serious doubt on the validity of existing interpretations of the crisis. The purpose of this paper is to show that the crisis was attributable chiefly to an unusually severe seasonal deterioration in the Canadian balance of payments, rather than to purely internal factors. The remainder of the paper is organized as follows. In Section 1, I chronicle the events that led up to the crisis. Section 2 demonstrates that existing studies have not correctly traced the causes of the financial stringency. Section 3 is devoted to an analysis of the seasonal pattern of the pre-1914 Canadian balance of payments, while the causes of the crisis are examined in Section 4.

---

[4] The government held a monopoly for issuing notes in denominations of $4 or less. On the whole, the circulation of Dominion notes outside the banking system was restricted to the small denominations. See Table 1 for data on the Canadian money stock.

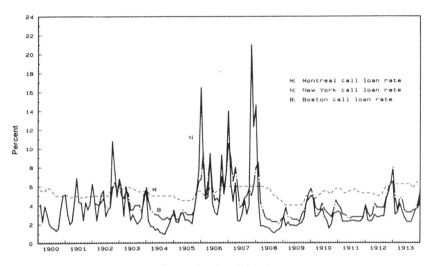

CHART 1.  See Table 1.

## 1. A CHRONICLE OF THE CRISIS

The financial crisis started in the United States. As a result of a strong cyclical expansion in economic activity, U.S. money markets tightened considerably, with a severe financial squeeze appearing in the summer of 1907. On October 22, the monetary stringency culminated in a veritable panic, due to the collapse of the Knickerbocker Trust Co. of New York. The failure of that institution triggered massive deposit withdrawals from banks throughout the United States. Numerous institutions were compelled to suspend specie payments and bank failures were an everyday occurrence. The scramble for liquidity caused interest rates in New York and other parts of the United States to surge to record levels (Chart 1).[5] The financial panic ushered in a drastic slump in U.S. economic activity. Although the recession was short-lived, the repercussions of the crisis were far-reaching. The panic greatly stimulated the debate on banking reform and led to the establishment of the U.S. National Monetary Commission, whose deliberations resulted in the creation of the Federal Reserve System.

In his path-breaking study of the New York money market, Goodhart (1969, p. 29) argues that the severity of the U.S. financial crisis was attributable to a coincidence of cyclical and seasonal peaks in money demand.[6] The evidence suggests that U.S. economic activity attained a

[5] Chart 1 understates the extent of the increase in the New York call loan rate immediately after the crash. In the fourth week of October 1907, that rate reached a high of 125% (Goodhart, 1969, p. 133).

[6] See Friedman and Schwartz (1963, pp. 156–168) and Goodhart (1969, Chap. 4) for excellent discussions of the New York panic.

cyclical peak in May 1907 (Burns and Mitchell, 1946, pp. 78–79). Furthermore, U.S. money demand tended to rise in the autumn, when the
crops were moved from the interior to the seaboard and to overseas
destinations. Since New York banks were heavily engaged in financing
agricultural trade, the seasonal fluctuations in U.S. money demand were
associated with corresponding movements in short-term interest rates in
New York and other U.S. financial centers. The New York call-loan
rate, for example, typically reached a seasonal peak in December and
a trough in the summer (Chart 1). When—as in the autumn of 1907—
the seasonal bulge in money demand came on top of a cyclical peak,
the New York money market tightened to such an extent that short-term
interest rates were pushed up to very high levels.

The U.S. financial stringency quickly developed into an international
crisis. The New York crash was followed by a drastic tightening of
Canadian and European money markets. As in the United States, money
demand in Canada invariably peaked during the crop moving season.
Owing to the strained financial conditions, the chartered banks in Canada
strove to cut back their lending even though the wheat crop was just
about to be shipped to the East. Western farmers' associations and grain
dealers complained that the chartered banks were unwilling to loan the
funds needed to move the crop. The difficulties were compounded by
the fact that, due to poor weather, the grain was harvested later than
usual. Moreover, a large part of the crop was damaged by frost and
could not be stored over the winter. In order to minimize the losses
from storage, it was imperative to ship the crop as quickly as possible.
In response to Western anxieties, the government, on November 20,
1907, decided to ease the credit squeeze and undertook to offer advances
to chartered banks involved in financing the grain trade. The advances
were made through the Bank of Montreal against the collateral of high-
grade securities.[7] The government provided the funds required to finance
the advances in the form of Dominion notes deposited with the Bank.
The additional notes were issued on an uncovered basis, that is, they
were not backed by gold in government vaults.[8] Although the government
was authorized to circulate $10 million worth of additional notes, the
banks only chose to borrow $5.3 million under the emergency scheme.

[7] The Bank of Montreal was charged by the government with setting the interest rate
on the advances. The Bank also administered the collateral and collected the interest on
behalf of the government. For a more detailed discussion of the emergency measures, see
the budget speech of March 17, 1908 (Canada, *Debates*, 1907–1908, pp. 5151–5158), Johnson
(1910, pp. 199–222), and Jamieson (1955, pp. 37–40).

[8] As a result of the increase in the uncovered note issue, the government failed to meet
the minimum gold reserve requirement (see Note 3). In 1908, Parliament sanctioned ret-
roactively the temporary breach of that requirement (Jamieson, 1955, pp. 38–39). The
emergency measures were authorized by an Order in Council, rather than by an act of
Parliament.

The advances were supplied between November 20, 1907, and January 2, 1908, and were fully repaid by the end of April 1908 (Jamieson, 1955, p. 38). Interestingly, the request for emergency assistance originated entirely with Western agricultural interests, whereas the chartered banks were reluctant to participate in the scheme. Despite the disturbed financial conditions in the United States, the chartered banks did not need government help. No Canadian bank was forced to suspend specie payments, nor did any bank failures take place.

Since the Canadian crisis reached its climax shortly after the New York crash, one would expect that the turbulence in the United States was a major cause of the Canadian credit squeeze. Nevertheless, existing studies of the 1907 crisis, surprisingly, do not attach much importance to the external causes of the Canadian difficulties, but tend to stress internal factors that allegedly were responsible for the credit squeeze. In the following section, I examine various possible internal and external causes of the crisis.

## 2. INTERNAL AND EXTERNAL CAUSES OF THE CRISIS

### 2.1. Internal Causes

The Canadian crisis—like the New York crash—occurred at the end of a vigorous business-cycle expansion that was associated with a marked tightening of the domestic money market. In Canada, economic activity began to pick up in June 1904, and attained a cyclical peak in December 1906, about half a year earlier than in the United States (Hay, 1966). As I have shown elsewhere (Rich, 1984), a cyclical upturn in Canadian economic activity was normally accompanied by a rise in short-term interest rates, prompted by a deterioration in the balance of payments and an attendant contraction of bank reserves (relative to trend). That increase in short-term interest rates typically set in near the midpoint of a business-cycle expansion and continued until the midpoint of the subsequent contraction. For this reason, the Montreal call-loan rate began to rise in the second half of 1905 and climbed by about $1\frac{1}{2}$ percentage points to a level of 6%, which was considered high by the standards of the pre-1914 period. As indicated by Chart 1, it remained at that level throughout 1907 and the first quarter of 1908.[9] Although interest rates were high, the cyclical tightening of the money market, by itself, does not explain why that business-cycle expansion developed into a financial crisis since Canadian banks up to that moment had never encountered

---

[9] The invariance of the Montreal call-loan rate in this period is puzzling but does not imply that there were legal restrictions on charging interest in excess of 6%. Canadian usury laws stipulated that the banks could charge any rate on their loans "but could not use legal process to recover interest in excess of 7%" (Neufeld, 1972, p. 88). Note that at the end of 1912 the Montreal call-loan rate rose above 6% (Chart 1).

major difficulties in absorbing cyclical losses of reserves. What was unusual about the situation in 1907 was not the monetary tightness as such, but the severity of the squeeze.

As far as the severity of the financial stringency is concerned, most contemporary observers believed that the source of the difficulties resided mainly in a decline in the seasonal elasticity of the bank-note circulation, besides the problems caused by poor weather. Canadian demand for bank notes invariably rose during the crop-moving season, attaining a seasonal peak in October or November (Curtis, 1931, p. 21). The chartered banks, in turn, accommodated the seasonal swings in note demand by corresponding changes in supply. The banks' ability to adapt their note issue to fluctuations in demand, however, was not unlimited. The Canadian Bank Act stipulated that a bank's note issue was not to exceed its paid-up capital. For a long time, the statutory ceiling imposed by the Bank Act did not constrain the supply of bank notes, for the note issue remained well below paid-up capital. But around the middle of the 1890s, the note issue began to rise relative to paid-up capital and gradually approached the statutory ceiling in the early 1900s (Curtis, 1931, pp. 20, 33).

In a study prepared for the U.S. National Monetary Commission, Johnson (1910, Chap. 8) analyzed the 1907 crisis in detail and argued that the statutory ceiling was a major cause of the difficulties. In his opinion, the banks were reluctant to expand lending during the last 3 months of 1907. They were concerned that the demand for bank notes would rise above the ceiling if they were too generous in accommodating the seasonal increase in activity. Since the penalty attached to excess issues was prohibitive,[10] the banks took pains to keep their note circulation within the limits of the Bank Act. Of course, they could have met the additional currency demand by paying out Dominion notes in lieu of their own notes, but this would have depleted their cash reserves and diminished their ability to accommodate the seasonal rise in activity. In Johnson's (1910, 118–119) own words,

> the banks dared not make large advances to the buyers of grain lest the depletion of their reserves or an excessive issue of notes should result . . . [N]o bank felt that it could authorize its branches to increase the issue of notes; the risk of being called upon to pay the penalty for excessive issue was too great.

The government apparently shared the views espoused by Johnson. In his budget speech of March 17, 1908 (see Note 7), Finance Minister Fielding outlined the emergency measures and ventured the opinion that the seasonal elasticity of the bank-note issue should be enhanced if similar

---

[10] The penalty depended upon the size of the excess issue. The maximum penalty, which was applicable to excess issues of over $200,000, amounted to $100,000 (Canada, *Statutes*, 53 Vict. Cap. 31, Section 51).

crises were to be avoided in the future. To this end, Parliament, in 1908, passed an amendment to the Bank Act, known as the crop-moving provisions, which permitted the banks to issue notes in excess of the statutory ceiling from September 1 to February 28.

Although the statutory ceiling, sooner or later, was bound to impinge on the banks' lending behavior, I doubt that the 1907 crisis was attributable to a decline in the seasonal elasticity of currency supply. The bank-note issue began to push against the statutory ceiling for the first time in October 1902, when it climbed to a seasonal high of 95% of paid-up capital. In the period 1903 through 1906, the autumnal peaks in the note issue remained near the ceiling, reaching a level of 91 to 94% of paid-up capital. The high of 93% attained in November 1907, was not exceptionally large as compared with the seasonal maxima recorded between 1902 and 1906.[11] Considering the patterns of the note issue and paid-up capital, I fail to see how the Johnson thesis accounts for the timing of the crisis.[12] Of course, it is possible that the statutory ceiling, if at all, did not constrain the banks' ability to accommodate the autumnal surge in the demand for credit and currency until 1907. In this event, the seasonal amplitude of the bank-note issue should have shrunk significantly in that year.

The seasonal amplitude of the note issue may be estimated from data on the largest amount of bank notes in circulation at any time during the month, with the spread between the months showing the largest and smallest amount of notes in circulation employed as a measure of seasonal amplitude. Between 1896 and 1906, that spread varied from 20 to 32% of the average annual note circulation. No significant reduction in the spread was recorded in 1907. The spread for that year amounted to 21%, a figure that was relatively low, but still within the normal range of fluctuations.[13]

Had the statutory ceiling served as a binding constraint, I would further expect that the banks were forced to pay out Dominion notes in lieu of their own notes, in order to meet the seasonal increase in currency demand. However, as will be shown later, the fourth quarter of 1907 did not witness an unusual rise in the circulation of Dominion notes

---

[11] The seasonal peak values of the bank-note issue are expressed as a percentage of paid-up capital at the beginning and end of the month in which a seasonal peak occurred. They are derived from monthly data on the largest amount of bank notes in circulation at any time during the month. These data were collected for the first time in July 1891 (Curtis, 1931, pp. 21, 33).

[12] During the crop-moving season of 1906, some banks already complained that the statutory ceiling impeded their ability to meet the increase in currency demand (Beckhart, 1929, pp. 382–383).

[13] See Note 11 for the data source. From 1892 to 1895, the spread was consistently smaller than 20%.

outside the banking system. All in all, it is hard to see how concern about the statutory ceiling could have precipitated the crisis of 1907.

## 2.2. External Causes

While the seasonal elasticity of the bank-note issue attracted a great deal of attention, possible external causes of the crisis went largely unnoticed. In particular, most contemporary observers failed to realize that immediately after the New York crash, the exceptionally high interest rates in New York caused the Canadian dollar price of New York exchange to rise above the gold export point. The premium on New York exchange provided an incentive to move gold to New York. On 30 November 1907, the *Monetary Times* (p. 871) reported that $2 million worth of gold had been shipped from Montreal to New York. It also pointed out that the government was worried about the gold drain and had taken steps to stem the flow of precious metal to New York.[14] Since a gold outflow tended to diminish bank cash reserves, it is possible that the New York crash compelled Canadian banks to curtail their lending in order to safeguard their liquidity position. Apart from a few financial journalists, contemporary observers did not believe that gold was exported from Canada in the wake of the New York crash. On the contrary, they claimed that international gold flows had served to moderate the Canadian monetary stringency. For example, Johnson (1910, p. 117) noticed that during October and November 1907, the Canadian banks had cut drastically their call loans to foreigners and had increased simultaneously their cash reserves. In his opinion, the chartered banks reacted to the New York crash by withdrawing gold from U.S. banks. Johnson's view is shared by Goodhart (1969, p. 152).

The belief that international gold flows tended to assuage the Canadian monetary stringency rests on the traditional view as to how the Canadian banks responded to seasonal fluctuations in money demand. Johnson (1910, pp. 94–99) succinctly summarized the traditional view. In his opinion, the banks satisfied the additional money demand during the crop-moving season by augmenting their domestic loans and liabilities. Moreover,

> as their liabilities increase . . . on account of expanding deposits and note circulation, they reduce their call loans in New York City, and so add a few million to their cash reserves. (1910, p. 95)

Consequently, the seasonal expansion in credit and deposits was sus-

---

[14] Normal practice was to redeem the Dominion notes in U.S. eagles (see also Note 2). In an effort to curb the gold drain, the government decided to pay out sovereigns in lieu of eagles. This reduced the profit from shipping gold to New York since sovereigns could be sold there only at a discount, while eagles were accepted at par. See Officer (1986, pp. 1048–1049) for estimates of the transaction costs of selling sovereigns in New York.

tained by a gold inflow from New York. Similar views were expressed by Finance Minister Fielding (Canada, *Debates,* 1907–1908, p. 4307), contemporary financial journalists (see *Monetary Times,* November 30, 1907, p. 865), and by Denison (1967, p. 295). In essence, the Canadian banks were thought to regard New York as a lender of last resort that could always be relied upon as a source of cash when money was scarce. New York's alleged lender-of-last-resort function led Viner (1924, p. 182) to reason that the Canadian banks, in periods of financial stringency, frequently compounded the liquidity problems of New York banks. If the traditional view of the seasonal adjustment mechanism were valid, it would not be sensible to trace the Canadian crisis to the New York crash. Rather, one would have to argue that liquidity management of the Canadian banks was one of many factors responsible for the monetary squeeze in New York.

Needless to say, there is nothing specifically Canadian about the views enunciated by Johnson. The same kind of adjustment mechanism was thought to operate within the United States. According to the traditional view as applied to the United States, the crop-moving season saw substantial flows of cash from New York to the interior in response to an increase in money demand by the agricultural sector, while during the slack season cash was returned to New York. The traditional view, however, has been challenged by Goodhart (1969). In his opinion, cash tended to flow from the interior to New York in the crop-moving season. Whatever the merit of Goodhart's assault on the traditional view as applied to the United States, a reexamination of the Canadian evidence suggests that Johnson's account of the adjustment mechanism is inconsistent with the facts. If the nature of that mechanism is properly understood, the severity of the 1907 crisis can be readily explained. An analysis of seasonal movements in the Canadian balance of payments provides the key to understanding the 1907 crisis.

## 3. SEASONAL MOVEMENTS IN THE CANADIAN BALANCE OF PAYMENTS

### 3.1. *The Seasonal Adjustment Mechanism: The Evidence*

Tables 1 to 3 help to explain the relationship between seasonal movements in the Canadian money stock and the balance of payments. The money stock is defined as the sum of bank notes, demand deposits, notice deposits, and Dominion notes held by the Canadian non-bank public. International monetary assets, as shown in Table 1, are employed as a measure of the cumulative overall balance-of-payments surplus (or deficit). They comprise monetary gold in government vaults, as well as monetary gold and secondary reserves on the books of the chartered banks. Secondary reserves—which consisted of call loans to foreigners and net claims

144                                        GEORG RICH

TABLE 1
Canadian International Monetary Assets and Money Stock—Quarterly Changes
(Millions of Dollars)

| | Int. monetary assets (1) | Money stock (2) | | Int. monetary assets (1) | Money stock (2) |
|---|---|---|---|---|---|
| | | | 1907 I | −21.6 | −11.3 |
| | | | II | 14.9 | 17.7 |
| | | | III | 9.2 | 1.4 |
| 1900 IV | 9.1 | 7.2 | IV | −19.6 | −36.4 |
| 1901 I | 3.1 | 5.5 | 1908 I | 13.8 | −11.9 |
| II | 5.0 | 15.4 | II | 25.1 | 12.5 |
| III | 15.6 | 15.9 | III | 63.6 | 42.4 |
| IV | −3.8 | 4.3 | IV | 15.7 | 34.7 |
| 1902 I | −7.0 | −0.3 | 1909 I | — | 9.8 |
| II | 11.3 | 9.8 | II | 5.7 | 35.3 |
| III | 7.5 | 20.6 | III | 21.9 | 41.8 |
| IV | −5.1 | 8.0 | IV | 0.5 | 45.9 |
| 1903 I | −12.2 | 2.1 | 1910 I | −5.4 | 11.6 |
| II | 6.5 | 6.6 | II | 9.3 | 31.9 |
| III | 10.1 | 18.7 | III | 6.7 | 30.1 |
| IV | −0.6 | 4.4 | IV | −40.1 | −3.6 |
| 1904 I | −3.2 | 7.8 | 1911 I | 0.8 | 6.5 |
| II | 1.7 | 16.2 | II | 25.1 | 42.7 |
| III | 25.7 | 21.0 | III | 17.9 | 34.7 |
| IV | 7.2 | 10.8 | IV | −8.6 | 20.5 |
| 1905 I | −3.2 | 0.9 | 1912 I | 5.1 | 18.2 |
| II | −7.3 | 11.9 | II | 34.9 | 69.1 |
| III | 22.1 | 31.7 | III | −19.1 | 2.6 |
| IV | −7.8 | 16.1 | IV | −27.4 | −12.3 |
| 1906 I | −5.4 | 18.0 | 1913 I | −0.5 | −11.4 |
| II | −2.8 | 10.5 | II | −2.2 | 0.4 |
| III | 17.1 | 28.0 | III | −9.9 | 17.3 |
| IV | −8.0 | 24.6 | IV | 39.7 | −10.6 |

*Source.* Rich (1988), Table A-2, columns (7) and (9).

(claims minus liabilities) on foreign correspondent banks—are assumed to be part of international monetary assets since banks regarded them as close substitutes for monetary gold (see Johnson, 1910, pp. 49–50; Viner, 1924; Beckhart, 1929, pp. 416–417, p. 430; Shearer, 1965, p. 331). Note that the data on international monetary assets employed in this study differ from those reported in existing published sources (e.g., Curtis, 1931).

The analysis is confined to the period 1900 to 1913 because reliable quarterly data on international monetary assets are unavailable for earlier years. Table 1 clearly indicates that the money stock and international

TABLE 2

Seasonal Movements in International Monetary Assets, Money Stock, and Domestic Bank Loans: 1901–1912

| Average stock at end of quarter | International monetary assets (adjusted) (1) | Money stock (adjusted) (2) | Domestic bank loans (adjusted) (3) |
|---|---|---|---|
| 1901–1911 | | | |
| IV | — | 2.8 | −2.1 |
| 1902–1912 | | | |
| I | −8.9 | −9.8 | 1.4 |
| II | −1.3 | −0.8 | 1.4 |
| III | 12.9 | 9.4 | −2.6 |
| IV | −1.1 | 3.2 | −0.5 |

*Sources.* Columns (1) and (2): See Table 1. Column (3): Total loans in Canada (Curtis, 1931, p. 50). This series covers loans to domestic borrowers and appears to be reasonably homogenous (Curtis, 1931, p. 12). It includes the following items: Current loans in Canada, call and short loans in Canada, loans to the Dominion government, loans to provincial governments, and from July 1913 onward, loans to cities, towns, municipalities, and school districts. Before July 1913, the last item was subsumed in "current loans in Canada."

*Estimation methods.* The data shown in the table are averages of end-of-quarter differences between the actual and smoothed values of the respective aggregate. The data are smoothed by a seven-quarter moving average. The averaging period equals one-half of the average length of a full Canadian business cycle. Therefore, this smoothing procedure filters much of the intracycle variation out of the data. Over the period starting with the peak of August 1895, and ending with the peak of November 1912, the average length of a full Canadian reference cycle amounted to 41.4 months or 13.8 quarters. See Hay (1966) for the dates of Canadian reference-cycle turning points.

monetary assets were subject to pronounced seasonal fluctuations. Moreover, there was a fairly close positive correlation between the seasonal swings in the two aggregates. The growth in both the money stock and international monetary assets typically started to accelerate in the spring and attained a seasonal peak in the second or third quarter. From October to December, the money stock normally increased further, but at a much lower rate than during the preceding quarter. The growth in international monetary assets also slowed down; the fourth quarter frequently saw them decline in absolute terms. Finally, in the first quarter, the money stock did not change much, while international monetary assets typically continued to shrink.

In Table 2, an attempt is made to determine and compare the seasonal amplitudes of international monetary assets and the money stock. To this end, the trend and cyclical fluctuations are eliminated from the data. The series, thus adjusted, will be termed adjusted international monetary assets (AI) and the adjusted money stock (AM). They capture mainly the seasonal swings in the data and, therefore, can be used for estimating

146                                    GEORG RICH

the seasonal amplitudes of the two aggregates. Table 2 shows the end-of-quarter averages of AI and AM for the years 1901 to 1912. The evidence suggests that AI fluctuated more strongly than AM, but the difference in the seasonal amplitudes of the two aggregates was small. Thus, the seasonal swings in the Canadian money stock were matched by corresponding swings in international monetary assets. The similarity of seasonal movements in the two aggregates is confirmed by the following regression equation:

$$AM = 0.79 + 0.78 \text{ AI}, \overline{R}^2 = 0.65, DW = 1.97, \qquad (1)$$
$$(0.25) \quad (9.06)$$

sample period: 1901IV to 1912IV.

Equation (1) is estimated on the basis of the Cochrane-Orcutt technique since the corresponding OLS estimates are marred by strong serial correlation in the residuals.[15] However, the two estimation procedures yield virtually identical parameter estimates for AI. Equation (1) corroborates my earlier result that the seasonal variance of AI was slightly higher than that of AM.

Unlike AI and AM, bank loans to domestic borrowers, surprisingly, did not fluctuate much over the year. As indicated by Table 2, adjusted domestic bank loans tended to decline somewhat during the harvest and crop-moving season, but it should be noted that their seasonal pattern was less regular than that of the adjusted money stock. Considering the importance attached by contemporary observers to seasonal movements in the demand for credit, I am puzzled by the evidence of Table 2. Apparently, contemporary observers were mistaken in their belief that the credit needs of the agricultural sector caused the demand for domestic bank loans to surge in the autumn.[16] During the harvest and crop-moving season, the chartered banks were called upon mainly to augment the money supply, but not to provide additional loans to domestic borrowers. The seasonal expansion in the money supply, in turn, was backed entirely by a rise in Canadian holdings of international monetary assets. Financing agricultural trade was a money problem, not a credit problem.

Table 3 shows how the various components of the Canadian balance of payments contributed to the seasonal movements in international monetary assets. It offers quarterly data on the overall balance-of-payments surplus (or quarterly first differences in international monetary assets), the merchandise trade surplus (deficit), and residual inflows. The latter cover the non-merchandise trade surplus and capital inflows, and are

---

[15] The numbers in parentheses stand for the $t$ values.

[16] The evidence of Table 2, of course, need not imply that credit demand by the agricultural sector failed to rise during the harvest and crop-moving season. It is possible that the increase in agricultural credit demand was offset by a reduction in credit demand by other sectors of the economy.

TABLE 3
Seasonal Movements in Balance of Payments and Monetary Base, 1901–1913 (Millions of Dollars)

| | Balance of payments | | | Overall surplus | | | Δ Monetary base | | |
| | | | | | | Δ Uncovered | | Of which | |
| Quarter | Merchandise trade balance[a] (1) | Residual inflows[b] (2) | Total (3) = (1) + (2) | Δ Monetary gold (4) | Δ Secondary reserves (5) | Dominion notes (6) | Total (7) = (3) + (6) = (5) + (8) + (9) | Bank cash reserves (8) | Dominion notes outside banks (9) |
|---|---|---|---|---|---|---|---|---|---|
| Average 1901–1913 | | | | | | | | | |
| I | −36.0 | 33.3 | −2.7 | −0.9 | −1.8 | −0.3 | −3.0 | −0.7 | −0.4 |
| II | −33.8 | 43.6 | 9.8 | 3.9 | 5.9 | — | 9.8 | 2.9 | 1.0 |
| III | −19.0 | 33.5 | 14.5 | 5.2 | 9.3 | — | 14.5 | 4.1 | 1.0 |
| IV | 1.3 | −5.8 | −4.5 | 2.0 | −6.5 | 0.5 | −4.0 | 3.2 | −0.7 |
| Year 1907 | | | | | | | | | |
| I | −41.7 | 20.1 | −21.6 | −1.7 | −20.1 | −0.6 | −22.2 | −2.1 | — |
| II | −46.9 | 61.8 | 14.9 | 5.0 | 10.0 | — | 14.9 | 4.4 | 0.6 |
| III | −11.5 | 20.7 | 9.2 | 3.5 | 5.8 | −0.3 | 8.9 | 2.7 | 0.4 |
| IV | −11.7 | −7.9 | −19.6 | −2.4 | −17.3 | 6.0 | −13.5 | 4.2 | −0.5 |

*Sources.* Column (1): 1901–1902: Canada, *Monthly Reports*, fiscal 1909. 1903–1913: Canada, Department of Customs, *Trade and Navigation. Unrevised Monthly Statements*, 1905–1913. These sources contain monthly data on merchandise exports and imports entered for consumption. The export and import data exclude trade in coin and bullion. Column (3): Overall surplus equals quarterly first differences in international monetary assets (See Table 1). Columns (4) and (5): Rich, (1288), Table A-2, sum of columns (1) and (3); column (6). Column (6): Aggregate stock of Dominion notes minus gold stock of the Dominion government [Rich, 1988, Table A-2. columns (2) and (1)]. Column (8): Bank holdings of gold [Rich, 1988, Table A-2, column (3)] and Dominion notes, including holdings in the central gold reserves (Curtis, 1931, pp. 35, 38). Column (9): Aggregate Dominion notes [Rich, 1988, Table A-2, column (2)] minus bank holdings of Dominion notes [see legend to column (8)].

[a] Merchandise exports minus imports. The latter do not include imports for re-export, for which monthly data are not available for the entire period 1901–1913.

[b] Overall surplus minus merchandise trade balance.

148                                   GEORG RICH

estimated by taking the difference between the overall and merchandise
trade surplus. Since the requisite quarterly data are unavailable, it is
impossible to separate capital inflows from the non-merchandise trade
surplus. Furthermore, the overall surplus is split up into inflows of monetary
gold and secondary reserves.

The 13-year averages presented in the top four rows of Table 3 clearly
reveal the seasonal attributes of the Canadian balance of payments. As
would be expected, the merchandise trade surplus increased strongly
during the second half of the year and reached a seasonal peak in the
fourth quarter.[17] Interestingly enough, the seasonal movements in the
overall surplus did not parallel those in the trade surplus. The seasonal
increase in the overall surplus from the first to the second quarter was
due mainly to an acceleration of residual inflows. The further expansion
from the second to the third quarter, by contrast, reflected the improvement
in the trade balance setting in after the start of the harvest season.
However, the overall surplus did not rise as much as the trade surplus
since the seasonal improvement in the trade balance was largely offset
by a decline in residual inflows. The movements in the overall surplus
between the third and fourth quarter, once again, were dominated by
residual inflows. Paradoxically, the overall surplus declined sharply, despite
a massive rise in the trade surplus. Thus, except for the changes between
the second and third quarter, the seasonal fluctuations in the overall
surplus were dominated by residual inflows.

Table 3 further indicates that the seasonal swings in the overall surplus
were settled both by flows of monetary gold and secondary reserves.
Much like the overall surplus, the growth of the monetary gold stock
and secondary reserves tended to accelerate between the first and second
quarter and to slow down between the third and fourth quarter. However,
the seasonal amplitude of secondary reserves was much stronger than
that of monetary gold. During the fourth quarter, secondary reserves
normally declined absolutely, while the monetary gold stock continued
to grow, albeit at a smaller rate than during the preceding quarter.

### 3.2. The Seasonal Adjustment Mechanism: An Interpretation

A reexamination of the seasonal adjustment mechanism suggests that
residual inflows were instrumental in generating seasonal fluctuations in
Canadian international monetary assets and the money stock. Thus, if
the working of the adjustment mechanism is to be understood, one must
explain the seasonal movements in residual inflows. In all probability,
these movements mirrored strong seasonal swings in Canadian net imports
of short-term capital, for it is hard to see how non-merchandise trade

---

[17] In 1907, the seasonal peak in the merchandise trade surplus fell into the third quarter.
However, the value for 1907III was virtually the same as that for 1907IV (Table 3).

could have accounted for the sharp temporary drop in residual inflows normally recorded in the fourth quarter.[18] Moreover, the seasonal movements in residual inflows were likely to be due to shifts in short-term foreign borrowing or lending by Canadian non-bank residents. Aside from secondary reserves, the Canadian banks' foreign assets and liabilities did not fluctuate much over the year and, therefore, do not account for the observed cyclical pattern of residual inflows.[19]

The significant role non-bank borrowing or lending appears to have played in the adjustment mechanism is surprising since existing research suggests that foreign short-term assets and liabilities of Canadian non-bank residents were negligible (Cairncross, 1968, pp. 169–170). It is probably true that Canadian non-banks did not hold foreign bank deposits and did not raise loans from foreign banks to any great extent. However, they might have lent funds to foreigners through leads and lags in export finance, a possibility overlooked in existing studies of Canadian capital flows. In my opinion, leads and lags were likely to be an important phenomenon since existing accounts of pre-1914 Canadian export finance do not make sense unless it is assumed that Canadian producers normally were paid for exports well after goods shipped to other countries had crossed the Canadian border.

According to contemporary observers, Canadian banks typically financed exports of grain up to the point at which the shipments reached the eastern seaports. After the harvest, western farmers transported their

---

[18] Among the various components of non-merchandise trade, freight, tourism, and non-commercial remittances were liable to display seasonal fluctuations. Payments and receipts on account of freight and tourism were unlikely to be responsible for the fourth-quarter drop in residual inflows. From 1901 to 1913, payments and receipts on account of the two components of non-merchandise trade were approximately balanced. Moreover, for both tourism and freight, payments and receipts probably displayed the same seasonal patterns, that is, net receipts did not vary significantly over the year. It is possible that Canadian non-commercial remittances to foreigners peaked in the fourth quarter. During the crop-moving season, farmers and merchants possessed ample funds for making such payments. However, for this item to explain the fourth-quarter drop in residual inflows, one would have to assume that the funds were remitted exclusively between October and December. Over the period 1901 to 1913, non-commercial remittances to foreigners averaged $40.3 million per year, a sum that roughly equalled the drop in residual inflows from the third to the fourth quarter (Table 3). It seems implausible to assume that non-commercial remittances were made exclusively in the fourth quarter. See Hartland (1955, Table XXXI) for annual data on the various components on non-merchandise trade.

[19] In addition to secondary reserves, the banks showed on their books other current loans to and deposits from foreigners (Curtis, 1931, pp. 21, 52). These two balance-sheet items did not fluctuate much over the year. For example, in the third and fourth quarter of 1907, net imports of capital by the banks, other than in the form of net reductions in secondary reserves, amounted to −$0.3 and −$4.0 million, respectively (Δ deposits abroad minus Δ other current loans abroad). Residual inflows, by contrast, shrank from $20.7 to −$7.9 million (Table 3). Thus, banks only accounted for 13% of the reduction in residual inflows between the second and third quarter of 1907.

grain to a nearby elevator or to Winnipeg, where it was purchased by milling companies or large dealers. The farmers were paid in bank notes, which the buyers of the grain obtained by raising loans from the chartered banks.[20] Grain destined for export to Europe was then shipped along the Great Lakes route to the eastern seaports. With the assistance of the chartered banks, Canadian dealers drew "inland" drafts on New York and other export houses charged with shipping the grain. These export houses in turn negotiated sterling or continental bills of exchange on behalf of their Canadian customers, who sold these bills in the New York money market, probably with the help of Canadian banks.[21] Thus, upon arrival of the grain at the eastern seaports, Canadian dealers received cash, which they used to repay their loans from the chartered banks.

This account of Canadian export finance possesses two features that are at variance with the empirical evidence. First, if Canadian grain dealers had cashed their sterling or continental bills of exchange upon arrival of their shipments at the eastern seaports, I would expect that seasonal peaks in the overall balance-of-payments surplus coincided with, or lagged somewhat, the corresponding peaks in the merchandise trade surplus. As indicated above, the overall surplus normally peaked roughly one or two quarters earlier than the merchandise trade surplus. Second, seasonal peaks in the money stock should have led, rather than coincided with, seasonal peaks in international monetary assets.

The above analysis may be reconciled with the empirical evidence if it is assumed that Canadian export credit was sensitive to (i) the merchandise trade balance, (ii) New York money market rates, and (iii) changes in the transactions demand for domestic money induced by seasonal movements in Canadian economic activity. The autumnal surge in the trade surplus might have been counteracted, at least in part, by a rise in export credit growth and, hence, by a decline in residual inflows. Moreover, the sharp increase in New York money market rates toward the end of the year might have lowered residual inflows further by prompting Canadian exporters to postpone cashing their sterling or continental bills of exchange. For these reasons, export receipts might have lagged exports. Finally, it is possible that Canadian exporters took account of their needs for transactions balances in timing their sales of bills of exchange. They might have met a seasonal rise in demand for transactions balances by substituting domestic money for export credit, thereby reducing the lag between export receipts and exports. Similarly, they might have accommodated a seasonal drop in money demand by lengthening that lag.

---

[20] For a good discussion of Canadian export finance, see the interview granted by Finance Minister Fielding to the *Monetary Times,* November 16, 1907, pp. 796–798. From that interview it is not entirely clear how the additional bank notes were brought into circulation. Fielding merely stated that the notes were "loaned" to the farmers.

[21] Fielding did not explain in detail how the bills of exchange were sold in New York.

The relationship between residual inflows (RES) and these three factors is explored in two steps because it is difficult to construct a satisfactory indicator of seasonal fluctuations in pre-1914 Canadian economic activity. In a first step, only factors (i) and (ii) are considered. For this reason, RES are regressed on the merchandise trade surplus (TS) and quarterly first differences in the New York call-loan rate (RN). The latter is employed as a measure of borrowing costs in the New York money market. The analysis rests on the assumption that levels of interest rates determined stocks, rather than flows, of foreign capital. Due to a marked increase in RES over the sample period, the regression equation also includes a linear time trend. OLS estimates for the period 1901I to 1913IV point to a highly significant inverse relationship between RES and TS:

$$RES = 0.37 - 0.61\,\Delta RN - 0.78\,TS + 0.30t,$$
$$\phantom{RES =}(0.07)(-0.99)\quad(-6.77)\quad\ \ (1.40) \qquad\qquad (2)$$
$$\bar{R}^2 = 0.70,\ DW = 1.91.$$

The size of the estimated parameter of TS suggests that movements in the trade balance—at least in the short run—were largely offset by capital flows. As a matter of fact, the null hypothesis that the parameter of TS equalled unity can be rejected only at the 90% and lower levels of significance. As would be expected, RES were also inversely related to $\Delta RN$, but the latter variable was not statistically significant. This result, however, need not imply that RES were insensitive to changes in New York money market rates because of multicollinearity between $\Delta RN$ and TS ($r = 0.28$). If TS is dropped from Eq. (2), $\Delta RN$ shows up as statistically significant variable (almost at the 99% level) with negative sign.[22]

The observed relationship between RES and TS implies that the overall balance-of-payments surplus and the growth in the domestic money stock were virtually invariant to seasonal movements in the trade balance. Over the period 1901I to 1913IV, the simple correlation between first differences in the money stock and the trade balance was indeed very small ($r = 0.04$). However, it appears that international monetary assets and the money stock responded to seasonal movements in domestic economic activity and New York money market rates. In Table 4, the seasonal pattern of the money stock is compared to that of quarterly merchandise exports, with the latter employed as an (probably imperfect) indicator of seasonal swings in domestic economic activity. The data presented in Table 4 are adjusted in the same way as those in Table 2.

[22] First differences in the Montreal call-loan rate (RM), if introduced in the estimated equations as an additional independent variable, always appear with a wrong sign. Moreover, the explanatory power of the equations is not improved much if RES are regressed on the differential, $\Delta RM - \Delta RN$. This piece of evidence—which confirms the message of Table 2—suggests that the autumnal increase in export credit was not financed by raising additional loans from the chartered banks.

152                                                   GEORG RICH

TABLE 4
Seasonal Movements in the Money Stock and Exports (Millions of Dollars)

| End of quarter | Money stock (adjusted) | | | Centered exports (adjusted) |
|---|---|---|---|---|
| | Total | Notes | Deposits | |
| Average 1901–1911 | | | | |
| IV | 2.8 | 2.4 | 0.4 | 9.6 |
| 1902–1912 | | | | |
| I | −9.8 | −4.6 | −5.2 | −26.0 |
| II | −0.8 | −2.7 | 1.9 | 1.2 |
| III | 9.4 | 4.4 | 5.0 | 14.3 |
| IV | 3.2 | 3.0 | 0.2 | 9.9 |
| 1903–1913 | | | | |
| I | −10.1 | −4.61 | −5.5 | −26.3 |
| Year 1907 | | | | |
| I | 3.4 | −0.4 | 3.8 | −28.8 |
| II | 19.4 | −0.4 | 19.8 | 3.6 |
| III | 21.3 | 5.3 | 16.0 | 20.1 |
| IV | −17.2 | 3.0 | −20.2 | 7.7 |
| 1908 | | | | |
| I | −37.7 | −6.2 | −31.5 | −24.1 |

*Sources and estimation methods.* The procedure for calculating the adjusted money stock is described in Table 2. The data shown in Table 4 are adjusted accordingly. See the legend to Rich (1988), Table A-2, column (9), for data on the two components of the money stock. The aggregate money stock is adjusted for float, that is, for notes and checks on other banks. Since notes and checks on other banks were reported under a single heading, they are deducted from deposits, while bank notes are not adjusted for float.

Since the money stock data represent end-of-quarter stocks, quarterly export flows are centered at the last month of the quarter in order to guard against spurious leads or lags between the two variables. For example, centered exports for the second quarter embrace the flows recorded for May, June, and July. Table 4 points to a fairly close correlation between seasonal movements in the *level* of the money stock and the *level* of centered exports, even though *first differences* in the money stock were unresponsive to changes in the *level* of exports (or of the trade surplus). The levels of both variables tended to reach a seasonal trough near the end of the first quarter and a peak near the end of the third quarter.[23]

Further insights into the seasonal adjustment mechanism are gained if the relationship between centered exports and the two principal components

---

[23] Over the period 1901IV–1912IV, the simple correlation between the adjusted money stock and adjusted centered exports amounted to 0.5. A similar result is obtained for the correlation between first differences in the unadjusted values of the two variables.

of the domestic money stock, that is, notes (Dominion and bank notes) and deposits, is examined. As indicated by Table 4, during the crop-moving season, notes were more closely correlated with centered exports than deposits. Both notes and centered exports only decreased slightly in the fourth quarter, but fell strongly in the subsequent 3 months.[24] Deposits, by contrast, decreased at a steady pace during both the fourth and the first quarter. A plausible explanation for the relatively strong fourth-quarter decrease in deposits—which occurred at the height of the crop-moving season—was the autumnal surge in New York money market rates, inducing Canadian exporters to substitute export credit for domestic deposits. Thus, while notes moved in sympathy with domestic economic activity, it is likely that deposits were responsive to seasonal movements in both domestic economic activity and New York money market rates.[25] As a result of timing their export receipts in accordance with seasonal movements in domestic economic activity and New York money market rates, Canadian exporters were largely responsible for the seasonal gyrations in international monetary assets and the money stock.

In contrast to Canadian exporters, the chartered banks, for the most part, played a passive role in the seasonal adjustment mechanism. According to Table 3, the seasonal swings in international monetary assets were mirrored by corresponding fluctuations in the monetary base and bank reserves. The monetary base is assumed to embrace cash (monetary gold and Dominion notes) and secondary reserves held by the chartered banks, as well as Dominion notes outside the banking system. Since Dominion notes were issued either against gold or on an uncovered basis, the monetary base may also be defined as the sum of international monetary assets and uncovered Dominion notes. As indicated by Table 3, uncovered Dominion notes were only a minor source of variation in the monetary base. Therefore, the seasonal movements in base-money growth paralleled those in the overall balance-of-payments surplus. Moreover, the seasonal swings in the monetary base mirrored mostly fluctuations in bank cash and secondary reserves. On the whole, a seasonal increase (decrease) in the money stock was balanced by an increase (decrease) in bank reserves of the same order of magnitude.

The similarity of seasonal movements in bank reserves and the money stock implies that the aggregate reserve ratio of the chartered banks (ratio of aggregate reserves to sum of bank notes, demand, and notice deposits) normally reached a seasonal peak at the end of the third quarter, as shown by the gap between the actual and smoothed values shown in

[24] As was the case for bank notes, merchandise exports tended to peak in October or November.

[25] In the spring and summer, notes were less closely correlated with exports than deposits. However, exports may not have been a reliable indicator of seasonal movements in economic activity at that time of the year.

154                                     GEORG RICH

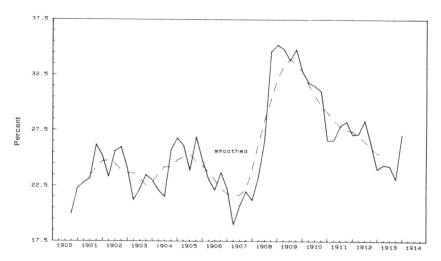

CHART 2.   Sum of the chartered banks' cash and secondary reserves [legend to Table 3, columns (8) and (6)] as a percentage of the difference between the money stock and Dominion notes outside the banking system [legend to Table 1, and Table 3, column (9)]. To derive the broken line, both aggregate reserves and monetary liabilities are smoothed by a seven-quarter moving average. See legend to Table 2 for a justification of the smoothing procedure.

Chart 2.[26] The banks did not react to the increase in their reserve ratios by augmenting their loan supply. They knew that their reserve ratios would go up only temporarily and, therefore, had no incentive to expand lending. Since neither the supply of nor the demand for bank loans was significantly affected by the seasonal rise in Canadian economic activity, Canadian bank loan rates did not vary much over the year. The stability of the Montreal call-loan rate, in particular, was remarkable in the face of the sharp seasonal swings in U.S. short-term interest rates. Even in London, the call-loan rate fluctuated more than in Montreal (Table 5).

   In summary, the traditional account of the seasonal adjustment mechanism must be modified in three respects. First, the seasonal movements in the money stock were backed by corresponding movements in international monetary assets, rather than by changes in domestic bank loans. The seasonal swings in the two monetary aggregates were generated by Canadian exporters varying the lags in export finance in response to changes in domestic economic activity and New York money market rates. Second, although the beginning of the harvest season normally saw Canadian imports of monetary gold accelerate, the seasonal advance in gold imports, contrary to Johnson's assertion, did not result from a

---

[26] For the period 1901–1913, the end-of-quarter averages of the aggregate reserve ratio assumed the following values (percentage): Quarter I: 25.0, II: 25.5, III: 27.1, IV: 26.2.

THE CRISIS OF 1907                                    155

TABLE 5
Seasonal Movements in Canadian, United States and British Short-Term Interest Rates
(Percentage)

| Averages of end-of-quarter rates during period 1902–1913 | Quarter | | | |
|---|---|---|---|---|
| | I | II | III | IV |
| Montreal call loans | 5.3 | 5.3 | 5.4 | 5.6 |
| New York call loans | 3.5 | 2.5 | 3.9 | 7.2 |
| New York time money | 4.1 | 3.4 | 4.8 | 5.5 |
| New York commercial paper | 4.8 | 4.4 | 5.3 | 5.5 |
| Boston call loans | 4.2 | 3.3 | 4.0 | 5.9 |
| Boston time money | 4.8 | 4.4 | 5.2 | 5.7 |
| Chicago commercial paper | 4.9 | 4.8 | 5.4 | 5.6 |
| London call loans | 2.7 | 1.7 | 2.2 | 2.8 |

*Sources.* The U.S. interest rates are monthly averages, while the Montreal call loan rate refers to the first day following the end of the month. Montreal: Canada, Board of Inquiry (1915), p. 739. New York: Macaulay (1938), Appendix, Table 10. Boston and Chicago: Goodhart (1969), Table 14. No quotation is available for the June 1909, Chicago commercial paper rate. I assume that rate to have amounted to 4% (equivalent to the quotations for May and July). London: Peake (1926), Appendix I. Interest rate on floating money for the first Friday following the end of the quarter.

shift in the composition of bank reserves, but went hand in hand with a sharp rise in inflows of secondary reserves. Third, it is too simplistic to argue that in periods of tight money Canada stepped up her gold imports from New York and, thus, compounded the liquidity problems of banks in that city. Only in the third quarter did a seasonal acceleration of gold imports (Table 3) coincide with a rise in short-term interest rates in New York (Table 5). In the fourth quarter—when the seasonal stringency in the New York money market reached a climax—Canada tended to curtail substantially her gold imports and, thus, alleviated the liquidity problems of New York banks. In other words, in periods of severe financial strain, Canada typically acted as a lender to the New York money market. Considering the relative size of the Canadian and United States economies, however, I doubt that the fourth-quarter decline in Canadian gold imports was large enough to make a strong imprint on the New York money market.

## 4. THE CAUSES OF THE 1907 CRISIS

As I pointed out in Section 1, the 1907 crisis broke out shortly after Canadian economic activity had passed a cyclical peak. International monetary assets, the monetary base, and aggregate reserves of the chartered banks normally reached a cyclical low near the midpoint of a business-

156                             GEORG RICH

cycle contraction. During the contraction of 1907–1908, which lasted
from December 1906 to July 1908, that trough was recorded in the autumn
of 1907 [Rich (1984, Chart 12.1)]. As may be seen from the smoothed
line in Chart 2, the aggregate reserve ratio—whose cyclical movements
were dominated by bank reserves—attained a cyclical low at about the
same time. Thus, upon eruption of the crisis, the Canadian banks' liquidity
position had already deteriorated as a result of a cyclical expansion in
economic activity and the attendant decline in the overall balance-of-
payments surplus.

The cyclical decline in the aggregate reserve ratio was reinforced by
an exceptionally large seasonal drop in international monetary assets
recorded in the fourth quarter of 1907. Therefore, adjusted international
monetary assets, expressed as a percentage of the corresponding smoothed
values, plunged to a record low (Chart 3). As a result of the outflow of
monetary gold and secondary reserves, the aggregate reserve ratio of
the chartered banks, at the end of 1907, amounted to only 21.1% (Chart
2), as compared with an end-of-year average of 26.2% for the period
1901–1913 as a whole (see Note 26). This ratio would have been even
lower without the emergency measures adopted by the government. As
indicated by Table 3, the loss of monetary gold in the fourth quarter of
1907 roughly corresponded to the figure quoted by the *Monetary Times*
(see p. 142). Thanks to the emergency issue of Dominion notes, the
banks were able to augment their cash reserves by $4.2 million despite
the gold outflow. This increase in cash reserves mirrored not only an
expansion in the banks' holdings of Dominion notes but also a rise in

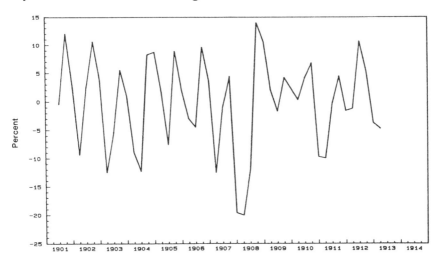

CHART 3.   Percentage deviation in international monetary assets from values smoothed
by a seven-quarter moving average. See legend to Table 2 for the source and for a
justification of the smoothing procedure.

their monetary gold stock. The banks apparently boosted their gold holdings by redeeming a portion of the additional Dominion notes issued by the government. The rise in bank holdings of gold recorded in the fourth quarter of 1907 explains why Johnson and Goodhart thought that Canada had imported gold after the New York crash. They overlooked the fact that the increase in these holdings, which amounted to $2.9 million, was more than offset by a $5.3 million loss of government gold (Rich, 1988, Table A-2).

An obvious explanation for the massive contraction in adjusted international monetary assets in the last quarter of 1907 was the surge in New York money market rates elicited by the October crash. As I showed in Section 3, it was normal for Canadian capital imports to shrink during the crop-moving season. Part of this decline was due to the improvement in the merchandise trade balance characteristic for this time of the year. The extent of the 1907 autumnal reduction in capital imports, however, was unusual. In contrast to the patterns typically observed for the period under study, the trade balance did not improve from the third to the fourth quarter. Nevertheless, residual inflows fell sharply (Table 3). In view of money market conditions in New York, this decline is not surprising. As a result of the October crash, the discount at which bills of exchange could be sold in New York was far greater than usual, inducing Canadian exporters to expand export credit. In November 1907, the financial press reported that it was practically impossible to sell sterling bills of exchange in New York (see *Monetary Times*, November 16, 1907, p. 794). In order to finance the additional trade credit, Canadian exporters ran down their domestic money holdings. For this reason, the drop in adjusted international monetary assets during the fourth quarter of 1907 was matched by an equally massive contraction in the adjusted money stock. This decrease in the money stock mirrored largely a fall in deposits, while the behavior of notes conformed closely to the pattern observed for the period 1901–1913 as a whole (Table 4). Thus, the evidence is consistent with the view that Canadian exporters substituted trade credit for deposits in the wake of the New York crash.

Through an expansion in trade credit, Canadian exporters assumed the role of lenders to the hard-pressed New York money market. The consequence of that role was the sharp reduction in bank reserves reported for the fourth quarter of 1907. While the drop in Canadian banks' secondary reserves did not make additional cash available to the New York money market, the gold outflow from Canada contributed somewhat to easing the financial squeeze in New York.[27] In view of the precarious state of

---

[27] According to Friedman and Schwartz (1963, p. 162), New York banks in November and December, 1907, imported over $130 million worth of gold. Inflows from Canada (of slightly over $2 million) only accounted for a small part of aggregate imports.

their liquidity, it is not surprising that the chartered banks took steps to cut back their lending.

Although the government passed its emergency measures with a view to enhancing the seasonal elasticity of the Canadian currency supply, their effect was to neutralize part of the reserve drain triggered by the New York crisis. As may be seen from Table 3, the drop in the Canadian monetary base in the fourth quarter of 1907 was much smaller than the overall balance-of-payments deficit because of the temporary expansion in the uncovered stock of Dominion notes. Thus, through the emergency issue of Dominion notes, the government eased the banks' liquidity problems. Normally, the banks managed to absorb the fourth-quarter cash drain to New York without being forced to curtail their lending. However, it appears that in times of financial distress, the ability of a laissez-faire banking system to supply cash to the New York money market was severely overtaxed unless the public was prepared to tolerate a significant reduction in domestic bank lending.

In contrast to Dominion notes in the hands of the chartered banks, non-bank holdings of government money decreased slightly in the fourth quarter of 1907, as was typical for the period under study. [Table 3, column (9)]. Since neither bank notes nor Dominion notes outside the banking system behaved abnormally in the autumn of 1907, it is unlikely that the statutory ceiling on the bank-note issue was the source of the difficulties.

## 5. SUMMARY AND CONCLUSIONS

In this paper I attempted to show that in periods of severe financial strain Canada acted as a lender to the New York money market. Prior to 1914, the money markets in New York and other financial centers typically tightened during the crop-moving season, with short-term interest rates attaining a seasonal peak in December. Contrary to the traditional view of the seasonal adjustment mechanism, Canada did not step up her gold imports when the financial stringency in New York reached its seasonal climax. Instead, the seasonal movements in Canadian gold imports were closely correlated with seasonal movements in the Canadian money stock. Canadian money demand normally peaked at the end of the third quarter, well before New York interest rates attained their seasonal highs. In this paper I argued that Canadian exporters responded to the autumnal surge in New York money market rates by lengthening the lag between export receipts and exports, thus, increasing their trade credit to foreigners. They financed the additional trade credit by running down their domestic money balances. Since this caused the Canadian money stock, bank reserves, and monetary gold holdings to shrink (relative to their trends), gold flows between Canada and the United States contributed to softening somewhat the autumnal financial squeeze in New York. Canadian banks

THE CRISIS OF 1907                                159

in turn did not attempt to stem the reserve loss by raising domestic interest rates, but simply allowed their reserve ratios to decline. Thus, in contrast to Viner's suggestion, Canadian banks, in periods of financial distress, did not compound the liquidity problems in New York.

The role played by Canadian exporters as lenders to the New York money market was particularly pronounced after the 1907 crash. As a result of soaring short-term interest rates in New York, Canadian capital imports shrank drastically, resulting in a massive balance-of-payments deficit, gold outflows, and reserve losses by the Canadian banks. The reserve drain triggered by the New York crash occurred at a time when a strong cyclical expansion in economic activity had already led to a substantial deterioration in the banks' liquidity position. In order to shore up their liquidity, the banks took steps to curtail their lending. The prospect of a credit squeeze prompted the government to provide liquidity assistance to the banks. Thus, the causes of the Canadian crisis were attributable directly to the New York crash. Most contemporary observers offered an alternative explanation of the crisis and argued that it was due to a decline in the seasonal elasticity of the Canadian bank-note issue. In this paper I show that the elasticity of the bank-note issue was unlikely to be the source of the difficulties.

The analysis presented in this paper suggests that seasonal movements in Canadian international monetary assets and capital flows are best explained by a variant of the monetary approach to balance-of-payments analysis. Seasonal movements in the trade balance did not significantly affect international monetary assets but were largely offset by capital flows. Instead, the seasonal swings in international monetary assets were attributable mainly to changes in domestic money demand, caused by seasonal fluctuation in domestic economic activity and New York interest rates. Trade credit by Canadian exporters to foreigners played a crucial role in generating seasonal movements in Canadian international monetary assets and the money stock.

## REFERENCES

Beckhart, B. H. (1929), *The Banking System of Canada*. New York: Holt.

Burns, A. F., and Mitchell, W. C. (1946), *Measuring Business Cycles*. New York: National Bureau of Economic Research.

Cairncross, A. K. (1968), "Investment in Canada, 1900–13." In A. R. Hall (Ed.), *The Export of Capital from Britain 1870–1914*. London: Methuen.

Canada. Board of Inquiry into Cost of Living in Canada. *Report of the Board*. Ottawa, 1915. Vol. 2.

Canada. *Canada Gazette*.

Canada. *Debates of the House of Commons*.

Canada. Department of Customs. *Trade and Navigation. Unrevised Monthly Statements of Imports Entered for Consumption and Export of the Dominion of Canada, 1905–1913*.

Canada. *Monthly Reports of the Department of Trade and Commerce*, various issues.

160 GEORG RICH

Canada. *Statutes of Canada.*

Curtis, C. A. (1931), "Banking statistics in Canada." In *Statistical Contributions to Canadian Economic History.* Toronto: Macmillan. Vol. 1.

Denison, M. (1967), *Canada's First Bank. A History of the Bank of Montreal.* Toronto/Montreal: McClelland and Stewart. Vol. 2.

Friedman, M., and Schwartz, A. J. (1963), *A Monetary History of the United States, 1867–1960.* Princeton: Univ. Press for NBER.

Goodhart, C. A. E. (1969), *The New York Money Market and the Finance of Trade.* Harvard Economic Studies. Cambridge, MA: Harvard Univ. Press. Vol. 132.

Hartland (Thunberg), P. (1955), *The Canadian Balance of Payments since 1868.* Unpublished manuscript. New York: National Bureau of Economic Research.

Hay, K. A. J. (1966), "Early Twentieth Century Business Cycles in Canada." *Canadian Journal of Economics and Political Science* **32**, 354–364.

Jamieson, A. B. (1955), *Chartered Banking in Canada.* Toronto: Ryerson.

Johnson, J. F. (1910), *The Canadian Banking System.* National Monetary Commission. Senate, 61st Congress, 2nd Session. Washington, DC: Govt. Printing Office.

Macaulay, F. R. (1938), *Some Theoretical Problems Suggested by the Movements of Interest Rates, Bond Yields and Stock Prices in the United States since 1856.* New York: National Bureau of Economic Research.

*The Monetary Times,* Toronto.

Neufeld, E. P. (1972), *The Financial System of Canada.* Toronto: Macmillan Co.

Officer, L. H. (1986), "The Efficiency of the Dollar-Sterling Gold Standard, 1890–1908." *Journal of Political Economy* **94**, 1038–1073.

Peake, E. G. (1926), *An Academic Study of Some Money Market and Other Statistics.* London: King. 2nd ed.

Rich, G. (1984), "Canada without a Central Bank: Operation of the Price–Specie–Flow Mechanism, 1872–1913." In M. D. Bordo and A. J. Schwartz (Eds.), *A Retrospective on the Classical Gold Standard.* Chicago/London: Univ. of Chicago Press for NBER. Chap. 12.

Rich, G. (1988), *The Cross of Gold. Money and the Canadian Business Cycle, 1968–1913.* Ottawa: Carleton Univ. Press.

Shearer, R. A. (1965), "The Foreign Currency Business of Canadian Chartered Banks." *Canadian Journal of Economics and Political Science* **31**, 328–357.

Shortt, A. (1922), "The Legislative Development of the Canadian Banking System." In V. Ross (Ed.), *The History of the Canadian Bank of Commerce.* Toronto: Oxford Univ. Press. Vol. 2, Chap. 7.

Viner, J. (1924), *Canada's Balance of International Indebtedness, 1900–1913.* Cambridge, MA: Harvard Univ. Press.

# [5]

Excerpt from *Economic Development in the Habsburg Monarchy and in the Successor States*, 89–113

## VII. THE CAUSES OF THE AUSTRIAN CURRENCY CRISIS OF 1931

Aurel Schubert
Austrian National Bank

Recent economic and financial developments, such as those of October 1987, have increased interest in financial crises, especially that of the early 1930s.[1] Austria played a very special role in this crisis, as the collapse of the largest bank of interwar Austria and of Europe east of Germany in May 1931, the Credit–Anstalt, is widely considered to have

> finally set a chain reaction in motion: the run on the German banks (June–July), the withdrawals from London and the devaluation of sterling (September), and another series of bank failures in the United States (October–January).[2]

In analyses of the events of the early 1930s the focus of attention usually shifts very quickly to the larger economies of Germany or Britain while the Austrian problems are only treated in connection with those in other countries. Therefore, the Austrian currency crisis of 1931 has only received marginal attention during the 1930s as well as in present day analyses of economic history. This aspect of the Austrian financial crisis of 1931, however, deserves more interest and research. At the time of its occurrence, as well as in many of the later accounts, it was considered as an irrational act by the panicy public, lacking any economic or rational foundation. After closer scrutiny, however, it appears as a good example of a rational and endogenously timed speculative attack on a currency.

We will argue and show some evidence that the public behaved rationally by using all the available information and drew—based on their experience, which was largely influenced by the hyperinflation of 1919–22—the right conclusions. The way the authorities handled the Credit–Anstalt crisis gave unambiguous signs to the public that a currency crisis was imminent and led them to attack the currency.

Therefore, this crisis should not be viewed as an exogenous event unforseeable by the authorities but rather as an endogenous consequence of the reactions of the authorities to the problems of that bank.

Therefore, the Austrian currency experience of 1931 fits very well into the recent literature on speculative attacks as rational and endogenously determined events.[3] During the crisis there was a clear asset shift in agents' portfolios generated by the belief that an asset price fixing scheme, the fixed parity of the schilling, was about to end. This would have caused a discontinuous downward shift in asset rates of return of schilling denominated assets and resulted therefore in a speculative attack on this currency. Although it appeared unexpected and irrational to the authorities, the speculative attack was rational, as the market recognized the fundamental inconsistencies in the policies which were not reversed by the authorities until the foreign reserves had approached complete depletion. The attempt of the authorities to resist a rational evaluation of the value of the schilling without changing the underlying policies resulted in the currency crisis.

First, the events of 1931 in Austria will be reviewed and then the causes of the currency crisis discussed. Some empirical evidence will be presented and finally some conclusions will be drawn.

*  *  *  *  *

On 8 May 1931, the Österreichische Credit–Anstalt für Handel und Gewerbe announced to the Austrian government and the Austrian National Bank (ANB) that its 1930 balance sheet had revealed a loss of 140 million schillings (20m dollars), amounting to about 85 percent of its equity.

The 1920s had already witnessed a series of Austrian bank failures, starting with the collapse of the stock exchange boom and the bear speculation against the French franc in 1924. These events were followed by a wave of bank collapses, eliminating most of the banks that had been established during the boom that had followed the end of the hyperinflation and the stabilization of the Austrian currency. Moreover, some of the older and larger institutions were also affected, as they suffered heavy losses themselves and had to absorb some of the collapsing banks. They emerged weakened from this crisis. What was so special about this particular bank failure in 1931 that it received so much attention that it was during the mid–1970s, still considered to be "the biggest ever bank collapse."[4]

First of all, the Credit–Anstalt (CA) was the largest bank in Austria with a 1930 total balance sheet equal to the federal budget. Its balance sheet accounted for about 53 percent of the balance sheet

totals of all twenty–five joint stock banks in the country. It had an
excellent international reputation, especially since a member of the
Rothschild family was its president, and it enjoyed better conditions
in the financial centers of the world than any of the large German
banks. More than 50 percent of its stocks were in foreign hands, while
a number of prominent foreigners sat on its supervisory board and
its creditors were the most reputable banks of the Western financial
world. The statement by a British official that "[if] even the Credit–
Anstalt cannot be relied on, everything in Austria must be rotten"
shows very dramatically that this was not considered to be just a
normal bank.[5] März concluded that the Credit–Anstalt was the most
important of Austrian banking houses and was treated very differently
than all the others.[6]

All the available reports of the events suggest that the collapse
was unexpected, even in the usually well informed financial circles of
London and New York. Barron's, for instance, reported on 18 May
1931 that

> the news of the difficulties [of the Credit–Anstalt] came as
> a considerable shock to London bankers where it was quite
> unexpected, as it had been thought the position had been
> cleared up when the Boden–Kreditanstalt was taken over
> some time ago [in 1929].[7]

As the "openly declared bankruptcy of Austria's foremost bank
was sure to be followed by numerous business failures"[8] the Austrian government decided to depart temporarily from its laissez–faire
orientation and—in order to avoid the negative externalities of such
a failure—accepted "socialization of [the] losses."[9] Within only three
days a reconstruction plan was put together, arranging for covering of
the losses by the state, the reserves, the shareholders, the Rothschilds,
and the Austrian National Bank, and the provision of new capital by
the state, the Austrian National Bank, and the Rothschilds.[10] The
most outstanding feature of the plan was that the shareholders were
treated very generously and that the state was to pay for the largest
share of the losses. The share capital was to be devalued by only 25
percent, instead of more than 80 percent, as would have been justified
by the volume of losses, and the state was to contribute 100 million
schillings to rescue and reconstruction.

When the problems of the bank were finally announced to the
public on 11 May 1931, together with the reconstruction plan, it was
thought that confidence in the troubled institution would be pre-
served. No interruption of the ordinary business had occurred and
the future of the bank on a new and larger capital basis seemed to

be secured.[11] The very optimistic announcements by the press, such
as *The Economist's* statement that "fortunately, it is already clear
that the difficulties of the Credit–Anstalt are already being taken
successfully in hand, and the very frank and reassuring statement
issued this week should go a long way to dispel doubts," were, however, premature.[12] So also were the congratulations to "all concerned
upon the frank, prompt and energetic manner in which the episode
has been dealt with."[13]

The inability of the reconstruction plan to dispel the doubts of
the public came just as unexpectedly as the problems of the bank.
During four days the Credit–Anstalt witnessed a run by its frightened
depositors, and so did most of the other Viennese banks.

In contrast to a widely held view, we now know that mainly
domestic and only to a smaller extent foreign creditors, withdrew
their money from the banks. In only two days the Credit–Anstalt
lost about one–sixth of its creditors, and within two weeks about
a third.[14] While foreign withdrawals during this period were estimated at about 120m schillings, withdrawals by domestic residents
amounted to roughly 300m schillings.[15]

This large scale run would have immediately rendered the ailing
bank illiquid, had not the Austrian National Bank accepted the role of
the lender of last resort. It freely rediscounted all the bills presented
by the Credit–Anstalt—initially just commercial bills, but soon afterwards financial bills, i.e., promissory notes. To accept the latter was
in violation of its own charter, but it did so "with the permission of
the government."[16]

Although the ANB's liberal discounting policy managed to allay
the fears of the public that means of payments would not be obtain-
able, the distrust of the Credit–Anstalt remained, especially when it
became more and more obvious that the reconstruction of the bank
was not completed and the true losses could be expected to run considerably higher than those initially reported.[17] Withdrawals slowed
down but did not stop.

In order to be able to finance its share in the reconstruction
plan, the Austrian government—without any budgetary funds at its
disposal—had planned to place two- and three-year treasury bonds
in foreign capital markets. In the meantime, it had approached the
Bank of England, and after having been rejected by it, the Bank
for International Settlements (BIS), for a credit amounting to 150m
schillings (approximately 21m dollars). It took the BIS, however,
about three weeks to arrange and forward such a loan, which was
granted for the reduced amount of 100m schillings. The loan was not
only too late and too small, but more importantly, its release was tied

to a state guarantee for the credits to the ailing bank. Although the guarantee was initially intended to apply only to new money lent to the bank, it later had to include old credits, in order to avoid that old credits were withdrawn (and then possibly redeposited). This, however, meant that the already financially strapped state accepted potential liabilities of an undetermined but very considerable amount. Therefore, Professor Kindleberger's correct observation that "the niggardliness of the sum [of the BIS credit] and the delay together proved disastrous" has to be extended to include the state guarantee.

The fact that the Austrian government gave such a guarantee, despite the poor state of its public finances, and the unfortunate way in which it was done proved to be counterproductive. Suddenly the banking problems affected the state of public finances and, therefore, the Austrian currency. Austrians, as well as some foreigners, started to convert (part of) their schilling holdings into foreign exchange, leading to large reductions in the reserve holdings of the Austrian National Bank. In less than a week the money lent by the BIS and several central banks was withdrawn by the concerned public. A further BIS credit was promised in anticipation of Austria's issue of treasury bonds in the international capital markets but French resistance to plans of an Austro–German customs union prevented both. France demanded political concessions that were unacceptable to Austria. In order to avoid foreign repercussions—especially on British claims—from a possible Austrian moratorium, the Bank of England intervened and extended an emergency short–term credit (for seven days, but renewable), amounting to 150m schillings.

Negotiations with the about 130 foreign creditor banks, which had formed the—so called—Austrian Credit–Anstalt International Committee, led to a standstill agreement.[18] For an interest charge of one percentage points above the discount rate in the respective home country these creditors agreed to prolong their credits for two years, until mid–1933. However, as a precondition for this agreement, they forced—with the support of the Austrian National Bank—the government to extend its guarantee to all foreign credits.[19]

From the end of June 1931 on, the state guarantee covered all liabilities of the ailing bank, so that the Austrian state with a federal budget of roughly 1,800m schillings stood guarantor for 1,200m schillings of Credit–Anstalt liabilities. The trust of the Austrian government officials that this generous guarantee would finally induce foreigners to place additional funds at the disposal of the bank proved to be not only overly optimistic, but outright incorrect. The foreign creditors, having rescued their endangered assets with a state guarantee, had no incentive to place new money into this bank. The Aus-

**94**    *Economic Development in the Habsburg Monarchy*

trians, on the other hand, had every reason to be concerned about the Austrian currency and to try to adjust their portfolios, reducing schilling assets and increasing foreign currency assets. The Credit–Anstalt had to continue to present financial bills to the Austrian National Bank for rediscounting, and the lender of last resort accepted them in order to keep the liquidity strapped bank afloat. This liberal discounting policy, however, was by no means undisputed within the National Bank. It was the cause of continuous disagreement within the management and even led to the resignation of one of the Vice–Presidents.

Large increases in the discount rate in June and July (from 5 to 10 percent) did not succeed in restricting the amount of rediscounting by the Credit–Anstalt, since it needed the liquidity irrespective of the cost involved, nor did it improve the position of the Austrian currency, since even a rate of 10 percent was insufficient to stop capital flight, despite the expectation that such a high rate would be able to "draw gold from the moon."[20]

As the government was unable to raise any long–term foreign loans, and as foreign reserves kept on declining, the Austrian currency became increasingly backed by financial bills of the ailing Credit–Anstalt. As a consequence, the government finally decided on 9 October 1931 to introduce exchange controls, de facto leaving the gold standard.[21] Great Britain had just suspended its adherence to the gold standard two weeks earlier, while other countries, such as Germany and Hungary had already introduced exchange controls in July and August, respectively.

In January 1933, about 20 months after the start of the Credit–Anstalt crisis, an agreement was reached with the foreign creditors, and the reconstruction of the Credit–Anstalt was finally started. The initially reported losses of 140m schillings turned out to be about 1,000m, with the Austrian state bearing about 90 percent of them—a sum equivalent to about 50 percent of the total state expenditures in 1930. It was not until the spring of 1934 that the devaluation of the schilling was finally officially accepted by the Austrian National Bank by a 28 percent revaluation of its gold stock.[22]

\* \* \* \* \*

Austria adhered during the 1920s—after the end of the hyperinflation in 1922—to a gold exchange standard with a dollar peg, i.e., a dollar exchange standard. Due to this fixed and stable peg to the dollar the Austrian schilling had been nicknamed "Alpine dollar."[23] As pointed out previously, the collapse of the Credit–Anstalt in May 1931 was followed by a currency crisis. The handling of the bank's problems led the public to expect a change in this fixed parity of the currency and it engaged in short term capital transfers out of schilling (assets). The Austrian National Bank, however, believed that the market's expectations were unfounded and incorrect and consequently took steps to keep the exchange rate within the gold points. Their respective actions resulted in large scale losses of foreign reserves for the ANB, and, as foreign exchange allocations became restricted, in the establishment of black markets. Finally, five months after the outbreak of the crisis in early October 1931 exchange controls were introduced. Inflationary fears by a large segment of the public led to a speculative attack on the schilling and forced an abandoning of the fixed exchange rate regime.

In order to understand this currency crisis the causes for the emergence of inflationary expectations and fears by the Austrian public have to be understood. The key to understanding the public's sensitivity with respect to inflation lies in the period 1919 to 1922, the period of the Austrian hyperinflation. The traumatic experience of that episode overshadowed all the later developments and left a distinctive mark on them.

In 1918, by the end of World War I, the price level in Austria was about 25 times as high as before the war. At the peak of the hyperinflation, in September 1922, it reached 14,153 times the prewar level.[24] At the same time, the exchange rate on the U.S. Dollar reached 16,877 times the 1913 value. In August 1922, however, the Austrian crown was abruptly stabilized and the "Austrian inflation was essentially stopped cold."[25]

The proximate cause for this unprecedented hyperinflation in Austria was the enormous increase in note circulation during and especially after the war. By the end of August 1922, bank–note circulation had reached 2,700 times the estimated prewar 1914 level. This was mainly due to the bank's policy of liberally discounting treasury bills presented by the cash strapped government.

The fundamental cause driving these developments was a chaotic budgetary situation. The Austrian state ran an enormous deficit. During the second half of 1921, for instance, the government's receipts could not cover more than 35.7 percent of its expenditures.[26] As no other means of financing were open to the government—as "every attempt to obtain credits from foreign banks or from foreign governments had met with failure,"[27] and as Viennese banks were not willing to lend to the state, either—it had to sell treasury bills to the Austrian administration of the Austro–Hungarian Bank.[27] This meant that up to two thirds of total federal government expenditures were covered by the printing press. As a consequence the amount of highpowered money and prices increased rapidly and people fled into currencies of those countries that did not suffer from hyperinflation and into real assets. The government felt obliged to introduce strict exchange controls.

> The depreciation of the Austrian crown was suddenly stopped by the intervention of the Council of the League of Nations and the resulting binding commitment of the government of Austria to reorder Austrian fiscal and monetary strategies dramatically.[28]

In particular, the Austrian government pledged to establish an independent central bank that would be forbidden to lend to the government, except on the basis of gold or foreign exchange security. It also promised to balance its budget within two years' time.[29] In exchange for these changes in the fiscal and monetary regimes, an internationally guaranteed loan of 650 million gold crowns was promised and raised in the international capital markets.[30] The government's willingness to abandon the old fiscal and monetary strategies and to follow fiscal and monetary policies compatible with maintaining convertibility of its liabilities into dollars, reinstated public confidence in the currency, even before the printing press was stopped or the loan was actually raised.

This experience with hyperinflation left the Austrian public with an increased sensitivity to, and even a constant fear of renewed inflation. At the same time it taught them a very painful but instructive lesson about the links between fiscal and monetary expansion, inflation and the exchange rate.

What kind of changes occurred in 1931 that made the public lose its trust and confidence in the "Alpine dollar"? Based on the previous discussion on the hyperinflation, we have to look for signals of a "perceived" return to policies similar to those of the 1919 to 1922 period.

As we recall, the initial rescue plan identified the Austrian government as the main contributor to the salvage of the failing bank, with a share of 100 million schillings in exchange for 33 percent of the bank's new share capital. In spite of its general laissez–faire philosophy, the government considered this move to be necessary in order to prevent much greater harm to Austrian industry and economy. This was not intended to be a policy change of any kind. Quite to the contrary, the government preferred intervention in this bank's affairs to potentially much wider reaching interventions at the level of individual industries and companies, since the latter approach would have been (perceived as) a complete break with its previous economic policy and philosophy. Help to the bank was considered to be an isolated action made necessary and justified by special circumstances. There is no indication that this action—per se—would already have created extensive adverse expectations with respect to the Austrian currency.

The state of public finance, namely the fact that the government did not even have the 100 million schillings it had pledged to contribute to the reconstruction of the ailing bank so that Viennese banks were eventually forced to advance that money might have influenced some people's expectations at this stage.[32]

No fundamental change in the fiscal regime had yet occurred. However, the events of 12 May 1931 and the following days had a strong impact on the monetary regime. Distrust in the Credit–Anstalt and, for that matter, in the other banks, had led to large–scale withdrawals by the public, and as the ANB followed a "lending freelypolicy," to a sharp increase in its bills portfolio and in the amount of high–powered money, as shown in Table 1 below.

In the course of only four days (12 May to 15 May) the amount of rediscounted bills increased by, at least, 328 percent,[33] while highpowered money expanded by no less than 19.4 percent.[34] Bank note circulation increased by 14.6 percent. These were rates of monetary expansion unknown during the preceding years and even unmatched at the height of the hyperinflation in the summer of 1922 when the highest weekly percentage increase in high–powered money had reached 18 percent.[35]

During the following weeks this unprecedented expansion was not reversed but rather reinforced, reigniting inflationary fears of the public. The *Wiener Börsen–Kurier*, (1 June 1931, p. 1) stated that "since inflation is usually combined with an increase in note circulation, inflationary fears have been created in the public due to the rise in currency," and one week late it reported that fears for the schilling had spread into wide circles of the public and had led to a flight of capital (8 June 1931, p. 1). By this time—less than one month after the outbreak of the crisis—the public had realized that the fixed exchange rate system was in danger as it was inconsistent with the rate of domestic credit expansion. As a reversal of the policies seemed unlikely, the collapse of the fixed rate was anticipated and a run on the foreign reserves developed. A speculative attack on the schilling, i.e., a discontinuous asset shift in agents' portfolios generated by the belief that an asset price fixing scheme was about to terminate, occurred.[36] When the public realized that capital gains could be made from hoarding foreign exchange they rationally demanded this increase in their holdings of foreign exchange.[37]

**98**        *Economic Development in the Habsburg Monarchy*

Table 1 shows the development of the reserves of the Austrian
National Bank and reflects this speculative attack very vividly. By 7

## Table 1.

Notes and Deposits, Foreign Reserves and Bills Discounted
at the Outbreak of the Crisis, weekly

| Day | High–powered Money | Foreign Reserves [+] | Bills ˙Discounted |
|---|---|---|---|
| April 30 | 1,048.5 | 860.0 | 89.2 |
| May 7 | 1,024.6 | 855.5 | 69.5 |
| May 15 | 1,223.8 | 826.4 | 297.6 |
| May 23 | 1,230.4 | 780.5 | 350.0 |
| May 31 | 1,282.9 | 732.2 | 451.3 |
| June 7 | 1,251.9 | 677.1 | 475.4 |
| June 15 | 1,286.4 | 698.7 | 488.2 |
| June 23 | 1,255.4 | 661.0 | 490.2 |
| June 30 | 1,290.9 | 658.6 | 528.7 |
| July 7 | 1,252.6 | 639.0 | 511.3 |
| July 15 | 1,259.7 | 622.4 | 533.9 |
| July 23 | 1,285.2 | 592.6 | 588.4 |
| July 31 | 1,299.7 | 566.7 | 632.1 |
| Aug. 7 | 1,261.9 | 546.7 | 614.3 |
| Aug. 15 | 1,217.0 | 524.3 | 591.8 |
| Aug. 23 | 1,192.2 | 504.5 | 586.5 |
| Aug. 31 | 1,215.7 | 490.3 | 624.3 |
| Sep. 7 | 1,193.7 | 472.3 | 620.3 |
| Sep. 15 | 1,162.8 | 456.4 | 604.9 |
| Sep. 23 | 1,141.9 | 407.0 | 630.3 |
| Sep. 30 | 1,185.5 | 391.7 | 688.5 |
| Oct. 7 | 1,201.7 | 358.9 | 736.2 |

[+] The data for "Foreign Reserves" do not include the foreign exchange assets that are part of "Other Assets" in the weekly reports of the ANB, nor the foreign exchange liabilities that are
part of "Other Liabilities."

**Source:** *Mitteilungen des Direktoriums der Oesterreichischen Nationalbank*, various issues.

June the stock of foreign reserves had declined—despite the foreign exchange credit by the BIS—by about one–fifth.

Since the stabilization of the currency in 1922, the ANB had followed a "real bills doctrine." In a speech in 1931 the president of the Austrian National Bank, Professor Reisch, pointed out that the note circulation was tied to real bills (commercial bills), as the volume of bills could be regarded as a good proxy for the level of capacity utilization of trade and industry, and therefore for the financial needs of the economy.[38] The pursuit of this "needs of trade" approach, was manifested in a relatively stable relationship between the note circulation and the nominal level of economic activity.[39] In May 1931, however, this ratio which had been previously kept within a rather narrow band, took a quantum leap upwards and remained at heights never reached before, indicating to the public that a sudden change in the monetary rule had occurred. The real bills doctrine and its implicit disciplinary effects on monetary growth had been abandoned in favor of the rescue of (the liquidity of) the banking sector as it collided with the lender of last resort function of the National Bank.

Other indicators of monetary policy that were used during those years showed a very similar picture and led to the same conclusions. We know from newspaper reports that the central bank's weekly statements had never before been studied as carefully as during that period in 1931.[40] The behavior of the note cover, the ratio between the sum of gold and foreign exchange reserves and currency in circulation, especially, received considerable interest. The note cover dropped considerably after the outbreak of the crisis (Table 2). Within the first days of the crisis it declined by about one–fifth or 16 percentage points. Despite the loans of the BIS and the Bank of England and the moratorium agreed with the foreign creditors of the Credit–Anstalt, it continued to decline.

The president of the ANB attempted to downplay the importance of the note cover and maintained that even a temporary fall below the statutory minimum cover would be unproblematic.[41] The markets, however, were not impressed by his arguments.

This perceived change in the monetary strategy then became the proximate reason for the currency crisis, since "any sort of fixed exchange rate is equivalent to a monetary growth rule" and consequently "implies a specific monetary discipline, which, if not followed for one reason or another, will precipitate an exchange rate collapse."[42]

*100*      *Economic Development in the Habsburg Monarchy*

## Table 2

### Note Cover in Austria, May–October 1931
### (in percent)[+]

| Month | Day 7 | 15 | 23 | Last Day |
|-------|-------|------|------|----------|
| May   | 83.5  | 67.5 | 63.8 | 57.1     |
| June  | 54.1  | 54.3 | 52.7 | 51.0     |
| July  | 51.0  | 49.4 | 46.1 | 43.6     |
| Aug.  | 48.7  | 43.1 | 42.3 | 40.3     |
| Sep.  | 39.6  | 39.3 | 35.6 | 33.0     |
| Oct.  | 29.9  | 29.1 | 28.7 | 28.1     |

[+] Note cover is here defined as the ratio of gold plus foreign exchange holdings of the ANB to currency in circulation (without coins) plus sight deposits at the ANB.

**Source:** *Mitteilungen des Direktoriums der Oesterreichischen Nationalbank,* various issues.

Movements in bills discounted (domestic credit) were offset by countermovements in foreign exchange reserves (Figure 1). A substitution between bills discounted and foreign exchange occurred in the portfolio of the National Bank.

Very restrictive allocations of foreign exchange, e.g., on some days—early June 1931—only 5 percent for dollar notes,[43] and some foreign short–term credits, prevented foreign reserves from converging towards zero at a rate faster than they actually did.

As the authorities failed to adjust their policies, and continued to rediscount bills of the Credit–Anstalt and to adhere at the same time to the fixed exchange rate, the flight out of the schilling continued until and even after exchange controls were introduced on 9 October 1931. The fixed exchange rate regime was made subject to collapse since it conflicted with the more important policy of bailing out the banking system, which forced the authorities to speed up domestic credit growth by more than had been anticipated.

The fundamental cause of the distrust in the currency, however, was the return to a chaotic state of the finances of the Austrian state. As we recall, the fundamental problem leading to the hyperinflation had been the complete imbalance between the Austrian government's revenues and expenditures. The League of Nations loan had been granted in order to restore a balanced budget and orderly public finance. The acceptance of this change in the fiscal regime, in exchange

## Figure 1
Foreign Reserves and Bills Discounted
in million schillings

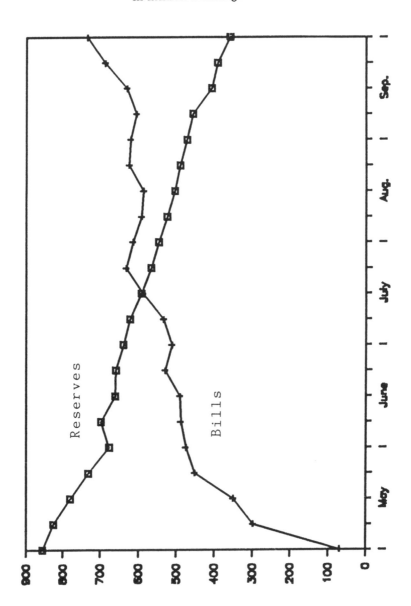

for the loan, had immediately stopped the currency's plunge in August 1922. Thereafter the government had pursued a policy of balanced budgets.

At the onset of the Credit–Anstalt crisis three adverse events— bad "fiscal news"—affected this policy regime. For one, 1930 had been the first year since stabilization, with a budget deficit on current account (17m schillings), as compared to a projected surplus. *The Wall Street Journal* (18 May 1931, p. 6) reported in this context that "the International Control Committee for the protection of Austrian loans . . . has issued a study indicating that the Austrian government, far from initiating economies, has allowed unnecessary expenditures." *The Daily Telegraph* (21 May 1931, p. 11), on the other hand, reported that "the Austrian governments, central and local, spend too much, as their budgets are higher than that of Czechoslovakia, which has 16,000,000 inhabitants, as against 6,000,000 Austrians." Both reports confirm conclusions made concerning the British situation in 1931, namely that ". . . the first thing at which foreigners look is the budgetary situation," and that "Continental observers looked immediately to the budget when confidence in the sterling was weakened." [44]

The budgetary predictions for 1931 that were issued at that time were even less encouraging. The Minister of Finance predicted a 150m sch. deficit for fiscal 1931, without accounting for any expenses in connection with the reconstruction of the Credit–Anstalt. [45] This sudden budgetary problem had been mainly caused by dwindling revenues due to the ongoing and deepening economic depression—which were only partly offset by new taxes—and by higher than expected outlays, due to high unemployment and the agricultural crisis of the fall of 1930.

Moreover, the practice of combatting the financial difficulties by means of fresh taxation was increasingly challenged, as the burden of taxation had increased fivefold since 1923. As *The Economist* (27 June 1931, p. 1379) reported, the Central Association of Industry had protested vigorously against further tax increases, and had claimed that taxation per head of population had increased from 14 schillings in 1923 to 70 schillings.

The second bad fiscal news was the fact that the Austrian treasury had no funds at its disposal, but as mentioned already, committed itself to contribute 100m schillings to the reconstruction of the Credit–Anstalt and thus had to force Viennese banks to advance the funds as the governmental vaults were empty.

The most important adverse fiscal news was the acceptance of a (first unclearly specified and then unlimited) state guarantee for the

liabilities of the Credit–Anstalt (on 28 May 1931 and then in mid–
and end–June). The potential fiscal implications of this (forced) guarantee constituted a clear departure from the balanced budget strategy
of the mid– and late–1920s. It created contingent liabilities for the
Austrian budget of amounts that could not be foreseen, at a time
when the continued business downturn was already threatening Austria's fiscal balance, and it increased the expected present value of
government debt in a discontinuous way. Moreover, by that time it
was already obvious that this crisis would become increasingly in-
termingled with international politics and that consequently foreign
credits could not be counted on to any large extent. As early as 16
May, *The Daily Telegraph* had reported that its correspondent had
been informed "by a high official of the French Foreign office that
naturally France would not agree to Austria obtaining such a loan
[i.e., from the League of Nations] in the face of the Austro–German
customs union plan."[46] Tax revenues, on the other hand, were declining as the business depression deepened, and the situation in the
domestic financial markets was judged to be unfavorable for a bond
issue.

   These were very clear signals for the public to be concerned about
a change in the fiscal regime and consequently, about a possible monetization of future government debt, as it had occurred during the
hyperinflation. The budget had emerged as the crucial determinant
of the state of confidence because of the popular association of budget
deficits with monetary expansion.[47] This regime change led to immediate doubts and fears by experts, and by the Bourse, as well as by the
general public as they recognized that the state could be forced under certain circumstances to borrow more than 1/2 billion schillings
from the National Bank—a policy which would lead to inflation.[48]
*The Economist* (28 November 1931, p.1009) characterized the situation this way: ". . . the government has committed itself far beyond
its strength."

   It is correct, however, that financing of the government by the
central bank was not allowed by law, but the bank had violated its
charter before, when it rediscounted financial bills. Moreover, by
that time, there had not yet been a test whether the government
and the central bank would really obey this restriction in such an
extraordinary situation.

   Capital flight received an additional impetus by the potential increase of current, but especially of future government deficits. Within
only 6 days (31 May to 5 June), the BIS credit of 100m sch. "was exhausted and the Austrian National Bank requested another,"[49] but
never received it. The BIS, although having assured the Austrians

that it would help them to protect their currency, should the need arise, did not fulfill this promise.

One 16 June, the government signed an extended guarantee and resigned, as there was "stiff internal opposition to such necessary measures."[50] This signaled to the concerned public that the government was—partly, at least—aware of the dangers of an unlimited guarantee for the Credit–Anstalt, possibly reinforcing and increasing concern in the population. *The Economist* (27 June 1931, p. 1379) reported that on several of the days following this extension of the guarantee and the resignation of the government "there was a panic demand for foreign values in Austria. The National Bank was hardly able to cope with the inquiry for notes, though at all times it naturally met demands for withdrawal." It stressed further that this run did not only affect the Credit–Anstalt, but that "big withdrawals were also made from savings banks in Vienna and in the provinces." Therefore, the driving force was more than only distrust in the ailing bank but rather distrust in the future of the Austrian currency. With the issue of the state guarantee the problem of the Credit–Anstalt became a problem of Austrian public finance and therefore of the Austrian currency.

Sargent's conclusion (1982, p. 47) about hyperinflations in general is consistent with the Austrian events since the perceived change in the government's strategy or regime resulted in a change in the public's strategies in choosing portfolios. The inflationary fears—based on the rapid extension of domestic credit and high–powered money— were reinforced. This led the public to dispose of their schilling holdings or schilling denominated assets and to try to acquire as much foreign exchange as possible, forcing the central bank—committed to a fixed peg—to reduce allocations and to support the exchange rate. Austria had become a prisoner of her inflation experience, since any sizeable budget deficit "would at that time immediately have been interpreted by the population as another destruction of the currency."[51]

Bankers, politicians and journalists alike, tried to emphasize that no danger to the stability of the currency existed, pointing out repeatedly that considerable exchange reserves were available at the central bank and that the note cover was far above the statutory minimum.[52] They disregarded, however, what Keynes had already emphasized during the 1920s, namely that the size of the government's gold reserves (and foreign exchange reserves) was not the key determinant of a country's ability to maintain convertibility into gold, but rather its fiscal policy was.[53] The gold reserves and international borrowing ceilings could only affect the length of time a currency could be defended or the time available to change fiscal policy in order to return it to consistency with the fixed exchange rate regime.

The fact that Austria's reserves were largely borrowed reserves—originating from short–term capital inflows that more than offset a persistent structural current account deficit—and therefore constituted outstanding callable debt to foreigners, greatly reduced the probability of a successful defense of the currency until a change in policy would occur. In this sense the adverse trade balance can be included as one of the factors contributing to the distrust in the exchange rate parity, since it influenced the probabilities attached to the different possible outcomes.

*  *  *  *  *

This reinterpretation of the causes of the currency crisis as it can be deduced from economic theory and supported by contemporary accounts of the events, can be substantiated, although not rigorously tested, by an investigation of the data available.

An efficient foreign exchange market should have anticipated this collapse very early in the crisis. A large discount on the forward rate of the Austrian schilling relative to strong currencies should have been observable. A comparison of the forward rates and the subsequent spot exchange rate—after the devaluation—would then reveal insight into the efficiency of the market in predicting the decline of the schilling. As far as the Austrian schilling in 1931 is concerned such a rigorous testing is not possible since no such forward exchange data is at our disposal and the spot rate was held almost constant by intervention. Therefore, we cannot test the efficient market hypothesis per se, but we can attempt to show that the market's behavior did not obviously contradict the efficiency postulate.

The asset holders' expectations of future exchange rates are largely influenced by their predictions of future supplies of domestic money relative to other national monies, adjusted for expected changes in the relative demands for them. The news, both fiscal and monetary, signaled to the market that the stability of the schilling was in jeopardy. Expected future supplies of the schilling were seen to be increasing strongly, without an equivalent change in the demand for them. This precipitated the run out of the schilling—in order to avoid capital losses or to secure capital gains. Foreign short–term credits by the BIS and the Bank of England, both intended to stabilize the currency, could not restore confidence in the Austrian currency. However, they increased the potential gains to speculators. These credits postponed the end of the authorities' interventions in the foreign exchange market, but did not prevent the sudden shift of reserves from the Austrian

National Bank to the public, as domestic credit expansion, which had triggered the collapse, and the problems of public finance continued.

There are mainly four sources of evidence for the public's expectations concerning the value of the Austrian schilling: (1) the official foreign exchange markets, (2) the behavior of the foreign reserves, (3) the gold and the bond markets, and (4) the black (unofficial) exchange markets.

Austria adhered to the gold exchange standard. The National Bank stood ready to supply all the foreign exchange demanded at the given parity, fixed to the U. S. dollar. Consequently, the official exchange rate hardly showed any variation, except a modest decline after the announcement of the bank's problems. It stayed well within the gold points.

In such a fixed exchange rate system, with the central bank observing its duty to protect the exchange rate, changes in the market's confidence in a currency are not reflected in the price of the currency but rather in changes in the level of foreign reserves of the respective central bank. The reserves of the Austrian National Bank were declining rapidly starting in May 1931 (Table 3). Between 30 April

### Table 3

Diminution of Foreign Exchange Holdings of the Austrian
National Bank, May–October 1931

(in million schillings)

|  |  | Stock |
|---|---|---|
| 30 April 1931 |  |  |
|  | Foreign Exchange | 860.0 |
|  | "Other Assets" | 106.0 |
|  | "Other Liabilities" | −14.5 |
|  | Total | 951.5 |
| 7 October 1931 |  |  |
|  | Foreign Exchange | 359.0 |
|  | "Other Assets" | 13.5 |
|  | Liabilities: |  |
|  | BIS | −90.0 |
|  | Bank of England | −100.0 |
|  | Other | −78.9 |
|  | Total | 103.6 |
|  | Decline | 847.9 |

**Source:** Oesterreichische Nationalbank, Bericht des Generalrates über die Geschäftsführung des Jahres 1931.

and 7 October 1931, foreign exchange holdings fell by almost 850m schillings.[54] These reserve losses reflected to a large extent the mounting distrust in the schilling and the expected devaluation, but they did not indicate the extend of the market's disagio.

Such information, however, can be obtained from the market for gold. The agio on the schilling price of gold reached about 20 percent even before the introduction of strict exchange controls in early October, and peaked at 44 percent at the end of November (Table 4)[55] By that time confidence in the schilling was at its lowest point and gold became a good inflation hedge.

## Table 4

Agio on the Schilling Price of Gold in 1931 and 1932

|  |  |  |  |  |  |
|---|---|---|---|---|---|
| **1931** | | | | | |
| September | 23 | 2% | November | 2 | 28% |
|  | 24 | 3% |  | 16 | 24% |
|  | 25 | 8% |  | 20 | 32% |
|  |  |  |  | 23 | 36% |
|  |  |  |  | 24 | 44% |
| October | 1 | 8% |  |  |  |
|  | 2 | 13% |  |  |  |
|  | 6 | 20% | December | 16 | 41% |
|  | 21 | 30% |  | 24 | 32% |
|  | 27 | 32% |  |  |  |
| **1932** | | | | | |
| January | 6 | 30% | April | 6 | 14% |
|  | 27 | 32% |  |  |  |
|  | 30 | 35% |  |  |  |
|  |  |  | May | 4 | 20% |
|  |  |  |  | 9 | 25% |
|  |  |  |  | 18 | 30% |
| February | 2 | 42% |  |  |  |
|  | 11 | 36% |  |  |  |
|  | 17 | 34% |  |  |  |
| March | 3 | 32% | June | 2 | 36% |
|  | 17 | 28% |  | 17 | 30% |
|  | 22 | 20% |  |  |  |
|  |  |  | July | 21 | 25% |
| 6 August until 31 December | | | 20% | | |

**Source:** *Wirtschaftsstatistisches Jahrbuch*, 1932, p. 364.

The price of gold did not start to rise until the introduction of controlled allocations of foreign exchange. Yet evidence from the bond market indicates that starting with the announcement of the bank's crisis, but especially so after the announcement of the state guarantee, the market's evaluation of the Austrian schilling deteriorated. Figure 2 shows the yield differential at the Viennese bourse between the 7 percent Austrian Government Guaranteed International Loan 1923–1943 (League of Nations bond) and the 7 percent Austrian International Loan 1930–1957. The main difference between these two bonds (in addition to their maturity dates) was the fact that the League of Nations issue had an international guarantee and its coupons were paid in U. S. dollars, while the 1930 issue was only backed by the Austrian state and its coupons were paid in schillings.

Since the interest rate risk was very similar for both bonds the differential in the current yields can be interpreted as an approximation for the required risk premium for the nonguaranteed schilling issue.[56] Variations in the risk premium can then be regarded as reflecting changes in the perceived credit rating (default risk) of the Austrian state and changes in the purchasing power of the schilling relative to the U.S. dollar. The curve shows the outbreak of the Credit–Anstalt crisis (11 May) very clearly, but the announcement of the state guarantee (28 May) resulted in a more pronounced jump in the yield differential. Overnight, the Austrian currency was considered more risky. Instead of calming the situation and contributing to a return to normalcy—as intended—the governmental guarantee for the bank's liabilities worsened Austria's credit rating and the prospects for its currency and reduced the likelihood of capital inflows at any given interest rate. The guarantee constituted unfavorable "fiscal news."[57] *The Review of Reviews* summarized the events of the day on which the initial guarantee was announced by stating that "the gravest twenty-four hours in the stormy twelve years of the Austrian Republic pass in doubt over the government's financial future."[58] This doubt left a clear mark in the bond market data.

We present in Table 5 the monthly prices of the 1923–1943 League of Nations bond in Vienna and New York for 1931. While the valuation of this security just prior to the start of the Credit–Anstalt crisis was about equal in both markets, a gap developed beginning in May, reflecting mainly the market's different evaluation of the Austrian and the U. S. currencies. As the coupons for this bond were paid in dollars they were desirable hedging instruments against exchange rate risk in Vienna. Therefore, their price on the Viennese market was pushed up by Austrians willing to pay a premium to hold a dollar denominated asset. However, no such increased demand occurred in New York. During September to December 1931 there was considerable correspondence between the relative bond price difference and the agio on the schilling price of gold, reflecting broad consistency in the market's valuation of the Austrian currency in both asset markets.

## Table 5

League of Nations Bond 1923–1943
Quotation in Vienna and New York

monthly averages in 1931

| Month | 1931 | | | 1932 | | |
| | Vienna | New York | Difference in % | Vienna | New York | Difference in% |
| --- | --- | --- | --- | --- | --- | --- |
| Jan. | 108.2 | 105.4 | 2.7 | 121.7 | 89.5 | 36.0 |
| Feb. | 1106.9 | 105.5 | 1.3 | 124.8 | 90.5 | 37.0 |
| Mar. | 106.7 | 107.2 | −0.5 | 124.3 | 93.7 | 32.7 |
| Apr. | 107.2 | 106.6 | 0.6 | 113.8 | 88.6 | 28.4 |
| May | 110.2 | 106.9 | 3.1 | 110.7 | 79.1 | 39.9 |
| June | 114.0 | 106.9 | 6.6 | 107.3 | 78.1 | 37.4 |
| July | 113.0 | 106.4 | 6.2 | 108.0 | 88.1 | 22.6 |
| Aug. | 111.0 | 104.8 | 5.9 | 107.0 | 86.8 | 23.3 |
| Sep. | 111.0 | 102.9 | 7.9 | 108.0 | 90.1 | 19.9 |
| Oct. | 118.6 | 94.0 | 26.2 | 106.9 | 92.2 | 15.9 |
| Nov. | 120.5 | 90.0 | 33.9 | 106.1 | 91.8 | 15.6 |
| Dec. | 126.8 | 82.7 | 53.3 | 108.4 | 89.8 | 20.7 |

Source: *Wirtschaftsstatistisches Jahrbuch*, 1932, p. 365.

The behavior of both the gold and the bond markets were very much the same. Early in the crisis the public started to believe that a change in the official parity was imminent and they were willing to pay a premium for gold, foreign exchange and assets denominated in foreign exchange. At times the value of this premium moved almost parallel in these markets, and it anticipated the eventual devaluation of the Austrian currency quite correctly.

While the Austrian National Bank was adhering to the official rates the market valued the schilling at a large discount, reaching a maximum of 44 percent in late November 1931. *The Economist* (3 October 1932, p. 615) reported that "the restricted allotment of notes . . . led, as always in such times, to growth of clandestine transactions, in which notes, gold and recently, also silver are negotiated at a premium." Transactions of any importance proceeded at a premium basis for gold currencies, and parallel markets developed. Following a Viennese tradition, the trading places for those black markets were—predominantly—coffee houses. Unfortunately, we do not have day–to–day data on the prices in those coffee–house markets, as it was forbidden to publish any such information. Ellis (1941, p. 40) reports that in September 1931 "the informal (but still legal) coffee–house dealings involved premia of 10–15 percent," while *The Economist* (10 October 1931, p. 661) states that "unofficial trade with foreign means of payment" was done in those markets at prices "up to 12 percent above official rates."

While the public fled into these parallel markets, businesses pursued a different approach as they recognized the potential depreciation and encountered problems with securing foreign means of payments for the use at a later date. They started to "add a gold clause to their invoices" while the government took the view "that the Austrian schilling [was] perfectly stable and that a gold clause [was] therefore of purely theoretical significance.[59]

Other signs of the public's fear for the currency were an unseasonal surge in imports in the summer of 1931 and a surge in investment in housing. Both were rather unusual phenomena in the midst of a business depression as deep as the one in mid–1931. Others rediscovered the stock market as a hedge against inflation, thus producing a stock market boom—again an atypical phenomenon during a severe depression. But the Austrian National Bank "probably regarded the rise in stock prices as an undurable symptom of fear for the schilling,"[60] and the boom was short lived.

In sum, there is considerable evidence that in spite of all efforts by the authorities to convince the public of the contrary, the market anticipated inflation and a currency crisis. The public recognized the fundamental inconsistencies of the adherence to the gold exchange standard in combination with the massive expansion of domestic credit and the inability of the Austrian government to preserve orderly public finances in light of the guarantees for the liabilities of the Credit–Anstalt.[61] Consequently, one price of the salvage of the Credit–Anstalt was the gold parity of the schilling, and that was clearly recognized by the market early in the crises. The authorities' attempts to resist a rational evaluation of the value of the Austrian schilling without changing the underlying policies had resulted in the currency crisis.

There is a general lesson to be learned from the Austrian experience of 1931, namely that if inconsistencies in economic policies of a country or among the policies of several countries exist, the market will discover them, and will act accordingly. If the authorities resist the necessary adjustments, the markets will bring them about. In the late 1980s this fact is, unfortunately—still more often than not—neglected, but it remains just as relevant as it was about sixty years ago.

## Figure 2
### Yield Spread of Bonds in Vienna

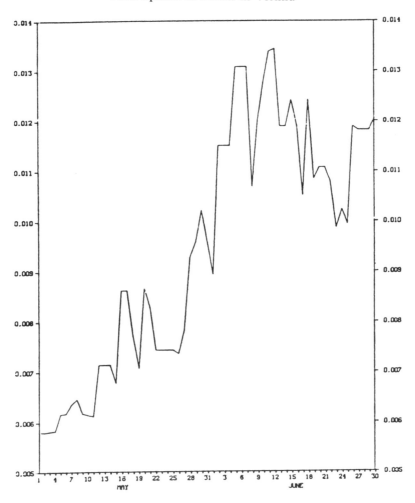

## References

Connolly, M. B., and Taylor, D. (1984). "The Exact Timing of the Collapse of an Exchange Regime and Its Impact on the Relative Price of Traded Goods." *Journal of Money, Credit, and Banking*, Vol. XVI, No. 2, May, pp. 194–207.

Eichengreen, B. J. (1981). "Bank Failures, Balance of Payments and the 1931 Sterling Crisis." Harvard University, Discussion Paper No. 869.

Ellis, H. S. (1941). *Exchange Control in Central Europe*. Harvard University Press, Cambridge.

Federn, W. (1932). "Der Zusammenbruch der Österreichischen Kreditanstalt." *Archiv für Sozialwissenschaft und Sozialpolitik*, Band 67, June, pp. 403–435. Translated by H. Jarecki in *Euromoney*, 1976, October, pp. 140–149, and November, pp. 68–80.

Flood, R. P. and Garber, P. M. (1984). "Collapsing Exchange–Rate Regimes, Some Linear Examples." *Journal of International Economics*, 17, pp. 1–13.

Garber, P.M. (1981). "The Lender of Last Resort and the Run on the Savings and Loans." National Bureau of Economic Research, Working Paper No. 823.

Garber, P. M. (1985). "The Collapse of Asset–Price–Fixing Regimes," in M. B. Connolly and J. McDermott (eds.) *The Economics of the Caribbean Basin*. Praeger, New York, pp. 287–301.

Gedye, G. E. R. (1931). "The Austro–German 'Bombshell'." *The Contemporary Review*, Vol. 139, No. 785, May, pp. 545–554.

Gratz, A. (1949). "Die österreichische Finanzpolitik von 1848 bis 1948," in Mayer, H. (ed.) *Hundert Jahre Österreichische Wirtschaftsentwicklung, 1848–1948*. Vienna.

Kernbauer, H. (1982). "The Policy of the Austrian National Bank before and during the 1931 Crisis." (not published).

Keynes, J. M. (1924). *Monetary Reform*. Harcourt, Brace & Co., New York.

Keynes, J. M. (1925). "The United States and Gold," in J. P. Young (ed.) *European Currency and Finance*. Vol. I, Government Printing Office, Washington, D.C.

Kindleberger, C. P. (1973). *The World in Depression, 1929–1939*. University of California Press, Berkeley.

März, E. (1982). "Comments," in C. P. Kindleberger and J.–P. Laffargue (eds.) *Financial Crises*. Cambridge University Press, Cambridge.

Oesterreichische Nationalbank (1932). Bericht des Generalrates über
    die Geschäftsführung des Jahres 1931, Vienna.

Reisch, R. (1931). "Schillingwaehrung und Österreichische National-
    bank." *Mitteilungen des Verbandes Oesterreichischer Banken
    und Bankiers,* July, pp. 213–220.

Sargent, T. J. (1982). "The Ends of Four Big Inflations," in R. E.
    Hall (ed.), *Inflation: Causes and Effects.* University of Chicago
    Press, Chicago.

Sokal, M. and Rosenberg, O. (1929). "The Banking System of Aus-
    tria," in P. H. Willis and B. II. Beckhart (eds.), *Foreign Banking
    Systems,* New York.

Stiefel, D. (1983). "The Reconstruction of the Credit–Anstalt," in A.
    Teichova and P. C. Cottrell (eds.), *International Business and
    Central Europe, 1918–1939.* Leicester University Press.

Stolper, G. (1967). *The German Economy, 1870 to the Present.* New
    York.

Vaubel, R. (1984). "International Debt, Bank Failures and the Money
    Supply: The Thirties and the Eighties." *The Cato Journal,* Vol.
    4, No. 1, Spring/Summer, pp. 249–267.

Walré de Bordes, J. van (1924). *The Austrian Crown, Its Deprecia-
    tion and Stabliization.* London.

Webb, St. B. (1986). "Fiscal News and Inflationary Expectations in
    Germany after World War I." *Journal of Economic History,* Vol.
    XLVI, No. 3, September, pp. 769–794.

Yeager, L. B. (1976). *International Monetary Relations: Theory,
    History and Policy,* second edition, Harper and Row, New York.

Yeager, L. B. (1981). *Experiences with Stopping Inflation.* American
    Enterprise Institute, Washington, D.C.

# Part II
# The International Transmission
# of Financial Crises

# [6]

Excerpt from *Keynesianism vs. Monetarism and Other Essays in Financial History*, 226–39

# 14

## International Propagation of Financial Crises: The Experience of 1888–93

I first met Wilfried Guth, if my memory serves, in 1939. A student interested in international capital movements, he had written to me because I had just finished and published my thesis on the subject. We met when I was at the Bank for International Settlements, on a visit from Basle to Frankfort. Since that time I have continued as a student of international capital movements and he has gone on to produce them – in government at the Kreditanstalt für Wiederaufbau, and at the Deutsche Bank. It may be appropriate then for me to honor him in recurring to capital movements in which we share a long-lived and keen, if perhaps diverging, interest.

There is another reason to study the crisis of 1890–93. Of all the crises in the last hundred years or so, it most closely resembles the difficulties the world is passing through in 1983. 1929 is the analogy that comes to the people's minds when they contemplate the present taut state of world credit. The comparison with 1888–93 seems to me, thus far, to run more closely parallel.

Some crises are clearly international; others, such as 1866 and 1907, appear to be national in extent, when they are in my judgement linked through an international propagation mechanism. It was no accident in 1866 that the collapse of the stock market in Berlin, the push of Italy off the gold standard, and the Overend, Gurney crisis in London all occurred within the first 11 days of May; this despite the assured statement of Clapham that the last was strictly British (1945, II, p. 267). In 1907, crises in New York and Turin were connected, not directly but through Paris and London, which kept largely unaffected. The timing need not be so tight-knit as in 1866. The wobbly backgrounds of crises in one country and another may develop independently or have a common origin in speculative euphoria. The contention, however, is that monetary tightness in one market is readily communicated to others and, when the credit system is stretched, may well propagate financial crisis from one market to another.

In what follows I hope to demonstrate a strong presumptive case – it is

*Reprinted with permission from Wolfram Engels, Armin Gutowski and Henry C. Wallich (eds), International Capital Movements, Debt and Monetary System (Mainz: v. Hase & Koehler Verlag, 1984), pp. 217–34. I acknowledge with thanks references kindly furnished by Knut Borchardt.*

virtually impossible to offer proof – that the series of financial crises from 1888 to 1893 were intimately connected. These crises include:

The Baring crisis running between London and Buenos Aires with repercussions in New York, Rio de Janeiro, and Santiago;

The Parisian Panama crisis starting in 1888 and ending in scandal in 1893, plus the copper corner and the collapse of the Comptoir d'Escompte in 1889;

The collapse of the market for diamond shares in 1881 and for gold shares in South Africa in 1889;

The collapse of a series of Italian banks running from 1887 to 1893;

The wave of bank suspensions in Australia in March and April 1893;

The gold panic in New York from July to October 1893 (following the lesser crisis of 1890 noted above);

Less certainly, the failure of two banks in Berlin in November 1891.

Most of these episodes are treated in economic history as separate. Both Lauck and Morgenstern, who pay some attention to international connections, emphasize the European connections, aside from Italy which they ignore, and tend to leave out the so-called periphery – Latin America, South Africa, and Australia (1907, ch. iv; 1959, esp. Chart 72, p. 548).

The mechanism of propagation of boom and crisis is largely capital movements and prices, including prices both of commodities and of financial assets. Morgenstern quotes Schumpeter to the effect that the chief channel through which influences are transmitted internationally is the interaction of stock markets (1959, p. 508, quoting Schumpeter, 1939, II, pp. 66–7). The connection can be direct as investors in one market buy or sell securities in another, or it can be psychological as two markets mark commodity or asset prices up or down in parallel, without transactions between them taking place. Psychological influences may in fact cross from one commodity to another. The attempted corner in copper was inspired, according to Wirth (1893, p. 222), by the success of the diamond syndicate in South Africa after the 1882 debacle in diamond shares, and by that of the Rothschild syndicate in mercury in Spain. There is no significant connection through national income, though not for the reason given by Morgenstern that there are no reliable data (1959, p. 566), but because the mechanism of exports, foreign-trade multiplier, national income and imports is too strung out with lags to explain the near simultaneity of upswings and crises.

The nature of capital movements differs rather widely between those among the financial centers of Europe, and those between Europe and the periphery, especially South Africa, Latin America, and Australia. Relations between the European financial centers and New York reflect both patterns. Within Europe, capital movements largely took the form of purchases and sales of existing securities, whereas with overseas areas the majority of capital flows went through newly issued securities. Like New York, the Russian connection with financial centers involved both new issues and existing securities, plus what lay between them,

228                          *Keynesianism vs. Monetarism*

maturing bonds that needed to be refunded. It is a curious phenomenon
that a major problem in international capital movements of the 1880s
and '90s was the shift of the Russian source of loans from Berlin to Paris,
a shift that took place relatively smoothly without involving Russia in
the financial crises that seized the major financial centers.


## II

The vortex of the world crisis was London. It financed the boom.
Cutting down on capital exports brought about the crisis. There were
whirlpools such as Paris and Berlin with their separate causes and
effects, related to the main source of tumult in London, but not central.
Part of the boom and bust was domestic in origin, part foreign. The
foreign crises were connected to London especially through the creation
of companies in London for investment in diamonds and gold in South
Africa, banks that operated especially in South Africa, Australia, and
Latin America, railroads in those continents and in the United States,
mortgage companies in Argentina and Australia, nitrates companies in
Chile, and the like.

The boom was incited by two domestic factors: the Goschen
conversion of 1888, which made investors search for higher-earning
assets, and the anticipation of a tightening of the company law of 1862,
which stimulated a number of private companies to go public before it
was too late to do so easily. The conversion under Viscount Goschen,
Chancellor of the Exchequer, occurred in March 1888 when three issues
of outstanding 3 percent government debt were changed for a single
issue bearing $2\frac{3}{4}$ percent coupon for 15 years and $2\frac{1}{2}$ percent for 20 years
thereafter (Spinner, 1973, p. 140). An attempt had been made at
conversion in 1884 and abandoned. By the time it took place in 1888 it
had long been anticipated. Some of the gains from lower interest rates
accrued to foreigners. In October 1888 the Brazilian government under
the Empire converted its sterling loans of 1865, 1871, 1875 and 1876, all
issued through the house of N. M. Rothschild and bearing 5 percent
interest, to 4 percent plus a $\frac{1}{2}$ percent amortization charge (Calogeras,
1910, p. 199). For the most part, the reduction in investor income in
Britain pushed private investors and trustees into foreign bonds to
prevent a decline in income.

The boom in private companies tended, like many manias, to run in
channels. The private brewing company, Guinness, sold a nominal £$3\frac{1}{2}$
million in October 1886, and the success of the issue acted like a starting
pistol, according to Cottrell. By November 1890, 86 other breweries had
gone public or increased their capital (1980, p. 169).

A contribution to the enthusiasm for beer in Britain was the
phylloxera which attacked French vineyards and reduced the
prospective supply of wine (Wirth, 1893, p. 220). Mathias claims
additionally that the size of brewing firms increased rapidly with
economies of scale in distribution (1969, pp. 369 ff, quoted in Edelstein,
1982, p. 60). The contagion soon crossed the Atlantic. Within the year

ended August 1, 1889, 14 American breweries had registered securities in England (M. Simon, 1955/1979, p. 450). The boom even extended to Canadian breweries, although as noted below Canada was left largely aside in the boom of the 1880s (Lauck, 1907, p. 41). In all, 12,068 companies with a nominal share capital of £1 billion went public between 1886 and 1890 (*ibid.*).

Table 1   *New Portfolio Investment, 1885–1893 (in millions of pounds sterling)*

|  | World Capital markets RR, Ind. (creations) | British foreign issues | British new issues by area | | | | | |
|---|---|---|---|---|---|---|---|---|
|  |  |  | Europe | NA | SA | Africa | Asia | Austr |
| 1885 | 124.7 | 52.7 | 3.4 | 14.1 | 7.1 | 4.7 | 11.0 | 14.9 |
| 1886 | 251.7 | 74.4 | 5.0 | 14.0 | 19.3 | 2.5 | 9.6 | 19.4 |
| 1887 | 190.0 | 83.7 | 12.9 | 23.9 | 18.9 | 1.5 | 10.5 | 16.5 |
| 1888 | 295.9 | 133.3 | 10.1 | 37.2 | 40.3 | 4.2 | 10.7 | 15.7 |
| 1889 | 501.9 | 138.5 | 11.2 | 37.2 | 40.2 | 8.9 | 11.2 | 14.2 |
| 1890 | 223.9 | 110.7 | 12.3 | 52.8 | 23.3 | 4.6 | 10.8 | 12.8 |
| 1891 | 225.5 | 51.8 | 5.0 | 18.7 | 9.4 | 6.6 | 5.7 | 12.3 |
| 1892 | 93.5 | 40.1 | 2.7 | 14.9 | 5.4 | 3.3 | 4.1 | 9.2 |
| 1893 | 134.7 | 31.5 | 1.7 | 13.1 | 5.4 | 2.6 | 2.5 | 6.7 |

*Source:* M. Simon (1967/1978), pp. 38, 40.

Table 2   *Balance of Payments on Current Account, 1885–1893 (in millions of specified units)*

|  | United Kingdom (pounds sterling) | France (French francs) | Germany (marks) |
|---|---|---|---|
| 1885 | 39.5 | 420 | 507 |
| 1886 | 60.9 | 505 | 486 |
| 1887 | 67.8 | 700 | 431 |
| 1888 | 74.6 | 805 | 686 |
| 1889 | 72.5 | 685 | 590 |
| 1890 | 94.4 | 590 | 430 |
| 1891 | 52.3 | 390 | 334 |
| 1892 | 37.4 | 490 | 185 |
| 1893 | 42.1 | 695 | 361 |

*Sources:* UK: Cairncross (1953), p. 180.
France: White (1933), p. 122.
Germany: Mitchell (1978), p. 437.

In addition there were foreign stimuli to the boom: the discoveries of diamonds in South Africa, of gold in South Africa and Australia, and of nitrates in Chile. Likewise, the clearing of Patagonia of Indians by Argentina during the early 1880s and the shift from grain to meat in both Argentina and Australia with the development of the refrigerator ship about 1875 both led to land booms in those countries, paralleled by similar booms in the Southern United States and in South Africa. Whether the push was stronger than the pull is probably unanswerable and in any event an idle subject for speculation as both were necessary.

230                        *Keynesianism vs. Monetarism*

Whatever the case, a substantial outflow of capital took place from London and from European capitals (see Table 1).

The World Capital Market new issues, taken from the Belgian publication, *Le Moniteur des intérêts matériels*, is incomparable with the British figure for the par value of issues. It is limited to railroads and industrial securities on the one hand, and includes domestic issues along with foreign on the other. British new issues by areas, moreover, differs from total capital flows since it excludes trade in existing securities, both listed on stock exchanges and unlisted. *Cedulas*, for example, the special sort of Argentine mortgage bond in which there was much speculation in the 1880s, were never listed (Ferns, 1960, p. 423). But there is some indication that the swing in British lending was wider than that of Germany on the upswing and of France on the downswing if one compares the 'outflow of capital' as measured by the balance of payments on current account (Table 2).

The booms in diamonds and gold in South Africa did not perhaps involve enormous amounts of capital, as Table 1 shows, but the psychological stimuli were great. The impact of the diamond cartel on the copper corner has been mentioned. Hobson observes that the boom in South African mines was the 'signal for unhealthy inflation in other countries, notably Australia and South America' (1914, p. 148) and goes on to remark that Continental investors 'went wild' over South African mining shares, even when they were not registered on local bourses. Most of the South African mining companies were headquartered and registered in London. Three hundred and ninety-six South African companies in mining, finance, exploration and landowning in 1880 had risen to 642 in 1889, and those having offices in London increased from 145 in 1888 with a paid-in capital of £5.8 million to 315 in 1890 with a paid-in capital of £44 million, although there was much duplication (Frankel, 1938/1969, p. 81).

British lending to Latin America peaked in 1888 and 1889 and started down in 1890. German investors seem to have taken alarm earlier. Hobson states that German investors participated in the Panama mania only to a slight extent, and became involved in Latin America when their enthusiasm for Russian securities had been curbed, as 'many of the most risky issues were wisely sold in Belgium when prices were still at a high level' (1914, p. 148). The caution of German investors and the hostility of the German government are noted by Ferns (1960, pp. xx, 433). One source claims that the Germans had been trained to regard Argentine securities as first-class but became uneasy in 1888 (Lauck, 1907, pp. 59–60) and sold all but 100 million marks worth by the end of 1890. Another view is that the German investor was troubled by the depreciation of the Argentine peso (Morgenstern, 1959, p. 523). Whatever the reason, here is one of the few cases where the enthusiasm of one class of investor for a security failed to communicate itself for long to another.

British investments in Argentina took the form of *cedulas*, that is mortgage bonds denominated in pesos, in railway securities and in bonds issued by the Argentine government and the provinces. The crisis came in stages, first when a series of new issues failed and were left on the underwriters' hands, and secondly when Baring Brothers was unable to make the payment due in 1890 on the Buenos Aires Water Supply bonds, which they had underwritten in 1888 and still held in considerable measure. Baring Brothers' reputation was so high from its successes in Anglo-American trade finance in the first half of the nineteenth century that the market in London was reassured by its continued involvement in Argentine securities. One analyst argues that the loans were sound in the long run, but the lending stopped before the investment projects could be completed, leaving high debt service without the exports to meet them (Ford, 1962, pp. 28, 142 n).

A general problem is how much to blame events in the overseas country for the crisis, and how much the cut-off of the capital flow from the center. A monetarist position tends to ascribe the crisis almost entirely to events in the periphery, especially new bank laws passed in Argentina in 1887 (and Brazil in 1888), plus political events such as revolutions or coups d'état. Williams' classic study of the depreciation of the Argentine peso insists that the cut-off of the capital flow produced the depreciation, rather than the expansion of the note issue. He goes further and suggests that the expansion was required by the depreciation, rather than being the cause of it (1920, pp. 103, 107). A recent study of the Brazilian crisis, I am told, makes the same point about Brazilian experience in 1889–91 (Franco, 1982). The issue is an old one, of course, in the debate between the Banking and the Currency School in England over the Bullion Report, and the similar controversy between monetarists and the balance-of-payments school over responsibility for the German hyperinflation of 1923. It is perhaps relevant that Williams adhered to the balance-of-payments school in the 1923 German debate (1922), as well as in his analysis of the Baring crisis in Argentina.

Brazilian borrowing overall was relatively modest, roughly $66 per capita, excluding the floating debt, compared to such numbers as $400 for Argentina and $412 for Australia (Wileman, 1896, p. 45, based on data of the French *Annuaire Statistique* for 1888). Most borrowing was for government account, but some was to expand coffee production and railroads. The borrowing helped bid up the milreis (which had fallen to 17½d in 1885 from par of 27d in 1875) back to par in 1889, when the lending stopped. How much the halt was owing to the Baring crisis, and how much to particular developments in Brazil – the fall in the price of coffee worldwide, the end of the Empire and its replacement by an unstable republic, a new banking law which provided for the issue of banknotes on the security of national government bonds (patterned after the US National Bank Act of 1863) – is a matter of some contention. Students of British banking in Latin America incline to believe that the crisis was communicated from one country to another through British banks (Joslin, 1963, pp. 123, 133; Jones, 1977, p. 24). Most current observers blamed the separate banking changes and the issue of more banknotes. A modern student raises the question whether the halt in lending might not have given rise to the need for new issues of banknotes

(Franco, 1982). Whether reason or excuse, when the Republic's finance minister appealed to Brazil's financial agents in London, N. M. Rothschild & Sons, for a loan after the 1891 coup d'état, stating that there was neither a political nor an economic crisis, he received a reply accepting his affirmation as to the political crisis, but differing on the financial: 'the decline on the exchange and the depression of Brazilian securities [in London] reveal a very grave crisis, caused principally by the fears of new issues of paper money' (Calogeras, 1910, p. 177).

The historiography of the Chilean crises of 1888 to 1893 focuses on monetary and political events local to the country, especially the war with Peru and the Civil War (Fetter, 1931). The depreciation of the peso in 1892 was precipitated by a withdrawal of capital, but loss of European investor confidence was the result of the landed classes insisting on inflation as a means of reducing the load of debt (*ibid.*, pp. 76, 85). There should, however, be some room for the preceding boom engineered by Colonel John Thomas North who created nitrate companies in 1883, 1885, and 1886. In all, 17 nitrate companies were organized between 1883 and 1889, of which four were created in 1888 and nine in 1889, including four in the single month of January 1889 (O'Brien, 1982, p. 115). Established companies sold out to the newcomers for high profits, and bought back in later in much the same way as shipping companies in London after World War I (Macrosty, 1927, quoted in Youngson, 1960, p. 45). Just as the brewery companies that had gone public in London could not meet their promised dividends (Wirth, 1893, p. 221), so six of nine nitrate companies reporting in June 1890 paid no dividends, and by December 1890 nitrate shares were quoted at one-quarter to one-eighth of the prices they had reached in 1889 (O'Brien, 1982, p. 122).

The Australian wave of bank and mortgage company failures occurred primarily in the spring of 1893. The data from which Table 1 is drawn show that Australia borrowed more in the first half of the 1880s than in the second. The boom went on into 1891, after the Baring crisis, but its ending was said to be 'inevitable' (Baster, 1929, p. 148); that is, merely the 'final explosion' of the banking crisis from 1891, the break in the boom of 1888 (Butlin, 1961, p. 279) and the 'eventuality which financial writers had prophesied for a decade or so' (Hall, 1963, p. 171). Most of these writers insist that the Australian boom had purely local causes in the land and mortgage company boom (e.g. Butlin, 1961, p. 280; Hall, 1963, p. 148; Boehm, 1971, chs 9, 10; Pressnell, 1982, p. 160), but all mention the leveling out of the capital inflow into Australia. Hall ascribes the slowdown in British lending partly to misgivings in London over the Argentine inflation, the Brazilian revolution and the Kaffir circus (1963, p. 159). But he blames it primarily on a 'breakdown in the marketing mechanism' for Australian securities in London, rather than a loss of investor interest in Australian issues (*ibid.*, pp. 101, 136, 171). The distinction seems overdrawn. Problems were found with the tendering system that awarded an entire issue to a particular syndicate, which might have much of the issue left on its hands, and a quarrel took place between the Bank of England and the Queensland government over a failure of an issue for the latter in 1891. The fact was, however, that the failure of syndicates to tender for Australian government bonds was not solely a technical question. Three provincial issues failed along with an Australian one, and the Queensland sum was ultimately raised only by a sharp reduction in the issue price. British investors could not but have been aware that the Australian and Argentine booms in land speculation were similar and that the failure of mortgage companies in Argentina might be paralleled in Australia. It is true that some lenders to Australia, such as the Scottish depositors in British offices of Australian banks, were slow to withdraw their deposits until after March 1893 (Hall, 1963, Table 20, p. 115). But these were time deposits for periods ranging from one to three years, and after 1893 they were drawn down as fast as they matured. I conclude that the Australian boom was part of the worldwide upswing of the 1880s fed by the flow of capital from London, and the crisis, while delayed, was part of the movement precipitated by the halt in that flow.

## III

France was connected with the boom and crisis centered in London in 1889–93 in two plus respects, and disconnected in two others. The attempted copper corner, as noted, derived its inspiration partly from the diamond syndicate of 1882. Its analogue today is the attempted corner in silver by Bunker Hunt that collapsed in 1980 (Fay, 1982). The Société des Métaux, supported by the Comptoir d'Escompte, one of the leading deposit banks of the country, tried to buy copper worldwide at a price up to £70 a ton and hoped to sell it for more than £80. New mines opened up as the price rose, and old copper was reclaimed and sold to the syndicate. By March 1889 the syndicate's holdings amounted to 160,000 tons, its financial resources were exhausted, and the price was declining, reaching £38 in 1889 before recovering to £60 in 1890. Isaac Denfert-Rocherau, who was also connected with financing the Panama canal and with an unsuccessful attempt to lend to Russia (Kennan, 1979, p. 386), committed suicide. The Bank of France organized a syndicate to underwrite the liabilities of the Comptoir, providing a precedent, according to Pressnell, for the guarantees of liabilities organized by the Bank of England and Rothschild to rescue Baring Brothers the following year (1968, p. 205). It was widely noted that this behavior contrasted with that of the banking establishment of Paris when in 1882 they allowed the Union Générale, an outsider upstart bank, to fail (Bouvier, 1960, pp. 151–3).

One relatively independent source of crisis in France was the financing of the Panama canal project of De Lesseps. The Universal Panama Interoceanic Company was floated in December 1880 with a three-day stampede for shares. In a short time, 5,000 franc shares were selling for 380,000 francs. Success in digging a sea-level canal, however, proved elusive as costs kept rising, and the Company borrowed four times in the first six years. The first two issues were enormously

234                    *Keynesianism vs. Monetarism*

successful, the second two found public interest drooping. The Company tried to revive investor interest with exotic issues. A straight lottery loan was refused authorization in 1886, and a substitute failed. A lottery loan was finally approved by a close vote in 1888, but that issue failed, and the company was forced to abandon the project. It was later revealed that enormous sums had been spent for publicity and bribing deputies. When the scandal was revealed in 1892, there was more financial turmoil in Paris markets. But the company had collapsed in 1889 (M. J. Simon, 1971).

The two other substantial French operations, one associated with the general financial crisis of the late 1880s and early 1890s and the other not, are surprisingly similar. Both involve Germany, and both involve recycling outstanding debt from one creditor to another. Both were also highly political. The first occurred when Bismarck sought to use financial weapons along with tariffs in cold war against Czarist Russia. In July 1887 Orphans Courts were forbidden to invest in Russian bonds; and in November a *Lombardverbot* instructed the Reichsbank to make no loans against the security of Russian bonds. But the prices of Russian bonds in Berlin did not fall substantially (Mai, 1970, p. 131). French investors were ready for economic and political reasons to buy Russian bonds in Berlin, to refund German issues of Russian bonds as they came due and to make new loans. In effect, German loans to Russia were recycled quietly, to the side of the financial crisis or crises, without major impact on other financial markets (Girault, 1973, 1977).

If one were to judge on the basis of lack of connection in the literature, the same would seem to have been the case in Italy. Here France backed away as the main lender, partly as a reaction to the Franco-Italian 'silent' tariff war of 1887, and Germany took over. There is no record of an explicit *Lombardverbot* as there had been in a similar episode in 1866 when the Bank of France refused to discount Italian loans for the Crédit Lyonnais and for a Paris banker, Erlanger (Gille, 1968, p. 190). But the German response was belated and intermittent, sometimes lead by Bleichröder, a private banker and Bismarck's confidant (Stern, 1977, pp. 432–4), and sometimes by Georg von Siemens of the Deutsche Bank (Helfferich, 1921–3/1956, pp. 125–8). A number of Turin banks had been speculating heavily in Roman real estate, and were squeezed when French borrowing stopped in 1887. The Banca Romana was then caught having violated its ceiling on note issues. French dumping of Italian foreign bonds in Paris in July 1889 led to the creation in September of that year of a German syndicate which provided 50 million lire in support of those bonds. The syndicate was organized by the Berliner Handelsgesellschaft and the Deutsche Bank, and in April 1890 by a group headed by Bleichröder (Luzzato, 1963, I, pp. 143–4). But support for Italian bonds in Paris helped France more than it did Italy, as recycling Russian debt from Germany to France helped Germany. In 1893 the Credito Mobiliaro and the Banca Generale collapsed under the weight of industrial loans, largely to the steel industry at Terni. New banks were started in 1894 with German help. The assistance was again limited as the German investors quickly sold out to French and Italian investors, but the initial stimulus this time was sufficient to lift Italian economic growth and activity until the new crisis in 1907.

I conclude that on balance Russian capital imports continued during the switch from German to French investing, but the Italian borrowing lapsed, as France turned away from lending to that country and Germany picked up the load only sporadically. While Italy is located in Europe, it was in financial terms, as Bonelli asserts with respect to 1907, a 'colonial country' at a time when 'colonial countries found themselves suddenly deprived of capital' (1971, p. 43).

Finally, it should be noted that France participated in the London–New York–Berlin–Paris group of connected financial markets in which a country in trouble could get help by selling securities abroad. This was especially the case with outstanding American securities, which were sold in New York by French during the copper-corner crisis in the summer of 1889, by British during the Baring crisis, and by German investors in November 1891 (M. Simon, 1955/1978, pp. 454, 473, 501). The 1890 financial crisis in the United States was entitled 'derivative' for such reasons (Sprague, 1910, p. 127). As the British dumped securities 7 to 9 percent below pre-panic levels, French sources reported that the British also sold huge quantities of US rails, both stocks and bonds, to Paris during the Baring crisis, with the Bank of England powerless to prevent the English investor from flooding the Paris market (Théry, 1908, quoted in Morgenstern, 1959, p. 526). This sort of distress selling is of course different from the anticipatory selling of Argentine bonds in the London market undertaken by Germans, as already mentioned.

I find little or no connection between the failure of two German banks in Berlin in November 1891, Bankhaus Hirschfeld u. Wolff and Friedlander und Sonnenfeld. These firms were not engaged in world trade, had only small depositors, and were totally different than the major D banks that operated worldwide. Their troubles doubtless came from the stock-market decline, which was worldwide. The stock-market index for domestic companies had dropped sharply from its high in December 1889 – the annual averages went from 126 in 1876 to 178 in 1889 and down to 149 in 1891 (Deutsche Bundesbank, 1976, p. 294). One banker was arrested after '60 years of Lucullan profligacy', and two brothers committed suicide (Kuczynski, 1961, ch. 3). Morgenstern's chart notes influences running from this Berlin panic to Paris and to Vienna (1959, Chart 72, p. 548).

The United States participated in international financial markets both as a major borrower for new issues and as a developed market in which other financial centers bought and sold existing securities. The crisis of 1890, as noted, derived from the second relationship and was an echo of European markets (mainly London) dumping good US securities in New York in order to be able to hold longer on to their speculative Latin American, South African, and Australian issues. The panic of 1893 was more like those of the periphery. In the first place, there had been a land boom akin to those in Argentina and Australia,

236                                    *Keynesianism vs. Monetarism*

largely concentrated in the Southern states (Sprague, 1910, p. 161). Excessive expansion had been undertaken by railroads, especially the Philadelphia and Reading and the Erie, and by the National Cordage Company, which paid a 100 percent stock dividend in January, but went into receivership in May. The Sherman Silver Purchase Act of 1890 led to fears that the country would be drained of gold and led to short-term capital withdrawals. Overall, the banking system of the country was fragile, with frequent panics occurring in the fall when credit was taut in order to move the crops, and when neither the Treasury (Taus, 1943) nor the money market banks had developed adequate monetary techniques to cope with the shortage. In 1873, 1884, and 1890, the Treasury had given aid to the money market by issuing more notes. In 1893, its position was endangered by the acquisition of silver and loss of gold, so that it added to rather than lessened the pressure. It is perhaps going too far to claim that the 1893 crisis in the United States was an integral part of the broad world financial crisis of 1888–93, but it would probably have been mitigated if credit conditions had been easier in Europe and the decline in new issues floated in Britain for North America had not been so sharp (see Table 1).

Having connected up so much of the world in a single financial crisis, a puzzle is provided by two countries, Canada and New Zealand, which, in spite of their similarities with South Africa, Argentina, Brazil, Chile, and Australia, were not connected with the 1893 crisis. Both were members of the Empire and both were regions of recent settlement. Both, moreover, participated in financial booms and crises on a large scale at other times, New Zealand in the period 1860–80 and Canada later, from 1904 to 1913 when it borrowed on the order of £300 million from London (Viner, 1924). New Zealand was a 'dependent economy' *par excellence*, the term having been applied to it relatively early (Simkin, 1951). New Zealand suffered from the Baring crisis, but did not enjoy the boom that preceded it, borrowing not even enough to pay the service on its earlier contracted debt. Its land boom had collapsed earlier, about 1880, and its credit position in London was poor, with no contagion coming from mining, railroads, or land in South Africa, Latin America and Australia. On the contrary, in the late 1880s, the Australian banks in New Zealand utilized funds there to feed the Australian boom (*ibid.*, ch. x).

The Canadian delay is more puzzling. One explanation is that the country was ice-bound half the year before the railroad connections with the United States, and direct access to Montreal was still blocked in 1904 when the investment boom of the sort earlier enjoyed by Argentina and Australia took place (Hall, 1963, p. 162). A further hypothesis, perhaps worth mention, is that the boom in international lending by London running from 1904 to 1913 would have resulted in another crisis, comparable to the Baring episode of 1890, had not the outbreak of war supervened to produce a crisis of a different sort. The crisis from 1888 to 1893 produced a depression that lasted to 1895 or 1896. It helps explain why the gold discoveries of California and Australia produced an immediate boom in the 1850s, whereas the 1886 discovery of the

Rand did not result in world monetary expansion for a decade. There are two critical counterfactual questions: whether a conscious effort on the part of London to stabilize lending rather than to halt it would have moderated the cycle, and whether a lender of last resort would have helped with or without stabilized British lending.

The fact is, of course, that the Bank of England operated the gold standard on a narrow margin, and shot bank rate up to 6 percent in December 1889 and again after the Baring crisis in December 1890. The lesson Goschen drew from the incident was that the London banks needed more reserves and less dependence on the Bank (Pressnell, 1968).

The Bank of France and the State Bank of Russia did come to the aid of the Bank of England as lenders of last resort for the pivot wheel of the world financial system. The Bank of France advanced £3 million in gold and the State Bank of Russia £1.5 million. In addition the State Bank of Russia agreed not to withdraw its deposit of £2.4 million. But this aid for the Bank of England did nothing to stabilize lending or to provide new loans for the periphery – for Argentina, Brazil, South Africa, the United States (in which J. P. Morgan rescued the US Treasury with gold).

In the USA children play a game called 'snap-the-whip'; a long line of children hold hands and run, and then one end stops. Centrifugal force leads the children at the other end to go faster and faster and then spin off into space. The surge of lending from 1886 to 1889 and its sudden stop in 1890 closely resembled that game.

## References

Baster, A. S. J. (1929), *The Imperial Banks* (London: P. S. King).

Bonelli, F. (1971), *La crisi del 1907: una tappa dello sviluppo industriale in Italia* (Turin: Einaudi).

Boehm, E. A. (1971), *Prosperity and Depression in Australia, 1887–1897* (Oxford: Clarendon Press).

Bouvier, J. (1960), *Le Krach de l'Union Générale, 1878–1885* (Paris: Prenes universitaires de France).

Butlin, S. J. (1961), *Australia and New Zealand Bank, the Bank of Australasia and the Union Bank of Australia, Limited* (Croydon, Australia: Longmans, Green).

Cairncross, A. K. (1953), *Home and Foreign Investment, 1870–1913: Studies in Capital Accumulation* (Cambridge: Cambridge University Press).

Calogeras, J. P. (1910), *La Politique monétaire du Brazil* (Rio de Janeiro: Imprimerie National).

Clapham, Sir John (1945), *The Bank of England: A History* (Cambridge: Cambridge University Press, 2 vols).

Cottrell, P. L. (1980), *Industrial Finance, 1830–1914* (London: Methuen).

Deutsche Bundesbank (1976), *Deutsches Geld- und Bankwesen in Zahlen, 1876–1975* (Frankfurt-am-Main: Fritz Knapp).

Edelstein, M. (1982), *Overseas Investment in the Age of High Imperialism: The United Kingdom, 1850–1914* (New York: Columbia University Press).

Fay, S. (1982), *Beyond Greed* (New York: Viking).

Ferns, H. S. (1960), *Britain and Argentina in the Nineteenth Century* (Oxford: Clarendon).

238 *Keynesianism vs. Monetarism*

Fetter, F. W. (1931), *Monetary Inflation in Chile* (Princeton, NJ: Princeton University Press).

Ford, A. G. (1962), *The Gold Standard, 1880–1914: Britain and Argentina* (Oxford: Clarendon).

Franco, G. H. B. (1982), 'Reforma monetaria e instabilidade durante a transico republicana', unpublished thesis, Department of Economics, Catholic University of Rio de Janeiro, July.

Frankel, S. H. (1938/1969), *Capital Investment in Africa: its Course and Effects* (London: Oxford University Press); reprint edn (New York: Howard Fertig).

Gille, B. (1968), *Les Investissements français en Italie (1815–1914)* (Turin: ILTE).

Girault, R. (1973), *Emprunts russes et investissements français en Russie, 1887–1914* (Paris: Colin).

Girault, R. (1977), 'Investissements et placements français en Russie, 1880–1914', in M. Lévy-Leboyer (ed.), *La Position internationale de la France* (Paris: Editions de l'Ecole des Hautes Etudes en Sciences Sociales).

Hall, A. R. (1963), *The London Capital Market and Australia, 1870–1914* (Canberra: ANV Social Science Monograph No. 21).

Helfferich, K. (1956), *Georg von Siemens: Ein Lebensbild aus Deutschlands großer Zeit*, revised and shortened edition of the 1921–23 three-volume work (Krefeld: Serpe).

Hobson, C. K. (1914), *The Export of Capital* (London: Constable).

Jones, C. (1977), 'Commercial Bank and Mortgage Companies', in D. C. M. Platt (ed.), *Business Imperialism 1840–1930: An Inquiry Based on British Experience in Latin America* (Oxford: Clarendon Press).

Joslin, D. (1963), *A Century of Banking in Latin America* (London: Oxford University Press).

Kennan, G. F. (1979), *The Decline of Bismarck's European Order: Franco–Russian Relations, 1875–1890* (Princeton, NJ: Princeton University Press).

Kuczynski, J. (1961), *Studien zur Geschichte der zyklischen Überproduktions-krisen in Deutschland, 1873–1914* (Berlin: Akademie Verlag).

Lauck, W. J. (1907), *The Causes of the Panic of 1893* (Boston, Mass.: Houghton Mifflin).

Luzzatto, G. (1963), *L'Economia italiana dal 1861 al 1914*. Vol. I: *1861–1894* (Milan: Banca Commerciale Italiana).

Macrosty, H. W. (1927), article in *Journal of Royal Statistical Society*.

Mai, J. (1970), *Das deutsche Kapital in Rußland, 1850–1894* (Berlin: VEB Deutsche Verlag).

Mathias, P. (1969), *The First Industrial Nation* (London: Methuen).

Mitchell, B. R. (1978), *European Historical Statistics, 1750–1950*, abridged edn (New York: Columbia University Press).

Morgenstern, O. (1959), *International Financial Transactions and Business Cycles* (Princeton, NJ: Princeton University Press, for the National Bureau of Economic Research).

O'Brien, T. F. (1982), *The Nitrate Industry and Chile's Crucial Transition, 1870–1891* (New York: New York University Press).

Pressnell, L. S. (1968), 'Gold Reserves, Banking Reserves and the Baring Crisis of 1890', in C. R. Whittlesey and J. S. G. Wilson (eds), *Essays in Money and Banking in Honour of R. S. Sayers* (Oxford: Clarendon).

Pressnell, L. S. (1982), 'The Sterling System and Financial Crisis before 1914', in C. P. Kindleberger and J. P. Laffargue (eds), *Financial Crises: Theory, History and Policy* (Cambridge and Paris: Cambridge University Press and Editions de la Maison des Sciences de l'Homme), pp. 148–64.

Schumpeter, J. A. (1939), *Business Cycles: A Theoretical, Historical, and*

*Statistical Analysis of the Capitalist Process* (New York: McGraw Hill).

Simkin, C. G. F. (1951), *The Instability of a Dependent Economy. Economic Fluctuations in New Zealand, 1840–1914* (Oxford: Oxford University Press).

Simon, M. (1955/1978), 'Cyclical Fluctuations and the International Capital Movements of the United States, 1865–1895', doctoral dissertation Columbia University; published (New York: Arno).

Simon, M. (1967/1968), 'The Pattern of New British Portfolio Foreign Investment, 1865–1914', in J. H. Adler (ed.), *Capital Movements and Economic Development* (London: Macmillan); reprinted in A. R. Hall (ed.), *The Export of Capital from Britain, 1870–1914* (London: Methuen).

Simon, M. J. (1971), *The Panama Affair* (New York: Charles Scribners Sons).

Spinner, T. J., Jr (1973), *George Joachim Goschen: The Transformation of a Victorian Liberal* (Cambridge: Cambridge University Press).

Sprague, O. M. W. (1910/1978), *History of Crises under the National Banking System*, reprint edn (New York: Kelley).

Stern, F. (1977), *Gold and Iron: Bismarck, Bleichröder and the Building of the German Empire* (London: Allen & Unwin).

Taus, E. R. (1943), *Central Banking Functions of the United States Treasury, 1789–1941* (New York: Columbia University Press).

Théry, E. (1908), *Les Progrès économiques de la France* (Paris: Economiste européen).

Viner, J. (1924), *Canada's Balance of International Indebtedness, 1900–1913. An Inductive Study in the Theory of International Trade* (Cambridge, Mass.: Harvard University Press).

White, H. D. (1933), *The French International Accounts, 1880–1913* (Cambridge, Mass.: Harvard University Press).

Wileman, J. P. (1896), *Brazilian Exchange: The Study of an Inconvertible Currency* (Buenos Aires: Galli Brothers).

Williams, J. H. (1920), *Argentine International Trade under Inconvertible Paper Money, 1880–1900* (Cambridge, Mass.: Harvard University Press).

Williams, J. H. (1922), 'German Foreign Trade and the Reparation Payments', *Quarterly Journal of Economics*, vol. 36.

Wirth, M. (1893), 'The Crisis of 1890', *Journal of Political Economy*, vol. I, no. 2 (March), pp. 214–356.

Youngson, A. J. (1960), *The British Economy, 1920–1957* (London: Allen & Unwin).

# [7]

MICHAEL D. BORDO

## The Impact and International Transmission of Financial Crises: Some Historical Evidence, 1870-1933 *

Recent fears of insolvency of major U.S. banks and the threat posed to world economic stability have raised considerable interest in the topic of financial crises and in financial crises of the past.[1] This study presents historical evidence for six countries in the period 1870-1933 on the impact of financial crises on economic activity and on the international transmission of financial crises.

Two approaches to financial crises predominate in the literature.[2] The monetarist approach of Friedman, Schwartz, and Cagan identifies financial crises with banking panics and views them as either producing or aggravating the effects of monetary contraction.[3] The second approach, associated with the work of Minsky and Kindleberger and the seminal work of Fisher, views financial crises as a key element of the upper turning point in the business cycle and as the inevitable consequence of the boom.[4]

Many financial crises in the past two hundred years have occurred worldwide although they have differed markedly in degree of severity. Monetary and real channels have been emphasized in the two approaches to international transmission.

According to the monetarist approach, financial crises (and also business fluctuations) are transmitted internationally primarily through the monetary standard.[5] Under a fixed exchange rate, such as the classical gold standard, a financial crisis in one country will reduce the money supply or velocity in that country and therefore attract gold flows from other countries. These countries will in turn suffer a contraction in their money supplies and a reduction in economic activity. Transmission can also occur through short-term capital flows, changes in real in-

* For helpful comments and suggestions I would like to thank: Robert Barro, Phillip Cagan, Ehsan Choudhri, Steve Easton, Milton Friedman, Lars Jonung, John McDermott, Jim Lothian, and Anna Schwartz. For excellent research assistance I am indebted to Fernando Santos.

Michael D. Bordo

come, and commodity arbitrage, but the way in which these channels affect activity is primarily through monetary change. Under flexible exchange rates, according to the monetarist approach, the transmission of financial disturbances should instead be considerably muted.

According to the Kindleberger-Minsky approach, financial crises are transmitted primarily through nonmonetary channels such as the portfolios of financial institutions, capital flows, commodity arbitrage, and changes in the balance of trade. Monetary factors are treated as of secondary importance.

Section 1 examines these two approaches to the role and importance of financial crises as disturbances to domestic and international economic activity. The two approaches can in some sense be treated as complements rather than substitutes. Both emphasize the role of monetary and nonmonetary factors in precipitating and transmitting crises, with different weights placed by each approach on each set of factors. In what follows we do not run a race between the two views but rather ascertain the extent to which historical evidence is compatible with elements of each of them.

Section 2 examines the evidence for six countries–the United States, Great Britain, France, Germany, Sweden, and Canada– on the relationship between monetary contraction, the sources of monetary change, declines in economic activity, and the incidence of financial crises. In a comparison of reference cycle contractions for the six countries over the period 1870-1933, severe contractions in economic activity were accompanied in all cases by monetary contraction, in most cases by stock market crashes, but (except for the United States) not by banking crises. The unique performance of the United States can be attributed to the absence of a nationwide branch banking system and to the less effective role played by the U.S. monetary authorities in acting as a lender of last resort.

Section 3 examines the evidence for the six countries on the international transmission of financial crises. The principal findings are two. The first is consistent with the monetarist approach: under the classical gold standard, in periods containing financial crises nations' money supplies were linked by gold flows and changes in high-powered money; with flexible exchange rates there is instead evidence of insulation of domestic monetary and real variables from foreign shocks.

The second is in sympathy with the Kindleberger-Minsky approach: the similarity between countries of stock market turning points, the common incidence of stock market crises, and the similar importance of the deposit-reserve ratio as the key determinant of monetary contraction in all countries (except the United States) suggest that arbitrage in stock prices was a channel for the international transmission of crises.

Section 4 contains a conclusion and discusses some implications of the historical record for the present situation.

## 1. *Theoretical approaches to financial crises*

The approach of Friedman, Schwartz, and Cagan identifies financial crises with banking panics.[6] Banking panics, in turn, may be a source of monetary contraction or may aggravate the effects of monetary contraction on economic activity.[7] The Fisherian approach views financial crises as a part of the normal functioning of the business cycle, and explains them as a natural consequence of "financial fragility" and "overindebtedness."

*The monetarist approach to financial crises.*    In their monumental *A Monetary History of the United State, 1867-1960*, Friedman and Schwartz devote considerable attention to the role of banking panics in producing monetary instability in the United States. For Friedman and Schwartz, banking panics (defined as banking runs, failures, and suspensions of payments) are important because of their effects on the money supply and hence on economic activity. Over the near-century studied, the United States had six severe contractions, of which four were marked by major banking or monetary disturbances.[8] Banking panics "have greatly intensified [severe] contractions, if indeed they have not been the primary factor converting what would otherwise have been mild contractions into severe ones."[9]

According to Friedman and Schwartz, banking panics arise out of the public's loss of confidence in the bank's ability to convert deposits into currency. A loss of confidence is typically precipitated by the failure of some important financial institution (as in 1873 and 1893). In a fractional reserve banking system, attemps by the public to increase the fraction of its money holdings held in currency can only be met by a multiple contraction of deposits. A banking panic, if not allayed by the suspension of convertibility of deposits into currency and the issuance of clearing house certificates (as was often the case before the establishment of the Federal Reserve in 1914) or by early intervention by the monetary authorities, will in turn produce massive bank failures, as otherwise sound banks are forced into insolvency by

44                                    Michael D. Bordo

a fall in the value of their assets induced by a mass scramble for liquidity.

Banking panics leading to widespread bank failures, such as occurred in 1929-33, have deleterious effects on economic activity primarily by reducing the money stock through a decline in both the deposit-currency and deposit-reserve ratios.

Friedman and Schwartz make an important distinction between the arithmetic and the economic aspects of a banking panic. In their discussion of the panic of 1893 they state that "the panic had important effects on the banking structure . . . and it undoubtedly affected the detailed timing, form, and impact of the economic adjustment. At the same time, it was at bottom simply the way in which an adjustment, forced by other considerations, worked itself out."[10]

Indeed, the nineteenth-century U.S. system of unit fractional reserve banking with reserves pyramided in New York was highly susceptible to banking panics. This vulnerability was finally ended by the introduction of federal deposit insurance in 1934, which removed the public's fear for its ability to convert deposits into currency.

Friedman and Schwartz highlight the importance in the pre-FDIC system of strong and responsible leadership exercising timely judgment in intervening to allay the public's fears. Before the advent of the Fed, such intervention by the New York clearing banks in suspending convertibility and issuing clearing house certificates and, on occasion, in conducting open-market purchases by the Treasury was generally successful, although not sufficient to prevent severe monetary contraction. The Federal Reserve System, established in part to provide such leadership, failed dismally in the 1929-33 contraction.

According to Friedman and Schwartz, had the Fed conducted open-market operations in 1930 and 1931 to provide the reserves needed by the banking system, the series of bank failures producing the unprecedented decline in the money stock would have been prevented.

Finally, according to Friedman and Schwartz, economic disturbances are spread internationally by the monetary standard. U.S. monetary disturbances during the 1929-33 contraction quickly spread abroad to other gold countries through the gold exchange standard. Only countries with flexible exchange rates, such as China and Spain, escaped its ravages.[11]

Cagan carefully analyzes the role of banking panics in the cyclical behavior of the U.S. money supply.[12] Like Friedman and Schwartz, Cagan explains the incidence of panics by events such as the failure of prominent financial institutions or railroads. The resulting decline in the public's confidence in the banks, by raising both the public's currency-money ratio and the banking system's reserve-deposit ratio, led to a contraction in the money supply." Cagan attributes the high incidence of banking panics in the United States "to the pre-World War I banking system with its inverted pyramid of credit resting on New York City banks and the absence of emergency reserves provided by a central bank" and to "sharp outflows of gold which sometimes forced banks to contract credit too fast." "

Finally, Cagan presents strong evidence that in the U.S. experience panics did not precipitate cyclical downturns, since they all followed peaks in economic activity. In several cycles, panics were important in reducing money growth more than would otherwise have happened, and in converting mild contractions into severe contractions. However, the evidence of two severe cyclical downturns not associated with banking panics—1920-21 and 1937-38—and two mild cyclical downturns that were associated with panics—1890 and 1914—leads Cagan to conclude that panics were neither a necessary nor a sufficient condition for producing a severe contraction.

Huffman and Lothian focus on the international transmission of business cycles under the pre-1933 gold standard." They view monetary shocks as the key sources of cyclical fluctuations, and the fixed-exchange-rate gold standard as the primary mechanism for transmission of shocks abroad. For example, an unexpected decline in the money supply in the United States will reduce income and prices and raise interest rates, leading to a balance-of-payments surplus and a gold and capital inflow from Great Britain. In Great Britain, the gold outflow will reduce the money supply, prices, and real output, and raise interest rates, leading to a new equilibrium. Empirical evidence based on Granger-Sims causality tests provides support for the paramount role of specie flows and money supplies in the pre-1933 gold standard transmission mechanism.

Since financial crises are important only to the extent that they affect the money supply, they should not be a crucial part of the transmission mechanism. In a comparison of common cycles in the United States and Great Britain, 1830-1933, Huffman and Lothian found panics in only three of twelve common cycles. This leads them to conclude that little importance should be attached to panics as a direct channel of international transmission of cyclical fluctuations.

Michael D. Bordo

*The Fisher-Minsky-Kindleberger approach.*   In contrast to the
monetarist approach, which regards financial crises as important
because they affect monetary aggregates, a tradition going back
to the nineteenth century regards financial crises as an essential
part of the upper turning point of the business cycle–as a necessary consequence of the "excesses" of the previous boom. The
modern proponents, Minsky and Kindleberger, basically extend
the views Irving Fisher expressed in *Booms and Depressions.*

According to Fisher the business cycle is explained by two key
factors: overindebtedness and deflation:[16]

> Disturbances in these two factors–debt and the purchasing power
> of the monetary unit–will set up serious disturbances in all, or nearly
> all, other economic variables. On the other hand, if debt and deflation
> are absent, other disturbances are powerless to bring on crises com-[17]
> parable in severity to those of 1837, 1873, or 1929-33.

The upswing in the cycle is precipitated by some exogenous
event that provides new, profitable opportunities for investment
in key sectors of the economy. Such "starters" can be new inven-
tions, gold discoveries, or wars. The exogenous shock encourages
new investment, thus increasing output and prices. Rising prices
raise profits and encourage more investment, but also encourage
speculation for capital gain. The whole process is debt-financed,
primarily by bank loans, which in turn increase deposits and the
money supply and raise the price level. An overall sense of optimism will raise velocity, fueling the expansion even further.
Moreover, the rising price level reduces the real value of outstanding debt, more than offsetting the increase in nominal debt,
and encourages further borrowing. The process continues until
a general state of "overindebtedness"–defined as "whatever
degree of indebtedness multiplies unduly the chances of becoming insolvent"–is reached.[18] When individuals, firms, and banks
have insufficient liquid assets to meet their liabilities, a crisis can
be triggered by errors in judgment by debtors or creditors. Debtors unable to pay debts when due and unable to refinance their
positions may be forced by creditors to liquidate their assets.

Such "distress selling," if widespread, triggers a "liquidity
crisis" that can in turn lead to a "debt crisis," a "banking crisis,"
and a deep depression unless the monetary authorities intervene.
Distress selling by the whole community produces a decline in the
price level because bank deposits decline as loans are extinguished
and not renewed. As the price level falls, the real value of
outstanding debt rises; because of money illusion both by debtors
and creditors, according to Fisher, it rises faster than nominal

debt is extinguished. Creditors see the nominal value of their collateral declining with the price level, and hence continue to call their loans; but the real debt burden of debtors rises, so they continue to liquidate. A fallacy of composition takes over: each individual joins the liquidation to avoid being worse off, but by reducing the price level the community as a whole actually becomes worse off. The process can proceed to involve bank runs as fears for their solvency rise, and to raise the demand for money as a sense of pessimism spreads.

Real economic activity is affected by falling prices that reduce net worth and profits, and lead to bankruptcy. Both factors contribute to a decline in output and employment. In addition, while nominal interest rates fall with deflation, real rates are increased, worsening the situation. The process can continue either until widespread bankruptcy has eliminated the overindebtedness, or until a reflationary monetary policy is adopted. However, once recovery begins, the whole process will repeat itself. Finally, depressions are transmitted from country to country by the monetary standard."[19]

In a series of articles since 1957, Minsky has elaborated Fisher's theory.[20] Basically, Minsky has extended the notion of overindebtedness, adding his concept of fragility.

According to Minsky, as the economy proceeds through the upswing of the business cycle, the financial structure becomes more fragile. A crisis occurs when a fragile financial structure receives a shock that triggers a sell-off of assets in a thin market, producing a sharp decline in asset prices.[21] The fragility or robustness of a financial structure is determined by three factors: the mix of hedge, speculative, and Ponzi finance; the liquidity of the portfolio; and the extent to which ongoing investment is debt-financed.

Minsky's terms are defined as follows: "if a unit's cash flow commitments on debts are such that over each significant period the cash receipts are expected to exceed the cash payments by a significant margin, the unit is said to be engaged in hedge financing." Speculative financing is defined as "cash flow payments over some period–typically near term–that exceed the cash flows expected over this period." A Ponzi finance unit "is a speculative unit for which the interest portion of its cash payment commitments exceeds its net income cash receipts. A Ponzi unit has to increase its debt in order to meet its commitments on outstanding instruments."[22] The importance of speculative and Ponzi finance is that a rise in the interest rate can convert a positive into a negative present value, precipitating insolvency.

In the upswing of the cycle, the demand for new investment in
response to improved profit opportunities leads to a demand for
finance. Part of the new investment is directly financed by short-
term bank loans, part by equity, and part by long-term debt. As
the economy expands it generates an excess demand for finance,
raising interest rates. However, the excess demand is partially
and temporarily offset by financial innovation, which in turn
fuels the finance of further investment." Thus, the investment
boom is fueled both by an endogenous (elastic) money supply and
by an elastic velocity.

As interest rates rise, four factors work to create a fragile
financial environment: an increase in debt finance; a shift from
long-term to short-term debt; a shift from hedge to speculative to
Ponzi finance; and a reduction in financial institutions' margin of
safety." Once a fragile environment is in place, a further rise in
interest rates can shift hedge to speculative to Ponzi financing
and precipitate a refinancing crisis where firms are unable to "roll
over" their debt. In that situation Fisher's "distress selling" process can be generated with all the attendant consequences. The
crisis can be aborted, however, if the central bank acts as a lender
of last resort to the money markets."

Finally, Minsky's thesis can also explain the international
transmission of crises. Commercial banks lending abroad face additional risks. The risks include greater economic and political
uncertainties that increase the likelihood of default and capital
losses from unexpected changes in exchange rates."

Kindleberger follows Minsky and Fisher, embellishing the
story with pages of anecdotes from history." Basically, some
displacement which improves profit opportunities leads to an investment boom, fueled by bank money and rising velocity. This
in turn produces a "speculative mania" involving a shift from
money to goods, "overtrading," and then "distress." At that
point some event triggers a massive shift from goods to money
and a "panic" results."

Kindleberger expands on the international transmission
mechanism. In addition to the traditional links of gold flows, the
balance of trade, and capital flows, he stresses the importance of
psychological factors, commodity arbitrage, and interest arbitrage
which, by linking the banking systems of different countries
directly, can offset the normal operations of the classical price-
specie-flow mechanism:

> Although Minsky's model is limited to a single country, overtrading
> has historically tended to spread from one country to another. The con-
> duits are many. Commodity prices may rise and so may the prices of

securities that are traded internationally. Speculation in exports, imports, or foreign securities furnishes direct links between markets of countries. By these means euphoria and overtrading in one country can be fed by capital inflows from foreign purchases of particular goods and assets. And if these capital flows lead to inflows of gold or silver, monetary expansion in the original country is enhanced as the boom is fueled by additional supplies of money on which higher pyramids of credit can be supported. In an ideal world, of course, a gain of specie for one country would be matched by a corresponding loss for another, and the resulting expansion in the first case would be offset by the contraction in the second. In the real world, however, while the boom in the first country might gain speed from the increase in the supply of reserves, or "high-powered money," it might also rise in the second despite the loss in monetary reserves, as investors respond to rising prices and profits abroad by joining in the speculative chase. In other words, the potential contraction from the shrinkage on the monetary side might be overwhelmed by the increase in speculative interest and the rise in demand. For the two countries together, in any event, the credit system is stretched tighter.[29]

Kindleberger views a flexible exchange rate as an important conduit for the international transmission of financial crises: "exchange appreciation and deflation, or exchange depreciation and inflation . . . can be connected with bankruptcies, bank suspensions and changes in the money supply."[30]

Finally, like Fisher and Minsky, Kindleberger assumes that a lender of last resort can abort the crisis; with his additional emphasis on the international nature of financial crises, he stresses the need for an international lender of last resort.[31]

*A comparison of the two approaches.*    The two approaches differ in two ways. The first difference concerns the importance of monetary change as the primary conduit through which financial crises affect economic activity. According to the monetarist approach, in a crisis the banking system has an impact on the economy primarily by reducing money growth. In contrast, in the Kindleberger-Minsky approach the importance of financial crises is largely independent of effects on the money supply.

The second difference concerns the importance of monetary factors in the international transmission of financial crises. According to the monetarist approach, transmission should occur primarily via the monetary standard, through international gold flows (or changes in international reserves) that affect monetary bases and hence money supplies. Under flexible exchange rates, transmission would be muted. In contrast, in the Kindleberger-Minsky approach transmission can occur through a wide variety of channels, including the monetary channel. One key channel stressed by Kindleberger and Minsky is the direct link between the banking systems of different countries. Moreover, flexible exchange rates may serve to accelerate transmission.

In what follows I examine the extent to which historical evidence for six countries in the period 1870-1933 conforms to each of these theories.

## 2. *Money, economic activity, and financial crises: the international evidence*

This section examines evidence on the behavior of money, its proximate determinants, and real activity during cyclical contractions marked by financial crises in the period 1870-1933. Because of data limitations, much of the focus is on annual data; this makes it more difficult to discuss the influence of a phenomenon such as a banking panic or a stock market crash than would be possible with monthly or weekly data.

Six countries are included in the sample. The United States, Great Britain, Germany, and France were the "core" countries in the period, with virtually all of the "crises" either originating in them or greatly amplified by them. The four countries were linked over much of the period by the gold standard and gold exchange standard as well as by close real trade and financial links. Unfortunately, reliable monetary data are available over the entire period for only two of the countries—the United States and Great Britain. For Germany coverage is limited to the pre-World War I period and for France to the post-World War I period; even then the data are spotty. Two "peripheral" but important countries with reliable data were added to the four core countries: Canada (for the period 1900-33) and Sweden (over the whole period). The two were closely linked to the core countries: Canada to the United States and Great Britain; Sweden to Great Britain and Germany.

*Incidence of financial crises.* Table 1 shows the incidence of crises in each of the six countries. To facilitate the comparison between countries, and to serve as a benchmark for our discussion, 12 "common international" reference cycles are demarcated. The common international cycles were chosen by picking turning points in the National Bureau of Economic Research reference chronology for each country that corresponded as closely as possible to the British reference cycle pattern." In the table the entries for each country for the incidence of crises are matched with the corresponding reference cycle chronology.

For the four core countries three kinds of crisis are identified: financial crises, according to Kindleberger's chronology of international financial crises; stock market crises, according to Morgenstern's chronology, classified as major or minor, international or local in scope; and finally banking crises, classified as panics (runs, failures, and suspensions of payments) or mere crises (runs or failures)." For the two peripheral countries, only minimal comparable evidence is available.

As can be seen from Table 1, the 63-year period was characterized by numerous financial crises, many of them international in scope, and even more numerous stock market crises affecting most of the core countries; but banking crises and especially banking panics were in the main confined to the United States.

*Money and real activity.*   Table 2 compares the behavior of real economic activity and the money supply over the cycle. Such a comparison sheds light on the possible importance of financial crises, especially banking crises, in exacerbating the effects of money on activity.

As a benchmark for comparison for each country Table 2 presents the annual, and in brackets the monthly, common international reference cycle chronology, for the peaks and troughs in business cycle contractions. Both annual and monthly data exist for all countries except Sweden, for which only annual data are available. The focus is on the cyclical contractions, since most financial, banking, and stock market crises have occurred at or shortly after the reference peak and have been associated with the severity of the ensuing cyclical contraction.

In addition, following Burns and Mitchell, six cyclical contractions are designated as severe (S): cycles (1), (2), (3), (7), (9), and (12)." As noted above, this chronology uses the British reference cycle pattern as the international standard. The five other countries in fact had more or fewer reference cycles than Great Britain (the United States had 16, Germany 11); but all these deviations in dating occurred within, or very close, to the British cycle." These deviations are characterized as subcycles to the common international cycle and the dates are presented in parentheses under the common international cycle dates."

Table 2 next presents the deviation of the average annual percentage change in real output from the long-run trend growth rate. This measures the severity of the decline in real economic activity in each country during cyclical contractions.

In general, the severity of the contractions in the common

Table 1  The Incidence of Financial Crises

### United States

| Common International Reference Cycle (trough to trough) (1) | Financial Crises (2) | Stock Market Crises (3) | Banking Crises (4) |
|---|---|---|---|
| 1. 1868-1879 | 9/1873 | 1873[c], 1875[b], 1879[a] | 9/1973[e] |
| 2. 1879-1886 | | 1880[a], 1881[a], 1882[b], 1884[a], | 5/1884[f] |
| 3. 1886-1894 | 5/1893 | 1887[b], 1889[a], 1890[c], 1891[b], 1893[a] | 1890[f], 7/1893[e] |
| 4. 1894-1901 | | 1899[a], 1900[b] | |
| 5. 1901-1904 | | 1901[a], 1904[a] | |
| 6. 1904-1908 | 8/1907 | 1907[c] | 10/1907[e] |
| 7. 1908-1914 | 8/1914 | 1912[b], 1914[a] | 8/1914[f] |
| 8. 1914-1919 | | | |
| 9. 1919-1921 | Spring 1921 | | |
| 10. 1921-1926 | | | |
| 11. 1926-1928 | | | |
| 12. 1928-1933 | 10/1929, 3/1931 | 1929[c], 1931[c] | 1930[f], 1931[f], 1933[e] |

### France

| Common International Reference Cycle (trough to trough) (12) | Financial Crises (13) | Stock Market Crises (14) | Banking Crises (15) |
|---|---|---|---|
| 1. 1868-1879 | 1871 | 1873[a], 1875[a], 1879[d] | |
| 2. 1879-1887 | 1/1882 | 1881[a], 1882[c] | 1882[f] |
| 3. 1887-1894 | | 1887[a], 1889[d], 1890[c], 1891[a] | 1889[f] |
| 4. 1894-1902 | | 1895[c], 1900[b] | |
| 5. 1902-1904 | | 1904[a] | |
| 6. 1904-1908 | 8/1907 | 1907[a] | |
| 7. 1908-1914 | 1914 | 1912[a], 1914[c] | |
| 8. 1914-1918 | | | |
| 9. 1918-1921 | | | |
| 10. 1921-1925 | 1926 | | |
| 11. 1925-1927 | | | |
| 12. 1927-1932 | | 1929[a], 1931[a] | 1930[f] |

[a] Crises affecting this country and other countries.
[b] This country not affected but major.
[c] Major international crisis sharply affecting this country.
[d] This country alone affected.
[e] Banking panic–runs, failures, suspensions of payments.
[f] Banking crises–runs or failures.

Source: W. A. Brown, jr., *The International Gold Standard Reinterpreted, 1914-1934* (New York, 1940), vol. 1; J. H. Clapham, *Economic Development of France and Germany 1815-1914* (Cambridge, 1966); M. Friedman and A. J. Schwartz, *A Monetary History of the United States* (Princeton, 1963); A.

### Great Britain

| Common International Reference Cycle (trough to trough) (5) | Financial Crises (6) | Stock Market Crises (7) |
|---|---|---|
| 1. 1868-1879 | 7/1870 | 1873*, 1875*, 1878[d] |
| 2. 1879-1886 | | 1880*, 1882*, 1884* |
| 3. 1886-1895 | 11/1890 | 1887*, 1890[c], 1892* |
| 4. 1895-1901 | | 1895[c], 1900* |
| 5. 1901-1904 | | 1901*, 1904* |
| 6. 1904-1908 | | 1907[b] |
| 7. 1908-1914 | 1914 | 1912*, 1914[c] |
| 8. 1914-1919 | | |
| 9. 1919-1921 | Spring 1921 | |
| 10. 1921-1926 | | |
| 11. 1926-1928 | | |
| 12. 1928-1933 | 9/1931 | 1929*, 1931[c] |

### Germany

| Common International Reference Cycle (trough to trough) (8) | Financial Crises (9) | Stock Market Crises (10) | Banking Crises (11) |
|---|---|---|---|
| 1. 1870-1878 | 5/1873 | 1873[c] | |
| 2. 1878-1886 | | 1880*, 1882[c], 1887* | |
| 3. 1886-1894 | | 1890[c], 1891*, 1893* | |
| 4. 1894-1902 | 1901 | 1895[c] | 1901[f] |
| 5. 1902-1904 | | 1900*, 1904* | |
| 6. 1904-1908 | | 1907[c] | |
| 7. 1908-1914 | | 1912*, 1914[c] | |
| 8. 1914-1919 | | | |
| 9. 1919-1923 | | | |
| 10. 1923-1926 | | | |
| 11. | | | |
| 12. 1926-1932 | 6/1931 | 1929*, 1931[c] | 1931[f] |

### Canada

| Common International Reference Cycle (trough to trough) (16) | Financial Crises (17) | Banking Crises (18) |
|---|---|---|
| 1. | | |
| 2. | | |
| 3. | | |
| 4. | | |
| 5. 1901-1904 | 1902 | |
| 6. 1904-1908 | 1907 | |
| 7. 1908-1915 | 1910 1914 | 1914[f] |
| 8. 1915-1919 | | |
| 9. 1919-1921 | 1921 | |
| 10. 1921-1924 | | 1924[f] |
| 11. | | |
| 12. 1924-1933 | 1931 | |

### Sweden

| Common International Reference Cycle (trough to trough) (19) | Financial Crises (20) |
|---|---|
| 1. 1866-1878 | |
| 2. 1878-1886 | |
| 3. 1886-1895 | |
| 4. 1895-1902 | |
| 5. 1902-1905 | |
| 6. 1905-1907 | 1907 |
| 7. 1907-1914 | 1914 |
| 8. 1914-1917 | |
| 9. 1917-1921 | |
| 10. | |
| 11. 1921-1928 | |
| 12. 1928-1931 | 1931, 1932 |

B. Jamieson, *Chartered Banking in Canada* (Toronto, 1959); L. Jonung, "The Depression in Sweden and the United States: A Comparison of Causes and Policies," in K. Brunner, ed., *The Great Depression Revisited* (Boston, 1981); C. P. Kindleberger, *The World in Depression 1929-39* (Berkeley, 1973), and *Manias, Panics and Crashes: A History of Financial Crises* (New York, 1978); P. McGouldrick, "Operations of the German Central Bank and the Rules of the Game, 1879-1913," in M. D. Bordo and A. J. Schwartz, eds., *A Retrospective on the Classical Gold Standard, 1821-1931* (Chicago, 1984); O. Morgenstern, *International Financial Transactions and Business Cycles* (New York, 1959); O. M. W. Sprague, "The Crisis of 1914 in the United States," *American Economic Review*, 5 (Sept. 1915), pp. 499-533; W. Thorp, *Business Annals* (New York, 1926); L. Yeager, *International Monetary Relations: Theory, History, and Policy* (2nd ed., New York, 1976).

54                          Michael D. Bordo

Table 2

The Money Supply and Real Economic Activity

United States

| Common International Reference Cycle | Annual [Monthly] Reference Cycle Contractions [Subcycles] | | Deviations from Trend of Average Annual Real Output Growth [a] (peak to trough) | Annual [Monthly] Specific Monetary Growth Cycle Contractions [Subcycles] | | Deviations from Trend of Average Annual Monetary Growth Rate [b] (peak to trough) |
|---|---|---|---|---|---|---|
| | Peak | Trough | | Peak | Trough | |
| | (1) | | (2) | (3) | | (4) |
| 1. 1868-1879 | 1873 (S)<br>[10/1873 | 1879<br>3/1879] | 0.5 | 1871<br>[7/1871 | 1878<br>5/1877] | −4.7 |
| 2. 1879-1886 | 1882 (S)<br>[3/1882 | 1885<br>5/1885] | −3.2 | 1880<br>[5/1881 | 1884<br>12/1883] | 2.6 |
| 3. 1886-1894 | 1890 (S)<br>[7/1890 | 1894<br>6/1894] | −2.6 | 1890<br>[12/1889 | 1893<br>12/1892] | −2.6 |
| | 1887<br>[4/1887<br>1890<br>[7/1890<br>1893 (S)<br>[1/1893 | 1888<br>4/1888]<br>1891<br>5/1891]<br>1894<br>6/1894] | { −6.7<br>0.78<br>−9.5 } | 1886<br>[12/1885<br>1890<br>[12/1889<br>1892<br>[12/1892 | 1888<br>12/1887]<br>1891<br>12/1890]<br>1893<br>12/1893] | { −0.78<br>−1.4<br>−9.3 } |
| 4. 1894-1901 | 1899<br>[6/1899 | 1900<br>12/1900] | 0.03 | 1899<br>[12/1898 | 1900<br>12/1899] | 2.6 |
| | 1896<br>[12/1896<br>1899<br>[6/1899 | 1897<br>6/1897]<br>1900<br>12/1900] | { 6.0<br>0.03 } | 1895<br>[12/1894<br>1899<br>[12/1898 | 1896<br>12/1895]<br>1900<br>12/1899] | { −7.8<br>2.6 } |
| 5. 1901-1904 | 1903<br>[9/1902 | 1904<br>8/1904] | −5.4 | 1901<br>[12/1900 | 1903<br>12/1903] | 2.0 |
| 6. 1904-1908 | 1907 (S)<br>[5/1907 | 1908<br>6/1908] | −14.7 | 1905<br>[12/1904 | 1908<br>12/1908] | −1.7 |
| 7. 1908-1914 | 1913<br>[1/1913 | 1915<br>12/1914] | −6.9 | 1912<br>[11/1911 | 1913<br>6/1913] | −1.5 |
| | 1909<br>[1/1910<br>1913<br>[1/1913 | 1911<br>1/1912]<br>1915<br>12/1914] | { −1.5<br>−6.9 } | 1909<br>[10/1908<br>1912<br>[10/1911 | 1910<br>4/1910]<br>1913<br>6/1913] | { −0.33<br>−1.5 } |
| 8. 1914-1919 | 1918<br>[8/1918 | 1919<br>3/1919] | 6.8 | 1916<br>[12/1916 | 1918<br>5/1918] | 7.0 |
| 9. 1919-1921 | 1920 (S)<br>[1/1920 | 1921<br>7/1921] | −7.6 | 1919<br>[12/1918 | 1921<br>1/1921] | −2.5 |
| 10. 1921-1926 | 1923<br>[5/1923 | 1924<br>7/1924] | −0.4 | 1923<br>[4/1922 | 1924<br>6/1923] | −0.13 |
| 11. 1926-1928 | 1926<br>[10/1926 | 1927<br>11/1927] | −2.2 | 1925<br>[7/1924 | 1927<br>12/1926] | −2.3 |
| 12. 1928-1933 | 1929 (S)<br>[8/1929 | 1932<br>3/1933] | −16.7 | 1928<br>[11/1927 | 1932<br>10/1932] | −11.7 |

## International Financial Crises, 1870-1933 55

| | Great Britain | | | | |
|---|---|---|---|---|---|
| Common International Reference Cycle | Annual [Monthly] Reference Cycle Contractions [Subcycles] | | Deviations from Trend of Average Annual Real Output Growth[a] (peak to trough) | Annual [Monthly] Specific Monetary Growth Cycle Contractions [Subcycles] | | Deviations from Trend of Average Annual Monetary Growth Rate[b] (peak to trough) |
| | Peak (5) | Trough | (6) | Peak (7) | Trough | (8) |
| 1. 1868-1879 | 1873 (S) [9/1872 | 1879 6/1879] | −0.09 | 1872 | 1878 | −3.12 |
| 2. 1879-1886 | 1883 (S) [12/1882 | 1886 6/1886] | −1.2 | 1881 | 1886 | −2.27 |
| 3. 1886-1895 | 1890 (S) [9/1890 | 1894 2/1895] | −0.19 | 1891 | 1893 | −2.51 |
| 4. 1895-1901 | 1900 [6/1900 | 1901 9/1901] | 2.5 | 1900 {1894 {1900 | 1901 1897} 1901} | −3.70 {0.09} {−3.70} |
| 5. 1901-1904 | 1903 [6/1903 | 1904 11/1904] | −0.65 | 1902 | 1903 | −4.02 |
| 6. 1904-1908 | 1907 (S) [6/1907 | 1908 11/1908] | −4.7 | 1906 | 1907 | −1.57 |
| 7. 1908-1914 | 1913 [12/1912 | 1914 9/1914] | −1.1 | 1910 | 1912 | 0.89 |
| 8. 1914-1919 | 1917 [10/1918 | 1919 4/1919] | −8.9 | 1917 | 1919 | 14.25 |
| 9. 1919-1921 | 1920 (S) [6/1920 | 1921 6/1921] | −6.9 | 1919 | 1922 | −5.06 |
| 10. 1921-1926 | 1924 [11/1924 | 1926 7/1926] | −0.9 | 1924 | 1925 | −3.72 |
| 11. 1926-1928 | 1927 [5/1927 | 1928 9/1928] | 0.46 | 1926 | 1928 | −0.49 |
| 12. 1928-1933 | 1929 (S) [7/1929 | 1932 8/1933] | −3.7 | 1928 {1928 {1930 | 1931 1929} 1931} | −4.27 {−4.20} {−8.95} |

*/continued overleaf*

(S) represents severe cyclical contractions.

[a] The trend growth rate in real output for each country was calculated from end point to end point. For the United States (NNP in 1929 prices) over 1870-1941, it was 3.22%; for Great Britain (NNP in 1929 prices) over 1870-1939, it was 1.48%; for Germany (NNP in 1913 prices) over 1870-1913 it was 2.66%; for France (GNP in 1938 prices) over 1900-1936 it was 1.36%; for Canada (GNP in 1949 prices) over 1900-1939 it was 3.10%; for Sweden (GNP in 1913 prices) over 1871-1939 it was 2.77%.

[b] The trend monetary growth rate ($M_2$ definition of money) was calculated from end point to end point. For the United States, it was 5.40%; for Great Britain, 2.71%; for Germany, 5.24%; for France, 7.34%; for Canada, 5.49%; for Sweden, 5.39%.

*continued* Table 2

| | Germany | | | | | |
|---|---|---|---|---|---|---|
| Common International Reference Cycle | Annual [Monthly] Reference Cycle Contractions [Subcycles] | | Deviations from Trend of Average Annual Real Output Growth[a] (peak to trough) | Annual [Monthly] Specific Monetary Growth Cycle Contractions [Subcycles] | | Deviations from Trend of Average Annual Monetary Growth Rate[b] (peak to trough) |
| | Peak (9) | Trough | (10) | Peak (11) | Trough | (12) |
| 1. 1870-1878 | 1872 (S) [1/1882 | 1878 2/1879] | −0.48 | 1872 { 1872 { 1876 | 1877 1875} 1877} | −2.9 { −0.6 } { −8.5 } |
| 2. 1878-1886 | 1882 (S) [1/1882 | 1886 8/1886] | 0.27 | 1881 { 1879 { 1881 { 1884 | 1885 1880} 1882} 1885} | −1.7 { −2.6 } { −4.1 } { −2.5 } |
| 3. 1886-1894 | 1890 (S) [1/1890 | 1894 2/1895] | −0.55 | 1889 { 1886 { 1889 { 1892 | 1893 1887} 1890} 1893} | −2.5 { −2.6 } { −3.4 } { −2.5 } |
| 4. 1894-1902 | 1900 [1/1900 | 1902 3/1902] | −2.04 | 1898 { 1895 { 1898 | 1900 1896} 1900} | 0.45 { −1.5 } { 0.45} |
| 5. 1902-1904 | 1903 [8/1903 | 1904 2/1905] | 2.5 | 1902 | 1903 | 1.1 |
| 6. 1904-1908 | 1907 (S) [7/1907 | 1908 12/1908] | −2.2 | 1906 { 1908 | 1907 1910} | −17.1 { 2.1 } |
| 7. 1908-1914 | 1913 [4/1913 | 1914 8/1914] | | 1910 | | |
| 8. 1914-1919 | 1918 [6/1918 | 1919 6/1919] | | | | |
| 9. 1919-1923 | 1922 (S) [5/1922 | 1923 11/1923] | | | | |
| 10. 1923-1926 | 1925 [3/1925 | 1926 3/1926] | | | | |
| 11. | | | | | | |
| 12. | 1929 (S) [4/1929 | 1932 8/1932] | | | | |

## International Financial Crises, 1870-1933  57

| | France | | | | |
|---|---|---|---|---|---|
| Common International Reference Cycle | Annual [Monthly] Reference Cycle Contractions [Subcycles] | | Deviations from Trend of Average Annual Real Output Growth^a (peak to trough) | Annual [Monthly] Specific Monetary Growth Cycle Contractions [Subcycles] | Deviations from Trend of Average Annual Monetary Growth Rate^b (peak to trough) |
| | Peak (13) | Trough | (14) | Peak    Trough (15) | (16) |
| 1. 1868-1879 | 1873 (S) [8/1873 1869 [8/1870 1873 [9/1873 1878 [3/1878 | 1879 9/1879] 1871 2/1872] 1876 9/1876] 1879 9/1879] | | | |
| 2. 1879-1887 | 1882 (S) [12/1881 | 1887 8/1887] | | | |
| 3. 1887-1894 | 1890 (S) [1/1891 | 1894 1/1895] | | | |
| 4. 1894-1902 | 1900 [3/1900 | 1902 9/1902] | | | |
| 5. 1902-1904 | 1903 [5/1903 | 1904 10/1904] | 6.43 | 1904    1905 | −3.1 |
| 6. 1904-1908 | 1907 (S) [7/1907 | 1908 2/1909] | −0.64 | 1906    1907 | −3.4 |
| 7. 1908-1914 | 1913 [6/1913 | 1914 8/1914] | | 1911    1912 { 1908    1910 { 1911    1912 | { −4.6 { −4.1 { −4.6 |
| 8. 1914-1918 | 1917 [6/1918 | 1918 4/1919] | | | |
| 9. 1918-1921 | 1920 (S) [9/1920 | 1921 7/1921] | −9.1 | 1920    1921 | −7.1 |
| 10. 1921-1925 | 1924 [10/1924 | 1925 6/1925] | −0.58 | 1923    1924 | −3.9 |
| 11. 1925-1927 | 1926 [10/1926 | 1927 6/1927] | −4.9 | 1925    1926 | 2.8 |
| 12. 1927-1932 | 1930 (S) [3/1930 | 1932 7/1932] | −7.2 | 1928    1929 | −4.6 |

*[continued overleaf*

58                           Michael D. Bordo

*continued* Table 2

| | | | Canada | | |
|---|---|---|---|---|---|
| Common International Reference·Cycle | Annual [Monthly] Reference Cycle Contractions \|Subcycles\| | | Deviations from Trend of Average Annual Real Output Growth[a] (peak to trough) | Annual [Monthly] Specific Monetary Growth Cycle Contractions \|Subcycles\| | Deviations from Trend of Average Annual Monetary Growth Rate[b] (peak to trough) |
| | Peak | Trough | | Peak          Trough | |
| | (17) | | (18) | (19) | (20) |
| 1. | | | | | |
| 2. | | | | | |
| 3. | | | | | |
| 4. | | | | | |
| 5. 1901-1904 | 1903 [12/1902 | 1904 6/1904] | 1.7 | 1901          1903 [4/1901      8/1902] | 2.8 |
| 6. 1904-1908 | 1907    (S) [12/1906 | 1908 7/1909] | −6.7 | 1906          1907 [1/1906     10/1907] | −9.7 |
| 7. 1908-1915 | 1913 [11/1912 | 1915 1/1915] | −7.5 | 1911          1914 [4/1912      5/1913] | −1.1 |
| | { 1910 [3/1910 | 1911 7/1911] } | { 2.5 | { 1909          1910 [12/1908    10/1910] } | { 2.8 |
| | 1913 [11/1912 | 1915 1/1915] } | −7.5 } | 1911          1914 [4/1912      5/1913] } | −1.1 } |
| 8. 1915-1919 | 1917 [3/1917 | 1919 4/1919] | 1.25 | 1917          1918 [10/1917     4/1918] | 0.8 |
| 9. 1919-1921 | 1920    (S) [6/1920 | 1921 9/1921] | −16.8 | 1919          1921 [9/1921      9/1922] | −7.1 |
| 10. 1921-1924 | 1923 [6/1923 | 1924 8/1924] | −6.9 | 1922          1923 [9/1922      9/1923] | −4.5 |
| 11. | | | | | |
| 12. 1924-1933 | 1929    (S) [4/1929 | 1932 3/1933] | −10.9 | 1927          1931 [10/1927    11/1931] | −7.8 |

## International Financial Crises, 1870-1933    59

| | Sweden | | | | |
|---|---|---|---|---|---|
| Common International Reference Cycle | Annual [Monthly] Reference Cycle Contractions [Subcycles] | | Deviations from Trend of Average Annual Real Output Growth[a] (peak to trough) | Annual [Monthly] Specific Monetary Growth Cycle Contractions [Subcycles] | | Deviations from Trend of Average Annual Monetary Growth Rate[b] (peak to trough) |
| | Peak | Trough | | Peak | Trough | |
| | (21) | | (22) | (23) | | (24) |
| 1. 1866-1878 | 1872 (S) | 1878 | −1.1 | 1876 | 1878 | −8.4 |
| | { 1872 | 1875 } | { −1.3 | | | |
| | { 1876 | 1878 } | { −5.0 } | | | |
| 2. 1878-1886 | 1883 (S) | 1886 | −1.4 | 1880 | 1886 | −1.3 |
| | | | | { 1880 | 1882 } | { −1.3 } |
| | | | | { 1883 | 1886 } | { −2.3 } |
| 3. 1886-1895 | 1889 (S) | 1895 | −0.6 | 1891 | 1894 | −2.9 |
| | { 1889 | 1890 } | { −1.5 } | { 1889 | 1890 } | { −3.5 } |
| | { 1891 | 1892 } | { −3.7 } | { 1891 | 1892 } | { −5.1 } |
| | { 1894 | 1895 } | { −5.6 } | { 1893 | 1894 } | { −3.2 } |
| 4. 1895-1902 | 1900 | 1902 | −3.3 | 1899 | 1902 | 2.7 |
| 5. 1902-1905 | 1903 | 1905 | −1.4 | 1903 | 1904 | −1.5 |
| 6. 1905-1907 | 1906 (S) | 1907 | −2.7 | 1907 | 1910 | −1.2 |
| 7. 1907-1914 | 1913 | 1914 | −5.2 | | | |
| 8. 1914-1917 | 1916 | 1917 | −11.9 | | | |
| 9. 1917-1921 | 1920 (S) | 1921 | −15.4 | 1918 | 1923 | −5.3 |
| 10. | | | | | | |
| 11. 1921-1928 | 1925 | 1928 | 0.22 | | | |
| 12. 1928-1931 | 1929 (S) | 1931 | −6.1 | 1930 | 1932 | −6.2 |

Source: *Reference Cycle Dates*: For the United States, Great Britain, Germany, and France: A. F. Burns and W. C. Mitchell, *Measuring Business Cycles* (New York, 1946). For Canada: K. A. J. Hay, "Money and Cycles in Post-Confederation Canada," *Journal of Political Economy*, 75 (1967), pp. 263-73. For Sweden: L. Jonung, "Studies in the Monetary History of Sweden," (Ph.D. diss., UCLA, 1975).

*Real Output*: For the United States and Great Britain: M. Friedman and A. J. Schwartz, *Monetary Trends in the United States and the United Kingdom: Their Relation to Income, Prices and Interest Rates, 1867-1975* (Chicago, 1982). For Germany: W. Hoffman, *Das Wachstum der Deutschen Wirtschaft seit der Mitte des 19. Jahrhunderts* (Berlin, 1965). For France: A. Sauvy, "Rapport sur le revenu national," *Journal Officiel. Avis et rapports du Conseil économique* (1954). For Canada and Sweden: M. D. Bordo and L. Jonung, "The Long-Run Behavior of the Income Velocity of Money in Five Advanced Countries, 1870-1975: An Institutional Approach," *Economic Inquiry*, 19 (Jan. 1981), pp. 96-116.

*Money Supply*: For the United States and Great Britain: Friedman and Schwartz, *Monetary Trends*. For Germany: R. Tilly, "Zeitreihen zum Geldumlauf in Deutschland, 1870-1913," *Jahrbücher für Nationaloekonomie und Statistik*, 87 (1973), pp. 360-63. For France: Insee, *Annuaire statistique* (1966). For Canada: Bordo and Jonung, "Long-Run Behavior of Velocity." For Sweden: Jonung, "Studies in the Monetary History of Sweden."

60                              Michael D. Bordo

cycles differed considerably across countries, reflecting differences in the level of economic development, differences in the
composition of output, and differences in the exchange rate
regime (to be discussed in Section 3 below). However, the six
cyclical contractions designated as severe had the greatest
declines in real activity in all the countries.

To compare the behavior of money with that of real economic
activity, a chronology of peaks and troughs of specific cycles
in monetary growth corresponding to the reference cycle chronology is developed for each country. Annual or monthly (depending on the frequency of the available data) turning points
were derived following procedures developed by Friedman and
Schwartz.[7]

For the United States, turning points in money growth
generally precede those in business by a calendar year. However,
as can be seen from the monthly series in brackets, the use of annual data greatly distorts the true measure of the lead. Nevertheless, since monthly data are available only for the United
States and Canada, the annual data are used for the other countries as a crude measure of timing. In these countries, the turning
points in money growth generally precede but often coincide
with the turning points in business.[58]

Finally, as a measure of the severity of the monetary contraction, Table 2 displays deviations from long-run trend of the
average rate of monetary growth between cycle peaks and
troughs. In virtually every case, with the principal exception of
World War I in Great Britain, declines in money growth below
trend are associated with declines in economic activity in the corresponding reference cycle contraction. Indeed the greater is the
deviation of money growth from trend, the greater the decline in
economic activity.

A comparison of Tables 1 and 2 reveals that the most severe
declines in both money and real output occurred in severe cycles
often characterized by financial and stock market crises. However, the greatest declines in all of the countries examined here
(except in 1920-21) occurred in the United States, in contractions associated with banking crises.

Table 3 examines in greater detail the role of monetary forces
in financial crises. Following the approach of Friedman, Schwartz
and Cagan, it shows the contributions to the specific cycle contractions in monetary growth of the three proximate determinants of the money supply: high-powered money ($H$); the
deposit-currency ratio ($D/C$); and the deposit-reserve ratio
($D/R$).[9]

In his pioneering study of the United States, Cagan found the currency-money ratio to be the key determinant of cyclical movements in the money supply, with high-powered money and the reserve ratio each having about one-half of the influence of the currency ratio.[40] For severe cycles, the order of magnitude remained the same but the influence of the currency ratio increased.[41] Cagan, Friedman, and Schwartz present evidence for the United States that in several severe cycles characterized by banking panics, declines in the deposit-currency ratio and hence (as banks increased their holdings of precautionary reserves) in the deposit-reserve ratio so reduced money growth as to produce a severe contraction in economic activity. Such results for the United States can be clearly seen for the banking panics of 1893, and the great contraction of 1929-33.

For Great Britain, in contrast to the United States, high-powered money was the key determinant of cyclical contractions in money, followed by the deposit-currency ratio and the deposit-reserve ratio.[42] For Great Britain, again in contrast to the United States, there were no banking crises in the period under consideration; yet the two ratios acting alone or jointly produced significant declines in money in several severe contractions associated with major stock market crises (1872-78, 1890-93, 1900-01, 1902-03, 1907-08, and 1928-31). However, except in 1930-31, none of the declines of the ratios were comparable to those observed in the U.S. case.[43]

For Germany, the deposit-currency ratio was the most important determinant of cyclical changes in money in specific cycle contractions. However, in contrast to other countries, money only declined in one specific cycle contraction (1906-07). With the exception of that episode, where a decline in $D/C$ produced a decline in $M$, the Reichsbank caused $H$ to vary countercyclically to offset the procyclical behavior of the ratios.[44] Germany's experience, like Great Britain's, was characterized by the absence of banking crises (with the exception of a mild crisis associated with several bank failures in 1901). Yet the decline in the ratios, especially $D/R$, seemed to coincide with major stock market crises.

In both Canada and Sweden $H$ and $D/R$ were the key determinants of changes in $M$ in cyclical contractions, with $D/C$ playing a minor role.[45] Both countries were characterized by stable banking systems and the absence of panics. In the Canadian case, the banking system's $D/R$ declined significantly in three severe contractions associated with financial crises abroad (1877-78, 1894-95, and 1927-31).[46]

Michael D. Bordo

The evidence suggests a number of conclusions on the relationship of money, financial crises, and real activity in the different countries. First, severe declines in economic activity in all countries are associated with (prior) declines in money growth. Second, most severe cyclical contractions in all the countries examined are associated with stock market crises but not, with the exception of the United States, with banking crises. Third, the junior partners to high-powered money as determinants of change in money–the $D/R$ and $D/C$ ratios–played an important role in reducing money growth in all countries, but not to the extent they displayed in the U.S. experience; this is especially true of the role played by the deposit-currency ratio in reducing the money supply during contractions involving banking panics.

Why was monetary contraction associated with financial crises

Table 3   The Proximate Determinants of the Money Supply

United States

| Common International Reference Cycle | Percentage Change in M, Specific Cycle (peak to trough) | Percentage Change in M if Determinants Indicated Alone Had Changed | | | Common International Reference Cycle | Percentage Change in M, Specific Cycle (peak to trough) |
|---|---|---|---|---|---|---|
| | | High-Powered Money | Deposit-Reserve Ratio | Deposit-Currency Ratio | | |
| | (1) | (2) | (3) | (4) | | (5) |
| 1. 1868-1879 | 5.2 | −1.9 | 4.2 | 2.7 | 1. 1868-1879 | −2.5 |
| 2. 1879-1886 | 32.2 | 23.8 | 2.8 | 5.2 | 2. 1879-1886 | −0.3 |
| 3. 1886-1894 | 8.3 {9.2, 4.0, −3.9} | 11.6 {8.3, 5.0, 1.8} | −3.8 {0.6, −1.4, −1.5} | 0.5 {0.3, 0.5, −4.3} | 3. 1886-1895 | 0.4 |
| 4. 1894-1901 | 8.0 {−1.8, 9.0} | 7.5 {−3.25, 7.5} | 1.3 {1.2, 1.3} | −0.8 {0.2, −0.8} | 4. 1895-1901 | 0.9 {8.4, −0.9} |
| 5. 1901-1904 | 14.9 | 8.3 | 4.5 | 1.9 | 5. 1901-1904 | −1.3 |
| 6. 1904-1908 | 11.0 | 21.7 | −8.3 | −2.65 | 6. 1904-1908 | 1.1 |
| 7. 1908-1914 | 3.9 {5.1, 3.9} | 2.2 {1.65, 2.2} | 1.6 {1.8, 1.8} | 0.1 {1.6, 0.1} | 7. 1908-1914 | 7.2 |
| 8. 1914-1919 | 24.8 | 39.3 | −14.8 | 3.7 | 8. 1914-1919 | 33.9 |
| 9. 1919-1921 | 5.8 | −1.35 | 4.2 | 2.8 | 9. 1919-1921 | −3.2 |
| 10. 1921-1926 | 5.3 | 2.7 | −0.2 | 2.8 | 10. 1921-1926 | −1.0 |
| 11. 1926-1928 | 6.2 | 1.6 | 1.6 | 2.9 | 11. 1926-1928 | 4.4 |
| 12. 1928-1933 | −25.2 | 8.1 | −8.3 | −27.4 | 12. 1928-1933 | −4.7 {−1.6, −6.2} |

International Financial Crises, 1870-1933 63

more severe in the United States than in other countries? One explanation is the greater instability of the U.S. banking system—a system composed largely of unit fractional reserve banks with reserves pyramided in the New York money market. Though numerous institutional reforms had been devised to strengthen the system over the years, the basic instability associated with potential threats to convertibility was not removed until the advent of federal deposit insurance in 1934. Until then, bank runs and panics occurred whenever a shock threatened the solvency of a few key banks or other financial institutions.

In contrast with the United States, the five other countries all developed nationwide branch-banking systems consolidated into a few very large banks. The system of bank branching, first successfully developed in Scotland in the eighteenth century and

| Great Britain | | | | Germany | | | |
|---|---|---|---|---|---|---|---|
| Percentage Change in M if Determinants Indicated Alone Had Changed | | | Common International Reference Cycle | Percentage Change in M, Specific Cycle (peak to trough) | Percentage Change in M if Determinants Indicated Alone Had Changed | | |
| High-Powered Money | Deposit-Reserve Ratio | Deposit-Currency Ratio | | | High-Powered Money | Deposit-Reserve Ratio | Deposit-Currency Ratio |
| (6) | (7) | (8) | | (9) | (10) | (11) | (12) |
| 7.1 | −4.8 | −5.2 | 1. 1870-1878 | 11.6<br>{ 13.8<br>{ −3.3 | −9.8<br>{ 0.1<br>{ −8.3 | 5.5<br>{ 3.4<br>{ 0.9 | 14.0<br>{ 9.6<br>{ 4.1 |
| −2.4 | −0.2 | 2.3 | 2. 1878-1886 | 14.2<br>{ 2.7<br>{ 1.2<br>{ 2.7 | −2.0<br>{ 2.0<br>{ −5.9<br>{ −3.5 | −0.9<br>{ −0.1<br>{ −1.1<br>{ −0.1 | 17.4<br>{ 3.0<br>{ 3.0<br>{ 6.7 |
| 2.7 | −0.1 | −2.2 | 3. 1886-1894 | 10.8<br>{ 2.7<br>{ 1.8<br>{ 3.1 | 4.3<br>{ −0.4<br>{ −1.5<br>{ −0.1 | −0.7<br>{ −0.3<br>{ −0.3<br>{ −0.2 | 7.4<br>{ 3.4<br>{ 3.8<br>{ 3.4 |
| 0.5<br>{ 5.6<br>{ 0.5 | −1.9<br>{ 0.5<br>{ −1.9 | 0.4<br>{ −2.3<br>{ 0.4 | 4. 1894-1902 | 11.3<br>{ 3.8<br>{ 11.3 | 8.2<br>{ −0.3<br>{ 8.2 | −6.0<br>{ −3.1<br>{ −0.5 | 3.8<br>{ 7.5<br>{ 3.8 |
| 0.5 | 2.2 | −3.8 | 5. 1902-1904 | 6.4 | 4.0 | 0.4 | 2.0 |
| 2.3 | 0.1 | −1.0 | 6. 1904-1908 | −11.8<br>{ 7.3 | 0.0<br>{ 3.2 | −3.4<br>{ −0.1 | −8.7<br>{ 4.3 |
| 3.1 | −0.1 | 4.2 | 7. 1908-1914 | | | | |
| 35.5 | 2.5 | −3.9 | 8. 1914-1919 | | | | |
| −13.7 | 2.0 | 4.5 | 9. 1919-1923 | | | | |
| 0.0 | −1.8 | 0.8 | 10. 1923-1926 | | | | |
| −2.2 | 2.9 | 3.6 | 11. | | | | |
| −4.1 | 0.6 | −1.3 | 12. 1926-1932 | | | | |
| { −2.1<br>{ −0.8 | { 0.7<br>{ −1.7 | { −0.2<br>{ −3.7 | | | | | |

/continued overleaf

Michael D. Bordo

emulated by other countries including Canada and Sweden, represented a method of pooling risks.[47] It proved quite effective in guarding against the "house of cards" effects common to the U.S. (and early nineteenth-century British) banking system.

A second explanation for the relatively poor performance of the United States stemming from the massive literature on the development of central banking and especially of the Bank of England–is the absence of an *effective* "lender of last resort."[48] Four of the six countries in our sample had central banks. By the beginning of this period, and in various degrees, they had learned in the face of a crisis to follow Bagehot's rule "to lend freely but at a penalty rate"; and to a certain extent they had learned to cooperate among themselves in times of severe international crisis, such as the Baring crisis of 1890.[49] Canada did not have a central bank until 1936; but with the compliance of the government the chartered banks had by 1890 established an effective self-policing agency, the Canadian Bankers' Association, which

*continued* Table 3

|  |  | Canada | | |
|---|---|---|---|---|
| Common International Reference Cycle | Percentage Change in M, Specific Cycle (peak to trough) | Percentage Change in M if Determinants Indicated Alone Had Changed | | |
|  |  | High-Powered Money | Deposit-Reserve Ratio | Deposit-Currency Ratio |
|  | (13) | (14) | (15) | (16) |
| 1. |  |  |  |  |
| 2. |  |  |  |  |
| 3. |  |  |  |  |
| 4. |  |  |  |  |
| 5. 1901-1904 | 16.5 | 21.8 | −6.6 | 1.5 |
| 6. 1904-1908 | −4.2 | 4.0 | −6.5 | −1.8 |
| 7. 1908-1915 | 13.8 | 21.6 | −10.3 | 2.1 |
|  | { 8.3 } { 13.1 } | { 7.8 } { 21.6 } | { 0.1 } { −10.3 } | { 0.4 } { 2.1 } |
| 8. 1915-1919 | 6.3 | 13.9 | −5.4 | −2.2 |
| 9. 1919-1921 | −3.1 | −14.3 | 5.8 | 4.9 |
| 10. 1921-1924 | 3.3 | 0.6 | −0.2 | 2.9 |
| 11. |  |  |  |  |
| 12. 1924-1933 | −9.3 | −20.6 | 9.1 | 2.0 |

Proximate determinants may not add up to total changes in M because of the omission of a small interaction term, and because of rounding errors.

successfully helped insulate the Canadian banks from the deleterious effects of U.S. banking panics in 1893 and 1907.[50] Such a mechanism could be provided by the government or by the private market; but once it proved effective it would educate the public and instill enough confidence to prevent incipient crises.[51]

In sum, the stark comparison of the United States with the other five countries tends to support the monetarist approach: financial crises involving banking crises seem to have played a major role in aggravating (if not producing) the effects of monetary contraction on the real economy.

### 3. *The international transmission of financial crises*

According to the monetarist approach, financial crises (and also business cycles) are transmitted internationally primarily

| Common International Reference Cycle | Sweden | | | |
|---|---|---|---|---|
| | Percentage Change in M, Specific Cycle (peak to trough) | Percentage Change in M if Determinants Indicated Alone Had Changed | | |
| | | High-Powered Money | Deposit-Reserve Ratio | Deposit-Currency Ratio |
| | (17) | (18) | (19) | (20) |
| 1. 1866-1878 | −6.1 | −11.8 | −8.0 | 15.2 |
| 2. 1878-1886 | 24.6 | 1.9 | 18.1 | 3.7 |
| | $\begin{Bmatrix} 8.2 \\ 9.2 \end{Bmatrix}$ | $\begin{Bmatrix} -7.0 \\ 8.2 \end{Bmatrix}$ | $\begin{Bmatrix} 14.5 \\ 0.9 \end{Bmatrix}$ | $\begin{Bmatrix} 0.6 \\ 0.3 \end{Bmatrix}$ |
| 3. 1886-1895 | 7.6 | 9.4 | −1.0 | 0.8 |
| | $\begin{Bmatrix} 1.9 \\ 0.3 \\ 2.2 \end{Bmatrix}$ | $\begin{Bmatrix} -0.1 \\ -1.0 \\ 5.1 \end{Bmatrix}$ | $\begin{Bmatrix} 1.7 \\ 0.4 \\ -1.1 \end{Bmatrix}$ | $\begin{Bmatrix} 0.4 \\ 0.9 \\ -1.7 \end{Bmatrix}$ |
| 4. 1895-1902 | 24.1 | 36.4 | 5.4 | −16.7 |
| 5. 1902-1905 | 3.9 | 9.0 | 0.5 | 5.6 |
| 6. 1905-1907 | 12.6 | 1.1 | 3.6 | 7.6 |
| 7. 1907-1914 | | | | |
| 8. 1914-1917 | | | | |
| 9. 1917-1921 | 0.6 | −19.1 | 2.6 | 16.6 |
| 10. | | | | |
| 11. 1921-1928 | | | | |
| 12. 1928-1931 | −1.6 | 8.7 | −11.0 | 0.8 |

Source: Same as Table 2.

66                              Michael D. Bordo

through the monetary standard. According to the Kindleberger-Minsky approach, financial crises are transmitted primarily through nonmonetary channels such as the portfolios of financial institutions.

Evidence supporting the Kindleberger-Minsky approach can be seen in Table 4, in the timing of the peaks and troughs of the long-term/short-term interest differential and of Morgenstern's stock price index for the four core countries. The interest differential chronology is reversed, reflecting financial pressure at the specific cycle trough and ease at the peak. In general, the troughs in this series for each country are very close to the corresponding reference cycle peaks (from Table 2), tending to follow them by only a few months. At the same time, peaks in

Table 4
International Variables

| | United States | | | | | |
|---|---|---|---|---|---|---|
| Common International Reference Cycle | Monthly Specific Cycle: Long-term Short-term Interest Differential | | Monthly Specific Cycle: Stock Price Index | | Percentage Change in Monetary Gold Stock | Exchange Rate Regime |
| | Trough | Peak | Peak | Trough | | |
| | (1) | | (2) | | (3) | (4) |
| 1. 1868-1879 | 9/1873 <br> { 9/1873 <br> 10/1877 | 8/1878 <br> 8/1876 <br> 8/1878 } | 5/1872 | 6/1877 | 64.9 | Flexible |
| 2. 1879-1886 | 6/1883 | 9/1885 | 6/1881 | 1/1885 | 45.7 | Fixed |
| 3. 1886-1894 | 12/1890 <br> { 7/1887 <br> 12/1890 <br> 7/1893 | 10/1894 <br> 11/1888 <br> 6/1892 <br> 10/1894 } | 5/1890 <br> { 5/1887 <br> 5/1890 <br> 8/1893 | 3/1895 <br> 6/1888 <br> 12/1890 <br> 3/1895 } | −21.0 <br> { −18.5 <br> −8.6 <br> −14.2 } | Fixed |
| 4. 1894-1901 | 3/1900 <br> { 10/1896 <br> 3/1900 | 11/1900 <br> 1/1899 <br> 11/1900 } | 4/1899 <br> { 9/1895 <br> 4/1899 | 9/1900 <br> 8/1896 <br> 9/1900 } | 6.4 <br> { −8.6 <br> 6.4 } | Fixed |
| 5. 1901-1904 | 8/1903 | 1/1905 | 9/1902 | 10/1903 | 11.4 | Fixed |
| 6. 1904-1908 | 12/1907 | 7/1909 | 9/1906 | 11/1907 | 27.7 | Fixed |
| 7. 1908-1914 | 6/1913 <br> { 6/1910 <br> 6/1913 | n/a <br> 11/1911 <br> n/a } | 12/1909 <br> { 12/1909 <br> 9/1912 | 12/1914 <br> 7/1910 <br> 12/1914 } | 2.9 <br> { −0.4 <br> 2.9 } | Fixed |
| 8. 1914-1919 | n/a | n/a | n/a | n/a | 25.9 | Fixed |
| 9. 1919-1921 | 10/1920 | 8/1922 | 7/1919 | 8/1921 | 4.6 | Fixed |
| 10. 1921-1926 | 5/1923 | 10/1924 | 3/1923 | 10/1923 | 10.5 | Fixed |
| 11. 1926-1928 | | | | | 4.8 | Fixed |
| 12. 1928-1933 | 8/1929 <br> { 8/1929 <br> 11/1931 | 9/1934 <br> 9/1931 <br> 9/1934 } | 9/1929 | 6/1932 | −6.3 | Fixed |

International Financial Crises, 1870-1933          67

the stock price index tend to precede reference cycle peaks, reflecting the stock market's role as a frequent leading indicator of economic activity.

Troughs in the interest differential series are more closely related among countries than the peaks, and closer links are found among the three European countries than between any of them and the United States." In addition, Morgenstern demonstrates that movements in the differential are largely explained by movements in short-term interest rates. According to Morgenstern, the behavior of this series is evidence for a tightly linked European short-term capital market. Morgenstern's evidence, and Lindert's on the relative pulling power of the discount rate in different financial centers, suggest that securities

Great Britain

| Common International Reference Cycle | Monthly Specific Cycle: Long-term Short-term Interest Differential | | Monthly Specific Cycle: Stock Price Index | | Percentage Change in Monetary Gold Stock | Exchange Rate Regime |
|---|---|---|---|---|---|---|
| | Trough | Peak | Peak | Trough | | |
| | (5) | | (6) | | (7) | (8) |
| 1. 1868-1879 | 11/1873 n/a {11/1873 8/1878 | 9/1879 8/1871 10/1876 9/1879} | 10/1873 | 7/1879 | n/a | Fixed |
| 2. 1879-1886 | 7/1883 | 6/1885 | 1/1880 | 11/1887 | −15.8 | Fixed |
| 3. 1886-1895 | 7/1890 { 7/1890 8/1893 | 10/1894 9/1892 10/1894} | 10/1889 | 4/1892 | 7.9 | Fixed |
| 4. 1895-1901 | 12/1899 | 10/1901 | 2/1900 | | 7.2 { 3.7 7.2} | Fixed |
| 5. 1901-1904 | 5/1903 | 10/1904 | | 8/1904 | −3.4 | Fixed |
| 6. 1904-1908 | 11/1907 | 4/1909 | 2/1907 | 3/1909 | 4.4 | Fixed |
| 7. 1908-1914 | 7/1913 { 4/1910 7/1913 | n/a 3/1911 } | 4/1911 | 6/1914 | 5.0 | Fixed |
| 8. 1914-1919 | n/a | n/a | | 1/1919 | 44.7 | Pegged/ Controls |
| 9. 1919-1921 | 5/1920 | 5/1923 | 1/1920 | 10/1921 | 0.2 | Flexible |
| 10. 1921-1926 | 5/1925 | | 6/1923 | 7/1924 | 1.7 | Fixed* |
| 11. 1926-1928 | | 7/1928 | | | 9.0 | Fixed |
| 12. 1928-1933 | 10/1920 { 10/1929 1/1932 | 7/1933 9/1920 7/1883} | 2/1929 | 5/1932 | −15.4 { −10.6 −10.2} | Fixed[b] |

* Great Britain returned to gold in April 1925.
[b] Great Britain left gold in September 1931.

/continued overleaf

markets were especially closely linked in time of financial pressure."

Turning points in the stock price index are very closely related among the four countries, although the links among the European countries are closer than those between the United States and Europe." A comparison of the peaks in this series and Morgenstern's chronology of stock market crises in Table 1 shows a remarkable coincidence for major crises that are international in scope. Such crises often originated in the United States and then spread quickly to Europe.

*continued* Table 4

| | Germany | | | | |
|---|---|---|---|---|---|
| Common International Reference Cycle | Monthly Specific Cycle: Long-term Short-term Interest Differential | | Monthly Specific Cycle: Stock Price Index | | Percentage Change in Monetary Gold Stock | Exchange Rate Regime |
| | Trough | Peak | Peak | Trough | | |
| | (9) | | (10) | | (11) | (12) |
| 1. 1870-1878 | | 5/1879 | 11/1872 | 6/1877 | 6.5 $\{\begin{matrix}15.3\\-10.2\end{matrix}$ | Fixed $^c$ |
| 2. 1878-1886 | 2/1882 $\{\begin{matrix}2/1882\\4/1885\end{matrix}$ | 9/1886 $\begin{matrix}2/1884\\9/1886\end{matrix}\}$ | 8/1881 | 1/1885 | -2.9 $\{\begin{matrix}-0.7\\1.0\\0.5\end{matrix}$ | Fixed |
| 3. 1886-1894 | 2/1890 $\{\begin{matrix}2/1887\\2/1890\\8/1893\end{matrix}$ | 12/1894 $\begin{matrix}1/1888\\5/1892\\12/1894\end{matrix}\}$ | 12/1889 | 11/1891 | 4.5 $\{\begin{matrix}1.7\\-1.6\\-0.7\end{matrix}$ | Fixed |
| 4. 1894-1902 | 3/1900 $\{\begin{matrix}8/1896\\3/1900\end{matrix}$ | 7/1902 $\begin{matrix}5/1897\\7/1902\end{matrix}\}$ | 5/1899 | 10/1901 | 7.2 $\{\begin{matrix}1.9\\7.2\end{matrix}$ | Fixed |
| 5. 1902-1904 | 8/1903 | 4/1905 | | | 2.1 | Fixed |
| 6. 1904-1908 | 7/1907 | 11/1908 | 9/1905 | 8/1908 | -2.6 $\{1.1\}$ | Fixed |
| 7. 1908-1914 | 2/1913 $\{\begin{matrix}6/1910\\2/1913\end{matrix}$ | | 9/1912 | 12/1913 | | Fixed |
| 8. 1914-1919 | | 7/1911 | | | | Flexible |
| 9. 1919-1923 | | | | 6/1924 | | Flexible |
| 10. 1923-1926 | | 7/1926 | 1/1925 | 12/1925 | | Fixed $^d$ |
| 11. | | | | | | Fixed |
| 12. 1926-1932 | 5/1929 $\{\begin{matrix}3/1928\\5/1929\\7/1931\end{matrix}$ | 6/1932 $\begin{matrix}1/1929\\6/1930\\6/1932\end{matrix}\}$ | 4/1927 | 4/1932 | | Fixed |

International Financial Crises, 1870-1933                69

Finally, a comparison of the turning points in the two financial variables with the chronology of financial, banking, and stock market crises suggests that crises in the gold standard era often tended to be international in scope; but the way in which they manifested themselves in different countries differed considerably, especially when the response of the banking system in the United States is compared to that of the other countries.

Evidence supporting the monetarist approach to international transmission via the monetary standard can also be seen in Table 4. Under the gold standard, which characterized much of the

| | France | | | |
|---|---|---|---|---|
| Common International Reference Cycle | Monthly Specific Cycle: Long-term Short-term Interest Differential | | Monthly Specific Cycle: Stock Price Index | Exchange Rate Regime |
| | Trough | Peak | Peak | Trough | |
| | (13) | | (14) | | (15) |
| 1. 1868-1879 | | 6/1879 | | | Fixed[e] |
| 2. 1879-1887 | 1/1882 | 6/1886 | | | Fixed |
| 3. 1887-1894 | 12/1888 {12/1883 3/1891 8/1898 | 8/1895 {2/1889 6/1892 8/1895} | | 1/1898 | Fixed |
| 4. 1894-1902 | 1/1900 | 9/1901 | 4/1900 | | Fixed |
| 5. 1902-1904 | 7/1903 | 8/1904 | | 2/1904 | Fixed |
| 6. 1904-1908 | 8/1907 | 5/1909 | 2/1907 | 10/1907 | Fixed |
| 7. 1908-1914 | 8/1913 | n/a | 9/1912 | 7/1914 | Fixed |
| 8. 1914-1918 | | | | 3/1919 | Flexible |
| 9. 1918-1921 | | | 4/1920 | 4/1922 | Flexible |
| 10. 1921-1925 | 4/1925 | 11/1925 | 10/1924 | 5/1925 | Flexible |
| 11. 1925-1927 | 10/1926 | 10/1927 | 9/1926 | 12/1926 | Flexible[f] |
| 12. 1927-1932 | 6/1929 | 6/1933 | 2/1926 | 5/1933 | Fixed |

[c] Germany was on a silver standard until 1873, and then on gold.
[d] Germany stabilized the mark in 1924.
[e] France was on a bimetallic silver standard until 1878, although gold was de facto the standard after 1872.
[f] France restored de facto gold convertibility at the end of 1926.

*/continued overleaf*

period for all the countries in Table 4, one would expect changes in the monetary gold stock to be the key source of changes in high-powered money over the cycle unless significant sterilization is occurring. Under perfectly flexible exchange rates no such link should prevail. To account for this, Table 4 presents for each country (except Sweden) the percentage change in monetary gold stock between the specific cycle peaks and troughs.

For the United States, there is a close correlation between changes in the monetary gold stock and changes in high-powered money in every specific cycle contraction except that of 1871-78, under flexible exchange rates; however, the link is far from one-to-one, reflecting periodic sterilization especially of gold outflows during contractions. For Great Britain the association, though positive, is much weaker; this agrees with the evidence of Bloomfield and others that the Bank of England engaged in active sterilization." For Germany, the association, though positive, is

---

*continued* Table 4

| | Canada | | | | Sweden | |
|---|---|---|---|---|---|---|
| Common International Reference Cycle | Percentage Change in Monetary Gold Stock | Exchange Rate Regime | | Common International Reference Cycle | | Exchange Rate Regime |
| | (16) | (17) | | | | (18) |
| 1. | | | | 1. 1866-1878 | | Fixed |
| 2. | | | | 2. 1878-1886 | | Fixed |
| 3. | | | | 3. 1886-1895 | | Fixed |
| 4. | | | | 4. 1895-1902 | | Fixed |
| 5. 1901-1904 | 38.4 | Fixed | | 5. 1902-1905 | | Fixed |
| 6. 1904-1908 | 11.7 | Fixed | | 6. 1905-1907 | | Fixed |
| 7. 1908-1915 | 11.8 | Fixed | | 7. 1907-1914 | | |
| 8. 1915-1919 | | Flexible | | 8. 1914-1917 | | Flexible |
| 9. 1919-1921 | | Flexible | | 9. 1917-1921 | | Flexible[i] |
| 10. 1921-1924 | −6.8 | Fixed[g] | | 10. | | |
| 11. | | Fixed | | 11. 1921-1928 | | |
| 12. 1924-1933 | −35.1 | Flexible[h] | | 12. 1928-1931 | | Fixed[i] |

[g] Canada returned to gold de jure in 1926.
[h] Canada left gold de facto in 1929.
[i] Sweden returned to gold de facto in 1922, de jure in 1924.
[j] Sweden left gold in 1931.

Source: *Interest Differential, Stock Price Indices*: Mongenstern, *International Financial Transactions. Monetary Gold Stock*: For the United States: P. Cagan, *Determinants and Effects of Changes in the Stock of Money* (New York, 1965). For Great Britain: M. D. Bordo, "The U.K. Money Supply," *Research in Economic History*, 6 (1981), pp. 107-25, and D. K. Sheppard, *The Growth and Role of U.K. Financial Institutions, 1880-1962* (London, 1962). For Germany: R. Tilly, "Zeitreihen zum Geldumlauf." For Canada: G. Rich, *The Cross of Gold: Money and the Canadian Cycle* (Ottawa, forthcoming), and R. A. Shearer, personal correspondence.

also weak. According to McGouldrick, this reflects the deliberate policy of the Reichsbank to shield the domestic money market from external influence."  For Canada, the few available observations suggest that the association is positive and quite strong. During this period, Canada did not have a central bank, and except for the interwar operation of the Finance Act did not engage in extensive intervention."

Such evidence, though rough, shows linkages between the money supplies of the different countries through gold flows and high-powered money, and agrees with Huffman and Lothian."

Finally, Table 4 distinguishes periods of fixed and flexible exchange rates. There are too few degrees of freedom to make other than very casual comparisons. The two significant periods of floating are 1862-78 for the United States and the early 1920s for all other countries. These provide some basis for comparing the insulating properties of fixed and flexible rates. Thus, for example, both the interest differential and stock price index cycles for the United States were more out of phase with those of the European countries in the 1873-79 contraction than in the rest of the period, and the U.S. contraction was then considerably milder than its European counterpart. However, the United States was affected by various European crises. Similarly in the 1920s, when France and Germany floated over much of the period, there were more business cycles in France and fewer in Germany than in other countries (Table 2). Moreover, in 1926 France experienced a major financial crisis that was not transmitted abroad.

A final piece of evidence consistent with the Kindleberger-Minsky view of transmission concerns the behavior of the deposit reserve ratio (Table 3) and the incidence of stock market crises (Table 1). In Great Britain, Germany, Canada, and Sweden, declines in the deposit-reserve ratio were key determinants of cyclical contractions in the money supply, and such contractions often occurred at the same time as stock market crises. This apparent association between declines in the $D/R$ ratio and the incidence of stock market crises suggests a possible additional channel whereby financial crises link money supplies between countries. The evidence indicates a link between turning points in money growth and stock price indexes (seen for the U.S. monthly data in a comparison of Tables 2 and 4)." The link may reflect early signs of the effects of changes in money growth on real economic activity. In combination with the evidence on the deposit-reserve ratio, the link suggests the following hypothetical scenario:

72                               Michael D. Bordo

A sharp decline in the money stock in one country (for example, the United States), produced initially by, say, a gold outflow,
leads to a sharp decline in stock prices (a "crash"). In the absence
of intervention, the stock market crash could in turn produce
both a liquidity crisis and a banking panic, resulting in declines in
the deposit-currency and deposit-reserve ratios. Concurrently,
given the tight linkage between stock exchanges in different
centers shown by Morgenstern (for example, through a decline in
the prices of U.S. securities traded in foreign markets), the
decline in securities prices of the initiating country are transmitted to the stock markets of other countries.[60] The decline in
securities prices in these countries could impact quickly on commercial banks that have extended call loans and brokers' loans to
the stock market and attempt to strengthen their liquidity by
calling these loans and thus reducing the loan-earning asset ratio.
At the same time the commercial banks increase their precautionary reserves, lowering the deposit-reserve ratio.

In other words, arbitrage in stock market securities may link
national money supplies directly through their effects on commercial bank reserve ratios. Such effects may occur before the
monetary shock has had time to spread its influence abroad
through the traditional price-specie flow mechanism.[61] Such a
link is inconsistent with the simple price-specie flow mechanism,
but perfectly compatible with a broader monetarist perspective
that stresses money supply linkages regardless of the channels.

Table 4 suggests that money flows adjust as indicated by the
monetarist approach, and that severe stock market crises occur
nearly simultaneously before severe economic contractions, as indicated by Kindleberger and Minsky. An alternative explanation
of this pattern may be derived from recent developments in the
theory of rational expectations.[62] If countries are linked by the
gold standard, and "news" that leads people to predict future
severe downturns throughout the world reaches the stock
markets in different countries almost simultaneously, then the
evidence may well be consistent with the monetarist scenario plus
efficient markets that predict the future.

### 4. *Conclusion*

This paper has examined two main theoretical approaches to
financial crises. Both receive a measure of support from the
historical evidence on the relationship of financial crises to the
money supply, the financial system, and real activity in six coun-

tries over the period 1870-1933. The evidence, though highly suggestive, yields the following conclusions.

The first is the important role of monetary institutions, particularly the banking system, in explaining why some countries had more serious monetary and real contractions in the face of crises. The absence of a nationwide branch banking system in the United States, and the less effective role played by the U.S. monetary authorities in acting as a lender of last resort, may explain why the United States experienced banking panics in a period when they were a historical curiosity in other countries.

The second is the difficulty in distinguishing between the monetarist approach and Minsky-Kindleberger approach to the international transmission of financial crises. The evidence is consistent with aspects of both theories. One possible reconciliation is an apparent connection in all the countries examined between crises in the stock market and a decline in the commercial banking system's deposit-reserve ratio. Such a relationship may provide a link between the money supplies of different countries in addition to the traditional linkages through gold flows and the balance of payments. Further research might thus use monthly data and time series analysis to examine the timing of the relationship between different international monetary linkages—between the stock market and other asset markets and commercial bank portfolios, on the one hand, and between gold and international reserve flows and the monetary base, on the other. Alternatively, the data may reflect the efficient transmission of "news" which allows asset markets to react before the monetary adjustment occurs.

What lessons does the record of financial crises from 1870 to 1933 have for the present-day situation? Key differences in institutional arrangements suggest that most of the factors conducive to financial crises, especially banking crises, and their international propagation have declined in importance.

First, the domestic banking systems of most major countries are more stable–less likely to be subject to runs and panics–than they were before 1933. This is especially true of the United States, following the adoption of the FDIC in 1934 and acknowledgment by the Federal Reserve System of its role as lender of last resort. Second, we no longer adhere to the fixed exchange rate gold standard which tended to transmit economic disturbances from country to country (although there is increasing evidence that flexible exchange rates may not insulate the economy as effectively as once believed).

74                          Michael D. Bordo

   This is not to say that financial crises can no longer occur; but
the likelihood of events such as the recent near-failure of the
Continental Illinois bank producing a worldwide series of financial crises (as often occurred before 1933) is much reduced.

[1] Indeed, in the last three years this interest has spawned three conference
volumes–C. P. Kindleberger and J. P. Laffargue, *Financial Crises: Theory,
History and Policy* (New York, 1982); P. Wachtel, ed., *Crises in the Economic and
Financial Structure* (Lexington, Massachusetts, 1982); F. Capie and G. E. Wood,
eds., *Financial Crises and the World Banking Systems* (London, 1985)–and a
number of important journal articles.

[2] A third recent approach is that of rational expectations, which views financial
crises as a consequence of rational behavior. According to this approach,
"manias" are viewed as examples of speculative bubbles (R. P. Flood, jr., and P.
M. Garber, "A Systematic Banking Collapse in a Perfect Foresight World,"
NBER working paper no. 691, 1981, and D. Blanchard and M. Watson, "Bubbles, Rational Expectations, and Financial Markets," in Wachtel, *Crises*); "runs
are defined as a speculative attack on an asset price fixing scheme" (P. Garber
and R. Flood, "Bubbles, Runs and Gold Monetization," in Wachtel, *Crises*); and
"panics" characterize a run whose timing was not perfectly foreseen (P. M.
Garber, "The Lender of Last Resort and the Run on the Savings and Loans,"
NBER working paper no. 823, 1981).

[3] M. Friedman and A. J. Schwartz, *A Monetary History of the United States 1867-
1960* (Princeton, 1963); P. Cagan, *Determinants and Effects of Changes in the
Stock of Money* (New York, 1965); A. J. Schwartz, "Real and Pseudo Financial
Crises," in Capie and Wood, *Financial Crises*.

[4] I. Fischer, *Booms and Depressions* (New York, 1932).

[5] See I. Fisher, "Are Booms and Depressions Transmitted Internationally
Through Monetary Standards?" *Bulletin of the International Statistical Institute*,
28 (1935), no. 1, pp. 1-29, and W. E. Huffman and J. R. Lothian, "U.S.-U.K.
Business Cycle Linkages Under the Gold Standard, 1834-1933," in M. D. Bordo
and A. J. Schwartz, eds., *A Retrospective on the Classical Gold Standard, 1821-
1931* (Chicago, 1984).

[6] Friedman and Schwartz, *A Monetary History*; Cagan, *Determinants*.

[7] B. S. Bernanke, "Non-Monetary Effects of the Financial Crisis in the Propagation of the Great Depression," *American Economic Review*, 73 (June 1983), pp.
257-76, and D. W. Diamond and P. H. Dybvig, "Bank Runs, Deposit Insurance
and Liquidity," *Journal of Political Economy*, 91 (June 1983), pp. 401-19, argue
that financial crises including bankruptcies have direct effects on economic activity over and above their effects on the money supply. To the extent that
financial crises produce losses in the financial sector of the economy, this raises
the cost of financial intermediation and hence reduces the efficiency of resource
allocation.

[8] Friedman and Schwartz, *A Monetary History*, p. 677.

[9] Ibid., pp. 441-42.

[10] Ibid., p. 110.

[11] See E. U. Choudhri and L. A. Kochin, "The Exchange Rate and the Interna-
tional Transmission of Business Cycle Disturbances: Some Evidence from the
Great Depression," *Journal of Money, Credit and Banking*, 12 (Nov. 1980), pp.
565-74, for evidence of the insulating properties of flexible exchange rates in the
Spanish case, and L. Jonung, "The Depression in Sweden and the United States:
A Comparison of Causes and Policies," in K. Brunner, ed., *The Great Depression
Revisited* (Boston, 1981), for the case of Sweden.

[12] Cagan, *Determinants*.

[13] According to G. Gorton, "Banking Panics and Business Cycles" (Wharton School, mimeo, 1985), banking panics are not a unique event but represent a rational response by depositors wishing to smooth out their consumption flows over time. Rational depositors wish to dissave in periods of expected low consumption, such as business cycle troughs; however, since the likelihood of suspensions of convertibility would also be highest at the trough, depositors will rush to convert their deposits to currency when they expect a trough to occur.

[14] Cagan, *Determinants*, pp. 226-27.

[15] Huffman and Lothian, "U.S.-U.K. Business Cycle Linkages."

[16] Fisher, *Booms and Depressions*, and I. Fisher, "The Debt Deflation Theory of Great Depressions," *Econometrica*, 1 (1933), pp. 337-57.

[17] Fisher, "The Debt Deflation Theory," p. 341.

[18] Fisher, *Booms and Depressions*, p. 9.

[19] See Fisher, "Are Booms and Depressions Transmitted," for evidence on the transmission of economic disturbances in the Great Depression.

[20] See the following, all by H. P. Minsky: "Central Banking and Money Market Changes," *Quarterly Journal of Economics*, 71 (1957), pp. 175-87; "Comment on Friedman and Schwartz's 'Money and Business Cycles'," *Review of Economics and Statistics*, 45 (1963); "A Theory of Systemic Fragility," in E. J. Altman and A. W. Sametz, eds., *Financial Crises: Institutions and Market in a Fragile Environment* (New York, 1977), pp. 138-52; "Financial Interrelations, the Balance of Payment and the Dollar Crisis," in J. Aron, ed., *Debt and the Less Developed Countries* (Boulder, Colorado, 1979); "Finance and Profits: The Changing Nature of Business Cycles," *Joint Economic Committee of the United States Congress, The Business Cycle and Public Policy, 1929-1980* (Washington, D.C., 1980); "Debt Deflation Processes in Today's Institutional Environment," *Banca Nazionale del Lavoro Quarterly Review*, 35 (Dec. 1982), pp. 375-93; "Financial Innovations and Financial Instability: Observations and Theory," *Seventh Annual Policy Conference of the Federal Reserve Bank of St. Louis* (St. Louis, Missouri, 1982); and "The Potential for Financial Crises" (Washington University, St. Louis, working paper no. 46, 1982).

[21] Minsky, "A Theory of Systemic Fragility."

[22] Ibid., p. 143.

[23] Minsky, "Central Banking."

[24] Minsky, "Debt Deflation Processes."

[25] Ibid.

[26] Minsky, "Financial Interrelations." Minsky's thesis has been criticized by A. Sinai, "Comment" in Altman and Sametz, *Financial Crises*, for not yielding any testable hypotheses, and by R. W. Goldsmith, "Comment on H. P. Minsky, 'The Financial Instability Hypothesis'," in Kindleberger and Laffargue, *Financial Crises*, on the grounds that the evidence of history is against a key implication of Minsky's view–that financial development and financial fragility are positively correlated. J. Melitz, "Comments on Minsky," in Kindleberger and Laffargue, *Financial Crises*, argues that Minsky's thesis is inconsistent with evidence on the behavior of the term structure of interest rates and the experience of countries with universal lenders of last resort, such as Sweden. Finally, J. Fleming, "Comments on Minsky," in Kindleberger and Laffargue, *Financial Crises*, argues that one implication of Minsky's thesis–that the boom lulls economic agents into taking a risky financial position conducive to a crisis–leads to the implausible suggestion that central banks should increase the amount of risk in the economic system.

[27] C. P. Kindleberger, *Manias, Panics, and Crashes: A History of Financial Crises* (New York, 1978).

[28] Ibid., p. 5.

[29] Ibid., p. 119.

[30] Ibid.

[31] In his discussion of the 1873, 1920-21 and 1931 crises, Kindleberger argues that the crises could have been aborted by the effective operation of a supernational monetary authority. See Kindleberger, *Manias*, and *The World in Depression 1929-1939* (Berkeley, 1973). However, D. E. Moggridge, "Policy in the Crises of 1920 and 1929," in Kindleberger and Laffargue, *Financial Crises*, effectively argues that in 1920-21 there was no crisis and hence no need for the lender of last resort, and that in 1931, though there was a considerable amount of international cooperation, the fundamental disequilibrium of the international monetary system could not have been alleviated by an international lender of last resort.

[32] For example, the second cycle for Great Britain has a peak in 1883 and a trough in 1886; the comparable cycle for the United States has a peak in 1882 and a trough in 1885.

[33] On financial crises, see Kindleberger, *Manias*. Also included are a number of extra "financial crises" based on W. Thorp, *Business Annals* (New York, 1926); L. Yeager, *International Monetary Relations: Theory, History, and Policy* (2nd ed., New York, 1976); and others. This demarcation of crises begs the question of whether all these events really were crises; on this point, see Schwartz, "Real and Pseudo Financial Crises." On stock market crises, see O. Morgenstern, *International Financial Transactions and Business Cycles* (New York, 1959). On banking crises, see Thorp, *Business Annals*, and Friedman and Schwartz, *A Monetary History*.

[34] A. F. Burns and W. C. Mitchell, *Measuring Business Cycles* (New York, 1946).

[35] For example, in the third cycle Great Britain has a peak in 1890, a trough in 1894; the comparable "common" U.S. cycle is designated as having a peak in 1890 and a trough in 1894. This dating involved combining for the United States three NBER reference cycles designated here as subcycles, taking the peak from the second NBER reference cycle and the trough from the third.

[36] The use of the common international cycle is purely descriptive, to facilitate international comparisons; much of the discussion for each country taken in isolation is based on the NBER reference cycle chronology.

[37] M. Friedman and A. J. Schwartz, "Money and Business Cycles," *Review of Economics and Statistics*, 45 (1963), no. 1, Part 2 / Supplement.

[38] The observed lead from the turning points in money growth to the reference cycle for the United States has been widely cited as an important piece of evidence for "causality" from money to business. See Friedman and Schwartz, "Money and Business Cycles"; W. Poole, "The Relationship of Monetary Decelerations to Business Cycle Peaks: Another Look at the Evidence," *Journal of Finance*, 30 (June 1975), pp. 698-712. For an opposing view, see J. Tobin, "Money and Income: Post Hoc Ergo Propter Hoc," *Quarterly Journal of Economics*, 84 (1970), and M. Friedman, "Comment on Tobin," *Quarterly Journal of Economics*, 84 (1970). Recent advances in the methodology of testing "for causality" confirm Friedman and Schwartz's evidence for a U.S. monetary cycle (the traditional quantity theory approach); see C. Sims, "Money, Income, and Causality," *American Economic Review*, 62 (Sept. 1972), pp. 540-52. The case is mixed for other countries. T. C. Mills and G. E. Wood, "Money Income Relationships and the Exchange Rate Regime," *Federal Reserve Bank of St. Louis Review*, 60 (Aug. 1978), pp. 22-27, and D. Williams, C. A. E. Goodhart, and D. H. Gowland, "Money, Income and Causality: The U.K. Experience," *American Economic Review*, 66 (June 1976), pp. 417-23, provide evidence for the United Kingdom of "causality" running from business to money in both the gold standard and subsequent Bretton Woods eras. These authors explain reverse causality by arguing that under fixed exchange rates the United Kingdom operated as a small open economy, according to the monetary approach to the balance of payments, with changes in its money supply through reserve flows caused by changes in money demand which in turn reflect changes in economic activity. This is compared to the United States, which in the same period is viewed essentially as a closed economy in which changes in the money supply interact with a stable money demand to produce changes in activity according to the traditional quan-

tity theory approach. However, A. Cassese and J. R. Lothian, "The Timing of Monetary and Price Changes and the International Transmission of Inflation," *Journal of Monetary Economics*, 10 (1982), pp. 1-23, present convincing evidence for a number of countries under fixed exchange rates consistent both with a dynamic stock adjustment version of the monetary approach to the balance of payments and with a monetary theory of the cycle.

[39] Friedman and Schwartz, *A Monetary History*; Cagan, *Determinants*. The arithmetic of the proximate determinants is derived in Friedman and Schwartz, *A Monetary History*, Appendix B. It is based on the equation $M^s = H \cdot (D/R (1 + D/C) / (D/R + D/C))$, where $M^s$ stands for the money supply, $D$ for deposits held by the public in commercial banks, $R$ for reserves in commercial banks, $C$ for currency held by the public. $H$ is determined by the behavior of the monetary authorities and the balance of payments, $D/R$ by the banking system, and $D/C$ by the nonbank public. Table 3 calculates what the percentage change in $M^s$ would be if each determinant held in isolation had changed.

[40] Cagan, *Determinants*.

[41] For the 16 reference cycles displayed here, the relative contributions of the determinants to cyclical contractions were: $H$, 67.6; $D/R$, 3.9; and $D/C$, 30.1. For the six severe cycles, it was $H$, 38.7; $D/R$, 16.2; and $D/C$, 47.6.

[42] Over the 12 British cycles the relative contributions of the determinants to cyclical contractions were $H$, 79.3; $D/C$, 18.9; and $D/R$, 9.1. For severe contractions, they were $H$, 109.0; $D/R$, 19.7; and $D/C$, -28.7.

[43] The commercial banks' loan-earning asset ratio, which in periods of financial stringency reflects the banks' desire for liquidity, declined in both Great Britain and the United States–countries for which data are available–during severe cycles characterized by crises. See M. D. Bordo, "Some Historical Evidence 1870-1933 on the Impact and Transmission of Financial Crises" (NBER working paper no. 160, April 1985).

[44] See P. McGouldrick, "Operations of the German Central Bank and the Rules of the Game, 1879-1923," in Bordo and Schwartz, *A Retrospective*.

[45] K. A. J. Hay, "Determinants of the Canadian Money Supply" (Carleton University, mimeo, 1968), and L. Jonung, "Sources of Growth in the Swedish Money Stock, 1871-1981," *Scandinavian Journal of Economics*, 78 (1976), pp. 611-27.

[46] In the gold standard period, the Canadian chartered banks kept a large proportion of their gold reserves in the New York and (to a lesser extent) London money markets. These outside reserves provided a direct link between financial conditions in these countries and Canada through the $D/R$ ratio. See Hay, "Determinants"; K. A. J. Hay, "Money and Cycles in Post-Confederation Canada," *Journal of Political Economy*, 75 (1967), pp. 263-73; and G. Rich, "Canada Without a Central Bank: Operation of the Price-Specie Flow Mechanism, 1872-1913," in Bordo and Schwartz, *A Retrospective*.

[47] For the Scottish banking experience see R. Cameron, *Banking in the Early Stages of Industrialization* (New York, 1967), and L. H. White, *Free Banking in Britain: Theory, Experience and Debate, 1800-1845* (New York, 1984). For Canada, see A. B. Jamieson, *Chartered Banking in Canada* (Toronto, 1959). For Sweden, see L. Jonung, "The Legal Framework and the Economics of Private Bank Notes in Sweden, 1831-1902," in G. Skogh, ed., *Law and Economics* (Lund, 1977). For a comparison between the U.S. and Canadian experiences, see E. N. White, *The Regulation and Reform of the American Banking System, 1900-1929* (Princeton, 1983).

[48] See for example R. S. Sayers, *Central Banking After Bagehot* (Oxford, 1957).

[49] See R. S. Sayers, *Bank of England Operations, 1890-1914* (London, 1936), and L. S. Presnell, "Gold Reserves, Banking Reserves, and the Baring Crisis of 1890," in C. R. Whittlesey and J. S. G. Wilson, eds., *Essays in Money and Banking in Honour of R. S. Sayers* (Oxford, 1968).

[50] This was done by quickly arranging mergers between sound banks and failing banks, by encouraging cooperation between strong and weak banks in times of

stringency, and by establishing a reserve fund to be used to compensate deposit holders in the event of failure. Friedman and Schwartz, *A Monetary History*, argue that the New York Clearing House performed a somewhat similar role in stemming incipient crises before 1914 by issuing clearing house certificates and by arranging for syndicates of strong banks to assist those in trouble. As Schwartz, "Real and Pseudo Financial Crises," argues, in most cases the system worked; but in two important exceptions, 1893 and 1907, it did not. These may be explained, she argues, by bad timing of relief in 1907 and public misinformation in 1893.

[51] See Schwartz, "Real and Pseudo Financial Crises."

[52] As discussed in detail in Morgenstern, *International Financial Transactions*.

[53] P. H. Lindert, *Key Currencies and Gold, 1900-1913*, Princeton Studies in International Finance, no. 24 (Princeton, 1969).

[54] Morgenstern's indexes include many securities which today would be called bonds. A significant fraction of the securities in the samples underlying the indexes for the European exchanges were foreign securities (both government and private). See Morgenstern, *International Financial Transactions*, pp. 507-28, for an extensive discussion of the several direct linkages between stock exchanges in the gold standard era.

[55] A. I. Bloomfield, *Monetary Policy Under the International and Gold Standard* (New York, 1959).

[56] McGouldrick, "Operations of the German Central Bank."

[57] R. A. Shearer and C. Clark, "Canada and the Interwar Gold Standard, 1920-1935: Monetary Policy Without a Central Bank," in Bordo and Schwartz, *A Retrospective*.

[58] Huffman and Lothian, "U.S.-U.K. Business Cycle Linkages." Additional evidence is provided by significant correlations between five successive pairs of countries, in periods characterized by severe cyclical declines in economic activity, of the year-to-year rates of change of high-powered money. The correlations are: United States–Great Britain, .45; United States–Germany, .53; United States–Sweden, .49; and Germany–Sweden, .79.

[59] See B. W. Sprinkel, *Money and Markets: A Monetarist View* (Chicago, 1971).

[60] Morgenstern, *International Financial Transactions*. As mentioned in note 54 above, the fact that many components of Morgenstern's stock price index would today be considered internationally traded bonds, as well as other special features of pre-1914 stock exchanges, may explain why stock exchanges appear to be more closely linked between countries 70 years ago than they are today.

[61] Or even possibly before raising short-term interest rates and causing short-term capital to flow. This would be consistent with Morgenstern's finding that peaks in the short-term interest rates cycle tended to follow peaks in business whenever the stock market index would precede it.

[62] See for example J. Frenkel, "Flexible Exchange Rates, Prices and the Role of 'News': Lessons from the 1970s," *Journal of Political Economy*, 89 (1981), pp. 665-705.

# [8]

Excerpt from *Threats to International Financial Stability*, 10–58

# 1    The anatomy of financial crises

BARRY EICHENGREEN and
RICHARD PORTES*

Much as the study of disease is one of the most effective ways to learn about human biology, the study of financial crises provides one of the most revealing perspectives on the functioning of monetary economies. Indeed, epidemiological metaphors like fever and contagion feature prominently in the literature on financial crises. Financial crises, like contagious disease, threaten not only the host organism, namely the financial market, but the entire economic environment in which that host resides.

There exists a voluminous historical literature concerned with episodes labelled financial crises.[1] Yet the usefulness of much of this literature is limited by the absence of any definition of the phenomenon under consideration and hence of a minimal structure around which historical observation can be organized.[2] This criticism is not limited to the historical literature, since recent theoretical analyses of financial crises are uniformly deficient in this same regard. While no single definition may be appropriate to all purposes, any work on financial crises should proceed on the basis of an explicit statement of meaning. Since our purpose in this chapter is to provide a perspective on the present and prospective danger of a serious disruption to the global financial system, which we propose to explore by comparing the last full-fledged financial crisis – that of the 1930s – with conditions prevailing today, we adopt the following definition. A financial crisis is a disturbance to financial markets, associated typically with falling asset prices and insolvency among debtors and intermediaries, which ramifies through the financial system, disrupting the market's capacity to allocate capital within the economy. In an international financial crisis, disturbances spill over national borders, disrupting the market's capacity to allocate capital internationally.

This definition suggests an agenda for research, of which the following

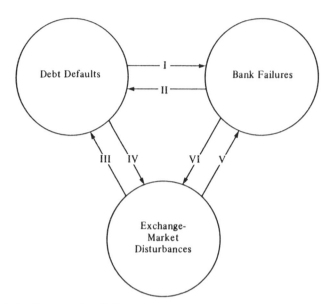

**Figure 1.1   Asset-market linkages**

questions form only a part. What are the distinguishing features of
disturbances which give rise to financial crises? Rather than the nature of
the disturbances, is it the financial system's response that differentiates
crises from perturbations to financial markets? What is the mechanism
through which a disturbance specific to a single market is generalized to
the entire system? In particular, what are the roles of asset prices and
solvency problems in the process of generalization and propagation?
How are the market's allocative capacities disrupted, and what are the
implications of this disruption for the course of the crisis itself?

Our definition implies a distinction between generalized financial crisis
on the one hand and bank failures, debt defaults and foreign-exchange
market disturbances on the other. This distinction is the presence of
linkages, which are represented schematically in Figure 1.1. These
linkages within the body economic give the essential anatomy of financial
crisis.

Consider two examples which play a leading role in our historical
analysis. Defaults on sovereign bonds, if sufficiently widespread and
disruptive, impede the ability of the bond market to allocate capital
across countries. But if these defaults are not accompanied by bank
failures (if in Figure 1.1 the linkage labelled 'I' is interrupted), there may

exist alternative channels, notably bank loans, through which the capital market's allocative functions may be carried out. Debt default need not give rise to financial crisis. But if, on the contrary, debt default heightens the commercial banks' susceptibility to failure, the danger of a generalized crisis is intensified. To take another example, an anticipated devaluation may threaten the banking system if depositors liquidate their accounts in an effort to avoid capital losses on their overseas assets (an example of the linkage labelled 'V'); but if they hold government securities instead, this linkage is broken and exchange-market difficulties need not be associated with financial collapse. Clearly, the extent and speed of transmission along these linkages depend on institutional arrangements in financial markets, including any institutionalized responses of policy-makers.

In this paper, we focus on the generalization and propagation of financial crises in an international setting. Ideally, these issues of generalization and propagation are studied historically: while all serious disturbances threaten the stability of financial institutions, it is only from the comparison of historical episodes during which different institutional arrangements prevailed that generalizations about the fragility or resilience of monetary economies can be derived. By analyzing the contrasting institutional arrangements of the 1930s and 1980s, we hope to identify configurations which render the international financial system particularly susceptible to collapse.

Our analysis of the generalization of financial disturbances underscores the critical role played by institutional arrangements in financial markets as a determinant of the system's vulnerability to destabilizing shocks. In both the 1930s and 1980s, the institutional environment was drastically altered by rapid change in foreign exchange markets, in international capital markets, and in the structure of domestic banking systems. But the implications of institutional changes have not all been similar. In the earlier period, they generally worked in the direction of heightening the system's vulnerability to shocks; recently, however, some have tended to work in the opposite direction. Our review of the course of crises suggests that the banking system and the linkages by which it is connected to the rest of the financial sector play a pivotal role in the propagation of crises. Our analyses highlight the importance of two sets of factors in the process of propagation: asset-market linkages running from debt defaults and exchange-market disturbances to the stability of the banking system (linkages I and V in Figure 1.1), and the role of economic policy in blocking these linkages and thereby insulating the banking system and the macroeconomy from threats to their stability.

## I   The international financial crisis of the 1930s

### A.   *The environment*

The 1920s were marked by three sets of developments which increased the international financial system's susceptibility to destabilizing shocks: flux in the foreign exchange market, rapid institutional change in the banking system, and dramatic shifts in the volume and direction of international lending. Each set of developments had its immediate origins in the dislocations associated with World War I.

*Foreign exchange markets*   The war and its aftermath marked the end of the classical gold standard. Most countries initially succeeded in maintaining their gold reserves and customary exchange rates by withdrawing gold coin from circulation and embargoing bullion shipments. But as hostilities dragged on and were financed through the issue of money and bonds, pressure mounted in foreign exchange markets. The German and Austrian exchanges collapsed by 1918. The British and French rates were propped up by American intervention but depreciated with the termination of support in 1919.[3] The postwar inflationary boom, the reparations tangle and deficit finance of reconstruction all wreaked havoc with national efforts to peg the domestic-currency price of gold.

Policymakers then confronted the question of the appropriate level at which to stabilize exchange rates. The history of subsequent efforts to reconstruct the system of fixed parities is familiar: Britain restored sterling's prewar parity in 1925 following a period of deflation; France opted against reversing half a decade of inflation, pegging the franc price of gold at five times the prewar level; Germany and other countries experiencing hyperinflation established new currency units; and Latin American countries reestablished gold standard parities in conjunction with budgetary reforms and newly independent central banks.[4]

The characteristics of the reconstructed gold standard added to the strains on the financial system. Paramount was the problem of misalignment, starting with the pound sterling, the traditional linchpin of the monetary mechanism. Due to high wages and to changes in the direction of trade, Britain's restoration of the prewar parity rendered the pound overvalued and difficult to defend with the Bank of England's slender reserves. Keynes (1925) estimated sterling's overvaluation at 10–15 per cent. In conventional accounts, an undervalued French franc figures also among the misaligned currencies.[5] Misalignment was related to the problem of maldistributed gold reserves, which came to be concentrated in the United States and France. This maldistribution gave rise elsewhere

14   **Barry Eichengreen and Richard Portes**

to complaints of a 'gold shortage', which induced countries to expand on prewar practice and supplement gold reserves with foreign deposits. The growth of foreign deposits rendered the reserve currencies increasingly vulnerable to destabilizing shocks.[6] Each of these difficulties reflected the failure of governments to coordinate their choice of exchange rates and to harmonize their monetary policies. Ultimately, the consequences of this failure would be far-reaching.[7]

*International lending*   The impact of the war on patterns of international lending and borrowing was equally profound.[8] The 1920s marked the rise of the United States and decline of Britain as external creditors. The transfer of business from London to New York, initiated by wartime closure of the London market to foreign borrowers and by the Liberty Loan campaign in the United States, was reinforced following the conclusion of hostilities by informal capital controls in the UK and abundant savings in the US. Before the war, Britain's foreign assets roughly matched the combined total of the remaining creditor countries, while the US was a creditor of negligible importance. In the 1920s (with the exception of 1923, when transfers to Europe were depressed by the Ruhr invasion), lending by the US, especially to countries outside the British Empire, consistently exceeded that by Britain.

The other side of this coin was rapidly mounting indebtedness in Central Europe and Latin America. Loans to Europe were used to finance the reconstruction of industry and infrastructure, the purchase of imported inputs and the provision of working capital. At the same time, the growth of lending can be understood as a response to the need to recycle German reparations in much the same way that OPEC investment in the US, in conjunction with US lending to LDCs, recycled oil revenues in the 1970s.[9] Loans to Latin America, in contrast, reflected favourable publicity and growing awareness of economic prospects in developing regions.[10] Table 1.1 summarizes the direction of US and British lending. American lending was widely distributed, going most heavily to Europe (where Germany was the leading debtor in absolute terms) and then to Latin America and Canada; British lending was directed predominantly towards the Empire, especially at the end of the decade.

Then, as recently, there was much discussion of the soundness of foreign loans, embellished by tales of loan pushing, excessive commissions, corrupt administration, and squandering of funds. Indeed, placing much of the business in relatively inexperienced American hands may have increased the market's tendency to fund risky projects.[11] It is important to note, therefore, that the macroeconomic performance of

Table 1.1. **US and British lending in the 1920s**

| | US lending abroad by region (millions of dollars) | | | |
|---|---|---|---|---|
| | Europe | Canada | Latin America | Far East |
| 1924 | 526.6 | 151.6 | 187.0 | 96.1 |
| 1925 | 629.5 | 137.1 | 158.8 | 141.7 |
| 1926 | 484.0 | 226.3 | 368.2 | 31.7 |
| 1927 | 557.3 | 236.4 | 339.7 | 151.2 |
| 1928 | 597.9 | 184.9 | 330.1 | 130.8 |
| 1929 | 142.0 | 289.7 | 175.0 | 51.5 |

| | British investment in government and municipal securities (millions of pounds) | |
|---|---|---|
| | Foreign | Dominion and Colonial |
| 1926 | 392.0 | 676.5 |
| 1927 | 406.7 | 703.3 |
| 1928 | 364.5 | 1036.0 |
| 1929 | 351.0 | 1061.6 |

*Sources:* For the US, Department of Commerce (1930); for Britain, Royal Institute of International Affairs (1937).

the debtors, and the consequent growth in their ability to service external debt, was more than respectable, and in the Latin American case rather impressive, during this period of large-scale foreign lending (1925–9). With the exception of Costa Rica and El Salvador, real GDP in those Latin American countries considered in Table 1.2 increased at then historically unprecedented rates in excess of five per cent per annum. Except for Brazil, Guatemala and (to a lesser extent) Costa Rica, the same is true of exports, despite a persistent decline in the prices of primary products. Initially, the ratio of debt service to exports (excluding reparations) remained manageable.[12]

Thus, in the 1920s as in the 1970s, foreign lending was associated with expanding trade and rosy prospects, at least in the short run, for economic growth in the borrowing regions. Whether the loans were sound in the sense that export receipts would prove adequate to service them is essentially the question whether it was realistic to assume that the growth rates and financial stability (e.g., absence of real interest rate

16   Barry Eichengreen and Richard Portes

Table 1.2.  **Annual growth rates of real GDP, industrial production and exports 1925–9, and debt/export ratio, 1929**

(in percentage points)

|  | GDP | Industrial production | Exports in US dollars | 1929 Central govt foreign debt as percent of exports |
|---|---|---|---|---|
| Germany | 1.7 | 5.0 | 9.9 | 6.6 |
| Austria | 2.7 | 6.3 | 4.0 | 77.5 |
| Hungary | 7.1 | −0.4*a* | 5.9 | 123.2 |
| Australia | −0.4 | 4.1 | −3.8 | 112.5 |
| Canada | 6.3*a* | 8.8 | −1.1 | 46.2 |
| Argentina | 5.7 | 5.2 | 4.8 | 41.8 |
| Brazil | 7.2 | 4.6 | −1.6 | 66.3 |
| Costa Rica | 0.2 | 1.6 | 3.1 | 95.4 |
| Chile | 10.8 | 0.0 | 5.8 | 101.7 |
| Colombia | 7.5 | 4.5 | 11.6 | 55.7 |
| Honduras | 5.6 | 6.8 | 20.2 | 43.3 |
| El Salvador | 1.7 | 5.9 | 12.4 | 105.4 |
| Guatemala | 5.5 | 3.0 | −3.4 | 54.0 |

*Note:* European figures exclude reparations. *a* indicates 1926–9. For Australia, industrial production is proxied by manufacturing production at constant prices. *Sources:* Latin American figures computed from Thorp (1984), Appendix Table 4. European figures computed from Mitchell (1976). Canadian figures computed from Urquhart and Buckley (1965). Australian figures computed from Butlin (1984).

shocks) of the 1920s would persist. The answer is surely more obvious with hindsight than it was at the time.

*Banking structure and regulation*   These changes in the direction of foreign lending were accompanied by equally profound developments in the structure and regulation of commercial banking. Following the lead of the United States, which had created the Federal Reserve System in 1914, in the 1920s many countries either established central banks or gave them added independence, in Latin America in conjunction with visits by US economic experts, in Central Europe as a condition of League of Nations stabilization loans.[13] One function of these central banks was to act as lender of last resort, although as we shall see there was considerable variation in the effectiveness with which they carried out this role. In a number of countries monetary reform was accompanied by new banking regulations patterned on the US model. In Chile, for example, a law of September 1925 established a 'Superintendencia de Bancos' charged with inspecting the books of banks and publishing a statement of their position annually. Banks were prohibited from extending individual loans in excess of ten per cent of the sum of paid-up capital and reserves and were required to observe minimum capital requirements which differed by city size and liability composition. Since there was considerable variation in the appropriateness of the US model, these reforms varied in their efficacy and implications for the stability of national banking systems.

A number of countries including Germany and Poland established publicly owned or controlled agricultural credit and mortgage banks which engaged in all forms of deposit and industrial banking and expanded rapidly.[14] Their implications for the stability of the financial system are not clear: on the one hand, public banks for political reasons sometimes extended loans to risky undertakings which did not attract private banks; on the other, the central authorities were particularly disinclined to let public enterprises fail.

A further feature of the development of banking structure in the 1920s was a pervasive amalgamation movement. While the immediate incentive for amalgamation was often savings on administrative costs, another advantage was the greater facility with which risk could be diversified and stability ensured through the dispersion of loans over different regions and sectors of the economy. Although present earlier, the amalgamation movement in commercial banking accelerated after World War I, spreading from England and Wales to Latin America, Hungary, Poland and Greece. In Germany and Czechoslovakia, large banks increasingly acquired control of their smaller counterparts, while in the US, restrictions on branch banking were circumvented through such mechanisms as the securities affiliate.

Along with the spread of the securities affiliate, financial innovation in the 1920s took the form of the adoption of 'investment' or 'industrial' banking on a national scale in the Succession States of what had been the Austro-Hungarian Empire. In English-speaking, Scandinavian and Latin American countries, intermediaries specialized in deposit banking, soliciting money on deposit and extending short-term advances to commerce and industry. The alternative of investment banking, which entailed long-term loans to industry, had traditionally prevailed in Central Europe. When the Succession States created new banking systems in the wake of World War I, they naturally emulated Austrian and German practice. Given the specialization of industry and agriculture in the newly partitioned Central European states, the fate of the

18   **Barry Eichengreen and Richard Portes**

Table 1.3.  **Business cycle indicators for advanced countries, 1929–38 and 1973–83**

|      | GDP   | Import volume | Terms of trade | Net capital outflow at 1929 prices $ million | World price level (US export unit values) |
|------|-------|---------------|----------------|----------------------------------------------|-------------------------------------------|
| 1929 | 100.0 | 100.0 | 100.0 | 355 | 100.0 |
| 1930 | 94.6  | 94.8  | 106.1 | −145 | 89.6 |
| 1931 | 89.3  | 89.5  | 111.8 | −1,422 | 69.4 |
| 1932 | 83.0  | 76.5  | 113.7 | −1,661 | 59.0 |
| 1933 | 84.0  | 78.4  | 114.8 | 1,006 | 61.9 |
| 1934 | 89.2  | 79.6  | 111.1 | −1,254 | 72.4 |
| 1935 | 94.3  | 81.8  | 108.0 | −406 | 74.6 |
| 1936 | 101.6 | 85.7  | 100.6 | −176 | 76.1 |
| 1937 | 107.0 | 97.4  | 103.9 | −1,677 | 80.6 |
| 1938 | 109.3 | 87.0  | 108.3 | −1,413 | 74.6 |
| 1973 | 100.0 | 100.0 | 100.0 | 8,919 | 100.0 |
| 1974 | 100.4 | 101.1 | 88.4  | 7,020 | 127.6 |
| 1975 | 99.8  | 92.7  | 90.3  | 12,507 | 142.6 |
| 1976 | 105.1 | 105.5 | 89.8  | 12,416 | 147.5 |
| 1977 | 109.1 | 109.5 | 88.7  | 13,429 | 152.7 |
| 1978 | 113.5 | 115.4 | 91.1  | 17,241 | 163.3 |
| 1979 | 117.3 | 124.0 | 87.3  | 16,265 | 185.9 |
| 1980 | 118.8 | 121.8 | 81.3  | 14,215 | 211.0 |
| 1981 | 120.4 | 118.4 | 80.2  | 15,792 | 230.4 |
| 1982 | 119.9 | 117.6 | 81.9  | 14,340 | 232.9 |
| 1983 | 122.8 | 122.0 | 83.4  | 11,702 | 236.5 |

*Notes:* GDP, import volume and terms of trade are weighted averages for 16 countries. The capital flows are deflated by the US export unit value index. The US export unit value in 1973 was 251 per cent of its 1929 level.
*Source:* Maddison (1985, p. 13).

banks' loan portfolios was tied to the fortunes of narrow industrial or agricultural markets. When a particular crop or industry was hit by the Depression, the shock to the banking system would prove severe.

*B.   The crisis and its management*

Our analysis of the financial crisis of the 1930s highlights two factors: first, the singular importance of linkages running from debt defaults and exchange market disturbances to the instability of banking systems; second, the critical role of policy in interrupting these linkages, thereby insulating the banking system and the macroeconomy from threats to their stability.

Table 1.4.  **Business cycle indicators for 11 developing countries, 1929–38 and 1973–83**

| | Latin America | | | | Asia | | | |
|---|---|---|---|---|---|---|---|---|
| | GDP | Export volume | Terms of trade | Import volume | GDP | Export volume | Terms to trade | Import volume |
| 1929 | 100.0 | 100.0 | 100.0 | 100.0 | 100.0 | 100.0 | 100.0 | 100.0 |
| 1930 | 96.1 | 81.2 | 81.5 | 77.4 | 101.1 | 91.3 | 90.4 | 89.5 |
| 1931 | 90.0 | 90.0 | 67.9 | 51.9 | 101.4 | 86.6 | 83.5 | 82.3 |
| 1932 | 86.7 | 73.0 | 71.4 | 39.5 | 103.8 | 77.7 | 84.2 | 78.5 |
| 1933 | 93.2 | 75.7 | 68.8 | 45.5 | 104.5 | 80.0 | 82.1 | 71.2 |
| 1934 | 101.0 | 85.4 | 76.5 | 52.5 | 99.4 | 82.6 | 86.6 | 76.7 |
| 1935 | 106.3 | 91.9 | 75.2 | 56.4 | 104.2 | 84.7 | 92.3 | 82.6 |
| 1936 | 113.4 | 93.3 | 80.6 | 61.7 | 109.9 | 94.1 | 94.9 | 81.0 |
| 1937 | 120.8 | 101.8 | 89.1 | 76.8 | 110.0 | n.a. | n.a. | n.a. |
| 1938 | 121.4 | (81.4) | (84.9) | (70.9) | 106.9 | n.a. | n.a. | n.a. |
| 1973 | 100.0 | 100.0 | 100.0 | 100.0 | 100.0 | 100.0 | 100.0 | 100.0 |
| 1974 | 106.7 | 100.4 | 95.8 | 126.4 | 101.6 | 101.7 | 97.5 | 109.1 |
| 1975 | 109.7 | 100.1 | 88.5 | 119.5 | 110.0 | 107.8 | 91.9 | 110.9 |
| 1976 | 116.0 | 112.1 | 94.1 | 112.0 | 110.2 | 132.0 | 97.0 | 121.9 |
| 1977 | 122.3 | 123.2 | 94.7 | 110.9 | 119.3 | 142.9 | 102.0 | 132.9 |
| 1978 | 127.3 | 141.2 | 87.9 | 121.2 | 131.7 | 163.6 | 97.7 | 157.5 |
| 1979 | 136.1 | 152.6 | 87.5 | 141.8 | 136.8 | 171.8 | 94.5 | 165.3 |
| 1980 | 143.9 | 167.7 | 92.1 | 169.7 | 145.2 | 189.6 | 91.2 | 176.3 |
| 1981 | 143.9 | 190.3 | 85.6 | 175.1 | 153.0 | 209.6 | 86.4 | 183.0 |
| 1982 | 142.3 | 194.0 | 83.1 | 132.3 | 161.6 | 220.4 | 81.2 | 176.5 |
| 1983 | 139.3 | 214.7 | 80.2 | 103.7 | 174.1 | 245.7 | 75.9 | 193.3 |

*Notes:* The above indices are all weighted averages. Latin America includes Argentina, Brazil, Chile, Colombia, Cuba and Mexico. Asia includes China, India, Indonesia, Korea and Taiwan.
*Source:* Maddison (1985, p. 14).

*Exchange market disturbances*   The first indication of serious financial distress was exchange-rate depreciation by primary producers starting in 1929. While misalignments within the North Atlantic community may have played some role in early exchange-market difficulties, the most disruptive pressures originated on the real side, notably in markets for agricultural commodities and primary products. So long as US import demands and foreign lending were maintained, these pressures remained tolerable. But in 1928–9 the indebted countries of Central Europe, Latin America and Oceania were subjected to dual shocks. First, the Wall Street boom both reflected and induced portfolio shifts by US investors, choking off American capital exports: after peaking in the summer of 1928, they fell by 46 per cent within a year (see Table 1.1). Next,

20   **Barry Eichengreen and Richard Portes**

commodity exports declined precipitously following the US cyclical downturn commencing in the summer of 1929 (see Table 1.3). Primary-producing countries were seriously affected (as shown in Table 1.4), since the US accounted for more than 40 per cent of the primary-product consumption of the 15 leading industrial countries.

The exchange rate and the external debt were directly linked through the government's reserve constraint. Gold and foreign-exchange reserves could be allocated either to debt service or to merchants and currency dealers who, under gold standard statutes, could demand gold for export. In principle, borrowing countries could have chosen to default on their external debts while defending the gold standard, to let their exchange rates go while maintaining debt service, or to default and depreciate simultaneously. Initially, they chose to sacrifice the exchange rate and honour the debt. One might speculate that policymakers viewed debt as even more sacrosanct than the gold standard, although that is doubtful in view of the frequency of default in the nineteenth century (matched only by the frequency of suspensions of convertibility). In fact, their motives were pragmatic: while default automatically precluded additional foreign borrowing, depreciation had less impact on credit-worthiness. It was even suggested that, insofar as depreciation stimu-lated exports, it might facilitate foreign bond flotations. Nevertheless, policymakers themselves saw depreciation as a threat to the national credit, albeit one less serious than default.

The pre-sterling depreciations were a Latin American and Antipodean phenomenon, starting with Uruguay in April 1929 and followed in rapid succession by Argentina, Paraguay, Brazil, Australia, New Zealand, Venezuela, Bolivia and Mexico. Australia's experience is especially revealing, since both default and devaluation were resisted so strongly.[15] The Australian economy was adversely affected by both declining wool and wheat prices and increasingly stringent London credit conditions. As early as the first semester of 1929, the Commonwealth Bank had been alarmed by the decline in its sterling balances and by its inability to float new loans in London. But despite the rising opportunity cost of debt service, little consideration was given to the option of default, in the hope that faithful maintenance of service might permit floating new loans in London. Instead, to curb imports the banks rationed foreign exchange and increased their rates against sterling while attempting to stay within the gold points. These expedients were viewed as temporary, and their reversal was anticipated as soon as new loans could be floated. The authorities obtained additional breathing space through the passage of legislation (patterned after the British Gold Standard and Currency and Bank Notes Acts of 1925 and 1928) which concentrated Australian gold holdings in the authorities' hands. Citizens were required to exchange gold for notes, and specie exports were discouraged by specifying a minimum quantity of gold (400 ounces fine) which could be obtained on demand. Hence there was additional scope for depreciation without destroying the gold standard facade.

To strengthen the trade balance and stave off depreciation, Australia adopted no fewer than seven new tariff schedules between April and December 1930. Exports were promoted by a 'Grow More Wheat Campaign' and by bounties or bonuses for wine-making and gold mining. Ultimately, these efforts proved inadequate due to deteriorating world market conditions and to resistance within Labour circles to further deflationary policies. When in December 1930 a political impasse over the budget deficit threatened to unleash a wave of capital flight, those in banking circles who viewed devaluation as damaging to Australian credit acceded to the others who insisted that devaluation would be acknowledged instead as a beneficial step 'towards recognition of the true state of affairs'.[16] In January the currency was depreciated substantially, at which point it held until sterling's devaluation the following September. The authorities continued to hope that additional borrowing on the London market might prove possible; hence little serious consideration was given to the alternative of default except by Labour heretics such as Jack Lang in New South Wales.

*Debt default*   Even after suspending convertibility, many countries found it difficult or impossible to maintain service on their external debt.[17] The debt crisis that followed fell into three phases.[18] The first, spanning calendar year 1931, is dominated by Latin American defaults. During the second, from January 1932 through June 1933, default spread to Southern and Eastern Europe. The third, whose opening coincided with the Monetary and Economic Conference of 1933, was dominated by Germany's reduction of service on its foreign debt.

Macroeconomic events, rather than disturbances limited to financial markets, played a leading role in the onset of the debt crisis. The Great Depression affected the ability of governments to generate both the tax revenues needed to service debt and the foreign exchange required to transfer revenues abroad. Plummeting economic activity and rising unemployment increased budgetary expenditures at the same time as revenues fell. The decline in export values and volumes led to a rapid contraction of foreign exchange earnings (see Table 1.4). In much the same manner that an isolated bank failure can be infectious given depositors' incomplete information about the solvency of other banks, defaults by a few countries caused investors to revise their expectations for continued debt service by others. International lending all but evaporated following Bolivia's January 1931 default, and with the collapse of lending, the incentive to keep debt service current was further reduced.[19]

The Latin American defaults that dominated the first phase of the crisis exhibited common features. Typically they resulted from the interaction of declining primary-commodity prices with government budget deficits (due both to expenditures on nonproductive projects and to the macroeconomic slump).[20] Debt crisis and domestic political instability interacted in a vicious circle: political instability hindered attempts to achieve fiscal reform, while the crisis environment and the draconian policies adopted to redress the debt and budget problems threatened to undermine the most stable of governments. Although Bolivia's default was in large part a function of a 40 per cent fall in the dollar price of tin, a long history of budgetary mismanagement culminating in the government's overthrow also played a role, as the British consul had recognised fully three months before default:

> The unlimited depredations on the State coffers by the late head of the country and his minions have left the country bled white, and there are no resources left on which to fall back. In fact there is every prospect that Bolivia will be obliged to default on her obligations in connection with foreign loans falling due in December.[21]

In Peru, as in Bolivia, the onset of the Depression exacerbated political unrest which culminated in revolution. While Peru's new government put a stop to what the British consul described as the previous administration's 'reckless squandering' of funds, it was still forced to halt debt service in March 1931 on the grounds that the Treasury was bare of funds.[22] Chile, which also experienced revolution and suffered greatly from the decline in nitrate and copper prices, defaulted four months later. Brazil, hit by a disastrous fall in coffee prices and similarly undergoing revolution, defaulted in October.

Default spread to Europe one year to the day after its appearance in Latin America. Compared with the Latin American republics, most Central and East European countries had suffered less from the collapse of primary-commodity prices (due to greater export diversification) and had pursued more austere budgetary policies. They were hesitant to interrupt service on the grounds that much of their debt had been arranged under League of Nations auspices. Nonetheless, Hungary's default in January 1932 was followed in rapid succession by those of Greece, Bulgaria and Yugoslavia.

The final phase of the crisis was ushered in by Germany's default. The German authorities had previously limited the transfer of funds to extinguish maturing loans but refrained from interfering with interest transfers. As in Latin America, default was associated with political upheaval. One of the first steps of the National Socialist Party upon taking power in 1933 was to convene a conference of bondholders' representatives with the intention of rescheduling the debt. Arrangements were made to transfer a share of accrued debt service into foreign currency, to issue scrip in place of the rest, and to convert maturing coupons into funding bonds. With few exceptions, the dollar obligations of German states, municipalities and corporations were brought under the control of the Reichsbank's Conversion Office.

Strikingly, debt default had limited repercussions in the foreign exchange market. The currencies of most defaulting Latin American countries had already depreciated, while the currencies of the major European debtors were under exchange control. Moreover, in contrast to the 1980s, the deterioration of long-term foreign assets posed no direct threat to the banking systems of the creditor countries. Links from debt default to bank failures were broken because foreign lending took place not through bank loans but through the issue of bonds, few of which were held by banks in the creditor countries. Banks might participate in the syndicate which organized the loan and serve as purchasers of last resort if the market failed to take up the entire issue. But even in such instances, banks could resell their share of the issue once bond-market conditions improved.

Commercial banks also purchased foreign bonds as investments, although information on the extent of this practice is sketchy and incomplete. For the United States, the Comptroller of the Currency provided only aggregated information on the foreign bond holdings of National Banks. According to these data, foreign bonds accounted for but a small share, on the order of 7.5 per cent, of the bond holdings of National Banks, and bonds for less than a third of total assets. The Comptroller provided no information which might be used to estimate what share of these foreign bonds were subject to default risk. But unlike the Comptroller, who listed foreign bonds only as a group, the Vermont Bank Commissioner in 1930 reported the book value of the individual foreign bonds held by each state-chartered bank and trust company.[23] Table 1.5 lists foreign government bonds held by mutual savings banks, trust companies and savings and loan associations in Vermont on 30 June 1930. *Ex post*, and perhaps also *ex ante* given the relatively small discounts from par, most of these bonds appear to have been subject to relatively little default risk. Of the 58 banks under the Commissioner's supervision, one closed its doors in 1930, but due to a bad domestic loan rather than foreign bonds, of which the bank in question in fact held

24   Barry Eichengreen and Richard Portes

Table 1.5.  **Foreign government bonds held by Vermont mutual savings banks and trust companies, 30 June 1930**

|  | Book value $000 |
|---|---|
| *National Debt* | |
| Dominion of Canada | 453 |
| Government of Argentina | 277 |
| Government of Newfoundland | 296 |
| Kingdom of Belgium | 1,083 |
| Kingdom of Denmark | 1,209 |
| Kingdom of Norway | 896 |
| Kingdom of Sweden | 4 |
| Republic of Chile | 751 |
| Republic of France | 54 |
| Republic of Uruguay | 437 |
| United Kingdom of Great Britain and Ireland | 159 |
| United Kingdom of Great Britain and Northern Ireland | 23 |
| *Provincial Debt* | |
| Province of Alberta | 317 |
| Province of British Columbia | 195 |
| Province of Manitoba | 69 |
| Province of New Brunswick | 20 |
| Province of Nova Scotia | 14 |
| Province of Ontario | 913 |
| Province of Quebec | 48 |
| Province of Saskatchewan | 245 |
| Miscellaneous Canadian bonds | 927 |

*Source:* State of Vermont (1930).

none. While foreign bonds accounted for a larger share of the portfolios of the banks of certain other states, it is hard to see how foreign defaults alone could have posed a serious threat to the US banking system. It is likely that the same conclusion holds for the UK and other creditor countries.

A more serious threat was posed by the liquidation of foreign bank deposits. The exception to the debtor-country rule of giving priority to debt over convertibility concerned the treatment of short-term credits. These credits typically originated in connection with commercial transactions. As the Depression deepened, not only did credits to finance international transactions become redundant, but financial uncertainty induced foreigners to convert them into domestic currency. Commercial banks in the indebted regions consequently experienced sudden withdrawals of foreign balances. Their governments responded with exchange control and prohibitions on the repatriation of short-term capital. For example, when in October 1931 Argentina experienced accelerating depreciation, it imposed exchange control and froze short-term liabilities, which were owed predominantly to British creditors. After nineteen months an agreement was reached with Britain, under the provisions of which a long-term loan was floated to provide funds to transfer the frozen accounts. What is noteworthy is that Argentina, at the same time as it faithfully maintained service on its long-term debt, did not hesitate to restrict foreign access to short-term liabilities. The difference is attributable to the higher costs of leaving short-term debt unfettered, given its volatility in response to changes in anticipated returns, and the greater benefits of leaving service on long-term debt uninterrupted in the hope that additional long-term borrowing might again prove possible for the creditworthy.[24]

### Short-term credits, bank failures and intervention

The preceding discussion has focused on links between exchange-rate convertibility and debt. A noteworthy aspect of Argentine experience is the absence of the next link in the chain, from debt and exchange rates to bank failures. While, as noted above, sovereign default was not a major source of instability of creditor-country banking systems, the same was not always true of debtor-country banks. Short-term debt was an important item on the liability side of many debtor-country-bank balance sheets, even if, due to their greater size, it represented a small item on the asset side of creditor-country-bank balance sheets.

In particular, foreign attempts to repatriate short-term credits in the summer of 1931 posed major threats to the solvency of the Austrian and German banking systems. Serious difficulties surfaced in Europe with the run on the Austrian Credit-Anstalt in May 1931. The problems of the Credit-Anstalt, while largely of domestic origin, were greatly complicated by its dependence on foreign credits. Austria had been the second European state (after Sweden) to stabilize its currency, and the early date of its stabilization in conjunction with League of Nations sponsorship promoted a sizeable inflow of foreign funds to the banking system. The Credit-Anstalt had participated fully in the amalgamation movement of the 1920s, absorbing the Bodenkreditanstalt and its portfolio of dubious industrial loans, and in 1929, when the market value of these loans declined precipitously, this amalgamation returned to haunt it.[25] Regulations forced the Credit-Anstalt to publish its 1930 balance sheet on 11 May 1931, revealing that it had lost more than half its capital, the criterion according to which it was officially declared insolvent. This announcement provoked large-scale withdrawals by domestic and

26  **Barry Eichengreen and Richard Portes**

Table 1.6. **Short-term indebtedness of selected European countries, 1930–3**

(millions of US dollars)

| Country | Date | Central Government | Local authorities | Central bank | Other banks | Other debtors | Total | Gross Foreign Debt |
|---|---|---|---|---|---|---|---|---|
| Austria | IX 1932 | 14.1 | 0.3 | 121.9 | | 19.4 | 156 | 583[a] |
| Hungary | XI 1931 | 42.8 | 21.8 | 25.3 | 106.7 | 124.0 | 320 | 695[a] |
| Bulgaria | XII 1931 | 4.2 | 3.4 | 1.1 | 10.3 | 23.4 | 42 | n.a. |
| Poland | XII 1931 | 0.4 | — | | 5.1 | 27.9 | 33 | 1,130[a] |
| Romania | 1932 | | | 13.5 | 23.7 | 41.9 | 79 | 965 |
| Denmark | XII 1932 | | — | 25.0 | | 36.2 | 61 | 361 |
| Finland | XII 1932 | 7.5 | 1.4 | 4.7 | 24.4 | 17.5 | 55 | 296 |
| Norway | I 1933 | | 2.2 | | 19.7 | 106.9 | 129 | 373 |
| Germany | IX 1932 | | 148.0 | 193.6 | 918.4 | 963.3 | 2,223 | 4,670 |

*Note:* [a] denotes 1930 value; n.a. denotes not available. Gross foreign indebtedness for Poland includes direct foreign investment.
*Sources:* League of Nations (1933, 1937, 1938) and Royal Institute of International Affairs (1937).

foreign creditors.[26] A $14 million credit obtained through the Bank for International Settlements was exhausted within five days, and a subsequent loan from the Bank of England lasted little longer. The government's next step was to freeze foreign balances, and on 16 June 1931 foreign creditors agreed to a two-year suspension of transfers provided that the Austrian Government guaranteed the debts. A second standstill between other Austrian banks and their creditors followed. Although this freeze of foreign transfers did not put a halt to domestic withdrawals, which continued through 1931, the Credit-Anstalt's doors remained open by virtue of large rediscounts with the National Bank. This aspect of Austrian experience suggests a lesson common to Europe and Latin America: shocks with the potential to destabilize the banking system did not lead to generalized collapse because central banks acted in lender-of-last-resort capacity and simply did not permit this to occur.[27]

The Austrian run alerted creditors to the precarious position of other countries dependent upon short-term credits from abroad, notably Germany and the Successor States of Eastern Europe. Table 1.6 indicates the extent of short-term foreign indebtedness of the German banking system. Even had German banks not shared many of the weaknesses of their Austrian counterparts, they would have suffered withdrawals given depositors' incomplete information about their position and the signal provided by the Credit-Anstalt crisis.[28] The Darmstadter Bank, which failed on 13 July 1931, had invested heavily in textiles in general and in the bankrupt Nordwolle firm in particular, as well as in the nearly insolvent municipalities of the Rhine–Ruhr region. Foreign deposits figured prominently on the liabilities side of its balance sheet. Between mid-1930 and July 1931, German statistics show withdrawals of 2.5 to 3 RM billion in short-term foreign credits, or roughly half of the gross short-term liabilities of the 28 most important German banks. In the six weeks ending 13 July 1931, the Darmstadter lost 30 per cent of its deposits, culminating in a run that forced the closure of all German financial institutions. As the price of state support, the Reich fused the Darmstadter with another bank and replaced its board of directors. To prevent capital flight, the Reichsbank was given a monopoly of trans-actions in foreign exchange. Under the provisions of an agreement coming into force in September, transfers of short-term debt were suspended for six months and then for a year starting February 1932. Nonperforming assets were written down and new capital was secured with the aid of the Treasury and, indirectly, the Reichsbank.

Next to Austria and Germany, Hungary was most seriously affected by the liquidation of short-term credits. In the Hungarian case, first the Credit-Anstalt disclosures led to a withdrawal of foreign credits, and then the German banking crisis precipitated a domestic run. The government declared a three-day bank holiday, limited withdrawals and instituted exchange control. Together with heavy rediscounts by the Central Bank, these measures prevented widespread failures. The experience of Romania, the next largest short-term external debtor, differed in that official exchange control was only introduced in May 1932, and in its absence rediscounts with the National Bank were provided even more liberally.

The role of the lender of last resort in containing bank failures is evident in Latin America as well. As noted above, Argentina escaped bank failures because of the substantial rediscount and other credits extended to commercial banks by the Banco de la Nacion: rediscounts rose from 80 million pesos at the end of 1928 to 160 million pesos in April 1931, while advances to banks against government bills rose from 190 to 250 million pesos. Where rediscounts were less liberally provided, instability was greater: in Peru, for example, the Banco del Peru y Londres suspended payments in October 1930, occasioning a banking moratorium lasting through the end of the year. The authorities

28   **Barry Eichengreen and Richard Portes**

Table 1.7.  **Indices of prices of bank shares and industrial shares, 1930–3
(1929 = 100)**

|  |  | VI 1930 | XII 1930 | VI 1931 | XII 1931 | VI 1932 | XII 1932 | VI 1933 | XII 1933 |
|---|---|---|---|---|---|---|---|---|---|
| Belgium | Banks | 66 | 55 | 47 | 36 | 30 | 35 | 35 | 35 |
|  | Industrial | 72 | 55 | 52 | 35 | 29 | 36 | 35 | 29 |
| Canada | Banks | 85 | 80 | 72 | 69 | 45 | 50 | 54 | 47 |
|  | Industrial | 62 | 45 | 34 | 28 | 18 | 22 | 39 | 40 |
| Denmark | Banks | 93 | 96 | 92 | 75 | 70 | 78 | 91 | 101 |
|  | Industrial | 92 | 90 | 88 | 81 | 71 | 74 | 85 | 90 |
| France | Banks | 89 | 76 | 73 | 46 | 47 | 54 | 52 | 50 |
|  | Industrial | 85 | 66 | 62 | 41 | 44 | 47 | 48 | 43 |
| Germany | Banks | 88 | 74 | 66 | n.a.[a] | 35 | 35 | 37 | ... |
|  | Industrial | 86 | 62 | 53 | n.a.[a] | 36 | 47 | 56 | 52 |
| Netherlands | Banks | 94 | 83 | 82 | 56 | 47 | 57 | 66 | 58 |
|  | Industrial | 73 | 51 | 43 | 30 | 21 | 30 | 33 | 32 |
| UK[b] | Banks[c] | 92 | 97 | 89 | 68 | 82 | 96 | 96 | 104 |
|  | Industrial | 75 | 64 | 56 | 49 | 45 | 57 | 63 | 70 |
| USA | Banks[d] | 67 | 43 | 38 | 21 | 14 | 23 | 21 | 15 |
|  | Industrial | 77 | 55 | 47 | 29 | 18 | 24 | 42 | 43 |
| Sweden | Banks | 104 | 101 | 93 | 70 | 50 | 53 | 53 | 58 |
|  | Industrial | 90 | 80 | 73 | 48 | 31 | 35 | 39 | 39 |
| Switzerland | Banks | 98 | 96 | 97 | 61 | 49 | 61 | 60 | 60 |
|  | Industrial | 89 | 75 | 77 | 50 | 45 | 54 | 68 | 66 |

*Notes:* [a]  No quotation.
      [b]  31.XII.1928 = 100.
      [c]  Banks and discount companies.
      [d]  New York bank shares.
*Source:* League of Nations (1934).

responded by encouraging amalgamations and, after 1931, by increasing rediscounts.

   The United Kingdom and the United States are the two prominent exceptions to this pattern, the UK because the banking system was not threatened, the US because of the extent to which it was. The relationship between the prices of industrial and bank stocks shown in Table 1.7 can be taken to indicate the condition of national banking systems relative to the condition of national economies. The table confirms that the British banking system weathered the crisis exceptionally well while the American banking system suffered profoundly.

   In the British case, external credits again play a role, but in a rather different fashion.[29] The extent of Britain's short-term liabilities, while known to experts, was heralded by the publication of the Macmillan Committee Report in the summer of 1931. Combined with uncertainty about the defensibility of the sterling parity due to a budgetary impasse and British creditors' inability to withdraw funds from Austria and Germany, it led to a run on the pound which forced Britain from the gold standard in September. But since the discount market and the Government, not only the banks, relied on foreign funds, and since the run took the form mainly of sales of foreign-owned Treasury bills and withdrawals of credits previously granted to the discount market, it posed little threat to the banking system. In the three months ending September 1931, total deposits of the ten London clearing banks fell by £70 million, not an insignificant amount but small in comparison with experiences on the Continent.

Even in the United States, where agricultural foreclosure and industrial insolvency are typically emphasized as explanations for bank failure, foreign credits played a role. Signs of widespread financial distress surfaced in June 1931, when foreigners reduced their holdings of dollar acceptances and transferred their deposits from commercial to reserve banks. With Britain's abandonment of the gold standard these movements accelerated. In part these withdrawals of foreign deposits reflected the imposition of exchange control abroad, which rendered the United States one of the few remaining sources of liquidity for foreigners scrambling for funds.

Foreign withdrawals were particularly damaging to the banking system because they reinforced domestic sources of weakness. In the course of the 1920s, US commercial banks had greatly augmented the security and real estate components of their portfolios.[30] Collapse of the security and mortgage markets therefore rendered their asset position especially vulnerable. Real estate loans, which tended to be geographically undiversified due to restrictions on branch banking, increased the vulnerability of thousands of small unit banks to sector-specific shocks. Their desperate attempts to restore liquidity induced them to call in open-market loans and sell securities. Similar responses occurred in other countries although, as Table 1.8 makes clear, the liquidity position of US banks had eroded particularly dramatically over preceding years.[31] In response, US banks restricted loans, giving rise to widespread complaints among manufacturing firms about a shortage of credit. The scramble for liquidity reinforced the collapse of the bond market. The prices of domestic bonds fell so dramatically that by June 1932, when the rate on 3-month acceptances had fallen below one per cent, domestic industrial bonds were quoted on an 11 per cent yield basis and second

30   **Barry Eichengreen and Richard Portes**

Table 1.8.   **Bank cash resources as percentage of total deposits, 1929–32**
             **(end of June)**

|                | 1929 | 1930 | 1931 | 1932 |
|----------------|------|------|------|------|
| France         | 7.4  | 9.7  | 13.9 | 33.6 |
| Switzerland    | n.a. | n.a. | 11.3 | 22.9 |
| United Kingdom | 11.3 | 11.5 | 11.7 | 11.5 |
| United States  | 7.3  | 7.4  | 7.6  | 8.2  |
| Italy          | 6.9  | 6.6  | 6.2  | 5.9  |
| Germany        | 3.1  | 2.7  | 3.6  | 3.4  |
| Poland         | 8.5  | 8.8  | 10.7 | 9.0  |
| Sweden         | 2.1  | 2.3  | 2.1  | 3.8  |
| Czechoslovakia | 6.7  | 7.3  | 7.2  | 7.4  |
| South Africa   | 10.3 | 10.0 | 9.1  | 10.1 |
| Argentina      | 17.9 | 14.2 | 13.4 | 17.5 |
| Australia      | 15.6 | 13.4 | 19.2 | 17.8 |
| Canada         | 13.3 | 12.1 | 10.9 | 12.2 |
| Chile          | 14.4 | 12.6 | 9.5  | 26.4 |
| Japan          | 9.1  | 9.0  | 10.1 | 9.8  |
| New Zealand    | 12.3 | 13.0 | 13.7 | 11.5 |

*Note:* n.a. signifies not available.
*Source:* League of Nations (1934).

grade rails yielded 19 per cent. While some component of these yields indicates the magnitude of the risk premium, their high level may also reflect distress sales and therefore the generalized effects of the financial crisis, which severely disrupted the domestic bond market's ability efficiently to allocate funds among competing uses in much the same manner that the collapse of the market in foreign bonds reduced international investment to a trickle.[32]

Although the literature on the American Depression emphasizes the two waves of bank failures in the late autumn of 1930 and early spring of 1933, in fact failures continued throughout. In October 1931, for example, 522 banks with deposits amounting to $470 million were forced to suspend payments, and in the 12 months ending in June 1932, 2,429 US banks failed. Again, the pattern of failure mirrors the actions of the authorities. In the spring of 1932 the incidence of bank failures declined as the Federal Reserve expanded credit through rediscounts and open market operations, but this expansionary initiative was reversed soon thereafter, permitting a resurgence of commercial bank insolvencies.[33]

The US case provides a graphic illustration of linkages running from bank failures to other markets and to the macroeconomy. Although it is still disputed whether monetary stringency, much of which resulted from bank failures, was a factor in the onset of the Great Depression, it is widely agreed that these monetary factors were central to its singular depth and long duration. The inability of the Federal Reserve to prevent widespread bank failures, along with its inability to interrupt the linkages running back from bank failures to financial markets and to the macro-economy, is a central explanation for the severity of the crisis in the United States. Thus, one reason for the exceptional depth of the Great Depression in the US was that policy was used less effectively than in other countries to prevent the transformation of financial market disturbances into a generalized financial crisis.

## II   Fifty years later

### A.   *The periods compared*

A summary of the apparent similarities and differences between our two periods will be useful background for our analysis. In the 1930s as in the 1980s, illiquidity was not confined to any one country or region. In neither instance can the problems of debtor countries be attributed exclusively to domestic causes – external shocks from the world economy were transmitted through sharp rises in real interest rates and falls in commodity prices and the economic activity of industrial countries. The burden of reparations inhibited expansion just as the burden of debt service does in many countries today (McNeil, 1986).

There can be no exact dating of recent troubles in international financial markets, nor *a fortiori* a precise correspondence between 1929 and 1979. Nevertheless, to take 1979 as the beginning of the contemporary period of interest is not merely a convenient metaphor. Admittedly, one cannot identify at that point a classical panic, preceded by 'mania', then 'distress', and followed by sharp, generalized price falls (Kindleberger, 1978). But conditions in the world economy and financial system clearly did deteriorate from the second oil shock to the Mexican collapse of August 1982, which marks the onset of the 'debt crisis' in popular consciousness.

Any simple analogy with 1932, however, would be equally inappropriate. For just as the contemporary debt crisis began the American economy entered a period of strong expansion which compensated, until recently, for the drag on world economic activity caused by the overhang of LDC debt and restrictive macroeconomic adjustment policies adopted to deal with it.

We have seen many debt reschedulings but not widespread, extended

32   **Barry Eichengreen and Richard Portes**

interruptions of service and amortization on the scale of the 1930s; even the deterioration of relations between Peru and the IMF in August 1986 is not strictly comparable to the defaults which began in January 1931. There have been wide swings in nominal and real exchange rates but no significant currency collapses, nor any resort to inconvertibility or new exchange controls to protect any major currency. Real interest rates rose to historically exceptional heights, but there was no worldwide dramatic fall of investment. Large government budget deficits in industrialized countries have in most cases (with a major exception!) been brought under control, with many crisis budgets but no collapse of government finances. There have been large trade imbalances and repeated threats of a plunge into overt protectionism, but in practice we have seen only the gradual accretion of non-tariff barriers to trade. Failures of individual financial institutions have been isolated, without generalized runs or significant contractions in the credit base. One authority judges that the crisis was worst in 1982–4 and is now over (Kindleberger, 1986).

We are less sanguine, and we stress in particular the need for continued and improved international policy coordination in providing the regulatory and macroeconomic environments necessary to prevent financial crisis. But despite greater interdependence in the world economy – and partly in response to it – institutional change and economic policies have tended to break, block or attenuate the linkages of Figure 1.1. A further difference from the 1930s is more difficult to analyse: the growing assertiveness of the United States and the political consensus among the major industrialized countries in dealing with international debt problems (Diaz Alejandro, 1984; Portes, 1986). It has been more difficult for any single debtor country, particularly in Latin America, to break ranks, and the cohesion of the creditors' cartel contrasts sharply with feeble efforts at coordination among debtors.

As noted, in both the 1930s and 1980s, the preceding decade had been marked by major changes in the structure and management of the international political economy. Before World War I, the United Kingdom played the pivotal role in the world economy, using its investment income to run a trade deficit that allowed other countries to pursue export-led growth. When World War I and its aftermath cut that income, the United States assumed the financial role of the world's leading creditor without taking on the corresponding responsibility of running an import surplus with open markets, thus leaving a structural weakness in the system. Now the transition from the United States to Japan as dominant lender is similarly occurring without a shift by Japan into import surplus (though in this case, with little immediate weakening of American political dominance).

Yet differences between the periods preclude simple generalizations. In the 1970s, the banks did not act merely as intermediaries in placing LDC bond issues among many dispersed bondholders, but rather took on very large direct exposure, with corresponding risk to themselves and the financial system.[34] Although there was significant cross-border lending among banks in the earlier period, the density of international interbank relationships now is incomparably greater. For both reasons, creditors have been much better organized in the 1980s than in the 1930s, a change that has favoured rescheduling rather than default.[35] But banks appear to have paid no more attention to sovereign risk in the lending of the 1970s than in that of the 1920s. And they lent at considerably shorter maturities than those of the 1920s bond issues.

An institutional difference of considerable practical importance is the International Monetary Fund. To some extent, the IMF acts as international lender of last resort, while also serving the capital market in a signalling capacity, providing information on domestic adjustment programmes and helping to differentiate among borrowers. There are also stronger domestic lenders of last resort (new, in some countries), with more extensive supervisory and regulatory roles now than fifty years ago despite recent moves towards deregulation; and there is deposit insurance in many countries. The macroeconomic background differs as well, with much greater experience of stabilization policies, a system of floating exchange rates in existence for over a decade, and extended international discussion of domestic macroeconomic policies in economic summits, the OECD and the EEC. Finally, there is greater political stability in relations among the industrialized creditor countries, and perhaps greater internal political stability in the LDC debtors.

### B.  The environment

Our description of the international financial environment begins with the breakdown of the Bretton Woods payments settlement and exchange rate systems in the early 1970s. A detailed history is not needed here. But the major events have brought deep structural change closely analogous to that of the 1920s, in the exchange rate system, in international lending, and in financial institutions.

The changes in the exchange rate system during 1971–73, while in the opposite direction to those of the mid-1920s, were equally profound and far-reaching.[36] Official convertibility of dollars into gold was abandoned in August 1971, and the adjustable-peg exchange-rate mechanism gave way to unrestricted floating in March 1973. The 'reform' negotiations of the C20 and its successors could not reconstruct or replace the constraints

34   **Barry Eichengreen and Richard Portes**

which Bretton Woods had imposed on the autonomy of national monetary authorities. The new freedoms and powers were *de jure* rather than *de facto*, however, as policy-makers, academic analysts and the markets soon discovered. The same capital mobility which made the old exchange rate system untenable also made true autonomy infeasible.

Among the many complementary explanations for the breakdown of the Bretton Woods exchange rate system, we stress capital mobility as fundamental. So did the architects of the system and their predecessors. Nurkse (1944) identified 'disequilibrating' capital flows as a major cause of the disturbances of the interwar period. Keynes insisted that controls over capital movements be an essential component of the postwar monetary order, and the Bretton Woods Agreement made no provision for convertibility for capital account transactions. But the progressive relaxation in the early 1950s did extend to capital flows. Their volume and speed grew dramatically as a function of technological innovation and profit opportunities. Since the authorities were unwilling to make the Bretton Woods exchange rate system their sole policy target, official convertibility and the adjustable peg could not withstand the pressures arising from the growing sophistication, scope and integration of international capital markets. This process has of course continued, and we return to it below.

Currency convertibility and the international institutions established at Bretton Woods survive. Moreover, the political relationship between France and Germany in the context of the European Community gave rise in 1979 to the European Monetary System, with its exchange rate mechanism providing a 'zone of (relative) monetary stability' among most of the EC currencies.[37] Even outside the exchange-market intervention in the EMS, the major currencies have not floated freely since 1973. Exchange rates have been regarded as important indicators or even targets for monetary policy, leading to intervention, whether unsterilized or sterilized.[38] This raises the question whether, by the end of the 1970s, the resulting exchange rate system was well-suited to absorb major macroeconomic and financial shocks, or whether the system propagated or even magnified such disorders, which might then be transmitted to capital markets and the financial system (linkages III and V in Figure 1.1).

The explosive growth of international lending in the 1970s is also familiar to contemporary observers.[39] Analysts still differ, however, in the importance they assign to supply and demand factors affecting international lending during the period. Econometric explanations of its volume and price perform no better than econometric models of exchange rate behaviour. It is clear that the 1970s saw a striking, unexpected growth of liability financing of balance-of-payments deficits under little apparent constraint for most countries; and that aggregate liquidity in the world economy was correspondingly demand-determined.

The process of institutional change in the banking system during the 1970s was also driven by the powerful forces of internationalization and the technological change which stimulated and facilitated it. The pace of internationalization may have slowed somewhat in the past five years.[40] This has not eased the regulatory authorities' task in keeping abreast of these changes. The problems of the banking system in 1974–5, from spectacular bank failures like Franklin National and Herstatt to many lesser difficulties, were surmounted.[41] But the Basle concordat of 1975 was just the beginning of a much more active, continuous process of consultation among central banks, in good part through the continuing work of the Cooke Committee. This internationalized prudential super-vision also forms an important part of the environment in which the events of the past several years have transpired.

## C.   *Disturbances and their management*

The two major sources of recent instability are those of fifty years earlier: disturbances in the foreign exchange market and sovereign debt.

Major exchange rate swings and misalignments, as well as sharp deterioration in the debt-servicing capacity of individual countries, have undoubtedly threatened domestic financial institutions and the inter-national financial system. There have been isolated, individual cases of bank failures, some quite spectacular, at least judging by the reaction of the media. Banco Ambrosiano, Johnson Matthey and Continental Illinois offered high-grade material to all from sensational journalists to sober academics. The scandals and political fallout were greater in Rome and London than in Chicago, but financially the most serious was Continental Illinois, then the twentieth largest US bank and a major participant in the international interbank market. Despite a classic run by foreign holders of its CDs, the bank was saved by the regulators (without bailing out its officers and shareholders), and there were no spread effects nor generalized financial crisis resembling the 1930s.

Stresses in foreign exchange markets, international lending and the banking system are striking, and they suggest analogies with the interwar period. These comparisons help to explain why there has so far been no collapse like that of the 1930s and shed light on the continuing vulnerabi-lity of the financial system. We shall therefore turn to data on the size of imbalances and shocks, on the capacity of the exchange-rate system to cope with misalignments and volatility, and on how the debt crisis has been managed. We then consider the linkages represented in Figure 1.1 and the roles of policy and institutional change in attenuating them.

*Exchange rates*   The exchange rate system operating since 1973 has survived both unexpectedly high volatility and substantial misalignments without exchange-market collapse or any overall drift towards controls.[42] Central bank intervention has doubtless helped; few would argue that it has been destabilizing, though many would judge its influence to be marginal. It has certainly not eliminated short-run volatility. Nor has market learning reduced volatility as the floating-rate period has gone on. Even the EMS has had only limited effects: among the major EMS currencies, only the Deutschmark and lira experienced clear declines in overall volatility (with respect to all currencies) from 1978 to 1984.[43] On most assessments, however, the EMS has succeeded in reducing volatility among the currencies participating in its exchange-rate mechanism, as one would expect.[44]

Yet more than a decade of learning among market participants and the authorities has apparently not delivered the supposedly stabilizing effects of speculative activity. The EMS may be interpreted as one response to this disappointment, while the rapidly developing forward and futures markets now provide ample opportunities to protect against exchange-rate instability. Recent evidence suggests, however, that these opportunities are not used fully to insulate trade, and that exchange-rate volatility does in fact have empirically significant effects on the volume of international trade.[45] And the new markets and instruments can be used not only to hedge but also to gamble. We must therefore regard short-run volatility still as evidence of instability which might itself spread through the financial and real economies.

Even more dangerous, however, are the large exchange-rate swings and misalignments of long duration which have characterized the period since 1973. Williamson (1985, p. 17) cites maximum swings in real effective exchange rates during 1973–82 of 22 per cent for the Deutschmark, 19 per cent for the French franc, 32 per cent for the US dollar, 35 per cent for the yen, and 60 per cent for the pound. His graph (reproduced as our Figure 1.2) is striking testimony to the magnitude of these gyrations and their extended duration. His calculations of misalignments give one measure, admittedly controversial, of the exchange-rate imbalances creating strains on other elements of the financial system. Table 1.9 gives these estimates of divergencies from 'fundamental equilibrium exchange rates' in 1984:Q4. One need not fully accept the methodology or conclusions to judge that the misalignments are likely to

Table 1.9. **Estimates of exchange-rate misalignments, 1984:Q4**

| | Effective exchange rate relative to estimated fundamental equilibrium | Fundamental equilibrium rate US dollar | Nominal appreciation needed against US dollar (percentage) |
|---|---|---|---|
| US dollar | 137 | n.a. | n.a. |
| Japanese yen | 89 | ¥ 198 | 24 |
| Deutschmark | 87 | DM 2.04 | 50 |
| French franc | 92 | FF 6.51 | 44 |
| Pound sterling | 107 | $ 1.52 | 25 |

*Note:* n.a.: not applicable.
*Source:* Williamson (1985, p. 79).

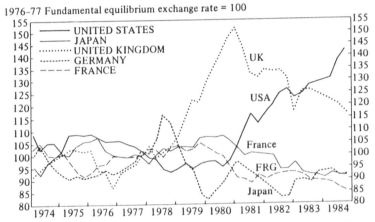

**Figure 1.2  Composite measures of real effective exchange rates, five major countries, 1974–84.**
*Source:* Williamson (1985, p. 103)

have been two to three times the magnitude of those estimated by Keynes for the 1920s.

Even in the absence of an agreed model of exchange-rate determination, there is consensus that changes in such fundamentals as the current account and purchasing power parities (or even 'safe haven' effects) cannot fully explain these shifts. Nor are they solely due to inappropriate monetary policies and exchange-rate targets (as represented by the pegs of the 1920s). An unbalanced *mix* of monetary and fiscal policies within the United States and among the major industrial countries is a more comprehensive explanation, especially insofar as it underlies the wide swings in nominal and real interest rates and international interest rate differentials. Yet it is increasingly agreed that speculative 'bubbles', with or without rational expectations, also played a role in accentuating recent exchange-rate swings.[46] If so, then the exchange rates are still highly uncertain for participants in trade and financial markets, however much they hedge.

This longer-run uncertainty may reduce trade volumes just as volatility appears to do, and direct investment may suffer as well. Large and sustained misalignments impede trade by encouraging protectionist policy responses. Since debt servicing capacity derives from trade flows, there is an indirect link from the exchange-market disturbances of the past decade to debt defaults (linkage III in Figure 1.1). Yet this differs from the link we identified for the earlier period, in which convertibility crises and the threat of exchange control induced withdrawals of short-term funds, which in turn could provoke default. Nor do exchange-rate misalignments appear to have threatened the banking systems in either creditor or debtor countries (linkage V). But exchange-rate uncertainty and volatility may have increased the importance of this link by offering banks new opportunities for speculation. Some have participated aggressively in these markets (often seeking to build up earnings depleted by bad loans), and some of these have not succeeded (Franklin National and Herstatt were early victims).

A more important example of linkage III can be found in the LDC debtor countries themselves. In several cases, exchange-rate over-valuation has led to massive capital flight by domestic residents, seriously exacerbating debt-servicing difficulties.[47] Insofar as overvaluation is a direct result of government policy, exchange-market intervention rather than post-1973 exchange-rate flexibility is the cause of the problem.

On balance, we are inclined to accept the judgment of Cooper (1983) that flexible exchange rates have served more as a shock absorber than as a source of destabilizing influences in the financial system or as a link in their transmission. The misalignments which this flexibility has permitted, by removing a constraint on monetary and fiscal policies, have not themselves provoked financial crisis or exacerbated financial instability, whatever their negative effects on trade and investment. Indeed, it is the process of correcting the misalignments without the appropriate coordination of macro policy mixes which might be highly destabilizing.[48]

*Debt*   As in the 1920s, the growth and export performance of major borrowing countries in the latter half of the 1970s gave some cause for optimism regarding the recycling process and the prospects for debt

Table 1.10. **Annual growth rates of real GDP and exports, 1975–9**

|  | GDP | Exports in US dollars |
|---|---|---|
| Argentina | 1.1 | 27.2 |
| Brazil | 6.6 | 15.9 |
| Chile | 7.4 | 25.7[a] |
| Mexico | 6.2 | 32.7[a] |
| Venezuela | 4.7 | 13.1[a] |
| Peru | 0.9 | 28.0[a] |
| Nigeria | 1.2 | 22.5[a] |
| India | 2.6 | 15.7 |
| Indonesia | 7.4 | 21.6 |
| Korea | 10.6 | 30.9 |
| Malaysia | 8.8 | 30.3 |
| Philippines | 6.6 | 18.6 |
| Egypt | n.a. | 6.9 |
| Turkey | 3.7 | 12.5 |
| Yugoslavia | 6.4 | 12.4 |

*Note:* [a] more than 50% increase in 1979 over previous year.
*Source: International Financial Statistics 1983 Yearbook.*

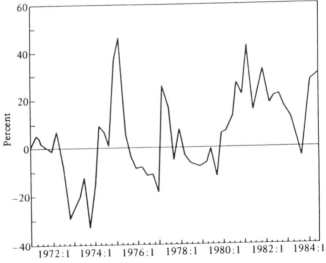

**Figure 1.3   The real interest rate of nonoil LDCs, 1971:1–1984:3.**
*Note:* The real rate is measured as the six-month lagged LIBOR adjusted with the three-month forward rate of inflation of export unit values of nonoil LDCs.
*Source:* Dornbusch (1985, p. 341)

service.[49] Table 1.10 gives data comparable with Table 1.2 for the earlier period. In both cases, however, the assumption that expansion would continue without major shocks proved to be false.

The problems which ensued were indeed similar. The major external shocks which hit the debtor countries were global, not country-specific. The second oil shock, the OECD recession and the industrialized countries' restrictive monetary policies created serious fiscal problems in the debtor countries (aggravated by domestic mismanagement) and cut the prices and volumes of commodity exports. Nominal interest rates finally rose to meet and exceed inflation, bringing a sharp switch from negative to positive real rates. Higher nominal rates also reduced debtor liquidity by shifting the burden of debt repayment towards the present (the tilt effect). Then as inflation subsided, nominal interest rates fell less quickly, and real rates rose further (see Figure 1.3).

Voluntary lending to LDCs by the commercial banks evaporated after the Mexican crisis of August 1982; the Polish debacle of early 1981 had already hit lending to Eastern Europe and put Hungary and Romania in deep trouble.[50] A wave of debt reschedulings followed: there were a total of 36 'multilateral debt renegotiations' in 1975–81 covering $19.6 billion of debt; then 10 in 1982 ($2.4 billion), 32 in 1983 alone ($51.7 billion), with some slackening in 1984, but a record number of 41 reschedulings signed in 1985 dealing with $92.8 billion of debt.[51] Lenders reacted to new information about global economic conditions and individual debtors with a generalized, discrete change of regime in credit markets. Rather than a continuous tightening of terms and constraints for borrowers, there was a shift to credit rationing.

This change of credit-market regime was a response to macroeconomic shocks exogenous to the credit markets whose effects conveyed new information to lenders.[52] Imperfect information about one or at most a few borrowers was generalized to others, and lenders' overall perceptions changed. The 'disaster myopia' emphasized by Guttentag and Herring (1984, 1985) was dispelled by such information; and when the disaster scenario suddenly took on a non-negligible subjective probability, lenders whose sole protection was to try to maintain short loan maturities could react only by pulling out of the market wherever possible.

The magnitude of the shocks which so dramatically affected lenders' behaviour can be seen in Tables 1.11–1.18 and Figures 1.3 and 1.4. The rise of 20 percentage points in real interest rates on floating-rate debt from 1980 to 1981 is extraordinary. The fall in the real commodity price (excluding oil) of 26 per cent from 1980:Q1 to 1983:Q1 is of a similar magnitude to fifty years previously. Although the terms of trade of

Table 1.11. **Average real percentage interest rate on LDC floating-rate debt, 1977–83**

| 1977 | 1978 | 1979 | 1980 | 1981 | 1982 | 1983 |
|------|------|------|------|------|------|------|
| −11.8 | −7.4 | −9.7 | −6.0 | 14.6 | 16.7 | 15.9 |

*Source:* Maddison (1985, p. 47).

Table 1.12. **Commodity price indices, 1979–85 (1980 = 100)**

|  | 1979 | 1980 | 1981 | 1982 | 1983 | 1984 | 1985 |
|--|------|------|------|------|------|------|------|
| Coffee (NY) | 112.5 | 100.0 | 76.8 | 83.4 | 84.9 | 93.7 | 88.6 |
| Copper (London) | 90.3 | 100.0 | 79.8 | 67.8 | 72.9 | 63.0 | 64.9 |
| Petroleum (Venezuela) | 60.8 | 100.0 | 116.1 | 116.1 | 101.6 | 97.9 | 97.9[a] |
| Rubber (Singapore) | 88.6 | 100.0 | 78.8 | 60.2 | 74.7 | 67.2 | 53.3 |
| Sugar (EEC Import price) | 87.4 | 100.0 | 83.7 | 82.0 | 79.5 | 72.6 | 72.4 |
| Tin (London) | 92.1 | 100.0 | 84.5 | 76.5 | 77.4 | 72.9 | 68.7 |

*Note:* [a] Quarter II.
*Source:* *International Financial Statistics 1985 Yearbook.*

Table 1.13. **External shocks, 1979–83**

|  | Percentage change in terms of trade from 1975–78 | Real income effect as percentage of GDP | Sum of real interest rate and terms of trade effects on GDP (percentage) |
|--|--------------------------------------------------|-----------------------------------------|-------------------------------------------------------------------------|
| Argentina | 3 | 0.2 | 1.6 |
| Brazil | −29 | −2.3 | −5.0 |
| Chile | −27 | −4.9 | −6.2 |
| Mexico | 26 | 1.8 | 1.2 |
| Peru | −22 | −3.7 | −4.2 |
| Venezuela | 64 | 15.9 | 16.2 |
| Colombia | −18 | −2.0 | −2.8 |
| Indonesia | 36 | 6.1 | 6.2 |
| Korea | −3 | −0.9 | −3.8 |
| Malaysia | 14 | 4.9 | 4.8 |
| Thailand | −14 | −2.9 | −3.3 |
| Philippines | −16 | −3.2 | −3.9 |

*Source:* Sachs (1985, pp. 527–28).

42   **Barry Eichengreen and Richard Portes**

Table 1.14. **Gross external liabilities and short-term component, 1978–83**

(billion US dollars, end-year)

|  |  | 1978 | 1980 | 1981 | 1982 | 1983 |
|---|---|---|---|---|---|---|
| Argentina | Total | 13.3 | 27.3 | 33.7 | 43.6 | 46.0 |
|  | S | 3.4 | 10.5 | 11.0 | 16.5 | 9.4 |
| Brazil | Total | 53.4 | 70.0 | 79.9 | 91.0 | 95.5 |
|  | S | 7.1 | 13.5 | 15.3 | 17.4 | 14.2 |
| Mexico | Total | 35.7 | 57.1 | 77.9 | 85.5 | 93.7 |
|  | S | 4.9 | 16.2 | 25.0 | 26.1 | 10.1 |
| Peru | Total | 9.7 | 10.0 | 10.3 | 12.2 | 12.4 |
|  | S | 2.1 | 2.1 | 2.5 | 3.1 | 1.4 |
| Venezuela | Total | 16.8 | 29.6 | 31.9 | 31.8 | 32.2 |
|  | S | 8.0 | 15.5 | 17.0 | 14.7 | 14.5 |
| Nigeria | Total | 5.5 | 9.0 | 11.9 | 14.2 | 19.7 |
|  | S | 2.4 | 3.5 | 4.4 | 4.3 | 6.7 |
| Korea | Total | 17.3 | 29.3 | 34.2 | 38.3 | 40.4 |
|  | S | 4.5 | 10.1 | 11.6 | 13.6 | 12.1 |
| Indonesia | Total | 18.0 | 29.9 | 22.7 | 26.5 | 30.2 |
|  | S | 1.8 | 2.8 | 3.3 | 4.8 | 4.6 |
| Philippines | Total | 10.8 | 17.4 | 20.8 | 24.2 | 23.9 |
|  | S | 3.9 | 7.6 | 9.4 | 11.3 | 9.4 |
| Yugoslavia | Total | 12.5 | 18.5 | 20.7 | 20.0 | 20.3 |
|  | S | 1.2 | 2.1 | 2.5 | 1.8 | 1.9 |

*Note:* Short-term liabilities S are those of *original* maturity less than one year.
*Source:* World Bank, *World Debt Tables*, 1985–86.

Table 1.15. **Ratio of gross external liabilities to exports of goods and services, 1978–84 (percentage)**

|  | 1978 | 1980 | 1981 | 1982 | 1983 | 1984 |
|---|---|---|---|---|---|---|
| Argentina | 169 | 244 | 285 | 449 | 471 | 464 |
| Brazil | 369 | 301 | 296 | 388 | 392 | 345 |
| Mexico | 313 | 232 | 256 | 310 | 327 | 301 |
| Peru | 401 | 206 | 243 | 292 | 323 | 331 |
| Venezuela | 154 | 133 | 130 | 158 | 186 | 182 |
| Nigeria | 45 | 33 | 61 | 110 | 179 | 160 |
| Korea | 101 | 130 | 125 | 135 | 133 | 128 |
| Indonesia | 159 | 94 | 91 | 125 | 151 | 147 |
| Philippines | 220 | 214 | 242 | 302 | 294 | 304 |
| Yugoslavia | 147 | 134 | 131 | 131 | 154 | 144 |

*Source:* World Bank, *World Debt Tables*, 1985–86.

Table 1.16.  **Exposure of US banks to LDC debtors, 1982 and 1986**

| | Percentage of capital | | | | Billion $US March 1986 |
|---|---|---|---|---|---|
| | June 1982 | | March 1986 | | |
| | 9 money center banks | All US banks | 9 money center banks | All US banks | All US banks |
| Mexico | 50 | 38 | 38 | 22 | 24.2 |
| Brazil | 46 | 31 | 37 | 22 | 23.7 |
| Korea | 19 | 14 | 11 | 9 | 9.4 |
| Venezuela | 26 | 16 | 16 | 9 | 9.7 |
| Argentina | 21 | 13 | 14 | 8 | 8.5 |
| Chile | 12 | 9 | 9 | 6 | 6.3 |
| Philippines | 14 | 8 | 8 | 5 | 5.0 |
| Colombia | 8 | 5 | 4 | 2 | 2.3 |
| Non-OPEC LDCs | 227 | 154 | 141 | 88 | 96.4 |
| OPEC | 35 | 60 | 33 | 18 | 19.4 |

*Note:* Banks' capital defined as equity, subordinated debt and loan-loss reserves. 'All US Banks' are those completing Country Exposure Report. Their total capital base rose from $66.2 b in June 1982 to $109.7 b in March 1986.
*Source:* Federal Reserve Board.

Table 1.17.  **Exposure of US and UK banks in Mexico, Brazil, Argentina and Venezuela as percentage of capital, 1982 and 1984**

| | End 1982 | End 1984 |
|---|---|---|
| Bank of America | 128 | 122 |
| Chase Manhattan | 139 | 142 |
| Manufacturers Hanover | 234 | 173 |
| Chemical | 155 | 134 |
| Bankers Trust | 131 | 114 |
| First Chicago | 123 | 103 |
| Citicorp | n.a. | 140 |
| National Westminster | n.a. | 73 |
| Barclays | n.a. | 62 |
| Lloyds | n.a. | 165 |
| Midland | n.a. | 205 |

*Sources:* Cline (1983, p. 34) for 1982 and Lever and Huhne (1985) for 1984.

44   Barry Eichengreen and Richard Portes

Table 1.18. **Bank share price/earnings ratio as percentage of overall market P/E for UK and US, 1970–86**

|                    | NYSE  | London |
|--------------------|-------|--------|
| 1970               | n.a.  | 66.9   |
| 1975               | n.a.  | 118.4  |
| 1980               | 62.0  | 52.5   |
| 1981               | 69.8  | 49.7   |
| 1982               | 48.8  | 39.7   |
| 1983               | 49.5  | 51.4   |
| 1984               | 45.5  | 47.5   |
| 1985               | 49.6  | 56.7   |
| 1986 (Jan–July)    | 56.8  | 46.1   |

At 15 August each year except 1986.

*Source:* Financial Times, Datastream.

non-oil LDCs (NLDCs) had peaked in 1977:Q1, the decline of 18 per cent from 1979:Q1 to 1983:Q1 was still substantial. The total effect in terms of real income is shown in Table 1.13; for the non-oil debtors (excluding Argentina), there were losses in GDP from three to six per cent. As a real income loss, this might be tolerable; as a required increase in transfer abroad, it was indeed onerous.[53]

Consequences for the debt burden are shown in Tables 1.14 and 1.15. Beginning in 1980, total indebtedness rose rapidly for the NLDCs, and by 1982 their debt-export ratios far exceeded the levels recorded in Table 1.2 for 1929 (which refer, however, only to central government debt, whereas the recent data cover all foreign liabilities). Most may still have been 'solvent' on a suitable long-run calculation,[54] but with uncertain expectations, the distinction between insolvency and illiquidity for a sovereign debtor is both theoretically imprecise and politically untenable. Certainly liquidity was impaired by the withdrawals of short-term funds in 1982–3 evident in Table 1.14; together with capital flight, they significantly increased the disaster probability. That reaction could have activated the linkages I, V and VI which proved so devastating in the 1930s. The 'debt strategy' was designed entirely to contain it.

The dangers are evident from the data on bank exposure in Tables 1.16 and 1.17 and on bank share prices in Table 1.18. The US banks did not begin to recover from the 1982 plunge in their relative price/earnings ratios until 1986, partly because of their subsequent problems with energy and real estate loans. The UK banks have fared somewhat better but show no sign of regaining the standing they enjoyed in the 1970s.

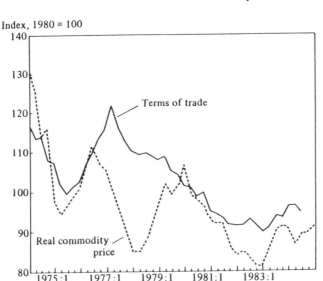

**Figure 1.4   The nonoil LDCs' terms of trade and the real commodity price, 1974:1–1985:1.**
*Note:* The real commodity price is the *Economist* index of commodities deflated by industrial countries' unit export values. Terms of trade are exports unit value index divided by imports unit value index. Terms-of-trade data extend through 1984:3.
*Source:* Dornbusch (1985, p. 324)

Many useful case studies treat the impact of the debt crisis on individual countries and regions and their responses.[55] Nevertheless, we require much more empirical evidence on the role of information about debt-servicing difficulties and their causes. How do the markets perceive such information, process it, and then react to individual borrowers and classes of borrowers? For example, we have two contradictory assessments of market evaluations of Mexican securities in the period leading up to August 1982, one finding a continuous deterioration from the previous winter, the other observing a discontinuous plunge shortly before the crisis became manifest.[56] How the market performs before a crisis is important in assessing whether shifting more sovereign debt into the market through securitization is likely to make the system more or less stable.

The response of policy-makers to the debt crisis assumed that it was essentially and almost everywhere a problem of liquidity rather than solvency, ignoring questions about the legitimacy of that distinction. This approach may have been adequate in the short run, when the key to avoiding financial crisis was maintaining confidence. On plausible assumptions about growth, interest rates, adjustment policies, industrial-country macro policies, and the provision of bridging loans, projections showed substantial improvement in the debt indicators during 1984–6 and a progressive dissipation of the crisis thereafter.[57]

The US government's optimism did not last; hence the Baker Plan in autumn 1985. For the objective of avoiding a financial crisis, however, the strategy has been almost completely successful so far in keeping both creditors and debtors on board. Neither the reasons nor the prospects for continued success are entirely obvious. There exist clear, level-headed, well-informed evaluations of the costs and benefits of default to debtors which imply that there are cases in which the benefits exceed the costs.[58] As long as rescheduling continues to eschew debt relief, this will remain the case; yet historical comparisons suggest the likelihood of some element of write-off, some ultimate sharing of the burden between creditors and debtors.[59] The question is whether there are circumstances in which debt relief or write-offs are possible without financial crisis.

The answer requires a judgment of the overall health of the international banking system and a scenario for how the authorities would react. Recently the banks have been building up their capital base while writing off some sovereign debt (see Table 1.16). There remain problems on the asset side. Keeping maturities short has little systemic advantage, since that just increases the competition, when trouble threatens, to exit first and leave the problem to other banks. It can be argued that some of the banks' off-balance-sheet activities that have grown so fast recently are relatively risky. On the other hand, securitization on the liability side of banks' balance sheets reduces their dependence on the highly volatile international interbank market.

*Linkages*   The discussion of recent disturbances and their management now permits a comparison between the two periods of the operation of the linkages we have stressed.

(1)   Whereas the events threatening debt default endangered the banks of some debtor countries in the 1930s, the creditor-country banks did not then hold enough sovereign debt to make it a problem for them. In the current period, there have been a few instances of the former linkage (Argentina had domestic financial difficulties at a critical juncture in its debt-servicing problems). The major effort today, with banks having assumed the credit risks formerly borne by purchasers of sovereign bonds, is to contain any menace this poses for the financial system. So far, direct policy intervention by national authorities and international institutions has succeeded almost entirely in protecting the banking system from major harm.

(ii)   There have been no bank failures so spectacular as themselves to provoke debt default.

(iii)   In the 1930s, withdrawals of short-term funds sometimes brought the authorities to restrict convertibility in order to avoid debt default. Recently, exchange-rate overvaluation without exchange controls has brought capital flight, which has played a greater role in the buildup to debt crisis than in the earlier period (although capital movements were important in the *propagation* of crises in both periods). Failure to block this linkage has been a key weakness in present-day arrangements relative to those of the 1930s. There is a further, indirect linkage from exchange-market disturbances to debt-servicing difficulties which is a major threat today: exchange-rate misalignments have caused pressures for protectionist trade policies, which impede the ability of debtor countries to earn the export surpluses they require.

(iv)   Whereas debt default did not generally force down the debtor's exchange rate in the 1930s, the burden of debt service has clearly had that effect even for non-defaulting debtors today. Pressures from the government budget and the need to run current account surpluses both work in this direction, insofar as depreciation relieves the financial burden of supporting an overvalued rate while raising net exports.

(v)   Instability in the foreign exchange markets was a major cause of generalized financial instability in the 1930s. In the recent period, it has endangered banks only insofar as some of them have sought too aggressively to profit from speculation in these markets.

(vi)   In the earlier period, bank failures caused pressures on the home country's currency by provoking capital flight, and occasionally on the currency of a major foreign creditor (recall how the pound weakened due to the problems of Austrian and German banks). Recently, tremors in the US banking system appear to have made the foreign exchange markets nervous, but this has not been a significant consideration.

### *Institutional change and public policy*

Partly in reaction to the problems faced by the banks, international credit flows have in the past few years shifted from bank lending towards direct credit markets. Simultaneously, there has been an explosion of new financial markets and financial instruments, primarily because technological innovation has substantially reduced transactions costs.[60]

In principle, reduction in interbank linkages should reduce systemic vulnerability. The 'Cross Report' (Bank for International Settlements, 1986), however, points out some countervailing aspects of recent trends: the quality of banks' loan assets may decline; the narrower base of the system may make it less responsive to sudden liquidity needs; non-bank capital markets may have less information on borrowers, less opportunity to screen and to monitor performance, and less capacity to arrange refinancing packages for those in debt-servicing difficulties; and many of the new services banks are providing appear to be underpriced, so that they are not providing earnings commensurate with their risks.

These trade-offs are complicated, and the pace of change has been so rapid that there is little contemporary experience from which to generalize. On the basis of interwar experience, these developments appear to be mainly positive from the viewpoint of financial stability. Our study of linkages suggests that incomplete and imperfect information favours the generalization of adverse shocks into full-fledged crises; that macroeconomic instability is the prime source of those shocks; and that appropriate action by the regulatory and monetary authorities can block the most dangerous linkages. Such action in the 'debt strategy' has avoided defaults and widespread bank failures to date. But it was the system of bank lending to sovereign borrowers that permitted the accumulation of excessive debt burdens, and the rescheduling process which has so far prevented defaults is maintaining almost the full weight of those burdens on the debtors.

In the 1930s, as during the century of international lending before World War I, creditors too assumed a share of the losses created by adverse shocks. The problem then was that when the shocks were global, the contagious, infectious nature of default contributed to financial crisis, disrupting the allocative mechanisms of the international capital market. We now have much more sophisticated public health measures, both macroeconomic and regulatory. They can cope with the dangers of securitization while the financial system switches from relationship- towards transaction-based banking.

Securitization will get more information into the market place. This should reduce adverse selection; substitute more frequent, smaller, visible shocks for the major upheavals which arise when relationships go wrong; and remove from the banking system the heavy burden of having to act as a buffer when shocks do occur. It is not evident that underpricing of new financial services exceeds the inadequacy of spreads in allowing for the default risk on bank lending to sovereign borrowers in the 1970s ('disaster myopia'); while the *ex-post* rates of return on international lending of the 1920s appear to have been relatively favourable for the lenders.[61]

Calls for more formal international-lender-of-last-resort (ILLR) arrangements[62] should not obscure the substantial development of both domestic and international LLR facilities over the past fifty years, as well as a much more sophisticated regulatory system. In the 1930s, financial weakness affected mainly the large banks in Europe, while in the United States it characterized the entire spectrum of the banking system. Now small banks are protected on the liability side by deposit insurance which limits runs,[63] and large ones in difficulty are handled directly by domestic LLRs. Internationally, the 'Paris Club' arrangements have for over two decades effectively handled rescheduling of official or government-guaranteed lending to sovereign debtors. The International Monetary Fund acts in a signalling capacity, providing the capital market with information on debtors and so reducing the risk that the difficulties of one will be transmitted infectiously to others who are creditworthy. IMF conditionality helps to maintain the standing of the debtor and its obligations, thereby limiting the risk of contagious transmission of financial illness to its creditors. And in contrast with the 1930s, the IMF can act to promote a rescheduling before default, whereas then default was needed to provoke direct negotiations between a sovereign debtor and representatives of its creditors.[64] This *ex ante* bargaining should in principle benefit both creditors and debtors; in practice, who gains how much from rescheduling is highly controversial.

Coordination of prudential supervision has taken place primarily under the auspices of the Bank for International Settlements. The Basle concordat of 1975, as revised in 1983, explicitly disclaims any ILLR responsibilities. The authorities' key principle is to exercise supervision on a consolidated basis. They do have a clear understanding of how responsibilities are shared between home and host central banks, and the individual regulatory authorities are much more experienced than they were fifty years ago. It has been difficult for them, however, to keep abreast of internationalization and financial innovation.

The key problem facing any LLR is moral hazard.[65] The classic answer is that the LLR is responsible for the money supply – avoiding financial crisis by containing any threat to the credit base – rather than for the survival of any particular financial institution. The internationalization of the interbank market has made this distinction harder to maintain, however, and no authority or institution currently has responsibility for the world money supply. There is no true ILLR, although the functions which one might fulfil are much better understood now than they would have been in the 1930s (as can equally be said of domestic LLRs).

Nevertheless, success in blocking the transmission of destabilizing shocks in the 1980s owes much to the ILLR-style activities of certain participants. The US Federal Reserve Board and Treasury sometimes seem to forget that the United States is supposed to have lost its hegemonic role. Whether by itself, as when domestic monetary policy was eased in autumn 1982 in response to signs of financial distress,[66] or in collaboration with the IMF, notably in dealing with Mexico in both 1982 and 1986, or coordinating its major Western partners, as at the Plaza Hotel in 1985, the United States has shown itself capable of leadership. Neither the commitment to 'hands-off' economic policies nor the decline of internationalism in the United States has inhibited decisive action when American vital interests are at stake.

Sometimes others play this role, as did the Governor of the Bank of England in arranging a bridging loan for Hungary through the BIS in spring 1982. Yet unless and until more formal institutional arrangements are established, the United States will continue to be the key player – if it wishes – in forcing action on debt strategy, exchange rates and macro-economic policy coordination, and hence in preventing financial crisis.

## III   The future

There are still plausible disaster scenarios. Marris (1985) on macro policy imbalances and their consequences (the 'hard landing') and Lever and Huhne (1985) on debt both permit the imagination to run to deep financial crisis. We believe, however, that greater understanding today of the linkages in financial crisis may have helped to reduce the danger of a serious crisis. Market participants and policy-makers may have learned from the experience of several smaller disturbances since the early 1970s that disaster probabilities are not negligible and appropriate precautions should be taken.

The main dangers lie not in disturbances originating in financial markets but in malfunctions of the real economy. Even though we have not experienced a crisis that seriously disrupted its allocative role, the international capital market still does not appear to be working properly, with the bulk of net flows now going from areas of high real marginal productivity to areas of lower productivity. Sustained high unemployment still fosters protectionism and threatens trade policy conflicts, with the 'inward-looking' consequences characteristic of the 1930s.[67] Although there has been more international macroeconomic policy cooperation recently, it is not fully institutionalized and may prove transient[68] – there is no international monetary constitution providing rules on exchange-market intervention and choice of reserve asset, constraints on fiscal and monetary policies, or responsibility for the ILLR function. Policy-makers still try to maintain their autonomy in an increasingly interdependent world. Paradoxically, even that objective, in the sense of expanding their opportunity set, might best be achieved through international economic policy coordination. Markets could not do the job, even if individual domestic policies were independently 'optimal'.

## IV   Conclusions

In this paper, we have contrasted the international financial crisis of the 1930s with the recent performance of the global financial system. We have sought to provide a perspective on the prospects for continued stability in international capital markets. While exhibiting fundamental differences in the operation of these markets currently and during the 1930s, our analysis nonetheless yields conclusions regarding conditions conducive to both the maintenance of stability and the onset of crisis.

The most important of these conclusions concern the roles of regulatory and stabilization policies. Financial crises spread most quickly when information is least complete, and they result in major externalities for particular sectors and the macroeconomy. On both imperfect information and externality grounds, there is a rationale for government intervention. Financial crises pose a greater threat under some institutional configurations than others. Even when the benefits of financial deregulation are apparent, there is a role for regulatory policy in channeling financial innovation in directions that leave the world economy less vulnerable to financial collapse. Finally, we have seen that financial crises are as much the result of macroeconomic shocks as they are of perturbations originating in financial markets. Perhaps the most important policy to prevent financial crises is therefore to provide a stable – and, in an increasingly interdependent world, internationally coordinated – macroeconomic environment within which financial markets may function.

The main difference between now and fifty years ago is that we have been there before and do not want to return. Informed policies can help us to avoid epidemic and keep our anatomy lesson to the conference room rather than the mortuary.

## NOTES

*  We thank H.M. Stationery Office for permission to cite documents from the Public Record Office, Anita Santorum for research assistance, and Jane Maurice for cheerful secretarial help beyond the call of duty. Anthony Harris, Joan Pearce and our discussants offered very useful comments, as did the seminar group at the Institute for International Economic Studies (Stockholm), where an early version of the work was presented in April 1986.
1  The most comprehensive recent survey is by Kindleberger (1978).

52   **Barry Eichengreen and Richard Portes**

2  This same point is made by Goldsmith (1982), p. 42.
3  Other exchanges, including those of Italy, the Netherlands, Spain, Sweden, Japan, Argentina and Brazil, remained stable even at the end of the war.
4  See the introduction to Eichengreen (1985a) for details.
5  Documenting the franc's undervaluation is problematic, however; see Eichengreen and Wyplosz (1986). Conventional accounts typically suggest that the franc was some 10 to 15 per cent undervalued relative to the dollar.
6  The transition from the gold to gold-exchange standard is analysed in Eichengreen (1985b). We return below to the role of foreign deposits.
7  Two views of the policy coordination problem are Clarke (1967) and Eichengreen (1985b).
8  The information summarized here is taken from Eichengreen and Portes (1986).
9  The parallels between the two experiences are explored by Balogh and Graham (1979).
10 Many articles in the financial press could be cited. An example is the *Financial Times* (18 December 1929), which even at this late date calls Peru 'apparently a country with a bright future.'
11 See for example Winkler (1933) or Securities and Exchange Commission (1937). Mintz (1950, ch. 4) presents evidence that a few aggressive issue houses were responsible for a disproportionate share of the loans which ultimately went into default.
12 The Table 1.2 data on ratios of public debt to GNP must be interpreted with care, since the importance of state and municipal borrowing varied enormously across countries. The low ratio for Germany, for example, reflects the tendency for borrowing to originate with municipalities and not the Reich.
13 Latin American experience is described in Eichengreen (1986) and Central European reforms in Nurkse (1946).
14 League of Nations (1931), p. 14.
15 Details are to be found in Schedvin (1970).
16 Schedvin (1970), pp. 166–7.
17 Insofar as exchange-rate fluctuations due to devaluation disrupted trade, a linkage to which contemporaries attached much importance, export receipts and debt capacity were reduced still further. For example, Condliffe (1933, p. 221) writes that 'exchange instability resulting from the breakdown of the international gold standard was one of the principal causes of further economic deterioration in 1932 and figured prominently among the factors which limited and checked the revival of prices and productive capacity in the third quarter of that year'. For similar comments, see Nurkse (1944). We return below to evidence on the impact of exchange-rate volatility on trade.
18 This periodization follows Condliffe (1933), chapter ix.
19 The situation in 1931 differs from Sachs's (1982) description of pre-World-War-I lending and default. Before World War I, Sachs argues, default by one country did little to interrupt the flow of capital to other borrowers. The difference between the periods may be that default in 1931 was seen as a response to global rather than country-specific shocks.
20 Eichengreen and Portes (1986) report regressions in which both the extent of terms-of-trade deterioration and the growth of the central government budget deficit are significantly correlated with the incidence and extent of default.

21  British Public Record Office (PRO) FO371/14198, Dispatch to Foreign Office by R. C. Mitchell, 'Political Situation in Bolivia', 22 September 1930.

22  PRO FO 371/14253, Dispatch from Mr Gurney (Lima), 'Annual Report of the Peruvian President to Congress', 18 September 1930; Madden *et al.* (1937), p. 111.

23  Bank Commissioner of the State of Vermont (1930). Vermont appears to be the only state for which this information is available. See White (1984) for further discussion of these data.

24  See Leguizamon (1933) for additional analysis.

25  Kindleberger (1984), p. 372. It is popularly thought that origins of the run were both economic, caused by the bank's uncertain liquidity, and political, caused by French alarm over the recently proposed Austro-German customs union.

26  A recent account of this episode is James (1984).

27  It could be argued that the provision of deposit insurance and improvements in bank regulation have reduced the extent of these externalities. We return to this point below.

28  See League of Nations (1934) for another statement of this view.

29  Details are to be found in Cairncross and Eichengreen (1983) and the references cited there.

30  Between June 1922 and June 1929, the real estate loans of commercial banks had risen by 128 per cent and their security loans by 77 per cent, in comparison with all other loans and investments, which rose by only 30 per cent.

31  The ratio of cash reserves to total deposits was consistently lower only in countries which ultimately turned to exchange control (Germany, Austria, Czechoslovakia) and in the exceptional Swedish case.

32  This is similar to the argument advanced by Bernanke (1983).

33  This episode is the subject of Epstein and Ferguson (1984).

34  Beenstock (1984) argues that this difference has no significant systemic consequences; and the 1970s may turn out to have been a quite exceptional period in this regard, with the growth of securitization and off-balance-sheet operations in the past few years.

35  There were negotiations between debtor countries and the bondholders' organizations after the defaults of the 1930s, but they were difficult to organize. See Eichengreen and Portes (1986).

36  See Williamson (1977) for an account of this period.

37  See Padoa Schioppa (1985) for background on the operation of the EMS and the detailed discussions and assessments in the report (and background documents) of the Treasury and Civil Service Committee of the UK House of Commons (1985).

38  The studies which supposedly showed the inefficacy of sterilized intervention were ignored when the United States changed its policy stance in September 1985.

39  Recent accounts, from somewhat different viewpoints, include Cline (1984) and Lever and Huhne (1985).

40  OECD (1983) describes the picture at the beginning of the 1980s, and Bryant (1987) offers a more recent and more analytical assessment.

41  See Kindleberger (1978, 1986) and Spero (1980).

42  Generally, capital controls have been progressively liberalized or removed, notably in the UK. It can be argued that they have played an important role in

54 **Barry Eichengreen and Richard Portes**

keeping the EMS together – or that the demands of keeping the system together have required capital controls (Giavazzi and Giovannini, 1986). This view is likely to be tested soon, as France and Italy proceed to relax exchange controls.

43 See Kenen and Rodrik (1986).
44 See Rogoff (1985), Padoa Schioppa (1985), and House of Commons (1985).
45 See de Grauwe and de Bellefroid (1986) and Kenen and Rodrik (1986).
46 See Frankel and Froot (1986) and references cited there.
47 The estimates in *World Financial Markets* (March 1986) are particularly striking, though controversial (according to the *Financial Times*, 21 August 1986, the Bank of Mexico estimates capital flight under the current government at $2 billion, in contrast to the Morgan Guaranty estimate of $17 billion). A more academic but still debatable analysis stressing the role of capital flight in Latin American debt problems, and the root cause of exchange rate overvaluation, is given by Sachs (1985).
48 The views of Marris (1985) are discussed below.
49 Diaz Alejandro (1984) argues that an observer in 1980–81 could not reasonably have foreseen a crisis of the magnitude experienced in 1982–4. On the other hand, Portes (1977) predicted a debt-servicing crisis for several East European countries in the early 1980s, beginning with a rescheduling for Poland in 1980–1.
50 See Portes (1982).
51 World Bank (1986).
52 As suggested by theory; see, for example, Guttentag and Herring (1984). Their argument that an extended period without adverse shocks creates conditions in which a shock will then provoke discontinuous market behaviour is more specific and rigorous than the 'financial instability hypothesis' of Minsky (1982), who argues that the danger of financial crisis builds up over an extended period of prosperous times.
53 Cf. note 20 above.
54 See Cohen (1985).
55 Notable among these are Kraft (1984), who gives an 'inside', circumstantial narrative of the negotiations which dealt with the initial Mexican crisis, and Fraga (1986), who makes an interesting comparison of Brazil's recent experience with Germany and reparations fifty years before.
56 Compare Guttentag and Herring (1985) with Edwards (1986).
57 'With reasonable recovery in the global economy, the problem of international debt should prove manageable and the degree of its current risk to the international system should decline' (Cline, 1983, p. 121).
58 See Kaletsky (1985) and Lever and Huhne (1985).
59 See Eichengreen and Portes (1986) for calculations of the *ex-post* rates of return earned by creditors in such cases.
60 Cooper (1986) describes these changes and argues convincingly that they are explained better by technical change than as innovative risk-sharing arrangements or as responses to cross-border differences in taxation and regulation.
61 Eichengreen and Portes (1986).
62 For example, see Guttentag and Herring (1983).
63 The models of the US Federal Deposit Insurance Corporation and Federal Savings and Loan Insurance Corporation have been increasingly followed in Europe and elsewhere.

64 Eichengreen and Portes (1986).
65 Solow (1982) provides a recent discussion of the theory relevant to LLR functions, which are treated further in Kindleberger (1978) and Kindleberger and Laffargue (1982). It can be argued that financial deregulation has led to more risk-taking by financial intermediaries, hence to more LLR intervention, exacerbating moral hazard (and weakening monetary control). This goes beyond our scope here.
66 See Carron (1982).
67 See Cooper (1983).
68 See Portes (1986).

## REFERENCES

Balogh, Thomas and Andrew Graham (1979). 'The Transfer Problem Revisited: Analogies Between the Reparations Payments of the 1920s and the Problem of the OPEC Surpluses', *Oxford Bulletin of Economics and Statistics* **41**, pp. 183–92.
Bank for International Settlements (1986). *Recent Innovations in International Banking*, Basle.
Beenstock, Michael (1984). *The World Economy in Transition*, London: Macmillan.
Bernanke, Ben S. (1983). 'Nonmonetary Effects of the Financial Crisis in the Propagation of the Great Depression', *American Economic Review* **73**, pp. 257–76.
Bryant, Ralph (1987). *International Financial Intermediation: Issues for Analysis and Public Policy*, Washington: Brookings Institution.
Buiter, Willem and Richard Marston (eds) (1985). *International Economic Policy Coordination*, Cambridge: Cambridge University Press.
Butlin, N. G. (1984). 'Select Comparative Economic Statistics, 1900–1940', Source Paper No. 4, Department of Economic History, Australian National University.
Cairncross, Alec and Barry Eichengreen (1983). *Sterling in Decline*, Oxford: Blackwell.
Carron, Andrew (1982). 'Financial Crisis: Recent Experience in US and International Markets', *Brookings Papers on Economic Activity*, No. 2, pp. 395–422.
Clarke, S. V. O. (1967). *Central Bank Coordination, 1924–31*, New York: Federal Reserve Bank of New York.
Cline, William (1983). *International Debt and the Stability of the World Economy*, Washington, DC: Institute for International Economics.
   (1984). *International Debt: Systemic Risk and Policy Response*, Washington, DC: Institute for International Economics.
Cohen, Daniel (1985). 'How to Evaluate the Solvency of an Indebted Nation', *Economic Policy* **1**, pp. 139–67.
Condliffe, J. B. (1933). *World Economic Survey, 1932–33*, Geneva: League of Nations.
Cooper, Ian (1986). 'Financial Markets: New Financial Instruments', paper presented to CEPR Workshop, London.

56 **Barry Eichengreen and Richard Portes**

Cooper, Richard (1983). 'Managing Risks to the International Economic System', in Herring, Richard, ed., *Managing International Risk*, Cambridge: Cambridge University Press.

Diaz Alejandro, Carlos (1984). 'Latin American Debt: I Don't Think We Are in Kansas Anymore', *Brookings Papers on Economic Activity*, No. 2, pp. 335–89.

Dornbusch, Rudiger (1985). 'Policy and Performance Links between LDC Debtors and Industrial Nations', *Brookings Papers on Economic Activity*, No. 2, pp. 303–56.

Edwards, Sebastian (1986). 'The Pricing of Bonds and Bank Loans in International Markets', *European Economic Review*, **30**, pp. 565–90.

Eichengreen, Barry (1985a), ed, *The Gold Standard in Theory and History*, London: Methuen.

(1985b). 'International Policy Coordination in Historical Perspective: A View from the Interwar Years', in Buiter and Marston (1985), pp. 139–78.

(1986). 'House Calls of the Money Doctor: The Kemmerer Missions to Latin America, 1923–1931', in Ronald Findlay *et al.* (eds), *Debt, Stabilization and Development: Essays in Honor of Carlos F. Diaz Alejandro*, Oxford University Press, forthcoming.

Eichengreen, Barry and Richard Portes (1986). 'Debt and Default in the 1930s: Causes and Consequences,' *European Economic Review* **30**, pp. 559–640.

Eichengreen, Barry and Charles Wyplosz (1986). 'The Economic Consequences of the Franc Poincare', unpublished manuscript.

Epstein, Gerald and Thomas Ferguson (1984). 'Monetary Policy, Loan Liquidation, and Industrial Conflict: The Federal Reserve and the Open Market Operations of 1932', *Journal of Economic History* **44**, pp. 957–86.

Frankel, Jeffrey and Kenneth Froot (1986). 'The Dollar as an Irrational Speculative Bubble', Marcus Wallenberg Papers on International Finance, **1**, No. 1.

Fraga, Arminio (1986). *German Reparations and Brazilian Debt*, Princeton Essays in International Finance No. 163, Princeton, NJ: International Financial Section, Princeton University.

Goldsmith, Raymond (1982). 'Comment on Minsky', in Kindleberger and Laffargue (1982), pp. 41–43.

Giavazzi, Francesco and Alberto Giovannini (1986). 'The EMS and the Dollar', *Economic Policy* 2, pp. 455–85.

de Grauwe, Paul and Bernard de Bellefroid (1986). 'Long-Run Exchange Rate Variability and International Trade', mimeo.

Guttentag, Jack and Richard Herring (1983). *The Lender-of-Last-Resort Function in an International Context*, Princeton Essays in International Finance No.151, Princeton, NJ: International Financial Section, Princeton University.

(1984). 'Credit Rationing and Financial Disorder', *Journal of Finance* **39**, pp. 1359–82.

(1985). *The Current Crisis in International Lending*, Washington, DC: Brookings Institution.

House of Commons, Treasury and Civil Service Select Committee (1985). *The Financial and Economic Consequences of UK Membership of the European Communities: The European Monetary System*, Vols. I, II, and Memoranda, London: HMSO.

James, Harold (1984). 'The Causes of the German Banking Crisis of 1931', *Economic History Review* **38**, pp. 68–87.

Kaletsky, Anatole (1985). *The Costs of Default*, New York: Twentieth Century Fund.

Kenen, Peter and Dani Rodrik (1986). 'Measuring and Analyzing the Effects of Short-Term Volatility in Real Exchange Rates', *Review of Economics and Statistics*, pp. 311–15.

Keynes, John Maynard (1925). 'Is Sterling Overvalued?' *The Nation and Athenaeum*, 4 April.

Kindleberger, Charles (1978). *Manias, Panics and Crashes*, New York: Basic Books.

   (1984). *A Financial History of Western Europe*, London: Allen & Unwin.

   (1986). 'Bank Failures: the 1930s and the 1980s', in *The Search for Financial Stability: The Past Fifty Years*, San Francisco, California: Federal Reserve Bank of San Francisco.

Kindleberger, Charles and Jean-Pierre Laffargue (eds) (1982). *Financial Crises: Theory, History and Policy*, London: Cambridge University Press.

Kraft, Joseph (1984). *The Mexican Rescue*, New York: Group of Thirty.

League of Nations (1931), *Commercial Banks, 1913–1929*, Geneva: League of Nations.

   (1934). *Commercial Banks, 1925–1933*, Geneva: League of Nations.

   (1937). *Balance of Payments 1936*, Geneva: League of Nations.

   (1938). *Balance of Payments 1937*, Geneva: League of Nations.

Leguizamon, Guillermo A. (1933). 'An Argentine View of the Problem of Exchange Restrictions', *International Affairs*, pp. 504–17.

Lever, Harold and Christopher Huhne (1985). *Debt and Danger: The World Financial Crisis*, London: Penguin.

Maddison, Angus (1985), *Two Crises: Latin America and Asia 1929–38 and 1973–83*, Paris: OECD.

McNeil, William C. (1986). *American Money and the Weimar Republic*, New York: Columbia University Press.

Marris, Stephen (1985). *Deficits and the Dollar: The World Economy at Risk*, Washington, DC: Institute of International Economics.

Minsky, Hyman (1982). 'The Financial Instability Hypothesis: Capitalist Processes and the Behaviour of the Economy', in Kindleberger and Laffargue (1982), pp. 13–38.

Mintz, Ilse (1950). *Deterioration in the Quality of Foreign Bonds Issued in the United States, 1920–1930*, New York: National Bureau of Economic Research.

Mitchell, B. R. (1976). *European Historical Statistics*, London: Macmillan.

Morgan Guaranty Trust Company of New York, *World Financial Markets*.

Nurkse, Ragnar (1944). *International Currency Experience*, Geneva: League of Nations.

   (1946). *The Course and Control of Inflation*, Geneva: League of Nations.

OECD (1983). *The Internationalization of Banking*, Paris.

Padoa Schioppa, Tommaso (1985). 'Policy Cooperation and the EMS Experience', in Buiter and Marston (1985), pp. 331–55.

Portes, Richard (1977). 'East Europe's Debt to the West', *Foreign Affairs* **55**, pp. 751–82.

   (1982). 'La crise polonaise et les relations économiques est-ouest', *Politique étrangère*, no. 1, pp. 75–90.

58   **Discussion by Robert F. Gemmill**

(1986). 'Finance, Trade and Development: Issues in Transatlantic Cooper-ation', *CEPR Discussion Paper No. 100.*

Rogoff, Kenneth (1985). 'Can Exchange Rate Predictability be Achieved without Monetary Convergence? Evidence from the EMS', *European Economic Review* **28**, pp. 93–116.

Royal Institute of International Affairs (1937). *The Problem of Foreign Invest-ment,* London: Oxford University Press.

Sachs, Jeffrey (1982). 'LDC Debt in the 1980s: Risk and Reforms', in *Crises in the Economic and Financial Structure,* ed. Paul Wachtel, Lexington, Mass.: D.C. Heath.

(1985). 'External Debt and Macroeconomic Performance in Latin America and East Asia', *Brookings Papers on Economic Activity* No. 2, pp. 523–64.

Schedvin, C. Boris (1970). *Australia and the Great Depression.* Sydney, Sydney University Press.

Securities and Exchange Commission (1937). *Report on the Study and Investi-gation of the Work, Activities, Personnel and Functions of the Protective and Reorganization Committees,* Washington, DC, GPO.

Solow, Robert (1982). 'On the Lender of Last Resort', in Kindleberger and Laffargue (1982), pp. 237–47.

Spero, Joan (1980). *The Failure of the Franklin National Bank,* New York: Columbia University Press.

State of Vermont (1930). *Annual Report of the Bank Commissioner of the State of Vermont for the Year Ending June 30, 1930,* Rutland, Vermont: The Tuttle Company.

Thorp, Rosemary (1984), ed., *Latin America in the 1930s,* London: Macmillan.

Urquhart, M. C. and K. A. H. Buckley (1965). *Historical Statistics of Canada,* Cambridge: Cambridge University Press.

U.S. Department of Commerce (1930). *American Underwriting of Foreign Securities,* Washington, DC: GPO.

White, Eugene (1984). 'A Reinterpretation of the Banking Crisis of 1930', *Journal of Economic History* **44**, pp. 119–38.

Williamson, John (1977). *The Failure of World Monetary Reform,* London: Nelson.

(1985). *The Exchange Rate System,* Washington, DC: Institute for Inter-national Economics.

Winkler, Max (1933). *Foreign Bonds: An Autopsy,* Philadelphia: Roland Swain.

World Bank (1986). *World Debt Tables,* Washington, DC: IBRD.

# [9]

Excerpt from *Financial Markets and Financial Crises*, 33–68

## 2    The Gold Standard, Deflation, and Financial Crisis in the Great Depression: An International Comparison

### Ben Bernanke and Harold James

### 2.1  Introduction

Recent research on the causes of the Great Depression has laid much of the blame for that catastrophe on the doorstep of the international gold standard. In his new book, Temin (1989) argues that structural flaws of the interwar gold standard, in conjunction with policy responses dictated by the gold standard's "rules of the game," made an international monetary contraction and deflation almost inevitable. Eichengreen and Sachs (1985) have presented evidence that countries which abandoned the gold standard and the associated contractionary monetary policies recovered from the Depression more quickly than countries that remained on gold. Research by Hamilton (1987, 1988) supports the propositions that contractionary monetary policies in France and the United States initiated the Great Slide, and that the defense of gold standard parities added to the deflationary pressure.[1]

The gold standard–based explanation of the Depression (which we will elaborate in section 2.2) is in most respects compelling. The length and depth of the deflation during the late 1920s and early 1930s strongly suggest a monetary origin, and the close correspondence (across both space and time) between deflation and nations' adherence to the gold standard shows the power of that system to transmit contractionary monetary shocks. There is also a high correlation in the data between deflation (falling prices) and depression (falling output), as the previous authors have noted and as we will demonstrate again below.

Ben Bernanke is professor of economics and public affairs at Princeton University and a research associate of the National Bureau of Economic Research. Harold James is assistant professor of history at Princeton University.

The authors thank David Fernandez, Mark Griffiths, and Holger Wolf for invaluable research assistance. Support was provided by the National Bureau of Economic Research and the National Science Foundation.

33

If the argument as it has been made so far has a weak link, however, it is probably the explanation of how the deflation induced by the malfunctioning gold standard caused depression; that is, what was the source of this massive monetary non-neutrality?[2] The goal of our paper is to try to understand better the mechanisms by which deflation may have induced depression in the 1930s. We consider several channels suggested by earlier work, in particular effects operating through real wages and through interest rates. Our focus, however, is on a channel of transmission that has been largely ignored by the recent gold standard literature; namely, the disruptive effect of deflation on the financial system.

Deflation (and the constraints on central bank policy imposed by the gold standard) was an important cause of banking panics, which occurred in a number of countries in the early 1930s. As discussed for the case of the United States by Bernanke (1983), to the extent that bank panics interfere with normal flows of credit, they may affect the performance of the real economy; indeed, it is possible that economic performance may be affected even without major panics, if the banking system is sufficiently weakened. Because severe banking panics are the form of financial crisis most easily identified empirically, we will focus on their effects in this paper. However, we do not want to lose sight of a second potential effect of falling prices on the financial sector, which is "debt deflation" (Fisher 1933; Bernanke 1983; Bernanke and Gertler 1990). By increasing the real value of nominal debts and promoting insolvency of borrowers, deflation creates an environment of financial distress in which the incentives of borrowers are distorted and in which it is difficult to extend new credit. Again, this provides a means by which falling prices can have real effects.

To examine these links between deflation and depression, we take a comparative approach (as did Eichengreen and Sachs). Using an annual data set covering twenty-four countries, we try to measure (for example) the differences between countries on and off the gold standard, or between countries experiencing banking panics and those that did not. A weakness of our approach is that, lacking objective indicators of the seriousness of financial problems, we are forced to rely on dummy variables to indicate periods of crisis. Despite this problem, we generally do find an important role for financial crises—particularly banking panics—in explaining the link between falling prices and falling output. Countries in which, for institutional or historical reasons, deflation led to panics or other severe banking problems had significantly worse depressions than countries in which banking was more stable. In addition, there may have been a feedback loop through which banking panics, particularly those in the United States, intensified the severity of the worldwide deflation. Because of data problems, we do not provide direct evidence of the debt-deflation mechanism; however, we do find that much of the apparent impact of deflation on output is unaccounted for by the mechanisms we

**35**    Financial Crisis in the Great Depression

explicitly consider, leaving open the possibility that debt deflation was important.

The rest of the paper is organized as follows. Section 2.2 briefly recapitu-
lates the basic case against the interwar gold standard, showing it to have been
a source of deflation and depression, and provides some new evidence consistent with this view. Section 2.3 takes a preliminary look at some mechanisms by which deflation may have been transmitted to depression. In section
2.4, we provide an overview of the financial crises that occurred during the
interwar period. Section 2.5 presents and discusses our main empirical results
on the effects of financial crisis in the 1930s, and section 2.6 concludes.

## 2.2   The Gold Standard and Deflation

In this section we discuss, and provide some new evidence for, the claim
that a mismanaged interwar gold standard was responsible for the worldwide
deflation of the late 1920s and early 1930s.

The gold standard—generally viewed at the time as an essential source of
the relative prosperity of the late nineteenth and early twentieth centuries—
was suspended at the outbreak of World War I. Wartime suspension of the gold
standard was not in itself unusual; indeed, Bordo and Kydland (1990) have
argued that wartime suspension, followed by a return to gold at prewar parities as soon as possible, should be considered part of the gold standard's normal operation. Bordo and Kydland pointed out that a reputation for returning
to gold at the prewar parity, and thus at something close to the prewar price
level, would have made it easier for a government to sell nominal bonds and
would have increased attainable seignorage. A credible commitment to the
gold standard thus would have had the effect of allowing war spending to be
financed at a lower total cost.

Possibly for these reputational reasons, and certainly because of widespread unhappiness with the chaotic monetary and financial conditions that
followed the war (there were hyperinflations in central Europe and more moderate but still serious inflations elsewhere), the desire to return to gold in the
early 1920s was strong. Of much concern however was the perception that
there was not enough gold available to satisfy world money demands without
deflation. The 1922 Economic and Monetary Conference at Genoa addressed
this issue by recommending the adoption of a gold exchange standard, in
which convertible foreign exchange reserves (principally dollars and pounds)
as well as gold would be used to back national money supplies, thus "econo-
mizing" on gold. Although "key currencies" had been used as reserves before
the war, the Genoa recommendations led to a more widespread and officially
sanctioned use of this practice (Lindert 1969; Eichengreen 1987).

During the 1920s the vast majority of the major countries succeeded in returning to gold. (The first column of table 2.1 gives the dates of return for the

countries in our data set.) Britain returned at the prewar parity in 1925, despite Keynes's argument that at the old parity the pound would be overvalued. By the end of 1925, out of a list of 48 currencies given by the League of Nations (1926), 28 had been pegged to gold. France returned to gold gradually, following the Poincaré stabilization, although at a new parity widely believed to undervalue the franc. By the end of 1928, except for China and a few small countries on the silver standard, only Spain, Portugal, Rumania, and Japan had not been brought back into the gold standard system. Rumania went back on gold in 1929, Portugal did so in practice also in 1929 (although not officially until 1931), and Japan in December 1930. In the same month the Bank for International Settlements gave Spain a stabilization loan, but the operation was frustrated by a revolution in April 1931, carried out by republicans who, as one of the most attractive features of their program, opposed the foreign stabilization credits. Spain thus did not join the otherwise nearly universal membership of the gold standard club.

The classical gold standard of the prewar period functioned reasonably smoothly and without a major convertibility crisis for more than thirty years. In contrast, the interwar gold standard, established between 1925 and 1928, had substantially broken down by 1931 and disappeared by 1936. An extensive literature has analyzed the differences between the classical and interwar gold standards. This literature has focused, with varying degrees of emphasis, both on fundamental economic problems that complicated trade and monetary adjustment in the interwar period and on technical problems of the interwar gold standard itself.

In terms of "fundamentals," Temin (1989) has emphasized the effects of the Great War, arguing that, ultimately, the war itself was the shock that initiated the Depression. The legacy of the war included—besides physical destruction, which was relatively quickly repaired—new political borders drawn apparently without economic rationale; substantial overcapacity in some sectors (such as agriculture and heavy industry) and undercapacity in others, relative to long-run equilibrium; and reparations claims and international war debts that generated fiscal burdens and fiscal uncertainty. Some writers (notably Charles Kindleberger) have also pointed to the fact that the prewar gold standards was a hegemonic system, with Great Britain the unquestioned center. In contrast, in the interwar period the relative decline of Britain, the inexperience and insularity of the new potential hegemon (the United States), and ineffective cooperation among central banks left no one able to take responsibility for the system as a whole.

The technical problems of the interwar gold standard included the following three:

1. *The asymmetry between surplus and deficit countries in the required monetary response to gold flows.* Temin suggests, correctly we believe, that this was the most important structural flaw of the gold standard. In theory, under the "rules of the game," central banks of countries experiencing gold

37    Financial Crisis in the Great Depression

**Table 2.1            Dates of Changes in Gold Standard Policies**

| Country | Return to Gold | Suspension of Gold Standard | Foreign Exchange Control | Devaluation |
|---|---|---|---|---|
| Australia | April 1925 | December 1929 | — | March 1930 |
| Austria | April 1925 | April 1933 | October 1931 | September 1931 |
| Belgium | October 1926 | — | — | March 1935 |
| Canada | July 1926 | October 1931 | — | September 1931 |
| Czechoslovakia | April 1926 | — | September 1931 | February 1934 |
| Denmark | January 1927 | September 1931 | November 1931 | September 1931 |
| Estonia | January 1928 | June 1933 | November 1931 | June 1933 |
| Finland | January 1926 | October 1931 | — | October 1931 |
| France | August 1926– June 1928 | — | — | October 1936 |
| Germany | September 1924 | — | July 1931 | — |
| Greece | May 1928 | April 1932 | September 1931 | April 1932 |
| Hungary | April 1925 | — | July 1931 | — |
| Italy | December 1927 | — | May 1934 | October 1936 |
| Japan | December 1930 | December 1931 | July 1932 | December 1931 |
| Latvia | August 1922 | — | October 1931 | — |
| Netherlands | April 1925 | — | — | October 1936 |
| Norway | May 1928 | September 1931 | — | September 1931 |
| New Zealand | April 1925 | September 1931 | — | April 1930 |
| Poland | October 1927 | — | April 1936 | October 1936 |
| Rumania | March 1927– February 1929 | — | May 1932 | — |
| Sweden | April 1924 | September 1931 | — | September 1931 |
| Spain | — | — | May 1931 | — |
| United Kingdom | May 1925 | September 1931 | — | September 1931 |
| United States | June 1919 | March 1933 | March 1933 | April 1933 |

*Source:* League of Nations, *Yearbook,* various dates; and miscellaneous supplementary sources.

inflows were supposed to assist the price-specie flow mechanism by expanding domestic money supplies and inflating, while deficit countries were supposed to reduce money supplies and deflate. In practice, the need to avoid a complete loss of reserves and an end to convertibility forced deficit countries to comply with this rule; but, in contrast, no sanction prevented surplus countries from sterilizing gold inflows and accumulating reserves indefinitely, if domestic objectives made that desirable. Thus there was a potential deflationary bias in the gold standard's operation.

This asymmetry between surplus and deficit countries also existed in the prewar period, but with the important difference that the prewar gold standard centered around the operations of the Bank of England. The Bank of England of course had to hold enough gold to ensure convertibility, but as a profit-making institution it also had a strong incentive not to hold large stocks of barren gold (as opposed to interest-paying assets). Thus the Bank managed the gold standard (with the assistance of other central banks) so as to avoid both sustained inflows and sustained outflows of gold; and, indeed, it helped ensure continuous convertibility with a surprisingly low level of gold reserves. In contrast, the two major gold surplus countries of the interwar period, the United States and France, had central banks with little or no incentive to avoid accumulation of gold.

The deflationary bias of the asymmetry in required adjustments was magnified by statutory fractional reserve requirements imposed on many central banks, especially the new central banks, after the war. While Britain, Norway, Finland, and Sweden had a fiduciary issue—a fixed note supply backed only by domestic government securities, above which 100% gold backing was required—most countries required instead that minimum gold holdings equal a fixed fraction (usually close to the Federal Reserve's 40%) of central bank liabilities. These rules had two potentially harmful effects.

First, just as required "reserves" for modern commercial banks are not really available for use as true reserves, a large portion of central bank gold holdings were immobilized by the reserve requirements and could not be used to settle temporary payments imbalances. For example, in 1929, according to the League of Nations, for 41 countries with a total gold reserve of $9,378 million, only $2,178 million were "surplus" reserves, with the rest required as cover (League of Nations 1944, 12). In fact, this overstates the quantity of truly free reserves, because markets and central banks became very worried when reserves fell within 10% of the minimum. The upshot of this is that deficit countries could lose very little gold before being forced to reduce their domestic money supplies; while, as we have noted, the absence of any maximum reserve limit allowed surplus countries to accept gold inflows without inflating.

The second and related effect of the fractional reserve requirement has to do with the relationship between gold outflows and domestic monetary contraction. With fractional reserves, the relationship between gold outflow and the reduction in the money supply was not one for one; with a 40% reserve requirement, for example, the impact on the money supply of a gold outflow was 2.5 times the external loss. So again, loss of gold could lead to an immediate and sharp deflationary impact, not balanced by inflation elsewhere.

2. *The pyramiding of reserves.* As we have noted, under the interwar gold-exchange standard, countries other than those with reserve currencies were encouraged to hold convertible foreign exchange reserves as a partial (or in some cases, as a nearly complete) substitute for gold. But these convertible reserves were in turn usually only fractionally backed by gold. Thus, just as a shift by the public from fractionally backed deposits to currency would lower the total domestic money supply, the gold-exchange system opened up the

possibility that a shift of central banks from foreign exchange reserves to gold might lower the world money supply, adding another deflationary bias to the system. Central banks did abandon foreign exchange reserves en masse in the early 1930s, when the threat of devaluation made foreign exchange assets quite risky. According to Eichengreen (1987), however, the statistical evidence is not very clear on whether central banks after selling their foreign exchange simply lowered their cover ratios, which would have had no direct effect on money supplies, or shifted into gold, which would have been contractionary. Even if the central banks responded only by lowering cover ratios, however, this would have increased the sensitivity of their money supplies to any subsequent outflow of reserves.

3. *Insufficient powers of central banks.* An important institutional feature of the interwar gold standard is that, for a majority of the important continental European central banks, open market operations were not permitted or were severely restricted. This limitation on central bank powers was usually the result of the stabilization programs of the early and mid 1920s. By prohibiting central banks from holding or dealing in significant quantities of government securities, and thus making monetization of deficits more difficult, the architects of the stabilizations hoped to prevent future inflation. This forced the central banks to rely on discount policy (the terms at which they would make loans to commercial banks) as the principal means of affecting the domestic money supply. However, in a number of countries the major commercial banks borrowed very infrequently from the central banks, implying that except in crisis periods the central bank's control over the money supply might be quite weak.

The loosening of the link between the domestic money supply and central bank reserves may have been beneficial in some cases during the 1930s, if it moderated the monetary effect of reserve outflows. However, in at least one very important case the inability of a central bank to conduct open market operations may have been quite destabilizing. As discussed by Eichengreen (1986), the Bank of France, which was the recipient of massive gold inflows until 1932, was one of the banks that was prohibited from conducting open market operations. This severely limited the ability of the Bank to translate its gold inflows into monetary expansion, as should have been done in obedience to the rules of the game. The failure of France to inflate meant that it continued to attract reserves, thus imposing deflation on the rest of the world.[3]

Given both the fundamental economic problems of the international economy and the structural flaws of the gold standard system, even a relatively minor deflationary impulse might have had significant repercussions. As it happened, both of the two major gold surplus countries—France and the United States, who at the time together held close to 60% of the world's monetary gold—took deflationary paths in 1928–29 (Hamilton 1987).

In the French case, as we have already noted, the deflationary shock took the form of a largely sterilized gold inflow. For several reasons—including a successful stabilization with attendant high real interest rates, a possibly undervalued franc, the lifting of exchange controls, and the perception that France was a "safe haven" for capital—beginning in early 1928 gold flooded into that country, an inflow that was to last until 1932. In 1928, France controlled about 15% of the total monetary gold held by the twenty-four countries in our data set (Board of Governors 1943); this share, already disproportionate to France's economic importance, increased to 18% in 1929, 22% in 1930, 28% in 1931, and 32% in 1932. Since the U.S. share of monetary gold remained stable at something greater than 40% of the total, the inflow to France implied significant losses of gold by countries such as Germany, Japan, and the United Kingdom.

With its accumulation of gold. France should have been expected to inflate; but in part because of the restrictions on open market operations discussed above and in part because of deliberate policy choices, the impact of the gold inflow on French prices was minimal. The French monetary base did increase with the inflow of reserves, but because economic growth led the demand for francs to expand even more quickly, the country actually experienced a wholesale price *deflation* of almost 11% between January 1929 and January 1930.

Hamilton (1987) also documents the monetary tightening in the United States in 1928, a contraction motivated in part by the desire to avoid losing gold to the French but perhaps even more by the Federal Reserve's determination to slow down stock market speculation. The U.S. price level fell about 4% over the course of 1929. A business cycle peak was reached in the United States in August 1929, and the stock market crashed in October.

The initial contractions in the United States and France were largely self-inflicted wounds; no binding external constraint forced the United States to deflate in 1929, and it would certainly have been possible for the French government to grant the Bank of France the power to conduct expansionary open market operations. However, Temin (1989) argues that, once these destabilizing policy measures had been taken, little could be done to avert deflation and depression, given the commitment of central banks to maintenance of the gold standard. Once the deflationary process had begun, central banks engaged in competitive deflation and a scramble for gold, hoping by raising cover ratios to protect their currencies against speculative attack. Attempts by any individual central bank to reflate were met by immediate gold outflows, which forced the central bank to raise its discount rate and deflate once again. According to Temin, even the United States, with its large gold reserves, faced this constraint. Thus Temin disagrees with the suggestion of Friedman and Schwartz (1963) that the Federal Reserve's failure to protect the U.S. money supply was due to misunderstanding of the problem or a lack of leadership; instead, he claims, given the commitment to the gold standard (and, presumably, the absence of effective central bank cooperation), the Fed had little choice but to let the banks fail and the money supply fall.

For our purposes here it does not matter much to what extent central bank choices could have been other than what they were. For the positive question of what caused the Depression, we need only note that a monetary contraction began in the United States and France, and was propagated throughout the world by the international monetary standard.[4]

If monetary contraction propagated by the gold standard was the source of the worldwide deflation and depression, then countries abandoning the gold standard (or never adopting it) should have avoided much of the deflationary pressure. This seems to have been the case. In an important paper, Choudhri and Kochin (1980) documented that Spain, which never restored the gold standard and allowed its exchange rate to float, avoided the declines in prices and output that affected other European countries. Choudhri and Kochin also showed that the Scandinavian countries, which left gold along with the United Kingdom in 1931, recovered from the Depression much more quickly than other small European countries that remained longer on the gold standard. Much of this had been anticipated in an insightful essay by Haberler (1976).

Eichengreen and Sachs (1985) similarly focused on the beneficial effects of currency depreciation (i.e., abandonment of the gold standard or devaluation). For a sample of ten European countries, they showed that depreciating countries enjoyed faster growth of exports and industrial production than countries which did not depreciate. Depreciating countries also experienced lower real wages and greater profitability, which presumably helped to increase production. Eichengreen and Sachs argued that depreciation, in this context, should not necessarily be thought of as a "beggar thy neighbor" policy; because depreciations reduced constraints on the growth of world money supplies, they may have conferred benefits abroad as well as at home (although a coordinated depreciation presumably would have been better than the uncoordinated sequence of depreciations that in fact took place).[5]

Some additional evidence of the effects of maintaining or leaving the gold standard, much in the spirit of Eichengreen and Sachs but using data from a larger set of countries, is given in our tables 2.2 through 2.4. These tables summarize the relationships between the decision to adhere to the gold standard and some key macroeconomic variables, including wholesale price inflation (table 2.2), some indicators of national monetary policies (table 2.3), and industrial production growth (table 2.4). To construct these tables, we divided our sample of twenty-four countries into four categories:[6] 1) countries not on the gold standard at all (Spain) or leaving prior to 1931 (Australia and New Zealand); 2) countries abandoning the full gold standard in 1931 (14 countries); 3) countries abandoning the gold standard between 1932 and 1935 (Rumania in 1932, the United States in 1933, Italy in 1934, and Belgium in 1935); and 4) countries still on the full gold standard as of 1936 (France, Netherlands, Poland).[7] Tables 2.2 and 2.4 give the data for each country, as well as averages for the large cohort of countries abandoning gold in 1931, for the remnant of the gold bloc still on gold in 1936, and (for 1932–35, when there were a significant number of countries in each category) for all gold standard and non–gold standard countries. Since table 2.3 reports data on four different variables, in order to save space only the averages are shown.[8]

The link between deflation and adherence to the gold standard, shown in table 2.2, seems quite clear. As noted by Choudhri and Kochin (1980), Spain's abstention from the gold standard insulated that country from the general deflation; New Zealand and Australia, presumably because they retained links to sterling despite early abandonment of the strict gold standard, did however experience some deflation. Among countries on the gold standard as of 1931, there is a rather uniform experience of about a 13% deflation in both 1930 and 1931. But after 1931 there is a sharp divergence between those countries on and those off the gold standard. Price levels in countries off the gold standard have stabilized by 1933 (with one or two exceptions), and these countries experience mild inflations in 1934–36. In contrast, the gold standard countries continue to deflate, although at a slower rate, until the gold standard's dissolution in 1936.

With such clearly divergent price behavior between countries on and off gold, one would expect to see similarly divergent behavior in monetary policy. Table 2.3 compares the average behavior of the growth rates of three monetary aggregates, called for short M0, M1, and M2, and of changes in the central bank discount rate. M0 corresponds to money and notes in circulation, M1 is the sum of M0 and commercial bank deposits, and M2 is the sum of M1 and savings bank deposits.[9] The expected differences in the monetary polices of the gold and non-gold countries seem to be in the data, although somewhat less clearly than we had anticipated. In particular, despite the twelve percentage point difference in rates of deflation between gold and non-gold countries in 1932, the differences in average money growth in that year between the two classes of countries are minor; possibly, higher inflation expectations in the countries abandoning gold reduced money demand and thus became self-confirming. From 1933 through 1935, however, the various monetary indicators are more consistent with the conclusion stressed by Eichengreen and Sachs (1985), that leaving the gold standard afforded countries more latitude to expand their money supplies and thus to escape deflation.

The basic proposition of the gold standard–based explanation of the Depression is that, because of its deflationary impact, adherence to the gold standard had very adverse consequences for real activity. The validity of this proposition is shown rather clearly by table 2.4, which gives growth rates of industrial production for the countries in our sample. While the countries which were to abandon the gold standard in 1931 did slightly worse in 1930 and 1931 than the nations of the Gold Bloc, subsequent to leaving gold these countries performed much better. Between 1932 and 1935, growth of industrial production in countries not on gold averaged about seven percentage points a year better than countries remaining on gold, a very substantial effect.

In summary, data from our sample of twenty-four countries support the

**Table 2.2**          **Log-differences of the Wholesale Price Index**

|  | 1930 | 1931 | 1932 | 1933 | 1934 | 1935 | 1936 |
|---|---|---|---|---|---|---|---|
| *1. Countries not on gold standard or leaving prior to 1931* | | | | | | | |
| Spain | −.00 | .01 | −.01 | −.05 | .03 | .01 | .02 |
| Australia (1929) | −.12 | −.11 | −.01 | −.00 | .04 | −.00 | .05 |
| New Zealand (1930) | −.03 | −.07 | −.03 | .03 | .01 | .03 | .01 |
| *2. Countries abandoning full gold standard in 1931* | | | | | | | |
| Austria | −.11 | −.07 | .03 | −.04 | .02 | −.00 | −.01 |
| Canada | −.10 | −.18 | −.08 | .01 | .06 | .01 | .03 |
| Czechoslovakia | −.12 | −.10 | −.08 | −.03 | .02 | .04 | .00 |
| Denmark | −.15 | −.13 | .02 | .07 | .09 | .02 | .05 |
| Estonia | −.14 | −.11 | −.09 | .02 | .00 | −.01 | .08 |
| Finland | −.09 | −.07 | .07 | −.01 | .01 | .00 | .02 |
| Germany | −.10 | −.12 | −.14 | −.03 | .05 | .03 | .02 |
| Greece | −.10 | −.11 | .18 | .12 | −.01 | .02 | .02 |
| Hungary | −.14 | −.05 | −.01 | −.14 | .00 | .08 | .03 |
| Japan | −.19 | −.17 | .05 | .11 | −.01 | .04 | .06 |
| Latvia | −.16 | −.18 | .00 | −.02 | −.01 | .05 | .04 |
| Norway | −.08 | −.12 | .00 | −.00 | .02 | .03 | .05 |
| Sweden | −.14 | −.09 | −.02 | −.02 | .06 | .02 | .03 |
| United Kingdom | −.17 | −.18 | −.04 | .01 | .04 | .04 | .06 |
| Average | −.13 | −.12 | −.01 | .00 | .02 | .03 | .04 |
| *3. Countries abandoning gold standard between 1932 and 1935* | | | | | | | |
| Rumania (1932) | −.24 | −.26 | −.11 | −.03 | .00 | .14 | .13 |
| United States (1933) | −.10 | −.17 | −.12 | .02 | .13 | .07 | .01 |
| Italy (1934) | −.11 | −.14 | −.07 | −.09 | −.02 | .10 | .11 |
| Belgium (1935) | −.13 | −.17 | −.16 | −.06 | −.06 | .13 | .09 |
| *4. Countries still on full gold standard as of 1936* | | | | | | | |
| France | −.12 | −.10 | −.16 | −.07 | −.06 | −.11 | .19 |
| Netherlands | −.11 | −.16 | −.17 | −.03 | .00 | −.02 | .04 |
| Poland | −.12 | −.14 | −.13 | −.10 | −.06 | −.05 | .02 |
| Average | −.12 | −.13 | −.15 | −.07 | −.04 | −.06 | .08 |
| *5. Grand averages* | | | | | | | |
| Gold standard countries | | | −.13 | −.07 | −.04 | −.05 | |
| Non-gold countries | | | −.01 | .00 | .03 | .04 | |

*Note:* Data on wholesale prices are from League of Nations, *Monthly Bulletin of Statistics* and *Yearbook,* various issues. Dates in parentheses are years in which countries abandoned gold, with "abandonment" defined to include the imposition of foreign exchange controls or devaluation as well as suspension; see table 2.1.

**44    Ben Bernanke and Harold James**

Table 2.3          Monetary Indicators

|  | 1930 | 1931 | 1932 | 1933 | 1934 | 1935 | 1936 |
|---|---|---|---|---|---|---|---|
| *1. Countries abandoning full gold standard in 1931* | | | | | | | |
| M0 growth | −.04 | −.02 | −.07 | .06 | .05 | .05 | .08 |
| M1 growth | .01 | −.11 | −.07 | .02 | .05 | .04 | .08 |
| M2 growth | .03 | −.08 | −.04 | .03 | .05 | .05 | .06 |
| Discount rate change | −0.8 | 0.4 | −0.2 | −1.2 | −0.4 | −0.1 | −0.1 |
| *2. Countries still on full gold standard as of 1936* | | | | | | | |
| M0 growth | .03 | .07 | −.06 | −.02 | .01 | −.03 | .03 |
| M1 growth | .05 | −.06 | −.07 | −.05 | .01 | −.06 | .08 |
| M2 growth | .08 | −.00 | −.02 | −.02 | .02 | −.03 | .05 |
| Discount rate change | −1.4 | −0.4 | 0.1 | −0.4 | −0.4 | 0.8 | −0.3 |
| *3. Grand averages: Countries on gold* | | | | | | | |
| M0 growth | | | −.04 | −.03 | .01 | −.02 | |
| M1 growth | | | −.09 | −.04 | −.01 | −.06 | |
| M2 growth | | | −.05 | −.01 | .01 | −.02 | |
| Discount rate change | | | 0.2 | −0.5 | −0.4 | 0.7 | |
| *4. Grand averages: Countries off gold* | | | | | | | |
| M0 growth | | | −.07 | .05 | .03 | .06 | |
| M1 growth | | | −.06 | .01 | .04 | .05 | |
| M2 growth | | | −.03 | .02 | .04 | .05 | |
| Discount rate change | | | −0.3 | −1.0 | −0.4 | −0.2 | |

*Note:* M0 is money and notes in cirulation. M1 is base money plus commercial bank deposits. M2 is M1 plus savings deposits. Growth rates of monetary aggregates are calculated as log-differences. The discount rate change is in percentage points. The data are from League of Nations, *Monthly Bulletin of Statistics* and *Yearbook,* various issues.

view that there was a strong link between adherence to the gold standard and the severity of both deflation and depression. The data are also consistent with the hypothesis that increased freedom to engage in monetary expansion was a reason for the better performance of countries leaving the gold standard early in the 1930s, although the evidence in this case is a bit less clear-cut.

## 2.3    The Link Between Deflation and Depression

Given the above discussion and evidence, it seems reasonable to accept the idea that the worldwide deflation of the early 1930s was the result of a monetary contraction transmitted through the international gold standard. But this

## 45    Financial Crisis in the Great Depression

**Table 2.4**              **Log-differences of the Industrial Production Index**

|                        | 1930  | 1931  | 1932  | 1933  | 1934  | 1935  | 1936  |
|------------------------|-------|-------|-------|-------|-------|-------|-------|
| *1. Countries not on gold standard or leaving prior to 1931* | | | | | | | |
| Spain                  | −.01  | −.06  | −.05  | −.05  | .01   | .02   | NA    |
| Australia (1929)       | −.11  | −.07  | .07   | .10   | .09   | .09   | .07   |
| New Zealand (1930)     | −.25  | −.14  | .05   | .02   | .13   | .09   | .14   |
| *2. Countries abandoning full gold standard in 1931* | | | | | | | |
| Austria                | −.16  | −.19  | −.14  | .03   | .11   | .13   | .07   |
| Canada                 | −.16  | −.18  | −.20  | .04   | .20   | .10   | .10   |
| Czechoslovakia         | −.11  | −.10  | −.24  | −.05  | .10   | .05   | .14   |
| Denmark                | .08   | −.08  | −.09  | .14   | .11   | .07   | .04   |
| Estonia                | −.02  | −.09  | −.17  | .05   | .17   | .10   | .10   |
| Finland                | −.10  | −.13  | .19   | .02   | .03   | .10   | .09   |
| Germany                | −.15  | −.24  | −.24  | .13   | .27   | .16   | .12   |
| Greece                 | .01   | .02   | −.08  | .10   | .12   | .12   | −.03  |
| Hungary                | −.06  | −.08  | −.06  | .07   | .12   | .07   | .10   |
| Japan                  | −.05  | −.03  | .07   | .15   | .13   | .10   | .06   |
| Latvia                 | .08   | −.20  | −.08  | .31   | .15   | .05   | .04   |
| Norway                 | .01   | −.25  | .17   | .01   | .04   | .10   | .09   |
| Sweden                 | .03   | −.07  | −.08  | .02   | .19   | .11   | .09   |
| United Kingdom         | −.08  | −.10  | −.00  | .05   | .11   | .07   | .09   |
| Average                | −.05  | −.12  | −.07  | .08   | .13   | .10   | .08   |
| *3. Countries abandoning gold standard between 1932 and 1935* | | | | | | | |
| Rumania (1932)         | −.03  | .05   | −.14  | .15   | .19   | −.01  | .06   |
| United States (1933)   | −.21  | −.17  | −.24  | .17   | .04   | .13   | .15   |
| Italy (1934)           | −.08  | −.17  | −.15  | .10   | .08   | .16   | −.07  |
| Belgium (1935)         | −.12  | −.09  | −.16  | .04   | .01   | .12   | .05   |
| *4. Countries still on full gold standard as of 1936* | | | | | | | |
| France                 | −.01  | −.14  | −.19  | .12   | −.07  | −.04  | .07   |
| Netherlands            | .02   | −.06  | −.13  | .07   | .02   | −.03  | .01   |
| Poland                 | −.13  | −.14  | −.20  | .09   | .12   | .07   | .10   |
| Average                | −.04  | −.11  | −.17  | .10   | .02   | .00   | .06   |
| *5. Grand averages* | | | | | | | |
| Gold standard countries |      |       | −.18  | .09   | .03   | .01   |       |
| Non-gold countries     |       |       | −.06  | .08   | .12   | .09   |       |

*Note:* Data on industrial production are from League of Nations, *Monthly Bulletin of Statistics* and *Yearbook,* various issues, supplemented by League of Nations, *Industrialization and Foreign Trade,* 1945.

raises the more difficult question of what precisely were the channels linking deflation (falling prices) and depression (falling output). This section takes a preliminary look at some suggested mechanisms. We first introduce here two principal channels emphasized in recent research, then discuss the alternative of induced financial crisis.

1. *Real wages.* If wages possess some degree of nominal rigidity, then falling output prices will raise real wages and lower labor demand. Downward stickiness of wages (or of other input costs) will also lower profitability, potentially reducing investment. This channel is stressed by Eichengreen and Sachs (see in particular their 1986 paper) and has also been emphasized by Newell and Symons (1988).

Some evidence on the behavior of real wages during the Depression is presented in table 2.5, which is similar in format to tables 2.2–2.4. Note that table 2.5 uses the wholesale price index (the most widely available price index) as the wage deflator. According to this table, there were indeed large real wage increases in most countries in 1930 and 1931. After 1931, countries leaving the gold standard experienced a mild decline in real wages, while real wages in gold standard countries exhibited a mild increase. These findings are similar to those of Eichengreen and Sachs (1985).

The reliance on nominal wage stickiness to explain the real effects of the deflation is consistent with the Keynesian tradition, but is nevertheless somewhat troubling in this context. Given (i) the severity of the unemployment that was experienced during that time; (ii) the relative absence of long-term contracts and the weakness of unions; and (iii) the presumption that the general public was aware that prices, and hence the cost of living, were falling, it is hard to understand how nominal wages could have been so unresponsive. Wages had fallen quickly in many countries in the contraction of 1921–22. In the United States, nominal wages were maintained until the fall of 1931 (possibly by an agreement among large corporations; see O'Brien 1989), but fell sharply after that; in Germany, the government actually tried to depress wages early in the Depression. Why then do we see these large real wage increases in the data?

One possibility is measurement problems. There are a number of issues, such as changes in skill and industrial composition, that make measuring the cyclical movement in real wages difficult even today. Bernanke (1986) has argued, in the U.S. context, that because of sharp reductions in workweeks and the presence of hoarded labor, the measure real wage may have been a poor measure of the marginal cost of labor.

Also in the category of measurement issues, Eichengreen and Hatton (1987) correctly point out that nominal wages should be deflated by the relevant product prices, not a general price index. Their table of product wage indices (nominal wages relative to manufacturing prices) is reproduced for 1929–38 and for the five countries for which data are available as our table 2.6. Like table 2.5, this table also shows real wages increasing in the early

**47    Financial Crisis in the Great Depression**

Table 2.5                  **Log-differences of the Real Wage**

|  | 1930 | 1931 | 1932 | 1933 | 1934 | 1935 | 1936 |
|---|---|---|---|---|---|---|---|
| *1. Countries not on gold standard or leaving prior to 1931* | | | | | | | |
| Spain | | | not available | | | | |
| Australia (1929) | .10 | .01 | −.05 | −.04 | −.03 | .01 | −.03 |
| New Zealand (1930) | .03 | .00 | −.00 | −.05 | −.01 | −.01 | .10 |
| *2. Countries abandoning full gold standard in 1931* | | | | | | | |
| Austria | .14 | .05 | −.04 | −.00 | −.05 | −.03 | .06 |
| Canada | .11 | .15 | .00 | −.06 | −.05 | .02 | −.01 |
| Czechoslovakia | .14 | .11 | .08 | .02 | −.04 | −.05 | −.00 |
| Denmark | .17 | .11 | −.03 | −.07 | −.09 | −.01 | −.04 |
| Estonia | .16 | .07 | .02 | −.06 | −.01 | .06 | −.03 |
| Finland | | | not available | | | | |
| Germany | .12 | .06 | −.03 | −.00 | −.07 | −.03 | −.02 |
| Greece | | | not available | | | | |
| Hungary | .14 | −.00 | −.07 | .09 | −.06 | −.11 | −.00 |
| Japan | .05 | .21 | −.04 | −.12 | .02 | −.05 | −.05 |
| Latvia | .20 | .18 | −.15 | −.05 | .01 | −.05 | −.02 |
| Norway | .08 | .08 | .02 | −.02 | −.01 | −.03 | −.02 |
| Sweden | .17 | .09 | .01 | −.02 | −.06 | −.01 | −.02 |
| United Kingdom | .17 | .16 | .02 | −.02 | −.03 | −.03 | −.03 |
| Average | .14 | .11 | −.02 | −.03 | −.04 | −.03 | −.02 |
| *3. Countries abandoning gold standard between 1932 and 1935* | | | | | | | |
| Rumania (1932) | .20 | .14 | −.10 | −.05 | −.02 | −.15 | −.12 |
| United States (1933) | .10 | .13 | −.01 | −.03 | .04 | −.03 | .02 |
| Italy (1934) | .10 | .07 | .05 | .07 | −.01 | −.11 | −.06 |
| Belgium (1935) | .19 | .10 | .07 | .04 | .01 | −.16 | −.02 |
| *4. Countries still on full gold standard as of 1936* | | | | | | | |
| France | .21 | .09 | .12 | .07 | .06 | .09 | −.06 |
| Netherlands | .12 | .14 | .09 | −.02 | −.04 | −.01 | −.06 |
| Poland | .11 | .06 | .05 | .00 | .01 | .02 | −.03 |
| Average | .15 | .10 | .09 | .02 | .01 | .03 | −.05 |
| *5. Grand averages* | | | | | | | |
| Gold standard countries | | | .05 | .03 | .01 | .02 | |
| Non-gold countries | | | −.02 | −.03 | −.03 | −.04 | |

*Note:* The real wage is the nominal hourly wage for males (skilled, if available) divided by the wholesale price index. Wage data are from the International Labour Office, *Year Book of Labor Statistics,* various issues.

**48    Ben Bernanke and Harold James**

Table 2.6              Indices of Product Wages

| Year | United Kingdom | United States | Germany | Japan | Sweden |
|------|----------------|---------------|---------|-------|--------|
| 1929 | 100.0 | 100.0 | 100.0 | 100.0 | 100.0 |
| 1930 | 103.0 | 106.1 | 100.4 | 115.6 | 116.6 |
| 1931 | 106.4 | 113.0 | 102.2 | 121.6 | 129.1 |
| 1932 | 108.3 | 109.6 | 96.8 | 102.9 | 130.0 |
| 1933 | 109.3 | 107.9 | 99.3 | 101.8 | 127.9 |
| 1934 | 111.4 | 115.8 | 103.0 | 102.3 | 119.6 |
| 1935 | 111.3 | 114.3 | 105.3 | 101.6 | 119.2 |
| 1936 | 110.4 | 115.9 | 107.7 | 99.2 | 116.0 |
| 1937 | 107.8 | 121.9 | 106.5 | 87.1 | 101.9 |
| 1938 | 108.6 | 130.0 | 107.7 | 86.3 | 115.1 |

*Source:* Eichengreen and Hatton (1987, 15).

1930s, but overall the correlation of real wage increases and depression does not appear particularly good. Note that Germany, which had probably the worst unemployment problem of any major country, has almost no increase in real wages;[10] the United Kingdom, which began to recover in 1932, has real wages increasing on a fairly steady trend during its recovery period; and the United States has only a small dip in real wages at the beginning of its recovery, followed by more real wage growth. The case for nominal wage stickiness as a transmission mechanism thus seems, at this point, somewhat mixed.

2. *Real interest rates.* In a standard IS-LM macro model, a monetary contraction depresses output by shifting the LM curve leftwards, raising real interest rates, and thus reducing spending. However, as Temin (1976) pointed out in his original critique of Friedman and Schwartz, it is real rather than nominal money balances that affect the LM curve; and since prices were falling sharply, real money balances fell little or even rose during the contraction.

Even if real money balances are essentially unchanged, however, there is another means by which deflation can raise ex ante real interest rates: Since cash pays zero nominal interest, in equilibrium no asset can bear a nominal interest rate that is lower than its liquidity and risk premia relative to cash. Thus an expected deflation of 10% will impose a real rate of at least 10% on the economy, even with perfectly flexible prices and wages. In an IS-LM diagram drawn with the nominal interest rate on the vertical axis, an increase in expected deflation amounts to a leftward shift of the IS curve.

Whether the deflation of the early 1930s was anticipated has been extensively debated (although almost entirely in the United States context). We will add here two points in favor of the view that the extent of the worldwide deflation was less than fully anticipated.

First, there is the question of whether the nominal interest rate floor was in fact binding in the deflating countries (as it should have been if this mechanism was to operate). Although interest rates on government debt in the United States often approximated zero in the 1930s, it is less clear that this was true for other countries. The yield on French treasury bills, for example, rose from a low of 0.75% in 1932 to 2.06% in 1933, 2.25% in 1934, and 3.38% in 1935; during 1933–35 the nominal yield on French treasury bills exceeded that of British treasury bills by several hundred basis points on average.[11]

Second, the view that deflation was largely anticipated must contend with the fact that nominal returns on safe assets were very similar whether countries abandoned or stayed on gold. If continuing deflation was anticipated in the gold standard countries, while inflation was expected in countries leaving gold, the similarity of nominal returns would have implied large expected differences in real returns. Such differences are possible in equilibrium, if they are counterbalanced by expected real exchange rate changes; nevertheless, differences in expected real returns between countries on and off gold on the order of 11–12% (the realized difference in returns between the two blocs in 1932) seem unlikely.[12]

3. *Financial crisis.* A third mechanism by which deflation can induce depression, not considered in the recent literature, works through deflation's effect on the operation of the financial system. The source of the non-neutrality is simply that debt instruments (including deposits) are typically set in money terms. Deflation thus weakens the financial positions of borrowers, both nonfinancial firms and financial intermediaries.

Consider first the case of intermediaries (banks).[13] Bank liabilities (primarily deposits) are fixed almost entirely in nominal terms. On the asset side, depending on the type of banking system (see below), banks hold either primarily debt instruments or combinations of debt and equity. Ownership of debt and equity is essentially equivalent to direct ownership of capital; in this case, therefore, the bank's liabilities are nominal and its assets are real, so that an unanticipated deflation begins to squeeze the bank's capital position immediately. When only debt is held as an asset, the effect of deflation is for a while neutral or mildly beneficial to the bank. However, when borrowers' equity cushions are exhausted, the bank becomes the owner of its borrowers' real assets, so eventually this type of bank will also be squeezed by deflation.

As pressure on the bank's capital grows, according to this argument, its normal functioning will be impeded; for example, it may have to call in loans or refuse new ones. Eventually, impending exhaustion of bank capital leads to a depositors' run, which eliminates the bank or drastically curtails its operation. The final result is usually a government takeover of the intermediation process. For example, a common scenario during the Depression was for the government to finance an acquisition of a failing bank by issuing its own debt; this debt was held (directly or indirectly) by consumers, in lieu of (vanishing) commercial bank deposits. Thus, effectively, government agencies became part of the intermediation chain.[14]

Although the problems of the banks were perhaps the more dramatic in the Depression, the same type of non-neutrality potentially affects nonfinancial

firms and other borrowers. The process of "debt deflation", that is, the increase in the real value of nominal debt obligations brought about by falling
prices, erodes the net worth position of borrowers. A weakening financial
position affects the borrower's actions (e.g., the firm may try to conserve financial capital by laying off workers or cutting back on investment) and also,
by worsening the agency problems in the borrower-lender relationship, im-
pairs access to new credit. Thus, as discussed in detail in Bernanke and Gertler (1990), "financial distress" (such as that induced by debt deflation) can in
principle impose deadweight losses on an economy, even if firms do not
undergo liquidation.

Before trying to assess the quantitative impact of these and other channels
on output, we briefly discuss the international incidence of financial crisis
during the Depression.

### 2.4   Interwar Banking and Financial Crises

Financial crises were of course a prominent feature of the interwar period.
We focus in this section on the problems of the banking sector and, to a lesser
extent, on the problems of domestic debtors in general, as suggested by the
discussion above. Stock market crashes and defaults on external debt were
also important, of course, but for the sake of space will take a subsidiary role
here.

Table 2.7 gives a chronology of some important interwar banking crises.
The episodes listed actually cover a considerable range in terms of severity, as
the capsule descriptions should make clear. However the chronology should
also show that (i) quite a few different countries experienced significant banking problems during the interwar period; and (ii) these problems reached a
very sharp peak between the spring and fall of 1931, following the Creditanstalt crisis in May 1931 as well as the intensification of banking problems in
Germany.

A statistical indicator of banking problems, emphasized by Friedman and
Schwartz (1963), is the deposit-currency ratio. Data on the changes in the
commercial bank deposit-currency ratio for our panel of countries are presented in table 2.8. It is interesting to compare this table with the chronology
in table 2.7. Most but not all of the major banking crises were associated with
sharp drops in the deposit-currency ratio; the most important exception is in
1931 in Italy, where the government was able to keep secret much of the banking system's problems until a government takeover was affected. On the other
hand, there were also significant drops in the deposit-currency ratio that were
not associated with panics; restructurings of the banking system and exchange
rate difficulties account for some of these episodes.

What caused the banking panics? At one level, the panics were an endogenous response to deflation and the operation of the gold standard regime.

**51**  Financial Crisis in the Great Depression

| Table 2.7 | | A Chronology of Interwar Banking Crises, 1921–36 |
|---|---|---|
| **Date** | **Country** | **Crises** |
| June 1921 | SWEDEN | Beginning of deposit contraction of 1921–22, leading to bank restructurings. Government assistance administered through Credit Bank of 1922. |
| 1921–22 | NETHERLANDS | Bank failures (notably Marx & Co.) and amalgamations. |
| 1922 | DENMARK | Heavy losses of one of the largest banks, Danske Landmandsbank, and liquidation of smaller banks. Landmandsbank continues to operate until a restructing in April 1928 under a government guarantee. |
| April 1923 | NORWAY | Failure of Centralbanken for Norge. |
| May 1923 | AUSTRIA | Difficulties of a major bank, Allgemeine Depositenbank; liquidation in July. |
| September 1923 | JAPAN | In wake of the Tokyo earthquake, bad debts threaten Bank of Taiwan and Bank of Chosen, which are restructured with government help. |
| September 1925 | SPAIN | Failure of Banco de la Union Mineira and Banco Vasca. |
| July–September 1926 | POLAND | Bank runs cause three large banks to stop payments. The shakeout of banks continues through 1927. |
| 1927 | NORWAY, ITALY | Numerous smaller banks in difficulties, but no major failures. |
| April 1927 | JAPAN | Thirty-two banks unable to make payments. Restructuring of 15th Bank and Bank of Taiwan. |
| August 1929 | GERMANY | Collapse of Frankfurter Allgemeine Versicherungs AG, followed by failures of smaller banks, and runs on Berlin and Frankfurt savings banks. |
| November 1929 | AUSTRIA | Bodencreditanstalt, second largest bank, fails and is merged with Creditanstalt. |
| November 1930 | FRANCE | Failure of Banque Adam, Boulogne-sur-Mer, and Oustric Group. Runs on provincial banks. |
| | ESTONIA | Failure of two medium-sized banks, Estonia Government Bank Tallin and Reval Credit Bank; crisis lasts until January. |
| December 1930 | U.S. | Failure of Bank of the United States. |
| | ITALY | Withdrawals from three largest banks begin. A panic ensues in April 1931, followed by a government reorganization and takeover of frozen industrial assets. |
| April 1931 | ARGENTINA | Government deals with banking panic by allowing Banco de Nacion to rediscount commercial paper from other banks at government-owned Caja de Conversión. |

*(continued)*

## 52    Ben Bernanke and Harold James

**Table 2.7**    (continued)

| Date | Country | Crises |
|------|---------|--------|
| May 1931 | AUSTRIA | Failure of Creditanstalt and run of foreign depositors. |
| | BELGIUM | Rumors about imminent failure of Banque de Bruxelles, the country's second largest bank, induce withdrawals from all banks. Later in the year, expectations of devaluation lead to withdrawals of foreign deposits. |
| June 1931 | POLAND | Run on banks, especially on Warsaw Discount Bank, associated with Creditanstalt; a spread of the Austrian crisis. |
| April–July 1931 | GERMANY | Bank runs, extending difficulties plaguing the banking system since the summer of 1930. After large loss of deposits in June and increasing strain on foreign exchanges, many banks are unable to make payments and Darmstädter Bank closes. Bank holiday. |
| July 1931 | HUNGARY | Run on Budapest banks (especially General Credit Bank). Foreign withdrawals followed by a foreign creditors' standstill agreement. Bank holiday. |
| | LATVIA | Run on banks with German connections. Bank of Libau and International Bank of Riga particularly hard hit. |
| | AUSTRIA | Failure of Vienna Mercur-Bank. |
| | CZECHOSLOVAKIA | Withdrawal of foreign deposits sparks domestic withdrawals but no general banking panic. |
| | TURKEY | Run on branches of Deutsche Bank and collapse of Banque Turque pour le Commerce et l'Industrie, in wake of German crisis. |
| | EGYPT | Run on Cairo and Alexandria branches of Deutsche Orientbank. |
| | SWITZERLAND | Union Financière de Genève rescued by takeover by Comptoir d'Escompte de Geneve. |
| | RUMANIA | Collapse of German-controlled Banca Generala a Tarii Românesti. Run on Banca de Credit Roman and Banca Romaneasca. |
| | MEXICO | Suspension of payments after run on Credito Espanol de Mexico. Run on Banco Nacional de Mexico. |
| August 1931 | U.S. | Series of banking panics, with October 1931 the worst month. Between August 1931 and January 1932, 1,860 banks fail. |
| September 1931 | U.K. | External drain, combined with rumors of threat to London merchant banks with heavy European (particularly Hungarian and German) involvements. |
| | ESTONIA | General bank run following sterling crisis; second wave of runs in November. |

*/continued overleaf*

**53**    Financial Crisis in the Great Depression

| Table 2.7 | (continued) | |
|---|---|---|
| Date | Country | Crises |
| October 1931 | RUMANIA | Failure of Banca Marmerosch, Blank & Co. Heavy bank runs. |
| | FRANCE | Collapse of major deposit bank Banque Nationale de Crédit (restructured as Banque Nationale pour le Commerce et l'Industrie). Other bank failures and bank runs. |
| March 1932 | SWEDEN | Weakness of one large bank (Skandinaviska Kreditaktiebolaget) as result of collapse of Kreuger industrial and financial empire, but no general panic. |
| May 1932 | FRANCE | Losses of large investment bank Banque de l'Union Parisienne forces merger with Crédit Mobilier Français. |
| June 1932 | U.S. | Series of bank failures in Chicago. |
| October 1932 | U.S. | New wave of bank failures, especially in the Midwest and Far West. |
| February 1933 | U.S. | General banking panic, leading to state holidays and a nationwide bank holiday in March. |
| November 1933 | SWITZERLAND | Restructuring of large bank (Banque Populaire Suisse) after heavy losses. |
| March 1934 | BELGIUM | Failure of Banque Belge de Travail develops into general banking and exchange crisis. |
| September 1934 | ARGENTINA | Bank problems throughout the fall induce government-sponsored merger of four weak banks (Banco Espanol del Rio de la Plata, Banco el Hogar Argentina, Banco Argentina-Uruguayo, Ernesto Tornquist & Co.). |
| October 1935 | ITALY | Deposits fall after Italian invasion of Abyssinia. |
| January 1936 | NORWAY | After years of deposit stability, legislation introducing a tax on bank deposits leads to withdrawals (until fall). |
| October 1936 | CZECHOSLOVAKIA | Anticipation of second devaluation of the crown leads to deposit withdrawals. |

When the peak of the world banking crisis came in 1931, there had already been almost two years of deflation and accompanying depression. Consistent with the analysis at the end of the last section, falling prices lowered the nominal value of bank assets but not the nominal value of bank liabilities. In addition, the rules of the gold standard severely limited the ability of central banks to ameliorate panics by acting as a lender of last resort; indeed, since banking panics often coincided with exchange crises (as we discuss further below), in order to maintain convertibility central banks typically *tightened* monetary policy in the face of panics. Supporting the connection of banking problems with deflation and "rules of the game" constraints is the observation that there were virtually no serious banking panics in any country after aban-

**54    Ben Bernanke and Harold James**

Table 2.8             Log-differences of Commercial Bank Deposit-Currency Ratio

| Country | 1930 | 1931 | 1932 | 1933 | 1934 | 1935 | 1936 |
|---|---|---|---|---|---|---|---|
| Australia | −.05 | −.12* | .05 | .01 | .05 | −.03 | −.01 |
| Austria | .17 | −.40* | −.06 | −.20* | −.07 | −.01 | −.02 |
| Belgium | −.13* | −.22* | −.10* | .07 | −.13* | −.27* | −.02 |
| Canada | .07 | −.01 | .03 | −.05 | .00 | .01 | −.06 |
| Czechoslovakia | −.11 | −.08 | .07 | .02 | .07 | −.03 | −.11* |
| Denmark | .08 | −.03 | .00 | −.07 | .02 | .02 | −.00 |
| Estonia | .16 | −.29* | −.02 | −.05 | .10 | .05 | .13 |
| Finland | .09 | −.05 | .14 | −.04 | −.06 | −.04 | −.09 |
| France | −.07 | −.12* | −.01 | −.10* | −.07 | −.10 | −.03 |
| Germany | −.11* | −.40* | .05 | −.09 | −.01 | −.08 | −.02 |
| Greece | .17 | .07 | −.27* | −.03 | .06 | −.04 | .02 |
| Hungary | .07 | −.07 | .10 | −.03 | −.08 | −.05 | −.03 |
| Italy | .04 | −.01 | .05 | .06 | .01 | −.20* | .08 |
| Japan | .09 | .03 | −.12* | −.04 | .03 | −.00 | .09 |
| Latvia | .03 | −.57* | .11 | −.06 | .12 | .10 | .45 |
| Netherlands | .10 | −.36* | −.05 | −.06 | −.05 | −.08 | .24 |
| Norway | .04 | −.15* | −.06 | −.09 | −.01 | .03 | −.23* |
| New Zealand | .04 | −.11* | .03 | .07 | .15 | −.08 | −.32* |
| Poland | .07 | −.29* | −.02 | −.08 | .10 | −.06 | .10 |
| Rumania | .11 | −.76* | −.05 | −.11* | −.28* | .10 | −.16* |
| Sweden | −.00 | −.00 | −.02 | −.06 | −.11* | −.08 | −.07 |
| Spain | .00 | −.24* | .08 | .03 | .01 | .06 | N.A. |
| United Kingdom | .03 | −.07 | .10 | −.07 | −.02 | .01 | −.03 |
| United States | .00 | −.15* | −.26* | −.15* | .14 | .05 | .02 |

*Note:* Entries are the log-differences of the ratio of commercial bank deposits to money and notes in circulation. Data are from League of Nations, *Monthly Bulletin of Statistics* and *Yearbook,* various issues.
*Decline exceeds .10.

donment of the gold standard—although it is also true that by time the gold standard was abandoned, strong financial reform measures had been taken in most countries.

However, while deflation and adherence to the gold standard were necessary conditions for panics, they were not sufficient; a number of countries made it through the interwar period without significant bank runs or failures, despite being subject to deflationary shocks similar to those experienced by the countries with banking problems.[15] Several factors help to explain which countries were the ones to suffer panics.

1. *Banking structure.* The organization of the banking system was an important factor in determining vulnerability to panics. First, countries with "unit banking," that is, with a large number of small and relatively undiversified banks, suffered more severe banking panics. The leading example is of course the United States, where concentration in banking was very low, but a high incidence of failures among small banks was also seen in other countries (e.g., France). Canada, with branch banking, suffered no bank failures during

the Depression (although many branches were closed). Sweden and the United Kingdom also benefited from a greater dispersion of risk through branch systems.[16]

Second, where "universal" or "mixed" banking on the German or Belgian model was the norm, it appears that vulnerability to deflation was greater. In contrast to the Anglo-Saxon model of banking, where at least in theory lending was short term and the relationship between banks and corporations had an arm's length character, universal banks took long-term and sometimes dominant ownership positions in client firms. Universal bank assets included both long-term securities and equity participations; the former tended to become illiquid during a crisis, while the latter exposed universal banks (unlike Anglo-Saxon banks, which held mainly debt instruments) to the effects of stock market crashes. The most extreme case was probably Austria. By 1931, after a series of mergers, the infamous Creditanstalt was better thought of as a vast holding company rather than a bank; at the time of its failure in May 1931, the Creditanstalt owned sixty-four companies, amounting to 65% of Austria's nominal capital (Kindleberger 1984).

2. *Reliance of banks on short-term foreign liabilities.* Some of the most serious banking problems were experienced in countries in which a substantial fraction of deposits were foreign-owned. The so-called hot money was more sensitive to adverse financial developments than were domestic deposits. Runs by foreign depositors represented not only a loss to the banking system but also, typically, a loss of reserves; as we have noted, this additional external threat restricted the ability of the central bank to respond to the banking situation. Thus, banking crises and exchange rate crises became intertwined.[17] The resolution of a number of the central European banking crises required "standstill agreements," under which withdrawals by foreign creditors were blocked pending future negotiation.

International linkages were important on the asset side of bank balance sheets as well. Many continental banks were severely affected by the crises in Austria and Germany, in particular.

3. *Financial and economic experience of the 1920s.* It should not be particularly surprising that countries which emerged from the 1920s in relatively weaker condition were more vulnerable to panics. Austria, Germany, Hungary, and Poland all suffered hyperinflation and economic dislocation in the 1930s, and all suffered severe banking panics in 1931. While space constraints do not permit a full discussion of the point here, it does seem clear that the origins of the European financial crisis were at least partly independent of American developments—which argues against a purely American-centered explanation of the origins of the Depression.

It should also be emphasized, though, that not just the existence of financial difficulties during the 1920s but also the policy response to those difficulties was important. Austria is probably the most extreme case of nagging banking problems being repeatedly "papered over." That country had banking prob-

lems throughout the 1920s, which were handled principally by merging failing banks into still-solvent banks. An enforced merger of the Austrian Bodencreditanstalt with two failing banks in 1927 weakened that institution,
which was part of the reason that the Bodencreditanstalt in turn had to be
forceably merged with the Creditanstalt in 1929. The insolvency of the Creditanstalt, finally revealed when a director refused to sign an "optimistic" financial statement in May 1931, sparked the most intense phase of the European crisis.

In contrast, when banking troubles during the earlier part of the 1920s were
met with fundamental reform, performance of the banking sector during the
Depression was better. Examples were Sweden, Japan, and the Netherlands,
all of which had significant banking problems during the 1920s but responded
by fundamental restructurings and assistance to place banks on a sound footing (and to close the weakest banks). Possibly because of these earlier events,
these three countries had limited problems in the 1930s. A large Swedish bank
(Skandinaviska Kreditaktiebolaget) suffered heavy losses after the collapse of
the Kreuger financial empire, and a medium-sized Dutch bank (Amstelbank)
failed because of its connection to the Creditanstalt; but there were no widespread panics, only isolated failures.

A particularly interesting comparison in this regard is between the Netherlands and neighboring Belgium, where banking problems persisted from 1931
to 1935 and where the ultimate devaluation of the Belgian franc was the result
of an attempt to protect banks from further drains. Both countries were heavily dependent on foreign trade and both remained on gold, yet the Netherlands did much better than Belgium in the early part of the Depression (see
table 2.4). This is a bit of evidence for the relevance of banking difficulties to
output.

Overall, while banking crises were surely an endogenous response to
depression, the incidence of crisis across countries reflected a variety of institutional factors and other preconditions. Thus it will be of interest to compare
the real effects of deflation between countries with and without severe banking
difficulties.

On "debt deflation," that is, the problems of nonfinancial borrowers, much
less has been written than on the banking crises. Only for the United States
has the debt problem in the 1930s been fairly well documented (see the summary in Bernanke 1983 and the references therein). In that country, large corporations avoided serious difficulties, but most other sectors—small businesses, farmers, mortgage borrowers, state and local governments—were
severely affected, with usually something close to half of outstanding debts
being in default. A substantial portion of New Deal reforms consisted of various forms of debt adjustment and relief.

For other countries, there are plenty of anecdotes but not much systematic
data. Aggregate data on bankruptcies and defaults are difficult to interpret
because increasing financial distress forced changes in bankruptcy practices

and procedures; when the League of Nations' *Monthly Bulletin of Statistics* dropped its table on bankruptcies in its December 1932 issue, for example, the reason given therein was that "the numerous forms of agreement by which open bankruptcies are now avoided have seriously diminished the value of the table" (p. 529). Perhaps the most extreme case of a change in rules was Rumania's April 1932 Law on Conversion of Debts, which essentially eliminated the right of creditors to force bankruptcy. Changes in the treatment of bankruptcy no doubt ameliorated the effects of debt default, but the fact that these changes occurred indicates that the perceived problem must have been severe. More detailed country-by-country study of the effects of deflation on firm balance sheets and the relation of financial condition to firm investment, production, and employment decisions—where the data permit—would be extremely valuable. A similar comment applies to external debt problems, although here interesting recent work by Eichengreen and Portes (1986) and others gives us a much better base of knowledge to build on than is available for the case of domestic debts.

## 2.5  Regression Results

In this section we present empirical results based on our panel data set. The principal question of interest is the relative importance of various transmission mechanisms of deflation to output. We also address the question, so far not discussed, of whether banking crises could have intensified the deflation process itself.

The basic set of results is contained in table 2.9, which relates the log-differences in industrial production for our set of countries to various combinations of explanatory variables. The definitions of the right-hand-side variables are as follows:

$\Delta \ln PW$: log-difference of the wholesale price index;

$\Delta \ln EX$: log-difference of nominal exports;

$\Delta \ln W$: log-difference of nominal wage;

*DISC*:  central bank discount rate, measured relative to its 1929 value (a government bond rate is used for Canada; since no 1929 interest rate could be found for New Zealand, that country is excluded in regressions including DISC);

*PANIC*:  a dummy variable, set equal to the number of months during the year that the country experienced serious banking problems (see below);

$\Delta \ln M0$: log-difference of money and notes in circulation.

Exports are included to control for trade effects on growth, including the benefits of competitive devaluation discussed by Eichengreen and Sachs (1986); and the wage is included to test for the real wage channel of transmission from deflation to depression. Of course, theory says that both of these

**58      Ben Bernanke and Harold James**

variables should enter in real rather than in nominal terms; unfortunately, in practice the theoretically suggested deflator is not always available (as we noted in our discussion of the real wage above). We resolve this problem by supposing that the true equation is, for example,

(1)    $\Delta \ln IP = \beta_e (\Delta \ln EX - \Delta \ln P_e) + \beta_w (\Delta \ln W - \Delta \ln P_w) + \text{error}$

where $P_e$ and $P_w$, the optimal deflators, are not available. Let the projections of log-changes in the unobserved deflators on the log-change in the wholesale price deflator be given by

(2)                          $\Delta \ln P_i = \psi_i \Delta \ln PW + u_i \quad i = e, w$

where the $u_i$ are uncorrelated with $\Delta \ln PW$ and presumably the $\psi_i$ are positive. Then (1) becomes

(3) $\Delta \ln IP = -(\beta_e \psi_e + \beta_w \psi_w) \Delta \ln PW + \beta_e \Delta \ln EX + \beta_w \Delta \ln W + \text{new error}$

This suggests allowing $\Delta \ln PW$ and the nominal growth rates of exports and wages to enter the equation separately, which is how we proceed.[18] Putting $\Delta \ln PW$ in the equation separately has the added advantage of allowing us to account for any additional effect of deflation (such as debt deflation) not explicitly captured by the other independent variables.

The discount rate *DISC* is included to allow for the interest rate channel and as an additional proxy for monetary policy. Since $\Delta \ln PW$ is included in every equation, inclusion of the nominal interest rate *DISC* is equivalent to including the actual ex post real interest rate, that is, we are effectively assuming that deflation was fully anticipated; this should give the real interest rate hypothesis its best chance.

In an attempt to control for fiscal policy, we also included measures of central government expenditure in our first estimated equations. Since the estimated coefficients were always negative (the wrong sign), small, and statistically insignificant, the government expenditure variable is excluded from the results reported here.

Construction of the dummy variable *PANIC* required us to make a judgment about which countries' banking crises were most serious, which we did from our reading of primary and secondary sources. We dated periods of crisis as starting from the first severe banking problems; if there was some clear demarcation point (such as the U.S. bank holiday of 1933), we used that as the ending date of the crisis; otherwise we arbitrarily assumed that the effects of the crisis would last for one year after its most intense point. The banking crises included in the dummy are as follows (see also table 2.7):

1. Austria (May 1931–January 1933): from the Creditanstalt crisis to the date of official settlement of the Creditanstalt's foreign debt.

2. Belgium (May 1931–April 1932; March 1934–February 1935): for one year after the initial Belgian crisis, following Creditanstalt, and for one

**59**     Financial Crisis in the Great Depression

year after the failure of the Banque Belge de Travail led to a general crisis.

3. Estonia (September 1931–August 1932): for one year after the general banking crisis.

4. France (November 1930–October 1932): for one year following each of the two peaks of the French banking crises, in November 1930 and October 1931 (see Bouvier 1984).

5. Germany (May 1931–December 1932): from the beginning of the major German banking crisis until the creation of state institutes for the liquidation of bad bank debts.

6. Hungary (July 1931–June 1932): for one year following the runs in Budapest and the bank holiday.

7. Italy (April 1931–December 1932): from the onset of the banking panic until the takeover of bank assets by a massive new state holding company, the Istituto por le Riconstruzione Industriale (IRI).

8. Latvia (July 1931–June 1932): for one year following the onset of the banking crisis.

9. Poland (June 1931–May 1932): for one year following the onset of the banking crisis.

10. Rumania (July 1931–September 1932): from the onset of the crisis until one year after its peak in October 1931.

11. United States (December 1930–March 1933): from the failure of the Bank of the United States until the bank holiday.

The inclusion of Austria, Belgium, Estonia, Germany, Hungary, Latvia, Poland, Rumania, or the United States in the above list cannot be controversial; each of these countries suffered serious panics. (One might quibble on the margin about the exact dating given—for example, Temin [1989] and others have argued that the U.S. banking crisis did not really begin until mid 1931—but we doubt very much that changes of a few months on these dates would affect the results.) The inclusion of France and Italy is more controversial. For example, Bouvier (1984) argues that the French banking crisis was not as serious as some others, since although there were runs and many banks failed, the very biggest banks survived; also, according to Bouvier, French banks were not as closely tied to industry as other banking systems on the Continent. For Italy, as we have noted, early and massive government intervention reduced the incidence of panic (see Ciocca and Toniolo 1984); however, the banks were in very poor condition and (as noted above) eventually signed over most of their industrial assets to the IRI.

To check the sensitivity of our results, we reestimated the key equations omitting first the French crisis from the *PANIC* variable, then the French and Italian crises. Leaving out France had a minor effect (lowering the coefficient on *PANIC* and its *t*-statistic about 5% in a typical equation); the additional exclusion of the Italian crisis has essentially no effect.[19]

As a further check, we also reestimated our key equations omitting, in separate runs, (i) the United States; (ii) Germany and Austria; and (iii) all eastern European countries. In none of these equations were our basic results substantially weakened, which indicates that no single country or small group of countries is driving our findings.

The first seven equations in table 2.9 are not derived from any single model, but instead attempt to nest various suggested explanations of the link between deflation and depression. Estimation was by OLS, which opens up the possibility of simultaneity bias; however, given our maintained view that the deflation was imposed by exogenous monetary forces, a case can be made for treating the right-hand-side variables as exogenous or predetermined.

The principal inferences to be drawn from the first seven rows of table 2.9 are as follows:[20]

1. Export growth consistently enters the equation for output growth strongly, with a plausible coefficient and a high level of statistical significance.

2. When wage growth is included in the output equation along with only wholesale price and export growth (row 5), it enters with the wrong sign.

Table 2.9      Determinants of the Log-difference of Industrial Production
               (dependent variable: $\Delta \ln IP$)

| Equation | Independent Variables | | | | | |
|---|---|---|---|---|---|---|
| | $\Delta \ln PW$ | $\Delta \ln EX$ | $\Delta \ln W$ | DISC | PANIC | $\Delta \ln M0$ |
| (1) | .855 | | | | | |
| | (.098) | | | | | |
| (2) | .531 | | | | − .0191 | |
| | (.095) | | | | (.0026) | |
| (3) | .406 | .231 | | | | |
| | (.121) | (.043) | | | | |
| (4) | .300 | .148 | | | − .0157 | |
| | (.111) | (.041) | | | (.0027) | |
| (5) | .364 | .231 | .272 | | | |
| | (.141) | (.046) | (.206) | | | |
| (6) | .351 | .150 | − .072 | | − .0156 | |
| | (.128) | (.044) | (.197) | | (.0029) | |
| (7) | .296 | .103 | − .119 | − .0358 | − .0138 | |
| | (.123) | (.044) | (.189) | (.0102) | (.0028) | |
| (8) | | .217* | − .015 | | − .0126 | .405 |
| | | (.048) | (.189) | | (.0031) | (.098) |

*Note:* For variable definitions, see text. The sample period is 1930–36. The panel consists of twenty-four countries except that, due to missing wage data, Finland, Greece, and Spain are excluded from equations (5)–(8). Estimates of country-specific dummies are not reported. Standard errors are in parentheses.

*Export growth is measured in real terms in equation (8).

Only when the *PANIC* variable is included does nominal wage growth have the correct (negative) sign (rows 6 and 7). In the equation encompassing all the various channels (row 7), the estimated coefficient on wage growth is of the right sign and a reasonable magnitude, but it is not statistically significant.

3. The discount rate enters the encompassing equation (row 7) with the right sign and a high significance level. A 100-basis-point increase in the discount rate is estimated to reduce the growth rate of industrial production by 3.6 percentage points.

4. The effect of banking panics on output is large (a year of panic is estimated in equation (7) to reduce output growth by $12 \times .0138$, or more than 16 percentage points) and highly statistically significant (*t*-statistics of 4.0 or better). The measured effect of the *PANIC* variable does not seem to depend much on what other variables are included in the equation.

5. There may be some residual effect of deflation on output not accounted for by any of these effects. To see this, note that in principle the coefficient on $\Delta \ln PW$ in equation (7) of table 2.9 should be equal to and opposite the weighted sum of the coefficients on $\Delta \ln EX$, $\Delta \ln W$, and *DISC* (where the weights are the projection coefficients of the respective "true" deflators on $\Delta \ln PW$). Suppose for the sake of illustration that each of the projection coefficients equals one (that is, the wholesale price index is the correct deflator). Then the expected value of the coefficient on $\Delta \ln PW$ should be approximately .052; the actual value is .296, with a standard error of .123. Thus there may be channels relating deflation to depression other than the ones explicitly accounted for here. One possibility is that we are simply picking up the effects of a simultaneity bias (a reverse causation from output to prices). Alternatively, it is possible that an additional factor, such as debt deflation, should be considered.

As an alternative to the procedure of nesting alternative channels in a single equation, in equation (8) of table 2.9 we report the results of estimating the reduced form of a simple aggregate demand–aggregate supply (AD-AS) system. Under conventional assumptions, in an AD-AS model output growth should depend on money growth and autonomous spending growth (represented here by growth in *real* exports[21]), which shift the AD curve; and on nominal wage growth, which shifts the AS curve. In addition, we allow *PANIC* to enter the system, since banking panics could in principle affect both aggregate demand and aggregate supply. The results indicate large and statistically significant effects on output growth for real export growth, money growth, and banking panics. Nominal wage growth enters with the correct sign, but the coefficient is very small and statistically insignificant.

We have so far focused on the effects of banking panics (and other variables) on output. There is an additional issue that warrants some discussion here; namely, the possibility that banking panics might have themselves worsened the deflationary process.

Some care must be taken with this argument. Banking panics undoubtedly had large effects on the composition of national money supplies, money multipliers, and money demand. Nevertheless, as has been stressed by Temin (1989), under a gold standard, small country price levels are determined by international monetary conditions, to which domestic money supplies and demands must ultimately adjust. Thus banking panics cannot intensify deflation in a small country.[22] Indeed, a regression (not reported) of changes in wholesale prices against the *PANIC* variable and time dummies (in order to isolate purely cross-sectional effects) confirms that there is very little relationship between the two variables.

The proposition that bank panics should not affect the price level does not necessarily hold for a large country, however. In econometric language, under a gold standard the price level of a large country must be cointegrated with world prices; but while this means that domestic prices must eventually adjust to shocks emanating from abroad, it also allows for the possibility that domestic shocks will influence the world price level. Notice that if banking panics led to deflationary shocks in a large country and these shocks were transmitted around the world by the gold standard, a cross-sectional comparison would find no link between panics and the price level.

The discussion of the gold standard and deflation in section 2.2 cited Hamilton's (1987) view that the initial deflationary impulses in 1928–29 came from France and the United States—both "big" countries, in terms of economic importance and because of their large gold reserves. This early deflation obviously cannot be blamed on banking panics, since these did not begin until at least the end of 1930. But it would not be in any way inconsistent with the theory of the gold standard to hypothesize that banking panics in France and the United States contributed to world deflation during 1931–32.[23]

Empirical evidence bearing on this question is presented in table 2.10. We estimated equations for wholesale price inflation in the United States and France, using monthly data for the five-year period 1928–32. We included an error-correction term in both equations to allow for cointegration between the U.S. and French price levels, as would be implied by the gold standard. This error-correction term is the difference between the log-*levels* of U.S. and French wholesale prices in period $t - 1$; if U.S. and French prices are in fact cointegrated, then the growth rate of U.S. prices should respond negatively to the difference between the U.S. price and the French price, and the French growth rate of prices should respond positively. Also included in the equations are lagged inflation rates (to capture transitory price dynamics), current and lagged base money growth, and current and lagged values of the deposits of failing banks (for the United States only, due to data availability).

The results are interesting. First, there is evidence for cointegration: The error-correction terms have the right signs and reasonable magnitudes, although only the U.S. term is statistically significant. Thus we may infer that shocks hitting either French or U.S. prices ultimately affected both price levels. Second, both U.S. base money growth and bank failures are important

**63    Financial Crisis in the Great Depression**

**Table 2.10        Error-correction Equations for U.S. and French Wholesale Prices**

| | Dependent Variable | |
|---|---|---|
| | $\Delta \ln USAWPI$ | $\Delta \ln FRAWPI$ |
| Constant | .044 $(t = 3.81)$ | $-.006$ $(t = 1.57)$ |
| Log $USAWPI$ $-$ log $FRAWPI$ (lagged once) | $-.166$ $(t = 2.77)$ | .071 $(t = 1.10)$ |
| Four lags of own WPI growth | $-.530$ $(F = 1.57; p = .202)$ | .320 $(F = 2.48; p = .057)$ |
| Current and four lags of base money growth | 1.412 $(F = 5.62; p = .0005)$ | .519 $(F = 0.78; p = .569)$ |
| Current and four lags of deposits of failing U.S. banks, in logs | $-.020$ $(F = 5.61; p = .0005)$ | |
| $R^2$ | .531 | .307 |
| D-W | 1.62 | 1.87 |

*Note:* Deposits of failing banks are from the *Federal Reserve Bulletin. USAWPI* and *FRAWPI* are wholesale price indexes for the United States and France, respectively. Monthly data from 1928 to 1932 are used.

determinants of the U.S. (and by extension, the French) deflation rates; these two variables enter the U.S. price equation with the right sign and marginal significance levels of .0005.

With respect to the effect of banking panics on the price level, then, the appropriate conclusion appears to be that countries with banking panics did not suffer worse deflation than those without panics;[24] however, it is possible that U.S. banking panics in particular were an important source of *world* deflation during 1931–32, and thus, by extension, of world depression.

## 2.6    Conclusion

Monetary and financial arrangements in the interwar period were badly flawed and were a major source of the fall in real output. Banking panics were one mechanism through which deflation had its effects on real output, and panics in the United States may have contributed to the severity of the world deflation.

In this empirical study, we have focused on the effects of severe banking panics. We believe it likely, however, that the effects of deflation on the financial system were not confined to these more extreme episodes. Even in countries without panics, banks were financially weakened and contracted their operations. Domestic debt deflation was probably a factor, to a greater or lesser degree, in every country. And we have not addressed at all the effect of deflation on the burden of external debt, which was important for a number of countries. As we have already suggested, more careful study of these issues is clearly desirable.

# Notes

1. The original diagnosis of the Depression as a monetary phenomenon was of course made in Friedman and Schwartz (1963). We find the more recent work, though focusing to a greater degree on international aspects of the problem, to be essentially complementary to the Friedman-Schwartz analysis.

2. Eichengreen and Sachs (1985) discuss several mechanisms and provide some cross-country evidence, but their approach is somewhat informal and they do not consider the relative importance of the different effects.

3. To be clear, gold inflows to France did increase the French monetary base directly, one for one; however, in the absence of supplementary open market purchases, this implied a rising ratio of French gold reserves to monetary base. Together with the very low value of the French money multiplier, this rising cover ratio meant that the monetary expansion induced by gold flowing into France was far less significant than the monetary contractions that this inflow induced elsewhere.

4. Temin (1989) suggests that German monetary policy provided yet another contractionary impetus.

5. There remains the issue of whether the differences in timing of nations' departure from the gold standard can be treated as exogenous. Eichengreen and Sachs (1985) argue that exogeneity is a reasonable assumption, given the importance of individual national experiences, institutions, and fortuitous events in the timing of each country's decision to go off gold. Strong national differences in attitudes toward the gold standard (e.g., between the Gold Bloc and the Sterling Bloc) were remarkably persistent in their influence on policy.

6. The countries in our sample are listed in table 2.1. We included countries for which the League of Nations collected reasonably complete data on industrial production, price levels, and money supplies (League of Nations' *Monthly Bulletin of Statistics and Yearbooks*, various issues; see also League of Nations, *Industrialization and Foreign Trade*, 1945). Latin America, however, was excluded because of concerns about the data and our expectation that factors such as commodity prices would play a more important role for these countries. However, see Campa (forthcoming) for evidence that the gold standard transmitted deflation and depression to Latin America in a manner very similar to that observed elsewhere.

7. We define abandonment of the gold standard broadly as occurring at the first date in which a country imposes exchange controls, devalues, or suspends gold payments; see table 2.1 for a list of dates. An objection to this definition is that some countries continued to try to target their exchange rates at levels prescribed by the gold standard even after "leaving" the gold standard by our criteria; Canada and Germany are two examples. We made no attempt to account for this, on the grounds that defining adherence to the gold standard by looking at variables such as exchange rates, money growth, or prices risks assuming the propositions to be shown.

8. In constructing the grand averages taken over gold and non-gold countries, if a

**65**    Financial Crisis in the Great Depression

country abandoned the gold standard in the middle of a year, it is included in both the gold and non-gold categories with weights equal to the fraction of the year spent in each category. We use simple rather than weighted averages in the tables, and similarly give all countries equal weight in regression results presented below. This was done because, for the purpose of testing hypotheses (e.g., about the relationship between deflation and depression) it seems most reasonable to treat each country (with its own currency, legal system, financial system, etc.) as the basic unit of observation and to afford each observation equal weight. If we were instead trying to measure the overall economic significance of, for example, an individual country's policy decisions, weighted averages would be more appropriate.

9. The use of the terms M1 and M2 should not be taken too literally here, as the transactions characteristics of the assets included in each category vary considerably among countries. The key distinction between the two aggregates is that commercial banks, which were heavily involved in commercial lending, were much more vulnerable to banking panics. Savings banks, in contrast, held mostly government securities, and thus often gained deposits during panic periods.

10. However, it must be mentioned that recent exponents of the real wage explanation of German unemployment invoke it to account for high levels of unemployment throughout the mid and late 1920s, and not just for the period after 1929 (Borchardt 1979).

11. In the French case, however, there may have been some fear of government default, given the large deficits that were being run; conceivably, this could explain the higher rate on French bills.

12. A possible response to this point is that fear of devaluation added a risk premium to assets in gold standard countries. This point can be checked by looking at forward rates for foreign exchange, available in Einzig (1937). The forward premia on gold standard currencies are generally small, except immediately before devaluations. In particular, the three-month premium on dollars versus the pound in 1932 had a maximum value of about 4.5% (at an annual rate) during the first week of June, but for most of the year was considerably less than that.

13. The effect of deflation on banks, and the relationship between deflation and bank runs, has been analyzed in a theoretical model by Flood and Garber (1981).

14. An important issue, which we cannot resolve here, is whether government takeovers of banks resulted in some restoration of intermediary services, or if, instead, the government functioned primarily as a liquidation agent.

15. In the next section we divide our sample into two groups: eleven countries with serious banking problems and thirteen countries without these problems. In 1930, the year before the peak of the banking crises, the countries that were to avoid banking problems suffered on average a 12% deflation and a 6% fall in industrial production; the comparable numbers for the group that was to experience panics were 13% and 8%. Thus, there was no large difference between the two groups early in the Depression. In contrast, in 1932 (the year following the most intense banking crises), industrial production growth in countries without banking crises averaged $-2\%$; in the group that experienced crises the comparable number was $-16\%$.

16. Although this correlation seems to hold during the Depression, we do not want to conclude unconditionally that branch banking is more stable; branching facilitates diversification but also increases the risk that problems in a few large banks may bring down the entire network.

17. Causality could run in both directions. For example, Wigmore (1987) argues that the U.S. banking panic in 1933 was in part created by a run on the dollar.

18. It has been pointed out to us that if nominal wages were literally rigid, then this approach would find no effect for wages even though changes in the real wage might

66     **Ben Bernanke and Harold James**

be an important channel for the effects of deflation. The reply to this is that, if nominal wages are completely rigid, the hypothesis that real wages are important can never be distinguished from an alternative which proposes that deflation has its effects in some other way.

19. In another sensitivity check, we also tried multiplying *PANIC* times the change in the deposit-currency ratio, to allow for differential severity of panics. The results exhibited an outlier problem. When Rumania (which had a change in the deposit-currency ratio of $-.76$ in 1931) was excluded, the results were similar to those obtained using the *PANIC* variable alone. However, inclusion of Rumania weakened both the magnitude and statistical significance of the effect of panics on output. The "reason" for this is that, despite its massive deposit contraction, Rumania experienced a 5% growth of industrial production in 1931. Whether this is a strong contradiction of the view that panics affect real output is not clear, however, since according to the League of Nations the peak of the Rumania crisis did not occur until September or October, and industrial production in the subsequent year fell by 14%. Another reason to downplay these results is that the change in the deposit-currency ratio may not be a good indicator of the severity of the banking crisis, as the Italian case indicates.

20. Results were unchanged when lagged industrial production growth was added to the equations. The coefficient on lagged production was typically small and statistically insignificant.

21. Deflation is by the wholesale price index.

22. A possible exception to this proposition for a small country might be a situation in which there are fears that the country will devalue or abandon gold; in this case the country's price level might drop below the world level without causing inflows of reserves. An example may be Poland in 1932. A member of the Gold Bloc, Poland's wholesale price level closely tracked that of France until mid 1931, when Poland experienced severe banking problems and withdrawals of foreign deposits, which threatened convertibility. From that point on, even though both countries remained on the gold standard, money supplies and prices in Poland and France began to diverge. From the time of the Polish crisis in June 1931 until the end of 1932, money and notes and circulation dropped by 9.1% in Poland (compared to a gain of 10.5% in France); Polish commercial bank deposits fell 24.5% (compared to a 4.1% decline in France); and Polish wholesale prices declined 35.2% (compared to a decline of 18.3% in France). Despite its greater deflation, Poland lost about a sixth of its gold reserves in 1932, while France gained gold.

23. This hypothesis does not bear on Temin's claim that there was little that central banks could do about banking crises under the gold standard; rather, the argument is that if, fortuitously, French and U.S. banking panics had not occurred, world deflation in 1931–32 would have been less severe.

24. Indeed, if banking panics induced countries to abandon gold, they may have indirectly contributed to an eventual rise in price levels.

# References

Bernanke, Ben. 1983. Non-monetary effects of the financial crisis in the propagation of the Great Depression. *American Economic Review* 73: 257–76.
———. 1986. Employment, hours, and earnings in the Depression: An analysis of eight manufacturing industries. *American Economic Review* 76: 82–109.
Bernanke, Ben, and Mark Gertler. 1990. Financial fragility and economic performance. *Quarterly Journal of Economics* 105: 87–114.

Board of Governors of the Federal Reserve System. 1943. *Banking and monetary statistics, 1919–41*. Washington, DC: Government Printing Office.

Borchardt, Knut. 1979. Zwangslagen und Handlungsspielraume in der grossen Wirtschaftskrise der fruhen dreissiger Jahren: Zur Revision des uberlieferten Geschichtesbildes. *Jahrbuch der Bayerische Akademie der Wissenschaften*, 87–132. Munich.

Bordo, Michael, and Finn Kydland. 1990. The gold standard as a rule. Typescript, Rutgers University and Carnegie-Mellon University.

Bouvier, Jean. 1984. The French banks, inflation and the economic crisis, 1919–1939. *Journal of European Economic History* 13: 29–80.

Campa, Jose Manuel. Forthcoming. Exchange rates and economic recovery in the 1930s: An extension to Latin America. *Journal of Economic History*.

Choudhri, Ehsan U., and Levis A. Kochin. 1980. The exchange rate and the international transmission of business cycle disturbances: Some evidence from the Great Depression. *Journal of Money, Credit, and Banking* 12: 565–74.

Ciocca, Pierluigi, and Gianni Toniolo. 1984. Industry and finance in Italy, 1918–40. *Journal of European Economic History* 13: 113–36.

Eichengreen, Barry. 1986. The Bank of France and the sterilization of gold, 1926–1932. *Explorations in Economic History* 23: 56–84.

———. 1987. The gold-exchange standard and the Great Depression. Working Paper no. 2198 (March). Cambridge, Mass.: National Bureau of Economic Research.

Eichengreen, Barry, and T. J. Hatton. 1987. Interwar unemployment in international perspective: An overview. In *Interwar unemployment in international perspective*, ed. B. Eichengreen and T. J. Hatton, 1–59. Boston: Kluwer Academic Publishers.

Eichengreen, Barry, and Richard Portes. 1986. Debt and default in the 1930s: Causes and consequences. *European Economic Review* 30: 599–640.

Eichengreen, Barry, and Jeffrey Sachs. 1985. Exchange rates and economic recovery in the 1930s. *Journal of Economic History* 45: 925–46.

———. 1986. Competitive devaluation in the Great Depression: A theoretical reassessment. *Economic Letters* 21: 67–71.

Einzig, Paul. 1937. *The theory of forward exchange*. London: Macmillan.

Fisher, Irving. 1933. The debt-deflation theory of great depressions. *Econometrica* 1: 337–57.

Flood, Robert P., Jr., and Peter M. Garber. 1981. A systematic banking collapse in a perfect foresight world. NBER Working Paper no. 691 (June). Cambridge, Mass.: National Bureau of Economic Research.

Friedman, Milton, and Anna J. Schwartz. 1963. *A monetary history of the United States, 1867–1960*. Princeton: Princeton University Press.

Haberler, Gottfried. 1976. *The world economy, money, and the Great Depression*. Washington, DC: American Enterprise Institute.

Hamilton, James. 1987. Monetary factors in the Great Depression. *Journal of Monetary Economics* 19: 145–69.

———. 1988. The role of the international gold standard in propagating the Great Depression. *Contemporary Policy Issues* 6: 67–89.

Kindleberger, Charles P. 1984. Banking and industry between the two wars: An international comparison. *Journal of European Economic History* 13: 7–28.

League of Nations. 1926. *Memorandum on Currency and Central Banks, 1913–1925*. Geneva.

———. 1935. *Commercial banks, 1929–1934*. Geneva.

———. 1944. *International currency experience: Lessons of the inter-war period*. Geneva.

Lindert, Peter. 1969. Key currencies and gold, 1900–1913. *Princeton Studies in International Finance*, no. 24.

Newell, Andrew, and J. S. V. Symons. 1988. The macroeconomics of the interwar years: International comparisons. In *Interwar unemployment in international perspective*, ed. B. Eichengreen and T. J. Hatton, 61–96. Boston: Kluwer Academic Publishers.

O'Brien, Anthony. 1989. A behavioral explanation for nominal wage rigidity during the Great Depression. *Quarterly Journal of Economics* 104: 719–35.

Temin, Peter. 1976. *Did monetary forces cause the Great Depression?* New York: W. W. Norton.

———.1989. *Lessons from the Great Depression.* Cambridge, Mass.: MIT Press.

Wigmore, Barrie. 1987. Was the Bank Holiday of 1933 a run on the dollar rather than the banks? *Journal of Economic History* 47: 739–56.

# Part III
# The Resolution of Financial Crises

# [10]

# The Lender of Last Resort:
# Alternative Views and Historical Experience

*Michael D. Bordo* *

## I. INTRODUCTION

Recent liquidity assistance to failing savings and loans and banks (some insolvent and some large) in the U.S. and similar rescues abroad have prompted renewed interest in the topic of the lender of last resort. Under the classical doctrine, the need for a lender of last resort arises in a fractional reserve banking system when a banking panic, defined as a massive scramble for high-powered money, threatens the money stock and, hence, the level of economic activity. The lender of last resort can allay an incipient panic by timely assurance that it will provide whatever high-powered money is required to satisfy the demand, either by offering liberal access to the discount window at a penalty rate or by open market purchases.

Henry Thornton (1802) and Walter Bagehot (1873) developed the key elements of the classical doctrine of the lender of last resort (LLR) in England. This doctrine holds that monetary authorities in the face of panic should lend unsparingly but at a penalty rate to illiquid but solvent banks. Monetarist writers in recent years have reiterated and extended the classical notion of the LLR. By contrast, Charles Goodhart and others have recently posited an alternative view, broadening the power of LLR to include aid to insolvent financial institutions. Finally, modern proponents of free banking have made the case against a need for any public LLR.

The remainder of this paper is organized as follows:

II. The LLR's role in preventing banking panics

III. Four views of the LLR: central propositions

IV. Historical evidence:

> Incidence of banking panics and LLR actions, U.S. and elsewhere
>
> Alternative LLR arrangements in the U.S., Scotland, and Canada
>
> Record of assistance to insolvent banks

V. Lessons from history in the context of the four views of the LLR

## II. BANKING PANICS AND THE LENDER OF LAST RESORT

The need for a monetary authority to act as LLR arises in the case of a banking panic—a widespread attempt by the public to convert deposits into currency and, in response, an attempt by commercial banks to raise their desired reserve-deposit ratios. Banking panics can occur in a fractional reserve banking system when a bank failure or series of failures produces bank runs which in turn become contagious, threatening the solvency of otherwise sound banks.

Two sets of factors, some internal and some external to banks, can lead to bank failures. Internal factors, which affect both financial and nonfinancial enterprises, include poor management, poor judgment, and dishonesty. External factors include adverse changes in relative prices (e.g., land or oil prices) and in the overall price level.

Of the external factors, changes in relative prices can drastically alter the value of a bank's portfolio and render it insolvent. Banking structure can mitigate the effects of relative price changes. A nationwide branch banking system that permits portfolio diversification across regions enables a bank to absorb the effects of relative price changes. A unit banking system, even with correspondents, is considerably less effective. The nearly 6000 bank failures that occurred during the decade of the 1920s in the U.S. were mostly small unit banks in agricultural regions. Canada, in contrast, had nationwide branch

* Research for this article began while the author was a Visiting Scholar at the Federal Reserve Bank of Richmond in Summer, 1988. Thanks go to the following for help on this paper and on an earlier draft: George Benston, Marvin Goodfriend, Bob Hetzel, Tom Humphrey, Allan Meltzer, Anna Schwartz, and Bob Graboyes. Paulino Texeira provided valuable research assistance. The views expressed are those of the author and not necessarily those of the Federal Reserve Bank of Richmond or the Federal Reserve System.

banking. Consequently, many bank branches in those regions closed, but no banks failed (with the exception of one, in 1923, due to fraud).

A second external factor that can lead to bank failures is changes in the overall price level (Schwartz, 1988). Price level instability (in a nonindexed system) can produce unexpected changes in banks' net worth and convert *ex ante* sound investments into *ex post* mistakes. Instability means sharp changes from rising to falling prices or from inflation to disinflation. It was caused by gold movements under the pre-1914 gold standard, and, more recently, by the discretionary actions of monetary authorities.

Given that bank liabilities are convertible on demand, a run on an insolvent bank is a rational response by depositors concerned about their ability to convert their own deposits into currency. In normal circumstances, according to one writer, bank runs serve as a form of market discipline, reallocating funds from weak to strong banks and constraining bank managers from adopting risky portfolio strategies (Kaufman, 1988). Bank runs can also lead to a "flight to quality" (Benston and Kaufman et al., 1986). Instead of shifting funds from weak banks to those they regard to be sound, depositors may convert their deposits into high-quality securities. The seller of the securities, however, ultimately will deposit his receipts at other banks, leaving bank reserves unchanged.

When there is an external shock to the banking system, incomplete and costly information may sometimes make it difficult for depositors to distinguish sound from unsound banks. In that case, runs on insolvent banks can produce contagious runs on solvent banks, leading to panic. A panic, in turn, can lead to massive bank failures. Sound banks are rendered insolvent by the fall in the value of their assets resulting from a scramble for liquidity. By intervening at the point when the liquidity of solvent banks is threatened—that is, by supplying whatever funds are needed to meet the demand for cash—the monetary authority can allay the panic.

Private arrangements can also reduce the likelihood of panics. Branch banking allows funds to be transferred from branches with surplus funds to those in need of cash (e.g., from branches in a prosperous region to those in a depressed region). By pooling the resources of its members, commercial bank clearing houses, in the past, provided emergency reserves to meet the heightened liquidity demand. A clearing house also represented a signal to the public that

help would be available to member banks in time of panic. Neither branch banking nor clearing houses, however, can stem a nationwide demand for currency occasioned by a major aggregate shock, like a world war. Only the monetary authority—the ultimate supplies of high-powered money—could succeed. Of course, government deposit insurance can prevent panics by removing the reason for the public to run to currency.[1] Ultimately, however, a LLR is required to back up any deposit scheme.

## III. ALTERNATIVE VIEWS ON THE LLR FUNCTION

Four alternative views on the lender of last resort function are outlined below, including:

- The Classical View: the LLR should provide whatever funds are needed to allay a panic;

- Goodfriend and King: an open market operation is the only policy required to stem a liquidity crisis;

- Goodhart (and others): the LLR should assist illiquid and insolvent banks;

- Free Banking: no government authority is needed to serve as LLR.

### The Classical Position

Both Henry Thornton's *An Enquiry into the Effects of the Paper Credit of Great Britain* (1802) and Walter Bagehot's *Lombard Street* (1873) were concerned with the role of the Bank of England in stemming periodic banking panics. In Thornton's time, the Bank of England—a private institution which served as the government's bank—had a monopoly of the note issue within a 26-mile radius of London, and Bank of England notes served as high-powered money for the English banking system.[2] For Thornton, the Bank's responsibility in time of panic was to serve

---

[1] In theory private deposit insurance could also be used. In practice, to succeed in the U.S., such arrangements would require the private authority to have the power, currently possessed by the FDIC, to monitor, supervise, and declare insolvent its members. Also the capacity of the private insurance industry is too limited to underwrite the stock of government-insured deposits. (Benston et al., 1986, ch. 3). Alternatives to deposit insurance include requiring banks to hold safe assets (treasury bills), charging fees for service, and one hundred percent reserves.

[2] Bank of England notes served as currency and reserves for the London banks. Country banks issued bank notes but kept correspondent balances in the London banks. From 1797 to 1821, Bank of England notes were inconvertible into gold.

as LLR, providing liquidity to the market and discounting freely the paper of all solvent banks, but denying aid to insolvent banks no matter how large or important (Humphrey, 1975, 1989).

Bagehot accepted and broadened Thornton's view. Writing at a time when the Bank had considerably enhanced its power in the British financial system, he stated four principles for the Bank to observe as lender of last resort to the monetary system:

* Lend, but at a penalty rate[3]: "Very large loans at very high rates are the best remedy for the worst malady of the money market when a foreign drain is added to a domestic drain." (Bagehot, 1873, p.56);

* Make clear in advance the Bank's readiness to lend freely;

* Accomodate anyone with good collateral (valued at pre-panic prices);

* Prevent illiquid but solvent banks from failing.[4,5]

Recent monetarist economists have restated the classical position. Friedman and Schwartz (1963), in *A Monetary History*, devote considerable attention to the role of banking panics in producing monetary

---

[3] Bagehot distinguished between the response to an external gold drain induced by a balance of payment deficit (raising the Bank rate) and the response to an internal drain (lending freely).

[4] Bagehot has been criticized for not stating clearly when the central bank should intervene (Rockoff, 1986), for not giving specific guidelines to distinguish between sound and unsound banks (Humphrey, 1975), and for not realizing that provision of the LLR facility to individual banks would encourage them to take greater risks than otherwise (Hirsch, 1977).

[5] In part, Humphrey's summary of the Classical position is:

". . . The lender of last resort's responsibility is to the entire financial system and not to specific institutions."

"The lender of last resort exists not to prevent the occurrence but rather to neutralize the impact of financial shocks."

"The lender's duty is a twofold one consisting first, of lending without stint during actual panics and second, of acknowledging beforehand its duty to lend freely in all future panics."

"The lender should be willing to advance indiscriminately to any and all sound borrowing on all sound assets no matter what the type."

"In no case should the central bank accommodate unsound borrowers. The lender's duty lay in preventing panics from spreading to the sound institutions, and not in rescuing unsound ones."

"All accommodations would occur at a penalty rate, i.e., the central bank should rely on price rather than non-price mechanisms to ration use of its last resort lending facility."

"The overriding objective of the lender of last resort was to prevent panic-induced declines in the money stock. . . ." (Humphrey, 1975 p.9)

stability in the United States (also see Cagan, 1965). According to them, the peculiarities of the nineteenth century U.S. banking system (unit banks, fractional reserves, and pyramiding of reserves in New York) made it highly susceptible to banking panics. Federal deposit insurance in 1934 provided a remedy to this vulnerability. It served to assure the public that their insured deposits would not be lost, but would remain readily available.

Friedman and Schwartz highlight the importance in the pre-FDIC system of timely judgment by strong and responsible leadership in intervening to allay the public's fear. Before the advent of the Fed, the New York Clearing House issued clearing house certificates and suspended convertibility, and, on occasion, the Treasury conducted open market operations. In two episodes, these interventions were successful; in three others, they were not effective in preventing severe monetary contraction. The Federal Reserve System, established in part to provide such leadership, failed dismally in the 1929-33 contraction. According to Friedman and Schwartz, had the Fed conducted open market operations in 1930 and 1931 to provide the reserves needed by the banking system, the series of bank failures that produced the unprecedented decline in the money stock could have been prevented.

Schwartz (1986) argues that all the important financial crises in the United Kingdom and the United States occurred when the monetary authorities failed to demonstrate at the beginning of a disturbance their readiness to meet all demands of sound debtors for loans and of depositors for cash. Finally, she views deposit insurance as not necessary to prevent banking panics. It was successful after 1934 in the U.S. because the lender of last resort was undependable. Had the Fed acted on Bagehot's principles, federal deposit insurance would not have been necessary, as the record of other countries with stable banking systems but no federal deposit insurance attests.

Meltzer (1986) argues that a central bank should allow insolvent banks to fail, for not to do so would encourage financial institutions to take greater risks. Following such an approach would "separate the risk of individual financial failures from aggregate risk by establishing principles that prevent banks' liquidity problems from generating an epidemic of insolvencies" (p. 85). The worst cases of financial panics,

20

according to Meltzer, "arose because the central bank did not follow Bagehotian principles."[6]

## Goodfriend-King and the Case for Open Market Operations

Goodfriend and King (1988) argue strongly for the exercise of the LLR function solely by the use of open market operations to augment the stock of high-powered money; they define this as monetary policy. Sterilized discount window lending to particular banks, which they refer to as banking policy, does not involve a change in high-powered money. They regard banking policy as redundant because they see sterilized discount window lending as similar to private provision of line-of-credit services; both require monitoring and supervision, and neither affects the stock of high-powered money.[7] Moreover, they argue that it is not clear that the Fed can provide such services at a lower cost than can the private sector. Goodfriend (1989) suggests that one reason the Fed may currently be able to extend credit at a lower cost is that it can make fully collateralized loans to banks, whereas private lenders cannot do so under current regulations. On the other hand, the availability of these fully collateralized discount window loans to offset funds withdrawals by uninsured depositors and others may on occasion permit delays in the closing of insolvent banks.[8] Goodfriend regards government-provided deposit insurance as basically a substitute for the portfolio diversification of a nationwide branch banking system. By itself, however, deposit insurance without a LLR commitment

---

[6] Meltzer (1986) succinctly restates Bagehot's four principles:

"The central bank is the only lender of last resort in a monetary system such as ours."

"To prevent illiquid banks from closing, the central bank should lend on any collateral that is marketable in the ordinary course of business when there is a panic . . ."

"Central bank loans, or advances, should be made in large amounts, on demand, at a rate of interest above the market rate."

"The above three principles of central bank behavior should be stated in advance and followed in a crisis." (Meltzer, 1986, p. 83)

[7] Like Goodfriend and King, Friedman (1960) earlier argued for use of open market operations exclusively and against the use of the discount window as an unnecessary form of discretion which "involves special governmental assistance to a particular group of financial institutions" (p. 38). Also see Hirsch (1977) and Goodhart (1988) for the argument that Bagehot's rule was really designed for a closely knit/cartelized banking system such as the London clearing banks.

[8] Cagan (1988) in his comment on Goodfriend and King makes the case for retention of discount window lending in the case of "a flight to quality". In that case, the discount window can be used to provide support to particular sectors of the economy which have had banking services temporarily curtailed.

---

to provide high-powered money in times of stress is insufficient to protect the banking system as a whole from aggregate shock.

## The Case for Central Bank Assistance to Insolvent Banks

Charles Goodhart (1985, 1987) advocates temporary central bank assistance to insolvent banks. He argues that the distinction between illiquidity and insolvency is a myth, since banks requiring LLR support because of "illiquidity will in most cases already be under suspicion about . . . solvency." Furthermore "because of the difficulty of valuing [the distressed bank's] assets, a Central Bank will usually have to take a decision on last resort support to meet an immediate liquidity problem when it knows that there is a doubt about solvency, but does not know just how bad the latter position actually is" (Goodhart, 1985, p. 35).

He also argues that by withdrawing deposits from an insolvent bank in a flight to quality, a borrower severs the valuable relationship with his banker. Loss of this relationship, based both on trust and agent-specific information, adds to the cost of flight, making it less likely to occur. Replacing such a connection requires costly search, a process which imposes losses (and possible bankruptcy) on the borrowers. To protect borrowers, Goodhart would have the central bank recycle funds back to the troubled bank.

Solow (1982) also is sympathetic to assisting insolvent banks. According to him, the Fed is responsible for the stability of the whole financial system. He argues that any bank failure, especially a large one, reduces confidence in the whole system. To prevent a loss of confidence caused by a major bank failure from spreading to the rest of the banking system, the central bank should provide assistance to insolvent banks. However, such a policy creates a moral hazard, as banks respond with greater risk-taking and the public loses its incentive to monitor them.

## Free Banking: The Case against Any Public LLR

Proponents of free banking have denied the need for any government authority to serve as lender of last resort. They argue that the only reason for banking panics is legal restrictions on the banking system. In the absence of such restrictions, the free market would produce a panic-proof banking system.

According to Selgin (1988, 1990) two of the most important restrictions are the prohibition of nation-wide branch banking in the U.S. and the prohibition everywhere of free currency issue by the commercial banking system. Nationwide branch banking would allow sufficient portfolio diversification to prevent relative price shocks from causing banks to fail. Free note issue would allow banks to supply whatever currency individuals may demand.

Free banking proponents also contend that contagious runs because of incomplete information would not occur because secondary markets in bank notes (note brokers, note detectors) would provide adequate information to note holders about the condition of all banks. True, such markets do not arise for demand deposits because of the agent-specific information involved in the demand deposit contract—it is costly to verify whether the depositor has funds backing his check. But, free banking advocates insist that clearing house associations can offset the information asymmetry involved in deposit banking.

According to Gorton (1985), and Gorton and Mullineaux (1987), clearing houses in the nineteenth century, by quickly organizing all member banks into a cartel-like structure, established a coinsurance scheme that made it difficult for the public to discern the weakness of an individual member bank. The clearing house could also allay a panic by issuing loan certificates which served as a close substitute for gold (assuming that the clearing house itself was financially sound). Finally, a restriction on convertibility of deposits into currency could end a panic. Dowd (1984) regards restrictions as a form of option clause.[9] In an alternative option (used in pre-1765 Scotland) banks had the legal right to defer redemption till a later date, with interest paid to compensate for the delay.

For Selgin and Dowd, the public LLR evolved because of a monopoly in the issue of currency. The Bank of England's currency monopoly within a 26-mile radius of London until 1826 and its extension to the whole country in 1844 made it more difficult than otherwise for depositors to satisfy their demand for currency in times of stress. This, in turn, created a need for the Bank, as sole provider of high-

powered money, to serve as LLR.[10] In the U.S., bond-collateral restrictions on state banks before 1863 and on the national banks thereafter were responsible for the well-known problem of currency inelasticity. Selgin and Dowd do not discuss the case of a major aggregate shock that produces a widespread demand for high-powered money. In that situation, only the monetary authority will suffice.

In sum, the four views—classical, Goodfriend/King, Goodhart, and free banking—have considerably different implications for the role of a LLR. With these views as backdrop, the remaining paragraphs now examine evidence on banking panics and their resolution in the past.

## IV. THE HISTORICAL RECORD

In this section, I present historical evidence for a number of countries on the incidence of banking panics, their likely causes, and the role of a LLR in their resolution. I then consider alternative institutional arrangements that served as surrogate LLRs in diverse countries at different times. Finally, I compare the historical experience with the more recent assistance to insolvent banks in the U.S., Great Britain, and Canada. This evidence is then used to shed light on the alternative views of the lender of last resort discussed in section III.

### Banking Panics and Their Resolution

The record for the past 200 years for at least 17 countries shows a large number of bank failures, fewer bank runs (but still a considerable number) and a relatively small number of banking panics. According to a chronology compiled by Anna Schwartz (1988), for the U.S. between 1790 and 1930, bank panics occurred in 14 years; Great Britain had the next highest number with panics occurring in 8 years between 1790 and 1866. France and Italy followed with 4 each.

An alternative chronology that I prepared (Bordo, 1986, Table 1) for 6 countries (the U.S., Great Britain, France, Germany, Sweden, and Canada) over the period 1870-1933 lists 16 banking crises (defined as bank runs and/or failures), and 4 banking

---

[9] A restriction of convertibility itself could exacerbate a panic because the public, in anticipating such restriction, demands currency sooner.

[10] Selgin (1990) argues that the Bank Charter Act of 1844 exacerbated the problem of panics because it imposed tight constraints on the issue of bank notes by the Issue Department. However, the Banking Department surely could have discounted commercial paper from correspondent banks without requiring further note issue. That is one of Bagehot's main points in *Lombard Street*.

panics (runs, failures, and suspensions of payments), all of which occurred in the U.S. It also lists 30 such crises, based on Kindleberger's definition of financial crises as comprising manias, panics, and crashes and 71 stock market crises, based on Morgenstern's (1959) definition.

The similar failure rates for banks and nonfinancial firms in many countries largely reflect that individual banks, like other firms, are susceptible to market vagaries and to mismanagement. Internal factors were important, as were the external factors of relative price changes, banking structure, and changes in the overall price level. The relatively few instances of banking panics in the past two centuries suggests that either (1) monetary authorities in time developed the procedures and expertise to supply the funds needed to meet depositors' demands for cash or (2) the problem of banking panics is exaggerated.

A comparison of the performances of Great Britain and the U.S. in the past century serves to illustrate the importance of the lender of last resort in preventing banking panics. In the first half of the nineteenth century, Great Britain experienced banking panics when the insolvency of an important financial institution precipitated runs on other banks, and a scramble for high-powered money ensued. In a number of instances, the reaction of the Bank of England to protect its own gold reserves worsened the panic. Eventually, the Bank supplied funds to the market, but often too late to prevent many unnecessary bank failures. The last such panic followed the failure of the Overend Gurney Company in 1866. Thereafter, the Bank accepted its responsibility as lender of last resort, observing Bagehot's Rule "to lend freely but at a penalty rate". It prevented incipient financial crises in 1878, 1890, and 1914 from developing into full-blown panics by timely announcements and action.

The United States in the antebellum period experienced 11 banking panics (according to Schwartz's chronology) of which the panics of 1837, 1839, and 1857 were most notable.[11] The First and Second Banks of the United States possessed some central banking powers in part of the period; some states

developed early deposit insurance schemes (see Benston, 1983; Calomiris, 1989), and the New York Clearing House Association began issuing clearing house loan certificates in 1857. None of these arrangements sufficed to prevent the panics.

In the national banking era, the U.S. experienced three serious banking panics — 1873, 1893, and 1907-08. In these episodes, the Clearing Houses of New York, Chicago, and other central reserve cities issued emergency reserve currency in the form of clearing house loan certificates collateralized by member banks' assets and even issued small denomination hand-to-hand currency. But these lender of last resort actions were ineffective. In contrast to successful intervention in 1884 and 1890, the issue of emergency currency was too little and too late to prevent panic from spreading. The panics ended upon the suspension of convertibility of deposits into currency. During suspension, both currency and deposits circulated freely at flexible exchange rates, thereby relieving the pressure on bank reserves. The panics of 1893 and especially 1907 precipitated a movement to establish an agency to satisfy the public's demand for currency in times of distrust of deposit convertibility. The interim Aldrich-Vreeland Act of 1908 allowed ten or more national banks to form national currency associations and issue emergency currency; it was successful in preventing a panic in 1914.

The Federal Reserve System was created in 1914 to serve as a lender of last resort. The U.S. did not experience a banking panic until 1930, but as Friedman and Schwartz point out, during the ensuing three years, a succession of nationwide banking panics accounted for the destruction of one-third of the money stock and the permanent closing of 40 percent of the nation's banks. Only with the establishment of federal deposit insurance in 1934 did the threat of banking panics recede.

Table I compares American and British evidence on factors commonly believed to be related to banking panics, as well as a chronology of banking panics and banking crises for severe NBER business cycle recessions (peak to trough) in the period 1870-1933.[12] The variables isolated include: deviations from trend of the average annual growth rate of real output; the absolute difference of the average annual rate of change in the price level during the preceding

---

[11] Selgin (1990), based on evidence by Rolnick and Weber (1986), argues that the episodes designated as panics in the antebellum Free Banking era are not comparable to these in the National Banking era because they did not involve contagion effects. Evidence to the contrary, however, is presented by Hasan and Dwyer (1988).

[12] For similar evidence for the remaining cyclical downturns in this period, see Bordo (1986, Table 6, 1A).

Table I

## Banking Panics (1870-1933): Related Factors, Incidence, and Resolution

Deviations from Trend of Average Annual Real Output Growth[a] (peak to trough)**

Absolute Difference of Average Annual Rate of Price Level Change (trough to peak minus peak to trough)*

Deviations from Trend of Average Annual Monetary Growth[b] (specific cycle peak to trough)**

Change in Money due to Change in Deposit-Currency Ratio (specific cycle peak to trough)**

Banking Crisis[c]**

Banking Panic[d]**

Existence of Clear and Credible LLR Policy***

Resolution***

Agency***

| | Peak | Trough | | | | | Banking Crisis | Banking Panic | LLR Policy | Resolution | Agency |
|---|------|--------|-------|--------|--------|--------|----------------|---------------|-----|------------|--------|
| United States | 1873 | 1879 | 0.5% | −7.1% | −4.7% | 2.7% | | 8/73 | No | Restriction of Payments | Clearing Houses/Treasury |
| | 1882 | 1885 | −3.2% | −12.2% | 2.6% | 5.2% | 5/84 | | Yes | Successful LLR | Clearing Houses/Treasury |
| | 1893 | 1894 | −9.5% | −9.0% | −9.3% | −4.3% | | 7/93 | No | Restriction of Payments | Clearing Houses/Treasury |
| | 1907 | 1908 | −14.7% | −6.1% | −1.7% | −2.7% | | 10/07 | No | Restriction of Payments | Clearing Houses/Treasury |
| | 1920 | 1921 | −7.6% | −56.7% | −2.5% | 2.8% | | | (?) | | |
| | 1929 | 1932 | −16.7% | −12.5% | −11.7% | −27.4% | 1930,1931,1932 | 1933 | No | Unsuccessful LLR | Federal Reserve |
| Great Britain | 1873 | 1879 | 0.9% | −7.1% | −3.1% | 5.2% | | | Yes | | |
| | 1883 | 1886 | −1.2% | −5.4% | −2.8% | 2.3% | | | Yes | | |
| | 1890 | 1894 | −0.2% | −4.4% | −2.5% | −2.2% | Baring Crisis 11/90 | | Yes | Successful | Bank of England |
| | 1907 | 1908 | −4.7% | −13.6% | −1.6% | −1.0% | | | Yes | | |
| | 1920 | 1921 | −6.9% | −68.0% | −5.1% | 4.5% | | | Yes | | |
| | 1929 | 1932 | −3.7% | −7.9% | −4.3% | −1.3% | | | Yes | | |

Data Sources:    *    See Data Appendix in Bordo (1981).

          **   See Data Appendix in Bordo (1986).

          *** Judgmental, based on this paper and other research.

Notes: (a) The trend growth rates of real output were 3.22% for the U.S. (1870-1941) and 1.48% for Great Britain (1870-1939). Each was calculated as the difference between the natural logs of real output in terminal and initial years divided by the number of years.

       (b) The trend monetary growth rates were 5.40% for the U.S. (1870-1941) and 2.71% for Great Britain (1870-1939). Each was calculated as in footnote (a).

       (c) Banking crisis—runs and/or failures. Source Bordo (1986).

       (d) Banking panic—runs, failures, suspension of payments. Ibid.

trough to peak and the current peak to trough as a measure of the effect of changes in the overall price level; deviations from trend of the average annual rate of monetary growth; and the percentage change in the money stock due to changes in the deposit-currency ratio.[13]

The table reveals some striking similarities in the behavior of variables often related to panics but a remarkable difference between the two countries in the incidence of panics. Virtually all six business cycle downturns designated by the NBER as severe were marked in both countries by significant declines in output, large price level reversals, and large declines in money-growth. Also, in both countries, falls in the deposit-currency ratio produced declines in the money stock in the three most severe downturns: 1893-94 (U.S.); 1890-1894 (G.B.); 1907-08; and 1929-32.

---

[13] In relating the changes in the money stock to changes in the deposit-currency ratio, we hold constant the influence of the other two proximate determinants of the money supply: the deposit-reserve ratio and the stock of high-powered money. It is calculated using the formula developed in Friedman and Schwartz (1963), Appendix B.

However, the difference in the incidence of panics is striking—the U.S. had four while Britain had none. Both countries experienced frequent stock market crashes (see Bordo, 1986, Table 6.1). They were buffeted by the same international financial crises. Although Britain faced threats to the banking system in 1878, 1890, and 1914, the key difference between the two countries (see the last three columns of Table I) was successful LLR action by the British authorities in defusing incipient crises.

Similar evidence over the 1870-1933 period for France, Germany, Sweden, and Canada is available in Bordo (1986). In all four countries, the quantitative variables move similarly during severe recessions to those displayed here for the U.S. and Great Britain, yet there were no banking panics. In France, appropriate actions by the Bank of France in 1882, 1889, and 1930 prevented incipient banking crises from developing into panics. Similar behavior occurred in Germany in 1901 and 1931 and in Canada in 1907 and 1914.

One other key difference was that all five countries had nationwide branch banking whereas the U.S.

had unit banking. That difference likely goes a long way to explain the larger number of bank failures in the U.S.

## Alternative LLR Arrangements

In the traditional view, the LLR role is synonymous with that of a central bank. Goodhart's explanation for the evolution of central banking in England and other European countries is that the first central banks evolved from commercial banks which had the special privilege of being their governments' banks. Because of its sound reputation, position as holder of its nation's gold reserves, ability to obtain economies by pooling reserves through a correspondent banking system, and ability to provide extra cash by rediscounting, such a bank would evolve into a bankers' bank and lender of last resort in liquidity crises. Once such banks began to act as lenders of last resort, "moral hazard" on the part of member banks (following riskier strategies than they would otherwise) provided a rationale for some form of supervision or legislation. Further, Goodhart argues that the conflict between the public duties of such an institution and its responsibilities to its shareholders made the transition from a competitive bank to a central bank lengthy and painful.

Though Goodhart (1985 Annex B) demonstrates that a number of central banks evolved in this fashion, the experiences of other countries suggests that alternative arrangements were possible. In the U.S. before the advent of the Fed, a variety of institutional arrangements were used on occasion in hopes of allaying banking panics, including:

* Deposit insurance schemes: relatively successful in a number of states before the Civil War (Benston, 1983; Calomiris, 1989);

* A variety of early twentieth century deposit insurance arrangements which were not successful (White, 1981);

* Clearing houses and the issue of clearing house loan certificates (Timberlake, 1984; Gorton, 1985);

* Restriction of convertibility of deposits into currency by the clearing house associations in the national banking era;

* Various U.S. Treasury operations between 1890 and 1907 (Timberlake, 1978);

* The Aldrich-Vreeland Act of 1908.

Two countries which managed successfully for long periods without central banks were Scotland and Canada. Scotland had a system of free banking from 1727 to 1844. The key features of this system were a) free entry into banking and free issue of bank notes, b) bank notes that were fully convertible into full-bodied coin, and c) unlimited liability of bank shareholders.

Scotland's record under such a system was one of remarkable monetary stability. That country experienced very few bank failures and very few financial crises. One reason, according to White (1984), was the unlimited liability of bank stockholders and strict bankruptcy laws that instilled a sense of confidence in noteholders.[14] Indeed, the Scottish banks would take over at par the issue of failed banks (e.g., the Ayr bank, 1772) to increase their own business. A second reason was the absence of restrictions on bank capital and of other impediments to the development of extensive branching systems that allowed banks to diversify risk and withstand shocks.[15] Faced with a nationwide scramble for liquidity, however, Scottish banks were always able to turn to the Bank of England as a lender of last resort (Goodhart 1985).

Although Canada had a competitive fractional reserve banking system throughout the nineteenth century, no central bank evolved (Bordo and Redish, 1987). By the beginning of the twentieth century, though, virtually all the elements of traditional central banking were being undertaken either by private institutions or directly by the government.

By 1890, the chartered banks, with the compliance of the Government, had established an effective self-policing agency, the Canadian Bankers Association. Acting in the absence of a central bank, it succeeded in insulating the Canadian banks from the deleterious effects of the U.S. banking panics of 1893 and 1907. It did so by quickly arranging mergers between sound and failing banks, by encouraging cooperation between strong and weaker banks in times of stringency, and by establishing a reserve fund to be used to compensate note holders in the event of failure.

In addition, the nationwide branch system overcame the problem of seasonal liquidity crises that characterized the United States after the Civil War,

---

[14] Sweden from 1830 to 1902 had a system of competitive note issue and unlimited liability. According to Jonung (1985), there is evidence neither of overissue nor of bank runs.

[15] Switzerland also had a successful experience with free banks 1826-1850 (Weber, 1988) but like Scotland's dependence on the Bank of England, she depended on the Bank of France as lender of last resort (Goodhart, 1985).

characterized the United States after the Civil War, thus lessening the need for a lender of last resort. However, the Bank of Montreal (founded in 1817) very early became the government's bank and performed many central bank functions.

Because Canadian banks kept most of their reserves on "call" in the New York money market, they were able in this way to satisfy the public's demand for liquidity, again precluding the need for a central bank. On two occasions, 1907 and 1914, however, these reserves proved inadequate to prevent a liquidity crisis and the Government of Canada had to step in to supplement the reserves.

The Finance Act, passed in 1914 to facilitate wartime finance, provided the chartered banks with a liberal rediscounting facility. By pledging appropriate collateral (this was broadly defined) banks could borrow Dominion notes from the Treasury Board. The Finance Act clause, which was extended after the wartime emergency by the Amendment of 1923, provided a discount window/lender of last resort for the Canadian banking system.

In sum, though Canada, Scotland, and several other countries did not have formal central banks serving as LLRs, all had access to a governmental authority which could provide high-powered money in the event of such a crisis.

## LLR Assistance to Insolvent Banks

The classical prescription for LLR action is to lend freely but at a penalty rate to illiquid but solvent banks. Both Thornton and Bagehot advised strongly against assistance to insolvent financial institutions. They opposed them because they would encourage future risk-taking without even eradicating the threat of runs on other sound financial institutions. Bagehot also advocated lending at a penalty rate to discourage all but those truly in need from applying and to limit the expansion in liquidity to the minimum necessary to end the panic.

Between 1870 and 1970, European countries generally observed the classical strictures. In the Baring Crisis of 1890, the Bank of England successfully prevented panic. It arranged (with the Bank of France and the leading Clearing Banks) to advance the necessary sums to meet the Barings' immediate maturing liability. These other institutions effectively became part of a joint LLR by guaranteeing to cover losses sustained by the Bank of England in the pro-

cess (Schwartz, 1986, p. 19). The German Reichsbank in 1901 prevented panic by purchasing prime bills on the open market and expanding its excess note issue, but it did not intervene to prevent the failure of the Leipziger and other banks (Goodhart, 1985, p. 96). The Bank of France also followed classical precepts in crises in 1881 and 1889.

The Austrian National Bank, however, ignored the classical advice during the Credit Anstalt crisis of 1931 by providing liberal assistance to the Credit Anstalt at low interest rates (Schubert, 1987). Then, a run on the Credit Anstalt and other Viennese banks in May 1931 followed the disclosure of the Credit Anstalt's insolvency and a government financial rescue package. The run degenerated into a speculative attack on the fixed price of gold of the Austrian Schilling.

The U.S. record over the same period is less favorable than that of the major European countries. Before the advent of the Federal Reserve System and during the banking panics of the early 1930s, LLR action was insufficient to prevent panics. By contrast, over the past two decades, panics may have been prevented, but LLR assistance has been provided on a temporary basis to insolvent banks and, prior to the Continental Illinois crisis in 1984, no penalty rate was charged. In the U.S. on three notable occasions, the Fed (along with the FDIC) provided liberal assistance to major banks whose solvency was doubtful at the time of the assistance: Franklin National in 1974, First Pennsylvania in 1980, and Continental Illinois in 1984. Further, in the first case, loans were advanced at below-market rates (Garcia and Plautz, 1988). This Federal Reserve policy toward large banks of doubtful solvency differs significantly from the classical doctrine.

The Bank of England followed similar policies in the 1974 Fringe Bank rescue and the 1982 Johnson Matthey affair. In 1985, the Bank of Canada arranged for the major chartered banks to purchase the assets of two small insolvent Alberta banks and fully compensate all depositors. In contrast to the Anglo-Saxon experience, the German Bundesbank allowed the Herstatt Bank to be liquidated in 1974 but provided LLR assistance to the market. Thus, although the classical doctrine has been long understood and successfully applied, recent experience suggests that its basic message is no longer always adhered to.

## V. CONCLUSION:
### SOME LESSONS FROM HISTORY

One can draw a number of conclusions from the historical record.

(1) Banking panics are rare events. They occurred more often in the U.S. than in other countries. They usually occurred during serious recessions associated with declines in the money supply and sharp price level reversals. The likelihood of their occurrence would be greatly diminished in a diversified nationwide branch banking system.

(2) Successful LLR actions prevented panics on numerous occasions. On those occasions when panics were not prevented, either the requisite institutions did not exist or the authorities did not understand the proper actions to take. Most countries developed an effective LLR mechanism by the last one-third of the nineteenth century. The U.S. was the principal exception.

(3) Some public authority must provide the lender of last resort function. The incidence of major international financial crises in 1837, 1857, 1873, 1890-93, 1907, 1914, 1930-33 suggests that in such episodes aggregate shocks can set in train a series of events leading to a nationwide scramble for high-powered money.

(4) Such an authority does not have to be a central bank. This is evident from the experience of Canada and other countries (including the U.S. experience under the Aldrich-Vreeland Act in 1914). In these cases, lender of last resort functions were provided by other forms of monetary authority, including the U.S. Treasury, Canadian Department of Finance, and foreign monetary authorities.

(5) The advent of federal deposit insurance in 1934 solved the problem of banking panics in the U.S. The absence of government deposit insurance in other countries that were panic-free before the 1960s and 1970s, however, suggests that such insurance is not required to prevent banking panics.

(6) Assistance to insolvent banks was the exception rather than the rule until the 1970s.[16] The monetary authorities in earlier times erred on the side of deficiency rather than excess. Goodhart's view is certainly not a description of past practice. The recent experience with assistance to insolvent banks is inconsistent with the classical prescription. Liberal assistance to insolvent banks, combined with deposit insurance which is not priced according to risk, encourages excessive risk-taking, creating the conditions for even greater assistance to insolvent banks in the future.

In sum, the historical record for a number of countries suggests that monetary authorities following the classical precepts of Thornton and Bagehot can prevent banking panics. Against the free banking view, the record suggests that such a role must be provided by a public authority. Moreover, contrary to Goodhart's view, successful LLR actions in the past did not require assistance to insolvent banks. Finally, the record suggests that the monetary authority's task would be eased considerably by allowing nationwide branch banking and by following a policy geared towards price level stability. Under such a regime, as Goodfriend and King argue, open market operations would be sufficient to offset unexpected scrambles for liquidity.

---

[16] Although in the U.S., the policy of purchase and assumption carried out by the FDIC and FSLIC before that date incorporated elements of public subsidy.

# REFERENCES

Bagehot, W. (1873). *Lombard Street: A Description of the Money Market*. London: H.S. King.

Benston, G. J. (1983). "Deposit Insurance and Bank Failures." Federal Reserve Bank of Atlanta *Economic Review*. (March), pp. 4-17.

Benston, G. J., et al. (1986). *Perspectives on Safe and Sound Banking: Past, Present, and Future*. Cambridge: MIT Press.

Bordo, M. D. (1981). "The Classical Gold Standard: Some Lessons for Today." Federal Reserve Bank of St. Louis *Review*. (May), 63: 2-17.

—————— (1986). "Financial Crises, Banking Crises, Stock Market Crashes and the Money Supply: Some International Evidence, 1870-1933." In F. Capie and G. E. Wood (eds.), *Financial Crises and the World Banking System*. London: MacMillan.

Bordo, M. D. and A. Redish (1987). "Why did the Bank of Canada Emerge in 1935?" *Journal of Economic History*. (June), 47(2): 401-17.

Cagan, P. (1965). *Determinants and Effects of Changes in the Stock of Money, 1875-1960*. New York: Columbia University Press.

—————— (1988). "Commentary." In W. S. Haraf and R. M. Kushmeider, (eds.) *Restructuring Banking and Financial Services in America*. Washington: American Enterprise Institute.

Calomiris, C. (1989). "Deposit Insurance: Lessons from the Record." Federal Reserve Bank of Chicago *Economic Perspectives*. (May-June), pp. 10-30.

Cowen, T. and R. Kroszner (1989). "Scottish Banking Before 1845: A Model for Laissez-Faire." *Journal of Money, Credit and Banking*. (May), 21(2): 221-31.

Dowd, K. (1988). *Private Money: The Path to Monetary Stability*. Institute of Economic Affairs Hobart Paper 112. London.

Friedman, M. (1960). *A Program for Monetary Stability*. New York: Fordham University Press.

Friedman, M. and A. J. Schwartz (1963). *A Monetary History of the United States*. Princeton: Princeton University Press.

Garcia, G. and E. Plautz (1988). *The Federal Reserve: Lender of Last Resort*. Cambridge: Ballinger Publishing Company.

Goodfriend, M. (1989). "Money, Credit, Banking, and Payments System Policy." In D. B. Humphrey (ed.), *The U.S. Payments Systems: Efficiency, Risk and the Role of the Federal Reserve*. Boston: Kluwer Academic Publishers.

Goodfriend, M. and R. A. King, (1988). "Financial Deregulation, Monetary Policy, and Central Banking." In W. S. Haraf and R. M. Kushmeider (eds.), *Restructuring Banking and Financial Services in America*. Washington: American Enterprise Institute.

Goodhart, C. A. E. (1985). *The Evolution of Central Banks*. London: London School of Economics and Political Science.

—————— (1987). "Why Do Banks Need a Central Bank?" *Oxford Economic Papers*. (March), 39:75-89.

Gorton, G. (1985). "Clearing houses and the Origins of Central Banking in the U.S." *Journal of Economic History*. (June), 45: 277-84.

Gorton, G. and D. J. Mullineaux (1987). "Joint Production of Confidence: Endogenous Regulation and 19th Century Commercial Bank Clearinghouses." *Journal of Money, Credit and Banking*. (November), 19(4): 457-68.

Hasan, I. and G. P. Dwyer, Jr. (1988). "Contagious Bank Runs in the Free Banking Period." (mimeo). Cliometrics Conference, Oxford, Ohio.

Hirsch, F. (1977). "The Bagehot Problem." *Manchester School of Economics and Social Studies*. (September), 45(3): 241-57.

Humphrey, T. (1975). "The Classical Concept of the Lender of Last Resort." Federal Reserve Bank of Richmond *Economic Review*. (January/February), 61:2-9.

—————— (1989). "Lender of Last Resort: The Concept in History." Federal Reserve Bank of Richmond *Economic Review*. (March/April), 75: 8-16.

Jonung, L. (1985). "The Economics of Private Money: the Experience of Private Notes in Sweden, 1831-1902." (mimeo) Lund University.

Kaufman, G. G. (1988). "The Truth about Bank Runs." In C. England and T. Huertas (eds.), *The Financial Services Revolution*. Boston: Kluwer Academic Publishers.

Kindleberger, C. (1978). *Manias, Panics and Crashes*. London: MacMillan.

Meltzer, A. (1986). "Financial Failures and Financial Policies." In G. G. Kaufman and R. C. Kormendi (eds.), *Deregulating Financial Service: Public Policy in Flux*. Cambridge: Ballinger Publishing Company.

Morgenstern, O. (1959). *International Financial Transactions and Business Cycles*. Princeton: Princeton University Press.

Rockoff, H. (1986). "Walter Bagehot and the Theory of Central Banking." In F. Capie and G. E. Wood (eds.), *Financial Crises and the World Banking System*. London: MacMillan.

Rolnick, A. and W. Weber. (1985). "Inherent Instability in Banking: The Free Banking Experience." *Cato Journal*, May.

Schubert, A. (1987). "The Creditanstalt Crisis of 1931—A Financial Crisis Revisited." *Journal of Economic History*. (June), 47(2).

Schwartz, A. J. (1988). "Financial Stability and the Federal Safety Act." In W. S. Haraf and R. M. Kushmeider (eds.), *Restructuring Banking and Financial Services in America*. Washington: American Enterprise Institute.

—————— (1986). "Real and Pseudo—Financial Crises." In F. Capie and G. E. Wood (eds.), *Financial Crises and the World Banking System*. London: MacMillan.

Selgin, G. A. (1988). *The Theory of Free Banking: Money Supply Under Competitive Note Issue*. Totowa, N. J.: Rowman and Littlefield.

—————— (1990). "Legal Restrictions, Financial Weakening, and the Lender of Last Resort." *Cato Journal*. forthcoming.

Solow, R. M. (1982). "On the Lender of Last Resort." In
C. P. Kindleberger and J. P. Laffargue (eds.), *Financial
Crises: Theory, History and Policy*. Cambridge: Cambridge
University Press.

Thornton, H. (1802). *An Enquiry into the Nature and Effects of
the Paper Credit of Great Britain*. Edited by F. A. Hayek.
Fairfield: Augustus M. Kelley.

Timberlake, R., Jr. (1984). "The Central Banking Role of
Clearing House Associations." *Journal of Money, Credit and
Banking*. (February), 16:1-5.

——— (1978). *The Origins of Central Banking in the
United States*. Cambridge: Harvard University Press.

Weber, E. J. (1988). "Currency Competition in Switzerland,
1826-1850." *Kyklos*. 41.4 (3):459-78.

White, E. N. (1981). "State Sponsored Insurance of Bank
Deposits in the United States, 1907-20." *Journal of Economic
History*. (March), 13(1): 33-42.

White, L. H. (1984). *Free Banking in Britain: Theory, Experience, and Debate 1800-1945*. Cambridge: Cambridge
University Press.

# [11]

Excerpt from *Financial Crises and the World Banking System*, 160–80

# 5 Walter Bagehot and the Theory of Central Banking[1]

## HUGH ROCKOFF

### INTRODUCTION

In the debate in monetary economics over 'rules' versus 'discretion' there is one issue that receives little attention because it appears to have been settled long ago – what to do in a crisis. Here, the textbooks tell us, Walter Bagehot proved that there is one and only one correct course of action – 'lend freely at high interest rates'.[2] The appropriate policies for non-crisis periods are debated, and the appropriate arrangements for assuring that the monetary authority has the power to act on Bagehot's principle are debated, but the rule itself and Bagehot's case for it are seldom discussed.

Part of the reason, I think, is that Bagehot dazzles us. He had in Clapham's (1944, V. 2, p. 283) words 'as good a head and as good a pen as any in England'. His works bristle with brilliant epigrams – his collected works contains an index of them, surely unique for an economist – while they display deep practical knowledge of the money market. He wrote widely on literature and politics as well as economics, and *The English Constitution* has attained a status in political science that rivals that of *Lombard Street* in economics. He was the confidant of the leading businessmen and statesmen of the day. Indeed, he was known as the 'spare chancellor', a phrase that became the title of one of his biographies (Buchan, 1959). No wonder we are tempted to accept his word on things. This, I hope to show, is unfortunate because *Lombard Street* contains a subtler analysis, and raises more questions than our memory of Bagehot's epigram suggests.

The main problem, I believe, is this. There are really two Bagehots, even though we remember only one. There is, of course, the Bagehot

160

who tells us to 'lend freely at high rates' in a panic, but there is also the Bagehot who tells us to 'protect the reserve' when the market is merely apprehensive. Both speak authoritatively, but to whom should we listen? It is here that Bagehot fails us, for nowhere does he supply an explicit guide for recognizing the state of the market that calls for one policy rather than the other.

This weakness is not obvious when we confine ourselves to the theoretical parts of *Lombard Street*, but it becomes apparent when we turn to the historical parts. Indeed, I will argue below that when we compare Bagehot's descriptions of the nineteenth-century crisis with those of other analysts, particularly those of Clapham based on the records of the Bank, the conclusion that forces itself upon us is that the problems of the Bank were seldom if ever due to an unwillingness to lend in a panic. Rather the problem was typically one of recognising the right moment for extreme actions, and of avoiding being pushed to take actions it thought were unnecessary. *Lombard Street*, in other words, for all its excellent qualities, and I will have occasion to notice many of them, did not create an exception to the general rule of monetary economics. In this area, as in others, the crucial issues are still controversial.

It is always worthwhile to take a fresh look from time to time at our economic classics. But current policy discussions make a fresh look at *Lombard Street* seem particularly worthwhile. There exists a mounting concern that the world financial system has grown fragile, while the inability of the less developed countries to meet their obligations has increased the probability of a shock to the system. Plans for reforms of the system are discussed frequently. One argument, pressed perhaps most notably by Charles Kindleberger (1978) for example, is that what is most needed is an international lender-of-last-resort with the freedom and power to follow Bagehot's formulae. At the other end of the spectrum is the school of thought that would have us return to the gold standard in order to return to a lost world of monetary stability. Bagehot wrote about a world on the gold standard in which the Bank of England was (it could be argued) in a position to perform as an international lender-of-last-resort. It makes sense, therefore, to attend closely to what he had to say about that world.

I have divided the paper as follows. In the next section I review the central themes of *Lombard Street*. In the third section I then review some of the traditional criticisms, and the weaknesses that I think have been neglected next in the fourth section. In the fifth section I examine Bagehot's use of historical evidence. In the sixth section I review the

162     *Financial Crises and the World Banking System*

remainder of the nineteenth century to see to what extent later episodes also reveal shortcomings in Bagehot's analysis. In the seventh section I take up the role of the gold standard. And in the eighth and final section I set out my main conclusions.


## THE CENTRAL THEMES OF *LOMBARD STREET*

Bagehot began writing *Lombard Street*, he tells us (1873, p. 46), in the autumn of 1870. The reason is not hard to find. The Franco-Prussian War had forced the Bank of France to suspend specie payments. Now more than ever any great demand for gold, including an indemnity, would fall on the Bank of England. The appropriate response was for the Bank of England to hold a larger reserve. But Bagehot was not convinced that this was appreciated at the Bank. The point had to be driven home to the Bank and to the world of opinion. Hence, *Lombard Street*.

The lend-freely rule was, in fact, a secondary theme of *Lombard Street*. This was the lesson that later writers, such as Hawtrey (1933), distilled from Bagehot. But they were writing with a different financial system in mind, with different preconceptions about how the economy works, and with different social concerns. The Bank had stilled the panic that followed the failure of Overend, Gurney & Co. in 1866 by lending freely, and had even admitted its responsibility to do likewise in future crises. There had been some backsliding in the form of statements by Thomson Hankey, one of the directors of the Bank, who denied the Bank had an unequivocal duty to lend widely in panics. And Bagehot intended to set this right in *Lombard Street*. But the point at which he hammered away the most, because he thought it was the least understood, was the duty of the Bank to maintain a large reserve in all 'seasons of trouble'.

There is obviously a potential contradiction between maintaining or augmenting a reserve and lending it freely. Bagehot resolved this conflict by distinguishing between periods in which the market was merely apprehensive and periods in which it was in a panic. When the market was apprehensive the chief concern in the City was, according to Bagehot, with the level of the Bank of England's reserves. The appropriate policy was to protect and if possible augment them by raising the discount rate and restricting credit. Higher reserves would calm the market's fears and restore credit to normal. But, if the Bank failed to calm the market and if apprehension became panic, then the only plan open to the Bank was the 'brave plan', to lend freely. In a panic each man fears that the next deny him credit if he cannot show that he has money. Only when he gets cash, and sees that men in debt to him can get it, will the panic end.

It was altogether natural that Bagehot should make a psychological distinction the key to his theory. As Keynes (1915) pointed out long ago, it is Bagehot's psychological approach that provides the common thread of his seemingly diverse interests. He was best, moreover, in Keynes' view, at analysing men like himself, active self-confident men of business or politics.[3] But note that Bagehot's schema makes everything depend on the Bank's 'psychoanalysis' of the market. If the Bank mistakes apprehension for real panic and lends freely, then the reserve will fall and the level of apprehension will rise. On the other hand, if the Bank mistakes panic (significantly, Bagehot referred to it as a species of 'neuralgia') for mere apprehension, the Bank will starve the market of funds and the panic will intensify.

Although he was confident that the psychology of the market could be accurately read, and the appropriate medicine prescribed, Bagehot was not confident that the Bank of England as it was then constituted could do it. It was for this reason that he suggested his famous reforms of the Bank of England. There should be, he thought, a permanent Deputy Governor, to provide a clear head in a crisis – when the Governor and the Directors might be engaged with their own affairs. (Did he have himself or, more likely, a friend in mind?) And he thought that bankers, as well as brokers and exchange dealers, should be admitted to the 'court' – the flow of correct information to the Bank was crucial.

Bagehot's policy, it should be noted, was harder to apply than one which simply held that the Bank's reserves could be gradually augmented in 'normal' times and then used when troubles loomed. Bagehot, for example (1861, pp. 20–22), favoured a policy of augmenting the reserve in ordinary times, but it is clear from his analysis of historical episodes that this would not necessarily be enough. There were also sensitive periods when the market was close to panic, and yet when the correct policy was a further augmentation of the reserve.

The distinction between augmenting the reserve in normal times and augmenting it in periods of trouble was stressed earlier by Henry Thornton (1802, pp. 161–7), and the contrast between his analysis and Bagehot's helps to clarify the distinction.[4] Thornton, writing in the aftermath of the crisis of 1797, saw no reason to augment the reserve once the feeling was widespread that the reserve was inadequate; this was like trying to increase the supply of grain when there was already a shortage. Thornton simply had not conceived of it as a purely psychological problem in which the state of credit was closely tied to the level of reserves. There was more sense, Thornton thought, in the idea that the Bank of England should have tried to increase the reserve in more normal times. But this was ruled out, Thornton believed, by the cost to the shareholders of the Bank. The shareholders had a right to a normal return, and this would have been precluded by a build-up of reserves.

Given the crucial role of a larger reserve in Bagehot's schema, it is surprising that he did not consider some way of defraying the costs of accumulating gold. It would be natural to argue that since the economy as a whole benefits from a larger reserve at the Bank, the Treasury should subsidise the reserve. The costs of such a subsidy might be met in turn through a tax on the joint stock banks since the larger reserve is going to be of greatest benefit to them. Implicit taxes had been imposed on the joint stock banks before to the benefit of the Bank of England – the limitations on the note issue. But such a recommendation might have seemed out of place in the heyday of *laissez-faire*. In any case, Bagehot noted the profit problems of the Bank (1873, pp. 66–7). But he evidently believed that it was sufficient to point out to the Bank its appropriate duties. This decision may have been based on a close reading of the kind of men that directed the Bank. But in retrospect it appears to have been a mistake to ignore the profit problem. As we will see below, it was years before the Bank accumulated the additional reserves that Bagehot advocated.

## TRADITIONAL CRITICISMS

Bagehot is not without his critics. Perhaps the point made most frequently is that the existence of a lender-of-last-resort creates a problem of moral hazard. If the banks know that someone is there to bail them out in a crisis, they are likely to take more chances – reserve ratios will be reduced, dividend pay-outs will be increased, risky loans will be undertaken – and as a result, panics will be more frequent than they would otherwise be.[5] Charles Kindleberger (1978, pp. 215–20) has referred to it as a familiar argument, although he does not put much weight on it. He has argued, for example, that the presence of a lender-of-last-resort may actually reduce the frequency of panics by removing fears that a rapid business expansion must end in a liquidity crisis.

How would Bagehot have responded to this point? Hirsch (1977) argues that Bagehot implicitly assumed that the problem could be solved through the paternalistic leadership of the Bank within the narrow confines (social as well as physical) of Lombard Street. This seems to be a good suggestion. It fits well with Bagehot's neglect of a mechanism for providing the Bank with a financial incentive for holding more reserves. Men who had been to the right schools could be counted on to do the right thing once it was pointed out to them. But we also have some direct testimony in *Lombard Street* that shows that Bagehot thought this to be a minor point in any case. Moral hazard was the heart of Thomson Hankey's objection to the Bank committing itself to the role of lender-of-last-resort, the statement that so irritated Bagehot. Bagehot's answer was simply that the joint stock banks already acted on the principle that the Bank was there to bail them out. Their reserves were already reduced to the point where they were insufficient to meet the extra demands of a panic (1873, pp. 133–5). Any further movement of the joint stock banks in the direction of greater risk probably did not seem very important to Bagehot, especially because panics were as likely to be started by an external shock – war, a bad harvest, and so forth – as by bad banking.

A number of other reservations have been expressed. Mints (1945, p. 249) and Sayers (1957) expressed a concern that Bagehot's recommendation of a high discount rate sometimes did more harm by keeping up rates than good by slowing the loss of bullion from the Bank or by drawing fresh supplies from abroad.[6] And Kindleberger (1981, pp. 297–300) has noted that there may be a problem of mopping up excess liquidity after the panic has subsided. But despite the willingness of many economists to think critically about Bagehot's message, the literature seems to ignore a number of thorny problems that follow from a policy that grants the Bank – and more particularly the 'permanent deputy governor' – unrestricted authority to declare a crisis and to shift radically the Bank's policies.

## SOME NEGLECTED PROBLEMS

A panic, Bagehot evidently believed, was something to be read from the furrowed brows of the brokers in Lombard Street, not something to be deduced from quantitative indicators. With only one exception, the reserve of the Bank, the variables that play such a large part in modern discussions of monetary policy – the stock of money, interest rates, the supply of credit, and so on – are ignored. Bagehot apparently assumes that it is easy (at least for the right man) to intuit the state of the market. And when it comes to a certain kind of crisis, he is probably right. If the market is sailing along smoothly, and suddenly without warning a giant bank with a reputation for soundness fails, and if there is a sudden demand for cash, there is not likely to be much disagreement with labelling the situation a panic. As it turns out, the crisis of 1866, the one that was one of the provocations for *Lombard Street*, could be described in these terms without doing very much violence to the facts; it was very much a bolt from the blue. But in earlier crises, I will try to show below, it was not so easy to decide the state of the market.

The problem with leaving the definition of a panic to the discretion of the Bank is that without objective criteria it becomes extremely difficult for the Bank to resist political pressures to define any period of distress as a panic. As a matter of political survival the Bank is likely to find itself embarking on a policy of lending freely when it doesn't want to. As we will see below, Bagehot criticised the Bank for having allowed its reserves to become dangerously low in pre-1866 crises. But he is somewhat vague on why these mistakes were made. A closer look at these episodes shows that the reason was that there were many qualitative signs of a panic, and the Bank was under strong pressure to act as if there was one.

A second difficulty with Bagehot's set of proposals, is that it assumes that the market always responds in a simple and predictable way to the policy chosen by the Bank. Thus, it ignores the likelihood that the market will learn to anticipate the sharp changes in Bank policy that Bagehot advocates. Once it is established that the Bank has adopted a Bagehotian policy, Lombard Street is likely to watch the Bank closely and react, possibly in counter-productive ways, to changes in the Bank's official perception of the market.[7] The decision to raise the discount rate in an apprehensive market may further alarm the market once it is understood that this is the Bank's standard policy in an incipient crisis.

In short, the psychological states of the market that lie at the core of Bagehot's schema appear to have been harder to diagnose, and less stable than Bagehot suggested.

Bagehot was aware that the market watched the Bank closely. But he tended to ignore the implications of this for his own proposals. This was especially true in his discussion of the Bank's reserve. Bagehot argued that the main cause of apprehension in the market in past crises, before the point of actual panic, was a concern with the level of the

Bank's reserves. He believed that at the time when he was writing apprehension would become acute when the reserve in the Banking Department reached £10 000 000. This was the 'apprehension minimum'. To prevent this level from ever being approached he suggested an effective minimum of £15 000 000. The reserve had been £10 320 000 in 1869, close to the apprehension minimum, and averaged £12 259 750 in the years 1869–73. So Bagehot was advocating an increase of perhaps £3 000 000, about 25 per cent. He undoubtedly had figures of this sort in mind. A figure of £10 million was also mentioned by Thomas Tooke (1838, V.2, pp. 330–1), and Bagehot may have been influenced by him, or the figure may have simply been part of the lore of the market.

In any event, the crucial question is what would have happened if the Bank had adopted these figures as a guide to policy? The obvious answer is that once the market learned that whenever the reserve approached £15 000 000 the Bank would take restrictive actions – raising the discount rate, allowing bills to run-off, and so on – the market would react to the approach of £15 000 000 by limiting credit. The approach of the minimum would itself produce a crunch. Bagehot recognised this problem in a slightly different context. In considering the American plan of fixed legal reserve ratios he pointed out that if this plan were adopted by the Bank of England then, 'In a sensitive state of the English money market the near approach to the legal limit of reserve would be a sure incentive to panic; if one-third fixed by law, the moment the banks were close to one-third, the alarm would begin and would run like magic (1873, p. 216). Granted that a legal reserve ratio would be worse than a voluntary level of reserves, why would not this argument apply to Bagehot's proposal as well, even if on only a limited scale?

Thus Bagehot failed to solve the classic problem of defining the appropriate guide for monetary policy. In the case of panics he proposed giving the monetary authority complete discretion without giving them any bulwark against pressures to upgrade periods of stress to the status of panics. In the case of apprehensive markets he proposed a guide, the level of reserves, but one which on his own reasoning was not likely to work well.

## BAGEHOT AS ECONOMIC HISTORIAN

Because the state of the market, in Bagehot's schema, is something to be recognised intuitively, the ex-post definition of the state of the market can become a mere tautology. If we observe a period in which the Bank followed a policy of liberal lending, and we observe that things got worse, we can say that the market was merely apprehensive, and the Bank should have been concentrating on building up its reserve. If we observe a period in which the Bank holds on to its reserve, and we observe that things got worse, we can say that the market was in a panic, and the Bank should have been lending freely. At points Bagehot comes very close to this sort of reasoning.

He supports his case with an examination of the five crises, after the restriction, that preceded *Lombard Street*: 1825, 1939, 1847, 1857, and 1866. The crisis of 1825 was, next to 1866, his most persuasive example. His analysis of 1825 is simple. The Bank failed to protect its reserve and so produced a panic. The reserves (total bullion in the Bank) fell from £10 721 000 in December 1824 to £1 260 000 in December 1825 and, to quote Bagehot, 'the consequence was a panic so tremendous that its results are well remembered after nearly fifty years' (1873, p. 138). The Bank then took the correct action and lent freely. In a passage that has become famous he quoted Jeremiah Harman.[8]

> 'We lent it,' said Mr. Harman, on behalf of the Bank of England, 'by every possible means and in modes we had never adopted before; we took in stock on security, we purchased Exchequer bills, we not only discounted outright, but we made advances on the deposit of bills of exchange to an immense amount, in short, by every possible means consistent with the safety of the Bank, and we were not on some occasions over nice. Seeing the dreadful state in which the public were, we rendered every assistance in our power.' (1873, p. 73)

But what was going on in 1825? Why did the Bank's reserve decline so precipitously? Well before December of 1825, and the fall of Sir Peter Pole & Co. that is associated with the actions that Harman mentions, there were signs of strain in the banking system. Clapham (1944, V.2, p. 98) writes of abnormal bankruptcies beginning at the end of September. Tooke and Newmarch (1838 +, v.2, p. 184) suggest that there were runs on the country banks by small noteholders 'after the summer' of 1825 (although the evidence they cite mentions the end of the year). Now couldn't we argue as follows, using Bagehot's own principles? The reserve had fallen from £11 787 430 in August 1824 to £3 634 320 in August 1825, and perhaps this was a mistake, perhaps the drain was an external one that could have been stopped without alarming the money market. But beginning in the fall of 1825 there was an internal drain prompted by the fears of noteholders that could only be stayed by following the policy of lending freely. I think that we could reason along these lines; the only problem is that the crisis got worse. It is only in hindsight that it is clear that the Bank was following the wrong policy by lending freely in the fall of 1825.

In recounting the crisis of 1825 Bagehot made an instructive error stressed by Frank Fetter (1967).[9] Bagehot refers to a letter from Peel to Wellington discussing the Government's quandary over whether to issue more Exchequer bills, to make borrowing from the Bank easier, or whether to force the Bank into lending directly on goods, the course ultimately followed. Bagehot suggests that this letter refers to the same moment in the crisis as the statement by Harman quoted above. In fact, Peel's letter refers to events some months later. It is a natural error, and perhaps Bagehot is not to be faulted too much for making it. But it does illustrate the problem of defining a panic. Should the Government have gone to any length to make borrowing easier, or was it right in allowing other concerns (in this case a rather dubious concern with out-of-pocket expenses) to take precedence? The heaviest demands on the Bank had passed, but failures were still high. The pressure on the Government to define the situation as one requiring extreme measures was obviously great.

To be sure, the Bank could not use the discount rate during the crisis in the manner suggested by Bagehot due to the usury law. The rate was kept at 4 throughout 1825 until it was raised to 5 per cent in December. Bagehot could have argued consistently that an earlier and more vigorous increase in Bank rate, had it been legal, might have reduced the outflow of cash from the Bank. But what would have been the effect of a rapid increase in the discount rate in 1825, and in particular what would have been the effect if the public realised that this was a sign that the Bank thought its own reserves were inadequate?

Of the crisis of 1839 all that Bagehot tells us is that 'the Bank was compelled to draw for £2 000 000 on the Bank of France; and even after that aid the directors permitted their bullion, which was still the currency reserve as well as the banking reserve, to be reduced to £2 404 000: a great alarm pervaded society' (1873, p. 138). Clapham (1944, V.2, p. 166) is more circumspect, but he also criticises the Bank for 'a rather shortsighted complacency [about reserves]' from the autumn of 1938 on.

The moment that Bagehot has in mind is July 1839. Before that date, presumably, the Bank should have been defending its reserve. But if we look at the period before the final humiliation (the loan from France!), it is easy to point to a number of similarities to a 'panic', and to show

170      *Financial Crises and the World Banking System*

that the Bank was following the policy that Bagehot recommended for a panic. (1) There was a banking panic on the Continent in 1838 marked by a major suspension of payments by a bank in Belgium, a run on a banking house in Paris, and a collapse of credit and wave of failures throughout France (Clapham 1944, V.2, p. 166). The Bank of England was not under any obligation in Bagehot's scheme to act as an international lender-of-last-resort. But the linking of currencies under the gold standard created strong pressures on the Bank to operate in this way. (2) Two years earlier there had been significant closures in Britain and the circumstances had suggested that British firms were vulnerable to financial instability centred in other countries. It seems possible that the English market remained sensitive to any evidence of an unwillingness on the part of the Bank to lend when financial conditions in a major trading partner were deranged.

With these events in the backround, the Bank followed essentially the sort of policy Bagehot recommended for a panic. (1) It raised the discount rate from 4 to 5 per cent in May 1839 and from 5 to 5.5 in June. (2) In February it repeated its offer to lend on securities other than bills of exchange, and in general it followed a policy of 'allowing the public to act upon the bank' – as the policy was later described to Parliament (Clapham 1944, V.2, p. 166). From the outward course of events, in other words, we can argue that the Bank was behaving as an international lender-of-last-resort, and we can regard the Bank's difficulties as a failure of that policy. In retrospect, of course, we can also argue with Bagehot that there was no genuine panic in late 1838 or early 1839, and that the Bank followed the wrong policy. But the point is how was the Bank to know, and how was it to avoid the pressure for labelling this as a period when lending should be easy?

'The next trial,' according to Bagehot (1873, p. 138), 'came in 1847, and then the Bank permitted its banking reserve (which the law had now distinctly separated) to fall to £1 176 000; and so intense was the alarm, that the executive government issued a letter of license, permitting the Bank, if necessary, to break the new law, and, if necessary, to borrow from the currency reserve.' Again, Bagehot has the most dramatic moment in mind, the 'week of terror', 16–23 October 1847. But there were signs of a crisis well before October. Failures of major commercial houses, according to Clapham (1944, V.2, p. 203), began in August, when Bank rate was raised from 5 to 5.5. On 1 October, the Bank announced a number of actions to defend its reserve – a rate of 6 per cent for bills longer than a month, and a discontinuance of loans on stock or Exchequer bills. And it was these actions which at the time were blamed for producing the panic (Clapham 1944, v.2, p. 205), rather than the fall in the Bank's reserve cited by Bagehot; a fair illustration of the potential for Bagehot's formulae to prove counter-productive.

With hindsight we can argue that it was too late to defend the reserve at the end of September, and that the time had come to lend freely. But again the question is how could the Bank have divined this at the time? There is nothing in Bagehot's schema to help the Bank to decide on which course to follow.

The panic of 1857 was the first observed directly by the mature Bagehot; he was then 31, and would become director of *The Economist* two years later. But he argues in the same way about this crisis as about earlier ones. In *Lombard Street* (1873, p. 138) he shows the banking reserve falling from £4 024 000 on 10 October 1857 to £957 000 on 13 November. The result was that 'a letter of licence like that of 1847 was not only issued, but used'. The clear implication of this passage is that the Bank should not have 'let' the reserve fall. At the time, incidentally, Bagehot wrote a piece for the *National Review* (1858) in which he took a more moderate view. He then argued that the panic was aggravated by Peel's Act, and that some regular way for relaxing it was needed. But he did not directly criticise the Bank for allowing the reserve to fall, although he may have done so indirectly in one hard to interpret passage (1858, p. 69).

But why, to return to the main point, were there such stupendous demands on the Bank during this period? The answer, which by now should be obvious, is that the panic was already on, and the Bank was trying to put out the fires. The panic began, it appears, in the USA in September. Late in October the Liverpool Borough Bank went down. The Bank of England was clearly following Bagehot's lend-freely policy. The discount rate was raised from 6 to 7 to 8 in October, and then to 9 and the unprecedented figure of 10 in November. The Bank used its reserves as 'bravely' as possible, but its resources proved inadequate. The crisis dragged on even with the help of the letter of licence to break the Act of 1844. Finally, Bank rate was lowered from 10 to 8 on Christmas Eve, and this may be taken as a symbol of the end of the acute phase of the crisis (Clapham 1944, V.2, pp. 227–34).

Bagehot could have argued that the Bank was remiss in not building up its reserves over the years after the crisis of 1847. Or he might have argued that the letter of licence should have been issued earlier, although this course of action seems less consistent with his basic faith in the long-run usefulness of the gold standard. But it is hard to credit the argument – implicit in his discussion of the movement of reserves in October and November – that the Bank should have prevented the crisis by refusing to lend. The Bank, in other words, was listening to the Bagehot who says to lend freely in a panic; it is just that in retrospect this was the wrong Bagehot.

The panic of 1866, the one immediately preceeding *Lombard Street*, raised the fewest questions about Bagehot's schema, and one cannot help thinking that his theory was essentially a generalisation of this experience. It would be wrong to suggest that there were no signs of danger before the failure of Overend, Gurney & Co. Ltd on 11 May 1866. Yet it appears that 'panic, true panic, came with unexpected violence that day' (Clapham 1944, V.2, p. 263). Bagehot did not blame the Bank of England's reserve policy for contributing to the crisis (1873, p. 140), and he thought (1873, p. 79) the Bank's response, on the whole, was correct, although it may have erred in permitting a rumour to circulate that it was not accepting consols.

If all crises were as simple as the crisis of 1866, then Bagehot's schema might be adequate. But our review of the earlier crises shows that despite Bagehot's jamming and pushing not all of them can be made to fit into the 1866 mould. In some cases the crisis struck first in foreign countries or at the English country banks. Was this a situation that demanded action by the lender-of-last-resort? Sometimes the crisis grew slowly over months or even years. Again, when did the situation change from 'apprehension' to 'panic'? Is it any wonder that in these periods of uncertainty the Bank allowed its reserves to fall, when perhaps it should have been conserving them against a more acute demand. Without an explicit guide for defining a panic, Bagehot's analysis really helps in only a small number of cases, and may make it harder to follow an appropriate policy in others.

## THE REMAINDER OF THE NINETEENTH CENTURY

What happened after *Lombard Street*? Did the Bank follow Bagehot's recommendations?[10] It is easiest to speak about the call for higher reserves. In the sixteen years between the publication of *Lombard Street* and the Baring crisis, the average yearly reserve exceeded Bagehot's minimum of £15 000 000 only four times: in 1876, 1880, 1881, and 1885. In those sixteen years, the Bank's reserves averaged £13 376 000 compared with £12 693 000 during the years *Lombard Street* was being written. Indeed, in half those years the Bank's reserves averaged less

than they had when Bagehot was working on *Lombard Street*. After the
early 1890s the reserve began to grow rapidly. But this was clearly due
to the flood of gold from South Africa, Australia, the US, and
elsewhere, and owed nothing to Bagehot. At least in the long run
Bagehot's call for higher reserves went unheeded.

The reason was probably the mundane factor which Bagehot decided
not to pursue in *Lombard Street*: the cost to the Bank of holding larger
reserves. The sums involved do not seem large. Holding an extra
£2 000 000 in gold during these years might have cost the Bank, say,
£100 000 per year, and so reduced its annual dividend (about £700 000),
if it were all to come out of dividends, by about 14 per cent. Not a high
price for Britain to pay for a smaller chance of a financial crisis, but too
high a price for the shareholders to pay.

In the years closer to *Lombard Street* there were some spells of
trouble in the money market. And Bagehot was able to assimilate those
that came in his time (he died in 1877) within his system. There was a
crop of commercial failures in 1875 – although none of the order of
Overend, Gurney & Co. – but the Bank was never faced with a panic.
Bagehot (1875, 1876) claimed that this was because the Bank had
maintained a large reserve. But the reserve was not really larger than it
had been in the years when he was writing *Lombard Street*: the reserve
averaged £10 037 000 in 1874, barely above the apprehension minimum, and £11 597 000 in 1875. Perhaps it was true that the reserve was
large given the demands placed upon it.

But the plain fact was that these years, as might be said of the rest of
the century, were relatively free of the sort of crisis that had repeatedly
shaken the system before *Lombard Street*. The reason is not really
clear, although I would lean to the view expressed by R. C. O.
Matthews (Kindleberger and Lafargue 1982, p. 2) that the relative
absence of major wars played a part, along with perhaps the rising
supply of gold at the end of the period. The next real test of the Bank
came with the Baring crisis in 1890, a crisis similar to 1866 in the sense
that it involved the sudden (although not completely unanticipated)
failure of a giant house in London.

The reserve on the eve of the Baring crisis was only £10 815 000,
close to the apprehension minimum defined by Bagehot seventeen years
earlier, and well below the working minimum of £15 000 000 he had
laid down. Bagehot could well have berated the Bank once again for
maintaining an inadequate reserve, but further events moved along
lines that Bagehot had not foreseen. Bank rate was raised from 5 to 6
per cent in November when the Bank learned of the difficulties of

174      *Financial Crises and the World Banking System*

Barings. But Clapham (1944, v.2, p. 330) conjectures that the Bank didn't want to raise the rate further because it might alarm the City, once again illustrating the problem of unwanted announcement effects that Bagehot had ignored in *Lombard Street*. Once bills on Barings began to come in it was time for the Bank, according to Bagehot, or more properly to one of the Bagehots, to stem the crisis by lending freely. Instead, the Bank resorted to a device completely outside Bagehot's rules – a collective guarantee of the liabilities of the Barings, provided by the Bank, the government, and leading financial institutions. As it turned out this device was effective, and a panic was avoided (Clapham 1944, V.2, 326–39; Presnell, 1968). The success of the guarantee showed one way towards greater financial stability. But it was not a triumph for Bagehot.

## THE GOLD STANDARD AND BAGEHOT'S DILEMMA

The weaknesses in Bagehot's schema which I have been discussing are clearly a product of the gold standard. It is the finite limit to the stock of high-powered money that forces the Bank of England constantly to look over its shoulder at its reserves. Under a fiat standard, by way of contrast, the Bank could never run out of high-powered money. It could always lend freely in a crisis.

If the Bank could draw on some other large supply of gold besides its own reserves, then it would be in a position to act something like a central bank with fiat powers. Several possibilities have been suggested to me as ways of reconciling Bagehot's two rules, but all seem to me to miss one of the main points of *Lombard Street*, that the supply of gold was truly limited. It could be argued, for example, that Bagehot counted on Peel's Act being suspended in a panic. Indeed, Bagehot argued, as we have seen, that there should be some formalised means of suspending the Act, and in parliamentary testimony he conceded that the Act might have to be suspended. But it is clear from his remarks on the crises of 1847 and 1857, quoted above, that he regarded the suspension of the Act as a failure of policy. Nor is it clear that suspending the Act would always have the desired effect. The amount of gold in the Bank would still be limited, and the alarm of the financial community, particularly note holders, might increase. Only going off gold altogether would really help and this was clearly anathema to Bagehot.

It has also been suggested to me that Bagehot might have been assuming that an increase in the discount rate could bring in gold, allowing the Bank to follow a lend-freely policy without worrying about the level of its reserves. But attracting gold to London was not the same as attracting it to the Bank. In these years, as Cramp (1961) has shown, the participants in the market treated an increase in the discount rate as a signal that stormy weather lay ahead. Firms tried to strengthen themselves, and one result was to pull gold from abroad. But the same consideration that led firms to bring gold home led them not to deposit it with the Bank. The Bank, as Bagehot repeatedly argued, was the one great reserve of gold in the world. It could not readily augment that reserve in times of trouble because there was no place for the gold to come from.

The gold standard, by linking currencies together, tends to force any national bank that acts as a lender-of-last-resort to act as an international lender-of-last-resort. It may choose to build its reserves to the point where it can act alone, or it may choose to act in concert with other central banks, but it cannot remain aloof from crisis in other countries. Bagehot was not comfortable, I believe, with this aspect of the gold standard. Consider, for example, his evident disgust when the Bank of England was forced to borrow from the Bank of France during the crisis of 1839. It would be fair, I think, to infer that Bagehot believed that as long as panic was confined to foreign countries, or even to the British countryside, the Bank of England should look towards its reserves; only when the panic spread to Lombard Street should the Bank begin to lend freely. But that this is the best course of action is, of course, an empirical proposition. By then it might be too late. And it is clear that the Bank would be under strong political pressures to abandon its defensive posture long before the panic hit the City itself.

Under a fiat standard, it might be thought, Bagehot's two rules (1) lend freely and (2) defend the reserve are effectively reduced to one, and the problem of deciding which to apply disappears. Undoubtedly, the eclipse of the gold standard explains why modern students of banking tend to remember only one of Bagehot's rules. But even under a fiat system a central bank is likely to have goals, such as maintaining the trend growth of the money supply, that conflict with its lender-of-last-resort duties when the latter are broadly defined. Typically, the central bank will find itself under heavy pressure to upgrade each period of stress to the status of panic. But if this is done repeatedly the long-run goal may be lost.

Thus, the dilemma posed by Bagehot's policy is in great measure a function of the attempt to formulate an adequate policy under a gold

176     *Financial Crises and the World Banking System*

standard. In a world of fiat monies and flexible exchange rates it would be easier to play the role of lender-of-last-resort. The immediate relevance, then, of a closer look at Bagehot is to the case for returning to a gold standard. Advocates of a return might argue that the nineteenth-century gold standard was plagued by crises, but that modern theories of central banking derived from Bagehot provide an adequate means for managing such crises. My point here is that Bagehot provides a clear guide only to the most obvious situations. Ambiguous cases will remain so even after they are examined in the light of *Lombard Street*. We cannot rely on central banks to prevent crises under a new gold standard.

CONCLUSIONS

The problem I have been discussing may be put this way. In Bagehot's day the Bank of England had to be concerned with its own liquidity as well as that of the rest of the financial system. Bagehot's advice was for the Bank to protect its reserve when the state of the reserve was the major source of alarm on Lombard Street (a period of apprehension), and to lend freely when the main source of alarm was each firm's fear that its own reserve would soon prove inadequate (a panic). But how was the Bank to distinguish between these two delicate states of the market? And how could it be sure that actions taken to cure an apprehensive market wouldn't produce a panic? The most one can derive from *Lombard Street* is the implicit assumption that the right course of action would be obvious once the facts were examined.

In a few cases this appears to have been true. In the crisis of 1866, one that hit almost without warning, few would dissent from Bagehot's prescription of 'lending freely'. But other cases were ambiguous. Sometimes the crisis evolved slowly (1837–9), and sometimes it was centred initially in foreign countries (1857) or outlying regions of the UK (1825). It was not clear which Bagehot the Bank should have listened to, and the pressure was to listen to the one who advised 'lend freely'. As it turns out, *Lombard Street* argues that this policy was the wrong one. But it is hard to see how the Bank could have avoided the course it chose on these occasions without an explicit guide to fall back on.

One approach to try to rectify this weakness might be to attempt to frame an explicit definition of a financial panic. It would be possible, for example, to 'fit' a definition to the historical episodes that Bagehot described as panics. Such a Bagehotian definition would be extremely narrow by some modern standards. Panics requiring free lending would be brief moments, not long periods. They would be domestic, rather than international; indeed it would not be a true panic until the crisis hit the financial centre itself. And they would be moments when the payments mechanism itself would be in danger, when the demand was for the means of exchange. But even such an explicit definition leaves considerable room for discretion and promises difficulties as the moment for switching policies approaches.

There is much to be said, therefore, for relying on a quantitative guide such as the stock of money even during a financial crisis. This would provide the central bank with some defence against the pressure to redefine the crisis as a panic. ('Our monetary aggregates remain within their targeted range despite the unfortunate recent events on the continent!') And it would provide for the automatic increase in the means of payment as the demand for it increased. But the main point is simply that when we begin to think about the practical problems in applying Bagehot's formulae, we are led back to the standard debates on monetary policy.

The gold standard, I should reiterate, is at the heart of Bagehot's dilemma. In his day the Bank of England could run out of base money. In an emergency Peel's Act could be suspended. But even this would not eliminate the strait-jacket imposed by the gold standard. That could be achieved only by eliminating convertibility, but Bagehot evidently believed that the gold standard was such an integral part of the system of credit that had grown up in England that any abridgement of it would impose serious costs on the financial system. Today, a central bank can adopt the 'lend freely' policy more frequently and with greater vigour than it could in Bagehot's day. But a similar problem remains. The modern central bank has goals, such as maintaining a low trend rate of growth of the stock of money, which are analogies of Bagehot's goal of maintaining the reserve.[11] Bagehot, in modern terms, advises the Bank to abandon such policies in a panic. The problem is to recognise when an apprehensive market has degenerated into a panic, and to avoid announcement effects that cause the very transformation of the market the Bank seeks to prevent. The solutions to these problems, unfortunately, are not to be found in *Lombard Street*.

I have been rather critical of *Lombard Street*. I have argued that Bagehot should have proposed a system of taxes and subsidies to assure that the Bank would accumulate the additional reserves he thought necessary. I have argued that he should have proposed better guides for

178     *Financial Crises and the World Banking System*

recognising the states of the market that were crucial to his theory. And I have argued that he should have proposed ways of preventing the potentially destabilising announcement effects that might have been created by adopting his policies. But I do not mean to disparage Bagehot's achievement. By asking the central questions – what is the Bank of England, and what should it do – and by providing a clearly stated answer, Bagehot made one of the most important contributions to the development of the theory of monetary policy in the nineteenth century. Rather, my point is that *Lombard Street* is a far more subtle book, a harder book to use Keynes' (1915) term, than the one suggested by the epigram 'lend freely at high rates'. After all, what better praise can there be for an author than to say that people are still thinking about his work more than a century after it was written?

## NOTES

1. I would like to thank Anna Jacobson Schwartz, Richard Sylla and Eugene White for a number of thought-provoking comments on an earlier draft. They are not responsible, of course, for any remaining errors.
2. I first learned to pronounce Bagehot's name correctly in a class given by Professor Stigler. He explained that despite the spelling, the name was not pronounced, as most Americans supposed, as Baggy-hot.
3. Bagehot came from a banking family (indeed, he was literally born in a bank), and he maintained an active interest in the firm. So his adult observations of the money market, made from his post at *The Economist*, were joined by personal observations, some possibly from far back in his childhood. See the biography by Norman St John-Stevas (1959) for a brief well-written account of his life.
4. Thornton and Bagehot were treated by Humphrey (1975) as co-founders of the concept of the lender-of-last-resort. How much, if anything, Bagehot owed to the earlier writer, however, is unclear. In this and similar cases it should be remembered that Bagehot was not an academic, and was not concerned with intellectual precedence.
5. Roger Hinderliter and I (1976) once tried to examine the effects of the Bank of England behaviour on reserve ratios in a comparative context.
6. The high discount rate that Bagehot recommended for panics probably played several roles in his thinking. But the most important was simply that of providing some protection for the reserve (1873, p. 187). Gold or notes would be given to those who were truly desperate.
7. The argument that participants in the market form expectations and base their behaviour in part on what they perceive the policies of the Government to be has, of course, become a central issue in modern macroeconomics. The classical reference is perhaps Lucas (1976). Intuitively, central banking seems to be a clear case where considerations of this sort appear to be highly plausible.

8. This passage is quoted, for example, by Friedman and Schwartz (1963, p. 395).
9. This error was also noticed by Hawtrey (1933, p. 122), but he did not draw any conclusions from it.
10. See Fetter (1965, chapter 9) for a more positive view of Bagehot's impact.
11. In the draft of the paper presented at the conference I went a bit further in pressing this analogy than was warranted, and this was the basis of some of the comments.

## REFERENCES

I have listed the references to Bagehot's writings separately so that I could cite them by their original date in the text. All are available in his *Collected Works*.

Bagehot, W. (1858) 'The monetary crisis of 1857'. Originally published in the *National Review*, reprinted in the *Collected Works of Walter Bagehot*, edited by Norman St John-Stevas, vol. 10 (London: *The Economist*, 1978): 49–76.
Bagehot, W. (1861) 'The duty of the Bank of England in times of quietude', reprinted in the *Collected Works of Walter Bagehot*, vol. 10: 20–2.
Bagehot, W. (1873) *Lombard Street: A Description of the Money Market* (London: H. S. King) Reprinted in the *Collected Works of Walter Bagehot*, vol. 9: 45–233.
Bagehot, W. (1875) 'The lesson of recent events in the money market', reprinted in the *Collected Works of Walter Bagehot*, vol. 11: 48–53.
Bagehot, W. (1876) 'The use of a large bank reserve', reprinted in the *Collected Works of Walter Bagehot*, vol. 11: 54–6.
Buchan, A. (1959) *The Spare Chancellor: The Life of Walter Bagehot* (London: Chatto & Windus).
Clapham, Sir J. (1944) *The Bank of England: A History*. 2 vols. (Cambridge: Cambridge University Press).
Cramp, A. B. (1961) *Opinion on Bank Rate, 1822–60* (London: The London School of Economics and Political Science).
Fetter, F. W. (1965) *Development of British Monetary Orthodoxy, 1797–1875.* (Cambridge, Mass.: Harvard University Press).
Fetter, F. W. (1967) 'An historical confusion in Bagehot's *Lombard Street*', *Economica*, New Series, 34 (February 1967): 80–3.
Friedman, M. and Schwartz, A. J. (1963) *A Monetary History of the United States* (Princeton: Princeton University Press).
Hawtrey, R. G. (1933) *The Art of Central Banking* (London: Longmans, Greene).
Hinderliter, R. and Rockoff, H. (1976) 'Banking under the gold standard: an analysis of liquidity management in the leading financial centres', *The Journal of Economic History* 36 (June 1976): 379–98.
Hirsch, F. (1977) 'The Bagehot problem', *The Manchester School of Economics and Social Studies* 45 (September 1977): 241–57.
Humphrey, T. M. (1975) 'The classical concept of the lender of last resort',

180     *Financial Crises and the World Banking System*

Federal Reserve Bank of Richmond, *Economic Review* 61 (January/ February, 1975): 1–7.

Keynes, J. M. (1915) 'The Works of Bagehot', *The Economic Journal* 25 (September 1915): 369–75.

Kindleberger, C. P. (1978) *Manias, Panics, and Crashes* (New York: Basic Books).

Kindleberger, C. P. (1981) *International Money: A Collection of Essays.* (London: George Allen & Unwin).

Kindleberger, C. P. and Laffargue, J. P. (eds) (1982) *Financial Crises: Theory, History, and Policy* (Cambridge: Cambridge University Press).

Lucas, R. E., Jr. (1976) 'Econometric policy evaluation: a critique', in *The Phillips Curve and Labor Markets*, edited by K. Brunner and A. H. Meltzer. Carnegie–Rochester Conference Series on Public Policy, vol. 1: 19–46.

Mints, L. W. (1945) *A History of Banking Theory in Great Britain and the United States* (Chicago: University of Chicago Press).

Pressnell, L. S. (1968) 'Gold reserves, banking reserves, and the banking crisis of 1890', in *Essays in Money and Banking in Honour of R. S. Sayers*, edited by C. R. Whittlesey and J. S. G. Wilson (Oxford: Clarendon Press).

St John-Stevas, N. (1959) *Walter Bagehot* (London: Eyre & Spottiswoode).

Sayers, R. S. (1957) *Central Banking after Bagehot.* (Oxford: Clarendon Press).

Thornton, H. (1802) *An Enquiry into the Nature and Effects of the Paper Credit of Great Britain*, edited by F. A. Hayek. (New York: Farrar & Rinehart, 1939).

Tooke, T. and Newmarch, W. (1838 + ) *A History of Prices, and the State of the Circulation from 1792 to 1856* (London: Longman, Orme, Brown, Green, and Longman) Reprinted with an introduction by T. E. Gregory (New York: Adelphi, 1928).

# [12]

*Oxford Economic Papers* 39 (1987), 75–89

# WHY DO BANKS NEED A CENTRAL BANK?*

*By* C. A. E. GOODHART

## 1. Introduction

IN my earlier monograph, *The Evolution of Central Banks,* (1985), especially Chapter 3, pages 28–35, I sought to examine the key features that distinguished banks from other financial intermediaries, and, in particular, necessitated the support of a Central Bank. This paper continues and extends that work.

Fama, in his paper on 'Banking in the Theory of Finance', *Journal of Monetary Economics,* (1980), describes banks as having two functions, the first being to provide transactions and accounting services, the second being portfolio management. Yet transactions services are carried out by other institutions, e.g. giro, Post Office, non-bank credit card companies, etc., without much need for special supervision, etc, by a Central Bank.[1] More important, I shall argue that it would be perfectly possible, generally safer, and a likely development, for transactions services to be provided by an altogether different set of financial intermediaries, i.e. intermediaries providing mutual collective investment in (primarily) marketable securities. If this was to occur, would it make such mutual investment intermediaries, e.g. unit trusts, open-end investment trusts, into banks? Would such intermediaries then become subject to the same risks as banks, and need to be subject to the same kind of supervision/regulation?

I shall argue, in Section 2, that there is no necessary reason why banks alone among financial intermediaries should provide transactions services, and in their role as portfolio managers, banks have much in common with other intermediaries acting in this capacity (though, as I shall argue later, in Section 3, certain crucial distinctions remain between the characteristic form of portfolios held by banks as compared with those held by non-bank financial intermediaries). Nevertheless, it is this *joint* role that is held to give a special character to banking, and to require special treatment for banks through the establishment of a Central Bank, e.g. to provide Lender of Last Resort (LOLR) and other support services for banks in difficulties, support which goes beyond the assistance envisaged for other financial intermediaries that get into trouble.

* This paper was originally prepared for the Manhattan Institute Conference in New York, March 1986, and was also presented at seminars at Nottingham University and Brasenose College, Oxford. I have benefitted greatly from comments made on those occasions, notably by Max Hall, Mervyn Lewis, Bennett McCallum and Lawrence White, and subsequently by Gavin Bingham and my referees, but they should not be blamed for my remaining idiosyncracies.
[1] Except insofar as the Central Bank has a direct concern for the smooth and trouble-free operation of the payments' system itself, e.g. the working of the clearing house(s) and the settlement system(s), as contrasted with the institutions providing the transactions services.

Thus Tobin (1985), states on page 20, that

"The basic dilemma is this: Our monetary and banking institutions have evolved in a way that entangles competition among financial intermediary firms with the provision of transactions media".

But what actually are the problems caused by this entanglement? The problem is often seen, and so appears to Tobin, as arising from the propensity of banks, acting as competing financial intermediaries, to run risks of default, which then, through a process aggravated by contagion, puts the monetary system, whose successful functioning is an essential public good, at risk.

I begin Section 2 by recording that Tobin's suggestion, in accord also with Friedman's views, is that institutions (banks) seeking to offer deposits involving payments' services should be required to segregate these in special funds held against risk-free earmarked safe assets. As historical experience shows, however, such a restriction would reduce the profitability, and not just the riskiness, of banking. An alternative method of providing protection against runs, and systemic crises, could, however, be obtained by basing the payments' on the liabilities of mutual collective investment funds, the value of whose liabilities varies in line with the value of their marketable assets. Since the banking system developed first, the banks established a branch system, clearing houses, etc., which provided them with economies of scale and familiarity in running the payments' system, but technological change is eroding, and could even be reversing, banks' advantages in this respect.

Indeed, non-bank mutual investment funds are already beginning to provide payments' services and there is no (technical) reason why this development should not proceed much further. It is often claimed, however, that people would be unwilling to make payments against asset balances which fluctuate in value over time. In practice, however, payments already often incorporate a probabilistic element, in the sense that the payer may have some uncertainty whether the balance, or overdraft facility, available will be sufficient for the bank drawn on to honour the cheque. The additional uncertainty involved could possibly be reduced sufficiently to make people prepared to use payments' services offered by non-bank investment funds.

Since these latter financial intermediaries would be protected from illiquidity by their holding of marketable assets, and from insolvency by the fact that the value of their liabilities varies in line with their asset values, a Central Bank should welcome their entry into the provision of payments' services and need impose no further supervisory/regulatory constraints on them. This development would, however, raise further questions about the meaning of money, since the estimated nominal value of balances capable of being used in payments would vary automatically with the prices of the assets held by these intermediaries. Indeed, the central intuition of Section

2 is that the monetization of assets is *not* necessarily limited to a restricted set of financial intermediaries, i.e. banks.

So, I demonstrate in Section 2 that the provision of payments' services jointly with portfolio management does *not, per se,* require the involvement of a Central Bank—if, for example, the joint function is undertaken by mutual collective investment funds. Clearly it is not so much the joint function, but rather the particular characteristics of banks' liabilities and asset portfolios that makes them especially vulnerable. Indeed I try to highlight this by enquiring, in Section 3, whether the banking system would still require Central Bank support even if banks were to withdraw altogether from providing payments' services, i.e. funding their asset books only through time deposits and C.D.s.

The reason why the answer to this question is 'Yes' lies in the fundamental raison d'être of banking. Why do borrowers seek loans from banks and depositors place savings with banks rather than transact directly through the market place? In part the answer lies in the costs of obtaining and assessing information on the credit worthiness of (most) borrowers. Banks have a specialized advantage in this function, but, even so, the costs and limitations of such information induce banks to extend (non-marketable) loans on a *fixed nominal value basis.* With their assets largely on such a fixed nominal value basis, it is less risky for banks also to have their deposit liabilities on the same, fixed nominal value, terms: and the same concerns with only having access to limited information about their bank's 'true' position also makes the depositor prefer fixed nominal value bank deposits.

The resulting combination of uncertain 'true' bank asset valuation, and fixed nominal value deposits, leads to the possibility of bank runs: lengthening the maturity of bank deposits slows down the potential *speed* of such runs, but does not prevent them. What is, however, particularly interesting in recent analysis of banking is that it has been realized that much of the economic damage caused by bank crises and failures rebounds on bank *borrowers.* The loss of wealth to depositors, and the dislocation of the payments' system, have already been fully appreciated in the literature. What is new now is the view that the added pressures placed on bank borrowers by such crises, e.g. the removal of access to new loans, the need to obtain facilities elsewhere at an awkward time, and, in some cases, the demand by receivers for the repayment of their outstanding borrowing, can represent an additional deleterious effect.

## 2. The provision of payments' services by banks and by other financial intermediaries

Tobin, *op. cit.,* (1985, *page* 23) *states*:

"Even if bank managers act with normal perspicuity in the interests of the stockholders, even if all temptations of personal gain are resisted, sheer chance will bring some failures—insolvency because of borrowers' defaults or other capital losses on assets, or inability to meet withdrawals of deposits even though the bank would be solvent if assets' present values could be immediately realized. The probability is multiplied by the essential instability of depositor confidence. News of withdrawals triggers more withdrawals, sauve qui peut, at the same bank, or by contagion at others. For these reasons the banking business has not been left to free market competition but has been significantly regulated".

On page 24 Tobin notes:

"Government deposit insurance in the U.S. protects not only means-of-payment deposits but all other deposits in eligible institutions, including non-checkable savings accounts and time deposits. Similar obligations of mutual funds and other debtors not covered by deposit insurance are not guaranteed. It is not clear why all kinds of liabilities of covered institutions should be insured, except that the assets are so commingled that withdrawals of non-insured deposit liabilities would imperil the insured deposits. That indeed is why the insurance guarantee was *de facto* extended beyond the statutory limit".

Tobin's suggestion is:

"This problem could be avoided by segregating and earmarking assets corresponding to particular classes of liabilities permitting a depositor in effect to purchase a fund which could not be impaired by difficulties elsewhere in the institution's balance sheet. In this way, a bank would become more like a company offering a variety of mutual funds, just as these companies—which are not insured—are becoming more like banks,"

In particular, Tobin, following an earlier suggestion made by Friedman, advocated 100% reserve-backed funds for checkable deposits, as has also Henry Wallich, in his paper, 'A Broad View of Deregulation', and several other US economists. Thus Tobin continues,

"The 100%—reserve deposit proposed, ... , would be one such [mutual] fund, but there could be others. For example, many households of modest means and little financial sophistication want savings accounts that are safe stores of value in the unit of account. *They can be provided in various maturities without risk by a fund invested in Treasury securities. They can be provided as demand obligations either by letting their redemption value fluctuate with net asset value* or by crediting a floating interest rate to a fixed value", [emphasis added here, not in original].

With such illustrious, and wide, support from economists why has this idea not had more practical success? The concept of a 100% segregated reserve against checkable deposits would, however, reverse the evolution of banking. Initially goldsmiths received deposits of gold coin from customers and acted purely as safety vaults. It was the realization that it would be profitable, and under most circumstances relatively safe, to loan out some proportion of these reserves to prospective borrowers, in addition to the loans made on the basis of their own capital, that transformed such entrepreneurs into bankers. Naturally when such early bankers did run into difficulties, by over-trading, proposals were made to force such commercial bankers back to stricter segregation. Thus the fore-runner of the Swedish Riksbank, founded by John Palmstruch in 1656, was organized on the basis of two supposedly separate departments, the loan department financing loans on the basis of longer-term deposits and capital, and the issue department supplying credit notes on the receipt of gold and specie. But even when Palmstruch's Private bank had been taken over by Parliament,

> "A secret instruction, however, authorized the advance by the exchange department to the lending department of the funds at its disposal, though on reasonably moderate terms".[2]

The reason why such segregation and hypothecation of certain safe assets to checkable deposits will not work in the case of commercial banks is that it largely removes the profitability of banking along with its risks. The regulatory constraint on the banks' preferred portfolio allocation, under such circumstances, would be seen—as historical experience indicates—as burdensome: attempts would be made to avoid, or to evade, such constraints, e.g. by the provision of substitute transactions' media at unconstrained intermediaries, which, being free of such constraints, could offer higher returns on such media. Only in the case of non-profit-maximising banks, such as the Bank of England, divided into two Departments on much the same theoretical basis by the 1844 Bank Charter Act, would such segregation be acceptable and not subject to avoidance and evasion. Of course, if the public sector were prepared to subsidize the provision of payments' services either by operating them directly itself, or

> "by paying some interest on the 100%—reserves"

held by private sector intermediaries, then it could be done; but, in the light of Congress' recent response to suggestions for paying interest on required reserves in the USA, it seems difficult to envisage the public being prepared to vote tax funds for this purpose.

Anyhow, there is a simpler, and less expensive, alternative which Tobin almost reaches when he comments that the public's savings accounts could be

> "provided as demand obligations, . . . , by letting their redemption value fluctuate with net asset value"

We are so used to having payments' services provided against checkable fixed nominal value liabilities, with 100% convertibility of demand deposits, that we have not—mostly—realized that payments' services could be just as easily provided by a mutual collective investment financial intermediary, where the liabilities are units representing a proportional claim on a set of marketable assets. The value of the units fluctuates, of course, with the underlying value of the assets in the portfolio. Because the (close-of-day)

[2] See A. W. Flux (1911), page 17, and also Goodhart (1985), pages 109–116 and 159–162.

market value of the portfolio is known, the value of the unit can be
published each morning, and each depositor then knows how much his or
her units are worth. Because there will be a period of float, during which
underlying asset values will change, and because the attempt by the mutual
funds to meet net outflows by net sales of assets could itself influence prices,
one would expect a mutual fund to limit payments services and convertibility by requiring some minimum balance in units to be held normally,
with a progressive penalty in terms of yield foregone for dropping below this
balance, plus some emergency arrangements for occasional overdrafts, say
from an associated bank. This concept of required minimum balance has
been adopted often enough, by commercial banks, and the public is familiar
with it. The cheques would, of course, have to be drawn in terms of the
numeraire—otherwise they would not be useful in clearing debts. The value
of the drawers' units would change between the date of writing the cheque
and of its being presented,[3] and—in a period of falling asset prices—there
would be a danger of the drawer being overdrawn at the latter date, while
having had funds to spare at the earlier date; but this problem would seem
also to be generally soluble by only providing guaranteed payments' services
up to a minimum credit balance in units, (plus an emergency overdraft
arrangement, perhaps with an associated bank).

I see no insuperable technical problem why payments' services could not
be provided by mutual collective investment intermediaries in this manner.
They would need to hold some liquid reserves, vault cash to pay depositors'
demanding currency, and liquid assets to meet net outflows at times when
the fund manager judged that it would be inopportune to realize investments, (n.b. this latter need is *neither* for liquidity *nor* for solvency
purposes. Liquidity is always available from the ability to sell marketable
assets, and solvency is assured because the value of liabilities falls with the
value of assets. Instead, the desire for liquid assets would arise from desire
to maximise the net asset value of units under varying market conditions,[4]
and thus improve reputation, service fees, and managerial earnings).
Nevertheless the need to hold vault cash, at least, might lower the expected
return on the intermediaries' assets, but the effect of this on the demand for
units should be (more than) counterbalanced by the improved liquidity to
the unit holder of his investments, and the associated advantages of being
able to use them for transactions purposes.

Be that as it may, the current trend already is for (limited) transactions'
services to be provided by investment-managing non-bank financial intermediaries on the basis of depositors' funds, the value of which varies with
the market value of the underlying assets. Merrill Lynch cash management
service is one example. Certain other unit trusts and mutual funds, such as

---

[3] It would, of course, be just as simple to keep the value of each unit constant, but alter the
number of units owned by each depositor as asset values changes. I cannot see why that shift in
presentation should affect people's behaviour in any way.
[4] The analysis, of course, stems from Tobin (1958).

money market mutual funds, are also providing (limited) payments' services. Similarly certain building societies and certain mortgage businesses in other countries are considering allowing borrowers to draw additional top-up mortgages up to a stated proportion of the market value of their house.[5]

A common response to this idea is that, whereas it would be perfectly possible, as a technical matter, to provide payments' services against liabilities with a varying market value, the public would not happily accept it, and it would not succeed in practice. It is argued, for example, that there is a large psychological gulf between being absolutely certain that one has the funds to meet a payment, and being 99% certain of that. But is such 100% certainty a general feature of our existing payments' system? Unless one monitors one's bank account, outstanding float, etc., continuously, and knows exactly what overdraft limits, if any, the bank manager may have set, the willingness of the bank to honour certain cheque payments will have a probabilistic element.

Lawrence White, (1984, page 707) put this general case, *against* basing payments' services on liabilities with a varying market value, most persuasively:

"Demand deposits, being ready debt claims, are potentially superior to mutual fund shares, which are equity claims, in at least one respect. The value of a deposit may be contractually guaranteed to increase over time at a preannounced rate of interest. Its unit-of-account value at a future date is certain so long as the bank continues to honor its obligation to redeem its deposits on demand. No such contractual guarantee may be made with respect to an equity claim. A mutual fund is obligated to pay out after the fact its actual earnings, so that the yield on fund shares cannot be predetermined. In the absence of deposit rate ceiling regulation, the range of anticipated possible returns from holding fund shares need not lie entirely above the deposit interest rate. Risk-diversifying portfolio owners might therefore not divest themselves entirely of demand deposits even given a higher mean yield on mutual funds. It is true that the characteristic pledge of money market mutual funds to maintain a fixed share price, or rather the policy of investing exclusively in short-term highly reputable securities so that the pledge can be kept makes fund shares akin to demand deposits in having near-zero risk of negative nominal yield over any period. The difference between predetermined and postdetermined yields—between debt and equity—nonetheless remains. The historical fact is that deposit banking did not naturally grow up on an equity basis."

Because the provision of payments' services by mutual funds, whose liabilities have a market-varying value, would not only be a somewhat novel concept, but would also worry those unused to any probabilistic element in

---

[5] Building societies, of course, will be entering more actively into the provision of payments' services, once the Building Societies Bill (December 1985), has been passed into law. But payments will normally be on the basis of their nominally fixed-value convertible liabilities. The example above, however, envisages building societies, in certain circumstances, also being prepared to monetize assets with a varying market value.

payments, I would expect its introduction to be gradual, and probably to start with richer customers better able to cope with such probabilistic concerns. Moreover, such a limited introduction could prevent the mutual funds making use of economies of scale in the provision of payments' services. There are, therefore, some observers who believe that this possible development will fail the practical test of success in the free, open market.

On the other hand there seems no technical reason why the trend towards the provision of payments' services against the value of units in a collective investment fund (up to a minimum balance) should not proceed much further, especially now that technological innovations in the provision of such services, e.g. shared automated teller machines (ATMs), electronic fund transfer (EFT) and home-banking, are transforming the production function of payments' services, especially in reducing the economies of scale to a network of manned branch buildings. White's arguments (*ibid*, page 707/8) that the provision of payments' services by non-bank (mutual fund) intermediaries has been more expensive could be reduced in force, or even reversed, by the new technologies in this field.

Moreover, there would seem considerable cause to welcome such a development, not only for the extra competition that this would inject in this area, but also because the characteristics of mutual, collective investment funds should serve to make them naturally *more suitable* purveyors of payments' services than banks. In particular, both the likelihood of a run on an individual bank, and of systemic dangers to the monetary system arising from a contagion of fear, would be greatly reduced if payments' services were provided by mutual collective-investment intermediaries, rather than by banks. For example, the announcement of bad news reducing the market value of such an intermediary's assets, assuming an efficient market, would immediately reduce the value of depositors' units. There would be no risk of insolvency for the intermediary, and no advantage, again assuming an efficient market, for any depositor to withdraw his funds from that intermediary.[6] Again, since the asset portfolios of such intermediaries are publicly reported and their value at any time exactly ascertainable, there would seem little scope for rumour or fear to take hold. Certainly if a particular fund manager did significantly worse (better) than average, depositors would find it difficult to distinguish bad (good) luck from bad (good) management, and would probably switch funds in sizeable amounts to the ex post more successful, but such switching of funds between funds would hardly damage the payments' system, rather the reverse.

[6] Mutual funds seeking to attract depositors, in part on the grounds of an offer to provide payments' services, face a trade-off in this respect. Because of depositors' familiarity with fixed-nominal-value convertible deposits as a basis for the payments' system, some mutual funds, to attract such depositors, have given some commitments to hold the value of their liabilities (normally) at such a fixed nominal value. But this opens them up to runs as soon as the publicly observable value of their assets falls towards, or below, the (temporarily) fixed value of their liabilities. This happened with the UK Provident Institute in April 1986. White (1984, page 707) and Lewis, in personal discussion, have reported such behaviour among mutual funds in the US and Australia respectively.

There would still be a possibility of a sharp general fall in market values leading depositors to shift en masse out of market valued unit holdings into the fixed nominal value numeraire, thereby forcing the collective investment funds to have to sell further assets, and thereby deepening the asset price depression. Unlike the case of a run on the banks, which raises the subjective probability of failure elsewhere, and thus reduces the expected return on holding deposits, at least the fall in market values on the assets in the portfolio of the mutual fund should tend to increase the expected running yield on such units, and thus act as an offset to the inducement to hold cash. Moreover, it would still be possible for the authorities, perhaps the Central Bank, to undertake open market operations to offset the shift of unit holders into cash, possibly by buying the assets, say equities, that the funds were selling. There are precedents for such actions: at one time the Japanese intervened to support Stock Exchange values.

Thus a monetary system in which transactions' services were provided to unit holders of collective investment mutual funds would seem inherently safer and more stable than the present system, in which such services are provided to (a sub-set of) bank depositors. Indeed, the nature of bank portfolios, largely filled with nonmarketable assets of uncertain true value held on the basis of nominally fixed value liabilities, would seem remarkably unsuited to form the basis of our payments' systems. Why did it develop in this way? The answer is, I think, to be found in the accidents of historical evolution. Broad, well-functioning, efficient asset markets are a reasonably recent phenomenon. Because of people's need both to borrow and to find a secure home for savings, banks developed well before mutual collective investment funds. The historical form of bank development led them inevitably into the payments' business. Thereafter, the economies of scale involved in the existing structure of the payments' system, the clearing houses, branch networks and the intangibles of public familiarity and legal and institutional framework, left the banks largely—indeed in some Anglo Saxon countries absolutely—unrivalled in the provision of payments' services.

Owing to the various innovations noted earlier, such bank monopoly of the payments' system may now be coming to an end. The authorities should welcome the opportunity to encourage the development of a safer payments' system. They should certainly not put obstacles in the way of properly-run collective investment funds offering payments' services. Indeed there is a question exactly what concern the authorities (and/or the Central Bank) needs to feel about the amount of monetary units thereby created, and with the state of the intermediaries creating them.[7] So long as such intermediaries abided by their deeds of establishment and restricted their investments to marketable securities, of a certain class, with the value of the units adjusted continuously in line, solvency should never be in

---

[7] There would still have to be protection against fraud, but that is a common requirement, not particularly related to the provision of transactions' services.

doubt, and would not be affected by the additional offer of payments'
services. Similarly liquidity would be assured by marketability. So it is not
clear why a Central Bank should need to impose *any* additional regulation/
supervision over mutual funds offering payments' services.

Moreover, in a world where payments' services were predominantly provided by monetary units of collective investment funds rather than by banks,[8]
why should the authorities pay any particular attention to the quantity of
money itself, particularly since its nominal value would shift automatically
with asset market prices? In such circumstances how would the quantity of
money be measured? Indeed, the intuition of this Section is that the
monetization of assets is *not* necessarily limited to a restricted set of
financial intermediaries, i.e. banks. A much wider range of financial
intermediaries could, in principle, monetize a much wider set of assets than
is currently done. Under these circumstances the definition of money would
either have to contract, to become synonymous with the dominant,
'outside', base money, assuming that such still continues to exist,[9] or
become an amorphous concept almost devoid of meaning.

## 3. Bank portfolios and central bank support

It would appear, therefore, that the provision of payments' (monetary)
services on units offered by collective investment intermediaries would *not*,
*ipso facto*, require the involvement of the authorities (the Central Bank) to
monitor and regulate the provision of such services. The next question is
whether the withdrawal of commercial banks from the provision of
payments' services, (so that demand deposits, NOW accounts, and the like
were no longer offered), would absolve the Central Bank from its central
concern with the well-being of the banking system. If banks offered only

---

[8] Something of a half-way house between a monetary unit and a bank demand deposit would
be an *indexed* demand deposit provided either by a bank or another intermediary. It might
actually be slightly *more* difficult technically to organize payments services on the basis of
these, than on mutual funds invested in marketable assets, since the latter are continuously
revalued while the former have (partly unanticipated) jumps on discrete occasions with the
publication of the (RPI/CPI) price index to which the deposit was related. Again payment
might only be guaranteed up to some minimum real, or nominal, balance. Some way would
also have to be found to allow continuous revaluing of the deposits through the month in line
with the anticipated change in the forthcoming RPI. Still, these technical problems should be
surmountable. Given that there are fiscal advantages to (most tax-brackets of) depositors in
holding indexed rather than nominal deposits, (i.e. no Capital Gains Tax on the inflation
element in the indexed deposit; whereas income tax on the whole nominal interest on ordinary
deposits is charged less the allowance given against bank charges), and that, in the UK, riskless
short-term assets for such an intermediary to hold exist in the form of Government indexed
bonds, it is surprising that no intermediary has yet started to offer indexed banking, with both
liabilities and assets in indexed form. Perhaps the most likely reason, besides inertia and set-up
costs, is that intermediaries basically require a combination of riskier and higher yielding
assets, together with safe assets, to hold against liabilities, all denominated in the same form.
The disincentive for intermediaries in the UK from setting up as indexed bankers is an
apparent absence of borrowers prepared to take loans in indexed form: why that should be so
is beyond the scope of this paper.
[9] For surveys of this latter issue, see White (1984) and McCallum (1985).

time deposits, C.D.s, etc., leaving payments' and transactions' services to others, would there be any need for special support for the banking system?

The answer to this, I believe, is that cessation of payments' services would make little difference to banks' riskiness or to the real basis of Central Bank concern with the banking system. There is little, or no, evidence that demand deposits provide a less stable source of funds than short-dated time deposits, C.D.s or borrowing in the inter-bank market; rather the reverse appears to be the case.[10] Recent occasions of runs on banks have *not* involved an attempt by the public to move out of bank deposits into cash, but merely a flight of depositors from banks seen as now excessively dangerous to some alternative placement (not cash). The Fringe Bank crisis in 1973/74 in the UK, and Continental-Illinois, are instances of this, and earlier U.S. historical experience examined by Aharony and Swary (1983) points in the same direction. Earlier, it was suggested that flows of funds from one collective investment fund to another would *not* have damaging repercussions for the payments' system, were such funds offering monetized units and providing the (bulk of) such services. Yet I shall argue that, even were banking to be entirely divorced from the provision of payments' services, such flows between banks would be extremely damaging for the economy, and would require a continuing support role for a Central Bank to prevent and, if necessary, to recycle such flows.

The reasons why this is so are to be found in the fundamental *raison d'etre* of banking itself. In particular, consider why there is a need for banks to act as intermediaries in the first place? Why cannot people simply purchase the same diversified collection of assets that the bank does? There are, of course, advantages arising from economies of scale, and the provision of safe-keeping services, but these could be obtained by investing in a collective investment fund. The key difference between a collective investment fund and a bank is that the former invests entirely, or primarily, in marketable assets, while the latter invests quite largely in non-marketable (or, at least, non-marketed) assets.

Why do borrowers prefer to obtain loans from banks rather than issue marketable securities? The set-up costs required to allow a proper market to exist have represented, in practice, formidable obstacles to the establishment of markets in the debt and equity obligations of persons and small businesses. Underlying these are the costs of providing sufficient public information to enable an equilibrium fundamental value to be established (e.g. the costs of issuing a *credible* prospectus), and the size of the expected regular volume

---

[10] Of course the risk of a run still depends, in part, on a maturity transformation by the bank, with the duration of liabilities being generally shorter than that of assets. But even if there was *no* maturity transformation, a fall of asset values relative to the nominally fixed value of liabilities would make depositors unwilling to roll-over, or extend, further funds to the bank, except on terms which made such depositors preferred, earlier creditors (than depositors with later maturities), a course which would be subject to legal constraint. So, the absence of maturity transformation would delay, and slow, the development of a run, but would not stop depositors from running when, and as, they could.

of transactions necessary to induce a market maker to establish a market in such an asset. In this sense, as Leland and Pyle (1977), Baron (1982) and Diamond (1984) have argued, the particular role of banks is to specialize[11] in choosing borrowers and monitoring their behaviour. Public information on the economic condition and prospects of such borrowers is so limited and expensive, that the alternative of issuing marketable securities is either non-existent or unattractive.

Even though banks have such an advantage (*vis à vis* ordinary savers) in choosing and monitoring propective borrowers, they too will be at a comparative disadvantage, compared with the borrower, in assessing the latter's condition, intentions and prospects.[12] Even though there would be advantages in risk sharing resulting from extending loans whose return was conditional on the contingent outcome of the project for which the loan was raised, it would reduce the incentive on the borrower to succeed, and the bank would have difficulties in monitoring the ex post outcome. Businessmen, at least in some countries, are sometmes said to have three sets of books, one for the tax inspector, one for their shareholders, and one for themselves. Which of these would the banks see, or would there be yet another set of books.[13]

In order, therefore, to reduce information and monitoring costs, banks have been led to extend loans on a fixed nominal value basis, irrespective of contingent outcome (with the loan further supported in many cases by collateral and with a duration often less than the intended life of the project to enable periodic re-assessment). Even so, both the initial, and subsequent, valuation of the loan by a bank does depend on information that is generally private between the bank and its borrowers, or, perhaps, known only to the borrower.[14] Thus the true asset value of the bank's (non-marketed) loans is

---

[11] An interesting question, suggested to me by Professor Mervyn Lewis, is to what extent banks obtain useful information about borrowers' conditions from their (complementary) function in operating the (present) payments system. In so far as banks do obtain information that is useful for credit assessment from the handling of payment flows, this would provide a stronger economic rationale for the present combination of banking functions. Research into, and analysis of, the customarily private and confidential question of (informational) relationships between banks and their borrowers needs to be developed further, and we cannot say with any confidence now how far banks benefit in seeking to assess credit worthiness from their provision of payments services.

[12] At least this will be so until, and unless, a large borrower runs into prospective problems in meeting contractual repayment obligations. To a casual observer, banks seem to try to limit the informational costs of making the initial loans, e.g. by resorting to standardized grading procedures; but once a (sizeable) borrower runs into difficulties, the bank responds by greatly increasing its monitoring activities, becoming often very closely involved with that borrower's future actions.

[13] This is not, as it happens, a purely hypothetical question. The Muslim prohibition on interest payments is causing certain Islamic countries to require their banks to issue Mushariqi loans, which do represent a form of equity share in the project being financed. Students of banking theory and practice might find it informative to give closer study to Islamic banking. See, for example, the article, 'Islam's Bad Debtors' in the *Financial Times*, April 8, 1986.

[14] Much recent literature on banking and credit has assumed that the borrower's selection and management of projects may not be observed by any outside party, even the banker himself: see, for example, Stiglitz and Weiss (1981, 1983).

always subject to uncertainty, though their nominal value is fixed, subject to accounting rules about provisions, write-offs, etc. Under these conditions it will benefit both bank and depositor to denominate deposit liabilities also in fixed nominal terms. The banks will benefit because the common denomination will reduce the risk that would arise from reduced covariance between the value of its assets and of its liabilities (as would occur, for example, if its liabilities were indexed, say to the RPI, and its assets were fixed in nominal value, or, alternatively if its assets fluctuated in line with borrowers' profits while its liabilities were fixed in nominal value). The depositor would seek fixed nominal deposits from the bank for the same reason that the bank sought fixed nominal value terms from borrowers: depositors cannot easily monitor the actual condition, intentions and prospects of their bank, so that information and monitoring costs are lessened, and the incentives on the bank to perform satisfactorily are increased, by denominating deposits in fixed nominal terms.

The combination, however, of the nominal convertibility guarantee, together with the uncertainty about the true value of bank assets, leads to the possibility of runs on individual banks and systemic crises. Moreover, once the nominal convertibility guarantee is established, the effect of better public information on banks' true asset values is uncertain. For example, 'hidden reserves' were once justified by practical bankers as likely to reduce the likelihood of runs and to maintain confidence. Again, Central Bankers have been, at most, lukewarm about allowing a market to develop in large syndicated loans to sovereign countries, whose ability to service and repay on schedule was subject to doubt, because the concrete exhibition of the fall in the value of such loans could impair the banks' recorded capital value, and potentially cause failures. An economist might ask who was being fooled? Yet on a number of occasions financial institutions have been effectively insolvent, but, so long as everyone steadfastly averted their gaze, a way through and back to solvency was achieved.

Be that as it may, under these conditions of private and expensive information, and fixed nominal value loans, any major flow of funds between banks is liable to have deleterious effects on *borrowers*, as well as on those depositors who lose both wealth and liquidity by having been left too late in the queue to withdraw when the bank(s) suspended payment. Even if the prospects of the borrower of the failed bank are at least as good as on the occasion when the borrower first arranged to loan, the borrower will have to undergo expensive search costs to obtain replacement funds. Assuming the borrower searched beforehand, and found the 'best' deal, the likelihood is now that the borrower will obtain less beneficial arrangements.

Bank runs, however, tend to happen when conditions for many borrowers have turned adverse. The suspicion, or indeed the knowledge, of that is what prompted the run in the first place. Accordingly the expected value of the loans of many borrowers will have fallen. If they are forced to repay the failing bank, by the receiver to meet the creditors' demands,[15] they would not be able to replace the funds required on the same terms, if at all, from other banks. Thus bank failures will place the economic well-being, indeed survival, of many borrowers at risk, as well as impairing depositors' wealth.[16] Consequently flows of funds from suspect banks to supposedly stronger banks can have a severely adverse effect on the economy, even when there is no flight into cash at all. A Central Bank will aim to prevent, and, if that fails, to recycle such flows—subject to such safeguards as it can achieve to limit moral hazard and to penalize inadequate or improper managerial behaviour.[17]

## 4. Conclusion

To summarize and conclude, it is often claimed that banking is special and particular, requiring additional regulation and supervision by a Central Bank, *because* it is unique among financial intermediaries in combining payments' services and portfolio management. I hope to have demonstrated that this is false. Monetary payments' services not only could be provided, (and are increasingly being provided), by other collective-investment funds, but could also be provided more safely than by banks. Moreover, the characteristics of such funds are such that their entry into this field (the provision of monetary services) need not cause the authorities (the Central Bank) any extra concern; they could be left to operate under their current regulations. Similarly, if banks were to abandon the provision of payments' services, and restrict their deposit liabilities to non-checkable form, it would not much reduce bank riskiness. They would still require the assistance of a Central Bank.

All this follows because the really important distinction between banks and other financial intermediaries resides in the characteristics of their asset portfolio, which, in turn, largely determines what kind of liability they can offer: fixed value in the case of banks, market-value-related for collective investment funds. It is these latter differences, rather than the special

---

[15] Insofar as constraints, either external or self-imposed, exist which stop the receiver from calling in loans outstanding at failed banks, this source of potential loss to society would be lessened. Even so, at a minimum, the borrower would lose the ability to obtain *additional* loans from the failing bank, and that ability could be crucial to survival in a cyclical depression.

[16] This feature of banking, whereby calling of loans by failed banks causes economic disruption, has been recently noted and modelled by Diamond and Dybvig (1983), and by Bernanke (1983).

[17] Even in the absence of a Central Bank there will be some incentives for commercial banks to act, either independently or collusively, in the same way, i.e. to recycle deposit flows to banks facing liquidity problems and to support, or to take over, potentially insolvent banks. But the public good aspect of such actions will be less compelling to competing commercial banks, (e.g. why help a competitor that got into trouble through its own fault?), and the risk to their own profit positions of such action more worrying to them than to a Central Bank. Moreover the usual circumstances of a rescue, at very short notice under conditions of severely limited information, makes it more difficult for commercial banks to act collusively, than for an independent Central Bank to act swiftly and decisively.

monetary nature of certain bank deposits, that will maintain in future years
the distinction between bank and non-bank financial intermediaries.

*London School of Economics*

## BIBLIOGRAPHY

AHARONY, J. and SWARY, I. (1983), 'Contagion Effects of Bank Failures: Evidence from
    Capital Markets', *Journal of Business,* Vol. 56, No. 3, 305–22.
BARON, D. (1982), 'A Model of the Demand for Investment Banking and Advising and
    Distribution Services for New Issues', *Journal of Finance,* Vol. 37, No. 4, 955–76.
BERNANKE, B. S. (1983), 'Non-monetary Effects of the Financial Crisis in the Propagation of
    the Great Depression', *American Economic Review,* Vol. 73, No. 3, 257–76.
DIAMOND, D. W. (1984), 'Financial Intermediation and Delegated Monitoring', *Review of
    Economic Studies,* Vol. 51, No. 3, 393–414.
DIAMOND, D. W. and DYBVIG, P. H. (1983), 'Bank Runs, Deposit Insurance, and Liquidity',
    *Journal of Political Economy,* Vol. 91, No. 3, 401–19.
FAMA, E. (1980), 'Banking in the Theory of Finance', *Journal of Monetary Economics,* 6, No.
    1, 39–57.
FLUX, A. W. (1911), 'The Swedish Banking System', from *Banking in Sweden and Switzerland,*
    National Monetary Commission, Vol. XVII, (Government Printing Office: Washington).
GOODHART, C. A. E. (1985), *The Evolution of Central Banks,* (LSE, STICERD monograph).
HOUSE OF COMMONS (1985), *Building Societies Bill,* (HMSO: London).
LELAND, H. E. and PYLE, D. H. (1977), 'Information Asymmetries, Financial Structure and
    Financial Intermediaries', *Journal of Finance,* Vol. 32, No. 2, 371–87.
McCALLUM, B. T. (1985), 'Bank Deregulation, Accounting Systems of Exchange, and the Unit
    of Account: A Critical Review', *Carnegie-Rochester Conference Series on Public Policy,*
    Vol. 23.
STIGLITZ, J. E. and WEISS, A. M. (1981), 'Credit Rationing in Markets with Imperfect
    Information', *American Economic Review,* Vol. 71, No. 3, 393–410.
STIGLITZ, J. E. and WEISS A. M. (1983), 'Incentive Effects of Terminations: Applications to
    the Credit and Labor Markets', *American Economic Review,* Vol. 73, No. 5, 912–27.
TOBIN, J. (1958), 'Liquidity Preference as Behavior Towards Risk', *Review of Economic
    Studies,* Vol. 25, No. 67, 65–86.
TOBIN, J. (1985), 'Financial Innovation and Deregulation in Perspective', *Bank of Japan
    Monetary and Economic Studies,* Vol. 3, No. 2.,
WALLICH, H. (1984), 'A Broad View of Deregulation', Paper presented at the FRB San
    Francisco Conference on Pacific Basin Financial Reform, mimeo, December.
WHITE, L. H. (1984), 'Competitive Payments Systems and the Unit of Account', *American
    Economic Review,* Vol. 74, No. 4, 699–712.

# [13]

Excerpt from *Restructuring Banking and Financial Services in America*, 216–253

# 6

# Financial Deregulation, Monetary Policy, and Central Banking

*Marvin Goodfriend and Robert G. King*

Financial deregulation is widely understood to have important economic benefits for microeconomic reasons. Since Adam Smith, economists have provided arguments and evidence that unfettered private markets yield outcomes superior to public sector alternatives. But financial regulations—specific rules and overall structures—are sometimes justified on macroeconomic grounds. This paper analyzes the need for financial regulations in the implementation of central bank policy. Dividing the actions of the Federal Reserve into monetary and banking policy, we find that financial regulation cannot readily be rationalized on the basis of macroeconomic benefits, especially those from monetary policy.

There is a consensus among professional economists that monetary policy can be executed without supporting financial regulations. This consensus reflects an understanding of the central role of open-market operations. Although economists disagree substantially on the nature and magnitude of monetary policy's influence on the price level and real activity, this disagreement should not mask agreement on the central role of open-market operations in the management of high-powered money. Nor should it obscure the general agreement that the public sector plays an important, even unique, role in the management of money.

Banking policy involves regular lending and emergency financial assistance to individual banks and other institutions. Many aspects of Federal Reserve lending resemble credit market relationships in the private sector. In particular, a useful analogy can be drawn between

The authors would like to thank Mark Flannery, Bennett McCallum, William Poole, Alan Stockman, and seminar participants at the Federal Reserve Bank of Richmond for valuable comments. Research support from the American Enterprise Institute and National Science Foundation is acknowledged. The views, however, are solely those of the authors and should not be attributed to any of the preceding institutions.

private lines of credit and Federal Reserve discount window lending. Its regulation and supervision support banking policy in much the same way as loan covenants and monitoring support private lending. The value of Federal Reserve regulation and supervision, then, depends on the need for banking policy. The Federal Reserve is only one of many competing entities in the credit market, however, and any rationale for intervention by the Federal Reserve must involve evidence of a relative advantage for the public sector or a market failure deriving from inappropriate private incentives. Moreover, banking policy may influence outcomes in banking and financial markets by subsidizing certain economic activities, eroding private arrangements for liquidity, and encouraging risk taking. On these grounds, we conclude that it is difficult to make a case for central bank lending policy and the public financial regulation that supports it.

We begin this chapter with definitions of monetary and banking policy. We then consider financial deregulation and monetary policy, beginning by considering monetary policy in a fully deregulated environment. We illustrate how a prominent feature of Federal Reserve monetary policy (interest rate smoothing) is undertaken in such an environment, pointing out the irrelevance for monetary policy of a well-known financial regulation, reserve requirements, given the Federal Reserve's preference for an interest rate as its monetary policy instrument.

We begin our discussion of deregulation and banking policy by considering a fully deregulated environment, outlining the character of private borrowing and lending transactions. Then we discuss the provision of line-of-credit services through the Federal Reserve discount window and go on to develop the distinction between illiquidity and insolvency as a means of judging the appropriateness of public line-of-credit services.

In our analysis of how monetary and banking policy could react to systemwide disturbances, including banking crises, we conclude that monetary policy can effectively and desirably limit crises arising from a widespread demand to convert deposits into currency. Illustrating our point, we interpret Walter Bagehot's "lender-of-last-resort" rule as an irregular interest rate smoothing policy. In contrast, banking policy can do little to influence such events. But we explore other potential roles for banking policy in response to systemwide disturbances.

## Monetary and Banking Policy

Our investigation requires that we distinguish between central bank monetary policy and banking policy actions. By monetary policy, we

DEREGULATION, MONETARY POLICY, AND CENTRAL BANKING

mean changes in the total volume of high-powered money (currency plus non-interest-bearing bank reserves). Other central bank actions involve changes in the composition of the central bank's assets, holding the total fixed, or regulatory and supervisory actions of the central bank.[1] In general, the other actions might be described as commercial policies. In the United States, however, central bank commercial policies concentrate largely on the banking sector, so we term them banking policy.[2]

When the Federal Reserve was established, the major goals of central banking in the United States were, first, the provision of sufficient liquidity for the needs of enterprise so as to avoid banking crises and business fluctuations; second, the maintenance of liquid markets for bank assets; and, third, the public supervision of banking. These goals are reflected in the preamble to the Federal Reserve Act, which states that the purposes of the Federal Reserve were "to furnish an elastic currency, to afford a means of rediscounting commercial paper, and to establish a more effective supervision of banking in the U.S." Broadly, we take the Federal Reserve Act as mandating that the central bank manage society's provision of liquidity through its own actions and by influencing the choices of private agents.

These primary objectives involve a mixture of monetary policy and banking policy. The provision of an elastic currency is a monetary policy of sorts, since it implies that the stock of currency should be varied in response to economic conditions. The other objectives fall into the category of banking policy. For example, by allowing its inventory of government securities to vary, a central bank can accommodate variations in discounting without any change in the stock of high-powered money.

The primary objectives are of particular interest precisely because they are independent of the choice of monetary standard. In particular, these objectives were important under the gold standard, which was in force when the Federal Reserve was established. Other objectives for central banking such as management of the revenue from money creation and stabilization policy aimed at the price level are highly constrained under the gold standard. An additional rationale for central banking emerged with the Employment Act of 1946, which indirectly required the Federal Reserve to employ active monetary policy to stabilize business conditions.

## Deregulation and Monetary Policy

Monetary policy involves the manipulation of high-powered money by the central bank to manage nominal variables like the price level, the inflation rate, and the nominal interest rate and possibly to influence outcomes for employment and output temporarily. We argue here that financial and banking regulations are not needed to conduct monetary policy, although their effects must be taken into account where they exist. We illustrate our point by discussing interest rate smoothing, an important feature of monetary policy in the United States, showing that such smoothing does not require financial regulation. Indeed, the practice of smoothing interest rates essentially eliminates the need for reserve requirements. We continue by considering the effect of financial deregulation on stabilization policy.

**Why Regulations Are Not Necessary.** There is a mainstream professional consensus that monetary policy can be accomplished without supporting financial regulations, although there is not a professional consensus on the efficacy of monetary policy or on desirable patterns of behavior for the monetary authority. For practical purposes most economists think of a fully deregulated environment as one in which the central bank has a monopoly on the issue of high-powered money but in which private markets are otherwise unregulated.

This view is based on the notion that currency and bank deposits are not perfect substitutes for transactions in which they are employed. For example, certain costs lead individuals to treat deposits and currency as distinct assets. Notably, when payments are made through bank deposits, costs are incurred to determine whether the payer has enough money to cover the transaction. Moreover, costs are incurred when securities are bought and sold to complete the desired wealth transfer. Bankers specialize in providing these transaction services. In a deregulated, competitive system banks have incentives to provide payment services at cost and to pay interest on deposits that reflects the net return on assets.

In contrast, when payments are made with currency, there is a relative saving on information and computation costs because the wealth value of currency is more easily verified than that of a check written against a bank deposit. Presumably, there is a substantial set of payments for which the verification cost saving from using currency more than offsets the interest forgone by using deposits. The privacy provided by currency is an advantage for some transactions, since currency does not leave a paper trail.

The implication that deposits are imperfect substitutes for currency is important for two reasons. First, the public has a determinate real stock demand for currency $(C/P)$, where $C$ is the aggregate nominal stock of currency supplied by the central bank and $P$ is the currency price of goods (the price level).[3] It follows that controlling the nominal stock of currency $(C)$ and its growth rate is sufficient to

DEREGULATION, MONETARY POLICY, AND CENTRAL BANKING

control the price level *(P),* the inflation rate, and the nominal interest rate (expected inflation plus the ex ante real rate).[4] Second, the banking system, then, can be completely deregulated without interfering with the ability of monetary policy to control nominal magnitudes. Open-market operations are sufficient to accomplish monetary objectives.[5]

To understand why banking regulations are not essential for monetary policy, consider the following two policy actions. In preventing a temporary increase in the real demand for currency from decreasing the price level, a central bank simply acquires securities temporarily in the open market, providing sufficient nominal currency to satisfy the higher real demand without a fall in prices. Alternatively, if a central bank wants to restore a lower price level after an inflationary period, it may do so by selling securities in the open market to reduce the stock of currency. The unchanged real demand for currency could be satisfied only at a lower price level; hence, prices would fall.

The view that financial and banking regulations—or even the structural details of the banking system—are not essential to understand the effectiveness of monetary policy is very widely held. This view is shared by major undergraduate and graduate macroeconomics texts.[6] Banking regulations in fact, however, influence the magnitude, timing, and targets of open-market operations necessary for a specific objective, such as changing the price level to some specified target. Banking regulations could influence policy implementation since they affect both the supply and the demand for currency. For instance, reserve requirements on bank deposits could absorb high-powered money made available through open-market operations, thereby influencing the effective quantity of currency supplied. Alternatively, by affecting the incentive to substitute currency for bank deposits and vice versa, a prohibition of interest on demand deposits would influence the magnitude of open-market operations necessary to minimize price effects of changes in market interest rates.[7] In short, although banking regulations are not needed for the execution of monetary policy, where they exist a central bank must take them into account in policy implementation.

**Interest Rate Smoothing.** We have emphasized that open-market operations are sufficient for a central bank to manage the price level, inflation, and nominal interest rates. Here we illustrate the point by describing how the Federal Reserve has employed monetary policy to smooth nominal interest rates against routine seasonal and cyclical variations in the demand for money and credit.

220

*Evidence.* One indicator of the Federal Reserve's success in changing the character of nominal interest rate movements is the behavior
of short-term interest rates, measured by the monthly average call
money rate on short-term broker loans in New York.[8] Before the
advent of the Federal Reserve in 1914, the most notable characteristic
of this short-term interest rate series was its irregular sharp, sudden,
and temporary increases. In October 1867, for example, after remaining between 4.3 and 7.2 for the prior three years, the call money rate
rose suddenly from 5.6 to 10.8 percent. Although this change seems
large by postwar U.S. standards, similar episodes of at least this
magnitude occurred twenty-six times between the end of the Civil
War and the founding of the Federal Reserve. Moreover, sudden
changes of over ten percentage points occurred with surprising frequency, on eight occasions during the same forty-nine-year period. In
September 1873, the call money rate jumped from 4.6 percent in
August to 61.2 percent, falling back to 14.9 percent in October and to
5.5 percent by January 1874. Accompanying these sudden upward
jumps in call money rates were similar, though much less severe,
movements in sixty- to ninety-day commercial paper rates. These
episodes were distinctly temporary, ranging from one to four
months, with many lasting no more than one month. Needless to say,
such extreme temporary spikes have been absent from interest rate
behavior since the founding of the Federal Reserve.

Another distinctive feature of the period before the Federal Reserve was the large seasonal movement in short-term interest rates.
For example, the average seasonal variation for the call money rate
from 1890 to 1908 ranged from a peak of +4.6 percent in January to a
trough of −1.39 percent in June.[9] Generally, rates were at their annual
mean in the spring, below it in summer, and at their highs in the fall
and winter. By the 1920s the prominent seasonal movements of interest rates had virtually disappeared.

*Definition and mechanics.* Broadly speaking, then, the Federal Reserve may be said to have smoothed interest rates in two senses. First,
it insulated nominal interest rates from regular seasonal movements
in money and credit markets. Second, it removed temporary nominal
interest rate spikes prompted by recurrent irregular tightness in
money and credit markets. For purposes of this discussion, interest
rate smoothing is a deliberate effort by the Federal Reserve to reduce
or eliminate temporary nominal interest rate fluctuations.[10] We shall
find the distinction between regular and irregular interest rate
smoothing useful when we characterize Bagehot's lender-of-last-resort rule in the section on banking crises, monetary policy, and the
Federal Reserve.

221

DEREGULATION, MONETARY POLICY, AND CENTRAL BANKING

There has been considerable controversy about whether interest rate smoothing by the central bank is feasible when the public understands policy, that is, when the public has rational expectations. To illustrate its feasibility we consider the simplest possible model.[11] The model has three basic equations: (1) a money demand function; (2) a money supply function; and (3) an expression equating the expected real return on nominal securities (that is, the nominal interest rate minus expected inflation) to the expected real rate.

The model embodies two principles that are key to understanding nominal interest rate smoothing. First, because the price level is determined by a money supply rule, there is a nominal anchor in the system. Second, the nominal rate is affected by expected inflation, allowing a central bank to translate price level and inflation policy into interest rate policy.

Nominal interest rate smoothing works as follows. The money supply rule pins down the expected future nominal stock of money. Together with expected future real demand for money, this implies an anchor for the expected future price level. In practice, central banks have employed interest rate policy instruments to smooth interest rates.[12] This amounts to running an adjustable nominal interest rate peg; we therefore illustrate how a central bank smooths the nominal interest rate by pegging it. To see what happens, we consider the response to two disturbances. In each case we first ask what happens when the stock of high-powered money remains constant, and then we see how high-powered money must change to be consistent with a nominal rate peg.

• *A temporary rise in real money demand.* With high-powered money constant, the current price level would fall, raising both expected inflation and the nominal interest rate. By assumption, the required expected real yield on nominal securities is unchanged. Therefore, under a nominal rate peg expected inflation would remain unchanged, which means the current price level would remain equal to the expected future price level. The Federal Reserve would merely provide enough high-powered money, through open-market purchases, to satisfy the initial rise in money demand.

• *A temporary rise in the real rate.* With high-powered money constant, the nominal rate would rise, real money demand would fall, and the current price level would rise. Under a nominal rate peg the required increase in the expected real rate on nominal securities would be achieved by a matching expected deflation due to temporarily high prices. The Federal Reserve would merely provide enough nominal high-powered money to satisfy the unchanged demand for real money balances at the higher price level.[13]

A number of important points emerge from this theoretical discussion.

• First, nominal interest rate smoothing is monetary policy, because the power of the Federal Reserve to create or destroy high-powered money through open-market operations is necessary and sufficient for it to smooth nominal interest rates. In particular, no financial or banking regulations are necessary.

• Second, interest rate smoothing is clearly feasible when the public has rational expectations.

• Third, the mechanics of interest rate smoothing are the same regardless of whether the disturbances are seasonal or irregular.

• Fourth, since the nominal interest rate is the private opportunity cost of holding high-powered money (as currency for hand-to-hand transactions or as bank reserves), the change in the seasonal and irregular pattern of nominal interest rates produces a corresponding change in the pattern of real money balances held by individuals and banks. Thus, we interpret interest rate smoothing as the means by which the Federal Reserve satisfies its statutory mandate to provide liquidity for the U.S. economy by means of an elastic currency.

• Fifth, Federal Reserve interest rate smoothing has in practice made reserve requirements unnecessary for executing monetary policy. The conventional view, of course, is that reserve requirements help the Federal Reserve to control the stock of money. This is the view implicit in the 1980 Monetary Control Act, which extended reserve requirements to all depository institutions, whether Federal Reserve members or not. If the Federal Reserve were operating with a total reserve instrument, reserve requirements would help determine how a change in high-powered money would influence the price level and the nominal interest rate. The Federal Reserve, however, has chosen to operate with an interest rate instrument, that is, to run an adjustable rate peg. As should be clear from the examples discussed above, under even a temporary peg the current price level is determined by the chosen nominal interest rate, the real rate, and the expected future price level. The Federal Reserve simply uses open-market operations to satisfy current money demand at current prices. In such circumstances reserve requirements merely help determine the volume of open-market operations that the Federal Reserve must undertake to provide the accommodation; they do not help determine the money stock or prices.[14]

**Financial Deregulation and Stabilization Policy.** Since the Employment Act of 1946, the Federal Reserve has had a mandate to employ monetary policy to stabilize real economic activity. Thus, a major

DEREGULATION, MONETARY POLICY, AND CENTRAL BANKING

question about continuing and prospective financial deregulation concerns its influence on stabilization policy. While macroeconomic textbooks agree broadly on the nature of the demand for money, they do not show a similar agreement on a number of central issues concerning monetary policy.

Traditional monetarist arguments—originating with Milton Friedman and Karl Brunner, as developed in texts by Michael Darby and William Poole—hold that while monetary policy exerts a powerful influence over the course of the business cycle, in practice it has worked to exacerbate swings in economic activity.[15] From this perspective, monetary policy increases cyclical volatility for three reasons: (1) its effects are subject to long and variable lags, which make the timing of monetary policy actions difficult; (2) it is difficult for policy makers to assess the state of economic activity promptly, because of the complexity of the forces that drive the economy in a given period; and (3) policy makers' focus on smoothing nominal interest rates against cyclical changes in real rates generally leads monetary aggregates to be procyclical.

Rational expectations monetarist arguments—developed by Robert Lucas, Thomas Sargent, and Robert Barro, as summarized in Barro's text—stress the distinction between unpredictable policy actions (shocks), which are taken to exert a powerful influence on real economic activity, and predictable policy responses, which are taken to exert no real effects.[16] This group argues that systematic monetary policy cannot influence real activity, such as employment, real gross national product, and real interest rates, because private agents rationally anticipate the systematic component of monetary policy and take actions that neutralize its potential effects, leaving it to influence nominal variables only.

Analysts of real business cycles—according to theory developed by Edward Prescott, John Long, and Charles Plosser, as summarized in Barro's text—deny any major influence of money, anticipated or unanticipated, on real economic activity.[17] From the perspective of real business cycle analysis, variations in real activity (arising from changes in technology, sectoral reallocations, energy shocks, taxes, and government spending) drive the monetary sector, reversing the traditional macroeconomic view.

Modern Keynesian analysts—led by Stanley Fischer, Edmund Phelps, and John Taylor, as summarized in texts by Rudiger Dornbusch and Fischer and Robert Hall and Taylor—see a powerful role for monetary policy, even with rational private anticipations, because the Federal Reserve can act after private agents have entered into wage and price agreements. According to this view, monetary policy is a powerful stabilization tool, which can offset potentially inefficient economic fluctuations arising from variations in the demand for money, autonomous changes in private spending, and supply shocks.

The disagreement about the feasibility and desirability of stabilization policy, however, should not obscure a consensus on the operation of monetary policy apparent in all the current texts. Whether monetary policy influences real activity or only nominal variables, the prominent textbooks view it as the manipulation of the stock of high-powered money. The major professional debates concerning monetary policy accept as common ground the notion that open-market operations are a necessary and sufficient policy instrument. Financial market regulations are not necessary for the conduct of the Federal Reserve's attempts at stabilization policy irrespective of how it ultimately influences the cyclical component of economic activity.

Not only is this the point of view in the textbooks, it is also a central component of the modern Federal Reserve policy perspective. In its early years the Federal Reserve relied extensively on the discount window as a means of managing the high-powered money stock, but it rapidly came to view the method by which it managed high-powered money as a tactical consideration of little fundamental importance. For example, in the early 1920s the Federal Reserve largely substituted open-market security purchases for discount window loans as the primary means of adjusting high-powered money.

### Deregulation and Banking Policy

Banking policy, as we defined it above, has three dimensions. It involves changing the composition of central bank assets holding their total (high-powered money) fixed, it involves financial regulation, and it involves bank supervision. When executing banking policy, a central bank functions like a private financial intermediary in the sense that its actions neither create nor destroy high-powered money. Banking policy merely involves making loans to individual banks with funds acquired by selling off other assets, usually government securities. The primary dimension of banking policy is provision by the central bank of line-of-credit services to private banks. Regulatory and supervisory components of banking policy may be understood in this regard. Private credit extension is accompanied by restrictions on the borrower to limit his ability to take risks and to protect the value of loan collateral. Private credit lines are accompanied by continuous monitoring of borrowers by lenders. Efficient

DEREGULATION, MONETARY POLICY, AND CENTRAL BANKING

central bank line-of-credit provision likewise requires regulation and supervision of potential credit recipients.

We have seen that banking and financial regulations are inessential for the execution of monetary policy. Here we ask whether banking policy needs supporting regulation and supervision. The analogy between private and central bank credit extension drawn above, however, suggests that our inquiry about banking policy will be somewhat different. If a central bank provides line-of-credit services, the analogy suggests that it must follow up with supervision and regulation to safeguard its funds and make sure its commitment is not abused. Ultimately we must ask, therefore, whether central bank line-of-credit services to banks are really necessary and desirable in the first place.

Our analysis follows the strategy employed earlier in the discussion of monetary policy, by initially considering a deregulated environment. After describing restrictions voluntarily agreed to by borrowers in private credit markets, we discuss the demand for line-of-credit services, emphasizing that by their very nature credit lines must be accompanied by continuous supervision by the banks. We then take up problems of central bank lending, particularly issues that arise for public lenders such as the Federal Reserve. To keep things concrete, we discuss this material in relation to Federal Reserve discount window lending practices. We emphasize how regulatory and supervisory actions taken by the Federal Reserve to safeguard its funds and ensure that its discount window facilities are not abused parallel those taken in private credit markets.

The Federal Reserve discount window functions most importantly as a source of, emergency credit assistance. It is a temporary source of funds, available on short notice, for financially troubled individual banks. No one argues that the discount window should be used to prevent insolvent banks from failing, only that the window be used to aid solvent banks. The distinction between illiquidity and insolvency is therefore crucial to the management of the discount window. First of all, the feasibility of such selective lending depends on the Federal Reserve's having an operational and timely means of distinguishing between insolvent and illiquid banks. Moreover, understanding the economic distinction between illiquidity and insolvency is necessary to decide whether discount window lending is desirable policy at all. We address these fundamental issues in the section on illiquidity and emergency credit assistance.

As was the case in our initial treatment of monetary policy, when we analyzed monetary responses to routine seasonal and cyclical macroeconomic disturbances, we confine our initial treatment of banking policy in this section to routine circumstances, that is, emergency credit assistance to individual troubled banks. In a later section we take up the feasibility and desirability of monetary and banking policy responses to systemwide banking and financial market crises.

**Private Lending and Private Regulation.** Lenders face many potential problems that arise from borrowers' ability to renege on loans. Thus, borrowers and lenders agree on sets of rules and restrictions to accompany loans. For example, in the case of a car loan the lender provides the borrower an initial amount of funds with which to purchase a car, and the borrower agrees to a regular pattern of loan repayments. But the car loan involves more than these financial flows. Typically, the car is collateral against the borrower's ability to pay back the loan. For this reason, as part of the contract the borrower gives up the right to sell the car for the duration of the loan.[18] Additional agreements may restrict other aspects of the borrower's behavior. For example, insurance against damage to the car may be required, or the borrower may be prohibited from renting the car to others. These additional restrictions further protect the lender against damage to the loan collateral.

It is important to note that restrictions on the borrower's range of actions are ultimately in his interest, since they lower the cost of the loan. For example, if someone wanted to borrow funds for a vacation and owned a debt-free car, then he could more cheaply borrow against the car, voluntarily accepting a set of restrictions on use or transfer of the car, than he could arrange an unsecured personal loan.

Issues concerning incentives for borrowers become far more important and sophisticated in corporate lending. For this reason, corporate loans typically require complex covenants (restrictive agreements) that limit the borrower's range of actions,[19] particularly covenants limiting risk taking. For example, it is naive to lend to a corporation engaged in a specific riskless line of business, using an appropriate rate of return for riskless loans, without any restrictions on how the funds are to be spent. Ultimately, the loan is a claim to the minimum of the stream of loan payments or the liquidation value of the corporation's assets if it fails. From the standpoint of its equity holders, the firm's taking on a risky project would thus be a good idea: if it is a success, the equity holders will get the rewards; if it is a failure, the losses will be the lender's, that is, the bondholder's. Thus, with managers of the corporation responsive to equity holders, the firm has incentive to use the borrowed funds to take on risky projects. This difficulty could be circumvented with a covenant restricting types of projects that the company could initiate.

**Private Lines of Credit.** Efficient loan design requires the costly accumulation of detailed information about borrowers, both to sort

DEREGULATION, MONETARY POLICY, AND CENTRAL BANKING

borrowers into risk classes and to design covenants. Like many other economic activities, information production is highly costly when undertaken quickly without development of systems and experience. For this reason, lending typically occurs in the context of long-term relationships, in which information can be produced less expensively.[20]

One sort of long-term lending arrangement is commonly known as a line of credit. The demand for line-of-credit services arises because firms often need funds suddenly, as a result of events that are difficult to predict. For example, a firm may discover a potentially lucrative investment opportunity that must be seized quickly to yield a high rate of return. The firm may not have a sufficient inventory of readily tradable assets such as U.S. Treasury bills from which to raise the necessary funds. Furthermore, the delay caused by making a public security offering may make that avenue of obtaining funds ineffective. In contrast, a line-of-credit arrangement is designed to make funds available on very short notice, possibly as a bridge loan until other arrangements can be made.

Alternatively, a firm might develop a sudden need for funds after suffering a bad shock. A decline in sales might force the firm to finance inventory accumulation, or the unexpected failure of a project might cause a sudden cutoff of revenue. Credit lines, of course, are specifically designed to make funds immediately available in such circumstances too.

The extension of credit in response to bad outcomes, however, is more troublesome for lenders. Bad outcomes might accompany information that a firm should be dissolved altogether, in which case the credit should not be extended. But credit lines are valuable precisely because they make funds immediately available. Thus lenders must protect themselves against such contingencies. For this reason, continual monitoring of potential borrowers is a particularly important feature of the provision of line-of-credit services.[21]

Lines of credit require the payment of a facility fee either on the full amount of the line or on the unused portion.[22] The fee is paid during normal periods to cover the cost of monitoring incurred by the bank. Often the fee is paid by holding a compensating balance, a bank deposit that pays a below-market rate of interest. Because the compensating balance allows a bank to observe the borrower's financial transactions, it helps reduce monitoring costs. In return for the fee, the line-of-credit recipient acquires an option to borrow funds, up to the amount of the line, at a predetermined interest rate spread above a market reference rate. The size of the fee and the rate spread are lowest for top borrowers, ranging higher for worse credit risks. For reasons discussed above, credit lines are also accompanied by restrictions and covenants, as well as specification of allowable collateral, if any is required, should a loan actually be taken down. Of course, since conditions affect the riskiness of the credit line from the lender's point of view, they will influence the fee and spread as well. More restrictions accepted by the borrower will, generally speaking, enable him to pay less. Finally, borrowers will differ according to the intrinsic ease of monitoring. Monitoring a mom-and-pop grocery store is relatively cheap compared with monitoring a firm with many employees, offices, and product lines. Higher monitoring costs would also be reflected in a higher fee or spread.[23]

Individual banks fund their credit lines by maintaining good credit ratings themselves so they can attract funds in the certificate-of-deposit market in a timely fashion and at relatively low cost.[24] To a lesser extent they hold inventories of readily marketable securities such as U.S. Treasury bills, which they can sell to acquire funds on short notice.[25] If the need for funds is expected to be particularly short-lived, borrowing federal funds may be most economical.[26]

**Discount Window Lending.** Discount window lending is the way central banks provide line-of-credit services.[27] There are thus important similarities between discount window operations and private lines of credit. There is, however, a potentially important difference because a central bank's liabilities are high-powered money. But while the discount window plays an essential role in the execution of banking policy, it is unnecessary for monetary policy. We develop these points below by describing discount window procedures actually followed by the Federal Reserve.

Discount window lending is the extension of credit, usually secured by collateral, from a central bank to a private institution. In the United States, Federal Reserve banks lend to individual banks or other depository institutions in their districts through their discount windows. Reserve banks can finance discount window credit with high-powered money or with funds obtained from securities sold in the open market. We define discount window lending that is deliberately allowed to create high-powered money as unsterilized. Under our definition, unsterilized discount window operations are, in part, monetary policy. We say that discount window lending is sterilized when it is accompanied by an open-market sale of equal value. Sterilized discount window operations are thus pure banking policy, with no monetary policy implications, since they leave high-powered money unchanged. In this case only a substitution of bank paper (that is, the loan collateral) for government paper on the books of the

DEREGULATION, MONETARY POLICY, AND CENTRAL BANKING

central bank has occurred, with no change in total central bank liabilities (that is, high-powered money).

As we made clear earlier, open-market operations are sufficient for the execution of monetary policy. It follows that unsterilized discount window lending is redundant as a monetary policy tool.[28] In contrast, sterilized discount window lending plays a distinctive role apart from monetary policy. It allows a central bank to lend selectively to individual banks without affecting aggregate monetary conditions. In other words, it enables a central bank to offer line-of-credit services to individual banks in much the same way as private banks provide credit lines to their customers.

The 1984 report of the Bush commission on financial regulation put the rationale for Federal Reserve provision of discount window services as follows:

> Operation of the FRB's discount window is a vital element in the public "safety net" supporting stability of the banking system. Particularly in the event of difficulties affecting a large financial institution, the FRB must remain available to provide potentially extremely large amounts of liquidity on extremely short notice, and it is the only government agency that is in a position to provide this type of support to the financial system.[29]

Earlier a 1971 Federal Reserve report reappraising the discount window stated:

> Under present conditions, sophisticated open market operations enable the System to head off general liquidity crises, but such operations are less appropriate when the System is confronted with serious financial strains among individual firms or specialized groups of institutions. At times such pressures may be inherent in the nature of monetary restraint, [which often has] excessively harsh impacts on particular sectors of the economy. At other times underlying economic conditions may change in unforeseen ways, to the detriment of a particular financial substructure. And, of course, the possibility of local calamities or management failure affecting individual institutions or small groups of institutions is ever-present. It is in connection with these limited crises that the discount window can play an effective role.[30]

The Federal Reserve discount window is understood and valued as a line-of-credit facility. Open-market operations are seen as capable of handling aggregate monetary conditions. Implicitly, this sterilized discount window lending is valued for its ability to direct potentially large quantities of funds, on very short notice, to individual troubled firms. Like private lenders, the Federal Reserve in its role as public provider of line-of-credit services would be expected to impose restrictions on potential borrowers and to engage in monitoring. It does. In the public sector, however, these activities are known as regulation and supervision.

As is the case for private lenders, the Federal Reserve too is concerned about pricing its loans according to risk.[31] According to Regulation A, the Federal Reserve classifies discount window loans into short-term adjustment credit, seasonal credit, and emergency credit assistance. Adjustment credit is, from time to time, temporarily employed by banks in basically good financial condition.[32] Seasonal credit is employed primarily by banks in agricultural areas. Its use is also rather routine. In contrast, emergency credit is the designation given to funds borrowed by troubled banks on what might be a rather protracted basis.[33] The discount rates on adjustment and seasonal credit are lower than for emergency credit because the riskiness of a loan is generally lower on adjustment and seasonal credit.

The riskiness of a discount window loan also depends critically on the collateral. The Federal Reserve has considerable latitude as to what it will accept and the "haircut" it will take.[34] Fully collateralizing a loan with prime paper such as U.S. Treasury bills, however, would make the value of the Federal Reserve's line of credit minimal. A bank could simply borrow privately on such collateral with no trouble. The Federal Reserve could still make its credit line attractive, however, by charging below-market rates or by taking less than a market haircut. At any rate, whatever the Federal Reserve might do in practice, our interest here is to analyze how a central bank that provides meaningful line-of-credit services, based on imperfect collateral, would operate.

In addition to setting the terms upon which a loan can be taken down, our discussion of private lines of credit emphasized the need for continuous monitoring of potential borrowers by the lender. This is no less necessary for public provision of line-of-credit services by the Federal Reserve. A 1983 Federal Reserve position paper on financial regulation stated:

> Central banking responsibilities for financial stability are supported by discount window facilities—historically a key function of a central bank—through which the banking system, and in a crisis, the economy more generally, can be supported. But effective use of that critically important tool of crisis management is itself dependent on intimate familiarity with operations of banks, and to a degree other finan-

DEREGULATION, MONETARY POLICY, AND CENTRAL BANKING

cial institutions, of the kind that can only be derived from continuing operational supervisory responsibilities.[35]

Our interpretation of "effective use" in this quotation is that the Federal Reserve should, on short notice, be able to discern the financial position of a bank requesting funds. Especially with respect to emergency credit assistance, such information is necessary to price loans appropriately and, even more important, to be sure that the borrower is still viable. If the Federal Reserve is too lax, lending to excessively weak borrowers, then it will be taken advantage of, possibly supporting banks that should be dissolved. If the Federal Reserve is too stingy, it will fail to support temporarily troubled but fundamentally sound banks, possibly causing them to fail unnecessarily. Only by continually supervising banks to which it has credit commitments can the Federal Reserve hope to lend funds efficiently on short notice.[36]

Along with designating the terms upon which it is prepared to lend and the associated supervisory requirements, the Federal Reserve needs to set eligibility rules. Unlike a private firm, it is not completely free to choose whom it wishes to serve. The logic of the quotations presented above suggests that the Federal Reserve ought to provide line-of-credit services to the entire economy, nonfinancial as well as financial firms, to say nothing of banks. To do so, however, would require the devotion of resources for regulation and supervision on a scale society could not accept. Hence, the Federal Reserve has had to choose a rather arbitrary rule to limit its commitment. Currently, only Federal Reserve member banks or depository institutions holding transaction accounts or nonpersonal time deposits are entitled to basic discount window borrowing privileges. This group corresponds closely to those institutions holding reserves at Federal Reserve banks. Indeed, society's recognition of the need to limit the Federal Reserve's line-of-credit commitment is indicated by the choice of "central bank" rather than "credit market authority" to describe its functions.

If we take this logic one step further, we can better understand the concerns of policy makers for maintaining some form of separation between banking on one hand, and finance and commerce on the other, and for limiting access to the payments system.[37] We interpret their argument with regard to banking and commerce as recognizing the need to limit the Federal Reserve's line-of-credit commitments and the regulation and supervision that must accompany them to a manageable subset of the economy, namely, depository institutions. Blurring the line between banking and commerce, or banking and finance, would make it difficult for the Federal Reserve to do that. Without a reasonable limit, the Federal Reserve would tend to be drawn into additional implicit commitments that it could not keep. Even worse, without the regulatory and supervisory resources to safeguard its funds, the Federal Reserve might have to withdraw from providing line-of-credit services entirely.

The argument for limiting access to the payments system is similar. In the process of making payments over its electronic funds transfer network, Fedwire, the Federal Reserve grants same-day credit to depository institutions in the form of daylight overdrafts on their reserve accounts.[38] Because they are imperfectly collateralized, daylight overdrafts create problems for the Federal Reserve analogous to those associated with discount window lending. Although quantitatively much less significant, Federal Reserve float generated in the process of clearing checks creates similar problems.[39] Hence, the Federal Reserve needs to limit access to protect its funds. Of course, in principle it would be possible for the Federal Reserve to protect its funds by not granting credit in the process of making payments. That would be good policy only if any inefficiencies from completely eliminating or perfectly collateralizing daylight overdrafts and float did not offset the savings in regulatory and supervisory costs. Of course, the Federal Reserve could privatize the payments system entirely.

In summary, it is not because the Federal Reserve is selfish in wanting to protect its funds that banking policy must be accompanied by regulation and supervision. We saw for the case of private lines of credit that restrictions on borrowers were in their own interest because they lowered borrowing costs. That would be true here too. Efficient borrowing necessarily imposes restrictions, whether private or public in nature. If banking policy in the form of discount window lending and the production of payments system credit is necessary, then it should be accompanied by central bank regulation and supervision in both society's and the Federal Reserve's interest.

**Illiquidity and Emergency Credit Assistance.** The preceding discussion makes clear that the Federal Reserve discount window is most important as an immediately available source of emergency credit assistance for individual banks. As we noted above, no one argues that the discount window should be used to rescue insolvent banks, only that the window be used to aid temporarily illiquid banks. The familiar rule of thumb—lend only to illiquid but solvent banks—both protects public funds and safeguards the freedom to fail, which is vital to the efficiency of our economy.[40] The purpose of this section is to evaluate that rule of thumb in two senses: Can it be feasibly

DEREGULATION, MONETARY POLICY, AND CENTRAL BANKING

implemented, and does it provide a rationale for the public provision of line-of-credit services through the discount window? The value of central bank regulation and supervision of banking and financial markets hinges critically on the answer to the second question.

First, we require an operational means of distinguishing between illiquid and insolvent banks. This distinction appears meaningful only in the presence of incomplete and costly information about the character of bank assets. If information were freely available about these assets, then private markets would stand ready to lend any bank the present value of the income streams from its assets, discounted at a rate appropriate for the risk. Thus, any bank would always be fully liquid, able to pay all claimants, as long as it was also solvent, that is, it had nonnegative economic net worth.

If information is incomplete and costly to obtain, then it becomes possible to imagine an illiquid but solvent bank.[41] Suppose that a disturbance arises that adversely affects the returns to some existing bank loans. There are a large number of banks, some of which have made poor loans that will yield little revenue. If the private market cannot distinguish between good and bad banks, then it will lend to any individual bank at a rate appropriate for the pool of borrowing banks. For any good bank needing to borrow funds, then, the private market will charge a higher rate under incomplete information than under complete information, because the rate implies a probability that the bank is bad, even though it may not be. Faced with a need for funds, a good bank may find itself in difficulty: although its loans are capable of supporting a borrowing rate under full information, it cannot meet the higher market rate prevailing under incomplete information. That is, at the full information borrowing rate, the bank has positive economic net worth, but the private market is willing only to lend at a higher rate, at which the bank's net worth is negative. We would describe this bank as illiquid but solvent. The higher rate that prevails in the market is an outcome of costly information—it could be either a result of pooling diverse risk groups or a result of an actual cost of auditing the underlying assets of the firm. Timely auditing over very short periods could be quite costly, sufficiently so that individual banks would not find it feasible to engage in "last minute" auditing as part of a program for raising funds.

To avoid this situation, private line-of-credit arrangements provide banks with the option of borrowing funds on short notice, based on a continuing relationship, with periodic credit evaluation so that the lender can sort good risks from bad in the event of a request for funds. This relationship develops because the overall costs of evaluation are lower, as with many other economic activities, when they are distributed over time. A line of credit includes a commitment to lend funds at a fixed rate or a fixed rate spread; a bank then obtains funds on its own initiative if it is a good credit risk, with knowledge of its status made possible through continuing evaluation.

In operating a discount window, the government faces the same general problem as a private lender in the presence of incomplete and costly information. It has the same range of choices. If, for example, it lends to a pool of undifferentiated risks, then it must lend at a penalty rate equal to the private market pooled rate to break even. If the discount window has to compete with private lines of credit, however, such a pricing policy would attract only bad banks. In fact, whatever rate it set would tend to attract unprofitable risks, including insolvent banks. Hence, indiscriminate lending would be undesirable.

Alternatively, a central bank could supervise banks and lend selectively based on the information generated by that supervision, providing funds to banks facing pooled private market prices leaving them illiquid but solvent. Distinguishing between banks on this basis, a central bank selectively aids illiquid banks, but it incurs supervision costs to discriminate between types of banks. From this perspective, it is no accident that discount window lending and bank supervision are jointly included in the primary rationales for the Federal Reserve. If these supervision costs are taken into account, and they are at least as great as those of the private sector, then this banking policy breaks even or subsidizes illiquid banks. It could not penalize illiquid banks that have the option of using competitive private credit lines.

As with many other areas of government intervention, then, the efficacy of discount window lending turns on the relative efficiency of the government and the private sector in undertaking a productive activity. We know of no analyses that document the relative advantage of the Federal Reserve in this area. Plausibly, the private market is superior because it is difficult for the government to lend only to illiquid but not insolvent banks, rather than succumbing to political pressure to support powerful banks.[42] From this perspective, selective discount window lending and necessary supervision of banks fulfill the second objective of the framers of the Federal Reserve Act. It is unclear that this is an appropriate government intervention, however, in contrast to the provision of elastic currency.

We are finally in a position to answer more completely the question whether regulation and supervision are essential for central banking. We emphasized earlier that regulations were not essential for the execution of monetary policy. In sharp contrast, we showed that banking policy needed supporting regulation and supervision.[43]

DEREGULATION, MONETARY POLICY, AND CENTRAL BANKING

The reason for the difference is that monetary policy can be carried out with open-market operations in riskless government securities. By its very nature, however, banking policy involves a swap of government securities for claims on individual banks. Just as private lenders must restrict and monitor individual borrowers, so must a central bank. Although we admit that more research needs to be done on it, we know of no compelling rationale for public provision of line-of-credit services to individual banks through a central bank discount window. The fiat monetary system we currently have requires central bank management of high-powered money. But today's financial markets provide a highly efficient means of allocating credit privately. Since central bank loan commitments do not appear to be necessary, neither do the supporting regulation and supervision.

We must, however, qualify our conclusion in two ways. First, this chapter does not analyze the benefits of Federal Reserve credit generated in the process of making payments. Provision of imperfectly collateralized daylight overdrafts and float requires regulation and supervision, too. Second, we have so far discussed banking policy only with respect to individual troubled banks. In the next section we ask whether banking policy has a useful role to play in response to systemwide disturbances.

## Systemwide Banking and Financial Market Crises

Drawing a sharp distinction between monetary and banking policy, the previous two sections of this chapter have analyzed central bank policy in routine circumstances. Policy was analyzed as it might be undertaken in response to the normal course of macroeconomic seasonal and cyclical disturbances and in response to individual bank problems. Here we address questions concerning central bank policy with respect to systemwide banking and financial crises.

We begin our discussion by describing the nature of banking crises in the United States before the establishment of the Federal Reserve, paying particular attention to the measures taken privately by clearinghouses to protect the banking system. We then use the discussion to motivate the idea that monetary policy (provision of high-powered money), not banking policy (provision of sterilized discount window loans), is both necessary and sufficient for a central bank to protect the banking system against such crises. We proceed to characterize Walter Bagehot's famous lender-of-last-resort policy prescription as an irregular nominal interest rate smoothing policy. We show how Bagehot's rule could automatically trigger high-powered money responses to protect against the sort of banking system crises experienced before the establishment of the Federal Reserve. Finally, we compare Bagehot's proposed rule with regular interest rate smoothing procedures practiced by the Federal Reserve.

Having pointed out that monetary policy has an important role to play in response to systemwide banking or financial crises, we turn to the question of whether banking policy has a useful role to play in such circumstances. Here we reason by analogy. As we will illustrate below, monetary policy is valuable during potential banking crises because it can supply currency elastically to depositors who may doubt the banking system's ability to do so. Since banking policy does not change high-powered money, however, it cannot do that. Banking policy is a swap of one sort of credit for another, as when a central bank makes a discount window loan financed by a sale of U.S. Treasury debt. Hence, we ask what sort of systemwide disturbances in the credit market banking policy might address. We are particularly interested in assessing the costs and benefits of pursuing aggregate banking policy in comparison with those of monetary policy.

**Banking Crises before the Federal Reserve.** In his *History of Crises under the National Banking System*, O. M. W. Sprague identified five banking crises between the end of the Civil War and the advent of the Federal Reserve.[44] Sprague's crises occur in 1873, 1884, 1890, 1893, and 1907. Each of these crises was accompanied by interest rate spikes of the sort described above, although not all interest rate spikes were associated with banking crises.

All these banking crises included an incipient, widespread desire on the part of the public to convert bank liabilities into currency. They were also accompanied by a defensive effort on the part of banks by which they built up their reserve-deposit ratios.[45] Under the fractional reserve system without a central bank, this widespread demand for currency could not be satisfied. Organized around clearinghouses, the banking system responded in two ways.[46] First, clearinghouses, associations of commercial banks, were initially established to clear checks and settle accounts among member banks. Given their central position in the clearing process, they subsequently assumed responsibility for overseeing individual banks and protecting the banking system as a whole. In times of crises, clearinghouses did two things. First, they coordinated general restrictions on convertibility of deposits into currency, while maintaining banks' ability to settle deposit accounts among themselves and undertake lending. Second, clearinghouses issued temporary substitutes for cash, known as clearinghouse loan certificates. These notes were issued against acceptable collateral, as clearinghouse liabilities rather than as individual bank

DEREGULATION, MONETARY POLICY, AND CENTRAL BANKING

liabilities. In that way, clearinghouse certificates facilitated the settlement of accounts among banks mutually suspicious of one another. The clearinghouse certificates were issued in each of the crises discussed by Sprague and remained outstanding for as little as four months in 1890 and as long as six months in 1907. Restrictions, however, accompanied the issue of clearinghouse certificates only in 1873, 1893, and 1907.

Because restrictions thwarted an increased demand to convert deposits into currency at par value, they involved temporary periods in which currency sold at a premium relative to deposits. For example, during the restriction in 1907, the premium on currency over deposits ranged as high as 4 percent. Taken together, the actions of the clearinghouse allowed member banks both to accommodate a higher private demand for currency by using certificates in place of currency for clearing purposes and to frustrate the demand by temporarily increasing the relative price of currency to deposits. At unchanged relative prices and without accommodation, the increased private demand for currency would have resulted in larger outflows of reserves from banks than actually occurred.

How well did these measures contain the harmful effects of banking crises? As calculated from data reported in *Historical Statistics of the United States* for the period 1875 to 1914, the mean annual bank failure rate was less than 1 percent. Moreover, it was comparable to a nonbank business failure rate that was only slightly higher. The annual bank failure rate exceeded 2 percent in only three years, 1877, 1878, and 1893. It exceeded 4 percent only in 1893, when it was 5.8 percent. Notably, the failure rate was 1.7 percent in the 1884 crisis year and only 0.5 and 0.4 percent in the 1890 and 1907 crisis years respectively.

The 1940 *Annual Report* of the Federal Deposit Insurance Corporation reports data on losses to bank depositors over the period 1868 to 1940. The estimated average rate of loss on assets borne by depositors in closed banks was $0.06 from 1865 to 1920, $0.19 from 1865 to 1880, $0.12 from 1881 to 1900, and $0.04 from 1901 to 1920, per year per $100 of deposits.

The relatively small losses borne by depositors reflected, in part, the high capital-asset ratios of banks, which cushioned depositors against loss in the event of a bank failure. Wesley Lindow reports a ratio of total bank capital to risk assets from 1863 to 1963.[47] The ratio falls from a high of 60 percent in 1880 to approximately 20 percent at the turn of the century, then rises to about 30 percent in the 1930s and 1940s, and falls to under 10 percent by the 1960s.[48]

In summary, this discussion should not suggest that bank failures before the advent of the Federal Reserve were not potentially very harmful to those involved. It does suggest, however, that even at their worst they were roughly of the same order of magnitude as nonbank business failures. Their aggregate effects appear to have been reasonably well contained by the private provision of bank capital and, most of all, by the collective protective behavior of the banking system by clearinghouses.

**Banking Crises, Monetary Policy, and the Lender of Last Resort.** Our reading of the banking crises before the Federal Reserve and the response of the clearinghouses to them suggests these important lessons. From a systemwide point of view, banking crises were dangerous because they were accompanied by a widespread demand to convert deposits into currency that could not be satisfied under the fractional reserve system without a central bank. The clearinghouses responded in two ways. They made more currency available to the nonbank public by using certificates in place of currency for clearing purposes; and they organized restrictions on cash payments that reduced the quantity of currency demanded by temporarily raising its price in terms of deposits. These measures were clearly monetary in the sense that they responded to temporarily high real demands for currency with policy actions influencing conditions upon which currency was supplied to the nonbank public. We take the evidence documented above, that the systemwide effects of banking crises appear to have been relatively small, as supportive of the view that the aggregate difficulties were monetary in nature, since policies focusing on currency supply seem to have been sufficient to contain them.

The preceding remarks underlie our view that central bank monetary policy would have been both necessary and sufficient to prevent banking crises before the creation of the Federal Reserve; banking policy, in contrast, would have been neither necessary nor sufficient. Why? The policy problem was to satisfy a temporary increase in currency demand, and only monetary policy could do that. Significantly, the effectiveness of monetary policy in this regard does not depend on whether the Federal Reserve makes high-powered money available by accepting bank assets as collateral at the discount window or by purchasing securities in the open market. By extension, it is clear that the power of the Federal Reserve to create currency remains sufficient today to contain any aggregate disturbances due to sudden sharp increases in currency demand, whether they result from banking or other difficulties.

We can make this point more concrete by using it to interpret Walter Bagehot's famous recommendation that a central bank should

DEREGULATION, MONETARY POLICY, AND CENTRAL BANKING

behave as a lender of last resort.[49] Bagehot's policy prescription—summarized as "lend freely at a high rate"—advocates that the discount rate or simply a rate for buying designated classes of securities in the open market be kept fixed suitably above the normal range of market rates. That rate would provide an interest rate ceiling and therefore an asset price floor to allow banks, in the event of crises, to liquidate their assets while remaining solvent. The proposal amounts to providing a completely elastic supply of currency at the fixed ceiling rate. Put still another way, it amounts to a suggestion for irregular use of nominal interest rate smoothing, in the event that market rates reach a certain height.

An important point about lender-of-last-resort policy in banking crises is that in our nomenclature it is not banking policy at all: it is monetary policy because it works by providing an elastic supply of high-powered money to accommodate precautionary demands to convert deposits into currency. Furthermore, lending, in the sense of advancing funds to particular institutions, is not even essential to the policy since it can be executed by buying securities outright.

One aspect of Bagehot's rule deserves some additional comment. He argued that the last-resort lending rate should be kept fixed above normal market rates, making borrowing generally unprofitable to minimize any government subsidies that might accrue to individual banks. He counted on nominal interest rate spikes accompanying banking crises to hit the ceiling rate, thereby automatically triggering the injection of currency into the economy.

In this regard, Bagehot's advice has not been followed by the Federal Reserve. Rather, as discussed earlier, the Federal Reserve has regularly chosen to smooth interest rates. It has done so either by using a federal funds rate policy instrument directly or by using targets for unsterilized borrowed reserves together with discount rate adjustments to achieve a desired federal funds rate path.[50] It is important to point out, however, that regular interest rate smoothing could still satisfy Bagehot's concerns: first, it could be free of subsidies to individual banks if carried out by purchases and sales of securities in the open market; second, it provides lender-of-last-resort services that are automatically triggered at the current central bank interest rate. If an increased demand for currency were generated by an incipient banking crisis, we might want to think of the Federal Reserve's provision of currency as last-resort lending. But routine seasonal and cyclical increases in currency demand are also accommodated at the same rate.

Thus Federal Reserve practice makes particularly clear that lender-of-last-resort policy and the routine provision of an elastic currency are essentially the same. Both are directed at insulating the nominal interest rate from disturbances in the demand for currency. Both are executed by using open-market operations to create and destroy high-powered money. Since both are monetary policy, we may extend our conclusion from the section on interest rate smoothing to make the point that banking and financial regulations are neither necessary nor sufficient for a central bank to pursue effective last-resort lending.

**Banking Policy and Credit Market Crises.** In the section on illiquidity and emergency credit assistance we described how banking policy could provide line-of-credit services to enable illiquid but solvent banks to remain operating. Implicitly, we assumed that the source of the trouble was limited. At worst only a few banks were insolvent; so when line-of-credit services sorted the good banks from the bad, there was a negligible effect on the interest rate. During general credit market crises associated with aggregate economic activity, however, interest rates will rise. If banking policy is to have a role, it will be in response to real interest rates, since banking policy is clearly an inappropriate response to monetary disturbances, including nominal interest rate spikes. What can banking policy accomplish in response to real rate disturbances?

For purposes of this discussion, the important effects of credit market disturbances are summarized by changes in the real rate of interest applicable to bank assets. This real rate is determined in part by macroeconomic conditions, including anticipated changes in the state of the economy and uncertainty in future prospects. It adjusts to equate aggregate supply and demand for output or, what is the same thing, to equate the aggregate supply and demand for credit. For example, an increase in future prospects that raises current consumption demand will induce a rise in the real rate to induce consumers both to save more out of a given income and to produce more, thereby restoring equilibrium in the goods market. Likewise, an increase in investment resulting from a perceived increased profit opportunity would induce a real rate rise to cut back somewhat on desired investment and induce additional saving. Finally, if individuals become more uncertain about the outcomes of investment projects, they require greater expected returns from those investments.

To investigate whether banking policy has a role, consider an unexpected rise in the real interest rate. Even a temporarily high real rate could cause previously profitable investment projects to become unprofitable.[51] This, in turn, would generate a rise in nonperforming bank loans, which could create insolvencies. The role for banking

DEREGULATION, MONETARY POLICY, AND CENTRAL BANKING

market intervention in such circumstances is usually formulated as "lend only to illiquid but solvent banks," as we discussed earlier. But we argued then that illiquidity arises only when financial markets cannot readily determine the status of a particular financial institution. An interest rate rise is observable in financial markets, however, unlike firm or bank-specific shocks, which are costly to uncover. If firms were alike on one hand and banks alike on the other, the distinction between illiquidity and insolvency would surely be irrelevant for real interest rate shocks. A real interest rate spike per se could not make banks illiquid unless it also made them insolvent. Of course, insofar as its effects were distributed unevenly across firms and banks, a real rate rise could cause some individual banks to be illiquid but solvent.

Thus aggregate disturbances can affect individual bank liquidity in addition to factors specific to a bank. But the fact that an aggregate disturbance is the source of the trouble does not alter the relative advantages of the central bank and private markets in providing liquidity. Central banks and private markets continue to face problems of screening good from bad banks. In practice, the rule of thumb "lend only to illiquid but solvent banks" could preclude the use of banking policy entirely. If banking policy did not respect this rule, however, it could well have important negative effects by subsidizing risk taking. Our conclusion must be that to avoid producing greater incentives for crises to occur, banking policy should not attempt to mitigate credit market disturbances.

We feel a bit uneasy about the implications of our result. While we think the familiar rule of thumb makes sense, we wonder whether discount window lending could be rationalized under an additional criterion: to prevent the disruption costs of widespread insolvencies associated with temporary real interest rate spikes. If the disruption costs resulting from widespread temporary insolvencies were large enough, temporary transfers to the banking system to avoid such costs could be in society's interest. We should point out, however, that a similar argument could be made for avoiding disruption costs of temporary insolvencies anywhere in the economy. Therefore, acceptance of the criterion for banking policy alone would need to be based on a demonstration that disruption costs are much larger in the financial industry than elsewhere.

At any rate, without an effect on supply of or demand for goods, banking policy could not reverse a real rate rise. Of course, a central bank's interest income could change as a result of banking policy, that is, exchanging government securities for claims on private banks. But that fiscal effect per se would have no implications for the real interest rate.[52]

242

What banking policy could do is support otherwise insolvent banks by temporarily swapping government securities for nonperforming bank loans. If the disturbance were temporary and the loans earned nothing for the central bank, then the size of its subsidy would be the lost interest on government securities that now goes to bank depositors. Alternatively, if the loans proved to be permanently bad, the subsidy would be the entire face value of the loans purchased by the central bank. The Treasury, in turn, would have to finance the revenue loss by cutting back purchases of goods, raising current taxes, or borrowing, that is, raising future taxes. Banking policy of this sort is clearly redistributive in nature, a contingent tax-and-transfer fiscal policy. It need not represent a subsidy to the banking system as a whole, however, if banks are taxed during normal times to finance any transfers during periods of high real rates. Significantly, to reduce the risk of insolvency effectively, the tax-and-transfer policy needs supporting regulations. Otherwise banks might simply restore the risk of insolvency to its initially optimal level by reducing capital accordingly or by restructuring contingent liabilities to offset the transfers.[53] Thus we have another example of how banking policy needs supporting regulation and supervision to be effective.

By no means are we advocating the use of banking policy to rescue insolvent banks or, more generally, the use of tax-and-transfer policies to rescue insolvent firms in other industries. In fact, we think such a policy has serious problems: it requires costly regulation and supervision; it opens the door to bank rescues, which would be extremely difficult to limit in practice; it would not be easy to choose when to intervene; and there would be political pressure to abuse the policy. Moreover, it is far from clear that disruption costs associated with widespread temporary insolvencies are large. Last, we are worried about perverse incentive effects of systematic banking policies. Designed to promote financial market stability, they encourage risk taking and lead to the deterioration of private liquidity provision. Thus, they are likely to contribute to much more severe financial market crises, particularly if there are limits to the extent of central bank loans and guarantees or if political conditions arise under which anticipated public provision of financial support does not materialize.

## Conclusion

This paper has analyzed the need for financial regulations in the implementation of central bank policy. To do so, it has emphasized that a central bank serves two very different functions. First, central banks function as monetary authorities, managing high-powered money to influence the price level and real activity. Second, central

DEREGULATION, MONETARY POLICY, AND CENTRAL BANKING

banks engage in regular and emergency lending to private banks and other financial institutions. We have termed these functions monetary and banking policies. Our analytical procedure was to investigate how a minimally regulated system would operate and then to consider the consequences of various forms of public intervention. The analysis drew on contemporary economic knowledge in finance, monetary economics, and macroeconomics.

Our conclusions regarding the need for supporting financial regulation were radically different for monetary and banking policy. We emphasized that regulations were not essential for the execution of monetary policy. The reason is that high-powered money can be managed with open-market operations in government bonds. By its very nature, however, banking policy involves a swap of government securities for claims on individual banks. Just as private lenders must restrict and monitor individual borrowers, a central bank must regulate and supervise the institutions that borrow from it.

Virtually all economists agree that there is an important role for public authority in managing the nation's high-powered money. In contrast, there is little evidence that public lending to particular institutions is either necessary or appropriate. Banking policy has been rationalized as a source of funds for temporarily illiquid but solvent banks. To assess that rationale, we developed the distinction between illiquidity and insolvency in some detail, showing the distinction to be meaningful precisely because information about the value of bank assets is incomplete and costly to obtain. Nevertheless, we saw that the costliness of information per se could not rationalize the public provision of line-of-credit services. Even if central bank lending served a useful purpose earlier in the century, today's financial markets provide a highly efficient means of allocating credit privately. On the basis of such considerations, we find it difficult to make a case for central bank lending, through either the discount window or the payments system, and the regulatory and supervisory activities that support it.

Consideration of the use of monetary and banking policy in response to systemwide crises led us to modify our conclusion only slightly. We saw that monetary policy, on the one hand, could play an important role in banking crises by managing the stock of high-powered money to smooth nominal interest rates. Moreover, it could do so without costly regulation and supervision. Banking policy, on the other hand, directly influences neither high-powered money nor the aggregate supply of and demand for goods. So banking policy could not influence either nominal or real interest rates. We recognized, however, that a role for banking policy in preventing banking crises might arise in response to real interest rate spikes, which could cause widespread insolvencies against which monetary policy would be ineffective. Such banking policy actions could have social value if the temporary disruption costs associated with widespread insolvencies were large. But central bank transfers to troubled financial institutions redistribute wealth between different classes of citizens at best. And inappropriate incentives for risk taking and liquidity management might lead to more severe and frequent financial crises at worst. Hence, it is by no means clear that there is a beneficial role for banking policy even in this case.

# Notes

1. One can easily imagine central bank actions that combine both monetary and banking policy. An increase in bank reserve requirements, coupled with an increase in high-powered money sufficient for banks to finance it, is one important example. The possibility of combination policies in no way diminishes the usefulness of our distinction.

2. Donald R. Hodgman, *Selective Credit Controls in Western Europe* (Chicago: Association of Reserve City Bankers, 1976), is a good survey of commercial policies executed by foreign central banks. In the United States, commercial policies executed through the credit market are extensive. Federal deposit insurance, farm credit programs, and pension guarantees fall into this category. In contrast to the other credit market activities, Federal Reserve banking policy emphasizes availability on very short notice, through line-of-credit services at the discount window and through daylight overdrafts and float extended in the payments system.

3. A brief survey of money demand theory may be found in Bennett McCallum and Marvin Goodfriend, "Theoretical Analysis of the Demand for Money," in John Eatwell et al., eds., *The New Palgrave: A Dictionary of Economics* (London: Macmillan Press, 1987), vol. 1, pp. 775–81.

4. This argument is due to Don Patinkin, "Financial Intermediaries and the Logical Structure of Monetary Theory," *American Economic Review*, vol. 51 (March 1961), pp. 95–116. It was later emphasized by Eugene Fama, "Banking in a Theory of Finance," *Journal of Monetary Economics*, vol. 6 (January 1980), pp. 39–57.

Patinkin pointed out that a central bank must fix both a nominal interest rate and a nominal quantity to make the price level determinate. These conditions are met if a central bank pays no interest on currency and controls its aggregate nominal quantity. The price level is determined as follows: Because currency earns zero nominal interest, the opportunity cost of holding it is the nominal interest rate on securities. It is efficient for people to hold a real stock of currency for which the marginal service yield just equals the interest rate. For a diminishing marginal service yield on currency with a sufficiently high initial threshold, there is a determinate real stock demand for currency and a determinate price level, that is, for any given nominal

DEREGULATION, MONETARY POLICY, AND CENTRAL BANKING

interest rate on securities. The nominal interest rate on securities is the sum of expected inflation plus a real interest rate component. The central bank can control inflation and thereby expected inflation by choosing a desired rate of currency growth. For example, it can choose zero currency growth and zero inflation, so that the nominal interest rate is simply the real rate and the price level is constant.

5. Notably, this point has been emphasized in Milton Friedman, *A Program for Monetary Stability* (New York: Fordham University Press, 1960), and in Eugene Fama, "Financial Intermediation and Price Level Control," *Journal of Monetary Economics*, vol. 12 (July 1983), pp. 7–28.

6. See texts by Robert Barro, Michael Darby, Rudiger Dornbusch and Stanley Fischer, Robert Gordon, Robert Hall and John Taylor, and Thomas Sargent. A notable exception is the view emphasized in Neil Wallace, "A Legal Restrictions Theory of the Demand for 'Money' and the Role of Monetary Policy," *Federal Reserve Bank of Minneapolis Quarterly Review*, vol. 1 (1983), pp. 1–7. Bennett McCallum, "The Role of Overlapping Generations Models in Monetary Economics," in Karl Brunner and Allan H. Meltzer, eds., *Carnegie-Rochester Conference Series on Public Policy*, vol. 18 (Spring 1983), pp. 9–44, which emphasizes the medium-of-exchange services of money, and Robert G. King and Charles I. Plosser, "Money as the Mechanism of Exchange," *Journal of Monetary Economics*, vol. 17 (January 1986), pp. 93–115, which emphasizes verification costs, may be read as responses to the arguments of Wallace.

7. For an analysis of how recent financial deregulation has influenced the demand for money, see Yash Mehra, "Recent Financial Deregulation and the Interest Elasticity of M1 Demand," *Federal Reserve Bank of Richmond Economic Review* (July/August 1986), pp. 13–24.

8. This series is reported in Frederick R. Macaulay, *Bond Yields, Interest Rates, and Stock Prices* (New York: National Bureau of Economic Research, 1938).

9. These numbers come from Jeffrey A. Miron, "Financial Panics, the Seasonality of the Nominal Interest Rate, and the Founding of the Fed," *American Economic Review*, vol. 76 (March 1986), pp. 125–40.

10. There are actually a number of ways that one can define a nominal interest rate smoothing policy. It can mean eliminating deterministic seasonals, as emphasized by Miron, referenced in note 9. It can mean minimizing interest rate surprises, as studied by Marvin Goodfriend, "Interest Rate Smoothing and Price Level Trend-Stationarity," *Journal of Monetary Economics*, vol. 19 (May 1987), pp. 335–48. Or it can mean using monetary policy to maintain expected constancy in interest rates as studied by Robert Barro, "Interest Rate Smoothing," University of Rochester, February 1987. Regardless of what nominal interest rate policy is followed, however, the theoretical mechanism by which it works is basically as described in the text.

11. We are drawing on Goodfriend's article referenced in note 10 for this discussion.

12. The method by which the Federal Reserve smooths interest rates has varied over the years. In the 1920s the Federal Reserve forced the banking

system to be "in the window" for a portion of high-powered money demanded. Since there was relatively little nonprice rationing, the discount rate tended to provide a ceiling to interest rates. The discount rate was raised and lowered to adjust the level of interest rates, with appropriate adjustments to nonborrowed reserves to keep banks marginally borrowing reserves. In the 1930s nominal rates were near their floor at zero, and in the 1940s they were pegged. In the 1950s and 1960s the Federal Reserve used procedures similar to those it used in the 1920s. Explicit federal funds rate targeting was used in the 1970s. Likewise, the nonborrowed reserve operating procedure employed from October 1979 to the fall of 1982 was in effect a noisy week-by-week funds rate peg. See Marvin Goodfriend, *Monetary Policy in Practice* (Richmond, Va.: Federal Reserve Bank of Richmond, 1987), pp. 40–41. Since then the Federal Reserve has employed a mixture of borrowed reserve and federal funds rate targeting.

13. Empirical evidence on the high-powered money and inflation responses associated with the elimination of nominal interest rate seasonals around 1914 may be found in Barro's article referenced in note 10.

14. This was true even under the Federal Reserve's post–October 1979 nonborrowed reserve operating procedure. See "A Historical Assessment of the Rationales and Functions of Reserve Requirements," in Marvin Goodfriend, *Monetary Policy in Practice*.

15. See, for example, William Poole, *Money and the Economy: A Monetarist View* (Reading, Mass.: Addison-Wesley, 1978).

16. See Robert E. Lucas and Thomas J. Sargent, *Rational Expectations and Econometric Practice* (Minneapolis: University of Minnesota Press, 1980).

17. See Robert G. King and Charles I. Plosser, "Money, Credit, and Prices in a Real Business Cycle," *American Economic Review*, vol. 74 (June 1984), pp. 363–80.

18. If the individual could sell the car without permission from the lender, then there would be no effective difference between car loans and an unsecured personal loan to be used, for example, to finance a vacation. In general, without the security provided by the physical asset (car), there would need to be a higher interest rate, reflecting the lender's lessened probability of receiving loan payments or the resale value of the car.

19. See Clifford W. Smith, Jr., and Jerold B. Warner, "On Financial Contracting: An Analysis of Bond Covenants," *Journal of Financial Economics*, vol. 7 (1979), pp. 117–61.

20. For example, George Benston and Clifford Smith, "A Transactions Cost Approach to the Theory of Financial Intermediation," *Journal of Finance* (May 1976), pp. 215–31, discusses why bundling of financial products can be efficient in a world of costly information. Joseph Haubrich, "Financial Intermediation, Delegated Monitoring, and Long-Term Relationships" (Working Paper, Wharton School, October 1986), provides a recent formal description of one set of gains from long-term relationships in financial intermediation.

21. A number of authors in recent years have emphasized monitoring as a key function of banks. See, for example, Douglas Diamond, "Financial Inter-

DEREGULATION, MONETARY POLICY, AND CENTRAL BANKING

mediation and Delegated Monitoring," *Review of Economic Studies*, vol. 51 (July 1984), pp. 393–414; and Eugene Fama, "What's Different about Banks?" *Journal of Monetary Economics*, vol. 15 (January 1985), pp. 29–39.

22. For descriptions of various aspects of lines of credit see Mitchell Berlin, "Loan Commitments: Insurance Contracts in a Risky World," *Federal Reserve Bank of Philadelphia Business Review* (May/June 1986), pp. 3–12; Dwight B. Crane, *Managing Credit Lines and Commitments* (Chicago: Association of Reserve City Bankers, 1973); Gerald Hanweck, "Bank Loan Commitments," in *Below the Bottom Line*, Staff Study, Board of Governors of the Federal Reserve System, January 1986, pp. 103–30; and Bruce Summers, "Loan Commitments to Business in United States Banking History," *Federal Reserve Bank of Richmond Economic Review* (September/October 1975), pp. 115–23.

23. Theoretical analysis of bank loan commitments is found in Gregory D. Hawkins, "An Analysis of Revolving Credit Arrangements," *Journal of Financial Economics*, vol. 10 (March 1982), pp. 59–81; and in Arie Melnik and Steven Plaut, "The Economics of Loan Commitment Contracts: Credit Pricing and Utilization," *Journal of Banking and Finance*, vol. 10 (June 1986), pp. 267–80.

24. See the chapter on certificates of deposit in Timothy Q. Cook and Timothy D. Rowe, eds., *Instruments of the Money Market*, 6th ed. (Richmond, Va.: Federal Reserve Bank of Richmond, 1986), as well as the chapter on repurchase agreements, a related bank funding source.

25. In recent years loan sales have apparently become more common. See Gary Gorton and Joseph Haubrich, "Loan Sales, Recourse, and Reputation: An Analysis of Secondary Loan Participations" (Working Paper, Wharton School, May 1987); and Christine Pavel, "Securitization," *Federal Reserve Bank of Chicago Economic Review* (July/August 1986), pp. 16–31. It is not clear, however, whether loan sales are being used as a funding source on short notice.

26. See the chapter on federal funds in Cook and Rowe, *Instruments of the Money Market*.

27. The name of the discount window arose from the following historical circumstances. In the eighteenth and nineteenth centuries, much of international and interregional trade was financed with bills of exchange, which were short-term securities without explicit interest. When sold or used as collateral, a security was discounted—or valued at less than its face value—to permit a return to its holder. The discount window thus took its name from the fact that its primary function was establishing a discount rate for securities purchased or used as collateral. Howard Hackley, *Lending Functions of the Federal Reserve Banks: A History* (Washington, D.C.: Board of Governors of the Federal Reserve System, 1973), contains a thorough discussion of the legal history of Federal Reserve lending. For many years virtually all Federal Reserve lending has taken the form of advances rather than discounts. Hackley describes the shift, as well as the evolution of other aspects of discounting such as eligible paper and the size of the basic borrowing privilege, that is, the amount of a temporary discount window loan that is permitted.

28. Nevertheless, over the years the Federal Reserve has extensively em-

ployed unsterilized discount window lending, together with discount rate adjustments, in the execution of monetary policy. See note 12. Though it remains puzzling, use of the discount window this way seems to be connected with the use of secrecy or ambiguity in monetary policy. See Alex Cukierman and Allan H. Meltzer, "A Theory of Ambiguity, Credibility, and Inflation under Discretion and Asymmetric Information," *Econometrica*, vol. 54 (September 1986), pp. 1099–1128; and Marvin Goodfriend, "Monetary Mystique: Secrecy and Central Banking," *Journal of Monetary Economics*, vol. 17 (January 1986), pp. 63–92. In a similar vein, Timothy Cook and Thomas Hahn, "The Information Content of Discount Rate Announcements and Their Effect on Market Interest Rates," *Journal of Money, Credit, and Banking*, vol. 20 (May 1988), pp. 167–80, provides extensive evidence that the discount rate has served as a monetary policy signal, signaling permanent changes in the federal funds rate.

29. Task Group on Regulation of Financial Services, *Blueprint for Reform* (Washington, D.C., 1984), p. 49.

30. *Reappraisal of the Federal Reserve Discount Mechanism* (Washington, D.C.: Board of Governors of the Federal Reserve, 1971), p. 19.

31. Notably, although the Monetary Control Act of 1980 directed the Federal Reserve to price many of its services, the discount window was exempted. There are some superficial similarities between Federal Reserve practices and private line-of-credit pricing. For instance, the non-interest-earning required reserves at the Federal Reserve are like compensating balances. But there is little evidence that the Federal Reserve prices line-of-credit services efficiently according to each bank's circumstances with respect to supervision cost, risk of insolvency, or collateral.

32. Since the early 1960s, the Federal Reserve has allowed the federal funds rate to move above the discount rate for long periods of time. To limit borrowing, the Federal Reserve has imposed a noninterest cost, which rises with the level and the duration of borrowing. In practice, higher and longer-duration borrowing increases the likelihood of triggering costly Federal Reserve consultations with bank officials. See Marvin Goodfriend, "Discount Window Borrowing, Monetary Policy, and the Post–October 1979 Federal Reserve Operating Procedure," *Journal of Monetary Economics*, vol. 12 (September 1983), pp. 343–56, for a discussion of how this means of administering the window has been employed in monetary policy.

33. For example, Continental Illinois Bank borrowed extensively at the Federal Reserve discount window from May 1984 to February 1985. It was in the window for over $4 billion during much of that period. See George Benston et al., *Perspectives on Safe and Sound Banking* (Cambridge, Mass.: MIT Press, 1986), pp. 120–24.

34. Hackley, *Lending Functions*, documents the history of legal collateral requirements in discount window lending. Although the Federal Reserve has wide discretion in what it can take, it has generally required very good collateral on its loans.

A "haircut" is a margin that is subtracted from the market or face value of a security for purposes of calculating its value as collateral in a loan transaction.

DEREGULATION, MONETARY POLICY, AND CENTRAL BANKING

For example, a 10 percent haircut off face value of a $100 security would value it at $90 for purposes of collateral.

35. U.S. Congress, House of Representatives, Committee on Government Operations, *Federal Reserve Position on Restructuring of Financial Regulation Responsibilities*, 99th Congress, 1st session, 1985, p. 235.

36. In fact, although Federal Reserve regulations apply to all banks, the Federal Reserve directly supervises and examines only state-chartered Federal Reserve member banks and bank holding companies. The comptroller of the currency, for example, supervises and examines nationally chartered banks. The Federal Deposit Insurance Corporation does so for insured state-chartered nonmember banks. Other agencies, however, make information available to the Federal Reserve.

Committee on Banking, Finance, and Urban Affairs, Staff Report, *Continental Illinois National Bank: Report of an Inquiry into Its Federal Supervision and Assistance*, contains a good discussion of the difficulties of government supervision of banks.

37. See E. Gerald Corrigan, "Financial Market Structure: A Longer View," *Federal Reserve Bank of New York Annual Report* (February 1987).

38. David Mengle, David Humphrey, and Bruce Summers, "Intraday Credit: Risk, Value, and Pricing," *Federal Reserve Bank of Richmond Economic Review* (January/February 1987), pp. 3–14, describes the creation of daylight overdrafts as follows:

> On Fedwire, transfers take place by debiting the reserve account of the sending bank and crediting the reserve account of the receiving bank. However, the sending bank is not required to have funds in its reserve account sufficient to cover the transfer at the time it is made. Rather, the transfer must be covered by the end of the day. Allowing reserve balances to become negative during the day leads to "daylight overdrafts," and it is these overdrafts that are the major source of risk to Federal Reserve Banks from Fedwire. Since a Fedwire transfer becomes final when the receiving institution is notified of the transfer, the Federal Reserve could not revoke the transfer if the sending institution failed to cover its overdraft by the end of the day. Thus, the receiving institution would have its funds while the Fed would be left with the task of collecting the payment for the defaulting sending bank. Credit risk in this case is borne by the Reserve Banks and possibly by the public.

Mengle, Humphrey, and Summers, p. 12, report total funds transfer daylight overdrafts of $76 billion per day. This is an enormous number when one considers that total reserve balances with reserve banks are around $35 billion. Daylight overdrafts are currently not priced. They are interest-free loans. Therefore, depository institutions have little incentive to economize on their use. To limit somewhat the use of intraday credit, the Federal Reserve monitors depository institutions according to "caps" and relatively informal guidelines, resorting to consultations with bank officials when necessary. This is reminiscent of administration of the discount window. See note 32.

39. Checks sent to reserve banks for collection are credited to the deposit-

ing institution's reserve or clearing account automatically, according to a schedule that allows time for the checks to be presented to the depository institutions on which they are drawn. The maximum deferral is two business days. The depository institution's account is credited regardless of whether the checks have reached the banks on which they are drawn. Because it may take longer than two days to process and collect some checks presented for collection, depository institutions receive credit to their accounts for those checks before the institutions on which the checks are drawn lose reserves. This "extra" amount of reserves in the banking system is called Federal Reserve float. The effect of float on high-powered money is usually sterilized, however, by offsetting open-market operations.

The Monetary Control Act of 1980 mandated that the Federal Reserve charge fees to recover the cost of providing check clearing and other services. In particular, the Federal Reserve was directed to charge for Federal Reserve float at the federal funds rate. Consequently, check float has fallen from $7.4 billion in the first half of 1979 to under $1 billion today. See "The Tug-of-War over Float," *Morgan Guarantee Survey* (December 1983), pp. 11–14; U.S. Congress, *The Role of the Federal Reserve in Check Clearing and the Nation's Payments System*, 1983; and John Young, "The Rise and Fall of Federal Reserve Float," *Federal Reserve Bank of Kansas City Economic Review* (February 1986), pp. 28–38.

40. Walker Todd, "Outline of an Argument on Solvency" (Memorandum, Federal Reserve Bank of Cleveland, March 1987), documents in detail the establishment of the principle that the central bank should lend only to illiquid but not to insolvent institutions.

41. Our analysis here involves the substantial work on private information economies stimulated by Michael Rothschild and Joseph Stiglitz, "Equilibrium in Competitive Insurance Markets: An Essay on the Economics of Imperfect Information," *Quarterly Journal of Economics*, vol. 90 (November 1976), pp. 629–50. Since we consider costly evaluation, however, our treatment of private information economies is closer to John Boyd and Edward Prescott, "Financial Intermediary Coalitions," *Journal of Economic Theory* (April 1986), pp. 211–32.

42. Irvine Sprague, *Bailout: An Insider's Account of Bank Failures and Rescues* (New York: Basic Books, 1986), and Todd, "Argument on Solvency," report numerous instances of government support for insolvent institutions. The Federal Reserve minimizes the risk of supporting insolvent banks by making discount window loans only on the best collateral. By doing do, however, it greatly reduces the value of its line-of-credit services too. For example, it took the best collateral when lending to Continental Illinois in 1984–1985. See note 33.

There is an additional reason why government emergency credit assistance might be necessary. Private markets would make arrangements to protect themselves against liquidity problems only if they believed that the government would not offer such services. Yet it might be impossible for the government to make credible its intention not to intervene in future crises. To do so, the government would have to precommit itself not to provide emergency credit assistance. The worst possible case would be one where the

DEREGULATION, MONETARY POLICY, AND CENTRAL BANKING

government announced its intention not to provide emergency credit assistance in the future, but the banks believed that in fact it would. Then if a liquidity problem arose, banks would not have prepared for it by holding sufficient capital and by arranging lines of credit. If the government remained true to its policy, then widespread insolvency could prevail.

43. If the Federal Reserve always perfectly collateralized its banking policy loans, then in principle it could need very little supporting regulation and supervision. If it lent at below-market rates, however, it would still need regulation and supervision to see that its policy was not abused.

44. E. W. Kemmerer, *Seasonal Variations in the Relative Demand for Money and Credit in the United States* (Washington, D.C.: National Monetary Commission, 1910), pp. 222–23, contains a more extensive classification of financial panics including more moderate episodes.

45. See Phillip Cagan, *Determinants and Effects of Changes in the Stock of Money 1875–1960* (Washington, D.C.: National Bureau of Economic Research, 1965).

46. In addition to O. M. W. Sprague, *History of Crises under the National Banking System* (Washington, D.C.: National Monetary Commission, 1910), see James Cannon, *Clearing-Houses* (New York: D. Appleton and Company, 1908); Gary Gorton and Donald Mullineaux, "The Joint Production of Confidence: Endogenous Regulation and 19th Century Commercial-Bank Clearinghouses," *Journal of Money, Credit, and Banking* (forthcoming); Richard Timberlake, "The Central Banking Role of Clearing Associations," *Journal of Money, Credit, and Banking* (February 1984), pp. 1–15; and Timberlake, *The Origins of Central Banking in the United States* (Cambridge, Mass.: Harvard University Press, 1978).

47. Wesley Lindow, "Bank Capital and Risk Assets," *National Banking Review* (September 1963), pp. 29–46.

48. The measure of total capital here is generally defined to include total equity, reserves for losses on loans and securities, and subordinated notes and debentures. Risk assets are defined as total assets, less cash, less government securities issued by the U.S. Treasury Department.

49. Thomas Humphrey and Robert Keleher, "The Lender of Last Resort: A Historical Perspective," *Cato Journal*, vol. 4 (Spring/Summer 1984), pp. 275–318, provides a historical perspective on the concept of the lender of last resort.

50. See notes 12 and 28.

51. Many investment projects involve the purchase of inputs—fuel, intermediate goods, and labor—today, but yield output only in the future. Production is profitable if the current value of future output discounted back to the present at the real interest rate is greater than the current cost of inputs. By pushing the present discounted value of output below its cost of production, even a temporarily high real interest rate could cause a project to be shut down temporarily.

52. If a central bank's remittances to the government Treasury changed as well and the Treasury adjusted its goods purchases accordingly, then there

could be a goods market effect. But that would involve more than banking policy.

53. This argument is analagous to those that arise in consideration of the Ricardian equivalence proposition, which states that under certain situations a substitution of public debt for taxation will have no effects on prices or quantities. Robert Barro's *Macroeconomics* (New York: John Wiley, 1986) provides an accessible introduction to Ricardian analysis. Louis Chan, "Uncertainty and the Neutrality of Government Financing Policy," *Journal of Monetary Economics*, vol. 11 (May 1983), pp. 351–72, provides a proof of Ricardian neutrality under conditions of uncertainty, stressing the analogy to Modigliani-Miller propositions in finance.

The ineffectiveness of credit policy, of which banking policy is an example, is well illustrated by the student loan program. Student loans need not result in increased expenditure on education. A loan may reduce the extent to which families draw down their own financial savings or sacrifice expenditure on other goods and services to pay for a student's education. Because loan funds are fungible, they cannot ensure a net increase in expenditure in the targeted area. The targeted effect would require provisions in the program to prevent substitution for private outlays and to restrict access to other credit sources.

# [14]

GARY GORTON
DONALD J. MULLINEAUX

# The Joint Production of Confidence: Endogenous Regulation and Nineteenth Century Commercial-Bank Clearinghouses

THE FEASIBILITY OF PRIVATE-MARKET ARRANGEMENTS for the production of money has resurfaced as an important research question (see King 1983 for a review essay). In an early and influential contribution to this literature, Benjamin Klein (1974) emphasized the critical role of consumer confidence in laissez-faire monetary arrangements, and he analyzed "brand names" as potential devices for insuring confidence in private monies.[1] He noted that if monies could not be differentiated, each producer would have incentive to over-issue and would do so, unless constrained by some mechanism involving monitoring and control of individual bank behavior. In this regard, Klein notes (p. 441) that "many banks became members of private protective and certifying agencies, which performed some functions similar to present-day central banks." Commercial-bank clearinghouses (CBCHs), for example, utilized regulatory-like tools such as reserve requirements, deposit-rate ceilings, and bank examinations to influence and control the behavior of member institutions.[2]

The authors thank the New York Clearinghouse Association for access to their archives, and Gertrude Beck of the NYCHA for assistance with the archives. They also thank Michael Bordo and members of the staffs of the Federal Banks of Philadelphia and Cleveland for comments on an earlier draft.

[1]Vaubel (1977) claims that guarantees, rather than brand name backing, are more likely to be provided in a competitive money-production environment.

[2]Gorton (1985b) and Timberlake (1984) have called still more explicit attention to the strong similarities between the activities of nineteenth century CBCHs and today's Federal Reserve System. Neither of these authors explored in depth the reasons why clearinghouses took on regulatory-like activities, however.

GARY GORTON *is assistant professor of finance, The Wharton School, University of Pennsylvania.*

DONALD J. MULLINEAUX *is the DuPont professor of banking and financial services, University of Kentucky.*

*Journal of Money, Credit, and Banking,* Vol. 19, No. 4 (November 1987)

Based on Klein's analysis, it is somewhat unclear: (1) what motivated commercial banks to voluntarily participate in such arrangements or, (2) why CBCHs were involved in the production of monetary confidence. In this paper, we argue that the evolution of the CBCH reflects an endogenous "regulatory" response to the problems associated with the asymmetric distribution of information in the banking industry. The nature of these information problems was related to the product mix in the banking sector—in particular, to the proportion of demand deposits relative to bank notes. The capacity of "the market" to monitor and control the behavior of bank managers was increasingly eroded as demand deposits came to supplant bank notes during the nineteenth century. The set of actions of the CBCH represent the substitution of hierarchy ("private regulation") for a market-based mechanism of control. That "organizations" may dominate markets as allocation and control devices is hardly a new idea (Coase 1937, Williamson 1975, and Stiglitz 1985).

In section 1, we discuss the importance of the banking product mix during the nineteenth century from the viewpoint of information costs. Section 2 describes the role of the CBCH as a monitor/supervisor which provides valuable "screening" services to both member banks and the public. Section 3 examines the behavior of the CBCH during financial panics. In response to the unusual information costs associated with a panic, the CBCH increased the amount of private regulation. The CBCH then reverted to its simpler organizational form following the conclusion of a panic. Private regulation declined and the role of "the market" as a control mechanism increased. Section 4 concludes.

## 1. BANK NOTES, BANK DEPOSITS, AND INFORMATION COSTS

Bank notes involved a contract between the bearer and the bank to redeem the face value of the note in specie at the bank. The specie value of a bank note to a seller accepting it in exchange was simply the expected value of a bank's specie promise less the costs of collecting specie at that bank. Even if the expected specie value of a note was par, the collection costs drove a wedge between the par value of a note and its value in exchange for goods. This wedge created an incentive for note-broker businesses to form offering to exchange bank notes for gold or the notes of other banks at discounted rates. Brokers could profit by collecting specie at par at the issuing bank. Such firms indeed did form, and a secondary market in bank notes emerged. The size of the discounts quoted on notes presumably varied with the geographic distance to the issuing bank, the perceived riskiness of that institution and the quantity of counterfeit notes of that institution believed to be in circulation relative to the total issue (Gorton 1986). In "bank-note reporters," brokers published information on counterfeits along with current quotes on various notes.

Secondary market makers also had strong incentives to monitor the quality of the assets backing bank notes since they collected specie in bulk as the source of their profitability. Their price quotations in turn revealed their information to

GARY GORTON AND DONALD J. MULLINEAUX : 459

buyers and sellers of bank notes. Indeed, merchants commonly consulted bank-note reporters in reaching judgments about the exchange values of particular bank notes. Competition among note brokers and publishers of note reporters presumably enhanced the information quality of these price signals (Dillistin 1949, White 1895). To the extent that brokers returned notes to the bank of issue, they also performed a clearing and collection function. Thus, while bank notes typically exchanged for goods and services at a discount, the overall variability in these discounts was constrained by the self-correcting responses of banks, note brokers, and consumers to the recurring signals provided by the secondary market in bank notes.

A demand deposit, unlike a bank note, is both a claim on a bank and on an agent's account at that bank. This complicates the information required to price a check claim on that deposit. In an exchange mediated by check, the seller of goods must consider (1) whether the check writer has sufficient funds for the check to be collected; (2) whether the check writer's bank can exchange for specie; and perhaps (3) whether his own bank can exchange for specie at par. While the identity of a buyer "doesn't matter" with use of a bank note (in the absence of counterfeits), a check-based transaction is agent-specific with respect to risk.

The contractual characteristics of demand deposits accordingly increased the transactions costs associated with this product. These costs in turn precluded the development of a secondary market in claims on such deposits. Such a market would require pricing agent-specific claims on a bank. It would prove extremely costly for specialist note brokers to acquire information on the reliability of individuals as well as banks. Yet such information is necessary to price such a claim since the agent issuing a check can overdraw his balances.

Banks were better able than note brokers to handle the information-related disadvantages of checks. Banks could delay specie payment on checks, for instance, until after checks were collected. This required an accounting system, but such a system was a necessary adjunct to producing demand deposits. Also, banks could assume that some proportion of the checks collected would be held as deposits rather than paid in specie. These deposits could fund income-producing assets. Brokers could not offer deposit-type accounts, at least not without the risk of being considered a bank, and therefore having to submit to chartering requirements and perhaps other regulations.

The contractual differences between bank deposits and notes effectively precluded brokers from competing with banks in the collection of deposits. Accordingly, no "secondary market" in check claims was formed. As a result, the information production of the note brokers concerning the "quality" of individual banks became increasingly less available as the volume of deposits increased relative to notes. Holders of bank liabilities therefore could monitor bank behavior only in a direct and costly fashion.

Banks in the cities had a larger proportion of their liabilities as deposits than as bank notes as early as the late eighteenth century. The Bank of New York reported in 1791 that it had 50 percent more deposits than notes outstanding. Data became regularly available in the 1830s and show a fairly steady decline in the notes/deposits ratio. In New York state, for example, the notes/deposit in ratio was 1.2 in 1837, 0.74 in 1847, and 0.31 in 1857 (Redlich 1951). Nationally, the trend was less pronounced. The ratio fell from 0.85 in 1835, to 0.79 in 1845, and to 0.67 in 1860 (see *Historical Statistics of the United States*, p. 995).

Given their informational disadvantages, it may seem curious that deposits came to dominate bank notes rather early in the century, even before the establishment of the first CBCH. But demand deposits do possess certain well-known advantages over bank notes. They are less subject to theft, for example. In addition, writing checks avoids the cost of making change and provides proof of payment. Another less commonly recognized feature of using checks rather than notes to make payments is that checks exchanged against currency or goods and services in local markets at a fixed price. While the specie price of a particular bank's notes could vary dramatically over time and space, deposits, when acceptable to sellers in transactions, exchanged at par in local transactions. But if deposits were to prove viable in exchange, some mechanism for providing confidence in performance by banks was necessary. This was especially the case since a uniform exchange rate for deposits created incentives for banks to "cheat" by backing deposits with inferior assets. There was no secondary market to "reveal" such behavior as there was with bank notes.

The formation of the CBCH not only reduced the costs of clearing checks, it solved the information problem created by the missing market, by *internalizing* the secondary market in a unique organizational form. With the CBCH, the apparent defects of the demand deposit product could be turned into distinct advantages.

## 2. THE CLEARINGHOUSE AS A MONITOR/MANAGER

The CBCH was not initially formed to deal with resource allocation problems which markets handle poorly. Its function was to economize on the costs of check clearing. Prior to the New York CBCH formation in 1853, commercial banks collected checks and other instruments by a daily exchange and settlement with each other bank. Once the clearinghouse formed, the exchange was made with only one party—the clearinghouse itself. Gibbons (1859) estimates that for New York City banks the cost of "conducting this vast amount of business did not exceed eight thousand dollars a year," which constituted roughly 0.02 percent of deposits in the New York CBCH at the end of 1854.

While the clearinghouse was organized to produce a simple product, check-clearing, it was also capable of producing a by-product—information. When demand deposits dominate bank notes, banks have an exploitable information advantage over their customers concerning the quality of bank liabilities. Banks face incentives to back deposits with high-yielding, risky assets. Customers want to obtain information about the true quality of bank deposits, but face free rider problems. The direct statement of the bank lacks credibility since a "bad" bank has no incentive to reveal its true condition. Customers would clearly gain if some form of credible supervisor monitored the quality of bank liabilities and disseminated relevant information. Such a supervisor would need enforcement powers to correct contract deviations. The supervisor, in other words, would act as a substitute for the price system; hierarchy (authority) would replace the market.

Such a system would be implemented if it were in the welfare interests of the banks as well as their customers. The gain to an individual bank from industry supervision is identical to that for employees in a firm: colleagues can shirk only at a higher cost. Even though workers see compulsion as costly, they are better off in a number of circumstances by accepting it (Stiglitz 1975). This becomes more true as shirking by colleagues reduces the return to an individual worker or increases his risk. When deposits dominate, banking is characterized by just such a condition, since shirking by one bank can lower the return to another directly. A "bad" bank's failure or suspension, for example, would induce bank customers to monitor the quality of their own bank's liabilities.[3] The cheapest way to monitor was to exercise the deposit contract. But if large numbers of customers chose to monitor at once (a bank run), even a "good" bank ran a substantial risk of failure. This externality problem strengthened the demand for supervision, other things equal. The "best" banks would favor monitoring even aside from externalities since disclosure of their status may allow them to capture "ability rents."

There are strong reasons in favor of quality measurement by the banks themselves. Bank measurement need occur only once per measurement period, for example, but customer measurement involves a great deal of duplication. In addition, bankers possess comparative advantages in judging the quality of the assets backing deposits.

The CBCH was well positioned to provide monitoring and supervision services to the banking industry. The form of the New York clearinghouse, embodied in its 1854 constitution, included a number of aspects similar to institutions commonly identified today as providing screening services, mainly educational institutions. The clearinghouse required, for example, that member institutions satisfy an admissions test (based on certification of adequate capital), pay an admissions fee, and submit to periodic exams (audits) by the clearinghouse. Members who failed to satisfy CBCH regulations were subject to disciplinary actions (fines) and, for extreme violations, could be expelled.

Expulsion from the clearinghouse was a clear negative signal concerning the quality of bank's liabilities. It suggested that in the collective judgment of the banking community, the probability of nonperformance in the exchange process by the expelled bank was uncomfortably high. The ability of the CBCH to audit a member's books (to measure quality) at any moment provided strong incentives for prudent behavior by each bank and thus strengthened the credibility of the CBCH signals.[4] Moreover, without access to the clearinghouse a bank had to

---

[3] Suspension was a temporary default on the contract to exchange bank liabilities for specie.

[4] Gibbons writes: "With knowledge of these facts (debits in excess of specie balances for a sustained period), the Committee visits the bank, and investigates its affairs. If they are found to be hopelessly involved, it is suspended from the exchange at the Clearing House—a last blow to its credit" (pp. 319–20). Dismissal from the clearinghouse required only a majority vote.

clear its checks in the more costly manner used prior to the existence of the CBCH. Consequently, expulsion was a potent enforcement threat.

The CBCH also increased the value of other information signals. Each bank in New York City was required by law to publish on each Tuesday morning a statement showing the average amount of loans and discounts, specie, deposits, and circulation for the preceding week. Banks were also required to publish quarterly statements of condition. The existence of the CBCH prevented banks from publishing inaccurate statements and from engaging in excessive "window dressing" of balance sheets.[5]

The advantage of the CBCH organization were such that within a decade a large number of new local clearinghouses were formed. These typically organized along lines similar to the New York CBCH, but some extended their roles beyond that of monitoring to regulating bank behavior. The Buffalo and Sioux City clearinghouses set interest-rate ceilings on deposits which could be paid by member banks (Cannon 1910).

The New York CBCH did not employ fixed reserve requirements as a supervisor-enforced constraint on members until 1858, when a 20 percent "coin requirement" was established against "net deposits of every kind" (Hammond 1957, p. 713). Reserve requirements were also soon thereafter established in Philadelphia. The reserve requirement did *not* apply against circulating *notes*. The CBCH also monitored the extent to which members purchased or borrowed specie from external sources to meet claims. Member banks were, in effect, under implicit contract to the CBCH to avoid "excessive liability management."[6]

These activities of CBCHs served to enforce the fixed local exchange rate of one-to-one between specie and demand deposits. By credibly supervising member bank activities and by reducing the costs of clearing checks, CBCHs helped demand deposits become the preferred bank product on the liability side. But one problem remained: how would bank liability holders monitor the monitor?

### 3. THE CLEARINGHOUSE DURING BANKING PANICS

The behavior of CBCHs was consistent with a hierarchical form of organization focused principally on supervisory kinds of activities. But, while the costs of

---

[5]"It was only when the Clearing House *records* were brought to such perfection as to give the means of analysis and test beyond dispute, that the positive integrity of those statements could be guaranteed to the public" (Gibbons 1859, p. 325). The CBCH would also investigate rumors about the states of particular member banks. In response to rumors, the CBCH would audit the bank and publish the results. There are many examples of this in the New York City Clearinghouse Association, Clearinghouse Committee *Minutes* (hereafter, *Minutes*).

[6]"A positive principle, or rule of financial government, has been demonstrated by this action of the Clearing House on the city banks—that is, the restriction of loans, by the necessity of maintaining a certain average of coin *from resources within the bank*. Borrowing from day to day will no longer do. It cannot be concealed." (Italics original, Gibbons 1859, p. 321.)

member-bank "cheating" were raised by the CBCH, it could not eliminate all incentives to cheat. Indeed, by raising the public's perception of the quality of the "average" bank, the CBCH raised the benefit of cheating along with the cost. There remained some incentive, therefore, for bank customers to engage in their own monitoring of bank behavior. A banking panic may be seen as an instance of customer monitoring. Exercising the deposit contract's option feature en masse represents a cheap way for bank customers to monitor the ability of their bank to perform, and, in effect, to monitor the monitoring of the CBCH.

Banking panics were large-scale attempts by bank customers to convert deposits into specie or currency. While the precise causes of banking panics remains a point of dispute, it seems clear that, because of the information asymmetry created by demand deposits, depositors had to rely on aggregate or nonbank-specific information to assess the riskiness of deposits. Increases in business failures or the failure of a single large financial firm could cause depositors to "run" on all banks seeking, in a single act, to withdraw deposits and measure the performance of their individual banks and, implicitly, the performance of the CBCH (Gorton 1984).

From a bank's point of view, there are potentially large costs to such measurement by its customers. The customers can only be convinced of the value of demand deposits if the banks can transform them into specie or currency. With bank notes, the secondary market signaled the value of bank portfolios in an efficient manner. But without a secondary note market, bank claim holders had to rely on nonmarket methods of evaluation. In part because of the high cost of obtaining information on the quality of bank loans, this portion of a bank's assets can be deemed illiquid. If the sale of such illiquid assets is required to meet depositors' demands, then a bank may incur substantial losses. In other words, the excessive measurement by customers which occurs during a panic effectively makes illiquidity the same as insolvency.

With costless, full information, the banking system would never face problems during panics because bank assets could easily be transformed into any other desired securities. But in that case there would never be a panic to start with because depositors would never need to monitor. With an information asymmetry, banks would value some mechanism which allowed for their assets to be transformed into some other security in such a way as to signal to depositors their value. The CBCH provided such a mechanism by inventing a new security, the clearinghouse loan certificate.

The first issue of clearinghouse loan certificates occurred during the panic of 1857; they were issued in every subsequent panic through 1914. The process was straightforward: a policy committee of the CBCH first authorized the issuance of loan certificates. Member banks needing specie or currency to satisfy customers' demands could then apply to the clearinghouse loan committee for certificates. Borrowing banks were charged interest rates varying from 6 to 7 percent and were required to present "acceptable collateral" to be "discounted" by the CBCH. The loan certificates had a fixed maturity of, typically, one to three months. The important feature of the certificates was that member banks could use the loan certificates in the clearing process in place of currency, freeing currency for the payment of depositors' claims.[7]

The mechanism of the loan certificate produced a more hierarchical organizational form of the CBCH during panics than existed otherwise. Indeed, during panics when the loan certificate process was operating, the CBCH behaved much like an integrated firm allocating resources by hiearchical decision. In fact, the loan certificates were claims on the clearinghouse, a joint liability of the member banks. If a member bank with outstanding loan certificates failed, the loss (in excess of the value of pledged collateral) was shared by the remaining members of the CBCH.[8]

The loan certificate process in effect internalized the missing market within a hierarchical form. While depositors faced an information asymmetry, the banks themselves were in a position to cope with this problem. The clearing process itself provided information on members, as did clearinghouse audits and member bank reports. Also, banks had the specialized knowledge to value bank assets. Most importantly, individual banks had an incentive to lower the probability of other members' failures because of the information externalities. This meant in practice that no member banks were allowed to fail during a period of panic. Instead, members were expelled from clearinghouse membership for failure to repay loan certificates after the panic had clearly ended and their failure would result in weaker externality effects.

The loan certificate process was available to all members, and consequently, is accurately described as a coinsurance arrangement. But this meant that resources had to be allocated to members, even those which the CBCH perhaps knew would certainly fail, in the interests of all members. Since the interest rate on loan certificates and the discount on collateral did not vary over banks or assets, the central decisions of selecting and approving collateral, and deciding on amounts of certificates were *quantity* decisions made by the CBCH. Moreover, the CBCH could, at its discretion, demand additional security and requisition aid for particularly troubled banks.[9] The CBCH clearly possessed a great deal of control. It regulated bank behavior substantially during a panic.

Another managerial decision in which the CBCH became involved was when and whether to suspend the right of deposit convertibility, that is, to suspend the

[7]The dates of issue, amounts issued, rate of interest, and nature of collateral can be found in the *Report* of the U.S. Treasury, 1914, p. 589. In the pre–Civil War, "bills receivable, stocks, bonds, and other securities" were acceptable. Also see Sprague (1910), pp. 432–33.

[8]In New York the first explicit record of how loan certificates were to function, *Minutes*, November 21, 1860, does not mention this. It was made clear during the Panic of 1907 (*Minutes*, October 31, 1907) which was apparently the only occasion when, after the panic, members (two banks) could not repay loan certificates. However, during the first panic the CBCHs faced after formation, a particularly lucid statement of this was adopted by the Boston CH (October 15, 1857). The agreement is quoted in Redlich (1951), p. 159.

[9]In Boston the original 1857 agreement included the following:

And it is further agreed  .  .  .  that the Clearing House Committee may at any moment call upon any bank for satisfactory collateral security, for any balance thus paid in bills instead of Specie; and each Bank hereby agrees with the Clearing House Committee, and with all and each of the other Banks to furnish immediately such security when demanded.
Quoted in Redlich (1951), p. 159.

option feature of deposit contracts. Suspension amounted to default on the deposit contract, and was a violation of banking law. Nevertheless, suspension occurred on eight occasions during the nineteenth century.[10] In banking panics after 1853, the CBCH played the central role in deciding whether and when suspension was appropriate.[11] Suspension signals that the CBCH believes further liquidation of bank assets to acquire currency or specie is not in the welfare interests of either the suspending banks or their customers (Gorton 1985a).

The transformation of the CBCH into a single firm-like organization during panics was signalled by suspending the weekly publication of individual bank statements, and instead, publishing the weekly statement of the clearinghouse itself.[12] In this way, the clearinghouse avoided identifying weak banks. But, more importantly, with the loan certificate process at work, the aggregate information was the appropriate information. Also, the CBCH did not publish the identity of banks borrowing through the loan-certificate process. Cannon (1910, p. 90) reports that "attempts on the part of the business community were made in vain to discover what banks had taken out in certificates."

For this organizational structure to be successful, the amount of currency released from use in the clearing process through use of loan certificates had to be large enough to signal to depositors that the one-to-one deposit exchange rate was, in fact, correct. But the amount of currency released was limited, and so, during the panics of 1893 and 1907, the clearinghouses directly monetized bank portfolios by issuing loan certificates, in small denominations (as low as 25¢), directly to the public. This allowed all the banks' assets to be monetized, if needed.[13]

Depositors were willing to accept loan certificates in exchange for demand deposits (rather than currency) because the loan certificates, being claims on the CBCH, insured depositors against individual bank failure. In this way, the problem of bank-specific risk arising from the information asymmetry was solved, leaving only the risk that the CBCH would fail. But the circulating loan certificates were neither bank- nor agent-specific, so a secondary market could and did quickly develop, allowing the risk of CBCH failure to be priced. This secondary

---

(footnote 9 continued): In New York the CH Committee had the "power to demand additional security either by an exchange or an increased amount at their discretion." (*Minutes*, November 21, 1860). But beyond this was power to directly allocate resources by making requisitions on individual banks (*Minutes*, October 21, 1907). Also, see *Minutes*, October 18, 1907; October 21–22, 1907; January 9, 28, 1907; February 1, 1908.

[10]Suspension of convertibility occurred during August 1814, Fall 1819, May 1837, October 1857, September 1873, July 1893, and October 1907. Suspension also occurred in the 1860s though this was not related to a major banking panic as in the other cases. Loan certificates were issued during every panic after the formation of the CBCH, including 1860 and 1884. During the crises of 1895 and 1896 the New York City CBCH authorized the issuance of loan certificates, but no member banks applied (*Loan Committee Minutes*, December 24–31, 1895; August 24, 1896).

[11]For example, the Marine National Bank was punished for acting on its own by unilaterally suspending in May, 1884 (*Minutes*, May 6, 1884). The New York CBCH avoided suspension during the Panic of 1884.

[12]E.g., *Loan Committee Minutes*, January 30, 1891; June 6, 1893; November 1, 1907; and *Minutes*, November 1, 1907.

[13]Gorton (1985b) computes that the U.S. money stock temporarily increased in this way by 2 1/2 percent during the Panic of 1893 and by 4 1/2 percent during the Panic of 1907.

market served as an index of confidence. Initially, a currency premium existed in exchanges of certificates for currency.[14] Over the period of suspension, it gradually subsided until reaching zero, whereupon suspension was lifted. In this way, a market signal was sent from depositors to CBCHs.

During banking panics, the CBCH was operating a miniature capital market, allocating resources by nonmarket means for the benefit of the collective of firms. But once the period of suspension was over, the CBCH reverted to its more limited organizational form. Only by reverting back to the more limited organizational form could the CBCH restore the proper incentives for banks to jointly monitor each other on a continuous basis.

Suppose that once the more hierarchical form of organization had been adopted during a panic, the CBCH did not revert back to its more limited form. Then individual banks, knowing that the loan certificates were available, would have an incentive to make riskier loans since each would believe that the risk could be spread over the other members through the loan certificate process. Clearly, this would not be viable. During the period of suspension when the risk pooling arrangement was in effect, however, banks have incentives to make more risky loans, free-riding on the CBCH. No mention of such a problem appears in the archives of the New York Clearinghouse Association or other sources. The problem apparently didn't exist because member banks had no funds to make new loans. During panics banks attempted to liquidate loans of existing customers to generate cash. If a member did engage in making riskier loans, however, it was exposed to the risk that the maturity of the loans would be longer than the suspension period, making free-riding less likely. Also, the CBCH required daily reporting of all balance-sheet changes during a panic period.

Only by reverting back to the more limited organizational form did individual banks have the incentives to monitor each other. The externalities from individual bank cheating provided the incentives, and the resulting monitoring made it possible for the panic-form of the CBCH to be effective since the risk exposure of the members had been limited during nonpanic times. Consequently, the changing organizational form and degree of regulation of the CBCH was an integral part of the production of demand deposit services. In the absence of a market to monitor product quality, bank firms were required to jointly produce "confidence" in deposits, but this required a delicate balance between hierarchy and maintenance of market incentives.

## 4. CONCLUSION

Analysis of the CBCH system focuses attention on the issue most critical to the discussion of competitive banking: the ability of "the market" to control the behavior of bank managers. Hayek (1976) and White (1984) have argued that market forces are capable of controlling banks, and consequently preserving

[14]See Sprague (1910), pp. 57, 187, 280–81.

confidence in the system, provided that bank liabilities are convertible into some outside money. Klein (1974) has emphasized the role of brand names in establishing and maintaining confidence concerning convertibility. We have argued, however, that, because of information asymmetries, the market's capacity to control bank behavior depends on the banking product mix. In particular, the rising ratio of deposits to bank notes during the nineteenth century resulted in (1) increased monitoring costs for bank customers, and (2) more significant externality problems among banks. The CBCH, originally formed as a simple collective to reduce the costs of collecting checks, became involved in monitoring activities and established mechanisms of managerial control. In fact, the CBCH "regulated" bank behavior.

Our analysis provides a more complete and consistent explanation for the role of private institutions such as the CBCH in the creation of monetary confidence, which has been noted by Klein (1974), Timberlake (1984), and Gorton (1985).[15] It also suggests that the conclusions of Hayek (1976) and White (1984) concerning the efficacy of markets as control mechanisms in banking may be valid only under certain conditions concerning information costs and monitoring technologies.

LITERATURE CITED

Cannon, James G. *Clearing Houses.* (U.S. National Monetary Commission) Washington: Government Printing Office, 1910.

Coase, Ronald H. "The Nature of the Firm." *Economica* 4 (November 1937), 386–405.

Dillistin, William. *Bank Note Reporters and Counterfeit Detectors, 1826–1866.* New York: American Numismatic Society, 1949.

Gibbons, James S. *The Banks of New York, Their Dealers, the Clearinghouses, and the Panic of 1857.* New York, 1859.

Gorton, Gary. "Banking Panics and Business Cycles." Mimeographed. The Wharton School, University of Pennsylvania, 1984.

———. "Bank Suspension of Convertibility." *Journal of Monetary Economics* 15 (March 1985), 177–94, (a).

———. "Clearinghouses and the Origins of Central Banking in the U.S." *Journal of Economic History* 42 (June 1985), 277–84, (b).

———. "Inside Money and Contracting Technologies: An Empirical Study." Mimeographed. The Wharton School, University of Pennsylvania, 1986.

Hammond, Bray. *Banks and Politics in America.* Princeton: Princeton University Press, 1957.

Hayek, Friedrich A. Von *The Denationalisation of Money.* London: Institute of Monetary Affairs, 1976.

King, Robert. "On the Economics of Private Money." *Journal of Monetary Economics* 12 (July 1983), 127–58.

---

[15]Mullineaux (1987) analyzes the role of a different private institution, the Suffolk Bank System, in maintaining confidence in bank notes in New England during the mid-nineteenth century.

468 : MONEY, CREDIT, AND BANKING

Klein, Benjamin. "The Competitive Supply of Money," *Journal of Money, Credit, and Banking* 6 (November 1974), 423–53.

Mullineaux, Donald J. "Competitive Monies and the Suffolk Bank System." *Southern Economic Journal* 53 (April 1987), 884–98.

Redlich, Fritz. *The Molding of American Banking.* New York: Hafner Publishing Company, 1951.

Sprague, Oliver M. W. *History of Crises under the National Banking System.* (U.S. National Monetary Commission). Washington: Government Printing Office, 1910.

Stiglitz, Joseph E. "Incentives, Risk and Information: Notes toward a Theory of Hierarchy." *Bell Journal of Economics* 6 (Autumn 1975), 552–79.

_____. "Credit Markets and the Control of Capital." *Journal of Money, Credit, and Banking* 17 (May 1985), 133–52.

Timberlake, Richard H., Jr. "The Central Banking Role of Clearinghouse Associations." *Journal of Money, Credit, and Banking* 16 (February 1984), 1–15.

Vaubel, Roland. "Free Currency Competition." *Weltwirtschafliches Archiv* 113 (September 1977), 435–59.

White, Lawrence H. *Free Banking in Britain: Theory Experience and Debate, 1800–45.* Cambridge: Cambridge University Press, 1984.

Williamson, Oliver. *Markets and Hierarchies: Analysis and Antitrust Implications.* New York: Free Press, 1975.

# [15]

## State-Sponsored Insurance of Bank Deposits in the United States, 1907–1929

EUGENE NELSON WHITE

Before the creation of the Federal Deposit Insurance Corporation in 1933, several states established deposit guarantee funds. The key factor influencing the adoption of deposit insurance by a state was the structure of its banking industry. In states where small unit banks were dominant, there was strong support for guarantee funds to protect deposits; in other states there was more interest in branch banking. The failure to design the guarantee funds in accordance with sound principles of insurance brought about their demise and led to increased branch banking.

CONGRESS and the state legislatures responded to the panic of 1907 with legislation aimed at strengthening the nation's banking system. Although most of the attention given to banking reform in this period has been focused on the Federal Reserve Act, state provision of deposit insurance deserves greater consideration. This legislation influenced the development of banking within the states adopting it, and the debate over the guarantee of deposits defined more sharply the points of conflict between the different schools of banking reform.

Although federal and state banking reforms took different directions, there was a certain similarity in their overall purpose. Neither tried to reverse the effects of past legislation that had promoted the growth of thousands of unit banks. Their legislation instead attempted to correct the banking system's malfunctioning while preserving the structure of the banking industry. The Federal Reserve Act sought to accomplish this by the provision of discounting facilities sufficient to prevent another liquidity crisis. Since the control of the monetary base was a prerogative of the federal government, states could not follow suit. One alternative for them was deposit insurance. States could remove the motive behind panics by guaranteeing depositors recovery of their assets. The public, alert to the potential benefits of deposit insurance, switched their deposits from uninsured national banks to insured state banks. Insurance of deposits thus increased the attractiveness of possessing a state bank charter and led to an expansion of the state banking systems at the expense of the National Banking System and later the Federal Reserve System. Eight states— Oklahoma, Kansas, Nebraska, South Dakota, Texas, Mississippi, North Dakota, and Washington—sought these advantages after the panic of

*Journal of Economic History* Vol. XLI, No. 3 (Sept. 1981). © The Economic History Association. All rights reserved. ISSN 0022-0507.

The author is Assistant Professor of Economics, Rutgers University, New Brunswick, New Jersey 08903. An early draft of this paper was presented to the 1980 Cliometrics Conference at the University of Chicago. The author would like to acknowledge the valuable comments received there and from Larry Neal, Jeremy Atack, Tom Ulen, Hugh Rockoff, and two anonymous referees.

1907 and established deposit guarantee funds.

PREVIOUS ATTEMPTS TO INSURE BANK LIABILITIES

This was not the first attempt by states to insure banking liabilities. Prior to the National Banking Act of 1864 and its amendments which demolished the antebellum state banking systems, several states had insurance schemes designed primarily to protect bank note issue. Pre-eminent among these was the New York Safety Fund created in 1829. Assessing banks on their capital, New York provided a fund that gave 100 percent protection to subscribing banks' liabilities. Financial crisis placed a heavy strain on it, but the Safety Fund and the systems of Indiana, Ohio, Michigan, and Iowa were able to withstand all the antebellum crises. Only the Vermont system failed to give insured claimants payment in full.[1] When the National banks were allowed to monopolize the issue of bank notes, they were required to back them with U.S. bonds and the total volume of notes was strictly limited. With bank notes secured in this fashion, insurance was superfluous.

The resurgence in the 1880s of state chartered banks was based on the development of deposit banking which circumvented the national bank monopoly of bank notes. The idea of insuring deposits was first widely considered after the panic of 1893. Unlike the crisis of 1907, there was no pre-emptive suspension of payments by banks and 491 commercial banks failed compared to a total of 243 for 1907–1908.[2] To alleviate the plight of the failed banks' depositors, William Jennings Bryan presented a bill to Congress in 1893 to establish a deposit insurance fund. Several state legislatures in the West also debated the issue, but there was no action taken, even though banks continued to fail at an alarmingly high rate after the panic.[3] This was primarily the result of an agricultural depression, and bank failures were significantly higher in the South and the West.[4] Deposit insurance could not prevent these failures, and interest in deposit insurance waned in the late 1890s when agriculture prices began to recover.

THE DEBATE OVER DEPOSIT INSURANCE

The panic of 1907 reawakened interest in deposit insurance, and nowhere did the idea enjoy greater currency than in the populist West. At the height of the crisis in December 1907, the Oklahoma legislature

---

[1] Carter H. Golembe, "The Deposit Insurance Legislation of 1933: An Examination of its Antecedents and Purposes," *Political Science Quarterly*, 75 (June 1960), 183–87.

[2] A. Piatt Andrew, "Substitutes for Cash in the Panic of 1907," *Quarterly Journal of Economics*, 22 (Aug. 1908), 513–14, and Board of Governors of the Federal Reserve, *Banking and Monetary Statistics* (Washington, D.C., 1943), p. 283.

[3] W.E. Kuhn, *History of Nebraska Banking: A Centennial Retrospect*, University of Nebraska Bureau of Business Research, Bull. No. 72 (Lincoln, 1968), p. 13.

[4] Hugh Rockoff, "Regional Interest Rates and Bank Failures, 1870–1914," *Explorations in Economic History*, 14 (Jan. 1977), 92.

## *State-Sponsored Insurance of Bank Deposits* 539

passed the first law since the Civil War to guarantee bank liabilities. Its example was followed shortly by the legislatures of Kansas, Nebraska, South Dakota, and Texas. The remaining state deposit insurance systems of Mississippi, North Dakota, and Washington were established after the founding of the Federal Reserve System. Deposit insurance legislation was passed by these states under a variety of circumstances, but their banking systems all had similar characteristics.

The states in which deposit insurance was adopted had, by previous legislation, all firmly established unit banking within their boundaries and were all in relatively undiversified regions where business prosperity in general depended on one or two commodities. Support for deposit insurance came primarily from small-town country bankers. The opposition to the guarantee of deposits was composed largely of city bankers. In states where city banks were the dominant element in the industry, deposit insurance was not seriously considered.

The divisions within the banking industry over the question of deposit insurance and reform arose principally from differences in the size and scope of banks' operations. These were, in turn, the product of differences in regional conditions and state regulations. The size of banks was determined by population density, minimum capital requirements, and branching restrictions. Widespread prohibition of branching meant the vast majority of banks were restricted to a single office. Population density limited to a large degree the potential number of depositors and borrowers of single-office banks. Minimum capital requirements imposed a lower bound on bank size. Rural states with low population densities typically had low capital requirements to ensure that small communities would not be deprived of bank offices. This created banking systems in the southern and western states dominated by hundreds of small unit banks. Greater population density coupled with higher capital requirements and some branching led to the establishment of larger, more diversified banks in the East.

In states where regulation and low population density had created many small unit banks, the banking industry was particularly vulnerable to economic fluctuations because the typical bank had a small number of depositors and undiversified loan portfolios. Country bankers often looked favorably on deposit insurance, viewing it as a means of protecting themselves and their depositors from the danger of a panic. The alternative was to allow increased branching. This would have permitted banks to insure themselves by gaining more depositors, lessening the probability of large unexpected withdrawals, and by offering loans to more types of business, decreasing the danger of investing too heavily in one type of activity.

Although most country bankers were unwilling to consider branch banking as an alternative, many contemporary observers recognized the superior safety offered by branch banking. In an article in the *Quarterly*

*Journal of Economics* in 1902, Oliver M. W. Sprague of Harvard argued that branch banking provided banks with a form of insurance:

> The larger the number of individual borrowers, the smaller is the likelihood, in general, of serious loss from their failure to meet obligations. The danger of heavy losses at any one time is further reduced if the bank is engaged in business over a wide geographical area, with loans based upon more kinds of business than is possible to local banks, except in large centers of population. . . . The larger the number of depositors and the more varied their business, the less likely are their demands to come at any one time. Such demands vary with the season of the year, both in different trades and different sections of the country . . . . The bank with many branches can concentrate its reserves whenever the demand arises.[5]

This potential for diversification enabled branching banks to reduce their exposure to risk, lessening their desire for government-provided insurance that might force them to join a system with smaller, less well-diversified banks.

Sprague recognized that correspondent banking served as a partial surrogate for branch banking in facilitating the clearing and collection of checks and interregional financial intermediation. Yet, although the system of bankers' balances in the reserve cities provided interior banks with fairly liquid secondary reserves, it failed to give them sufficient liquidity in periods of acute distress. Sprague wrote:

> It is possible for the banks of a city to unite upon some common policy to allay a panic; but experience shows that at such times country banks withdraw deposits to protect themselves even when they are in no immediate danger. The credit structure as a whole is weakened, reserves become unavailable at points of greatest danger and banks fail which might have survived with a little timely assistance.[6]

The panic of 1907 followed this pattern. The country banks drew down their correspondent balances, and in attempting to hoard currency they forced a general suspension of payments.[7]

In spite of its recognized benefits, branch banking was severely limited at the turn of the century. The National Banking Act of 1864 forbade national banks from branching. In 1910 only nine states allowed statewide branching and four permitted limited branching.[8] Branch bank offices accounted for only 3.4 percent of total bank offices, and branching banks constituted a modest 1.2 percent of all commercial banks holding 8.9 percent of commercial bank loans and investments.[9] Most of the nation's

---

[5] Oliver M. W. Sprague, "Branch Banking in the United States," *Quarterly Journal of Economics*, 27 (Feb. 1903), 243.

[6] Ibid., p. 244.

[7] A. Piatt Andrew, "Hoarding in the Panic of 1907," *Quarterly Journal of Economics*, 22 (Feb. 1908), 296–99.

[8] Frederick A. Bradford, *The Legal Status of Branch Banking in the United States* (New York, 1940).

[9] Board of Governors of the Federal Reserve, *Banking and Monetary Statistics*, p. 297; Board of Governors of the Federal Reserve, *All Bank Statistics, 1896-1955* (Washington, D.C., 1963), pp. 34-35.

## State-Sponsored Insurance of Bank Deposits 541

banks were small unit banks spread out over the country. This dispersion also reduced the possibility of interbank cooperation that might have substituted for the intrabank coordination that strengthened branching banks. Deposit insurance appeared to offer an alternative to branching and interbank cooperation; thus it was promoted as protecting the small country banks from panics. Deposit holders in these banks wanted to protect their assets, and the guarantee of deposits offered a solution that was acceptable to their bankers, holding at bay the populist menace of the large bankers' "Money Trust."

Deposit insurance was never seriously considered in any of the states in which large banks were dominant. Relatively higher capital requirements and some provision for branching ensured the growth of larger banks that could manage financial crises more easily. Bankers in the Northeast and the Mid-Atlantic states were adamantly opposed to deposit insurance. They feared that they would have to pay for the weakness and recklessness of other bankers. The opinion of bankers in the major financial centers was reflected in an editorial published by the *Philadelphia Enquirer* in 1909 when several states were considering deposit insurance legislation. The author anathematized deposit insurance:

The idea of furnishing a guarantee for bank deposits is one of those crude, half-baked, ill-digested notions in which the populist West is so prolific. A bad deposit is a debt like any other and there is no more reason why it should be guaranteed by law than there is in the case of any other kind of indebtedness.[10]

Many of these bankers thought that the only way to strengthen the banking system was to increase branching. One of the first major reform bills considered by Congress was introduced by Representative Charles Fowler of New Jersey in 1902 with the support of the Midwest reserve city bankers. One major provision of the bill would have legalized branching in the interest of strengthening the banking system and equalizing interest rates.[11]

The American Bankers' Association, whose leadership was dominated by the Chicago bankers, moved to approve the Fowler plan at their annual convention, but it aroused the opposition of the country bankers who stood firmly against any form of branch banking. Against the wishes of the organization's executives, the country bankers defeated the motion and in its place a resolution was substituted that condemned branching because "individualism in management would cease, local taxes [would] be evaded, [there would be] no home distribution of profits, and local progress [would be] retarded."[12] The leaders of the ABA were able to prevent this from becoming the association's official stand only by a parliamentary maneuver. Undaunted, the country bankers returned home and

[10] Golembe, "Deposit Insurance Legislation," 196.
[11] Robert Craig West, *Banking Reform and the Federal Reserve 1863–1923* (Ithaca, 1977), pp. 46–50.
[12] Robert H. Wiebe, *Businessmen and Reform: A Study of the Progressive Movement* (Cambridge, MA, 1962), p. 24.

attacked the Fowler Plan and branch banking, in particular, at their annual state conventions. The state associations of Kansas, Illinois, Iowa,
Minnesota, Missouri, Nebraska, South Dakota, and Wisconsin passed
lengthy resolutions to this effect.[13]

The argument that the adoption of deposit insurance by a state was determined by the interests of its banking community is supported by the
"economic" theory of regulation. As laid out by Stigler and Posner, the
economic theory of regulation posits that regulation is a good like any
other that will be supplied to those who value it the most.[14] In place of
price signals in the market place, political pressure is applied in the legislature. The more highly valued a particular type of regulation is by an industry or interest group, the greater the lobbying effort it makes will be. In
contrast to the theory of cartels, which posits that an industry will be more
successful at setting a joint price and securing its subsequent enforcement
if the number of firms is small, it appears that an industry will be more
likely to obtain favorable regulation (and hence, prices and profits) when
there are many firms in it. The costs of forming and maintaining a cartel
are too high when there is a large number of firms; however, the existence
of many firms may enhance an industry's ability to lobby. In banking
there were thousands of firms well distributed throughout the country;
banks were therefore able to exert considerable pressure on Congress and
the state legislatures. Another factor likely to increase political activity is
an asymmetry of interests within an industry.[15] If there are divisions in the
industry, each group will tend to be drawn into politics. In the banking industry the interests of the larger banks often conflicted with those of the
smaller banks, and this created an additional incentive for banks to try to
influence the legislatures.

The struggle by each section of the banking industry to protect its position is revealed in the legislative struggles over deposit insurance. The
smaller, usually rural banks eager to have the state legislatures establish
deposit insurance encountered strong opposition from the larger, more
conservative banks. The Texas legislature made membership in the state
guarantee fund compulsory but sought to accommodate both parties by
giving its state banks a choice between joining the Deposit Guaranty
Fund where they paid in annually 1 percent of their average daily deposits, or the Bond Security System where they posted a bond of indemnity
equal to their capital with a surety company.[16] In Nebraska and Mississippi, the state bankers' associations organized by the larger state banks

---

[13] Ibid., pp. 24-25.

[14] George Stigler, "The Theory of Economic Regulation," *Bell Journal of Economics and Management Science*, 2 (Spring 1971), 3-21; Richard Posner, "Theories of Economic Regulation," *Bell Journal of Economics and Management Science*, 5 (Autumn 1974), 335-58.

[15] Stigler, "The Theory of Economic Regulation," 10-14.

[16] Joseph Grant and Lawrence Crum, *The Development of State Chartered Banking in Texas* (Aus-
tin, 1978), pp. 82-83.

## *State-Sponsored Insurance of Bank Deposits* 543

vigorously lobbied their state legislatures to block deposit insurance laws but to no avail. The Nebraska Bankers' Association challenged the constitutionality of their state's statute, but the law was upheld by the supreme court in 1911.[17] The larger state banks in Nebraska and other states responded by taking out national bank charters to avoid compulsory insurance. Kansas, South Dakota, and Washington avoided these battles by offering voluntary deposit insurance. Apart from the eight states which passed deposit insurance legislation and several others which seriously considered it, 150 bills for guaranteeing deposits were submitted to Congress between 1907 and 1933. Most of these came from the representatives of the southern and western states where unit banking was firmly established. One third of the bills were sponsored by representatives from the states of Oklahoma, Nebraska, Texas, and Kansas.[18] In contrast to other western states, California responded to the panic of 1907 by passing the most liberal contemporary branch banking law. It is important to note also that at the same time the state of Washington adopted deposit insurance it abandoned branch banking.[19]

Banking reformers thus were divided into two hostile camps, one bent on preserving, the other upon eliminating, unit banking. These positions were maintained and sharpened in succeeding years, and the debate over the creation of the Federal Deposit Insurance Corporation reflected this division. The Comptroller of the Currency, John Pole, commenting on the Banking Act of 1933, said:

I am in agreement with the ultimate purpose of this bill, namely, greater safety to the depositor. The method proposed by the bill and the principles which I advocate stand at opposite poles. A general guaranty of bank deposits is the very antithesis of branch banking.[20]

A key supporter of the bill, Representative Henry Steagall, Chairman of the House Committee on Banking and Currency, agreed with this interpretation, arguing, "this bill will preserve independent dual banking in the United States. . . that is what this bill is intended to do."[21]

### THE STRUCTURE OF THE BANKING INDUSTRY AND THE DEMAND FOR DEPOSIT INSURANCE

If the characterization of the division on the question of banking reform presented above is correct, then the disposition of each state's legislature toward deposit insurance should have been influenced by existing bank-

---

[17] Thomas B. Robb, *The Guaranty of Bank Deposits* (New York, 1921), pp. 162-70.

[18] Golembe, "Deposit Insurance Legislation," pp. 181-200.

[19] *Annual Report of the State Bank Examiner of the State of Washington* (Olympia, WA, 1919), p. 8ff.

[20] Golembe, "Deposit Insurance Legislation," p. 197.

[21] Ibid., 198.

ing legislation and the banking structure it created. States where the small unit bank was uncontested probably would have considered seriously or adopted deposit insurance, whereas states in which larger banks predominated and some branching was allowed would have opposed the guarantee of deposits.

To test the hypothesis that a state's existing banking structure conditioned its response to deposit insurance proposals, a probit analysis was employed. Qualitative-response analysis is appropriate here since the dependent variable, the establishment of deposit insurance, is a dichotomous variable. There are two approaches to examining the choice of deposit insurance. The first formulation examines individual factors that affected a bank's ability to diversify its activity to insure itself and hence its desire for state-provided deposit insurance. It includes as independent variables the three major regulatory provisions that determined the structure of the banking industry: the minimum capital requirements for non-reserve city banks, a dummy variable for branch banking, and the reserve requirement for non-reserve city banks.[22] It was hypothesized that higher capital requirements and provision for some branching, which would tend to eliminate smaller unit banks, would make deposit insurance less likely, whereas a higher reserve requirement would make deposit insurance more probable since it reduced the profitability of banking. A fourth variable was the ratio of rural to total state population taken from the 1910 Census.[23] The hypothesis here was that the lower the population density, the smaller the average size of banks and the more vulnerable they would be to irregularities in withdrawals of deposits, increasing the need for deposit insurance. The last variable was the ratio of assets in the failed state banks to the total assets of state banks for the period 1903–1909, and it was expected that the higher this failure rate was the more likely a state would be to adopt deposit insurance.[24] The second formulation of the model has as its independent variables the average size of state and national banks in 1908 using data in the Comptroller of the Currency's *Annual Report* for that year. The hypothesis here was that the smaller the average size of a bank, the greater would be the pressure applied by banks to the legislature to secure deposit insurance.

The forty-eight states and territories constituted the sample. A maximum likelihood technique that ensures asymptotically consistent estimators was used to obtain the estimates of the probit coefficients and standard errors presented in Table 1. In order to test the significance of the

---

[22] These data were obtained from Samuel Welldon, *Digest of State Banking Statutes* (Washington, D.C., 1910), supplemented by the *Federal Reserve Bulletin* for 1917 and 1924, and the Comptroller of the Currency's *Annual Reports* for various years.

[23] Department of Commerce, *Historical Statistics of the United States* (Washington, D.C., 1975), pp. 24–37. Rural population is defined as those people living in towns of 2500 inhabitants or less.

[24] *Annual Report of the Comptroller of the Currency*, various years. For states adopting deposit insurance later, the failure rate was for a seven-year period prior to the passage of their laws.

## State-Sponsored Insurance of Bank Deposits                    545

TABLE 1

VARIABLES AFFECTING STATE SELECTION OF DEPOSIT INSURANCE:
PROBIT ESTIMATES

| Variable | Estimated Coefficient | Estimated Standard Error | Approximate t-Statistic |
|---|---|---|---|
| | Model 1 | | |
| Intercept | −0.706 | 1.649 | −0.428 |
| Minimum Capital Requirement | −0.074 | 0.047 | −1.559 |
| Branch Banking | −5.493 | 3.787 | −1.454 |
| Reserve Requirement | 0.0562 | 0.039 | 1.415 |
| Ratio of Rural to Total Population | −0.075 | 1.6406 | −0.045 |
| State Bank Failure Rate | 30.429 | 23.569 | 1.291 |
| | Model 2 | | |
| Intercept | 0.438 | 0.582 | 0.752 |
| Average Size of National Banks | −0.290 | 0.724 | −0.401 |
| Average Size of State Banks | −4.569 | 2.868 | −1.593 |

Source: Regressions are based on data described in the text.

variables, the coefficients were divided by the standard errors yielding probit "t-tests" which are asymptotically normally distributed. The significance of the whole equation was tested using a log likelihood ratio test that has an asymptotic chi-square distribution. The statistic for Model 1 was 13.18 and for Model 2 was 11.27. These are both significant at the 5 percent level.[25]

The results in Table 1 support the hypothesis that a state's banking regulation or structure determines its response to deposit insurance. For Model 1 all the estimated coefficients had the correct expected sign except the ratio of rural to total population. Branch banking, minimum capital requirements, and reserve requirements were all significant at less than 10 percent, whereas the ratio of rural to total population and the failure rate were not. Additionally, alternative measures of the last two variables were employed to determine if the estimates were sensitive to any particular

[25] The likelihood ratio index, a measure of the goodness of fit suggested by McFadden, was calculated and found to be equal to 0.305 and 0.261 for Model 1 and Model 2. While these may appear to be on the low side, McFadden found that the index tends to produce a number that is smaller than the multiple correlation coefficient. For information on probit and the test statistics, see George G. Judge, et al., *The Theory and Practice of Econometrics* (New York, 1980), pp. 590–601; Daniel McFadden, "Conditional Logit Analysis of Qualitative Choice Behavior," in P. Zarembka, ed., *Frontiers of Econometrics* (New York, 1974), pp. 105–42.

measure. Population density measured as inhabitants per square mile in 1910 and national, nonnational, and commercial bank failure rates in terms of assets or the number of banks were substituted for the insignificant variables, but they did not substantially alter the results.[26] Multicollinearity may be responsible for the insignificance of the population density variable as it was closely correlated (-0.618) with minimum capital requirements.

One possible explanation for the insignificance of the bank failure rate may be that to the extent that differences in failure rates were a consequence of differences in the structure of the banking industry in each state, the regulation variables would pick this up directly. Only other sources of failure would be indicated by this coefficient, and these may have been slight. Agriculture's prosperity after the turn of the century helped to diminish regional differences in failure rates. The marked convergence of failure rates in all regions thus may have led to this variable's weakness.[27]

In Model 2 the average size of state banks is significant. Although the coefficient for the average size of national banks does have the correct sign, it is insignificant. It seems plausible to find that national banks did not exert an influence on the choice of deposit insurance, for they were prohibited by the U.S. Attorney General from joining the state deposit guarantee systems in 1908.

It is not surprising that both models perform equally well. The average size of state banks can be explained to a large degree by the regulations imposed by each state on its banking industry. In an ordinary least squares regression of the average size of state banks on the minimum capital requirements, the branching dummy, and the ratio or rural to total population, all contributed significantly (at the 5 percent level) to explaining average bank size. The coefficient on reserve requirements was insignificant. The equation explained 58 percent of the variance in the average size of banks.[28]

The explanatory power of the model may also be gauged by its ability to predict which states actually adopted deposit insurance. Prediction is based on the estimated probit coefficients. (For a description of the technique employed see the Appendix.) Thhe probabilities of any state passing a law guaranteeing deposits given its index $I_i$ are presented in Table 2 for Model 1 and in Table 3 for Model 2. States allowing some form of branch banking are designated by an asterisk.

---

[26] *Historical Statistics*, pp. 24–37, and *Annual Report of the Comptroller of the Currency* (Washington, D.C., 1920).

[27] Rockoff, "Regional Interest Rates," p. 92.

[28] The dependent variable was the total assets of state banks in thousands of dollars divided by the number of banks of "size." The regression equation was: Size = 0.530 + 0.025 minimum capital requirement + 0.330 branching dummy − 0.005 total reserve requirement + 0.009 vault cash reserve requirement − 0.84 population density. All estimates were significant at the 5 percent level except for reserve requirements. The f statistic was equal to 13.6, being significant at 5 percent, and the $R^2$ was equal to 0.058.

TABLE 2
MODEL 1: PROBABILITY THAT A STATE WILL SELECT DEPOSIT
INSURANCE GIVEN THE ESTIMATE VALUE OF ITS PROBIT INDEX

| 0 to 5 percent | 6 to 10 percent | 11 to 20 percent | 21 to 30 percent | 31 to 40 percent | 41 to 50 percent | 51 percent and above |
|---|---|---|---|---|---|---|
| Arizona | Illinois | Michigan | Arkansas | Wisconsin | Minnesota | North Carolina |
| California* | Iowa | Pennsylvania | South Carolina | *North Dakota* | *South Dakota* | Montana |
| Delaware* | New Mexico | Kentucky | Idaho | *Kansas* | Wyoming | *Texas* |
| Florida* | *Mississippi* | Alabama | *Nebraska* | | *Washington* | |
| Georgia* | Ohio | | Nevada | | | |
| Louisiana* | Virginia | | *Oklahoma* | | | |
| Maine* | Colorado | | Utah | | | |
| Massachusetts* | Indiana | | Maryland | | | |
| Missouri* | | | | | | |
| New Jersey | | | | | | |
| New York* | | | | | | |
| Oregon | | | | | | |
| Rhode Island* | | | | | | |
| Tennessee* | | | | | | |
| Vermont | | | | | | |
| New Hampshire | | | | | | |
| Connecticut | | | | | | |
| West Virginia | | | | | | |

Note: In each category the states are listed in ascending order of probability. States adopting deposit insurance are in italics. States marked with an asterisk permitted some form of branching.

Source: The probabilities are calculated from the estimates of Model 1 in Table 1 using the method described in the Appendix.

TABLE 3
MODEL 2: PROBABILITY THAT A STATE WILL SELECT DEPOSIT
INSURANCE GIVEN THE ESTIMATED VALUE OF ITS **PROBIT** INDEX

| 0 to 5 percent | 6 to 10 percent | 11 to 20 percent | 21 to 30 percent | 31 to 40 percent | 41 to 50 percent | 51 percent and above |
|---|---|---|---|---|---|---|
| California* | Maryland | Wisconsin | Florida* | Colorado | Wyoming | *North Dakota* |
| Connecticut | West Virginia | Virginia | South Carolina | Idaho | *Texas* | *Oklahoma* |
| Delaware* | Arizona | Iowa | Georgia* | Minnesota | *South Dakota* | |
| Illinois | Montana | Alabama | *Mississippi* | North Carolina | | |
| Maine* | | Kentucky | | Arkansas | | |
| Massachusetts* | | Indiana | | New Mexico | | |
| Michigan | | Tennessee* | | *Kansas* | | |
| New Jersey | | New Hampshire | | *Nebraska* | | |
| New York* | | Vermont | | | | |
| Ohio | | | | | | |
| Pennsylvania | | | | | | |
| Rhode Island* | | | | | | |
| Utah | | | | | | |
| Louisiana* | | | | | | |
| Missouri* | | | | | | |
| Nevada | | | | | | |
| *Washington* | | | | | | |
| Oregon | | | | | | |

Note: In each category the states are listed in ascending order of probability. States adopting deposit insurance are in italics. States marked with an asterisk permitted some form of branching.

Source: The probabilities are calculated from the estimates of Model 2 in Table 1 using the method described in the Appendix.

## *State-Sponsored Insurance of Bank Deposits* 549

In Table 2 it is striking that no state with branch banking had greater than 5 percent probability of adopting deposit insurance, and in Table 3 there are only three exceptions. Those states that set their minimum capital requirement greater than or equal to the National Banking system's $25,000 minimum never had greater than an 11 percent probability of guaranteeing deposits. The appearance of Mississippi and Washington as outliers is explained by the fact that in both cases deposit insurance was hastily imposed by the state legislature in response to crises other than panics. Although there had been some support in the state of Washington for deposit insurance after the panic of 1907, bills before the legislature were routinely defeated. In 1917, while the bill was being debated, however, banks in the city of Seattle failed, and the opposition to the bill was overwhelmed.[29] Washington had relatively large banks compared to other states in the West at the time its act to guarantee deposits was passed. Until that time there was a limited form of branching permitting the growth of fairly large commercial banks. The large average size of state banks in Washington accounts for the state's low probability of adopting deposit insurance (see Table 3). Mississippi adopted deposit insurance not in response to a panic but to the disastrous failure of the cotton crop in 1913 which caused many banks to fail. The states that had high probabilities of guaranteeing deposits but failed to do so may also be accounted for. Although information on agitation for deposit insurance in each state is scant, it does appear that many of those states that had high probabilities of guaranteeing deposits had strong movements pressing for such legislation. There was considerable sentiment in Minnesota and Montana for the establishment of deposit guarantee funds; and the Wisconsin legislature seriously considered deposit insurance but rejected the bill before it when, in the midst of hearings on a projected fund, the Oklahoma system of insurance broke down.[30] Thus it may be concluded that states which favored unit banking through their legislation were inclined to adopt deposit insurance to provide banks with additional protection.

### A COMPARISON BETWEEN THE UNITED STATES AND CANADIAN BANKING SYSTEMS

It is instructive to compare how Canada, a country similar to the United States in many ways, resolved the problem of guaranteeing the convertibility of deposits. In the early twentieth century there was no interest in insuring deposits in Canada. This may be attributed to the fact that Canada had a banking system in which there was free nationwide branching. The minimum capital requirement of $500,000 was greater than that for any class of state or national bank in the United States. This

---

[29] Robb, *The Guaranty of Bank Deposits*, pp. 170–72.
[30] Ibid., pp. 161–62; Charles S. Popple, *Development of Two Bank Groups in the Central Northwest* (Cambridge, MA, 1944), p. 101.

promoted a system of large branching banks whose offices were spread across the country.[31] Branching was well established and spreading rapidly. In 1890 there were 38 chartered banks with 426 branches, and in 1910 there were 28 banks with a total of 2367 branches.[32] Compared to the American system, Canadian banking was virtually unregulated. There were neither reserve requirements nor extensive governmental supervision. The most important requirement was that a chartered bank's issue of bank notes could not exceed the par value of its capital. Banks recognized their interdependence and their small numbers made cooperation relatively easy. As the economic theory of regulation predicts, a cartel-like association rather than government provision of insurance was the means by which Canadian banks guaranteed their deposits and notes. In 1892, the chartered banks formed the Canadian Bankers' Association, which served to coordinate the reform efforts of bankers. In 1900 this voluntary association was given status as a public corporation with its primary purpose that of superintending the issue of notes. Banks agreed to open enough provincial redemption centers to ensure that their notes would not be discounted but would circulate at par.[33]

The same factors that in the United States caused money markets to tighten and precipitate the panic of 1907 were present in Canada. Although credit became very tight and there were some bank failures, no panic occurred in Canada. Canadian banks were well aware of their mutual interdependence and how the failure of one bank to meet its obligations in a time of financial stringency could prejudice the interests of the others and cause a run on the banks to begin. When the Bank of Ontario failed in October 1906, bankers were afraid that this bank's failure to sustain convertibility might endanger all banks. To prevent this, the Bank of Montreal agreed to take over the Bank of Ontario's assets and pay all liabilities, provided the other banks would agree to accept a share of its losses. This was done behind closed doors on the day of the bank's demise. The next day the bank and all its branches opened as part of the Bank of Montreal. Similarly, when the Sovereign Bank was close to suspending its operations in 1908, its business was taken over by twelve other institutions.[34] Most of Canada's mergers in this period were begun when small banks approaching insolvency solicited offers from larger banks.[35]

Private cooperative action by the Canadian banking industry contrasts what happened in the United States in 1907. When the Knickerbocker Trust (the second largest trust company in New York) tried to obtain a

---

[31] Joseph French Johnson, *The Canadian Banking System* (Washington, D.C., 1910), pp. 18–19.

[32] Benjamin Haggot Beckhart, "The Banking System in Canada," in H. Parker Willis and B.H. Beckhart, eds., *Foreign Banking Systems* (New York, 1929), pp. 327 and 362.

[33] Roeliff Morton Breckenridge, *History of Banking in Canada* (Washington, D.C., 1910), pp. 131–34.

[34] Johnson, *The Canadian Banking System*, pp. 124–27.

[35] Beckhart, *The Banking System in Canada*, p. 340.

loan from another city bank to improve its weak liquidity position, the denial of the loan precipitated a run on Knickerbocker Trust and ignited the panic.[36]

Comparison of the American and Canadian banking systems strengthens the propositions of the economic theory of regulation and suggests that how a banking industry seeks to insure its liabilities may depend on the number of firms. Because the number of Canadian banks was small, they were able to cooperate mutually to guarantee their note issues and deposits. In the United States it was almost impossible for banks to cooperate when a panic threatened because there were so many independent institutions. The larger banks sought to increase branching to strengthen the industry but met opposition from the smaller banks. Anxious to protect themselves from absorption by larger banks, the small country banks promoted deposit insurance as a means of guaranteeing bank liabilities. Which of these was a better form of dealing with the danger of panics, the cartel-produced or the regulation-produced outcome? The Canadian solution seems to have been the better of the two solutions when the subsequent histories of the American and Canadian systems are examined and compared.

### THE DESIGN AND DEMISE OF THE STATE GUARANTEE FUNDS

The American experiment with deposit insurance had two phases. In the first, the state banking authorities learned from bitter experience what modern economists have established on a theoretical basis. Provision of deposit insurance where the premium or assessment is fixed and free of the risk characteristics of a bank's portfolio, and where the bank's asset choice is left free and unsupervised, will create an incentive to hold very risky portfolios.[37] The "moral hazard" created by fixed-premium insurance encouraged banks to substitute state-supplied insurance for self-insurance in the form of greater capital and surplus.[38] The insurer—the state—thus found itself faced with a rising number of bank failures and imposed additional regulations on capital as well as other controls to limit

---

[36] Milton Friedman and Anna J. Schwartz, *A Monetary History of the United States, 1867-1960* (Princeton, 1963), pp. 159-63. Interbank cooperation was not unknown in the United States. When three prominent Chicago banks were about to suspend operations in 1905, the city's leading bankers organized by James Forgan, head of the Chicago Clearing House, took over the banks' assets and paid their depositors. The Chicago bankers reasoned that it would be less costly to do this than to risk the possible danger of a panic. See Fritz Redlich, *The Molding of American Banking* (New York, 1968), pp. 285-86.

[37] John H. Karekan and Neil Wallace, "Deposit Insurance and Bank Regulation: A Partial Equilibrium Exposition," *Journal of Business*, 51 (July 1978), 413-38.

[38] The theory is laid out in Issac Ehrlich and Gary Becker, "Market Insurance, Self-Protection, and Self-Insurance," *Journal of Political Economy*, 80 (July/Aug. 1972), 623-48. In his article, "Capital Investment in Commerical Banking and Its Relationship to Portfolio Regulation," *Journal of Political Economy*, 78 (Jan./Feb. 1970), 1-26, Sam Peltzman found that, in spite of capital-to-asset restrictions, Federal Deposit Insurance has led banks to substitute deposit insurance for capital.

the risk to which the banks exposed themselves. In the second phase, the state legislatures were forced to terminate deposit insurance when the rising number of bank failures brought about by a regional depression bankrupted the guarantee funds.

The first state to establish deposit insurance, Oklahoma, discovered the principles at great cost. Oklahoma had rushed to establish a deposit guarantee system in 1907 and little attention was given to its design. An assessment on bank capital was levied to create an insurance fund, all deposits were insured, and immediate payment upon closure was promised. The Oklahoma legislature had intended the fund to provide protection for all commercial banking institutions, but the United States Attorney General ruled in 1908 that national banks could not join the system. Deposit insurance, therefore, was limited to state banks and trust companies.[39] With virtually no supervision or further regulation, deposit insurance absolved banks from a considerable degree of risk and led to a rapid expansion of state banks. Between March 1908 when the legislation went into effect and November 1909, the number of state banks increased from 470 to 662 with their deposits rising from $18 million to $50 million. National banks, on the other hand, declined from 312 to 220 as banks took out state charters. Their deposits rose slightly from $38 million to $42 million.[40] These developments offer a striking contrast to the slower nationwide growth of banks after the panic of 1907. State banks had increased in number at a rate of 15.9 percent per annum and national banks at 7.8 percent per annum during the period 1897-1907, but this slowed to 4.9 percent per annum and 2.4 percent per annum during 1907-1914.[41] Meanwhile, during 1908-1909 membership in Oklahoma's banking system jumped 40.8 percent in less than two years.

This frenzy of activity resulted in severe problems for the deposit guarantee fund. The crisis began with the collapse of the Columbia Bank, which had overextended itself, expanding its deposits from $365,000 in September 1908 to $2,806,000 in September 1909. The Columbia Bank's demise in 1909 immediately threatened the insurance fund, which had only $400,000, and a special levy on all other member banks was required to pay off the depositors.[42]

This was only the first in a rising number of failures that undermined the system of deposit insurance. The Oklahoma legislature responded to the crisis by overhauling the deposit guarantee law in 1909. The new law tried to ensure that the fund would not be exhausted. It provided for fixed annual assessments of one fourth of 1 percent of average daily deposits to

[39] Thornton Cooke, "The Insurance of Bank Deposits in the West," *Quarterly Journal of Economics*, 33 (Nov. 1909), reprinted in George Barnett, *State Banks and Trust Companies* (Washington, D.C., 1911).

[40] Robb, *The Guaranty of Bank Deposits*, pp. 82–87.

[41] These were calculated from tables in *Historical Statistics*, pp. 1025–30.

[42] Cooke, "The Insurance of Bank Deposits," 286–90.

## State-Sponsored Insurance of Bank Deposits 553

raise the fund gradually from its original 1 percent to 5 percent of average daily deposits, and special assessments of up to 2 percent a year were allowed to maintain the fund.[43] The legislature also imposed additional restraints on banks to reduce the possibility of failure. Banks henceforth were to have aggregate deposits up to, at most, ten times their capital and surplus. Supervision of banks was also improved. A stiff fine was imposed on banks that endeavored to attract new depositors by advertising that deposits were guaranteed by the state rather than by the deposit guarantee fund. The state bank commissioner was also given considerable discretion to determine which new banks merited charters. The reorganization of state institutions and the new regulations slowly brought the situation under control, and by 1920 the fund was restored to solvency.[44] Increased assessments necessary to cover the failure of smaller banks, however, drove the larger banks out of the state system. By 1914 only two state banks remained that had capital greater than the minimum required of national banks.[45] This flight from the state's banking system automatically increased the burden on those remaining in the system and threatened the deposit guarantee fund's operation.

The lessons of Oklahoma's experience were learned slowly. All states adopting deposit insurance after Oklahoma attempted to limit the morally hazardous expansion of loans and deposits by setting capital to deposit ratios. These regulations did not constrain banks, however, and the number of state banks and the size of their operations grew rapidly. Between 1909 and 1914, the number of state banks rose at a rate of 17.3 percent per annum in Texas and 12.6 percent in Nebraska compared to a national average of 4.9 percent. Kansas established a more tightly regulated system of voluntary deposit insurance and consequently had a lower growth rate of 5.4 percent per annum.[46]

The closer regulation of banks in Kansas tended to exclude the smaller banks with more risky portfolios, and the larger banks dominated the Kansas Deposit Guarantee Fund. One half of the state banks subscribed to the fund but they held over 80 percent of the state banks' deposits.[47] The state of Washington's deposit insurance law was modeled after the Kansas statute; it, too, kept out smaller banks by imposing rather strict regulations.[48]

Although most state insurance schemes were set up to maintain the confidence of depositors and diminish the danger of a run on the banks, the systems of Washington and Mississippi were created in response to bank failures. What these states did not foresee was that although deposit

---

[43] Ibid., 283–40.

[44] Robb, *The Guaranty of Bank Deposits*, pp. 105–06.

[45] Ibid., p. 87.

[46] *All Bank Statistics*, figures are calculated from the data provided for each state.

[47] Robb, *The Guaranty of Bank Deposits*, p. 123.

[48] Ibid., pp. 170–72.

insurance, if properly designed, could prevent bank failures by reducing the convertibility worries that led to a depositors' panic, it could not stop the wave of closures that resulted when a new agriculture depression began in the West and the South.

In Mississippi, the boll weevil did its part to promote deposit insurance. The destruction of a large part of the cotton crop in 1912 and 1913 brought down 29 banks in the state.[49] Other deposit insurance statutes had been passed largely in response to the need to curtail panics, but the passage of the Mississippi act at the outset of a depression indicated a serious misunderstanding of the purpose behind the guarantee of deposits. Deposit insurance could only allay a loss of depositor confidence and successfully operate by itself at times when the economy was in good health. If a depression gripped the local or national economy, some other instrument, open market operations or massive discounting, would be necessary to prevent banks from going under. The decline in agricultural prices in the 1920s spelled trouble for the banks in the West and the South. In 1923 the first wave of bank failures that crippled the deposit insurance funds hit these regions. The governing boards were forced either to default on payments or levy increasingly high assessments on the remaining banks in the system. The voluntary system began to melt away. For the state of Washington, 1922 was the last year when receipts from assessments exceeded the disbursements to depositors from failed banks. A year later, membership had fallen off and the guarantee fund was exhausted, paying out only a fraction of the value of insured deposits.[50]

The compulsory systems struggled on for a little longer. In Texas, when agricultural prices began to fall in the 1920s, many small rural banks began to fail, placing a heavy burden on the Deposit Guaranty Fund. Additional levies on the remaining members became necessary. Eventually the legislature was pressured by the banks to alter the 1909 statute and allow banks to switch to the Bond Security System. Banks abandoned the Deposit Guaranty Fund *en masse.* By 1926, a year after the law was changed, there were only 75 banks left in the Fund and they were subjected to an 8.5 percent levy on their capital to replenish the fund. The odium of this heavy tax and widespread hostility to the bond scheme forced the legislature to abolish both types of deposit insurance in 1927.[51]

In Nebraska, the bank commission tried to cope with the situation by refusing to levy a special assessment to replenish the fund. Instead, it took over the operation of technically insolvent banks, if creditors would agree, in the expectation that liabilities could be reduced without resorting to the deposit guarantee fund. By 1928 even these extraordinary measures failed, and a special assessment had to be levied. This was resisted tooth and nail

---

[49] Ibid., pp. 165–70.
[50] *Annual Report of the State Bank Examiner of the State of Washington* (Olympia, 1922, 1923).
[51] Grant and Crum, *The Development of State Chartered Banking,* pp. 123–84.

by the state banks who obtained a court injunction to halt the assessment. The legislature, acknowledging defeat, repealed the deposit insurance law in 1930.[52] The agriculture depression wrecked the rest of the systems as liabilities of the guarantee funds greatly exceeded their assets. By 1929, South Dakota's fund, for example, had $1 million of resources and $37.8 million worth of claims against it. The state legislature dissolved the fund, and after administrative expenses were met the fund paid out less than 1 percent on its outstanding debts.[53]

### BANK FAILURES AND BRANCH BANKING

Banks might have been strengthened and the number of failures decreased if there had been more branching in the 1920s. This assertion is supported by evidence from several sources. An inverse relationship was found to exist between branching and bank failures. The correlation coefficients between failures and two measures of branching, the ratio of branching banks to all commercial banks and the ratio of branch bank offices to all commercial banks in each state for 1925, were −0.196 and −0.214. These correlations were significant at the 9 percent and 7 percent levels. When the bank suspension variable was replaced by the ratio of deposits of suspended banks to the deposits of all commercial banks in a state, the coefficients were −0.211 and −0.203; these were significant at the 7 percent and 8 percent levels.[54] Although these correlations do not evince a particularly strong inverse relationship, they do suggest that branching did impart additional strength to the banking systems of those states that permitted it. Detection of a relation between branch banking and failures is difficult because branching was still quite limited in the 1920s. In 1925, for example, only 2.5 percent of all banks were branching banks and 10.5 percent of all offices were branch bank offices.

Another means of assessing the importance of branching is to examine those states where branch banking was well developed. In 1927, the *Federal Reserve Bulletin* singled out six states—California, Louisiana, Massachusetts, Michigan, New York, and Ohio—where branching was firmly established.[55] In these states in 1925, branching banks were 9.1 percent of all commercial banks and branch bank offices were 30.7 percent of all bank offices. Banks in these six states held $20,346 million in deposits; 13 banks with deposits of $6.1 million failed. Total deposits in banks in the rest of the states were $27,223 million. These states had 618 bank failures with deposits of $167.5 million in 1925. The eight states with deposit in-

[52] Kuhn, *History of Nebraska Banking*, pp. 15–20.

[53] *South Dakota Biennial Report of the Superintendent of Banks* (Pierre, 1930, 1932,), pp. 306; 345.

[54] The data used for this analysis came from *Banking and Monetary Statistics*, pp. 296–300 and *All Bank Statistics*.

[55] *Board of Governors of the Federal Reserve System, Federal Reserve Bulletin* (Washington, D.C., May 1927), p. 317ff.

surance systems suffered from an expansion of banking and a decline in demand for their agricultural products. The result was that they bore a disproportionate share of the bank failures. Their total deposits amounted to only $3,379 million, but in 1925 they had 204 banks with deposits of $46.9 million fail.[56]

The Canadian experience also suggests that branch banking reduced the incidence of bank failures. Between 1920 and 1926 only one bank with liabilities of $18.5 million closed its doors in Canada compared to 3,063 banks with liabilities of $1,085 million that failed in the United States in the same period. The average annual ratio of liabilities of failed banks to total banking liabilities in this period was 0.27 percent for the United States and 0.09 percent for Canada.[57] The Canadian system offered greater safety than the American system. The depositors of the failed Hamilton Bank lost nothing as that bank was absorbed by the Canadian Bank of Commerce.[58] Furthermore, in contrast to the United States banking system which was plagued by bank failures in the 1930s, the Canadian system emerged from the ravages of the Great Depression relatively unscathed.[59]

### CONCLUSION

The failure of state deposit guarantee systems to stem the bank failures of the 1920s and the weakness of the banking industry during the crises of the 1930s were what finally turned banking reform away from efforts to shore up unit banking and toward branching as a means of strengthening the industry and providing increased offices.

State deposit insurance schemes all ended in dismal failure. They had contributed to the rapid growth of many small and vulnerable unit banks in the least economically diversified areas of the country. With no means to counter the agricultural depression of the 1920s, the insuring states saw a rising tide of bank failures cripple their deposit guarantee funds. Unable to protect their unit banking systems from this and the more severe crises of the 1930s, states began to ease restrictions on branch banking. By 1939, Washington and South Dakota allowed statewide branch banking, and Mississippi and North Dakota permitted limited branch banking.[60] This turn of events marked the beginnings of a national shift away from unit banking toward branch banking. The major beneficiary of state experimentation with deposit insurance was the Federal Deposit Insurance Corporation, whose design avoided the errors of previous legislation.[61]

---

[56] *Banking and Monetary Statistics*, pp. 284–85, and *All Bank Statistics*.

[57] Calculated from the data in Beckhart, *The Banking System*, p. 483; *All Bank Statistics*, pp. 24–25; and M. C. Urquhart and K.A.H. Buckley, *Historical Statistics of Canada* (Toronto, 1965), pp. 240–41.

[58] Beckhart, *The Banking System*, p. 338.

[59] George Morrison, *Liquidity Preferences of Commercial Banks* (Chicago, 1966), pp. 63–77.

[60] Bradford, *The Legal Status*, pp. 22–23.

[61] Golembe, "Deposit Insurance Legislation," pp. 195–200.

## State-Sponsored Insurance of Bank Deposits            557

The establishment of state and later federal deposit insurance was a consequence of nineteenth century anti-branching statutes that created a banking system dominated by unit banks. Self-insurance and interbank cooperation to prevent panics via the growth of a nationwide system of branch banking along Canadian lines was unacceptable to the smaller banks, and they sought government insurance instead. The problem-plagued banking structure engendered a weak solution in the form of state deposit insurance. The inherent weaknesses of the state guarantee funds in turn contributed to the problems of banking industry.[62] It was appropriate that the federal government should finally assume the job of insuring banks. With a well designed system, an individual state could insure banks only as long as a deflation or other general financial disturbance did not bring about widespread bank failures. The Federal Deposit Insurance Corporation's successful operation was not threatened by this problem because the risk to which the entire banking system was exposed could be controlled by the Federal Reserve System's open market operations or discounting. This, however, was not the only policy alternative; another was the easing of the constraints on branching by the state legislatures. The irony is that the federal insurance of deposits, which had long been promoted by its supporters to protect unit banking, was installed by the Congress even as state legislatures began to ease the constraints on branching. Federal deposit insurance was an expedient solution. As the states had belatedly realized, however, it was inferior to the establishment of a system of branch banking which, in conjunction with the proper use of other monetary instruments, could have allayed more easily the danger of a panic.

### APPENDIX

The probit procedure assumes that there is some index $I_i$ equal to $X_i'B$, that is, the data matrix times the true response coefficients for each state. If it is assumed the larger $I_i$ is the greater the probability that a state would adopt deposit insurance, then there is a monotonic relationship between the value of $I_i$ and the probability of its legislating deposit insurance. The "true" probability function will then have the characteristics of a cumulative density function (CDF), which probit analysis assumes to be normal. The conditional probability of adopting deposit insurance E given $I_i$ is $P(E/I_i) = F(X_i'B)$ where $F(\cdot)$ is the normal CDF evaluated at $X_i'B = I_i$. In the estimation, the dependent variable was $P_i$ or the probability that a state adopts deposit insurance where $P_i = 1$ if it established a deposit guarantee fund and $P_i = 0$ if it did not. Once the estimation was performed, the estimates of the response coefficient $\hat{B}$ were used to obtain the estimated probabilities $\hat{P}_i = F(X_i'\hat{B}) = F(\hat{I}_i)$. The higher $\hat{I}_i$ was, the greater the likelihood that deposit insurance was adopted.

---

[62] The limitations on branching probably prevented many banks from attaining their optimal size. There appear to have been substantial economies of scale in banking. See John A. James, "Cost Functions of Postbellum National Banks," *Explorations in Economic History*, 15 (Apr. 1978), 184–95, and George Benston, "Economies of Scale in Financial Institutions," *Journal of Money, Credit and Banking*, 4 (May 1972), 312–41.

# [16]

## Deposit insurance: Lessons from the record

The successful state-run bank deposit insurance schemes were broad enough to give near-universal coverage, yet narrow enough to insure tight self-monitoring by banks—a neat trick, and one we may need to emulate

Charles W. Calomiris

The deterioration of the federal deposit insurance funds, particularly the Federal Savings and Loan Insurance Corporation (FSLIC), has become a common theme in the press and a major concern of financial regulators. Estimates of the amount necessary to reimburse depositors' losses in FSLIC member institutions range above $100 billion. The Federal Deposit Insurance Corporation (FDIC) is in much better condition, but some fear that the structural flaws that led to the losses in FSLIC are present in FDIC insurance as well. At the state level, deposit insurance funds for thrifts have been collapsing at a rapid rate. The insolvencies of Mississippi's fund in 1976 and Nebraska's in 1983 have been followed by four others since 1984, and three other state systems are winding down. Only three state-level funds remain, and these have limited their scope.[1]

Recent studies of deposit insurance funds have focused on banks' incentives to take on risky investments when deposit insurance is not fairly priced. It is argued that banks will choose to hold high risk-return portfolios because their losses are shared while their gains are private. Depositors, who would normally withdraw funds from high-risk banks and thus prevent such behavior, have little incentive to do so when their deposits are insured.

This article considers possibilities for deposit insurance reform in the light of historical successes and failures of bank liability

insurance in the United States. I address four central questions: What was the motivation for bank liability insurance historically? Is this concern justified by the historical record? Which "safety nets" for bank liability holders were most successful, and why? What are the lessons of the historical record for current reforms?

### U.S. bank liability insurance before the FDIC

Prior to the creation of the FDIC, bank liability insurance was organized at the state level. These insurance schemes differed in important respects but they had the same essential motivation: to insulate the economy's payments system from the risk of bank failures.[2]

When bankers and depositors have different (asymmetric) information about the safety of banks, concerns about bank solvency can induce "unwarranted" withdrawals from banks and contraction of bank lending. In extreme cases, when banks respond to economy-wide runs by suspending convertibility of their liabilities on demand, asymmetric information can render bank claims useless as a medium of exchange, if uninformed traders become unwilling to accept them.[3]

Charles W. Calomiris is assistant professor of economics at Northwestern University and a consultant to the Federal Reserve Bank of Chicago. He is currently on leave to the Economics Department of Stanford University. He thanks Herbert S. Baer, Charles Kahn, and Edward Nash for helpful comments.

For example, during a recession, the solvency of banks may come to be questioned. Even when the initial disturbance to bank portfolios is small in the aggregate, if depositors are unable to determine precisely *which* banks have suffered from the shock, all banks may be perceived as riskier. Fears of bank insolvency can become self-fulfilling if withdrawal orders and forced asset sales (or the calling of loans) lead to the collapse of banks, and the contraction of credit and the medium of exchange. As a defensive action, banks would often suspend convertibility on demand during such economy-wide runs. Once banks have done this, the uninformed may be unwilling to accept bank claims, or accept them only at a large discount, in fear that the claims were "lemons" being unloaded by knowledgeable insiders.

Deposit insurance removes much of the incentive for economy-wide runs, and if suspension does occur, it eliminates the incentive for insiders to dump bad deposits on the unsuspecting. Thus, bank claims can continue to be a medium of exchange.[4]

What makes the payments system vulnerable to disturbances is that banks historically have performed two tasks simultaneously: They make "information-intensive" loans (loans that are not easily valued in centrally traded markets) and they issue checks and bank notes. If banks did not hold information-intensive loans, then their portfolios could be "marked to market," and the liquidity of their claims would not be reduced during disturbances. Similarly, if banks issued long-term claims that were not used for transactions, shocks to their portfolios would not threaten the payments system. Recent research suggests that demandable debt banking was useful as a disciplinary device to limit the discretion of bankers; this, in turn, helped to make bank claims more liquid.[5]

Reasonable fears of insolvency of a subset of banks, and confusion as to which banks have suffered most from the shock, underlay most financial panics from the Roman bank run of 33 A.D. to those in the U.S. in the nineteenth and twentieth centuries.[6] It is worth noting that a classic lender of last resort, who freely discounts acceptable assets at a market (or penalty) rate, would not provide the same protection to the payments system against

these disturbances as deposit insurance. A lender of last resort can offset shocks to the relative supply of money and marketable assets, but does not insure banks, or resolve the information problem of determining which banks' information-intensive assets have fallen in value, and by how much.

Several recent studies see the development of nineteenth-century clearing houses (beginning in the 1850s) as one means to prevent financial collapse and ensure the continuing flow of transactions through the banking system during crises.[7] Clearing houses performed many of the functions of state liability insurance funds, including the insulation of the payments system from individual or economy-wide bank runs. Clearing house banks banded together during crises to "make a market" in each others' deposits and maintain the interbank check-clearing system, even when the withdrawal of deposits from the system was restricted. By developing self-imposed regulations, including reserve ratios and the restrictions on portfolio holdings, these associations ensured that banks would not take advantage of such co-insurance. Banks had strong incentives to monitor the actions of their partners in the clearing house, and to eject members who broke the rules.

The co-insurance of risk required ease of communication and monitoring among participants to ensure compliance with regulations. Unit banking laws in the North, which created a large number of banks scattered throughout the state, prevented the benefits of private coordination from spreading beyond the cities, and made regional or national clearing houses impracticable.[8]

In the South, the existence of large branching banks made such formal arrangements less necessary. Southern banks were able to maintain liquidity during crises as well as or better than their neighbors to the North. The South's large branching banks used interbank loans and simultaneous region-wide bank suspension in much the same way as the clearing house system.

Self-regulation occurred in the South as in the North, though it could be more informal, due to the smaller number of parties involved. Coordination was facilitated by the clear leader-follower relationship between the large branching banks and the smaller banks.

Branching also reduced the fragility of the system by making it less vulnerable to confusion over the dispersion of solvency risk.

Historians have frequently pointed out that unit banking, which dominated the U.S. experience, made the system particularly vulnerable to crises and encouraged the development of deposit insurance.[9] Both Carter Golembe and Eugene White argue that deposit insurance and unit banking reinforced each other: Without branch banking, an alternative to protect the payments system was necessary; once enacted, deposit insurance removed some of the pressure to allow branch banking.[10]

### Patterns of success and failure

To compare performance it is necessary to settle on a measure of success. I define an ideally successful deposit insurance system as one that fully protects the payments system, without encouraging any excessive risk-taking. Systems that fail to protect the payments system, or those that collapse due to incentive incompatibility, therefore, are complete failures. The various insurance schemes I describe here can be adequately categorized either as complete failures, or as (qualified) successes.

### Three Pre-Civil War failures

*New York* enacted the first government-sponsored insurance plan for bank liabilities in 1829. The Safety Fund Banking System required that all banks renewing charters in New York state join the system. Member banks were required to pay an annual assessment of 1/2 percent of capital until their total payments equaled 3 percent of capital. The accumulated funds would be used to redeem in full the notes and deposits of member banks that failed whenever the failed bank's assets were insufficient. Special assessments were authorized in the event of a shortfall but these were limited to 1/2 percent of capital per year. Note issues were restricted as a function of bank capital, and a board of commissioners was established to examine member banks. By the end of 1837 almost all of New York's banks were members.

New York's Safety Fund failed to provide lasting protection to the payments system. The Panic of 1837 and the subsequent panic and depression of 1839–41, both induced by constrictions of foreign credit by the Bank of England, prompted asset and commodity price declines, immediate bank suspensions, merchant failures, and subsequent bank liquidations. The bank failures experienced by the Safety Fund during the Panic were primarily the result of economy-wide "debt-deflation" shocks, rather than the fault of the insurance system.[11]

But the failure to protect the payments system from 1839 to 1841, and subsequently, was the fault of the Fund and not of the Panic. New York's system failed because it was neither credible nor broadly based, and did not create the proper incentives for prudent risk-taking. The failure is particularly disturbing because the losses of liquidated member banks, and of non-member free banks in New York from 1837 to 1860, were a small portion of aggregate bank capital.[12]

The system was undercut by a 1838 law which allowed entry into banking by uninsured "free banks," whose notes were backed by reserve holdings of bonds, but whose deposit issues were unregulated and uninsured. After the establishment of free banking, no new Safety Fund charters were granted, and upon expiration of charter, banks were invited to join the free banking system. In 1840 more than 90 percent of bank liabilities were covered by the Safety Fund; by 1860, only 2 percent were covered.[13] The protection to the payments system was even less than these proportions indicate, because an attack on any unprotected part of the system sufficient to disrupt interbank check and note clearing threatened the whole.

Further, by limiting the fees paid by member banks to an annual assessment of 1/2 percent, the Safety Fund could not credibly guarantee the value of member banks' notes and deposits and, therefore, could not adequately ensure liquidity of member bank's obligations. In 1842, when the claims of noteholders and depositors on the Fund exceeded available resources, payment was delayed. Later failures by banks in the Fund led to large market discounts on failed banks' notes, indicating that noteholders perceived the insurance to be virtually worthless. Although the Fund was able to make good on all outstanding claims by 1866, this ex post success was not anticipated by the market (Safety-Fund banks' notes traded at high discount rates), and insurance did not provide any protection to the payments system during crises.[14]

After the Fund became delinquent in 1842, the law was amended to protect only noteholders in subsequent bank failures. Thus, the growing deposit base of the insured banks, which financed some 30 percent of bank assets in Safety-Fund and free banks alike, was uninsured. Sudden depositor withdrawals proved particularly important in the onset of the Panic cf 1857 and later panics. The exclusion of demandable deposits and the notes of free banks left the state's banks vulnerable to disintermediation, and eventually to depositor runs, when losses by bank borrowers dependent on the fortunes of the declining bond market of September and October 1857 caused mounting uncertainty about the solvency of New York City banks.[15]

The New York system was also plagued by fraud and excessive risk-taking, resulting in part from inadequate supervision. The Fund failed to levy risk-based premiums, and thus removed the incentives of depositors to avoid risky banks. The resulting additional risk-taking could only be offset by more efficient examination. While regular examinations were called for under the law, they do not seem to have offset the decrease in depositor monitoring. Prior to 1842, when the Safety Fund was perceived by depositors as providing insurance, bank fraud and "unsafe practices" were a far more important cause of failure than afterwards. Sixteen of the twenty-one failures of Safety-Fund banks occurred prior to the end of 1842, and ten of these were traced to fraud or unsafe practices. Of the five post-1842 failures, only two were so described.[16]

The failure of the Safety Fund cannot be blamed on the severity of the shocks that buffeted the banking system. If the Safety Fund had been broad-based in membership and liability coverage, if it had effectively guaranteed payment (say, through unlimited mutual liability of banks), and if it had provided for thorough bank supervision, it could have offered adequate protection to the payments system and prevented crises like the Panic of 1857.[17]

New York's bank liability insurance plan spread to other states in the North. Vermont enacted similar legislation in 1831, and Michigan adopted the New York plan in 1836.

*Vermont's* insurance fund suffered many of the weaknesses of New York's system. Like New York's, its coverage was only partial. While the Vermont system insured notes and deposits of member banks, it did not require bank membership in the system. In 1839, Vermont exempted several banks from joining the system, and in 1840 liability insurance became voluntary. Banks could withdraw from the system with the full value of their contributions to the fund.[18] The establishment of a free banking statute in 1851 created a further alternative to insured banking in Vermont.

The insurance fund covered 56 percent of bank liabilities in 1840; this rose to 78 percent in 1845 and fell to 8 percent by 1858. In 1859, the last bank withdrew and the fund was closed. Outstanding obligations of $17,000— some 28 percent of total claims on the fund — were never paid.

The Vermont fund was a failure, not only because it failed to insure creditors ex post, but because, like New York's system, it failed to provide credible backing for bank liabilities ex ante. As in New York, the upper bound placed on annual assessments implied that bank liabilities could exceed the ceiling on fund resources. This was compounded by provisions giving solvent banks the option to withdraw. Thus, depositors could not reasonably have expected that losses to a few banks would be covered by remaining banks. In fact, the Vermont system collapsed under the weight of only two bank failures in its 29-year history, one in 1839, the other in 1857. These failures were sufficient to force other banks out of the system.

By allowing banks to join and depart at will, the fund suffered, and was ultimately undone by, the problem of *adverse selection*. Adverse selection takes place when the insurance encourages only the worst risks to participate. When failures occur they force up premiums, raising the cost of remaining in the system. The best banks — which stand to gain the least — opt out and the average riskiness of insured banks rises. Subsequent failures lead to further selection against the best banks, until finally only the worst risks remain.

In Vermont, adverse selection also operated at the point of entry into the system. While the first failure resulted from fraud at a

# TABLE 1

Pre-Civil War insurance systems

| State and period | Supervisory agency | Enforcement powers | Funding method | Non-member banks |
|---|---|---|---|---|
| New York 1829–1866 | 1829–37 Three bank commissioners; one appointed by Governor, two by banks. | Could apply to court for injunction to stop operation of insolvent banks or banks in violation of law. | Safety fund, with upper bound on annual assessments. | Free banks, after 1838. |
| | 1837–43 Three bank commissioners; appointed by Governor. | | | |
| | 1843–51 State comptroller. | | | |
| | 1851–66 State Banking Dept. | | | |
| Vermont 1831–1858 | 1831–37 Three banks commissioners; one appointed by Governor, two by banks. | Could close insolvent banks or banks in violation of law. | Safety fund with upper bound on annual assessments. | Member banks could join and leave at will. Free banks, after 1851. |
| | 1837–58 One bank commissioner appointed by legislature. | | | |
| Michigan 1836–1842 | 1836–40 Bank commissioners appointed by Governor. | Could close insolvent banks or banks in violation of law. | Safety fund with upper bound on annual assessments. | All state banks (including free banks) participated in system. |
| | 1840–42 State's Attorney General. | | | |
| Indiana 1834–1865 | Board of Directors; four appointed by legislature and one by each insured bank. | Could close banks in violations of law or regulations. Could regulate ratio of assets to capital. Could regulate dividend payments. | Mutual guarantee without limit. | Free banks, after 1851. |
| Ohio 1845–1866 | Board of Control; one member appointed by each insured bank | Could close banks at will for violations of regulations. Could regulate total notes outstanding, or total liabilities. Could regulate dividend payments. Could regulate notes of vault cash to total reserves. Could require banks to make interbank loans. | Mutual guarantee without limit and safety fund. | "Independent" banks after 1845, and free banks, after 1851. |
| Iowa 1858–1866 | Board of Control; three appointed by legislature, one by each insured bank. | Could close banks at will for violations of regulations. Could regulate total notes or liabilities. Could regulate dividend payments. | Mutual guarantee without limit and safety fund. | No free banks chartered under free banking statute. |

SOURCE: Golembe and Warburton, *Insurance of Bank Obligations in Six States, passim.*

long-time member, the second failure was that of a new entrant that joined the fund only after its prospects worsened.[19]

A successful, broadly based insurance program in Vermont was feasible. The actual obligations incurred by the fund could have been paid if withdrawal had not been allowed. Golembe and Warburton estimate that, had the fund been expanded to cover all banks, its insurance liability would have been increased by roughly $100,000, and that this could easily have been covered by surviving banks.[20]

*Michigan's* program extended coverage to all liabilities and all banks (including free banks). Unlike the Vermont system, however, Michigan's was established on the eve of a financial crisis, and there was no time to accumulate funds with which to meet its first obligations. In the absence of a mutual-guarantee commitment or state lending to reimburse borrowers, the fund could not maintain its commitments or keep the payments system afloat. Under pressure by healthy banks, mandatory membership was dropped, and uninsured free banking became the alternative system of choice. There were no banks left in the fund by 1841, and it was closed in 1842.

The failures of these three pre-Civil War insurance systems reflected basic flaws in their design. Protection of the payments system requires an insurance fund that is broad in its coverage of demandable claims. Alternative free-bank chartering or voluntary insurance precludes protection of the payments system and weakens deposit insurance through adverse selection. Furthermore, fixed premiums, with upper bounds for special assessments and no state guarantees, cannot provide a credible guarantee to depositors. Finally, in the absence of effective regulation and supervision, fixed-fee deposit insurance involves *moral hazard* — that is, the potential for fraud or excessive risk-taking — because it subsidizes risk-taking by individual banks. While all three insurance systems limited bank assets as a proportion of capital and loans to insiders and provided for examinations of bank records by government officials, supervision was ineffectual; unsound banking practices were not detected until after banks had failed.

### Pre-Civil War success stories

*Indiana* enacted a different kind of liability insurance plan in 1834. Unlike the systems of New York, Vermont, and Michigan, the Indiana system charged no advance fees, and special assessments were made as needed without limit. Liabilities of failed banks not covered by liquidated assets were redeemable by surviving banks without limit. Both notes and deposits were insured. This "mutual guarantee" system became the basis for similar legislation in Ohio in 1845 and Iowa in 1858.

The banks in the Indiana system, though separately owned and operated, were called "branches" of the State Bank of Indiana.[21] From its inception in 1834 until the chartering of free banks began in 1851, the system covered virtually all the liabilities of banks in Indiana. After that date, the two systems existed side by side.

Rapid growth by free banks meant that by the beginning of January 1854, 25.7 percent of the obligations and only 12.6 percent of the banks in the state were insured. But the financial crises of 1854–1855 and 1857 wrought havoc on the state's free banks, and the proportion of insured banks rose and remained high until the enactment of the national banking system. Between 1858 and 1864 over half the state's banks, and an average of three-fourths of the liabilities, were in the insured system.[22]

The system's president and board of directors had broad powers to investigate bank operations and to close banks if necessary. Examinations were required at least every six months. Upon a two-thirds majority vote of the board, any bank could be closed, without recourse to the courts. The board also had power to set limits on the volume of member bank assets relative to capital.[23]

Most board members were appointed by the individual banks; the president initially was appointed by the legislature, but later was appointed by the board. Thus, control of the supervisory authority was in the hands of the member banks. This was an important feature, because it gave regulatory authority to those with a strong interest in monitoring the behavior of member banks. Member banks had access to a particular bank's records at any time and could limit risk-taking by restricting a bank's loans relative to capital or, in extreme cases, by closing the bank.

Regulation served to limit the potential for excessive risk-taking by members. Dividend payment policy, loans to officers and directors, loan interest rates, and loans in excess of $500 were all regulated in ways that served to protect the system. Stockholders were liable for bank losses up to twice their capital contribution and officers and directors of failed banks were presumed guilty of fraud until they proved otherwise. If they failed to prove their innocence, their liability was unlimited.[24]

The Indiana system was well conceived. Its coverage was thorough (until 1851) and credible. It established strong supervisory authority to eliminate the problem of moral hazard, and gave that authority to the banks themselves, which (because of mutual liability) had an incentive to implement it properly. The board was quick to take disciplinary action to enforce compliance and corrected problems before they threatened bank solvency.[25]

Indiana's system was extraordinarily successful. During its thirty years of operation no insured bank failed, and only one was briefly suspended at the behest of the board, in response to perceived irregularities in its loan portfolio.

The Indiana system weathered the Panic of 1837 admirably, even though the Panic came only three years after the system was enacted. The mutual-guarantee provision removed the dependence on pre-existing funds that proved fatal to Michigan's system. Indiana's insured banks were not able to avoid nationwide suspensions of convertibility that occurred from May 1837 to August 1838 and November 1839 to June 1842. But this was the last suspension for insured banks. When the regional panic of 1854–1855 hit, the insured banks all survived without suspending convertibility, while 55 of Indiana's 94 newly created free banks failed. When the Panic of 1857 came, the insured banks again avoided failure and suspension of convertibility, while 14 of the 32 free banks in Indiana failed.[26]

***Ohio's*** insured banking system was organized later, in 1845. Ohio was already a mature state with a long history of banking under special chartering. The weakening of the system after the Panic of 1837 and the lapsing of several charters in 1843 and 1844 provided an opportunity for restructuring.

Like Indiana, Ohio adopted limitations on loans to insiders and restrictions on loan interest rates. Banks were required to maintain

reserves equal to 30 percent of their outstanding notes. In addition to unlimited mutual guarantee, Ohio banks were required to deposit with the Board of Control assets equal to ten percent of their outstanding notes. This "safety fund" ensured rapid redemption of any liabilites incurred by the system. Bank circulation was also bounded as a proportion of capital. Thus, for example, a bank issuing $700,000 in notes was required to maintain a level of capital in excess of $500,000 and a liquid reserve in excess of $215,000.

The Board of Control had virtually unlimited authority over individual banks, with voting power by board members commensurate with bank size (a proxy for the degree of insurance provided by a bank under mutual liability). The board could compel banks to reduce their notes or deposits. The board could close banks on its own authority, or alternatively, it could recapitalize the banks, using the resources of the fund. In six of ten cases of bank difficulty the board chose aid or a combination of aid and reorganization instead of liquidation. More than half of the amount actually expended by the board was for aid rather than payments to noteholders.

The Ohio system was established alongside eight pre-existing banks and a new alternative system of "independent" banks was chartered in 1845 as well. A free banking statute was passed in 1851, providing an additional alternative to insured banking. Furthermore, insurance did not guarantee all liabilities, but was limited to the notes of member banks. From 1850 to 1864 insured banks accounted for between 60 and 70 percent of bank liabilities in Ohio. Roughly two-thirds of insured banks' liabilities took the form of bank notes. Thus, the system guaranteed about half the Ohio payments system.

While insurance was limited to the bank notes of member banks *de jure*, it acted *de facto* to insure deposits of member banks as well through the discretionary actions of the Board of Control. The board had authority to call on member banks to loan money to each other during times of crisis. During the Panic of 1857 the board used this authority to coordinate the banking system's response through interbank transfers, thereby preventing the national financial crisis from crippling Ohio's banking sector. In fact, by keeping the insured banks from suspending, the board avoided failures throughout the system, as insured banks seem to have provided liquidity to uninsured independent and free banks. Thus, the board acted to protect the entire payments system from precisely the kind of economywide disturbances that prompted the establishment of deposit insurance.

Ohio was one of the very few states to avoid general suspension of specie convertibility during the Panic of 1857, and only one Ohio bank failed.[27] Ohio's success is remarkable, because many Ohio banks had substantial deposits on account with the Ohio Life Insurance and Trust Company, whose failure in August of 1857 marked the beginning of the financial crisis. Moreover, each member of the insured system was obligated to redeem all other member banks' notes on demand, a move which could have accelerated the rate of disintermediation.

This exceptional performance can be traced to the wise and timely policies of the Board of Control. First, the board acted quickly to insulate the banks from the Ohio Life and Trust's failure. Assets of the failed bank were transferred directly to its depositor banks to secure their deposits. This effectively subordinated the debts of individual depositors and other creditors of the Ohio Life and Trust to those of the Ohio banks. Some of these assets were liquidated to help keep the banks afloat during the crisis.

Next, the board established a program of mutual assistance among the banks. Within a few days after the failure of the Ohio Life and Trust, the first letter from the secretary of the board was dispatched instructing the Commercial Branch in Cleveland to render aid to the Merchants Branch of Cleveland. Over the next two months four insured banks received $56,000 in assistance. All of these transactions were treated explicitly as interest-bearing loans, backed by collateral in the form of time notes or paper currency, and guaranteed by the insurance system as a whole.[28] More important than the amount transferred, however, was the clear signal the board's policy sent. The risk of runs on banks would be borne collectively.

The stability of the insured banks proved "contagious;" the collective action of the large insured banks reduced the threat to the pay-

ments system. In addition, evidence suggests that the insured banks came to the aid of uninsured banks. As a result, Ohio had the lowest bank-failure rate in the North.

*Iowa's* bank insurance legislation, enacted in 1858, was the last of the pre-Civil War period. The success of Ohio's system led to imitation in Iowa, and many of the key political figures backing the plan had been residents in Ohio with experience in its insured system. Features of the Iowa plan included: mutual guarantee protection, a "safety fund," limitation of insurance to bank notes, self-regulation by the Board of Directors of the State Bank, co-insurance, and par convertibility of members' notes.

In addition to a 25 percent specie reserve against notes outstanding, banks had to maintain a 25 percent reserve on their deposits. Note issues were limited as a decreasing proportion of capital. Loans to stockholders and directors were limited. Stockholders were made to assume double liability in the event of bank failure. Interest charged on loans was limited, and violation of the law was penalized by cancellation of the debt. The supervisory board has broad powers of enforcement, including closure and limitations of dividend payments. Board records indicate thorough regular examination of banks, and willingness to force compliance by restricting dividends.

The state-insured system comprised the entire chartered banking system of Iowa. Its coverage of the banking system was virtually complete.[29] During its seven years of operation no insured bank failed in Iowa. Two banks experienced difficulties during this period, one due to fraudulent activities by a cashier, the other due to portfolio deterioration. The case of fraud was solved quickly with a change in management, and the other case was solved with a collateralized loan. Neither resulted in losses to the system.

Iowa's system was unique among pre-Civil War insurance plans in that it was never tested by an economy-wide financial crisis. However, its close resemblance to Ohio's plan makes it likely that it would have done as well as Ohio.

The lessons of success

The successful liability insurance schemes of Indiana, Ohio, and Iowa shared common features with each other and with private clear-

## TABLE 2

### Insurance systems after 1907

| State and period | Supervisory agency | Enforcement powers | Funding method | Non-member banks |
|---|---|---|---|---|
| Oklahoma 1907–1923 | 1907–1913 State banking board consisted of Governor, Lt. Governor, Auditor, Treasurer, and President of Agriculture Board. | Bank commissioner could take possession of and liquidate banks, or revoke bank charter for cause. | 1907–1909 Safety fund with unlimited special assessments. | National banks. |
|  | 1913–1923 State banking board consisted of three members chosen by Governor from a list of banks' nominees, and the banking commissioner and assistant commissioner. |  | 1909–1923 Safety fund with upper bound on annual assessments. |  |
| Texas 1909–1925 | State banking board consisted of Attorney General, Commissioner of Insurance and Banking, and Treasurer of State. | Bank commissioner could take possession of and liquidate banks, remove officials from member banks, and adopt rules and regulations as needed | Safety fund with upper bound on annual assessments. | National banks and state banks that chose private insurance. |
| Kansas 1909–1929 | Governor appointed Commissioner of Banking and Insurance and his deputies. | Commissioner of banking and insurance could close and take possession of banks and appoint receiver. | Safety fund with upper bound on annual assessments. | National banks or state banks that chose not to participate. |
| Nebraska 1909–1930 | State banking board consisted of Governor, Attorney General, and auditor of public accounts. | Board could take possession of bank and apply for receiver. | Safety fund with upper bound on annual assessments. | National banks. |
| South Dakota 1909–1931 | Depositors Guaranty Fund Commission composed of public examiner and three members appointed by Governor from a list of twelve bank nominees. | Commission could take possession and liquidate. | Safety fund with upper bound on annual assessments. | National banks, or state banks that chose not to participate. After 1916, compulsory for state banks. |
| North Dakota 1917–1929 | Depository Guaranty Fund Commission composed of Governor, State Examiner, and three appointees of Governor. | Commission could take possession and apply for receiver. | Safety fund with upper bound on annual. assessments. | National banks. |
| Washington 1917–1929 | Guaranty Fund Board consisted of Governor, State Examiner, three appointees of Governor, two of which were be officers of director of member banks. | State examiner could take possession and apply for receiver, or cancel insurance for violation of law. | Safety fund with upper bound on annual assessments. | State banks choosing not to join. National banks. |
| Mississippi 1914–1930 | Three independent district examiners elected by popular vote. | Examiners could take possession and liquidate banks. | Safety fund with upper bound on annual assessments. | National banks. |

SOURCES: Robb, *The Guaranty of Bank Deposits*; Barnett, *State Bank and Trust Companies*; Cooke, "The Insurance of Bank Deposits;" *Laws of Kansas,* 1909; *Laws of Nebraska,* 1909; *Laws of Oklahoma,* 1907-1908; *Laws of Mississippi,* 1914; *Session Laws of South Dakota,* 1909; *Supplement to the 1913 laws of North Dakota*; *General Laws of the State of Texas,* 1909; *Pierce's Washington Code, 1919: Annotated Cyclopedic.*

ing house arrangements. These included thorough coverage of the payments system (whether *de jure* or *de facto*) made credible by the mutual guarantee commitment of member banks, provisions for sufficient reserves to ensure liquidity during crises, and the effective co-insurance of liquidity risk. Thoroughness of coverage due to limited competition by other forms of banking and compulsory membership without the opportunity for contingent entry and exit also limited the potential for adverse selection. Moral hazard was avoided by effective supervision of individual banks.

An especially important feature of the three successful insurance schemes and clearing houses was the alignment of the incentive to regulate and the authority to regulate. The mutual guarantee feature made it in the interest of members to establish effective means to discipline each other. By giving members control over the supervisory authorities, the legislators provided them with the means to act in their own interest and in the collective interest, by restricting excessive risk-taking and free riding. The vigilance of the three bank-operated supervisory bodies, as compared with those in the unsuccessful systems, is attested to by the number of fraudulent or risky practices that were detected and corrected early. Furthermore, by granting the supervisory authority to banks (which presumably had a comparative advantage in monitoring each other) the government could benefit from bankers' expertise in identifying unsafe or dishonest practices. Finally, by giving bankers the choice whether to liquidate or reorganize troubled banks, legislators ensured that this decision would be made by the best informed parties, who also had an interest in minimizing the cost.

While these systems were successful in providing protection to the payments system, they did so at some cost. Reserve requirements entail foregone earnings, and restrictions on portfolio investments reduce the asset opportunities of banks, and may cause scarcity of credit for some worthy enterprises. Supervision entails costs as well. The similarities, however, with privately developed schemes of regulation through clearing houses suggest that the state systems were not far in cost from privately determined (and presumably cost-minimizing) alternatives.

### Bank note insurance under the National Banking System

The National Banking System was enacted in 1863 primarily as a war-financing measure to increase the demand for government bonds. Its 10 percent federal tax on state-chartered bank notes effectively put an end to the antebellum liability insurance systems, all of which had ceased operations by 1866. The advantage of joining the state-insured systems, rather than the free-banking system, had been the low cost of note issues, given the high reserve requirements of the other state-chartered (free) banks.[30] When this advantage was removed, banks opted either for uninsured state charters or national charters, and most of the previously insured banks chose national charters.

The National Banking System probably reduced the safety of the payments system. It drove out the successful state insurance programs and precluded further imitation of their success by other states. It substituted the narrower insurance of national bank notes, backed by government bonds and guaranteed by the Treasury, for the broader coverage of notes and deposits found in the successful state systems. Furthermore, bank runs by noteholders were not the primary threat to banks by the 1850s. Bond and specie reserve requirements against note issues and subordination of deposits to notes made noteholders' risks minimal. Even during suspensions of convertibility, discounts on notes were small, and bank failures often resulted in little or no loss for noteholders.[31] These considerations explain why conversion to the national system was slow initially, and had to be induced by the 10 percent tax on state bank note issues.

### Later deposit insurance systems

Deposits were not insured under the National Banking System. But, partly in response to the increased (regulatory) cost of note finance, and partly because of developments in the technology of processing checks, banks turned more and more to deposits as the principal means of financing bank activities.[32] The ratio of deposits to currency rose from 1.0 in 1860 to 1.5 in 1870. By 1900, deposits were five times currency in circulation.[33]

As uninsured deposits became a larger part of the banking system's balance sheet, financial crises and the risks to the payments system came to be identified with runs by depositors and difficulties in the transactability of deposits. As early as 1857, runs by depositors had become the primary threat to the liquidity of banks.[34] Under the National Banking System and its federally insured currency, crises were exclusively deposit-related.

One option to insulate banks from such disturbances was branch banking, and a movement arose to eliminate restrictions on branching. The political forces of unit banking, however, proved too powerful. When, in the aftermath of the Panic of 1907, branching was increasingly advocated, eight states established insurance funds instead.

I evaluate the performance of four of these systems below. Because the other states' systems were organized just before, or in the midst of, adverse economic shocks, their failures are less instructive about the relative advantages of different plans and the potential for excessive risk-taking.

*Oklahoma* was the first state to initiate deposit insurance following the Panic of 1907. It established a fixed-premium system with a provision for emergency assessments. The fund promised full immediate payment to bank depositors upon bank failure. Deposit insurance was compulsory for state-chartered banks and voluntary for national banks. National bank participation was precluded, however, by a Comptroller of the Currency ruling in 1908 that prohibited membership in state insurance schemes. Entry and exit from the system, therefore, accompanied change of charter.

The Oklahoma system provides nearly perfect conditions to examine the potential for moral hazard and adverse selection. Entry and exit into the system were essentially voluntary, and the actions of member banks were virtually unfettered.

When Oklahoma enacted its deposit insurance scheme, there were many private banks that had never been subject to any regulation. Deposit insurance was one of the first pieces of legislation passed in the state, which had achieved statehood only in 1907. The existence of the private banks meant that potential members of the insurance system included banks with which regulators had virtually no experience, in addition to existing banks chartered by the territory and national banks that

wished to convert to state charters in order to join the system.

The authority to examine banks was vested in the Bank Commissioner. All banks were examined before being admitted to the system. The entry examinations were superficial. Within sixty days thirty-one bank examiners evaluated the solvency of 468 banks. Because there were no limits on leverage or clear standards of banking practice, virtually all banks passed their examinations.[35]

Although the Bank Commissioner also had authority to limit the rate of interest paid on deposits (thereby limiting a bank's ability to attract funds for high-risk investments), these ceilings were not effective. Bankers found it easy to disguise larger-than-legal payments to depositors.[36] Binding regulations on banks in the system were virtually non-existent.

Banks hurried to take advantage of the plan. From June 1907[37] to June 1909, deposits in state-chartered banks rose from $17.3 million to $45 million. The number of banks in the state system rose from 470 to 662, while the number of national banks fell from 294 to 242.

The first failure of an insured bank occurred in September of 1909. The Columbia Bank and Trust Company, the largest bank in the state, failed with nearly $3 million dollars in liabilities, some 6 percent of all bank deposits covered by the fund. The existing balance of the fund was insufficient to pay depositors, whose losses were met by a special assessment on member banks.

The experience of the Columbia Bank and Trust is instructive. Prior to passage of the insurance law, the bank had operated an unexceptional banking business. In October 1908, the bank was taken over by an oil speculator, W. L. Norton, who used the bank to finance his speculative oil enterprises. A decline in the oil market brought down his thinly leveraged enterprises, and with them, the bank.

In one year, Norton had increased bank liabilities from $365,000 to $2.8 million. He attracted depositors by offering insured deposits and paid more than the legally allowed rate of interest. Some of the largest depositors in the bank were smaller banks, which failed along with Columbia when regulators decided to pay individual depositors before paying other banks.[38]

Almost immediately, under pressure from surviving banks, new legislation, which took effect in June 1909, sought to deal with the problems of the fund. In part, the changes served to protect low-risk banks at the expense of reducing coverage of the payments system. Deposits were limited to ten times capital. The liability of members for assessments was limited to 2 percent per year of deposits. After 1916, this upper bound was further reduced to 0.25 percent of deposits.

Table 3 shows that the 1909 law did not eliminate the risk differential between the state and national systems, as indicated by the differing failure rates of state and national banks. During the period the insurance plan was in operation, 180 state banks, or some 35.6 percent of the average number of insured banks, failed, compared with 27 national bank failures, representing 7.6 percent of national banks. The higher risk-taking of state banks is also visible in the extraordinarily high average dividend payments that stockholders of state banks were receiving (which presumably reflected the funding of high-risk projects). In 1914, Oklahoma's insured banks paid a 17.9 percent dividend, compared with a 12.6 percent dividend by national banks in the state. The national average dividend rates of state and national banks were 10 and 11.4 percent, respectively, and the average for state banks in Western states was 12.5 percent.[39]

The 1909 limitation on special assessments meant that the fund no longer guaranteed the liquidity of the payments system. After 1914, depositors of failed banks did not receive immediate reimbursement; only in 1920 did the fund's resources catch up to its liabilities. In the interim, the probability of repayment was far from certain, and the fund did not provide effective insurance to the payments system. The fund's positive net balance was short-lived. After 1920 the fund remained illiquid, with increasing failures caused by the agricultural depression in the Southwest. In 1923, the insurance legislation was repealed with outstanding obligations to depositors of $7.5 million.[40]

Without being able to force banks to remain in the system, the state had little chance of stabilizing the banking system by increasing the payments of members. Increasing the costs of membership simply encouraged more

low-risk banks to join the national system. Indeed, adverse selection caused a decline in membership, even under the limited assessments of the law as amended in 1909 and 1916. From 1910 to 1914, the number of national banks in Oklahoma rose from 225 to 343, while the number of state banks fell from 692 to 574.

There is little doubt that drastic price declines in oil in 1909 and wheat in 1920 precipitated the bank failures that brought an end to the system. Furthermore, it is in the nature of a state-level insurance system that such region-specific shocks may be practically uninsurable. The resources of a state deposit fund, or even a state government, are, after all, ultimately limited by the resources of the state itself. In contrast, a federal insurance system can pool risks of specific regions, and can rely on the ability of the federal government to create money during liquidity, or even solvency, crises.[42]

Still, it would be wrong to view the failure of Oklahoma's system as inevitable. Moral hazard and adverse selection were clearly important. The differential failure rates of insured and national banks, which became most pronounced during the agricultural crisis, indicate that excessive risk-taking during the price booms played an important role in the Oklahoma system's collapse. From 1909 to 1921, 4.8 percent of the average number of insured banks failed, compared with 0.9 percent of national banks. During the agricultural decline, from 1922 to 1924, 24.1 percent of state banks failed, while only 6.1 percent of national banks failed. The liberal lending policies of the insured banks promoted excessive leveraging of farmers and banks and made the system susceptible to price shocks.

*Kansas'* system took effect on July 1, 1909. Like the amended Oklahoma plan, the Kansas fund was financed by annual assessments with an upper bound. The Kansas plan contained three important features, however, that made it different: the degree of regulation and enforcement was higher; reimbursement of depositors was not immediate; and membership was voluntary. Regulatory provisions served to protect Kansas from the extremes of moral hazard experienced in Oklahoma's first years, but voluntary exit and entry invited problems of adverse selection.

## TABLE 3

### Membership and failures of national and state-chartered banks in four post-1907 insured states

| | OKLAHOMA | | TEXAS | | KANSAS | | | NEBRASKA | |
| --- | --- | --- | --- | --- | --- | --- | --- | --- | --- |
| | State | National | State | National | Insured state | Uninsured state | National | State | National |
| Insurance begins | 1908 | – | 1910 | – | 1909 | – | – | 1911 | – |
| Number of banks in year before operation of insured system | 393 | 294 | 616 | 528 | – | 749 | 208 | 670 | 232 |
| Number of banks in year after beginning of insured system | 613 | 242 | 828 | 511 | 456[1] | 443[1] | 207 | 693 | 245 |
| Number of banks | | | | | | | | | |
| 1915 | 558 | 351 | 997 | 537 | 526 | 427 | 215 | 803 | 212 |
| 1920 | 612 | 348 | 1,125 | 556 | 676 | 420 | 249 | 1,037 | 188 |
| 1923 | 446 | 459 | 1,071 | 561 | 681 | 357 | 266 | 968 | 182 |
| 1925 | 381[2] | 393 | 943 | 642 | 611 | 381 | 258 | 939 | 172 |
| 1930 | 322[2] | 278[2] | 762[2] | 593[2] | 0 | 806 | 245 | 625 | 171 |
| Insurance ends | 1923 | – | 1925 | – | 1929 | – | – | 1930 | – |
| Number of failures | | | | | | | | | |
| up to 1920 | | | 17 | 4 | | | | | |
| up to 1921 | 29[3] | 3 | 51 | 12 | 5 | 11 | 2 | 20 | 5 |
| 1920–1922 | | | | | 17 | 6 | 0 | | |
| 1920–1923 | 68 | 7 | | | | | | | |
| 1920–1925 | | | 98[4] | 14 | | | | | |
| 1922–1924 | 106 | 27 | 44 | 6 | 42 | 12 | 4 | 58 | 11 |
| 1924–1926 | | | | | 35 | 10 | 2 | | |
| 1921–1930 | | | | | | | | 329 | 31 |
| Percent failing[5] | | | | | | | | | |
| up to 1920 | | | 1.8 | 0.8 | | | | | |
| up to 1921 | 4.8 | 0.9 | 5.1 | 2.3 | 0.9 | 2.4 | 0.9 | 2.6 | 2.4 |
| 1920–1922 | | | | | 2.5 | 1.4 | 0.0 | | |
| 1920–1923 | 12.5 | 1.7 | | | | | | | |
| 1920–1925 | | | 9.1 | 2.4 | | | | | |
| 1922–1924 | 24.1 | 6.1 | 4.1 | 1.1 | 5.9 | 3.0 | 1.5 | 6.0 | 6.1 |
| 1924–1926 | | | | | 5.3 | 2.6 | 0.7 | | |
| 1921–1930 | | | | | | | | 38.5 | 18.2 |

[1] Data are for 1912.
[2] Insurance no longer in effect.
[3] 95 banks closed, but 66 were reorganized with no loss to the insurance fund.
[4] 150 banks closed, but 52 were reorganized with no loss to the insurance fund.
[5] Percent of banks failing is defined as the number of failures divided by the average number of banks in existence during the period.
SOURCE: *Annual Reports*, U.S. Comptroller of the Currency, 1909-1930; *All Bank Statistics: U.S., 1896-1955*, Board of Governors; Robb, *The Guaranty of Bank Deposits*; *Annual Report*, 1956, Federal Deposit Insurance Corporation, pp. 66-70.

By not endeavoring to reimburse depositors until after the liquidation of bank assets, the legislation failed to provide effective protection of the payments system. Liquidity crises are aggravated by delaying depositors' access to liquid resources. Moreover, when ultimate reimbursement is not certain, delays reduce the expected value of protection (and depositors' current net worth).

The key regulatory provisions intended to enhance soundness included: limitation of membership to banks in operation for at least one year; limitation of interest on deposits to 3 percent; a maximum deposit-to-capital ratio of ten; and double liability for bank stockholders (which had a similar effect to doubling the capital requirement). Perhaps most important, the law threatened to withdraw deposit insurance from banks found to be violating these regulations. This created an incentive for depositors to be concerned about the operation of the bank and thus discouraged bank violations of regulations, since offending banks would find it difficult to attract depositors.

Early growth under the voluntary Kansas plan was moderate compared to that of Oklahoma, and followed earlier trends, indicating less potential for abuse of insurance protection. In the five years prior to the legislation state banks increased from 572 to 778; from 1909 to 1914 their number (insured and uninsured) had risen to 932. Still, state-system growth was large relative to the national banks which showed virtually no growth in number or assets from 1909 to 1914.

The wartime boom of wheat and livestock prices initially masked the higher riskiness of insured banks' portfolios. As Table 3 shows, the percentage of failures from 1909 to 1921 was 0.9 for both insured and national banks. Uninsured state banks had a higher failure rate, but this seems due to the selection bias of the system, which excluded banks until they had been in operation for a year. Non-member state banks tended to be smaller and younger and, hence, more vulnerable. As farm incomes declined and borrower losses mounted, however, the insured-bank failure rate rose.

By 1925 healthy insured banks were leaving the system at a rapid rate, and by the end of 1926 only a handful remained. From 1922 to 1924, 5.9 percent of insured banks failed, compared with 3.0 percent of uninsured state banks, and 1.5 percent of national banks. From 1924 to 1926, 5.3 percent of insured banks failed, compared with 2.6 percent of other state banks and 0.7 percent of national banks.

In 1929 the insurance legislation was repealed with $7.2 million in outstanding claims.[43] While the regional agricultural crisis of the 1920s triggered the demise of the system, as in Oklahoma the relative failure experiences of national banks, non-participating state-chartered banks, and insured banks indicate that excessive risk-taking and adverse selection increased the fragility of the insured system. As one would expect, loan risk differentials became increasingly visible during bad times.

*The Nebraska law* came into full force in July 1911. In most respects Nebraska followed the lead of Kansas. However, unlike Kansas, membership was compulsory for state-chartered banks. Thus adverse selection was less of a problem in Nebraska than in Kansas.

Apparently bankers found the system attractive. From 1911 to 1914, the number of state banks rose from 661 to 910, and the assets of state banks tripled. Over the same period, the number of national banks declined from 246 to 191.

As in Kansas and Oklahoma, the greater risk-taking of the insured banks became increasingly visible in Nebraska as agricultural income fell. As Table 3 shows, from 1911 to 1924 the failure rates of state and national banks were virtually identical. As falling incomes became translated into bank loan losses, the state bank failure rate rose dramatically relative to the national bank rate. From 1921 to 1930, 38.5 percent of average state bank membership failed, compared to 18.2 percent of national banks. Declining membership from 1922 to 1930 contributed to the high state failure rate in the 1920s, but most of the difference was due to the greater risk-taking of state banks. The Nebraska law was repealed in 1930 with $20 million in unpaid depositor claims.[44]

*The Texas system* began operation in January 1910. Texas legislators tried to avoid the problems of Oklahoma's early experience by limiting deposits to between five and ten times capital. Special assessments were limited to a maximum of 2 percent of deposits per year. As in Oklahoma, the Texas law provided for immediate payment of depositors at failed banks. Although the Texas statute did not limit interest on deposits, it restricted coverage to deposits receiving no interest.

A unique feature of the Texas law was the establishment of two separate deposit insurance systems. Banks could either join the guarantee fund, or opt for a different plan in which they would secure insurance privately and place the private bond with the state authorities. In the second plan, insurance could take the form of "a bond, policy of insurance, or other guaranty of indemnity in an amount equal to their capital stock." In no case, however, could the amount of the bond be lower than one-half of average deposits for the preceding year.[45] Once banks had joined, the law did not permit them to switch from one plan to the other. The potential benefits of free-riding and the opportunity costs of investing in bonds seem to have favored the guaranty plan over the bond plan or national charters. Some 541 banks joined the guaranty system, while only 43 joined the bond plan in the first year.

Predictably, the Texas plan suffered the same problems as that of Oklahoma. Initially, growth was rapid. From 1908 to 1912, state banks increased in number from 506 to 878, while national charters fell from 533 to 515. But the combination of lax regulation and enforcement and the potential for moral hazard undermined the system. The problems in Texas came earlier than those in Kansas. Texas, like Oklahoma, was a cotton-producing state, and suffered from the poor harvests and falling prices of cotton from 1913 to 1915. Texas also followed Oklahoma's example in admitting many newly organized banks into the insured system with minimal examination.[46] From 1910 to 1920 the failure rate among member banks was 1.8 percent, while the failure rate for national banks was 0.8 percent.

The fund managed to reimburse depositors at 17 failed banks in full from 1910 to 1920. However, as Table 3 shows, there was a steady migration of members to the national system. When the fall in agricultural prices came in the 1920s, the insurance system was unable to support deposits of failed banks. From 1920 to 1925, 9.1 percent of insured banks failed, while 2.4 percent of national banks failed.

Under the pressure of surviving banks that did not wish to bear the burden of other bank's failures, the legislature allowed banks to switch to the bond plan in 1925, leaving outstanding depositors' claims of $15 million, which were gradually repaid by special assessments on remaining banks.[47] As in the other states, the agricultural crisis, combined with excess risk-taking and adverse selection, dealt the guaranty fund its final blow.

**Repeating the mistakes of the past**

With respect to supervision, these later systems differed in the extent to which bankers participated in appointing, or served as, regulators. In no state were banks given as dominant a role as in the three successful pre-Civil War systems, but in several cases there was a conscious effort to insulate bank supervision from political considerations by appointing bankers to state banking boards. For example, in its early years Oklahoma witnessed a politically motivated bank closure of a solvent institution, and a politically motivated intervention of the Governor to protect a member bank. In 1913, the legislature changed the composition of the state's banking board to limit such politicizing and give a greater role to member banks.[48] South Dakota and Washington followed Oklahoma's example, as shown in Table 2.

In part, the desire to include bankers on the supervisory boards reflected a belief that bankers would find it in their interest to promote supervision and monitor one another. This belief was based in part on the successful self-regulating clearing houses that existed at the time. Regulators were surprised to find, however, that members of the insurance system had little interest in monitoring one another or reporting on misconduct under the insurance systems. Robb writes that:

> One of the fascinating arguments for bank guaranty was that, if all banks were required to contribute toward a fund with which to meet losses, the honest and conservative banks would keep watch on the reckless and dishonest, and that the inside pressure would force the rascals out of business. Practically every failure in Oklahoma, Texas, and Kansas has been caused by incompetency or dishonesty, and there is not a case on record where another banker has raised his finger against the proceedings.[49]

Robb goes on to argue that in many cases banks did not inform regulators of fraudulent practices about which they clearly had information.

How can one explain the absence of inter-bank monitoring in this period and the indifference of bankers to each other's behavior, even when they were involved in the supervisory system? Certainly, the difference in the success of pre-Civil War and later self-regulation was not due to differences in enforcement power, as the later authorities had as much power to close and liquidate banks as did those in Ohio, Indiana, and Iowa.

The difference, it seems, can be traced to the incentives provided by a mutual guarantee system of a small number of banks, as contrasted with a fixed-fee system of a large number of banks. In the pre-Civil War mutual-guarantee states, banks had both the authority and the incentive to keep a close eye on their neighboring banks and to identify and put a stop to unsound practices early on. Under the limited assessment programs of the early 20th century, incentives to monitor and enforce were far less, since the cost of a bank's choosing not to monitor its neighbor was bounded by the maximum annual assessment. Furthermore, even if the premium was below the maximum allowed by law, the effect of any one bank's behavior on the assessment was likely to be small in a system with hundreds of banks.

### Building a deposit insurance system that works

Adverse selection and moral hazard are more than theoretical constructs; deposit insurance systems that failed to deal effectively with these problems were undone by them. Banks vary with respect to their abilities and opportunities (hence the potential for adverse selection), and they have latitude in choosing among investments of different risk characteristics (hence moral hazard). When alternatives to membership exist or entry and exit are permitted on a voluntary basis, adverse selection becomes pronounced. Without proper safeguards against excessive risk-taking, banks will choose to free-ride on collective deposit insurance.

Excess risk-taking that accompanies poorly designed insurance schemes is not as visible during good times when risky investments yield high returns. During bad times, however, when risky investments collapse, the riskiness of insured banks' portfolios reveals itself. Policymakers should not infer, therefore, that bank failures are "exogenous" to bank behavior just because they occur during bad times. Neither should they conclude that risk-taking is solely a response to bad times. It is likely that insured banks will take on riskier loans during bad times, since such loans offer the potential to avoid failure at little cost for the owners of a bank that already faces likely liquidation; but without assuming an *ex ante* bias toward risk on the part of many insured banks, one cannot explain the relative failure differences observed in the post-1907 period between state and national banks at the onset of adverse real shocks.

For deposit insurance to be effective, of course, it must do more than preserve the solvency of its members—it must protect the payments system from liquidity crises. A limited fund with upper bounds on emergency contributions will not prevent an economy-wide run. Only substantial borrowing power with a credible future asset stream to back it up or a mutual guarantee commitment among banks can provide the credibility needed to prevent systemic runs. Also, the resources of the system must be sufficiently liquid to meet large short-run withdrawals.

There are also lessons concerning effective and efficient supervision of banks. Self-regulation of banks, in privately organized clearing houses and in state-run mutual guarantee systems, worked very well. It aligned the incentives to monitor, the authority to monitor, and the ability to use information to the advantage of the system as a whole through disciplinary action and early closure or reorganization to reduce exposure to risk. Moreover, it established an efficient system in which those with a comparative advantage in gathering and interpreting information and deciding on bank closure and reorganization policy, actually performed those functions.[50]

History does not provide adequate guidance concerning the optimal size of self-regulating organizations. On the one hand, when an insurance system is confined to a few banks in a small area, each bank has a strong incentive to monitor other banks and report unusual

# The panic of A.D. 33

A few months after the panic of 1907, *Moody's Magazine* published an account by A. W. Ferrin of an earlier panic, that of A.D. 33, which brought the sophisticated financial and business world of Rome to the brisk of disaster. To the businessmen and investors of 1908, the tale must have been startling in its parallels. It is still instructive; here is the story:

As with most panics, the causes were not obvious. About a year before, the firm of Seuthes & Son of Alexandria, lost three richly laden spice ships on the Red Sea in a hurricane. Their ventures in the Ethiopian caravan trade also were unprofitable, owing to a falling market in ostrich feathers and ivory. Rumors that they were insolvent were circulated in Rome. A little later the well-known house of Malchus & Co. of Tyre, with branches at Antioch and Ephesus, suddenly became bankrupt as the result of a strike among their Phoenician workmen and the defalcation of a trusted manager. It was learned that the great Roman banking house of Quintus Maximus & Lucius Vibo had loaned heavily to both Suethes and Malchus. The depositors of Maximus & Vibo began a run on the bank and distrust spread throughout the Via Sacra (the Roman Wall Street), with the rumor that the still larger house of Pettius Brothers was involved with Maximus & Vibo.

The two threatened establishments might have pulled through had they been able to realize on their other securities. Unfortunately the Pettii had placed much of their deposits in loans among the Belgians. In normal times such loans commanded a very profitable interest, but a rebellion among the semi-civilized Belgians had caused the government to decree a temporary suspension of processes for debt. The Pettii were therefore unable to liquidate. Maximus & Vibo closed their doors first but Pettius Brothers suspended the same afternoon. There were grave rumors that owing to the interlacing of credit many other banks were involved.

The crisis might still have been localized at Rome but for a new and very serious factor. The Senate, in a laudable desire to revive declining Italian agriculture had, with the consent of the Emperor, ordered one-third of every Senator's capital to be invested in lands in Italy. Failure to obey this law was punishable with heavy penalties. The time for compliance with the decree had almost expired, with many rich Senators awoke to the fact that they had barely time to effect the required relocation of their funds and avoid the wrath of the law. To obtain capital to buy land it was necessary for them to call in all their private loans and to draw down their balances at their bankers. Publius Spinther, for instance, notified Balbus & Ollius that they must pay him back the 30,000,000 sesterces ($1,350,000) he had deposited with them two years before. Two days later Balbus & Ollius closed their doors.

The same day a notice in the Acta Diurna, the official gazette posted daily in the Forum, reported the suspension of the great Corinthian bank of Leucippus' Sons. A few days later came word that a big bank in Carthage had suspended. On receipt of this alarming information, all the surviving

---

activities to the supervisory authority, because it shares significantly in the costs of failing to do so. As a system becomes wider in its range, the costs of monitoring other members rises, and the benefits from identifying unsafe or dishonest bank practices fall with the number of banks participating. On the other hand, there are advantages to a wider geographical range of coverage that follow from interregional connections in the payments system and opportunities for diversification.

The geographical range of clearing house members was governed by the private interests of member banks, and did not adequately take into account the public benefits of expanded coverage. The range of coverage of the various state systems was limited by state borders.

A challenge for applying the lessons of the past is constructing a system which is national in its protection of the payments system and diversification of risk, but decentralized in its self-regulation. Below I explore how this might be achieved.

### Restructuring deposit insurance

There are two valid reasons that guide the desire for insurance of bank obligations: protecting scarce information capital contained in the banking system (thereby maintaining the flow of credit to information-intensive borrowers) and preserving the payments system. It is quite possible that deposit insurance is no longer the best way to achieve these objectives. Unfettered interstate branch banking

banking houses in the Via Sacra gave notice that they would enforce the time clause on all deposits. The arrival of the corn fleet from Alexandria temporarily relieved the situation, but immediately afterwards came the news that two banks in Lyons and one in Byzantium were in trouble. From the provincial towns in Italy and the farming districts, where creditors had long allowed their loans to run at profitable interest but were now suddenly calling them in, arose cries of distress and tidings of bankruptcy after bankruptcy. After this nothing seemed able to check the panic at Rome. One bank closed after another. The legal 12% rate of interest was set at naught by any lucky man with ready money to lend. Courts were crowded with creditors demanding the seizure and sale by auction of debtors' houses, slaves, stocks or furniture; but the auctions were thinly attended, nobody had any money to buy anything. Valuable villas and racing studs went for a song. Men of excellent credit and seeming fortunes were reduced to beggars.

The panic was spreading all through the Empire and threatening suspension of all commerce and industry when Gracchus, the praetor, before whom most of the bankruptcy cases were being tried, sought help from the Senate which, after a hurried debate, dispatched a fast messenger to the Emperor Tiberius who was taking a vacation at Capri.

While Caesar's reply was awaited Rome held its breath. In four days the messenger returned. The Senate assembled with incredible celerity. A vast crowd in which slaves and millionaires rubbed elbows filled the Forum while the Emperor's letter was read, first to the Senate, and then from the open Rostrum to the waiting throng. The situation reminds one of October 24, 1907, when New York bankers and brokers, with call money unobtainable, stood on the steps of J. P. Morgan's office awaiting word of their fate from the arbiter of American finance.

The solution of the crisis by Tiberius was similar to that made by the United States Treasury Department through J. P. Morgan & Co. on the fateful day of the 1907 panic. Secretary Cortelyou, it will be remembered, deposited $19,000,000 in the New York banks, and J. P. Morgan & Co. loaned $25,000,000 at 10%, breaking the deadlock. Similarly, the Emperor Tiberius ordered the distribution of 100,000,000 sesterces from the Imperial Treasury among reliable bankers, to be loaned to needy debtors, no interest to be collected for three years. He also suspended the decree forcing the investment of Senatorial capital in land.

The Government's action stemmed the tide and private bankers soon began to offer money at reasonable rates. Dispatches from Alexandria, Carthage and Corinth indicated that the panic had been stopped there. The Via Sacra resumed its normal aspect. A few banking houses and individuals never recovered, but the majority escaped permanent suspension and the panic of A.D. 33 passed into half forgotten history.

---

may provide a better approach for maintaining the smooth functioning of the payments system and eliminating the risk of bank runs.

Some advocates of deposit insurance reform propose limiting insurance to a narrowly defined monetary deposit backed by "marked-to-marketable" securities.[51] While such a system would insulate the money supply from financial disturbances, it would not protect the banking system and the supply of commercial credit from liquidity crises. Commercial lending is likely still to be financed by short-term claims, and the potential for disintermediation and credit contraction still would exist.[52] If, for economic or political reasons deposit insurance is to continue, the historical record offers some insight into how to protect against moral hazard and adverse selection. Under the three successful mutual-guarantee insurance systems of the pre-Civil War period and, to a lesser extent, private clearing houses, banks worked to establish firm guidelines on portfolio composition, reserve holdings, loan practices, and capital. They also participated in enforcing these regulations and were far more successful in doing so than were government-appointed regulators. This approach worked because banks were adept at restricting risk-taking and at identifying least-cost regulatory structure (the optimal combination of reserve requirements, risk-based insurance premiums, capital and subordinated debt requirements, etc.). Because of their constant contact with neighboring banks, they also were in an excellent position to monitor each other. The key to establishing an incentive-compatible deposit insurance system may well be to give banks expanded authority in regulating themselves as a group.

Expanding the authority of banks to determine and enforce their own regulations, of course, will only be successful if individual banks have an incentive to establish and enforce regulations that are in the collective interest of the system. The difficulty here is that when the insured system becomes very large, the benefits to any individual bank from monitoring its neighbors become small relative to the costs of doing so, because the reduction in each bank's risk exposure is not much affected by any one bank's monitoring behavior.

The solution to this problem may be a two-tier regulatory system of deposit insurance in which the government provides national protection, but relies on local incentives to monitor.[53] By making insurance premiums for banks in any region depend on the failure experience of their neighbors, for example, the government can make monitoring incentive-compatible. The size of such a basic region would have to be large enough to preclude collusion by a handful of banks and small enough to encourage only low-cost monitors to do the monitoring (say, one or two groups per state on average), and the conditional increase in the insurance premium would have to be large enough to make monitoring worthwhile.[54] Collusive behavior among members of groups can be further discouraged by allowing geographical overlap and, hence, competition among groups.

Some regulations governing banks (including the geographic limits on bank groups) could be determined at the national level by a mainly bank-appointed commission, and other regulations might be allowed to vary at the level of the individual groups.

A successful self-regulating system of bank liability insurance is much more than a pipedream; it is the mechanism that characterizes the only successful liability insurance systems in the historical record. The deposit insurance lawmakers of the post-1907 period failed to learn from the pre-Civil War experience and, hence, repeated the mistakes of insufficient and delayed coverage of bank deposits and promoted systemic insolvency through moral hazard and adverse selection. The goal of this paper has been to help current policymakers start paying attention to history.

## FOOTNOTES

[1]For an excellent study of the incentive-incompatibility problems in the state-level systems, see Edward J. Kane, "How Incentive-Incompatible Deposit-insurance Funds Fail," mimeograph, Ohio State University, 1988.

[2]In his survey of the legislative history of bank insurance, Carter Golembe notes that the statements and actions of state legislators indicate that insurance of wealth was a secondary, incidental, achievement of bank liability insurance. See Carter Golembe, "The Deposit Insurance Legislation of 1933: An Examination of its Antecedents and its Purposes," *Political Science Quarterly (June 1960), pp. 189-95.*

[3]See George Akerlof, "The Market for 'Lemons': Qualitative Uncertainty and the Market Mechanism," *Quarterly Journal of Economics* (1970), pp. 488-500; Gary Gorton and George Pennacchi, "Transactions Contracts," mimeograph, University of Pennsylvania, 1988; and Charles Jacklin, "Demand Equity and Deposit Insurance," mimeograph, Stanford University, 1988.

[4]During normal times, in the absence of deposit insurance, the percentage of "lemons" was small, and the liquidity of bank claims was ensured by their demandability. The first-come-first-serve nature of demandable debt provided an

incentive for some depositors (particularly other banks) to monitor the actions of banks. Informed monitors made a market in the notes and deposits of banks through the interbank clearing of checks and the note brokerage market. As long as a bank was open (as long as informed monitors had not yet run on the bank), non-monitors were able to transact in bank claims with reasonable certainty about their value. Once banks had suspended, however, this sort of information sharing was no longer possible. See Charles W. Calomiris and Charles M. Kahn, "The Role of Demandable Debt in Structuring Optimal Banking Arrangements," mimeograph, Northwestern University, 1988. Of course, deposit insurance eliminates the first-come-first-serve preference for early withdrawals and ensures liquidity during normalcy and crisis through the government guarantee of deposits. Some current proposals for reforming deposit insurance emphasize the benefits of uninsured depositors or bondholders for disciplining bank behavior, as in the pre-insurance regime.

[5]See Calomiris and Kahn, "The Role of Demandable Debt."

[6]For a theoretical discussion of the problems created by depositors' inability to sort out the distribution of an adverse disturbance among banks, see Gary Gorton, "Self-Regulating Bank Coalitions," mimeograph, University of

Pennsylvania, 1989. Empirical evidence on the importance of this type of confusion for propagating the crisis of 33 A.D. can be found in A. W. Ferrin, "The Business Panic of A.D.33," Moody's Magazine (August 1908), pp. 81-2. For a discussion of this same problem during the Panic of 1857, see Charles W. Calomiris and Larry Schweikart, ":Was the South Backward? North-South Differences in Antebellum Banking During Crisis and Normalcy," mimeograph, Northwestern University, 1988.

[7]See James G. Cannon, *Clearing Houses* (Washington, D.C.: 1910); Gary Gorton, "Self-Regulating Bank Coalitions," and Calomiris and Schweikart, "Was the South Backward?"

[8]The Suffolk System was wide ranging in that it operated throughout New England. While it succeeded in the more limited task of establishing a regional interbank network for clearing notes, it did not provide effective protection for the payments system as a whole. See Charles W. Calomiris and Charles M. Kahn, "Interbank Monitoring as Seignorage Sharing: The Suffolk System," mimeograph, Northwestern University, 1989.

[9]For discussions of the connection between unit banking and financial system fragility, see G.M.W. Sprague, *History of Crises Under the National Banking System* (National Monetary Commission: 1910); Milton Friedman and Anna J. Schwartz, *A Monetary History of the United States* (Princeton: 1963); and Charles W. Calomiris, R. Glenn Hubbard, and James Stock, "The Farm Debt Crisis and Public Policy," *Brookings Papers on Economic Activity*, vol 2 (1986).

[10]In *The Regulation and Reform of the American Banking System, 1900-1929* (Princeton: 1983), pp. 206-07, Eugene N. White argues that early twentieth-century Canadian banks used branch banking and informal coordination as an effective substitute for other measures (pp. 206-207). White also argues (pp. 218-22) that the bank failure experiences of the various states in the U.S. in the 1920s indicate that branching provided more effective protection than deposit insurance of unit banks. In "The Political Economy of Bank Regulation," *Journal of Economic History* (March 1982), pp 33-42, White claims that deposit insurance was pushed by unit banking interests which saw it as an alternative to branch banking. Carter Golembe argues that unit banking favored the use of deposit insurance and that deposit insurance reduced the costs of unit banking. He traces this political symbiosis from 1829 to 1933. See "The Deposit Insurance Legislation of 1933," pp. 195-99.

[11]For a discussion of the causes of the Panic of 1837, see Peter Temin, *The Jacksonian Economy* (New York, 1969).

[12]See Calomiris and Schweikart, "Was the South Backward?"; Golembe and Warburton, *Insurance of Bank Obligations in Six States During the Period 1829-1866,* (Federal Deposit Insurance Corporation: 1958) Chapter II, pp. 55-7; and Robert E. Chaddock, *The Safety Fund Banking System in New York, 1829-1866* (National Monetary Commission: 1910).

[13]Golembe and Warburton, *Insurance of Bank Obligations,* chapter II, p. 33.

[14]See Calomiris and Schweikart, "Was the South Backward?"

[15]See Calomiris and Schweikart, "Was the South Backward?" Consistent with the lack of effective insurance, we find there is little evidence of moral hazard as a cause for bank failures during the panic of 1857.

[16]See Golembe and Warburton, *Insurance of Bank Obligations,* chapter II, pp. 35-7.

[17]Gorton, "Self-Regulating Bank Coalitions," argues that panics are often caused by depositor confusion over which banks are most affected by a given disturbance. Calomiris and Schweikart, "Was the South Backwards?" argue that the panic of 1857 began with a small aggregate disturbance that was propagated, and turned into a panic, by precisely this type of confusion. A deposit insurance system or an alternative means of dispersing risk (like branch banking) would have prevented the Panic.

[18]Some withdrawals were allowed even before the expiration of member bank charters, which was contrary to law, but the courts did not force the banks or the government to reimburse the fund. See Golembe and Warburton, *Insurance of Bank Obligations,* chapter III, pp. 16.

[19]The Danby Bank had operated outside the insured system from 1850 to 1856. It joined the fund in 1856 and failed on September 4, 1857 before the Panic of 1857.

[20]See Golembe and Warburton, *Insurance of Bank Obligations,* chapter V.

[21]The state constitution only provided for the chartering of a state bank and its branches, which required that this language be used in the insured banking system. See Golembe and Warburton, *Insurance of Bank Obligations,* chapter IV, p. 1.

[22]See Golembe and Warburton, *Insurance of Bank Obligations,* chapter IV, p. 14.

[23]See Golembe and Warburton, *Insurance of Bank Obligations,* chapter IV, p. 6-7.

[24]See Golembe and Warburton, *Insurance of Bank Obligations,* chapter IV, p. 9.

[25]These included the forced resignation of bank officials and forced reductions of loans to insiders. See Golembe and Warburton, *Insurance of Bank Obligations,* chapter IV, pp. 17-24.

[26]See Calomiris, "Falling Bond Prices, Contagion, and Bank Failures."

[27]As I have noted, Indiana avoided a general suspension, but at the cost of many free bank failures.

[28]See Golembe and Warburton, *Insurance of Bank Obligations*, chapter IV, p. 29.

[29]Iowa had long prohibited the chartering of banks, and so the insured system had no competition from existing banks. While Iowa enacted a free banking law in 1858, the terms of these charters were prohibitively costly and no free bank was ever established under the law.

[30]See Calomiris and Schweikart, "Was the South Backward?"

[31]See Calomiris and Schweikart, "Was the South Backward?," for a discussion of note discount rates during the panic of 1857.

[32]This is not to say that the technological changes in check clearing were entirely exogenous; they were likely motivated in part by the costs of note issue. Still, the two effects—the rising costs of note finance, and the decreasing costs of deposits finance—were separate influences.

[33]See Milton Friedman and Anna J. Schwartz, *Monetary Statistics of the United States: Estimates, Sources, Methods*, (New York: 1970), pp. 4, 8, 224.

[34]The Panic of 1857 became a panic when depositors of banks in New York City ran their banks on October 13. This was first system-wide bank run precipitated by depositors in U.S. banking history, according to contemporary chroniclers. See James Cook, "The Report of the Superintendant of the Banking Department of the State of New York," *House of Representatives Executive Document no. 107*, 35th Congress, First Session.

[35]See Thorton Cooke, "The Insurance of Bank Deposits in the West," in George E. Barnett, *State Banks and Trust Companies* (National Monetary Commission: 1910), pp. 261-303, and Thomas B. Robb, *The Guaranty of Bank Deposits* (New York: 1921), pp. 40-41.

[36]Cooke, "The Insurance of Bank Deposits", p. 273

[37]In May of 1908 the International Bank of Colgate was closed by the Commissioner, but it was reorganized and reopened soon thereafter, without imposing any loss on the fund. See Cooke, "The Insurance of Bank Deposits", pp. 281-2.

[38]See Robb, *The Guaranty of Bank Deposits*, pp. 50-53.

[39]See the Annual Report of the Comptroller of the Currency, 1914, volume 2, pp. 752-3.

[40]See American Bankers Association, *The Guaranty of Bank Deposits*, (New York: 1933), p. 12.

[41]Additionally, higher assessments without supervision can make matters worse by forcing banks to finance this tax on deposits with higher return, higher risk loans.The printing of money to finance payments to banks offers banks direct and indirect relief. First, banks receive actual payments from the government. Second, banks receive the benefit of inflationary reductions in the value of nominal debts, which increase the probability of borrower solvency.

[42]The printing of money to finance payments to banks offers banks direct and indirect relief. First, banks receive actual payments from the government. Second, banks receive the benefit of inflationary reductions in the value of nominal debts, which increase the probability of borrower solvency.

[43]See American Bankers Association, *The Guaranty of Bank Deposits*, p. 35.

[44]See American Bankers Association, *The Guaranty of Bank Deposits*, p. 20.

[45]See Cooke, "The Insurance of Bank Deposits," p. 322.

[46]See Robb, *The Guaranty of Bank Deposits*, p. 155.

[47]See American Bankers Association, *The Guaranty of Bank Deposits*, pp. 37.

[48]See Robb, *The Guaranty of Bank Deposits*, pp. 28-9.

[49]See Robb, *The Guaranty of Bank Deposits*, pp. 185.

[50]Edward Kane particularly stresses the poor performance of bank regulators in the state and federal savings and loan insurance funds in detecting and correcting unsound practices. He argues that this poor performance can be traced to the incentives of the regulators to conceal problems. See Kane, "How Incentive-Incompatible Deposit-Insurance Funds Fail.

[51]Note that the theoretical motivation for demandable debt discussed above (a disciplinary device on bank behavior) does not arise when bank assets can be "marked to market." Furthermore, confusion would not occur when assets backing share accounts are marked to market.

[52]The maturity mismatch of commercial lending predates the transactability of bank claims (see Calomiris and Kahn, "The Role of Demandable Debt"). The potential for credit contraction during liquidity crises has been apparent even in commercial paper markets, where borrowed quality is very high. See Charles W. Calomiris, "The Motivations for Loan Commitments Backing Commercial paper," *Journal of Banking and Finance*, forthcoming.

[53]Marvin Goodfriend, in "Money, Credit, Banking, and Payments System Policy," (Federal Reserve Bank of Richmond; August 1988), also advocates a two-tier system.

[54]Of course, unit banks in states with a non-diversified income base will still be vulnerable to cataclysmic regional shocks, even if the value of their transactable claims is guaranteed. Only branch banking, or improvements in information sharing that allow banks to hold interests in loans across state lines, can reduce that risk. If the government were to suspend insurance premiums penalties during regional crises, that would only encourage banks to take region-specific risks (which proved disastrous in the postbellum state systems), and would provide no incentive for other banks to prohibit or detect such practices.

# Name Index